Middle School 3-1
학교시험 완벽대비

1학기 전과정
적중 100plus

영어 기출문제집

중3

시사 | 박준언

Best Collection

구성과 특징

교과서의 주요 학습 내용을 중심으로 학습 영역별 특성에 맞춰 단계별로 다양한 학습 기회를 제공하여
단원별 학습능력 평가는 물론 중간 및 기말고사 시험 등에 완벽하게 대비할 수 있도록 내용을 구성

Words & Expressions

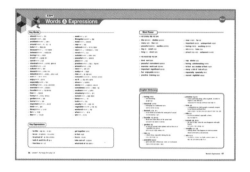

Step1	Key Words 단원별 핵심 단어 설명 및 풀이
	Key Expression 단원별 핵심 숙어 및 관용어 설명
	Word Power 반대 또는 비슷한 뜻 단어 배우기
	English Dictionary 영어로 배우는 영어 단어
Step2	실력평가 단원별 수시평가 대비 주관식, 객관식 문제풀이
Step3	서술형 대비 학업성취도 및 수행능력평가 대비 서술형 문제풀이

Conversation

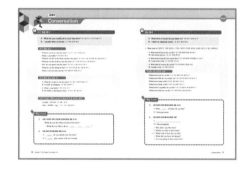

Step1	핵심 의사소통 소통에 필요한 주요 표현 방법 요약
	핵심 Check 기본적인 표현 방법 및 활용능력 확인
Step2	대화문 익히기 교과서 대화문 심층 분석 및 확인
Step3	교과서 확인학습 빈칸 채우기를 통한 문장 완성 능력 확인
Step4	기본평가 시험대비 기초 학습 능력 평가
Step5	실력평가 단원별 수시평가 대비 주관식, 객관식 문제풀이
Step6	서술형 대비 학업성취도 및 수행능력평가 대비 서술형 문제풀이

Grammar

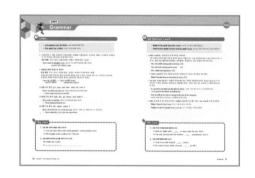

Step1	주요 문법 단원별 주요 문법 사항과 예문을 알기 쉽게 설명
	핵심 Check 기본 문법사항에 대한 이해 여부 확인
Step2	기본평가 시험대비 기초 학습 능력 평가
Step3	실력평가 단원별 수시평가 대비 주관식, 객관식 문제풀이
Step4	서술형 대비 학업성취도 및 수행능력평가 대비 서술형 문제풀이

Reading

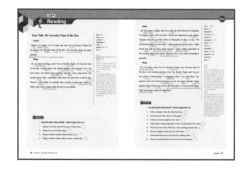

Step1	구문 분석 단원별로 제시된 문장에 대한 구문별 분석과 내용 설명
	확인문제 문장에 대한 기본적인 이해와 인지능력 확인
Step2	확인학습A 빈칸 채우기를 통한 문장 완성 능력 확인
Step3	확인학습B 제시된 우리말을 영어로 완성하여 작문 능력 키우기
Step4	실력평가 단원별 수시평가 대비 주관식, 객관식 문제풀이
Step5	서술형 대비 학업성취도 및 수행능력평가 대비 서술형 문제풀이
	교과서 구석구석 교과서에 나오는 기타 문장까지 완벽 학습

Composition

|영역별 핵심문제|

단어 및 어휘, 대화문, 문법, 독해 등 각 영역별 기출문제의 출제 유형을 분석하여 실전에 대비하고 연습할 수 있도록 문제를 배열

|단원별 예상문제|

기출문제를 분석한 후 새로운 시험 출제 경향을 더하여 새롭게 출제될 수 있는 문제를 포함하여 시험에 완벽하게 대비할 수 있도록 준비

|서술형 실전 및 창의사고력 문제|

학교 시험에서 점차 늘어나는 서술형 시험에 집중 대비하고 고득점을 취득하는데 만전을 기하기 위한 학습 코너

|단원별 모의고사|

영역별, 단계별 학습을 모두 마친 후 실전 연습을 위한 모의고사

교과서 파헤치기

- **단어Test1~3** 영어 단어 우리말 쓰기, 우리말을 영어 단어로 쓰기, 영영풀이에 해당하는 단어와 우리말 쓰기
- **대화문Test1~2** 대화문 빈칸 완성 및 전체 대화문 쓰기
- **본문Test1~5** 빈칸 완성, 우리말 쓰기, 문장 배열연습, 영어 작문하기 복습 등 단계별 반복 학습을 통해 교과서 지문에 대한 완벽한 습득
- **구석구석지문Test1~2** 지문 빈칸 완성 및 전문 영어로 쓰기

Lesson

1

All about Me

 의사소통 기능

- 궁금증 표현하기
  Can you tell me about yourself?
- 가장 좋아하는 것 말하기
  What I like most is to take pictures.

 언어 형식

- 동사의 강조
  I **do feel** good when I walk in the forest.
- 관계대명사 what
  Having fun is **what I want most.**

Words & Expressions

Key Words

- **advise**[ædváiz] 동 조언하다, 충고하다
- **among**[əmʌ́ŋ] 전 … 중에서
- **automatically**[ɔ̀:təmǽtikəli] 부 자동으로
- **barbecue**[bá:rbikjù:] 명 바비큐
- **basement**[béismənt] 명 지하층[실]
- **cartoon**[kɑ:rtú:n] 명 만화
- **check**[tʃek] 동 확인하다
- **choice**[tʃɔis] 명 선택
- **comfortable**[kʌ́mfərtəbl] 형 편안한
- **contest**[kántest] 명 대회
- **cool**[ku:l] 형 멋진
- **countryside**[kʌ́ntrisaid] 명 시골 (지역)
- **create**[kriéit] 동 만들다
- **designed**[dizáind] 형 그려진, 디자인된
- **designer**[dizáinər] 명 디자이너
- **different**[dífərənt] 형 다른, 다양한
- **do**[du] 조 (동사를 강조) 정말로
- **draw**(–drew–drawn)[drɔ:] 동 (그림을) 그리다
- **early adopter** 얼리 어답터 (남들보다 먼저 신제품을 사서 써 보는 사람)
- **enter**[éntər] 동 들어가다
- **exciting**[iksáitiŋ] 형 흥미로운
- **fantastic**[fænstǽstik] 형 환상적인, 매우 멋진
- **favorite**[féivərit] 형 가장 좋아하는
- **floor**[flɔ:r] 명 (건물의) 층
- **forest**[fɔ́:rist] 명 숲
- **forward**[fɔ́:rwərd] 부 앞으로
- **free**[fri:] 형 한가한, 다른 계획이 없는
- **furniture**[fə́:rnitʃər] 명 가구
- **garden**[gá:rdn] 명 정원
- **goal**[goul] 명 목표
- **guest**[gest] 명 손님

- **hero**[híərou] 명 영웅, 히어로
- **homeroom teacher** 담임 선생님
- **humorous**[hjú:mərəs] 형 재미있는, 유머러스한
- **imagine**[imǽdʒin] 동 상상하다
- **interest**[íntərəst] 명 관심, 흥미
- **interesting**[íntərəstiŋ] 형 흥미로운, 재미있는
- **join**[dʒɔin] 동 가입하다
- **kind**[kaind] 명 종류
- **language**[lǽŋgwidʒ] 명 언어
- **motto**[mátou] 명 좌우명, 모토
- **nature**[néitʃər] 명 자연
- **nickname**[níknèim] 명 별명
- **not just** …: 단지 …가 아닌
- **others**[ʌ́ðərz] 대 다른 사람들
- **pet**[pet] 명 애완동물
- **photographer**[fətágrəfər] 명 사진사
- **photo-taking** 사진촬영
- **poster**[póustər] 명 포스터
- **practice**[prǽktis] 동 연습하다
- **pretty**[príti] 부 매우, 꽤
- **product**[prádʌkt] 명 제품
- **real**[rí:əl] 형 진짜의
- **recognize**[rékəgnàiz] 동 인식하다
- **refreshed**[rifréʃt] 형 (기분이) 상쾌한
- **save**[seiv] 동 구하다, 절약하다
- **scene**[si:n] 명 장면
- **SF movie** 공상 과학 영화
- **skill**[skil] 명 기술
- **subject**[sʌ́bdʒikt] 명 과목, 주제
- **technology**[teknálədʒi] 명 기술
- **theater**[θíːətər] 명 극장
- **wake up** (잠에서) 깨다, 일어나다

Key Expressions

- **be full of** …: …로 가득 차다
- **be filled with** …: …로 가득 차다
- **be good at**: …을 잘하다
- **be interested in**: …에 관심이 있다
- **go traveling**: 여행을 가다
- **get along with**: …와 잘 지내다

- **have free time**: 여가 시간을 가지다
- **here are**+복수명사: 여기에 …가 있다
- **look like**+명사: …처럼 보이다
- **stop –ing**: …하는 것을 그만두다
- **thank A for B**: B 때문에 A에게 감사하다
- **would like to**+동사원형: …하고 싶다

Word Power

※ 서로 반대되는 뜻을 가진 어휘
- □ **forward**(앞으로) ↔ **backward**(뒤쪽으로)
- □ **interesting**(재미있는) ↔ **uninteresting**(재미없는)
- □ **different**(다른) ↔ **same**(같은)
- □ **construct**(건설하다) ↔ **destroy**(파괴하다)

※ 서로 비슷한 뜻을 가진 어휘
- □ **enter** : **go into**(들어가다)
- □ **draw** : **sketch**(그리다)
- □ **humorous** : **funny**(재미있는)
- □ **recognize** : **identify**(인식하다, 확인하다)
- □ **fantastic** : **wonderful**(환상적인, 멋진)
- □ **advise** : **counsel**(조언하다, 충고하다)

English Dictionary

- □ **advise** 충고하다
  → to tell someone that they should do something
  누군가에게 무언가를 해야 한다고 말하다

- □ **among** ~ 중에서
  → in the middle of a group
  어떤 그룹의 한 가운데에

- □ **basement** 지하실[층]
  → part of a building that is under the level of the ground
  지면 아래에 있는 건물의 일부

- □ **choice** 선택
  → the possibility of choosing between two or more things
  두 가지 이상의 것 중에서 선택하는 가능성

- □ **countryside** 시골
  → land that is not in towns or cities and may have farms, fields, etc.
  도시에 있지 않고 농장, 밭 등이 있는 땅

- □ **create** 만들다, 창출하다
  → to make something happen or exist
  어떤 일이 일어나거나 존재하게 만들다

- □ **enter** 들어가다
  → to go into a place
  어떤 장소에 들어가다

- □ **fantastic** 환상적인
  → extremely good, attractive, or enjoyable
  매우 좋거나 매력적이거나 즐길 만한

- □ **forest** 숲
  → a large area of land that is covered with trees
  나무로 덮여 있는 넓은 지역의 땅

- □ **forward** 앞으로
  → towards a place or position that is in front of you
  당신 앞에 있는 장소나 위치를 향하여

- □ **furniture** 가구
  → things such as chairs, tables, and beds that you put into a room or building
  방이나 건물에 두는 의자, 탁자, 침대와 같은 물건

- □ **hero** 영웅
  → a very brave person, often a man, that a lot of people admire
  많은 사람들이 존경하는, 종종 남자로, 매우 용감한 사람

- □ **imagine** 상상하다
  → to form or have a mental picture or idea of something
  어떤 것에 대한 마음 속의 그림이나 생각을 형성하거나 가지다

- □ **motto** 좌우명, 모토
  → a short sentence or phrase that expresses a belief or purpose
  믿음이나 목적을 표현하는 짧은 문장이나 문구

- □ **pet** 애완동물
  → an animal that is kept in the home as a companion and treated kindly 집에서 동반자로 길러지고 친절하게 대접받는 동물

- □ **photographer** 사진사
  → a person who takes photographs, either as a job or hobby
  직업이나 취미로 사진을 찍는 사람

- □ **recognize** 인식하다, 알아차리다
  → to know someone or something because you have seen or heard him or her or experienced it before
  이전에 보거나 듣고 경험했기 때문에 사람이나 사물을 알다

01 다음 문장의 빈칸에 주어진 영어 설명에 해당하는 말을 쓰시오.

• My dream house has a theater in the _____.

part of a building that is under the level of the ground

02 다음 빈칸에 들어갈 말로 가장 적절한 것은?

Nature is my good friend. I do feel good when I walk _____.

① in the building　② in the forest
③ on the street　④ across the road
⑤ with my pet dog

[03~04] 다음 설명에 해당하는 단어를 고르시오.

03

to know someone or something because you have seen or heard him or her or experienced it before

① imagine　② enter
③ advise　④ recognize
⑤ create

04

the possibility of choosing between two or more things

① choice　② check
③ motto　④ poster
⑤ goal

05 다음 우리말에 맞게 빈칸에 알맞은 단어를 쓰시오.

나의 꿈의 집에서, 나의 가족은 안전하고 편안하게 느껴.

➡ In my dream house, my family _____ safe and _____.

06 다음 빈칸에 공통으로 들어갈 말로 알맞은 것은?

(A) I am an early _____ of new technology.
(B) France is the biggest _____ of Korean orphans in Europe.

① plan　② choice
③ adopter　④ promise
⑤ condition

서답형
07 다음 짝지어진 단어의 관계가 같도록 빈칸에 알맞은 말을 쓰시오.

enter : go into = advise : _____

08 다음 빈칸에 들어갈 말로 알맞게 짝지어진 것은?

I like to use new technology. I do like to use new products and technology (A) _____ others. When I get near my house, the front door (B)_____ my face and opens automatically.

① with – captures　② after – recognizes
③ after – works　④ before – closes
⑤ before – recognizes

⭐**01** 다음 빈칸에 들어갈 말을 〈보기〉에서 찾아 쓰시오. (필요하면 변형하여 쓰시오.)

┌─ 보기 ┼─────────────────┐
│ furniture advise excite technology │
└───────────────────────────────┘

(1) I like the scenes made with computer _____.

(2) The room is full of old _____.

(3) My dream house is filled with _____ things.

(4) Would you _____ me what I should do?

02 〈보기〉의 단어를 이용하여 문장의 빈칸을 완성하시오.

┌─ 보기 ┼─────────────────┐
│ along interest good stop │
└───────────────────────────────┘

(1) My goal this year is to _____ _____ fast food.

(2) I'm _____ _____ playing the drums.

(3) I'm _____ _____ the stars. I usually go out to see stars at night.

(4) I want to _____ _____ _____ everyone in the club.

03 다음 우리말과 같은 표현이 되도록 문장의 빈칸을 채우시오. (철자가 주어진 것은 주어진 철자로 시작하여 쓸 것.)

(1) 내가 가장 좋아하는 것은 새로운 언어를 배우는 것이다.
　➡ What I like most is to learn a new _____.

(2) 너의 별명은 뭐니?
　➡ What is your _____?

(3) 오늘 수업 시간에, 우리는 꿈의 집을 만들었다.
　➡ Today, in class, we c_____ our dream house.

04 다음 영영풀이에 해당하는 단어를 〈보기〉에서 찾아 첫 번째 빈칸에 쓰고, 두 번째 빈칸에는 우리말 뜻을 쓰시오.

┌─ 보기 ┼─────────────────┐
│ imagine fantastic forward forest │
└───────────────────────────────┘

(1) _____ : extremely good, attractive, enjoyable: _____

(2) _____ : towards a place or position that is in front of you: _____

(3) _____ : to form or have a mental picture or idea of something: _____

05 다음 빈칸에 공통으로 알맞은 단어를 주어진 철자로 시작하여 쓰시오.

(1) • What k_____ of things do you want in your future?
　• The k_____ man helped us.

(2) • Our g_____ is to reduce our trash by ten percent.
　• Liverpool won by three g_____s to one.

교과서

Conversation

Can you tell me about yourself? 나에게 너에 대해 말해 줄 수 있니?

■ 'Can you tell me about + 명사[대명사]?' 또는 'Can you tell me 의문사+주어+동사 ~?'로 사실이나 원인, 어떤 상황에 대한 궁금증을 설명해 달라고 요청할 수 있다.

• Can you tell me about your family? 당신의 가족에 대해 얘기해 줄래요?
• Can you tell me about what happened? 무슨 일이 있었는지 말해 줄래요?
• Can you tell me why you were late yesterday? 어제 왜 늦었는지 말해 줄래요?
• Can you tell me why you don't love me? 왜 날 사랑하지 않는지 말해 줄래요?

■ 궁금증을 표현하는 다른 방법

'I'm really curious about ~.'은 '나는 ~에 대해서 정말 궁금해.'라는 의미로 새로운 정보에 대하여 궁금증을 표현하거나 보다 많은 정보를 알고 싶을 때 사용하는 표현이다. 'I'd like to know more about ~.', 'be interested in ~, want to know ~' 등으로도 표현할 수 있다.

• The cat was naturally curious about its new surroundings. 그 고양이는 원래 새로운 환경에 호기심이 있었다.
• We are curious about why you never called us. 우리는 왜 네가 우리에게 전화를 하지 않았는지 궁금하다.

핵심 Check

1. 다음 대화의 빈칸에 공통으로 들어갈 알맞은 것은?

• **A:** Can you tell me _____ the Wright Brothers?

  B: They invented the airplane.

• **A:** I am curious _____ this movie.

  B: So am I.

① in   ② of   ③ for
④ with   ⑤ about

2 가장 좋아하는 것 말하기

What I like most is to take pictures. 내가 가장 좋아하는 것은 사진을 찍는 것이다.

- 'What I like most is ~.'는 '내가 가장 좋아하는 것은 ~이다.'라는 의미로 자신이 가장 좋아하는 것을 말할 때 사용하는 표현이며, 여기서 what은 관계대명사로 '~하는 것'의 의미를 가진다. 관계대명사 what은 the thing(s) that[which]로 바꾸어 쓸 수 있다. 즉, 'What I like most'는 'The thing that I like most'로 바꿀 수 있다.

- 가장 좋아하는 것을 말하는 다른 표현은 'My favorite ~ is ...' / 'I like ... most.' / 'I prefer ...' 등이 있다.

  - My favorite movie is *Titanic*. 내가 가장 좋아하는 영화는 *Titanic*이야.
  - I like pizza most. 나는 피자를 가장 좋아해.

- 가장 좋아하는 것을 묻는 표현

  'What's your favorite ~?'은 상대방이 가장 좋아하는 것을 묻는 표현으로 'Which[What] ~ do you like most?'나 'What do you like most?'라고 말할 수도 있다.

  - What's your favorite movie? 네가 가장 좋아하는 영화는 무엇이니?
  - Which food do you like most? 너는 어떤 음식을 가장 좋아하니?

- 가장 좋아하는 것 묻고 표현하기

  A: What's your favorite subject? 네가 가장 좋아하는 과목이 뭐니?

  B: My favorite subject is English. / What I like most is English. 내가 가장 좋아하는 과목은 영어야.

핵심 Check

2. 다음 우리말에 맞도록 빈칸에 들어갈 알맞은 말을 쓰시오.

내가 가장 좋아하는 것은 보드 게임을 하는 거야.

_____ I like most is to play board games.

① Which   ② How   ③ What

④ When   ⑤ Whether

Conversation 교과서 대화문 익히기

Listen & Speak 1 A-1

G: Jiho, how was your first day of third grade?

B: It was ❶pretty good. The teachers and my new classmates are all good.

G: That sounds good. Who is your homeroom teacher?

B: My homeroom teacher is Mr. Kim. He teaches math.

G: ❷Can you tell me more about him?

B: Yes. He is humorous and ❸told us some fun stories about math. It was interesting.

G: Cool! I hope you enjoy studying math.

G: 지호야, 너의 3학년 첫 날은 어땠어?

B: 꽤 좋았어. 선생님들과 새로운 반 친구들 모두 좋아.

G: 그거 좋네. 담임 선생님은 누구셔?

B: 내 담임 선생님은 김 선생님이셔. 그는 수학을 가르치셔.

G: 나에게 그에 대해 좀 더 말해 줄 수 있니?

B: 응. 그는 재미있고 우리에게 수학에 대한 재미있는 몇 가지 이야기를 해 주셨어. 그것은 흥미로웠어.

G: 멋지네! 네가 수학 공부를 즐기기 바라.

❶ 여기서 'pretty'는 부사로 '매우, 꽤'의 의미이다.
❷ 'Can you tell me about + 명사[대명사]?'는 궁금증을 표현할 때 사용하는 말이다.
❸ 'tell+간접목적어(…에게)+직접목적어(~을)' 형태이다.

Check(√) True or False

(1) Jiho's homeroom teacher is a math teacher. T ☐ F ☐

(2) Jiho's homeroom teacher isn't funny. T ☐ F ☐

Listen & Speak 2 A

1. G: I often go traveling with my family. ❶What I like most about traveling is trying new foods.

2. B: My favorite subject is music. I can play the drums and guitar. Among them, ❷playing the guitar is what I like most.

3. G: This is a picture of Dora. She is my best friend, not just a pet. ❸ Playing with her in my free time is what I like most.

1. G: 나는 가끔 나의 가족들과 여행을 가. 여행에 관해 내가 가장 좋아하는 것은 새로운 음식들을 먹어보는 거야.

2. B: 내가 가장 좋아하는 과목은 음악이야. 나는 드럼과 기타를 연주할 수 있어. 그것들 중에서, 기타를 연주하는 것이 내가 가장 좋아하는 거야.

3. G: 이것은 Dora 사진이야. 그녀는 단순히 애완동물이 아니라, 나의 가장 친한 친구야. 여가시간에 그녀와 함께 노는 것이 내가 가장 좋아하는 거야.

❶ 'What I like most is ~.'는 '내가 가장 좋아하는 것은 ~이다'라는 의미로 자신이 가장 좋아하는 것을 말할 때 사용하는 표현이다.
❷ playing the guitar는 동명사 주어로 '기타를 연주하는 것은'으로 해석한다. what I like most는 보어 자리에 사용된 관계대명사절로 '내가 가장 좋아하는 것'이라는 뜻이다.
❸ Playing with her는 동명사 주어이고, her는 애완동물인 'Dora'를 가리키는 말이다.

Check(√) True or False

(3) G likes going traveling with her family. T ☐ F ☐

(4) B prefers playing the drums to playing the guitar. T ☐ F ☐

(5) What G likes most is playing with Dora. T ☐ F ☐

Listen & Speak 1 B

A: ❶Can you tell me about your plan for this weekend?

B: Yes. ❷I am going to have a birthday party.

A: ❸Can you tell me about your goal for the year?

B: Yes. I want to ❹stop eating fast food.

A: 나에게 너의 이번 주말 계획에 대해 말해 줄 수 있니?

B: 응. 나는 생일 파티를 할 거야.

A: 나에게 너의 올해 목표에 대해 말해 줄 수 있니?

B: 응. 나는 패스트푸드를 그만 먹고 싶어.

❶ 이번 주의 미래의 계획을 묻는 표현이다.

❷ 'be going to+동사원형'은 '~할 예정이다'라는 의미로 미래의 계획을 말할 때 사용한다.

❸ 궁금증을 표현하는 표현이다.

❹ 'stop+동명사(v-ing)'는 '~하는 것을 그만두다'라는 의미이다. 'stop+to v'는 '~하기 위해 멈추다'라는 의미가 된다.

Check(√) True or False

(6) B is planning to have a birthday party this month.　　　　　　T ☐ F ☐

(7) B wants to stop eating fast food this year.　　　　　　　　　T ☐ F ☐

Real Life Talk

Seho: Nice to meet you. ❶I'd like to join your photo club.

Bora: ❷Thank you for your interest in the club. Can you tell me about yourself?

Seho: Yes. My name is Kim Seho. I am in the third grade, class 8.

Andy: Tell me more. ❸What do you like to do most in your free time?

Seho: Well, ❹what I like most is to take pictures.

Bora: That's great. What is your dream for the future?

Seho: I want to be a photographer.

Andy: Then you made the right choice. You can learn a lot of photo-taking skills here. Welcome to our club.

Seho: Thank you. I'm so glad!

세호: 만나서 반가워. 나는 너희의 사진 동아리에 가입하고 싶어.

보라: 동아리에 관심을 가져 줘서 고마워. 너에 대해 말해 줄래?

세호: 응. 내 이름은 김세호야. 나는 3학년 8반이야.

Andy: 좀 더 말해 줘. 너는 여가 시간에 무엇을 하는 걸 가장 좋아하니?

세호: 음, 내가 가장 좋아하는 건 사진 찍는 거야.

보라: 멋지다. 너의 장래 희망은 뭐니?

세호: 나는 사진 작가가 되고 싶어.

Andy: 그러면 너는 정말 좋은 선택을 했구나. 너는 여기서 사진 찍는 기술을 많이 배울 수 있어. 우리 동아리에 온 걸 환영해.

세호: 고마워. 나도 기뻐!

❶ 'would like to v'는 '~하고 싶다'라는 의미이다.

❷ 'thank A for B' 구문으로 'B 때문에 A에게 고마워하다'라는 의미이다.

❸ 상대방이 가장 좋아하는 것이 무엇인지 묻는 표현이다.

❹ what은 관계대명사로 'the thing(s) that[which]'로 바꾸어 쓸 수 있다. 'to take pictures'는 보어 자리에 사용된 명사적 용법이다.

Check(√) True or False

(8) What Seho likes most in his free time is to take pictures.　　　T ☐ F ☐

(9) Seho learned many photo-taking skills in the photo club.　　　T ☐ F ☐

Warm Up

B1: Hello, my name is Kim Chanho. ❶I want to tell you about myself. I'm interested in music. ❷I'm good at playing the drums.

G1: Hi! I am Teri. I like running in the evening. ❸I feel refreshed when I exercise.

B2: Hello, my name is Jack. I'm interested in the stars. I ❹usually go out to see stars at night.

G2: I am Lee Bora. I want to be a designer in the future, so I ❺practice drawing when I have free time.

B3: I am Mark. I like dancing. I want to win first prize in the dance contest.

❶ want는 to부정사를 목적어로 취하는 동사이고, myself는 주어와 목적어가 같을 때 사용하는 재귀대명사이다.

❷ be good at은 '~을 잘하다'는 뜻이고, 전치사 at 뒤에는 동명사 playing을 사용한다.

❸ 'feel+형용사'로 '~하게 느끼다'라는 의미이다.

❹ 빈도부사 usually는 일반동사 앞에 사용한다.

❺ practice는 동명사(drawing)를 목적어로 취하는 동사이다.

Listen & Speak 1 A-2

G: Ted, look at this movie poster. I want to see this movie.

B: ❶It looks interesting. Can you tell me about it, Amy?

G: Yes. It is about a hero ❷who saves the Earth.

B: It ❸looks like an SF movie.

G: Yes, it is. Actually, SF is my favorite kind of movie. I like the scenes ❹made with computer technology. They are fantastic and look real.

B: That's cool. I am free this weekend. ❺Let's go to see it together.

G: Sounds good.

❶ 'look+형용사'는 '~하게 보이다'는 의미이다.

❷ 관계대명사절로 선행사 a hero를 수식하는 역할을 한다. 선행사가 단수명사인 a hero이므로 주격 관계대명사 뒤에 단수동사 saves를 사용해야 한다.

❸ 'look like+명사'로 '~처럼 보이다'는 의미이다.

❹ made는 '만들어진'의 의미로 명사 the scenes를 수식하는 수동의 의미를 가진 과거분사이다.

❺ 'Let's+동사원형' 형태로 '~하자'라는 권유의 표현이다.

Communication Task Step 2

A: What is your nickname?

B: My nickname is Speedy ❶because I can run fast.

C: What do you like most?

B: What I like most is to play baseball.

D: Can you tell me about your dream job?

B: I want to be a baseball player.

A: What is your motto?

B: My motto is "You can go ❷forward slowly, but never go back."

❶ because는 이유의 부사절 접속사로 뒤에 '주어+동사'가 온다. 'because of'는 전치사구로 뒤에 명사가 온다.

❷ forward는 부사로 '앞으로'의 의미로 동사 go를 수식한다.

Wrap Up

W: Today, we have a new student Hojun. Hojun, can you please introduce yourself to the class?

B: Yes. Hi, my name is Kim Hojun. I am from Busan. Nice to meet you.

W: ❶Can you tell us more about yourself?

B: Yes. I like sports, especially soccer. I want to join a sports club.

W: Is there anything else ❷you want to tell your new friends?

B: I want to get along with everyone. Please help me because I'm new here.

W: Thanks, Hojun. Welcome to our class.

❶ 궁금증을 표현하거나 보다 많은 정보를 알고 싶을 때 사용하는 표현이다. 'I'd like to know more about ~.'으로 표현할 수도 있다.

❷ anything else와 you 사이에 목적격 관계대명사 that이 생략되어 있다.

다음 우리말과 일치하도록 빈칸에 알맞은 말을 쓰시오.

Warm Up

B1: Hello, my name is Kim Chanho. I _____ _____ _____ you about _____. I'm _____ _____ music. I_____ _____ _____ _____ the drums.

G1: Hi! I am Teri. I like running in the evening. I feel _____ _____ I exercise.

B2: Hello, my name is Jack. I'_____ _____ in the stars. I _____ go out _____ _____ stars at night.

G2: I am Lee Bora. I want to be a _____ in the future, so I _____ _____ when I have free time.

B3: I am Mark. I like dancing. I want to _____ first prize in the dance _____.

Listen & Speak 1 A

1. **G:** Jiho, _____ was your first day of third _____?
   B: It was _____ good. The teachers and my new classmates are all good.
   G: That sounds _____. Who is your _____ _____?
   B: My homeroom teacher is Mr. Kim. He _____ math.
   G: _____ _____ _____ _____ _____ more _____ him?
   B: Yes. He is _____ and _____ us some _____ _____ about math. It was _____.
   G: Cool! I hope you _____ _____ math.

2. **G:** Ted, look at this movie poster. I want _____ _____ this movie.
   B: It _____ interesting. Can you tell me about it, Amy?
   G: Yes. It is _____ a hero _____ _____ the Earth.
   B: It _____ _____ an SF movie.
   G: Yes, it is. Actually, SF is my _____ kind of movie. I like the _____ with computer technology. They are _____ and look _____.
   B: That's _____. I am free this weekend. Let's go to see it together.
   G: _____ good.

해석

B1: 안녕, 내 이름은 김찬호야. 너에게 나에 대해 말해주고 싶어. 나는 음악에 관심이 있어. 나는 드럼을 잘 쳐.

G1: 안녕. 나는 Teri야. 나는 저녁에 달리는 것을 좋아해. 나는 달릴 때 상쾌함을 느껴.

B2: 안녕, 내 이름은 Jack이야. 나는 별들에 관심이 있어. 나는 보통 밤에 별을 보러 나가.

G2: 나는 이보라야. 나는 미래에 디자이너가 되고 싶어서, 시간이 날 때 그림 그리는 연습을 해.

B3: 나는 Mark야. 나는 춤추는 걸 좋아해. 나는 춤 대회에서 1등을 하고 싶어.

1. **G:** 지호야, 너의 3학년 첫 날은 어땠어?
   B: 꽤 좋았어. 선생님들과 새로운 반 친구들 모두 좋아.
   G: 그거 좋네. 담임 선생님은 누구셔?
   B: 내 담임 선생님은 김 선생님이셔. 그는 수학을 가르치셔.
   G: 나에게 그에 대해 더 말해 줄 수 있니?
   B: 응. 그는 유머가 있으시고 우리에게 수학에 대한 재미있는 몇 가지 이야기를 해 주셨어. 그것은 흥미로웠어.
   G: 멋지네! 네가 수학 공부를 즐기기 바라.

2. **G:** Ted, 이 영화 포스터 좀 봐. 이 영화 보고 싶어.
   B: 그거 재미있어 보이네. 나에게 그것에 관해 말해 줄 수 있니, Amy?
   G: 응. 그것은 지구를 구하는 영웅에 대한 거야.
   B: 공상 과학 영화 같네.
   G: 응, 맞아. 사실 공상 과학은 내가 가장 좋아하는 영화 장르야. 나는 컴퓨터 기술로 제작된 장면들을 좋아해. 그 장면들은 환상적이고 진짜 같아 보여.
   B: 그거 멋지네. 나 이번 주말에 시간 있어. 같이 그거 보러 가자.
   G: 좋아.

Listen & Speak 1 B

A: Can you tell me _____ your plan for this weekend?

B: Yes. I am going to _____ a birthday party.

A: Can you tell me about your _____ for the year?

B: Yes. I want to _____ _____ fast food.

A: 나에게 너의 이번 주말 계획에 대해 말해 줄 수 있니?
B: 응. 나는 생일 파티를 할 거야.
A: 나에게 너의 올해 목표에 대해 말해 줄 수 있니?
B: 응. 나는 패스트푸드를 그만 먹고 싶어.

Listen & Speak 2 A

1. **G:** I often _____ _____ with my family. _____ I like _____ about traveling is trying new foods.

2. **B:** My _____ subject is music. I can play the drums and guitar. _____ them, _____ the guitar is _____ I like most.

3. **G:** This is a picture of Dora. She is my best friend, _____ _____ a pet. _____ with her in my free time is _____ I like most.

1. **G:** 나는 가끔 나의 가족들과 여행을 가. 여행에 관해 내가 가장 좋아하는 것은 새로운 음식들을 먹어보는 거야.

2. **B:** 내가 가장 좋아하는 과목은 음악이야. 나는 드럼과 기타를 연주할 수 있어. 그것들 중에서, 기타를 연주하는 것이 내가 가장 좋아하는 거야.

3. **G:** 이것은 Dora 사진이야. 그녀는 단순히 애완동물이 아니라, 나의 가장 친한 친구야. 여가시간에 그녀와 함께 노는 것이 내가 가장 좋아하는 거야.

Real Life Talk

Seho: Nice to meet you. I'_____ _____ _____ join your photo club.

Bora: Thank you _____ your interest in the club. Can you tell me _____ _____?

Seho: Yes. My name is Kim Seho. I am _____ the _____ grade, class 8.

Andy: Tell me _____. _____ do you like to do _____ in your free time?

Seho: Well, _____ I like most is _____ _____ pictures.

Bora: That's great. What is your dream for the future?

Seho: I want to be a _____.

Andy: Then you made the right _____. You can learn a lot of _____ skills here. Welcome to our club.

Seho: Thank you. I'm so _____!

세호: 만나서 반가워. 나는 너희의 사진 동아리에 가입하고 싶어.
보라: 동아리에 관심을 가져 줘서 고마워. 너에 대해 말해 줄래?
세호: 응. 내 이름은 김세호야. 나는 3학년 8반이야.
Andy: 좀 더 말해 줘. 너는 여가 시간에 무엇을 하는 걸 가장 좋아하니?
세호: 음, 내가 가장 좋아하는 건 사진 찍는 거야.
보라: 멋지다. 너의 장래 희망은 뭐니?
세호: 나는 사진 작가가 되고 싶어.
Andy: 그러면 너는 정말 좋은 선택을 했구나. 너는 여기서 사진 찍는 기술을 많이 배울 수 있어. 우리 동아리에 온 걸 환영해.
세호: 고마워. 나도 기뻐!

Communication Task Step 2

A: What is your _____?

B: My nickname is Speedy _____ I can run fast.

C: What do you like _____?

B: _____ _____ _____ _____ is to play baseball.

D: _____ _____ _____ _____ _____ your dream job?

B: I want to be a baseball player.

A: What is your _____?

B: My _____ is "You can go _____ slowly, but never go _____."

해석

A: 너의 별명이 뭐니?

B: 내 별명은 스피디인데 나는 빨리 달릴 수 있기 때문이야.

C: 너는 무엇을 가장 좋아하니?

B: 내가 가장 좋아하는 것은 야구를 하는 거야.

D: 나에게 네가 꿈꾸는 직업에 대해 말해 줄 수 있니?

B: 나는 야구 선수가 되고 싶어.

A: 너의 좌우명은 뭐니?

B: 나의 좌우명은 "앞으로 천천히 나아갈 수 있지만, 절대 물러설 수는 없다"야.

Wrap Up

W: Today, we have a _____ _____ Hojun. Hojun, can you please _____ _____ to the class?

B: Yes. Hi, my name is Kim Hojun. I am _____ Busan. Nice to meet you.

W: _____ _____ _____ _____ _____ about yourself?

B: Yes. I like sports, _____ soccer. I want to join a sports club.

W: Is there _____ else you want to tell your new friends?

B: I want to _____ _____ _____ everyone. Please help me _____ I'm new here.

W: Thanks, Hojun. _____ to our class.

W: 오늘, 새로 온 학생 호준이가 있어요. 호준아, 반 친구들에게 너를 소개해 주겠니?

B: 네. 안녕, 내 이름은 김호준이야. 나는 부산에서 왔어. 만나서 반가워.

W: 너에 대해 더 말해 줄 수 있니?

B: 네. 나는 스포츠, 특히 축구를 좋아해. 나는 스포츠 동아리에 가입하고 싶어.

W: 너의 새로운 친구들에게 더 말하고 싶은 게 있니?

B: 모두와 함께 잘 지내고 싶어. 나는 이곳에 새로 왔으니 도와주길 바라.

W: 고마워, 호준아. 우리 반에 온 것을 환영한단다.

01 우리말에 맞도록 주어진 단어를 이용하여 5단어로 쓰시오.

> • 그녀에 관해 말해 줄 수 있니? (tell, about)

➡ _____ _____ _____ _____ _____ her?

02 다음 대화의 빈칸에 공통으로 들어갈 말로 알맞은 것은?

> A: _____ your plan for this weekend?
> B: Yes. I am going to have a birthday party.
> A: _____ your goal for the year?
> B: Yes. I want to stop eating fast food.

① Are you curious about
② What's your favorite
③ What would you like for
④ Can you tell me about
⑤ Are you interested in

03 다음 글의 빈칸에 들어갈 말로 가장 알맞은 것은?

> My favorite subject is music. I can play the drums and guitar.
> Among them, _____ .

① I'd like to know how to play the drums
② I am having trouble with playing the guitar
③ my favorite subject is music
④ I wonder if I can play the guitar well
⑤ playing the guitar is what I like most

04 다음 대화의 밑줄 친 우리말에 맞게 문장의 빈칸을 채우시오.

> Hi! I am Teri. I like running in the evening. <u>운동을 할 때 상쾌함을 느껴</u>.

➡ I feel _____ _____ I exercise.

[01~02] 다음 글을 읽고 물음에 답하시오.

Teri: I often go traveling with my family. (A)
_____ I like most about (a)(travel) is
trying new foods.

Sumi: This is a picture of Dora. She is my
best friend, not just a pet. (b)(Play) with
her in my free time is (A)_____ I like
most.

 01 위 글의 빈칸 (A)에 공통으로 들어갈 말로 알맞은 것을 모두
고르시오.

① That[that]　　　② How[how]

③ What[what]　　④ Whether[whether]

⑤ The[the] thing that

서답형
02 위 글의 괄호 (a)와 (b)의 단어를 알맞은 형태로 고치시오.

➡ (a) _____　(b) _____

서답형
03 다음 대화의 밑줄 친 우리말에 맞게 주어진 어구를 이용하
여 영어로 쓰시오. (어형 변화 필수)

G: Ted, look at this movie poster. I want to
see this movie.

B: It looks interesting. Can you tell me
about it, Amy?

G: Yes. 그것은 지구를 구하는 영웅에 관한 것이
야.

B: It looks like an SF movie.

G: Yes, it is.

it / about / a hero / who / save / the Earth / is

➡ _____

[04~05] 다음 대화를 읽고 물음에 답하시오.

A: We would like to know more about you,
Minho. (A)_____

B: I like pizza most.

C: Can you tell me about your favorite
subject?

B: Art is (B)내가 가장 좋아하는 것. I want to
become an art teacher like Mr. Kim.

D: What do you like to do after school?

B: I like to practice taegwondo and sing
songs.

04 위 대화의 빈칸 (A)에 들어갈 말로 알맞은 것은?

① Do you like pizza?

② What's your favorite music?

③ What do you think of Italian food?

④ What is your favorite food?

⑤ What do you want to eat?

서답형
05 위 대화의 빈칸 (B)의 우리말에 맞게 4단어로 쓰시오.

➡ _____

06 다음 대화의 밑줄 친 부분의 의도로 알맞은 것은?

G: Who is your homeroom teacher?

B: My homeroom teacher is Mr. Kim. He
teaches math.

G: Can you tell me more about him?

B: Yes. He is humorous and kind.

① 알고 있는지 묻기　　② 의무 표현하기

③ 확신 표현하기　　　④ 궁금증 표현하기

⑤ 의견 묻기

[07~08] 다음 대화를 읽고 물음에 답하시오.

Seho: Nice to meet you. I'ⓐd like to join your photo club.

Bora: Thank you ⓑfor your interest in the club. Can you tell me about yourself?

Seho: Yes. My name is Kim Seho. I am in the third grade, class 8.

Andy: Tell me more. What do you like to do most in your free time?

Seho: Well, ⓒthat I like most is to take pictures.

Bora: That's great. What is your dream for the future?

Seho: I want ⓓto be a photographer.

Andy: Then you made the right choice. You can learn ⓔa lot of photo-taking skills here. Welcome to our club.

Seho: Thank you. I'm so glad!

07 위 대화의 밑줄 친 ⓐ~ⓔ 중 어법상 어색한 것은?

① ⓐ   ② ⓑ   ③ ⓒ   ④ ⓓ   ⑤ ⓔ

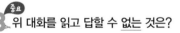
08 위 대화를 읽고 답할 수 없는 것은?

① What does Seho want to do?
② What does Seho like to do most in his free time?
③ What skills does Andy have?
④ What is Seho's dream for the future?
⑤ What can Seho learn in the photo club?

서답형
09 다음 글의 빈칸에 들어갈 말에 대한 영어 풀이를 보고 주어진 철자로 시작하여 쓰시오.

My favorite subject is music. I can play the drums and guitar. _____ them, playing the guitar is what I like most.

---

in the middle of a group

➡ A_____

10 주어진 문장에 이어질 대화의 순서를 바르게 배열하시오.

Can you tell me about your plan for this weekend?

(A) Can you tell me about your goal for the year?
(B) Yes. I am going to have a birthday party.
(C) Yes. I want to stop eating fast food.

➡ _____

11 다음 두 사람의 대화가 어색한 것은?

① A: Can you tell me about your dream job?
B: I want to be a soccer player.
② A: Can you tell us about yourself?
B: My friends are all kind to me.
③ A: What is your favorite food?
B: I like pizza most.
④ A: What do you like to do most in your free time?
B: Well, what I like most is to take pictures.
⑤ A: I'd like to join your photo club.
B: Thank you for your interest in the club.

서답형
12 다음 글의 밑줄 친 우리말에 맞게 주어진 단어를 알맞은 순서로 배열하시오.

I often go traveling with my family. 여행에 관해 내가 가장 좋아하는 것은(traveling / what / like / most / I / about) is trying new foods.

➡ _____

[01~02] 다음 대화를 읽고 물음에 답하시오.

W: Today, we have a new student Hojun. Hojun, can you please introduce yourself to the class?

B: Yes. Hi, my name is Kim Hojun. I am from Busan. Nice to meet you.

W: (A)너에 관해 더 말해 줄 수 있니?

B: Yes. I like sports, especially soccer. I want to join a sports club.

W: Is there anything else you want to tell your new friends?

B: (B)나는 모두와 잘 지내고 싶어. Please help me because I'm new here.

W: Thanks, Hojun. Welcome to our class..

01 위 대화의 밑줄 친 (A)의 우리말에 맞게 주어진 단어를 활용하여 영작하시오.

> can / tell / us / more / yourself

➡ _____

02 위 대화의 밑줄 친 (B)의 우리말에 맞게 'get'과 'everyone'을 활용하여 영작하시오.

➡ _____

03 다음 대화의 빈칸에 들어갈 말로 자연스러운 것을 〈보기〉에서 찾아 쓰시오.

A: What is your nickname?
B: My nickname is Speedy (A)_____
C: What do you like most?
B: (B)_____
D: Can you tell me about your dream job?
B: I want to be a baseball player.
A: (C)_____
B: My motto is "You can go forward slowly, but never go back."

┤ 보기 ├
• What I like most is to play baseball.
• because I can run fast.
• What is your motto?

➡ (A) _____
(B) _____
(C) _____

[04~05] 다음 대화를 읽고 물음에 답하시오.

G: Ted, look at this movie poster. I want to see this movie.

B: It looks interesting. Can you tell me about it, Amy?

G: Yes. _____

B: It looks like an SF movie.

G: Yes, it is. Actually, SF is my favorite kind of movie. I like the scenes made with computer technology. They are fantastic and look real.

B: That's cool. I am free this weekend. Let's go to see it together.

G: Sounds good.

04 위 대화의 밑줄 친 질문에 대한 답을 주어진 단어를 활용하여 조건에 맞게 영작하시오.

┤ 조건 ├
• 전치사 about을 사용할 것
• 관계대명사를 사용할 것.
• 현재시제를 사용할 것
(a hero, save, the Earth)

➡ It's _____ .

05 위 대화의 내용을 정리할 때 빈칸에 알맞은 말을 쓰시오.

• What Amy wants to see: a (a)_____
• When Amy is going to see it with Ted: (b)_____

Grammar

교과서

① 동사 강조

- I **do love** swimming in the lake. 나는 호수에서 수영하는 것을 정말 좋아한다.
- Sumin doesn't like horror movies, but she **does like** animated films.
  수민이는 공포 영화를 좋아하지 않지만, 애니메이션 영화는 정말 좋아한다.

■ 문장에서 동사의 앞에 do를 배치해서 동사의 의미를 강조할 수 있다. 주어의 인칭과 수 및 시제에 맞춰 do/does/did 등을 활용하며, really의 의미로 해석한다.

- Ted **did see** the accident. Ted가 그 사고를 정말 봤다.
- Jane **does prefer** the mineral water. Jane은 미네랄 워터를 정말 선호한다.

■ 명령문을 강조할 때도 앞에 Do를 사용할 수 있다.

- Be kind to others! = **Do** be kind to others! 다른 사람들에게 정말 친절하게 대하라!

■ do는 동사를 강조하는 반면에 재귀대명사는 주어를 강조한다.

- Mary will do it **herself**. = Mary **herself** will do it. Mary가 직접 그것을 할 것이다.

■ It ~ that 강조구문에서는 주어와 목적어 및 부사(구/절)를 강조한다. 강조하려는 대상에 따라 that을 관계대명사 who/which 등으로 대체할 수 있다.

- Kevin stole the book from Susan's house yesterday. Kevin이 어제 Susan의 집에서 그 책을 훔쳤다.
  → **It was** Kevin **that[who]** stole the book from Susan's house yesterday.
    어제 Susan의 집에서 그 책을 훔친 것은 바로 **Kevin**이었다.
  → **It was** the book **that[which]** Kevin stole from Susan's house yesterday.
    Kevin이 어제 Susan의 집에서 훔친 것은 바로 **그 책**이었다.
  → **It was** yesterday **that** Kevin stole the book from Susan's house.
    Kevin이 Susan의 집에서 그 책을 훔친 것은 바로 **어제**였다.
  → **It was** from Susan's house **that** Kevin stole the book yesterday.
    어제 Kevin이 그 책을 훔친 것은 바로 **Susan의 집에서**였다.

핵심 Check

1. 괄호 안에서 알맞은 단어를 고르시오.
   (1) I (am / do) feel bad when I pass by smokers.
   (2) He (do / does) want to meet you today.

② 관계대명사 what

- Tom gave her **what** he had bought. Tom은 그가 산 것을 그녀에게 줬다.
- This is **what** she has wanted. 이것은 그녀가 원해 왔던 것이다.

■ what은 선행사를 포함하는 관계대명사이다.
  - I will do **what** I can. = I will do **(all) the thing(s) that** I can. 나는 내가 할 수 있는 (모든) 것을 할 것이다.
  - **What** she told me yesterday is true. = **The thing that** she told me yesterday is true. 그녀가 어제 나에게 말했던 것은 사실이다.

■ 관계대명사 what은 명사절을 이끈다.
  - **What he said** to me was shocking. 그가 내게 말해 준 것은 충격적이었다. (주어)
  - I can't believe **what she did** in such a short time. 그렇게 단시간에 그녀가 해낸 것을 나는 믿을 수 없다. (목적어)
  - They are familiar with **what is baked** now. 그들은 지금 구워지는 것에 익숙하다. (전치사의 목적어)
  - This is **what I told you** last Friday. 이것이 지난 금요일에 너에게 말한 것이다. (보어)

■ 의문대명사 what과 문장의 구조는 동일하며, 구분은 해석으로 한다. 관계대명사 what은 '~하는 것'으로, 의문대명사 what은 '무엇(을/이)'로 해석한다.
  - She asked me **what** I hid in my hand. 그녀는 내가 손에 무엇을 감췄는지 물어보았다. (의문대명사)
  - **What** I brought here is a puppy. 내가 여기 가져온 것은 강아지이다. (관계대명사)

■ 관계대명사 what의 관용적인 표현들
  - A man should not be judged by **what he has**. 사람은 그의 재산으로 판단하면 안 된다.
  - Abe is **what is called** a lazy worm. Abe는 말하자면 게으른 벌레이다.
  - **What's better[worse]** is that she doesn't know the news. 더욱 좋은[나쁜] 것은 그녀가 그 소식을 모른다는 것이다.

핵심 Check

2. 다음 우리말에 맞게 괄호 안의 어구를 바르게 배열하시오.

(1) Janet은 그녀가 만든 것을 나에게 주었다. (what, had, me, made, Janet, she, gave)

➡ _____

(2) 그 공장에서 생산되는 것은 자동차이다. (the factory, what, cars, are, produced, in, are)

➡ _____

01 다음 문장에서 어법상 어색한 부분을 바르게 고쳐 쓰시오.

(1) She judged him by which he had.

_____ ➡ _____

(2) They does love the work of Gustav Climt.

_____ ➡ _____

(3) Shakira did felt very proud of her son.

_____ ➡ _____

(4) All what he said was a lie.

_____ ➡ _____

02 다음 중 어법상 바르지 않은 것은?

① What was taken by her camera was a UFO.
② The workers did built the museum about 100 years ago.
③ John does love what she paints.
④ What the letter says is that I should go back home.
⑤ They all do like her novel.

03 다음 대화의 밑줄 친 부분 중에서 어법상 잘못된 곳을 고르시오.

> A: ①Are you ②tired ③from the trip to Vietnam?
> B: No. I ④do ⑤feeling good.

04 다음 우리말에 맞게 주어진 단어를 바르게 배열하시오. (필요하면 어형을 바꿀 것)

(1) 그가 종이에 쓴 것은 흥미로웠다. (was, the paper, he, on, what, interesting, write)

➡ _____

(2) 그녀는 그녀의 엄마가 만드는 것을 정말 자랑스럽게 느낀다. (she, of, mother, feel, do, proud, her, make, what)

➡ _____

01 다음 빈칸에 알맞은 것은?

Is this _____ you want to buy?

① which ② those
③ where ④ what
⑤ for what

02 다음 문장에서 어법상 틀린 부분을 찾아 바르게 고쳐 쓰시오.

He failed in his business, and that was worse, he fell ill.

➡ _____ ➡ _____

03 다음 중 두 문장의 뜻이 같지 않은 것은?

① I do spend a lot of time watching TV these days.
→ I really spend much time watching TV these days.
② Jenny will show me what she took with her camera.
→ Jenny will show me the pictures that were taken with her camera.
③ Mom made me what I don't want.
→ Mom made me the thing that I don't want.
④ Sarah did break her leg at the basketball game.
→ Sarah really broke her leg at the basketball game.
⑤ King Arthur did find the legendary sword.
→ King Arthur was able to find the legendary sword.

04 다음 빈칸에 알맞은 말이 순서대로 바르게 짝지어진 것은?

• Jina _____ love skiing.
• _____ I hope is to hear from you.

① was – That ② did – How
③ does – What ④ is – What
⑤ does – That

05 다음 빈칸에 알맞은 것은?

It is the most boring magazine _____ I have ever read.

① who ② where ③ what
④ that ⑤ whom

06 다음 빈칸에 공통으로 들어갈 말로 알맞은 것은?

• Kevin _____ feel at ease with her.
• Mom always _____ the dishes right after dinner.

① does ② has ③ do
④ have ⑤ doesn't

07 다음 중 밑줄 친 부분이 어법상 올바른 것은?

① The officer did warned them immediately.
② Do be quiet!
③ The girl did changed her mind.
④ She does believed it was not a dream.
⑤ Sam's uncles do looks happy.

다음 밑줄 친 what 중에서 나머지 넷과 용법이 다른 것은?

① <u>What</u> he said inspired the audience.
② Susan received <u>what</u> he had sent her.
③ I do like <u>what</u> was shown by the magician.
④ I don't know <u>what</u> Mother is cooking.
⑤ This is <u>what</u> they suggested at the meeting.

09 다음 중 어법상 옳은 문장은?

① Is this dog what you were looking for?
② He bought a new car his wife.
③ All the students think what the teacher is giving them special lessons.
④ The boy likes the toy what his aunt bought for him yesterday.
⑤ What she said him was really touching.

10 다음 중 어법상 어색한 문장을 모두 고르면?

① The fans believe what BTS said.
② That is not the thing which the president was trying to say.
③ She will see the movie that the director filmed.
④ This is not the book what she wanted to read.
⑤ Which he told his students at the graduation ceremony made them cry.

11 다음 밑줄 친 부분 중 어법상 어색한 것은?

① All of them <u>do think</u> he is guilty.
② James <u>does teach</u> art six years ago at the school.
③ He <u>did cut</u> his hair this morning.
④ She <u>did find</u> him behind the curtain soon.
⑤ Running a hotel <u>does require</u> a lot of time and energy.

12 다음 빈칸에 들어갈 말로 어색한 것은?

> A: Scott, you don't play Star Craft any longer, do you?
> B: No, but I _____ when I was young.

① used to play a lot
② played it a lot
③ did played it a lot
④ did play a lot
⑤ would play it a lot

 13 다음 중 어법상 옳은 문장을 모두 고르면?

> ⓐ The kids are expected to do which their parents want them to do.
> ⓑ Taking a walk is an exercise what gives you more energy.
> ⓒ The thing cannot be cured must be endured.
> ⓓ That will make them think about what they should or shouldn't do.
> ⓔ I can't believe that I've just read in this book.
> ⓕ Making a plan for holidays, you should consider what you can do.
> ⓖ What you teach can be different from that you know.

➡ _____

14 다음 문장의 밑줄 친 부분을 강조하는 문장으로 알맞은 것은?

> Sandra <u>made</u> the plan yesterday.

① Sandra made the only plan yesterday.
② Sandra did made the plan yesterday.
③ Sandra made the very plan yesterday.
④ Sandra did make the plan yesterday.
⑤ Sandra makes did the plan yesterday.

15 다음 중 밑줄 친 부분의 쓰임이 주어진 문장의 밑줄 친 <u>do</u>와 같은 것은?

> The students <u>do</u> feel that something worse than before will happen today.

① Mom has lots of things to <u>do</u>.
② They <u>did</u> their role as extras.
③ I don't eat it, but she <u>does</u> enjoy it.
④ Everyone agrees you <u>did</u> your best at the contest.
⑤ I <u>do</u> not have much information.

16 다음 우리말을 영작할 때, 빈칸에 들어갈 알맞은 말을 쓰시오.

> 이제 그는 과거의 그가 아니다.

➡ Now, he is not _____ he _____.

17 다음 밑줄 친 what의 용법이 나머지 넷과 <u>다른</u> 것은?

① The girl started to eat <u>what</u> they had given her.
② That volunteer work is <u>what</u> she wants to do.
③ She accepted <u>what</u> he offered.
④ I wonder <u>what</u> he gave her.
⑤ That's <u>what</u> I meant to say.

18 다음 중 어법상 옳은 문장은?

① What she do like to have right now is a piece of pizza.
② Frank did made what his father designed.
③ Sean does love what he is doing.
④ Tony did play the game what he was good at.
⑤ He does show her what he invented it.

19 Which of the following has the same usage as the underlined part below?

> He knows I <u>do</u> feel nervous on the stage.

① He doesn't teach how to swim, <u>does</u> he?
② The college students are <u>doing</u> some research on the bacteria.
③ What Kitty <u>did</u> was to jump off the roof into the pool.
④ Jane folds her ears and so <u>do</u> I.
⑤ I'm sure that I <u>did</u> lock the safe.

20 다음 우리말을, 주어진 단어들을 배열하여 영작할 때, 네 번째로 오는 단어는?

> 그녀가 하고 있는 말에 집중하라.
> (to, is, pay, she, saying, attention, what)

① pay   ② is   ③ she
④ what   ⑤ attention

21 다음 중 어법상 <u>어색한</u> 문장은?

① He forgot the thing what she did.
② They know the reason why it's cold.
③ She knew the way he solved the problem.
④ This is how he killed the big bear.
⑤ That is what Mike wants to buy.

01 다음 대화의 빈칸을 채우되, 동사를 강조하는 'do'를 활용하시오.

(1) A: Did the old man really build the huge sand castle by himself? It's amazing.

B: Yeah. He _____ _____ it.

(2) A: She doesn't look good. Don't you think that she overworked yesterday?

B: I _____ _____ so. I'm so worried about her.

(3) A: Can you believe Cindy wrote this letter to her boyfriend?

B: She _____ _____ this letter to him, though he can't read it yet.

02 다음 문장에서 어법상 <u>어색한</u> 부분을 찾아 바르게 고쳐 다시 쓰시오.

(1) I don't believe that they said to me the other day.

➡ _____

(2) Show her that you put in your mouth.

➡ _____

(3) She did felt friendly to Mike.

➡ _____

(4) I do loved Susan, but she left me forever.

➡ _____

(5) What she asked him to help her was not true.

➡ _____

03 주어진 두 문장을 관계대명사 what을 이용하여, 하나의 문장으로 만드시오.

(1) • Sarah bought the things.
• They were comic books.

➡ _____

(2) • Robert couldn't believe the thing.
• The researchers explained it.

➡ _____

(3) • The thing was discussed.
• It was shocking.

➡ _____

04 우리말과 일치하도록 괄호 안에 주어진 어휘를 활용하여, 글자 수에 맞게 영작하시오.

(1) 그녀가 동굴 안에서 발견한 것이 세상을 놀라게 했다. (find, cave, surprise, 10 단어)

➡ _____

(2) 이 방에서는 정말 조용해라! (quiet, do, 6 단어)

➡ _____

(3) 그녀가 시장에서 사온 것들은 모두 비싼 것이었다. (buy, expensive, from, all, 9 단어)

➡ _____

05 다음 각 문장을 밑줄 친 부분을 강조하는 문장으로 바꿔 쓰시오.

(1) Charlie <u>found</u> his missing child.

➡ _____

(2) He <u>knows</u> many K-pop singers.

➡ _____

(3) Jeremy <u>wrote</u> those essays last year.

➡ _____

06 다음 문장을 각각의 주어진 조건에 맞게 강조하는 문장으로 바꿔 쓰시오.

> • Carl bought the hamster yesterday.

(1) Carl 강조. 재귀대명사 사용.

➡ _____

(2) the hamster 강조. It ~ that 구문 사용.

➡ _____

(3) bought 강조.

➡ _____

(4) yesterday 강조.

➡ _____

07 다음 문장에서 어법상 <u>어색한</u> 부분을 찾아 바르게 고쳐 다시 쓰시오.

(1) She finally accepted that he offered.

➡ _____

(2) He did felt satisfied with the result.

➡ _____

(3) It is quite different from which they have been waiting for.

➡ _____

(4) What I saw him yesterday is not true.

➡ _____

(5) What people believed in the past does surprises me.

➡ _____

08 다음 우리말을 영작할 때, 빈칸에 들어갈 알맞은 단어를 쓰시오.

(1) 그녀는 재즈 음악을 정말 좋아한다.

→ She _____ like jazz music.

(2) 그 회의에서 논의되는 것은 현재의 경제 상황에 매우 중요하다.

→ The thing _____ is being discussed at the meeting is critical for the current economic situation.

(3) 그 곰이 개를 정말 죽였다.

→ The bear did _____ the dog.

(4) 너에게 중요한 것들이 나에게는 중요하지 않다.

→ _____ are important to you _____ not important to me.

09 다음 그림을 보고, 우리말에 맞게 빈칸을 채우되, 괄호 안의 어휘를 이용하시오.

> _____ (John은 정말 치통을 느꼈기 때문에), he went to the dentist for treatment. (feel, do, as, a toothache)

➡ _____

Reading

My Dream House

Have you ever thought about your dream house? Today, in class, we
현재완료 – 경험
created our dream house. Here are some of the dream houses that we
Here are + 복수 주어　　　　　목적격 관계대명사(생략 가능)
made.

A House in Nature - Minho

Nature is my good friend. I do feel good when I walk in the forest.
feel 강조
I'd like to have a dream house in the countryside. It should have a big
~하고 싶다　　　　　　　　　　　　= The dream house
garden with many flowers and trees. I am always excited by the sound
~이 있는　　　　　　　　　　감정을 느낄 때 과거분사
of birds. It will be wonderful to wake up in the morning and listen to
가주어　　　　　진주어　　　　　　　wake up과 병렬구조
the songs of the birds. Also, I'd like to have many pets. It will be fun to
　　　　　　　　　　　　　　　　　　　　가주어　　　진주어
play with them!

A Fun Place - Julie

Welcome to my dream house! Having fun is what I want most, so my
동명사 주어　　관계대명사 what(~하는 것)
dream house is full of exciting things. It has a theater in the basement.
신나는 감정을 유발할 때 현재분사
There, I can eat cookies and enjoy my favorite movies. My dream
= In the theater
house has a game room on the second floor. I can play many different

kinds of games there.
= in the game room

create: 만들다, 창작하다
forest: 숲
would like to V: ~하고 싶다
countryside: 시골 지역, 전원 지대
excited: 신이 난
wonderful: 아주 멋진, 신나는, 훌륭한
basement: 지하실, 지하층
floor: 층
favorite: 가장 좋아하는

확인문제

● 다음 문장이 본문의 내용과 일치하면 T, 일치하지 않으면 F를 쓰시오.

1　The students made their dream house in class. ☐

2　Minho thinks that nature is his good friend. ☐

3　Walking in the forest makes Minho feel lonely. ☐

4　Minho's dream house has a theater. ☐

5　Julie's dream house enables her to play various kinds of games. ☐

My house also has a swimming pool. I want to do fun things with my
friends in my house. You can be my guest!

A Place for Family - Misun

My family is the most important thing to me. In my dream house,
my family feels safe and comfortable. At the gate, you can find
a beautifully designed sign with my family's picture on it. When
you enter the house, you will see a large living room. My family
sometimes plays board games and sings there. It will have a garden
with a large picnic table for family picnics. There, we will enjoy
barbecues. Do you like my dream house?

A House with New Technology - Bryan

I am an early adopter of new technology. I do like to use new
products and technology before others. When I get near my house, the
front door recognizes my face and opens automatically. The furniture
checks the weather conditions and advises me on what to wear. The
bathroom mirror tells me my weight and the condition of my health.
A robot cleans the house and cooks for me. This is what I can imagine
about my dream house.

swimming pool: 수영장
guest: 손님
comfortable: 편안한
gate: 정문, 대문
picture: 사진
enter: ~로 들어가다
living room: 거실
early adopter: 남들보다 먼저 신기술을 사용하는 사람
product: 물건, 제품
technology: 기술
get near: 가까이 가다, 접근하다
recognize: 알아보다, 인식하다
automatically: 자동으로
furniture: 가구
advise: 조언하다
weight: 무게, 체중
imagine: 상상하다

 확인문제

● 다음 문장이 본문의 내용과 일치하면 T, 일치하지 않으면 F를 쓰시오.

1 Julie doesn't want anyone to come to her dream house. ☐

2 Misun didn't make a living room in her dream house. ☐

3 Misun wants to enjoy barbecues with her family in her dream house. ☐

4 Bryan wants a house where the latest technologies are used. ☐

5 In Bryan's dream house, he has to clean the house and cooks for himself. ☐

● 우리말을 참고하여 빈칸에 알맞은 말을 쓰시오.

My Dream House

1 _____ you _____ _____ about your dream house?

2 Today, in class, we _____ our dream house.

3 Here _____ some of the dream houses _____ we made.

A House in Nature - Minho

4 _____ is my good friend.

5 I _____ _____ _____ when I walk in the forest.

6 I'd _____ _____ _____ a dream house _____ the countryside.

7 It _____ _____ a big garden _____ many flowers and trees.

8 I _____ always _____ _____ the sound of birds.

9 It will be _____ _____ _____ _____ in the morning and _____ _____ the songs of the birds.

10 Also, I'd _____ _____ _____ many pets. It will be fun _____ _____ with them!

A Fun Place - Julie

11 Welcome _____ my dream house!

12 _____ _____ is _____ I want most, so my dream house _____ _____ _____ exciting things.

13 It has a theater _____ _____ _____ .

14 There, I can eat cookies and _____ my favorite _____ .

15 My dream house _____ a game room _____ the second _____ .

내가 **꿈꾸는 집**

1 여러분은 꿈의 집에 대해 생각해 본 적이 있나요?

2 오늘, 우리는 수업 시간에 우리가 꿈꾸는 집을 만들었습니다.

3 여기 우리가 만든 몇몇 꿈의 집이 있습니다.

자연 속의 집 – 민호

4 자연은 나의 좋은 친구입니다.

5 나는 숲속에서 걸을 때 기분이 정말 좋습니다.

6 나는 시골에 꿈의 집을 갖고 싶습니다.

7 집에는 많은 꽃과 나무가 있는 큰 정원이 있을 것입니다.

8 나는 항상 새소리에 신이 납니다.

9 아침에 깨어나서 새들의 노래 소리를 듣는 것은 멋질 것입니다.

10 또한 나는 많은 애완동물을 갖고 싶습니다. 그들과 노는 것은 매우 재미있을 것입니다!

재미있는 장소 – Julie

11 나의 꿈의 집에 온 것을 환영합니다!

12 즐겁게 지내는 것은 내가 가장 원하는 것입니다. 그래서 내 꿈의 집은 흥미로운 것들로 가득합니다.

13 집에는 지하에 영화관이 있습니다.

14 그곳에서 나는 쿠키를 먹을 수 있고 내가 좋아하는 영화들을 즐길 수 있습니다.

15 내 꿈의 집에는 2층에 게임방이 있습니다.

16 I can play many different _____ _____ _____ there.

17 My house also has _____ _____ _____.

18 I want to _____ _____ _____ with my friends in my house. You can be _____ _____!

A Place for Family - Misun

19 My family is _____ _____ _____ to me.

20 In my dream house, my family _____ _____ and _____.

21 _____ the gate, you can find a _____ _____ _____ with my family's picture _____ it.

22 When you _____ the house, you will _____ _____ _____ _____ _____.

23 My family sometimes plays _____ _____ and sings there.

24 It will have a garden with _____ _____ _____ for family picnics.

25 There, we will _____ barbecues. _____ _____ my dream house?

A House with New Technology - Bryan

26 I am _____ _____ _____ of new technology.

27 I _____ _____ to use new products and technology _____ others.

28 When I _____ _____ my house, the front door _____ my face and _____ automatically.

29 The furniture _____ the weather _____ and _____ me _____ what to wear.

30 The bathroom mirror _____ _____ my weight and the _____ of my health.

31 A robot _____ the house and _____ _____ me.

32 This is _____ _____ _____ _____ _____ about my dream house.

16 나는 그곳에서 많은 다양한 종류의 게임을 할 수 있습니다.

17 나의 집에는 또한 수영장이 있습니다.

18 나는 나의 집에서 친구들과 함께 즐거운 일들을 하고 싶습니다. 여러분도 나의 손님이 될 수 있습니다!

가족을 위한 장소 – 미선

19 나의 가족은 나에게 가장 중요한 것입니다.

20 내 꿈의 집에서 가족은 안전하고 편안함을 느낍니다.

21 현관에서 여러분은 가족 사진이 있는 아름답게 디자인된 문패를 발견할 수 있습니다.

22 여러분이 집에 들어서면 여러분은 큰 거실을 보게 될 것입니다.

23 나의 가족은 때때로 그곳에서 보드 게임도 하고 노래를 부르기도 합니다.

24 가족 소풍을 위한 커다란 피크닉 테이블이 있는 큰 정원을 갖게 될 것입니다.

25 그곳에서 우리는 바비큐를 즐길 것입니다. 내 꿈의 집이 마음에 드나요?

신기술이 있는 집 – Bryan

26 나는 남들보다 먼저 신기술을 써 보는 것을 좋아하는 사람입니다.

27 나는 새로운 제품이나 기술을 다른 사람보다 먼저 사용하는 것을 정말 좋아합니다.

28 내가 집 근처에 도착할 때, 현관문은 내 얼굴을 인식하고 자동으로 문을 엽니다.

29 가구는 날씨 상태를 확인하여 내게 무엇을 입을지 조언해 줍니다.

30 욕실 거울은 나에게 체중과 건강 상태를 알려 줍니다.

31 로봇은 집을 청소하고 나를 위해 요리합니다.

32 이것이 내가 나의 꿈의 집에 대해 상상할 수 있는 것입니다.

● 우리말을 참고하여 본문을 영작하시오.

My Dream House

1 여러분은 꿈의 집에 대해 생각해 본 적이 있나요?

➡ _____

2 오늘, 우리는 수업 시간에 우리가 꿈꾸는 집을 만들었습니다.

➡ _____

3 여기 우리가 만든 몇몇 꿈의 집이 있습니다.

➡ _____

A House in Nature - Minho

4 자연은 나의 좋은 친구입니다.

➡ _____

5 나는 숲속에서 걸을 때 기분이 정말 좋습니다.

➡ _____

6 나는 시골에 꿈의 집을 갖고 싶습니다.

➡ _____

7 집에는 많은 꽃과 나무가 있는 큰 정원이 있을 것입니다.

➡ _____

8 나는 항상 새소리에 신이 납니다.

➡ _____

9 아침에 깨어나서 새들의 노래 소리를 듣는 것은 멋질 것입니다.

➡ _____

10 또한 나는 많은 애완동물을 갖고 싶습니다. 그들과 노는 것은 매우 재미있을 것입니다!

➡ _____

A Fun Place - Julie

11 나의 꿈의 집에 온 것을 환영합니다!

➡ _____

12 즐겁게 지내는 것은 내가 가장 원하는 것입니다. 그래서 내 꿈의 집은 흥미로운 것들로 가득합니다.

➡ _____

13 집에는 지하에 영화관이 있습니다.

➡ _____

14 그곳에서 나는 쿠키를 먹을 수 있고 내가 좋아하는 영화들을 즐길 수 있습니다.

➡ _____

15 내 꿈의 집에는 2층에 게임방이 있습니다.

➡ _____

16 나는 그곳에서 많은 다양한 종류의 게임을 할 수 있습니다.

➡ _____

17 나의 집에는 또한 수영장이 있습니다.

➡ _____

18 나는 나의 집에서 친구들과 함께 즐거운 일들을 하고 싶습니다. 여러분도 나의 손님이 될 수 있습니다!

➡ _____

A Place for Family - Misun

19 나의 가족은 나에게 가장 중요한 것입니다.

➡ _____

20 내 꿈의 집에서 가족은 안전하고 편안함을 느낍니다.

➡ _____

21 현관에서 여러분은 가족 사진이 있는 아름답게 디자인된 문패를 발견할 수 있습니다.

➡ _____

22 여러분이 집에 들어서면 여러분은 큰 거실을 보게 될 것입니다.

➡ _____

23 나의 가족은 때때로 그곳에서 보드 게임도 하고 노래를 부르기도 합니다.

➡ _____

24 가족 소풍을 위한 커다란 피크닉 테이블이 있는 큰 정원을 갖게 될 것입니다.

➡ _____

25 그곳에서 우리는 바비큐를 즐길 것입니다. 내 꿈의 집이 마음에 드나요?

➡ _____

A House with New Technology - Bryan

26 나는 남들보다 먼저 신기술을 써 보는 것을 좋아하는 사람입니다.

➡ _____

27 나는 새로운 제품이나 기술을 다른 사람보다 먼저 사용하는 것을 정말 좋아합니다.

➡ _____

28 내가 집 근처에 도착할 때, 현관문은 내 얼굴을 인식하고 자동으로 문을 엽니다.

➡ _____

29 가구는 날씨 상태를 확인하여 내게 무엇을 입을지 조언해 줍니다.

➡ _____

30 욕실 거울은 나에게 체중과 건강 상태를 알려 줍니다.

➡ _____

31 로봇은 집을 청소하고 나를 위해 요리합니다.

➡ _____

32 이것이 내가 나의 꿈의 집에 대해 상상할 수 있는 것입니다.

➡ _____

[01~03] 다음 글을 읽고 물음에 답하시오.

My Dream House

Have you ever thought about your dream house? Today, in class, we created our dream house. Here are some of the dream houses that we made.

A House in Nature - Minho

Nature is my good friend. I do feel (A)_____ when I walk in the forest. I'd like to have a dream house in the countryside. It should have a big garden with many flowers and trees. I am always excited by the sound of birds. It will be wonderful to wake up in the morning and listen to the songs of the birds. Also, I'd like to have many pets. It will be fun to play with them!

01 다음 중 빈칸 (A)에 들어갈 말로 가장 적절한 것은?

① embarrassed   ② scared

③ terrible   ④ bored

⑤ good

 What is Minho mainly talking about?

① the forest he visited last weekend

② the house that he lives in now

③ his dream for the future

④ a dream house he wants to have

⑤ pets that he raises

서답형

03 According to the passage, where does Minho want to have his dream house? Answer in English with a full sentence.

➡ _____

[04~06] 다음 글을 읽고 물음에 답하시오.

A Fun Place - Julie

Welcome to my dream house! ① Having fun is what I want most, so my dream house is full of exciting things. ② It has a theater in the basement. ③ There, I can eat cookies and enjoy my favorite movies. ④ My dream house has a game room on the second floor. ⑤ My house also has a swimming pool. I want to do fun things with my friends in my house. You can be my guest!

 ①~⑤ 중 다음 주어진 문장이 들어가기에 가장 적절한 곳은?

I can play many different kinds of games there.

①   ②   ③   ④   ⑤

05 다음 중 Julie의 꿈의 집을 잘못 이해한 사람은?

① Amy: The house is perfect for Julie because she likes having fun.

② Brian: The house is filled with many exciting things.

③ Chris: It is a very good idea to have a theater on the ground floor.

④ David: It must be really exciting to have a game room in her house.

⑤ Emily: I want to swim in her swimming pool.

서답형

06 다음과 같이 풀이되는 말을 위 글에서 찾아 쓰시오.

someone who is visiting you because you have invited them

➡ _____

[07~09] 다음 글을 읽고 물음에 답하시오.

(A)_____ - Misun

My family is the most important thing to me. In my dream house, my family feels safe and comfortable. At the gate, you can find a beautifully designed sign with my family's picture on it. When you enter the house, you will see a large living room. My family sometimes plays board games and sings there. It will have a garden with a large picnic table for family picnics. There, we will enjoy barbecues. Do you like my dream house?

07 빈칸 (A)에 들어갈 말로 가장 적절한 것은?

① The Place Where I Live Now
② A Place for Family
③ Let Me Introduce My Family
④ Building a Safe House
⑤ A Comfortable Place for Herself

08 다음 중 위 글을 읽고 답할 수 있는 것은?

① How do Misun's friends feel about her dream house?
② How many family members does Misun have?
③ How large is the living room?
④ What does Misun's family do in the living room?
⑤ When did Misun make the dream house?

서답형
09 According to the passage, what is the most important thing to Misun? Answer in English with a full sentence.

➡ _____

[10~12] 다음 글을 읽고 물음에 답하시오.

A House with New Technology - Bryan
I am an early (A)[adapter / adopter] of new technology. I do like to use new products and technology before others. When I get (B)[near / away] my house, the front door recognizes my face and opens automatically. The furniture checks the weather conditions and advises me on (C)[when / what] to wear. The bathroom mirror tells me my weight and the condition of my health. A robot cleans the house and cooks for me. This is ⓐ_____ I can imagine about my dream house.

10 다음 중 빈칸 ⓐ에 들어갈 말과 같은 말이 들어가는 것은?

① This is the tip _____ I want to give you.
② The book _____ she read is here.
③ A bag is _____ Mary wants to have.
④ The man _____ is walking over there is famous in our town.
⑤ _____ she lied to us doesn't change.

11 (A)~(C) 중 글의 흐름상 적절한 것이 바르게 짝지어진 것은?

① adaptor – near – when
② adaptor – away – when
③ adopter – near – when
④ adopter – away – what
⑤ adopter – near – what

서답형
12 What does a robot do for Bryan in his dream house? Answer in English with a full sentence.

➡ _____

[13~16] 다음 글을 읽고 물음에 답하시오.

My Dream House

Have you ever thought about your dream house? Today, in class, we created our dream house. Here are some of the dream houses that we made.

A House in Nature - Minho

Nature is my good friend. I do feel good when I walk in the forest. I'd like to have a dream house in the countryside. It should have a big garden with many flowers and trees. I am always excited by the sound of birds. It will be wonderful to wake up in the morning and listen to the songs of the birds. (A)Also, I'd like to have many pets. It will be fun to play with them!

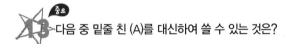 다음 중 밑줄 친 (A)를 대신하여 쓸 수 있는 것은?

① However　　② Nevertheless
③ Therefore　　④ For example
⑤ In addition

14 다음 중 위 글에 이어질 내용으로 가장 적절한 것은?

① the reason why walking in the forest is good for our health
② how to get to Minho's dream house
③ the dream house that another student created
④ some reasons why Minho doesn't like to live in the city
⑤ benefits of waking up early in the morning

15 When did the students create their dream house? Answer in English.

➡ _____

 다음 중 위 글을 바탕으로 알 수 있는 민호의 성향으로 가장 적절한 것은?

① selfish and greedy
② nature friendly
③ wise and considerate
④ talkative and generous
⑤ lonely and boring

[17~19] 다음 글을 읽고 물음에 답하시오.

A Fun Place - Julie

Welcome to my dream house! Having fun is what I want most, so my dream house is full (A)_____ exciting things. It has a theater in the basement. There, I can eat cookies and enjoy my favorite movies. My dream house has a game room on the second floor. I can play many different kinds of games there. My house also has a (B)swimming pool. I want to do fun things with my friends in my house. You can be my guest!

17 다음 중 빈칸 (A)에 들어갈 말과 같은 말이 들어가는 것은?

① He is interested _____ playing with toys.
② They didn't pay attention _____ his presentation.
③ The girl depended _____ her brother.
④ Who does this watch belong _____?
⑤ I want to get rid _____ this headache.

18 Write the things that Julie's dream house has. Answer in English.

➡ _____

19 다음 중 밑줄 친 (B)와 쓰임이 같은 것은?

① Did you see the crying baby?
② Where is my sleeping pill?
③ Is he riding a bike?
④ The dancing boy is my cousin.
⑤ The surprising news made us sad.

[20~21] 다음 글을 읽고 물음에 답하시오.

A Place for Family - Misun

My family is the most important thing to me. In my dream house, my family feels safe and comfortable. At the gate, you can find a beautifully designed sign with my family's picture on it. When you enter the house, you will see a large living room. My family sometimes plays board games and sings there. It will have a garden with a large picnic table for family picnics. There, we will enjoy barbecues. Do you like my dream house?

20 다음 중 위 글에서 반의어를 찾을 수 <u>없는</u> 것은?

① dangerous   ② small
③ big   ④ uncomfortable
⑤ unimportant

21 다음 중 위 글의 내용과 일치하는 것은?

① Misun thinks she will live in her dream house by herself.
② Misun thinks her family feels unpleasant in the dream house.
③ There is no living room in Misun's house.
④ Misun will enjoy barbecues in the garden with her family.
⑤ The picnic table is for birthday parties for friends.

[22~25] 다음 글을 읽고 물음에 답하시오.

A House with (A)_____ - Bryan

I am an early adopter of new technology. I do like to use ①new products and technology ②after others. When I get near my house, the front door ③recognizes my face and opens ④automatically. The furniture checks the weather conditions and ⑤advises me on what to wear. The bathroom mirror tells me my weight and the condition of my health. A robot cleans the house and cooks for me. This is (B)_____ I can imagine about my dream house.

서답형
22 빈칸 (A)에 알맞은 말을 위 글에서 찾아 쓰시오.

➡ _____

23 다음 중 빈칸 (B)에 들어갈 말로 가장 적절한 것은?

① that   ② how   ③ when
④ why   ⑤ what

24 ①~⑤ 중 글의 흐름상 어색한 것은?

①   ②   ③   ④   ⑤

25 다음 중 위 글을 읽고 답할 수 있는 것은?

① How many stories does the house have?
② What made Bryan become an early adopter?
③ What happens when Bryan gets near his dream house?
④ How many times a day does a robot clean the house?
⑤ How many rooms does the house have?

[01~04] 다음 글을 읽고 물음에 답하시오.

My Dream House

Have you ever thought about your dream house? Today, in class, we created our dream house. Here are some of the dream houses that we made.

A House in Nature - Minho

Nature is my good friend. I do feel good when I walk in the forest. I'd like to have a dream house in the countryside. It should have a big garden with many flowers and trees. I am always excited by the sound of birds. It will be wonderful to wake up in the morning and listen to the songs of the birds. Also, I'd like to have many pets. It will be fun to play with (A)them!

01 According to the passage, how does Minho feel when he walks in the forest? Answer in English with a full sentence.

➡ _____

02 What did they make in class today?

➡ _____

03 What can we find in the garden of Minho's house?

➡ _____
_____

04 밑줄 친 (A)가 가리키는 것을 위 글에서 찾아 쓰시오.

➡ _____

[05~08] 다음 글을 읽고 물음에 답하시오.

A Fun Place - Julie

Welcome to my dream house! Having fun is what I want most, so my dream house is full of exciting things. It has a theater in the basement. There, I can eat cookies and enjoy my favorite movies. My dream house has a game room on the second floor. I can play many different kinds of games there. My house also has a swimming pool. I want to do fun things with my friends in my house. You can be my guest!

05 According to the passage, what does Julie want most? Answer in English with a full sentence.

➡ _____

06 Where can we find a theater in Julie's dream house?

➡ _____

07 다음 중 위 글의 내용과 일치하지 <u>않는</u> 것을 찾아 바르게 고쳐 쓰시오.

Julie's dream house is filled with strange things. It has a theater and a swimming pool. She wants to do fun things in her dream house.

➡ _____

08 Where can we find the game room? Answer in English with a full sentence.

➡ _____

[09~11] 다음 글을 읽고 물음에 답하시오.

A Place for Family - Misun

My family is the most important thing to me. In my dream house, (A)my family feels safe and comfortable. At the gate, you can find a beautifully designed sign with my family's picture on it. When you enter the house, you will see a large living room. My family sometimes plays board games and sings there. (B)It will have a garden with a large picnic table for family picnics. There, we will enjoy barbecues. Do you like my dream house?

09 밑줄 친 문장 (A)의 동사를 강조하여 다시 쓰시오.

➡ _____

10 What can we see at the gate of Misun's dream house? Answer in English with a full sentence.

➡ _____

_____

11 밑줄 친 (B)가 가리키는 것을 영어로 쓰시오.

➡ _____

[12~13] 다음 글을 읽고 물음에 답하시오.

A House with New Technology - Bryan

I am an early adopter of new technology. I do like to use new products and technology before others. When I get near my house, the front door recognizes my face and opens automatically. The furniture checks the weather conditions and advises me on what to wear. The bathroom mirror tells me my weight and the condition of my health. A robot cleans the house and cooks

for me. This is what I can imagine about my dream house.

12 다음 빈칸에 들어갈 알맞은 말을 위 글에서 찾아 쓰시오.

Early adopters are people who _____

_____.

13 What does the furniture do in Bryan's dream house?

➡ _____

_____

[14~15] 다음 글을 읽고 물음에 답하시오.

To Jina, at some future time

(A)_____ I want to put into my memory box are my soccer ball, my school newspaper, and a letter from my best friend, Semin. I want to put in the soccer ball because I spend a lot of time playing soccer. I want to put in the school newspaper because I do want to remember what happened in my middle school days. Finally, I want to put in the letter from Semin because it shows what good friends we are. What I hope from you is to keep these three things forever.

From Jina

14 빈칸 (A)에 들어갈 알맞은 말을 쓰시오.

➡ _____

15 Write the reason why Jina wants to put the school newspaper in the memory box. Use the words 'It's because and 'does'.

➡ _____

_____

After You Read -Read and Match

I like to use new products and technology.
목적어(to부정사의 명사적 용법)

There are many items that use new technology in my dream house. Every day
관계대명사(주격)   선행사가 items이므로 복수동사 use를 사용

my furniture checks the weather and tells me (□what to do / ☑what to wear).
확인하다. 점검하다   의문사+to부정사(무엇을 입을지): 명사구

A robot (☑ cooks / □cleans my classroom) for me.

해석

나는 새로운 제품과 기술을 사용하는 것이 좋다.

내가 꿈꾸는 집에는 새로운 기술을 이용하는 물건들이 많이 있다. 매일 내 가구들은 날씨를 확인해서 내가 무엇을 입을지 말해 준다. 로봇은 나에게 요리를 해 준다.

Project Step 1

A: We would like to know more about you, Minho.
would like to+V: ～하고 싶다

What is your favorite food?
상대방이 가장 좋아하는 것 묻기

B: I like pizza most.
'가장 (많이)'라는 최상급 표현

C: Can you tell me about your favorite subject?

B: Art is what I like most.
관계대명사로 the thing that[which]으로 바꾸어 쓸 수 있다. '～하는 것'으로 해석한다.

I want to become an art teacher like Mr. Kim.
전치사로 '～처럼, ～와 같은'

D: What do you like to do after school?

B: I like to practice taegwondo and sing songs.
practice와 sing은 병렬 관계다.

구문해설 • **favorite**: 가장 좋아하는 • **subject**: 과목. • **after school**: 방과 후에 • **practice**: 연습하다

A: 우리는 너에 대해서 더 많이 알고 싶어, 민호야. 네가 가장 좋아하는 음식은 뭐니?
B: 나는 피자를 가장 좋아해.
C: 나에게 네가 가장 좋아하는 과목에 대해 말해 줄 수 있니?
B: 미술이 내가 가장 좋아하는 거야. 나는 김 선생님과 같은 미술 선생님이 되고 싶어.
D: 너는 방과 후에 무엇을 하는 것을 좋아하니?
B: 나는 태권도를 연습하고, 노래 부르는 것을 좋아해.

Project Step 3

We made an M and an H with what Minho likes. Minho likes art and pizza, so
관계대명사(～하는 것)   결과를 이끄는 접속사(그래서)

we made an M with a paint brush, colored pencils, and a piece of pizza. We

made an H with a musical note and taegwondo.
수단을 나타내는 전치사(～로, ～을 써서)

구문해설 • **art**: 예술, 미술 • **paint brush**: 붓 • **colored pencil**: 색연필

우리는 민호가 좋아하는 것으로 M과 H를 만들었습니다. 민호는 미술과 피자를 좋아합니다. 그래서 우리는 붓, 색연필, 그리고 피자 조각으로 M을 만들었습니다. 우리는 음표와 태권도로 H를 만들었습니다.

Words & Expressions

01 다음 주어진 두 단어의 관계가 같도록 빈칸에 알맞은 단어를 쓰시오.

> wide : narrow = backward : _____

02 다음 글의 빈칸 (a)와 (b)에 들어갈 단어가 바르게 짝지어진 것은?

> • Today, in class, we (a)_____ our dream house. Here are some of the dream houses that we made.
> • My dream house is full of exciting things. I want to do fun things with my friends in my house. You can be my (b) _____!

① destroyed – host ② destroyed – guest
③ created – host ④ created – guest
⑤ made – pet

[03~04] 다음 영영 풀이에 해당하는 것을 고르시오.

03

> an animal that is kept in the home as a companion and treated kindly

① puppy ② furniture
③ pet ④ swallow
⑤ subject

04

> a short sentence or phrase that expresses a belief or purpose

① motto ② sign
③ photographer ④ hero
⑤ forest

05 (A)와 (B)의 빈칸에 공통으로 들어갈 말을 쓰시오.

> (A) There are many items that use new _____ in my dream house. Every day my furniture checks the weather and tells me what to wear.
> (B) Romans had very advanced _____ in producing concrete.

06 다음 밑줄 친 부분의 뜻이 잘못된 것은?

① You made the right choice. (선택)
② I like the scenes made with computer technology. (장면)
③ This is what I can imagine about my dream house. (상상하다)
④ I'd like to have many pets. (애완동물)
⑤ My dream house has a theater in the basement. (오락실)

Conversation

07 다음 글의 빈칸에 들어갈 말로 적절한 것은?

> **G1:** Hi! I am Teri. I like running in the evening. I feel (a)_____ when I exercise.
> **B2:** Hello, my name is Jack. I'm (b) _____ in stars. I usually go out to see stars at night.

	(a)	(b)
①	bored	uninterested
②	tired	interested
③	tired	uninterested
④	refreshed	interested
⑤	refreshed	pleased

08 주어진 문장에 이어질 대화를 순서에 맞게 바르게 배열한 것은?

> G: Jiho, how was your first day of third grade?

(A)

> B: Yes. He is humorous and told us some fun stories about math. It was interesting.
> G: Cool! I hope you enjoy studying math.

(B)

> B: My homeroom teacher is Mr. Kim. He teaches math.
> G: Can you tell me more about him?

(C)

> B: It was pretty good. The teachers and my new classmates are all good.
> G: That sounds good. Who is your homeroom teacher?

① (A) – (B) – (C)　　② (B) – (A) – (C)
③ (B) – (C) – (A)　　④ (C) – (A) – (B)
⑤ (C) – (B) – (A)

[09~11] 다음 대화를 읽고 물음에 답하시오.

> Seho: Nice to meet you. I'd like to join your photo club. (①)
> Bora: Thank you for your interest in the club. Can you tell me about yourself? (②)
> Seho: Yes. My name is Kim Seho. I am in the third grade, class 8.
> Andy: Tell me more. (③)
> Seho: Well, what I like most is to take pictures. (④)
> Bora: That's great. (A)_____
> Seho: I want to be a photographer. (⑤)
> Andy: Then you made the right choice. You can learn a lot of photo-taking skills here. Welcome to our club.
> Seho: Thank you. I'm so glad!

09 주어진 문장이 들어갈 위치로 알맞은 것은?

> What do you like to do most in your free time?

①　　　②　　　③　　　④　　　⑤

10 위 대화의 빈칸 (A)에 들어갈 말로 알맞은 것을 <u>모두</u> 고르시오.

① Can you tell me about your dream job?
② What do you like most?
③ Can you tell me about your goal for next year?
④ What is your dream for the future?
⑤ What do you think of a photographer?

11 위 대화의 내용과 일치하지 <u>않는</u> 것은?

① Seho wants to join the photo club.
② Bora wants to know about Seho.
③ Seho already knows a lot of photo-taking skills.
④ Bora and Andy belong to the photo club.
⑤ The photo club teaches lots of photo-taking skills.

12 다음의 제시된 〈조건〉에 맞게 Carol의 질문에 대한 답을 완성하시오.

> ┤ 조건 ├
> (1) 관계대명사 what을 사용할 것
> (2) to부정사를 사용할 것
> (3) 'play baseball'을 이용할 것

> Andy: What is your nickname?
> Becky: My nickname is Speedy because I can run fast.
> Carol: What do you like most?
> Becky: _____
> Dan: Can you tell me about your dream job?
> Becky: I want to be a baseball player.

➡ _____

13 다음 중 어법상 옳은 문장은?

① Jenny do look lovely.

② They are look handsome on the stage.

③ He does believes she's crazy.

④ I do met my cousins in Suwon.

⑤ She did make a fortune.

14 다음 우리말의 내용을 주어진 조건에 맞게 강조하는 문장으로 영작했을 때, 빈칸에 적절한 말을 쓰시오.

> • Peter가 지난 수업에서 그 문제들을 풀었다.
>
> (1) Peter 강조
>
> = It was _____
>
> in the last class.
>
> (2) '풀었다'라는 동사 강조
>
> = Peter _____ .
>
> (3) '지난 수업에서' 강조
>
> = It was _____
>
> _____ .

15 다음 빈칸에 알맞은 말이 바르게 짝지어진 것은?

> • The photographer showed me _____
>
> were taken in front of the White House.
>
> • Janet _____ start her own business.

① what – did   ② that – does

③ whose – does   ④ what – do

⑤ that – did

16 Which of the followings are grammatically <u>incorrect</u>? Choose all.

① The room does feel too cold.

② Do be careful when you drive.

③ Sam did believe what Will said.

④ My uncle do likes playing with me.

⑤ It did took three hours and a half.

17 다음 두 문장의 의미가 같도록 빈칸에 들어갈 알맞은 말을 쓰시오.

> • I didn't see the thing that he had done.
>
> = I didn't see _____ he had done.

[18~19] 다음 그림을 보고 빈칸에 맞는 단어를 채우시오.

18

➡ *The Old Man and the Sea* by Ernest Hemingway _____ make me impressed.

19

➡ The pyramids showed _____ the ancient Egyptians believed.

20 다음 밑줄 친 부분의 쓰임이 나머지와 <u>다른</u> 것은?

① The guards <u>do</u> protect well the actor.

② Can I <u>do</u> some laundry over there?

③ Barbara <u>does</u> work for the bank.

④ Paul <u>did</u> eat kimchi last night.

⑤ Laura <u>does</u> play the villain role.

21 다음 중 각각의 (A)와 (B)에서 밑줄 친 부분의 쓰임이 서로 일치하는 것을 고르면?

① (A) What should we <u>do</u> now?
  (B) He knows that I <u>do</u> believe her.

② (A) She <u>did</u> keep the promise.
  (B) They <u>did</u> something to correct it.

③ (A) Emily <u>does</u> as she wants.
  (B) He <u>does</u> buy the sneakers of the brand.

④ (A) <u>Do</u> be nice to others.
  (B) <u>Do</u> you know when he will come?

⑤ (A) Everyone wonders how he <u>did</u> it.
  (B) All the villagers don't trust him even if he <u>does</u> good things.

22 다음 중 어법상 어색한 문장을 모두 고르면?

① What Robert really wanted at that moment was to be left alone on the stage.

② Susan's cold face was what made her husband nervous.

③ That you said was dangerous, and we were all worried about it.

④ There are about 6 different songs what the musician composed.

⑤ Asking questions and finding out the answers are what scientists do.

[23~27] 다음 글을 읽고 물음에 답하시오.

My Dream House
Have you ever thought about your dream house? Today, in class, we created our dream house. Here are some of the dream houses (A)_____ we made.
  A House in Nature - Minho
Nature is my good friend. I do feel good when I walk in the forest. I'd like to have a dream house in the countryside. (B)It should have a big garden with many flowers and trees. I am always excited by the sound of birds. It will be wonderful to wake up in the morning and listen to the songs of the birds. Also, I'd like to have many pets. (C)It will be fun to play with them!

23 다음 중 빈칸 (A)에 들어갈 말로 적절한 것을 <u>모두</u> 고르시오.

① which   ② why   ③ what
④ that   ⑤ who

24 밑줄 친 (B)가 가리키는 것을 위 글에서 찾아 쓰시오.

➡ _____

25 According to the passage, what always makes Minho excited? Answer in English with a full sentence.

➡ _____

26 다음 중 밑줄 친 (C)와 쓰임이 같은 것은?

① It is not that far from here to the mart.

② It was cold and windy outside.

③ It looks like a cucumber.

④ It is interesting to read the novel.

⑤ It is flying high in the sky.

---

27 다음 중 위 글의 내용과 일치하지 <u>않는</u> 것은?

① Minho's dream house was made in class today.

② Minho likes to walk in the forest.

③ Minho wants his dream house to be in the middle of a city.

④ Lots of flowers and trees can be found in the garden.

⑤ Minho wants to have many pets in his dream house.

[28~31] 다음 글을 읽고 물음에 답하시오.

To Jina, at some future time

Hi, Jina. What I want to ①<u>put into</u> my memory box are my soccer ball, my school newspaper, and a letter ②<u>from</u> my best friend, Semin. I want to put in the soccer ball because I spend a lot of time ③<u>to play</u> soccer. I want to put in the school newspaper because I ④ <u>do</u> want to remember what happened in my middle school days. (A)<u>Finally</u>, I want to put in the letter from Semin because it shows ⑤ <u>what</u> good friends we are. What I hope from you is to keep these three things forever.

From Jina

28 ①~⑤ 중 어법상 바르지 <u>않은</u> 것은?

①   ②   ③   ④   ⑤

29 다음 중 밑줄 친 (A)를 대신하여 쓸 수 있는 것은?

① Fortunately   ② At first

③ Lastly   ④ Interestingly

⑤ Hardly

30 Write the reason why Jina wants to put in the letter from Semin. Use the phrase 'It's because.'

➡ _____

31 다음 중 위 글을 읽고 답할 수 <u>없는</u> 것은?

① How many things does Jina want to put into the box?

② How many letters does Jina want to put into the box?

③ Who is Jina's best friend?

④ Why does Jina want to put her soccer ball into the box?

⑤ When did Jina start to play soccer?

32 주어진 단어를 바르게 배열하여 다음 글의 주제를 쓰시오.

To Jina, at some future time
Hi, Jina. What I want to put into my memory box are my soccer ball, my school newspaper, and a letter from my best friend, Semin. I want to put in the soccer ball because I spend a lot of time playing soccer. I want to put in the school newspaper because I do want to remember what happened in my middle school days. Finally, I want to put in the letter from Semin because it shows that what good friends we are. What I hope from you is to keep these three things forever.

From Jina

(Jina / put / wants / into / memory / her / things / to / box)

➡ _____

출제율 90%

01 다음 짝지어진 단어의 관계가 같도록 빈칸에 알맞은 말을 쓰시오.

> answer : reply = counsel : _____

출제율 90%

02 다음 영영 풀이에 해당하는 단어는?

> land that is not in towns or cities and may have farms, fields, etc.

① ground   ② countryside
③ space   ④ forest
⑤ castle

출제율 95%

03 다음 대화의 밑줄 친 (A)와 같은 의미의 문장을 주어진 단어를 활용하여 쓰시오.

> A: What is your nickname?
> B: My nickname is Speedy because I can run fast.
> C: What do you like most?
> B: What I like most is to play baseball.
> D: (A)Can you tell me about your dream job?
> B: I want to be a baseball player.

➡ I'm _____.
(really / curious)

[04~05] 다음 대화를 읽고 물음에 답하시오.

> W: Today, we have a new student Hojun. Hojun, can you please introduce yourself to the class?
> B: Yes. Hi, my name is Kim Hojun. I am from Busan. Nice to meet you.
> W: Can you tell us more about yourself?
> B: Yes. I like sports, especially soccer. I want to join a sports club.
> W: (A)새 친구들에게 더 할 말 없니?
> B: I want to get along with everyone. Please help me because I'm new here.
> W: Thanks, Hojun. Welcome to our class.

출제율 100%

04 위 대화를 읽고 다음 빈칸에 Hojun에 관한 정보를 완전한 문장의 영어로 쓰시오.

(1) Hojun의 출신지: _____
(2) Hojun이 좋아하는 운동: _____
(3) Hojun이 새 친구들에게 하고 싶은 말:
_____

출제율 90%

05 위 대화의 밑줄 친 우리말에 맞게 주어진 어구를 알맞게 배열하시오.

> (there / anything / is / you / want / else / to tell / your new friends / ?)

➡ _____

출제율 90%

06 What does each student like most? (What으로 문장을 시작하여 쓰시오.)

> (1) Jiho: I often go traveling with my family. What I like most about traveling is trying new foods.
> (2) Bora: My favorite subject is music. I can play the drums and guitar. Among them, playing the guitar is what I like most.
> (3) Jenny: This is a picture of Dora. She is my best friend, not just a pet. Playing with her in my free time is what I like most.

➡ (1) _____
     (2) _____
     (3) _____

[07~08] 다음 대화를 읽고 물음에 답하시오.

G: Ted, look at this movie poster. I want to see this movie.

B: It looks (a)interesting. Can you tell me about it, Amy?

G: Yes. It is about a hero (b)who saves the Earth.

B: It (c)looks like an SF movie.

G: Yes, it is. Actually, SF is my favorite kind of movie. I like the scenes (d)making with computer technology. They are fantastic and (e)look real.

B: That's cool. I am free this weekend. Let's go to see it together.

G: Sounds good.

출제율 95%

07 위 대화의 밑줄 친 부분 (a)~(e) 중 어법상 어색한 것은?

① (a) ② (b) ③ (c) ④ (d) ⑤ (e)

출제율 100%

08 위 대화의 내용과 일치하지 않는 것은?

① They are talking about a movie.

② Amy wants to see the movie.

③ The movie is about a hero who helps people in need.

④ Amy likes SF movies a lot.

⑤ They are going to see the movie this weekend.

[09~11] 다음 대화를 읽고 물음에 답하시오.

Seho: Nice to meet you. I'd like to join your photo club. (①)

Bora: Thank you for your interest in the club. (A)_____

Seho: Yes. My name is Kim Seho. (②) I am in the third grade, class 8.

Andy: Tell me more. What do you like to do most in your free time? (③)

Seho: Well, (B)내가 가장 좋아하는 것은 사진을 찍는 거야.

Bora: That's great. What is your dream for the future? (④)

Seho: I want to be a photographer.

Andy: (⑤) You can learn a lot of photo-taking skills here. Welcome to our club.

Seho: Thank you. I'm so glad!

출제율 95%

09 위 대화의 빈칸 (A)에 들어갈 말로 알맞은 것은?

① What's your favorite club?

② Can you tell me about yourself?

③ Let me introduce myself to you.

④ Do you know who I am?

⑤ Do you mind telling me about yourself?

출제율 85%

10 위 대화의 밑줄 친 (B)의 우리말에 맞게 주어진 조건을 활용하여 대화를 완성하시오.

┤ 조건 ├

(1) 관계대명사 what을 사용할 것

(2) to부정사를 사용할 것

➡ _____

출제율 100%

11 위 대화의 (①)~(⑤) 중 주어진 문장이 들어갈 위치로 알맞은 것은?

Then you made the right choice.

① ② ③ ④ ⑤

출제율 95%

12 다음 두 문장의 의미가 같도록 빈칸을 채우시오. (단, book과 that은 사용 불가)

• What she bought at Sam's bookstore were the books about making hip-hop music.

= The _____ _____ she bought at Sam's bookstore were the books about making hip-hop music.

출제율 95%

13 다음 중 어색한 문장을 모두 고르시오.

① You are the only one what makes me happy.

② Edvard Munch did painted *The Scream* in 1893.

③ Jeremy did take good care of his youngest sister.

④ It were the books that he bought for Sumi yesterday.

⑤ All the citizens understood what the mayor announced.

출제율 100%

14 다음 주어진 문장의 밑줄 친 what과 같은 용법으로 쓰인 것을 모두 고르시오.

> • That is <u>what</u> she has taught for decades.

① <u>What</u> did you come here for?

② I don't know <u>what</u> these words mean.

③ <u>What</u> upset me was his attitude.

④ I wonder <u>what</u> you are interested in.

⑤ <u>What</u> was considered polite in the past is not always seen as such today.

출제율 90%

15 다음 두 문장을 관계대명사 what을 이용하여, 하나의 문장으로 만드시오.

(1) • That is not the thing.
   • Harry has always wanted it.
   ➡ _____

(2) • My parents already know the things.
   • They happened three weeks ago.
   ➡ _____

(3) • Tell her the things.
   • They have been bothering you.
   ➡ _____

[16~18] 다음 글을 읽고 물음에 답하시오.

To Jina, at some future time

What I want to put into my memory box are my soccer ball, my school newspaper, and a letter from my best friend, Semin. I want to put in ⓐ _____ because I spend a lot of time playing soccer. I want to put in ⓑ _____ because I do want to remember what happened in my middle school days. Finally, I want to put in ⓒ _____ from Semin because it shows what good friends we are. (A)내가 너에게 바라는 것 is to keep these three things forever.

From Jina

출제율 90%

16 빈칸 ⓐ~ⓒ에 들어갈 알맞은 말을 위 글에서 찾아 쓰시오.

➡ ⓐ _____
   ⓑ _____
   ⓒ _____

출제율 95%

17 주어진 단어를 활용하여 밑줄 친 우리말 (A)를 영어로 쓰시오.

> (hope / from)

➡ _____

18 출제율 95%

다음 중 위 글의 내용과 일치하는 것은?

① Jina is making a memory box to send to Semin.

② Jina used to wite letters to Semin.

③ Jina puts in more than three things.

④ Jina would like to keep the memory box forever.

⑤ Jina wants Semin to accept the memory box.

[19~20] 다음 글을 읽고 물음에 답하시오.

A Place for Family - Misun

My family is the most important thing to me. In my dream house, my family feels ①<u>safe and comfortable</u>. ②<u>At</u> the gate, you can find a beautifully ③<u>designed</u> sign with my family's picture on it. When you ④<u>enter into</u> the house, you will see a large living room. My family sometimes plays board games and sings there. It will have a garden with a large picnic table ⑤<u>for</u> family picnics. There, we will enjoy barbecues. Do you like my dream house?

19 출제율 95%

밑줄 친 ①~⑤ 중 어법상 바르지 <u>않은</u> 것은?

①   ②   ③   ④   ⑤

20 출제율 100%

다음 중 위 글에서 찾아볼 수 <u>없는</u> 것은?

① the gate with a beautifully designed sign

② a large living room where Misun's family can sing

③ a kitchen with a large picnic table

④ a garden where Misun's family will enjoy barbecues

⑤ a large picnic table for her family picnics

[21~23] 다음 글을 읽고 물음에 답하시오.

A House with New Technology - Bryan

I am an early adopter of new technology. I do like to use new products and technology before others. When I get near my house, the front door recognizes my face and opens automatically. The furniture checks the weather conditions and advises me on what to wear. The bathroom mirror tells me my weight and the condition of my health. A robot cleans the house and cooks for me. This is what I can imagine about my dream house.

21 출제율 100%

다음 중 위 글의 내용과 일치하는 것은?

① Bryan is not interested in using new technology.

② Bryan opens the front door by using a remote control.

③ The front door can identify Bryan's face.

④ Bryan gets some advice on what to wear from the bathroom mirror.

⑤ A robot answers the phone for Bryan.

22 출제율 90%

다음과 같이 풀이할 수 있는 말을 위 글에서 찾아 쓰시오.

> to know who someone is or what something is

➡ _____

23 출제율 90%

What does the bathroom mirror tell Bryan? Answer in English with a full sentence.

➡ _____

_____

01 다음 대화를 아래 〈조건〉에 따라 완성하시오.

> G: Jiho, (A) _____
>
> B: It was pretty good. The teachers and my new classmates are all good.
>
> G: That sounds good. Who is your homeroom teacher?
>
> B: My homeroom teacher is Mr. Kim. He teaches math.
>
> G: (B) _____
>
> B: Yes. He is humorous and told us some fun stories about math. It was interesting.
>
> G: Cool! I hope you enjoy studying math.

> ┤ 보기 ├
>
> (A) how를 이용하여 3학년 첫 날이 어떠했는지 묻는 말을 쓸 것.
> (B) Mr. Kim에 대해 더 많이 알고 싶어 하는 궁금증을 표현하는 말을 쓸 것.

02 다음 대화의 밑줄 친 우리말을 주어진 어휘를 배열하여 완성하시오.

> B: This movie looks like an SF movie.
>
> G: Yes, it is. Actually, SF is my favorite kind of movie. 나는 컴퓨터 기술로 만들어진 장면을 좋아해. They are fantastic and look real.

> I / made / the scenes / with / computer technology / like

➡ _____

03 다음 대화를 읽고 물음에 영어로 답하시오.

> Seho: Nice to meet you. I'd like to join your photo club.
>
> Bora: Thank you for your interest in the club. Can you tell me about yourself?
>
> Seho: Yes. My name is Kim Seho. I am in the third grade, class 8.
>
> Andy: Tell me more. What do you like to do most in your free time?
>
> Seho: Well, what I like most is to take pictures.
>
> Bora: That's great. What is your dream for the future?
>
> Seho: I want to be a photographer.
>
> Andy: Then you made the right choice. You can learn a lot of photo-taking skills here. Welcome to our club.
>
> Seho: Thank you. I'm so glad!

(1) What does Seho like to do most in his free time?

➡ _____

(2) What can Seho learn in the photo club?

➡ _____

04 다음 우리말과 같은 뜻이 되도록 주어진 단어들을 이용하여, 제시된 글자 수에 맞게 영작하시오.

(1) 나는 내가 가진 것을 최대한 이용해야 한다. (most, make, must, of, have, 9 단어)

➡ _____

(2) 당신이 하는 것이 당신이 말하는 것보다 훨씬 중요하다. (say, than, much, important, 11 단어)

➡ _____

05 다음 주어진 문장을 밑줄 친 부분을 강조하는 문장으로 바꾸어 쓰시오.

(1) People in Hong Kong <u>love</u> freedom.

➡ _____

(2) Did he break the door <u>yesterday</u>?

➡ _____

(3) The wall was painted by <u>Mr. Lee</u>.

➡ _____

[06~08] 다음 글을 읽고 물음에 답하시오.

A House with New Technology - Bryan

I am an early adopter of new technology. I do like to use new products and technology before others. When I get near my house, the front door recognizes my face and opens automatically. The furniture checks the weather conditions and advises me on what to wear. The bathroom mirror tells me my weight and the condition of my health. A robot cleans the house and cooks for me. This is what I can imagine about my dream house.

06 다음 역할에 맞게 빈칸에 알맞은 말을 쓰시오.

(1) _____ : checking weather conditions

(2) _____ : cooking for Bryan

(3) _____ : telling the condition of Bryan's health

07 다음 물음에 조건에 맞게 답하시오.

Q: Does the front door really open automatically?

A: Yes. _____ by recognizing my face.
(동사를 강조하여 쓸 것)

08 다음 중 위 글의 내용과 일치하지 <u>않는</u> 것을 두 군데 찾아 바르게 고쳐 쓰시오.

There are many items that use new technology in my dream house. Every day my furniture checks the weather and tells me what to do. A robot cleans my classroom for me.

➡ _____

➡ _____

[09~10] 다음 글을 읽고 물음에 답하시오.

A Place for Family - Misun

My family is the most important thing to me. In my dream house, my family feels safe and comfortable. At the gate, you can find a beautifully designed sign with my family's picture on (A)<u>it</u>. When you enter the house, you will see a large living room. My family sometimes plays board games and sings there. It will have a garden with a large picnic table for family picnics. There, we will enjoy barbecues. Do you like my dream house?

09 밑줄 친 (A)가 가리키는 것을 위 글에서 찾아 쓰시오.

➡ _____

10 According to the passage, where will the family enjoy barbecues? Answer in English with a full sentence.

➡ _____

01 아래 표를 보고 (A)는 주말 계획을, (B)는 올해 목표에 관해 묻는 말과 답을 하나 골라 쓰시오.

(A) Plan for This Weekend	(B) Goal for the Year
• have a birthday party	• stop eating fast food
• go to a concert	• get good grades
• take a day trip	• make many friends

A: _____ your plan for this weekend?
B: Yes. I am going _____ .
A: _____ your goal for the year?
B: Yes. I want to _____ .

02 〈보기〉에 주어진 어휘를 활용하여, 관계대명사 what이 들어간 문장을 3개 이상 만드시오. 단, 각 그룹에서 하나 이상의 단어가 각 문장에 포함되어야 함.

> 보기
>
> A 그룹: see / look for / find / know / buy
> B 그룹: Jane / Brian / Ms. Smith / Kathy
> C 그룹: book / the bag / at the market / at the library / in the kitchen

(1) _____
(2) _____
(3) _____

03 지민의 추억 상자에 넣을 물건과 그 이유를 살펴보고 다음 편지를 완성하시오.

> dancing shoes – They are related to my future dream.
> the first prize from a dancing performance – I can remember my happiest moment.
> some pictures with friends – I don't want to forget my friends from middle school.

> To Jimin, at some future time
> Hi, Jimin. What I want to put into this memory box are _____, _____
> _____, and _____. I want to put in _____
> because _____. I want to put in _____
> because _____. Lastly, I want to _____
> because _____.

단원별 모의고사

01 다음 단어에 대한 영어 설명이 <u>어색한</u> 것은?

① hero: a very brave person, often a man, that a lot of people admire

② furniture: things such as chairs, tables, and beds that you put into a room or building

③ photographer: a person who takes photographs, either as a job or hobby

④ save: to make something happen or exist

⑤ advise: to tell someone that they should do something

02 다음 짝지어진 단어의 관계가 같도록 빈칸에 알맞은 말을 쓰시오.

enter : go into = sketch : _____

03 다음 영영풀이에 해당하는 단어를 고르시오.

a large area of land that is covered with trees

① forest
② countryside
③ farm
④ wood
⑤ furniture

04 다음 중 짝지어진 대화가 <u>어색한</u> 것은?

① A: Can you tell me about your plan for this weekend?
   B: Yes. I am going to have a birthday party.

② A: What is your dream for the future?
   B: I want to be a doctor.

③ A: Can you tell me about your goal for the year?
   B: Yes. I want to stop eating fast food.

④ A: Can you tell me about your favorite subject?
   B: I want to become an art teacher.

⑤ A: Can you please introduce yourself to the class?
   B: Yes. Hi, my name is Kim Hojun.

[05~06] 다음 대화의 빈칸에 들어갈 말로 알맞은 것을 고르시오. (06은 정답이 2개)

05

A: What is your nickname?
B: My nickname is Speedy because I can run fast.
C: _____
B: What I like most is to play baseball.

① What do you do in your free time?
② What are you doing?
③ What do you like most?
④ Do you like to play baseball?
⑤ Why do you like sports?

06

A: We would like to know more about you, Minho. What is your favorite food?
B: I like pizza most.
C: _____
B: Art is what I like most. I want to become an art teacher like Mr. Kim.

① What is your favorite color?
② Can you tell me about your favorite subject?
③ Who's your favorite teacher?
④ How about Korean art?
⑤ What subject do you like most?

[07~08] 다음 대화를 읽고 물음에 답하시오.

W: Today, we have a new student Hojun. Hojun, can you please introduce yourself to the class?

B: Yes. Hi, my name is Kim Hojun. I am from Busan. Nice to meet you.

W: Can you tell us more about yourself?

B: Yes. I like sports, especially soccer. I want to join a sports club.

W: Is there anything else you want to tell your new friends?

B: (A)_____ Please help me because I'm new here.

W: Thanks, Hojun. Welcome to our class.

07 빈칸 (A)에 들어갈 말로 알맞은 것은?

① I want to know more about you.
② I'm really curious about soccer.
③ I want to get along with everyone.
④ I want to know about Busan.
⑤ I don't feel like talking to you.

08 What does Hojun want to do? (7단어로 답할 것)

➡ _____

09 다음 대화의 빈칸에 'tell me'를 사용하여 상대방의 가장 친한 친구에 관한 궁금증을 나타내는 표현을 쓰시오.

> A: _____
>
> B: Yes. My best friend is Jiwoo. He is very good at surfing.

10 다음의 〈보기〉를 보고 Andy와 Teri가 가장 좋아하는 것을 묻고 답하는 문장을 완성하시오.

> ┌─ 보기 ─
> Andy: listen to K-pop music
> Teri: travel by train

Andy: _____, Teri?

Teri: _____ is to travel by train. How about you?

Andy: _____ is to _____ K-pop music.

11 (A)와 (B)에 공통으로 들어갈 말로 알맞은 것은?

> (A)
> My favorite subject is music. I can play the drums and guitar. Among them, playing the guitar is _____.
> (B)
> This is a picture of Dora. She is my best friend, not just a pet. Playing with her in my free time is _____.

① what I don't want to do
② that I want to know what a friend is for
③ why I like music
④ what I like most
⑤ how we know each other

12 다음 대화의 빈칸에 들어갈 말로 적절하지 않은 것은?

> A: Can you tell me about your dream job?
> B: I want to be a baseball player.
> A: What is your motto?
> B: My motto is "_____."

① Actions speak louder than words
② Working hard is the mother of good luck
③ If you do not walk today, you will have to run tomorrow
④ You can go forward slowly, but never go back
⑤ There is no place like home

13 다음 두 문장을 같은 의미의 한 문장이 되도록 관계대명사 what을 사용하여 쓰시오.

(1) • I will read the words.
• Sarah wrote them in her mail.
= I will read _____ .

(2) • Australia is the place.
• Gloria wants to visit it someday.
= Australia is _____ .

14 다음 중 어법상 어색한 것을 고르시오.

① It was at the park that Mr. and Ms. Anderson first had a date.

② It was four months ago that Mary borrowed some books from me.

③ It was very hungry that Paul became after hard work.

④ Chinese people do love the number 8.

⑤ Sam Smith did compose all the songs.

15 다음 주어진 문장의 밑줄 친 부분과 쓰임이 같은 것을 모두 고르면?

> • Robert's mom does worry about his vision due to the PC games he is crazy for.

① She doesn't have any plans.

② Do we have to know your schedule?

③ They do think it's not fair.

④ Do not move an inch.

⑤ Susan did wash the dishes by herself.

16 우리말과 일치하도록 괄호 안의 어구를 바르게 배열하시오.

(1) 이것이 그녀가 작년에 일본인 목수로부터 구매한 것이다. (from, last year, she, a, what, this, carpenter, is, purchased, Japanese)

➡ _____
_____

(2) 그 무거운 상자를 옮겨 준 것은 바로 영어 선생님이었다. (the English teacher, moved, heavy, it, the, who, box, was)

➡ _____
_____

(3) John이 그 사무실에서 수리한 것은 복사기 한 대였다. (machine, office, in, John, photocopy, a, fixed, what, the, was)

➡ _____
_____

[17~19] 다음 글을 읽고 물음에 답하시오.

A House in Nature - Minho

[A] It will be wonderful to wake up in the morning and listen to the songs of the birds. Also, I'd like to have many pets. It will be fun to play with them!

[B] It should have a big garden with many flowers and trees. I am always excited by the sound of birds.

[C] Nature is my good friend. I do feel good when I walk in the forest. I'd like to have a dream house in the countryside.

17 다음과 같이 풀이되는 말을 위 글에서 찾아 쓰시오.

> an animal that you keep in your home to give you company and pleasure

➡ _____

18 자연스러운 글이 되도록 [A]~[C]를 바르게 배열한 것은?

① [A] – [C] – [B]   ② [B] – [A] – [C]
③ [B] – [C] – [A]   ④ [C] – [A] – [B]
⑤ [C] – [B] – [A]

19 According to the passage, when does Minho feel good?
Answer in English with a full sentence.

➡ _____

[20~21] 다음 글을 읽고 물음에 답하시오.

A: My name is Tanabat Suasawathe, but people call me Chang. It means an elephant.
B: My name is Alina Ivanovna Dmitrieva. My middle name Ivanovna says that my father's name is Ivan.
C: My name is Carl Hansen. My parents didn't make my name, but chose it from a list.
D: My name is Han Sujin. My sister's name is Han Mijin. Our family name is Han, and both of our names end with jin.

20 위 글의 내용과 일치하지 않는 것을 모두 고르시오.

① People call Tanabat by his name.
② By her middle name, we can guess what the name of Alina's father is.
③ Carl's name is made by his parents.
④ Sujin's family name is Han.
⑤ Sujin has a sister whose name ends with jin like her.

21 What does Chang mean? Answer in English with a full sentence.

➡ _____

[22~24] 다음 글을 읽고 물음에 답하시오.

A Fun Place - Julie
    Welcome to my dream house! Having fun is what I want most, so my dream house is full of exciting things. It has a theater in the basement. There, I can eat cookies and enjoy my favorite movies. My dream house has a game room on the second floor. I can play many different kinds of games there. My house also has a swimming pool. I want to do fun things with my friends in my house. You can be my guest!

22 다음 중 위 글의 내용과 일치하지 않는 것은?

① It is easy to find exciting things in her dream house.
② The theater is located in the basement.
③ In order to enjoy her favorite movies, she has to go to the basement.
④ She wants to play various kinds of games in the game room.
⑤ The swimming pool is on the same floor as the game room.

23 Write the reason why Julie's dream house is full of exciting things. Use the phrase 'It's because.'

➡ _____

24 What can Julie do in the theater in her dream house?

➡ _____

Lesson 2

Experience Different Cultures!

 의사소통 기능

- 조언 구하기
  Can I get your advice on what to bring?
- 경고하기
  Make sure you don't wrap the present in white or black paper.

 언어 형식

- 현재완료진행시제
  I **have been living** in America for three years.
- 분사
  You can wave to and smile at an elderly man **walking** on the street.

Words & Expressions

Key Words

- **address** [ədrés] 몡 주소
- **advice** [ədváis] 몡 충고, 조언
- **baht** [ba:t] 몡 바트(태국의 화폐 단위)
- **bowl** [boul] 몡 그릇
- **bring** [briŋ] 동 가져오다
- **bump** [bʌmp] 동 부딪치다
- **China** [tʃáinə] 몡 중국
- **Chinese** [tʃainíːz] 혱 중국(어)의 몡 중국어, 중국인
- **correctly** [kəréktli] 뮈 정확하게, 올바르게
- **cultural** [kʌ́ltʃərəl] 혱 문화의, 문화적인
- **death** [deθ] 몡 죽음
- **differ** [dífər] 동 다르다
- **difference** [dífərəns] 몡 차이
- **difficult** [dífikʌlt] 혱 어려운
- **elderly** [éldərli] 혱 나이 든
- **entrance fee** 입장료
- **exchange** [ikstʃéindʒ] 동 교환하다, 환전하다
- **expensive** [ikspénsiv] 혱 비싼
- **experience** [ikspíəriəns] 동 경험하다
- **finally** [fáinəli] 뮈 마지막으로
- **goods** [gudz] 몡 상품, 제품
- **greet** [gri:t] 동 ~에게 인사하다
- **guest** [gest] 몡 손님
- **hand** [hænd] 동 건네주다
- **invite** [inváit] 동 초대하다
- **Japan** [dʒəpǽn] 몡 일본
- **mean** [mi:n] 동 의미하다
- **negative question** 부정의문문
- **pack** [pæk] 동 (짐을) 싸다, 꾸리다

- **pay** [pei] 동 지불하다
- **place** [pleis] 동 놓다
- **positive question** 긍정의문문
- **postal code** 우편 번호
- **present** [préznt] 몡 선물
- **prepare** [pripέər] 동 준비하다
- **price tag** 가격표
- **rate** [reit] 몡 율, 비율
- **receive** [risíːv] 동 받다
- **rude** [ru:d] 혱 무례한
- **Russia** [rʌ́ʃə] 몡 러시아
- **sales tax** 판매세
- **serve** [sə:rv] 동 제공하다, 대접하다
- **share** [ʃɛər] 동 나누다, 공유하다
- **shorts** [ʃɔːrts] 몡 반바지
- **since** [sins] 접 …한 이후로
- **soup** [su:p] 몡 국, 수프
- **surprising** [sərpráiziŋ] 혱 놀라운
- **state** [steit] 몡 주
- **stay** [stei] 동 머물다
- **tag** [tæg] 몡 꼬리표, 태그
- **Taiwan** [tàiwáːn] 몡 대만, 타이완
- **tax** [tæks] 몡 세금
- **temple** [témpl] 몡 사원
- **tongue** [tʌŋ] 몡 혀
- **traditional** [trədíʃənl] 혱 전통적인
- **uncomfortable** [ənkʌ́mfətəbəl] 혱 불편한
- **wave** [weiv] 동 (손을) 흔들다
- **wrap** [wæp] 동 포장하다, 싸다

Key Expressions

- **a pair of** 한 벌의
- **at first** 처음에
- **be regarded as** …로 여겨지다
- **between A and B** A와 B 사이에
- **each other** 서로
- **get off** 내리다
- **get used to ...** …에 익숙해지다
- **have a bad effect on** …에 나쁜 영향을 미치다
- **in response to** …의 대답으로

- **make sure (that)** +주어+동사 ... 반드시 …하다
- **place** 목적어 **together** …을 모으다
- **range from A to B** (범위가) A에서 B에 이르다
- **remember to V** …할 것을 기억하다
- **take a picture** 사진을 찍다
- **take off** …을 벗다
- **the same as ...** …와 똑같은
- **Why don't you** +동사원형...? …하는 게 어때?
- **would like to V** …하고 싶다

Word Power

※ 명사(국가 이름) – 명사(국민, 언어) / 형용사

- **China**(중국) – **Chinese**(중국인, 중국어) / 중국의
- **Japan**(일본) – **Japanese**(일본인, 일본어) / 일본의
- **Korea**(한국) – **Korean**(한국인, 한국어) / 한국의
- **Russia**(러시아) – **Russian**(러시아인, 러시아어) / 러시아의
- **Taiwan**(대만) – **Taiwanese**(대만인, 대만어) / 대만의
- **France**(프랑스) – **French**(프랑스인, 프랑스어) / 프랑스의

※ 서로 비슷한 뜻을 가진 어휘

- **elderly** : **aged** (늙은, 나이 먹은)
- **hand** : **give** (건네주다)
- **rude** : **impolite** (무례한)
- **death** : **dying** (죽음, 사망)

※ 서로 반대되는 뜻을 가진 어휘

- **negative** (부정적인) ↔ **positive** (긍정적인)
- **expensive** (비싼) ↔ **cheap** (값싼)
- **difference** (차이) ↔ **similarity** (닮음)
- **bring** (가져오다) ↔ **take** (가져가다)

English Dictionary

- **address** 주소
  → the number of the house, name of the road, and name of the town where a person lives or works, and where letters can be sent
  집의 번호, 도로의 이름, 사람이 살거나 일하는 마을의 이름, 그리고 편지가 발송될 수 있는 곳

- **advice** 충고, 조언
  → an opinion that someone offers you about what you should do or how you should act in a particular situation
  어떤 상황에서 무엇을 해야 하는지, 어떻게 행동해야 하는지에 대해 누군가가 제안하는 의견

- **bump** 부딪히다
  → to hurt part of your body by hitting it against something hard
  무언가 단단한 것에 부딪혀서 신체의 일부를 다치게 하다

- **correctly** 올바르게, 맞게
  → in a way that is in agreement with the true facts or with what is generally accepted
  사실 또는 일반적으로 받아들여지는 것과 일치하는 방식으로

- **entrance fee** 입장료
  → an amount of money that you pay in order to be allowed into a cinema, theater, etc.
  영화관, 극장 등에 들어갈 수 있도록 지불하는 돈

- **exchange** 교환하다
  → to give something to someone and receive something from that person
  누군가에게 무언가를 주고 그 사람에게서 무언가를 받다

- **goods** 상품, 제품
  → things for sale, or the things that you own
  판매용 물건이나 당신이 소유한 물건

- **invite** 초대하다
  → to ask or request someone to come to an event
  누군가에게 어떤 행사에 오도록 부탁하거나 요청하다

- **postal code** 우편번호
  → a short series of letters and numbers that is part of an address, and shows exactly where a place is
  주소의 일부이며 장소가 정확히 어디에 있는지 보여주는 짧은 일련의 문자 및 숫자

- **rude** 무례한
  → not polite 공손하지 않은

- **sales tax** 판매세
  → a tax paid by people when they buy goods or services 상품이나 서비스를 살 때 지불하는 세금

- **tag** 꼬리표
  → a small piece of paper, cloth, or metal with information on it, tied or stuck onto something larger 더 큰 무언가에 묶여 있거나 붙어 있는, 그 위에 정보가 있는 종이나 천, 금속의 작은 조각

- **tax** 세금
  → money paid to the government that is based on your income or the cost of goods or services you have bought 당신의 수입이나 구입한 상품이나 서비스의 비용에 근거해서 정부에 지불되는 돈

- **traditional** 전통적인
  → following or belonging to the customs or ways of behaving that have continued in a group of people or society for a long time without changing
  오랜 기간 동안 사람들 또는 사회에서 변하지 않고 계속되어 온 관습이나 행동 방식을 따르거나 속해 있는

- **uncomfortable** 불편한
  → not feeling comfortable and pleasant, or not making you feel comfortable and pleasant 편안하고 쾌적하지 않거나, 편안하고 쾌적하지 못하도록 하는

- **wave** 흔들다
  → to raise your hand and move it from side to side as a way of greeting someone
  누군가에게 인사하기 위한 방법으로 손을 들고 좌우로 움직이다

- **wrap** 포장하다
  → to cover or surround something with paper, cloth, or other material
  종이, 천 또는 기타 재료로 뭔가를 덮거나 둘러싸다

서답형

01 다음 글의 빈칸에 주어진 철자로 시작하는 단어를 쓰시오.

> Since Minhee's family moved to America, they have experienced many cultural d_____ between Korea and America.

02 다음 대화의 빈칸에 들어갈 말로 가장 적절한 것은?

> A: Can I get your _____ on how to write an address in English?
> B: Sure. You should write the street address first.

① letter   ② choice
③ advice   ④ tax
⑤ report

[03~04] 다음 설명에 해당하는 단어를 고르시오.

03

> an amount of money that you pay in order to be allowed into a cinema, theater, etc.

① sale   ② tag
③ rate   ④ sales tax
⑤ entrance fee

04

> not feeling comfortable and pleasant, or not making you feel comfortable and pleasant

① uncomfortable   ② rude
③ traditional   ④ cultural
⑤ colorful

서답형

05 다음 우리말에 맞게 빈칸에 알맞은 어휘를 쓰시오.

> 미국에서, 나이든 사람에게 손을 흔드는 것은 무례하다고 여겨지지 않는다.

➡ In America, waving to an older person is not _____ _____ rude.

06 다음 글의 빈칸에 공통으로 들어갈 말로 알맞은 것은?

> (A) Americans often ask _____ questions, such as "Aren't you coming?"
> (B) Scientists have a fairly _____ attitude to the theory.

① positive   ② easy
③ different   ④ negative
⑤ difficult

서답형

07 다음 짝지어진 단어의 관계가 같도록 빈칸에 알맞은 말을 쓰시오.

> Korea - Korean : China - _____

08 다음 빈칸에 들어갈 말이 알맞게 짝지어진 것은?

> Here in America, in most states, people pay a (A)_____ when they buy goods. It is called a sales tax. Sales tax rates differ by state. They (B)_____ from less than one percent to more than ten percent.

① tip – pay   ② money – range
③ tip – differ   ④ tax – pay
⑤ tax – range

01 다음 빈칸에 들어갈 말을 〈보기〉에서 찾아 쓰시오. (필요하면 변형하여 쓰시오.)

보기
tag   stay   make   share   culture

(1) I bought a present for Ms. Han. I _____ at her house here in Korea.

(2) _____ sure you don't ask a person's age in Western cultures.

(3) In America, you usually need to pay more than the price on the _____.

(4) I have been learning about _____ differences since I came to America.

02 다음 글의 밑줄 친 우리말에 해당하는 말을 주어진 단어 개수에 맞게 쓰시오.

(A) ~의 대답으로(3단어) negative questions, such as "Don't you like apple pie?" you should answer "No," if you don't like it. And you should answer "Yes," if you like it. These answers are (B) ~와 같은(3단어) the answers to (C) 긍정의 questions, such as "Do you like apple pie?"

➡ (A) _____   (B) _____
   (C) _____

03 다음 우리말과 같은 표현이 되도록 문장의 빈칸을 채우시오.

(1) 연장자에게 한 손으로 무언가를 주는 것은 무례한 것으로 여겨진다.
➡ Giving something to older people with one hand is regarded as _____.

(2) 그를 위해 작은 선물을 준비하고 싶어.
➡ I want to _____ a small gift for him.

(3) 사원을 방문할 때 반바지를 입어서는 안 된다.
➡ You shouldn't wear _____ when you visit a _____.

04 다음 영영풀이에 해당하는 단어를 〈보기〉에서 찾아 첫 번째 빈칸에 쓰고, 두 번째 빈칸에는 우리말 뜻을 쓰시오.

보기
exchange   wave   correctly

(1) _____ : to raise your hand and move it from side to side as a way of greeting someone: _____

(2) _____ : in a way that is in agreement with the true facts or with what is generally accepted: _____

(3) _____ : to give something to someone and receive something from that person: _____

05 빈칸에 공통으로 알맞은 단어를 주어진 철자로 시작하여 쓰시오.

(1) • They also take g_____ care of us and protect us.
   • The shop put all its g_____s in the shopwindow that day.

(2) • Make sure you use two h_____s when you h_____ it to her.

Conversation

교과서

1 조언 구하기

> **Can I get your advice on what to bring?** 무엇을 가져갈지에 대해 너의 조언을 구할 수 있을까?

- 충고를 구할 때는 어려운 상황을 말한 다음 'Can I get your advice on ~?'으로 말할 수 있다. Can I get your advice on my bad habit?(내 나쁜 버릇에 대해서 충고 좀 해줄래?)

- 조언을 구하는 다양한 표현들
  - How can I speak English well? 어떻게 하면 영어를 잘할 수 있을까?
  - What should I do to pass the exam? 시험에 합격하기 위해 무엇을 해야 하니?
  - What can I do to lose weight? 체중을 줄이기 위해 무엇을 할 수 있니?
  - What's your advice? 네 충고는 무엇이니?
  - What do you advise me to do? 넌 내가 무엇을 하라고 충고하니?
  - If you were me, what would you do? 네가 나라면 어떻게 할래?

- 조언을 할 때
  - (I think) You should apologize. (내 생각에는) 넌 사과해야 해.
  - Make sure you wash your hands. 손을 꼭 닦도록 해.
  - I suggest you read it again. 넌 그것을 다시 읽어야 해.
  - You need to read a lot. 넌 독서를 많이 할 필요가 있어.
  - You have to go to bed early. 넌 일찍 잠자리에 들어야 해.

  - Why don't you ~?나 How[What] about ~?의 제안하는 표현을 이용하여 조언을 할 수도 있다.
  - Why don't you help her? 그녀를 도와주지 그래?
  - How about inviting Ann? Ann을 초대하는 게 어때?

핵심 Check

1. 다음 대화의 빈칸에 들어갈 말로 <u>어색한</u> 것은?

   A: You look worried. What's wrong?
   B: I can't get a good grade. _____
   A: How about making a study plan?
   B: That's a good idea.
   ① What should I do?
   ② What can I do to get a good grade?
   ③ What do you advise me to do?
   ④ If you were me, what would you do?
   ⑤ Make sure you study harder.

2 경고하기

Make sure you don't wrap the present in white or black paper. 절대 선물을 흰색이나 검
정색 종이로 포장하지 않도록 해.

- 상대방에게 경고나 당부하는 표현으로 '반드시 ~하도록 하다, ~을 확실히 하다'라는 의미의 'make sure ~'를 사용한다. make sure 다음에 접속사 that을 생략할 수 있고 당부하고자 하는 내용을 주어와 동사를 갖춘 문장으로 쓴다. 다시 말해, sure 다음에는 '(that+)주어+동사'를 쓴다. 유사한 의미를 가진 표현으로 'had better+동사원형 ~', 'Don't forget to+동사원형 ~', 'remember to+동사원형 ~' 등이 있다.

- 경고하기 표현
  - **A:** Make sure you don't cook it for over ten minutes. (그것을 10분 넘게 조리하지 마.)
    B: Okay, I will. (알겠어요. 그럴게요.)
  - **A:** I think I caught a cold. (나 감기에 걸린 것 같아.)
    B: That's too bad. Make sure you take some medicine and relax. (안됐구나. 꼭 약을 먹고 쉬렴.)
  - Remember to call me when you leave. (떠날 때 나에게 전화하는 것을 기억해라.)
  - Don't forget to call me when you arrive. (도착하면 나에게 전화하는 것을 잊지 마.)
  - You had better call me when you arrive. (너는 도착하면 나에게 전화하는 것이 좋겠다.)

- 상대방의 경고나 당부를 받아들일 때 make sure 다음에 긍정문이 오면 'OK. I will.'로 답하고, 부정문이 오면 'OK. I won't.'로 답한다.
  - **A:** Make sure you give me a call when you get home. (집에 도착하면 내게 꼭 전화해.)
    B: Okay, I will. (응. 그렇게 할게.)
  - **A:** Make sure you won't be late for the class again. (다시는 지각하지 마.)
    B: Okay, I won't. (네, 안 할게요.)

핵심 Check

2. 다음 대화의 빈칸에 들어갈 알맞은 것은?

A: Mom, can I play soccer with my friends after school?
B: Sure, but _____.

① you don't have to play soccer
② you can't play soccer
③ you had better not play soccer
④ don't forget to stay home after school
⑤ make sure you come home before dinner

 Listen & Speak 1 A-1

G: I want to send this to my aunt in the USA.

B: What is it?

G: It's her *hanbok*. ❶Can I get your advice on how to write an address in English?

B: Sure. You should write the street address first.

G: ❷Like this?

B: Yes. ❸Then, write the name of the city and the state and then the postal code. Finally, write the country.

G: Thanks for your help.

G: 나는 이것을 미국에 계신 이모에게 보내고 싶어.

B: 그게 뭔데?

G: 이모의 한복이야. 영어로 주소를 어떻게 쓰는지에 대해 너의 조언을 구할 수 있을까?

B: 물론이지. 먼저 거리 주소부터 적어야 해.

G: 이렇게?

B: 응. 그리고 나서, 도시 이름과 주 그리고 그 다음에 우편 번호를 적어. 마지막으로 국가를 적어.

G: 도와줘서 고마워.

---

❶ 충고를 구할 때 쓰는 표현으로, 'how to+동사원형'은 '어떻게 ~하는지, ~하는 방법'으로 해석한다.

❷ like는 전치사로 '~처럼'의 뜻이다.

❸ 순서대로 해야 할 일을 열거할 때 사용하는 표현이다.

Check(√) True or False

(1) G knows how to write an address in English.　　　　　　　　　　　　　　T ☐ F ☐

(2) G has to write the name of the country finally when she writes an address in English.　　　T ☐ F ☐

 Listen & Speak 2-1

B: Sena, I bought a present for Ms. Han. I have stayed at her house here in Korea.

G: That's great. What did you buy her?

B: ❶I bought her a hat. Do you think she'll love it?

G: Yes. ❷Make sure you use two hands when ❸you hand it to her.

B: Why?

G: ❹Because giving something to older people with one hand is regarded as rude in Korea.

B: Okay. I'll remember that.

B: 세나야, 나 한 씨 아주머니께 드릴 선물을 샀어. 이곳 한국에서 그녀의 집에 머물고 있거든.

G: 그거 잘 됐네. 그녀를 위해 무엇을 샀니?

B: 모자를 샀어. 그녀가 그것을 좋아할 거라고 생각하니?

G: 응. 그녀에게 그것을 건넬 때 반드시 두 손으로 건네도록 해.

B: 왜?

G: 연장자에게 한 손으로 무언가를 주는 것은 한국에서 무례한 것으로 여겨지거든.

B: 알겠어. 그걸 기억할게.

---

❶ buy+간접목적어(~에게)+직접목적어(~을)'의 4형식으로 'I bought a hat for her.'로 바꾸어 쓸 수 있다.

❷ 상대방에게 경고하는 표현으로 '반드시 ~하도록 하다'라는 의미이다. Make sure 뒤에 '(that+)주어+동사'를 사용한다.

❸ hand는 동사로 '건네주다'라는 의미이다. 직접목적어가 대명사(it)일 때는 'you hand her it.'처럼 4형식으로 사용하지 않는다.

❹ 이유의 부사절 접속사로 'Because+주어+동사 ~'의 어순을 취한다. giving은 동명사 주어로 동사는 단수 is가 온다. be regarded as는 '~로 여겨지다'라는 의미이다.

Check(√) True or False

(3) Sena will give a hat to Ms. Han.　　　　　　　　　　　　　　　　　T ☐ F ☐

(4) Koreans should not give something to the elderly with one hand.　　　　　　T ☐ F ☐

Listen & Speak 1 B

G: Look at the people ❶wearing traditional Moroccan clothes. They are really beautiful. I want to take pictures of them.

M: Wait. ❷There is an important thing you need to know before taking pictures.

G: Oh, really? Can I get your advice on it?

M: Yes. You shouldn't take pictures of Moroccan people ❸without asking.

G: Why?

M: They believe it may ❹have a bad effect on them when someone takes their picture.

G: 모로코 전통 의상을 입고 있는 사람들을 보세요. 그들은 매우 아름다워요. 그들의 사진을 찍고 싶어요.

M: 잠깐. 네가 사진을 찍기 전에 알아야 할 중요한 것이 있어.

G: 오, 정말요? 그것에 대해 조언을 구할 수 있을까요?

M: 응. 너는 물어보지 않고 모로코 사람들의 사진을 찍으면 안 돼.

G: 왜요?

M: 그들은 누군가가 자신의 사진을 찍으면 그것이 그들에게 나쁜 영향을 끼칠 것이라고 믿어.

❶ wearing은 명사 the people을 수식하는 현재분사이다.

❷ thing과 you 사이에 목적격 관계대명사 that[which]이 생략되어 있다. There is an important thing (that) you need to know ~. before는 전치사로 뒤에 동명사 taking이 온다.

❸ 전치사 without+동명사(asking): 물어보지 않고서

❹ have an effect on ~: ~에 영향을 미치다

Check(√) True or False

(5) G wants to take pictures of the people wearing traditional Moroccan clothes. T ☐ F ☐

(6) In Morocco, you can take pictures of Moroccan people freely. T ☐ F ☐

Listen & Speak 2 A-2

B: ❶Did you pack everything you need for the trip to Thailand tomorrow?

G: Not yet. What should I take?

B: ❷Remember to bring a pair of long pants or a long skirt.

G: Why? It's very hot in Thailand, ❸isn't it?

B: Yes, but there are many temples in Thailand. You shouldn't wear shorts when you visit a temple.

G: Okay. Is there anything else?

B: ❹Make sure you exchange Korean won to Thai baht.

B: 너는 내일 태국 여행에 필요한 모든 것을 챙겼니?

G: 아니 아직. 무엇을 가져가야 할까?

B: 긴 바지나 긴 치마를 한 벌 가져가는 것을 기억해.

G: 왜? 태국은 매우 덥잖아, 그렇지 않니?

B: 응, 하지만 태국에는 절이 많아. 너는 절을 방문할 때 반바지를 입으면 안 돼.

G: 알겠어. 다른 것이 또 있니?

B: 반드시 한국 원화를 태국 바트로 환전하도록 해.

❶ everything과 you 사이에 목적격 관계대명사 that[which]이 생략되어 있다.

❷ remember+to부정사: ~할 것을 기억하다 / remember+V-ing(동명사): ~한 것을 기억하다

❸ 평서문이 be동사의 긍정문이므로, 부가의문문에는 부정문 isn't와 대명사 it을 사용한다.

❹ 상대방에게 경고하는 표현으로 '반드시 ~하도록 하다'라는 의미이다. Make sure 뒤에 '주어+동사'를 사용한다.

Check(√) True or False

(7) G packed everything she needs for the trip to Thailand. T ☐ F ☐

(8) G shouldn't wear shorts when she visits temples in Thailand. T ☐ F ☐

Warm Up

1. People show their tongues in Tibet.
2. ❶People place their hands together and say "Namaste" in India.
3. ❷Men bump their noses in the United Arab Emirates.

❶ place+목적어+together: ～을 모으다   ❷ bump: 부딪히다

Listen & Speak 1 B

A: ❶Can I get your advice on visiting the Netherlands?
B: Sure. ❷You shouldn't stand on a bike path.
A: Can I get your advice on visiting the USA?
B: Sure. You should sit in the back seat in the taxi.

❶ 상대방의 조언을 구할 때 사용하는 표현이다. 전치사 on 뒤에 동명사가 와야 한다.
❷ shouldn't는 조동사의 부정문으로 '～해서는 안 된다'라는 의미이다.

Communication Task-Step 2

A: ❶Which country would you like to visit?
B: ❷I'd like to visit Malaysia. Can I get your advice on traveling there?
C: Sure. Make sure you don't use ❸your left hand to hand something to someone.
B: Okay. Thanks.

❶ which는 의문사로 명사 country를 수식하는 역할을 한다.
❷ 'I'd(=would) like to'는 '～하고 싶다'라는 뜻이다.
❸ your left hand의 'hand'는 명사로 '손'이고, to hand의 'hand'는 동사로 '건네주다'라는 뜻이다.

Real Life Talk

Seho: My Chinese friend invited me to his house for dinner this Friday.
Bora: That's good. ❶I hope you enjoy having dinner at his house.
Seho: I want to prepare a small gift for him. You lived in China for several years. Can I get your advice on what to bring?

Bora: How about some tea?
Seho: Tea?
Bora: Yes. Most Chinese people like to receive tea ❷as a present. They enjoy drinking tea. Also, they usually serve tea to guests.
Seho: Oh, thanks. Is there anything else that I need to know?
Bora: ❸Make sure you don't wrap the present in white or black paper. White and black mean death in China.
Seho: Okay. I'll remember that. Thank you for the advice.

❶ 'I hope (that+)주어+동사 ～'로 접속사 that이 생략되어 있다. enjoy는 목적어로 동명사(having)를 취한다.
❷ as는 전치사로 '～로'의 의미이다.
❸ 상대방에게 경고하는 표현으로 '반드시 ～하도록 하다'라는 의미이다. Make sure 뒤에 '(that+)주어+동사'를 사용한다.

Wrap Up 1

B: I'm going to Japan this summer. Can I get some advice on visiting there?
G: Make sure you pay when you get off the bus.
B: Oh, I didn't know that. Are there any other things I should remember?
G: Pick up the bowl and hold it ❶while eating. Also, ❷when having soup, you should drink it without a spoon.
B: Okay. Thanks

❶ 'while eating'은 '～하는 동안'의 의미로 'while you are eating'에서 주어와 be동사가 생략된 형태이다.
❷ when having soup는 when you are having soup에서 주어와 be동사가 생략된 형태이다.

Wrap Up 2

M: ❶I want to give flowers to my friend from Russia. ❷Is there anything I should remember?
W: Make sure you don't give flowers in even numbers.

❶ give A to B: B에게 A를 주다, from: ～출신인
❷ anything과 I 사이에는 목적격 관계대명사 that[which]이 생략되어 있다.

● 다음 우리말과 일치하도록 빈칸에 알맞은 말을 쓰시오.

Warm Up

1. People _____ _____ _____ in Tibet.
2. People _____ their hands _____ and say "Namaste" in India.
3. Men _____ _____ _____ in the United Arab Emirates.

1. 티베트 사람들은 그들의 혀를 보여준다.
2. 인도 사람들은 손을 모으고 "나마스테"라고 말한다.
3. 아랍에미리트에서 남자들은 코를 부딪친다.

Listen & Speak 1 A

1. G: I want _____ _____ this to my _____ in the USA.

   B: _____ is it?

   G: It's her *hanbok*. Can I _____ your _____ on _____ _____ _____ an _____ in English?

   B: Sure. You should write the _____ _____ first.

   G: _____ this?

   B: Yes. Then, write the name of the city and the _____ and then the _____ _____. _____, write the country.

   G: Thanks for your help.

2. G: _____ _____ the people _____ _____ Moroccan clothes. They are really beautiful. I want _____ _____ _____ _____ them.

   M: Wait. _____ _____ an important thing you need to know _____ _____ pictures.

   G: Oh, really? Can I get your _____ _____ it?

   M: Yes. You shouldn't _____ _____ _____ _____ people _____ _____.

   G: Why?

   M: They believe it may have _____ _____ _____ them _____ someone takes their picture.

1. G: 나는 이것을 미국에 계신 이모에게 보내고 싶어.
   B: 그게 뭔데?
   G: 이모의 한복이야. 영어로 주소를 어떻게 쓰는지에 대해 내가 너의 조언을 구할 수 있을까?
   B: 물론이지. 먼저 거리 주소부터 적어야 해.
   G: 이렇게?
   B: 응. 그러고 나서, 도시 이름과 주 그리고 그 다음에 우편 번호를 적어. 마지막으로 국가를 적어.
   G: 도와줘서 고마워.

2. G: 모로코 전통 의상을 입고 있는 사람들을 보세요. 그들은 매우 아름다워요. 그들의 사진을 찍고 싶어요.
   M: 잠깐. 네가 사진을 찍기 전에 알아야 할 중요한 것이 있어.
   G: 오, 정말요? 그것에 대해 조언을 구할 수 있을까요?
   M: 응. 너는 물어보지 않고 모로코 사람들의 사진을 찍으면 안 돼.
   G: 왜요?
   M: 그들은 누군가가 자신의 사진을 찍으면 그것이 그들에게 나쁜 영향을 끼칠 것이라고 믿어.

Listen & Speak 1 B

A: _____ _____ _____ your _____ on _____ the Netherlands?

B: Sure. You _____ stand on a bike _____.

A: Can I _____ _____ _____ _____ _____ the USA?

B: Sure. You _____ in the _____ _____ in the taxi.

A: 네덜란드를 방문하는 것에 대해 너의 조언을 구할 수 있을까?
B: 물론이지. 너는 자전거 도로에 서 있으면 안 돼.

A: 미국을 방문하는 것에 대해 조언을 구할 수 있을까?
B: 물론이지. 택시에서는 뒷좌석에 앉아야 해.

Listen & Speak 2 A

1. **B:** Sena, I bought a _____ for Ms. Han. I _____ _____ at her house here in Korea.

   G: That's great. _____ did you _____ her?

   B: I _____ her a hat. Do you think she'll love it?

   G: Yes. _____ _____ you use two hands when you _____ it _____ her.

   B: Why?

   G: Because _____ something to older people with one hand _____ _____ _____ _____ _____ in Korea.

   B: Okay. I'll remember that.

2. **B:** Did you _____ everything you need for the trip to Thailand tomorrow?

   G: Not _____. What should I _____?

   B: _____ _____ _____ a pair of long pants or a long skirt.

   G: Why? It's very hot in Thailand, _____ it?

   B: Yes, but _____ _____ many _____ in Thailand. You shouldn't wear _____ when you visit a _____.

   G: Okay. Is there anything _____?

   B: _____ _____ you _____ Korean won _____ Thai baht.

Listen & Speak 2 B

A: Is there anything I need to _____ when I eat in _____?

B: Yes. _____ _____ you _____ your hands _____ the table _____ _____ _____.

A: Is there _____ I need to remember _____ I eat in Uzbekistan?

B: Yes. _____ _____ you don't _____ _____ your hat or shoes _____ _____ a meal.

Real Life Talk

Seho: My _____ friend _____ me to his house for dinner this Friday.

Bora: That's good. I hope you enjoy _____ dinner at his house.

1. **B:** 세나야, 나 한 씨 아주머니께 드릴 선물을 샀어. 이곳 한국에서 그녀의 집에 머물고 있거든.
   G: 그거 잘 됐네. 그녀를 위해 무엇을 샀니?
   B: 모자를 샀어. 그녀가 그것을 좋아할 거라고 생각하니?
   G: 응. 그녀에게 그것을 건넬 때 반드시 두 손으로 건네도록 해.
   B: 왜?
   G: 연장자에게 한 손으로 무언가를 주는 것은 한국에서 무례한 것으로 여겨지거든.
   B: 알겠어. 그걸 기억할게.

2. **B:** 너는 내일 태국 여행에 필요한 모든 것을 챙겼니?
   G: 아니 아직. 무엇을 가져가야 할까?
   B: 긴 바지나 긴 치마를 한 벌 가져가는 것을 기억해.
   G: 왜? 태국은 매우 덥잖아, 그렇지 않니?
   B: 응, 하지만 태국에는 절이 많아. 너는 절을 방문할 때 반바지를 입으면 안 돼.
   G: 알겠어. 다른 것이 또 있니?
   B: 반드시 한국 원화를 태국 바트로 환전하도록 해.

A: 내가 프랑스에서 식사할 때 기억해야 할 것이 있니?
B: 응. 반드시 항상 손을 식탁 위에 올려두도록 해.

A: 내가 우즈베키스탄에서 식사할 때 기억해야 할 것이 있니?
B: 응. 식사할 때 모자나 신발을 절대 벗지 않도록 해.

세호: 나의 중국인 친구가 이번 주 금요일 저녁 식사에 나를 집으로 초대했어.
보라: 좋네. 그 친구 집에서 네가 즐거운 저녁 식사하기를 바라.

Seho: I want to _____ a small gift for him. You lived in China for _____ years. Can I get your _____ on _____ _____ _____?

Bora: _____ _____ some tea?

Seho: Tea?

Bora: Yes. _____ Chinese people like to _____ tea _____ a _____. They enjoy _____ tea. Also, they usually _____ tea to _____.

Seho: Oh, thanks. Is there anything else _____ I need to know?

Bora: _____ _____ you don't _____ the present in white or black paper. White and black _____ _____ in China.

Seho: Okay. I'll remember that. Thank you for the _____.

Communication Task Step 2

A: _____ country would you like to visit?

B: I'd like to visit Malaysia. Can I _____ your _____ on _____ there?

C: Sure. _____ _____ you don't use your left _____ to hand something to someone.

B: Okay. Thanks.

Wrap Up

1. **B:** I'm _____ to Japan this summer. Can I _____ some advice on _____ there?

   G: Make sure you _____ when you _____ _____ the bus.

   B: Oh, I didn't know that. Are there any other things I should _____?

   G: _____ up the bowl and hold it _____ _____. Also, _____ _____ soup, you should drink it _____ a spoon.

   B: Okay. Thanks.

2. **M:** I want _____ _____ flowers to my friend _____ Russia. Is there anything I should _____?

   W: _____ _____ you don't give flowers in even numbers.

01 우리말에 맞도록 주어진 단어를 이용하여 쓰시오.

> • 무엇을 입을지에 대해 제가 당신의 조언을 구할 수 있을까요?
> (can / get / advice / to / wear)

➡ _____

02 다음 대화의 빈칸에 들어갈 말로 <u>어색한</u> 것은?

> A: Is there anything I need to remember when I eat in France?
> B: Yes. _____ on the table at all times.

① Remember to keep your hands
② You'd better keep your hands
③ Make sure you keep your hands
④ Don't forget to keep your hands
⑤ Don't keep your hands

03 다음 대화의 빈칸에 들어갈 말로 알맞은 것은?

> A: _____
> B: Sure. You should never stand on a bike path.

① Do you know when to visit the U.S.A?
② Can I get your advice on what to bring?
③ Can I get your advice on visiting the Netherlands?
④ Which country would you like to travel to?
⑤ Did you enjoy riding a bike?

04 다음 우리말과 같도록 문장의 빈칸을 채우시오.

> 인도에서는 사람들이 손을 모으고 '나마스테'라고 말한다.

➡ People _____ their hands _____ and say "Namaste" in India.

[01~02] 다음 대화를 읽고 물음에 답하시오.

Girl: I want to send this to my aunt in the USA.

Boy: What is it?

Girl: It's her *hanbok*. Can I get your advice on (A)_____?

Boy: Sure. You should write the street address first.

Girl: Like this?

Boy: Yes. Then, write the name of the city and the state and then the postal code. Finally, write the country.

01 위 대화의 빈칸 (A)에 들어갈 말로 알맞은 것은?

① what to wear
② how to wear *hanbok*
③ how to write an address in English
④ what gift to buy
⑤ which way to go

02 위 대화의 내용과 일치하지 <u>않는</u> 것은?

① The girl's aunt lives in the USA.
② The girl wants to decide whether to wear *hanbok*.
③ The girl wants to know how to write an address in English.
④ The boy knows how to write an address in English.
⑤ The girl has to write the street address first.

03 다음 주어진 문장에 이어질 대화 순서로 알맞은 것은?

A: Which country would you like to visit?

(A) Okay. Thanks.
(B) I'd like to visit Malaysia. Can I get your advice on traveling there?
(C) Sure. Make sure you don't use your left hand to hand something to someone.

① (A)–(B)–(C)　　② (B)–(A)–(C)
③ (B)–(C)–(A)　　④ (C)–(A)–(B)
⑤ (C)–(B)–(A)

04 다음 대화의 빈칸에 들어갈 말로 알맞은 것을 고르시오.

A: _____
B: Sure. You should never chew gum on the street.

① Can I get your advice on getting a job in Singapore?
② Do you think I should visit Singapore?
③ Can you tell me when you will visit Singapore?
④ What would you like to do in Singapore?
⑤ Can I get some advice on visiting Singapore?

서답형
05 다음 대화의 빈칸에 들어갈 두 단어의 말을 쓰시오.

M: I want to give flowers to my friend from Russia. Is there anything I should remember?
W: _____ _____ you don't give flowers in even numbers.

*even number 짝수

06 다음 대화 중 **어색한** 것은?

① A: Which country would you like to visit?

B: I'd like to visit Malaysia.

② A: Can I get your advice on visiting the USA?

B: Sure. You should sit in the back seat in the taxi.

③ A: Can I get your advice on making Mattang?

B: Sure. Don't add too much sugar.

④ A: Do you think she'll like it?

B: Make sure you use two hands when you hand it to her.

⑤ A: Can I get some advice on visiting Japan?

B: Make sure you pay when you get off the bus.

07 다음 대화의 밑줄 친 우리말에 맞게 주어진 단어를 이용하여 영어로 쓰시오. (어형 변화 필수)

> B: Did you pack everything you need for the trip to Thailand tomorrow?
>
> G: Not yet. What should I take?
>
> B: 긴 바지나 긴 치마를 한 벌 가져가는 것을 기억해.

> remember / bring / a long skirt / long pant / a pair of / or

➡ _____

08 다음 대화의 밑줄 친 부분의 의도로 알맞은 것은?

> A: Can I get your advice on traveling there?
>
> B: Sure. Make sure you don't use your left hand to hand something to someone.
>
> A: Okay. Thanks.

① 조언 구하기　　　② 경고하기

③ 확신 표현하기　　④ 궁금증 표현하기

⑤ 가능성 묻기

[09~10] 다음 대화를 읽고 물음에 답하시오.

Seho: My Chinese friend invited me to his house for dinner this Friday.

Bora: That's good. I hope you enjoy having dinner at his house. (①)

Seho: I want to prepare a small gift for him. You lived in China for several years. Can I get your advice on what to bring? (②)

Bora: How about some tea?

Seho: Tea? (③)

Bora: Yes. Most Chinese people like to receive tea as a present. They enjoy drinking tea. Also, they usually serve tea to guests.

Seho: Oh, thanks. (④)

Bora: Make sure you don't wrap the present in white or black paper. White and black mean death in China. (⑤)

Seho: Okay. I'll remember that. Thank you for the advice.

09 위 대화의 ①~⑤ 중 주어진 문장이 들어갈 위치로 알맞은 것은?

> Is there anything else that I need to know?

①　　②　　③　　④　　⑤

10 위 대화를 읽고 답할 수 **없는** 것은?

① Who invited Seho to dinner?

② What did Bora suggest as a present for Seho's Chinese friend?

③ Why did Bora suggest some tea as a gift?

④ Why shouldn't Seho wrap the present in white or black paper?

⑤ In what color should Seho wrap the present?

[01~02] 다음 대화를 읽고 물음에 답하시오.

Seho: My Chinese friend invited me to his house for dinner this Friday.

Bora: That's good. I hope you enjoy having dinner at his house.

Seho: I want to prepare a small gift for him. You lived in China for several years. (A)
_____

Bora: How about some tea?

Seho: Tea?

Bora: Yes. Most Chinese people like to receive tea as a present. They enjoy drinking tea. Also, they usually serve tea to guests.

Seho: Oh, thanks. Is there anything else that I need to know?

Bora: (B)선물을 흰색이나 검은색 종이로 포장하지 않도록 해. White and black mean death in China.

Seho: Okay. I'll remember that. Thank you for the advice.

01 위 대화의 빈칸 (A)에 주어진 조건에 맞게 영어로 쓰시오.

┤ 조건 ├
• 조언을 구하는 표현을 쓸 것.
• 'can, get, on, what, bring'을 사용할 것.
• to부정사를 사용할 것.

➡ _____

02 위 대화의 밑줄 친 (B)의 우리말을 보고 주어진 조건에 맞게 영어로 쓰시오.

┤ 조건 ├
• Make sure를 사용하여 경고하는 표현을 쓸 것.
• 'the present', 'in', 'or'를 사용할 것.

➡ _____
_____

03 다음 대화의 빈칸에 들어갈 말로 자연스러운 것을 〈보기〉에서 찾아 문장을 쓰시오.

B: Did you pack everything you need for the trip to Thailand tomorrow?

G: Not yet. (A)_____

B: Remember to bring a pair of long pants or a long skirt.

G: Why? It's very hot in Thailand, isn't it?

B: Yes, but there are many temples in Thailand. (B)_____
_____

G: Okay. Is there anything else?

B: (C)_____

┤ 보기 ├
• You shouldn't wear shorts when you visit a temple.
• What should I take?
• Make sure you exchange Korean won to Thai baht.

04 다음 대화의 'Ben'의 조언에 맞게 주소를 알맞은 순서로 배열하시오.

Jihee: I want to send this to my aunt in the USA.

Ben: What is it?

Jihee: It's her _hanbok_. Can I get your advice on how to write an address in English?

Ben: Sure. You should write the street address first.

Jihee: Like this?

Ben: Yes. Then, write the name of the city and the state and then the postal code. Finally, write the country.

USA, California 94101, San Francisco, 123 Van Ness Street

➡ _____

Grammar

① 현재완료진행시제

> • They **have been searching** for the missing child for 3 days. 그들은 미아를 3일간 수색 중이다.
> • Mom **has been knitting** since last winter. 엄마는 작년 겨울부터 뜨개질을 하고 있는 중이다.

■ 과거에 시작한 일이 현재까지 계속 진행되고 있는 경우를 나타낼 때 사용한다.
  • My sister Sumi **has been running** on the ground for 6 hours. 내 동생 Sumi는 6시간 동안 운동장을 달리고 있는 중이다.
  • Two giant typhoons **have been heading** toward Japan. 거대한 태풍 2개가 일본을 향해 가고 있는 중이다.

■ 현재완료 '계속' 용법과 비슷하지만, 현재완료진행은 '상태'가 아닌, '동작'을 나타낸다.
  • Tommy and Susan **have known** each other since they were young. (상태의 계속 – 현재완료진행 불가)
  • Jonathan **has been studying** quantum physics. Jonathan은 양자물리학을 공부해 오고 있는 중이다. (동작의 계속 – 현재완료진행 가능)

■ 현재완료진행형 문장과 자주 쓰이는 부사구는 'for(~ 동안)'와 'since(~ 이후로)'이다.
  • John's family **have been staying** at Highclass Hotel **since** last Friday. John의 가족은 지난 금요일 이후로 Highclass 호텔에 체류하는 중이다.
  • Mom **has been talking** on the phone with Aunt Mary **for** four hours. 엄마는 Mary 이모와 4시간 동안 전화로 얘기하는 중이다.

■ 현재완료진행형은 의미상 두 문장으로 나누어 쓸 수 있다. (과거+현재진행)
  • The members of the committee **have been discussing** the issue for 2 days.
    → The members of the committee **began** to discuss the issue **2 days ago**. (과거) + They're still **discussing** it. (현재진행형)

■ 현재완료시제는 과거에서 현재까지의 동작의 완료, 경험, 결과 또는 계속을 의미한다.
  • Susan **hasn't finished** her part of the project yet. Susan은 아직 프로젝트에서의 그녀 몫을 끝내지 못했다. 〈완료〉
  • **Have** you ever **been** to Science Fair? 과학 박람회에 가본 적 있나요? 〈경험〉
  • My wife **has just lost** her traffic card. 내 아내가 방금 교통카드를 잃어버렸다. 〈결과〉
  • It **has rained** since last weekend. 지난 주말부터 계속 비가 오고 있다. 〈계속〉

 핵심 Check

1. 괄호 안에서 알맞은 것을 고르시오.
  (1) I have been feeling bad (for / since) I saw Abe.
  (2) He has been playing the trumpet (for / since) two and half hours.

2 분사

> Look at the dog **barking** at the strangers. 낯선 사람들을 향해 짖고 있는 개를 보아라.
>
> I know the girls **smiling** at me over there. 나는 저기에서 나를 향해 미소 짓고 있는 소녀들을 안다.

- 현재분사는 '동사원형+-ing' 형태로 형용사처럼 명사를 앞 또는 뒤에서 꾸며준다. 일반적으로는 명사 앞에서, 다른 어구와 함께 구(phrase)를 이룰 때는 명사 뒤에서 꾸민다.
  - The **crying** baby kicked the blanket. 울고 있는 아기가 이불을 발로 찼다.
  - Do you know the baby **crying** in the blanket? 이불 속에서 울고 있는 아기를 아니?

- 현재분사(-ing)는 능동/진행, 과거분사(p.p.)는 수동/완료의 의미를 갖는다.
  - The researchers are **searching** for the evidence of evolution. 연구진들은 진화의 증거를 찾고 있는 중이다.
  - Would you introduce me to the girl **dancing** on the stage? 무대에서 춤추고 있는 소녀를 소개해 주실래요?
  - Watch out the **broken** window! 깨진 창문을 조심하세요!
  - Some actors **invited** to the film festival didn't show up. 영화제에 초대된 일부 배우들이 나타나지 않았다.

- 명사를 뒤에서 꾸며 주는 분사구는 '주격 관계대명사+be동사'가 생략된 것으로 볼 수 있다.
  - The girl (**who is**) **wearing** her school uniform is my niece. 교복을 입고 있는 그 소녀는 내 조카딸이다.
  - The professor wants to buy the book (**which was**) **written** by Leonardo da Vinci. 그 교수는 Leonardo da Vinci에 의해 쓰인 책을 사고 싶어한다.

- 분사는 명사를 꾸며주는 역할 외에도, 주어나 목적어의 보충 설명을 하는 서술 용법이 있다. 이 경우, 주격 보어 또는 목적격 보어가 된다.
  - A lady stood **looking** at the picture. 한 숙녀가 그림을 보며 서 있었다.
  - The injured soldier lay **surrounded** by the enemies. 그 부상당한 군인이 적들에게 둘러싸인 채로 누워 있었다.
  - I am sorry to have kept you **waiting** so long. 그렇게 오래 기다리시게 해서 미안합니다.
  - Forest Gump heard his name **called**. Forest Gump는 그의 이름이 불리는 것을 들었다.
  - Finally, Sandra had her dream house **built** in her hometown. 마침내 Sandra는 그녀의 고향에 자신의 꿈의 집이 건축되도록 했다.

핵심 Check

2. 괄호 안에서 알맞은 것을 고르시오.

(1) I must have the car (repaired / repairing) by noon.

(2) Julie had her leg (breaking / broken) in the bike accident.

01 다음 문장에서 어법상 <u>어색한</u> 부분을 바르게 고쳐 쓰시오.

(1) She wants to make herself understanding in French.

_____ ➡ _____

(2) I have gone to Washington D.C. before.

_____ ➡ _____

(3) Shane has been studied mathematics since last year.

_____ ➡ _____

(4) The leader of the boy band received a letter writing in Spanish.

_____ ➡ _____

02 다음 중 어법상 바르지 <u>않은</u> 것은?

① My daughter has been using the smartphone for six hours.
② Roberto has been singing since this morning.
③ John's friends have been watching a horror movie.
④ The two families have been knowing each other since 1990s.
⑤ They all have been digging the hole to survive.

03 다음 대화의 밑줄 친 부분 중에서 어법상 <u>잘못된</u> 것을 고르시오.

> A: ①Are you ②tiring ③from the trip to Switzerland?
> B: No. I ④do ⑤feel good.

04 다음 우리말에 맞게 주어진 단어를 바르게 배열하시오. (필요하면 어형을 바꿀 것)

(1) Peter가 찍은 사진은 흥미로웠다. (was, by, the, Peter, picture, take, interesting)

➡ _____

(2) Billy의 엄마는 네 시간째 요리를 해오고 있는 중이다. (cook, hours, mom, been, have, for, five, Billy)

➡ _____

01 다음 빈칸에 알맞은 것은?

> Jimin began writing a poem half an hour ago, and she is still writing it now.
> = Jimin _____ a poem for half an hour.

① has begun   ② has wrote
③ has been writing   ④ has been
⑤ has been written

서답형
02 다음 문장에서 어법상 틀린 부분을 찾아 바르게 고쳐 쓰시오.

> She bought a bag making in Philippines.

_____ ➡ _____

서답형
03 다음 예시와 같이 두 문장을 한 문장으로 연결할 때, 빈칸에 알맞은 말을 넣으시오.

> • The little girl is reading a book in an armchair. She is my cousin.
>   → The little girl reading a book in an armchair is my cousin.

(1) There were many people.
    They were watching fireworks.
    → There were _____
        fireworks.
(2) The warehouse is very large.
    It was built by my father.
    → The warehouse _____ _____
        _____ very large.

04 다음 괄호 안의 단어의 알맞은 형태가 순서대로 바르게 짝 지어진 것은?

> • The girl (pick) up trash is my daughter.
> • The money (spend) for our vacation is too much.
> • The lecture was (bore) for the kids.

① picking – spending – boring
② picking – spent – bored
③ picking – spent – boring
④ picked – spending – bored
⑤ picked – spent – boring

서답형
05 다음 두 문장을 한 문장으로 표현할 때, 빈칸에 들어갈 알맞은 말을 쓰시오.

> • Sam started to play the cello 16 years ago.
> • He's still playing the cello now.

➡ Sam _____ _____ _____ the cello _____ 16 years.

06 다음 중 밑줄 친 부분의 쓰임이 다른 하나는?

① The girl standing next to me is Julie.
② They tried opening the box.
③ The sleeping lion seemed like a baby.
④ The boy watching TV got excited.
⑤ We saw a talking horse in Thai.

서답형
07 Translate the following Korean into English as directed below.

> • 노란 티셔츠를 입고 있는 아이가 단풍나무 아래에 앉아 있다.

<Directions>
• Use the words: T-shirt, the, wear, maple, be, under (Change the form if necessary.)
• Complete it with 12 words in total.

➡ The kid _____ _____ _____
_____ _____ _____ _____
_____ _____ tree.

08 다음 밑줄 친 ⓐ, ⓑ를 어법상 알맞게 고친 것이 차례대로 짝 지어진 것은?

> - She warned the baby not to touch the ⓐburn fire.
> - The students ⓑpass by bowed to the principal politely.

① burning – passed
② burnt – have been passing
③ burning – having been passed
④ burnt – being passed
⑤ burning – passing

09 다음 중 어법상 어색한 것을 모두 고르면?

① The little girl reads a storybook under the big tree is Sally.
② Kahn has been searching for a new item for his business since last year.
③ The member of the committee raising her hand was Jenny.
④ Sam Smith has been lied to all of us.
⑤ The people my family meeting there were so kind and gentle.

10 다음 중 어법상 옳은 것은?

① Steve has been losing his first job.
② The old man who sitting next to Mr. Brown was the mayor of the city.
③ The boy rides a horse over there is Frank.
④ There was no cake leaving for me.
⑤ This is the road leading to the castle.

11 다음 각 문장에서 어법상 어색한 부분을 하나씩 찾아서 알맞게 고치시오.

(1) William bought a book writing in ancient Greek from a second-hand bookstore.
➡ _____

(2) These are the cookies making with the oven James bought last week.
➡ _____

(3) Who will take care of the baby cried alone in the dark room?
➡ _____

12 다음 중 밑줄 친 부분의 쓰임이 〈보기〉와 다른 것은?

> ┤ 보기 ├
> She has been elected mayor twice.

① David hasn't heard of the word "ZZang-Nan-Dah" before.
② My family has been to Europe many times.
③ Have you witnessed the crime scene even once?
④ Michael has driven a jet-boat before.
⑤ Emily has gone to Hawaii with her family.

13 다음 중 밑줄 친 부분의 쓰임이 어색한 것을 모두 고르면?

① Yesterday was the most excited day of my life.
② The lecture by Professor Thomas may be the most boring one in this college.
③ The children were so curious that they tried to open the locked door.
④ Most of the audience there thought the film had lots of touched scenes.
⑤ My aunt Mariah loves collecting fallen leaves every autumn.

14 다음 문장의 빈칸에 들어갈 말로 가장 알맞은 것은?

It _____ since last weekend.

① rained　　　　② is raining
③ was raining　　④ has been rained
⑤ has been raining

15 다음 문장의 빈칸에 들어갈 수 <u>없는</u> 것을 고르시오.

The kids in the kindergarten have been playing block games _____.

① since 1 o'clock　② all this afternoon
③ for an hour　　　④ up to now
⑤ until 30 minutes ago

16 다음 〈보기〉에서 알맞은 동사를 한 번씩만 선택하여, 현재완료진행형으로 빈칸을 채워 문장을 완성하시오.

┤ 보기 ├
paint listen take travel teach

(1) James _____ _____ _____ to the radio program since last summer.
(2) The volunteers _____ _____ _____ the walls of the underdeveloped village for 15 years.
(3) Sumin _____ _____ _____ math for free to help the poor children since last spring.
(4) The patient with a heart problem _____ _____ _____ the medicine as her family doctor advised.
(5) The newlyweds _____ _____ _____ in Europe since they got married last year.

17 다음 〈보기〉에 주어진 동사를 한 번씩만 사용하여 어법에 맞게 바꿔 빈칸을 완성하시오.

┤ 보기 ├
know, relate, write, name

I'd like to introduce you to the novel (A)_____ about a pianist. She is well (B)_____ as a role model among young people. She is one of the most promising pianists in Europe (C)_____ Ebony Janelle. A film (D)_____ to her will also be made.

18 다음 중 밑줄 친 부분의 쓰임이 〈보기〉와 <u>다른</u> 것은?

┤ 보기 ├
The Jacksons <u>have lived</u> in this city since 1990s.

① We <u>have known</u> each other since we're born at the same hospital.
② Father <u>has finished</u> cleaning all the tables.
③ Thomas and Butler <u>have been</u> friends for 20 years.
④ It <u>has been</u> quite windy these days.
⑤ Sean <u>has stayed</u> in Austria since he went there to study music 4 years ago.

19 다음 우리말을 아래의 어휘들을 배열하여 현재완료진행시제를 이용하여 영작할 때, 4번째와 9번째 단어를 쓰시오.

• 당신은 여기에 차분하게 앉아 있으면서, 그들을 돕기 위해 아무것도 안하고 있는 건가요?
(nothing / sitting / here / doing / have / to / been / calmly / them / and / help / you)?

➡ _____, _____

01 괄호 안의 어구들을 바르게 배열하여 우리말을 영작하시오.

(1) David은 저녁식사를 하고 나서 1시간 동안 계속 껌을 씹고 있는 중이다.

(has / after / gum / been / David / chewing / an hour / dinner / for)

➡ _____

(2) Margaret은 인터넷을 처음 시작한 이후, 계속 블로그를 해 오고 있는 중이다.

(since / has / she / been / blogging / first / the Internet / Margaret / started)

➡ _____

_____

(3) 우리 팀원들은 6시간이 넘도록 체육관에서 계속 운동을 하고 있는 중이다.

(out / working / in / six hours / team / the gym / been / members / for / our / over / have)

➡ _____

_____

02 다음에 주어진 각 두 문장을 현재완료진행시제를 이용하여 한 문장으로 만드시오. 단, 반드시 전치사 for를 사용할 것.

(1) • Yujay started to practice playing the drums 6 weeks ago.

• He is still practicing it nowadays.

➡ Yujay _____

_____ .

(2) • Rachel began writing letters at 9:00 this morning.

• She keeps writing letters until now, at noon.

➡ Rachel _____ .

03 다음 우리말을 참고하여 빈칸에 알맞은 말을 쓰시오.

(1) I often take a picture of _____ birds. (날고 있는 새들의 사진)

(2) Look at the man _____ the car. (세차하고 있는 남자)

(3) The woman _____ in front of me is Ms. Brown. (내 앞에 서 있는 여인)

(4) The dog _____ in the corner is cute. (구석에 앉아 있는)

(5) She looked out of the _____ window. (닫힌 창문에서)

(6) Keep all the e-mails _____ to you. (너에게 보내진 모든 이메일)

(7) The story _____ by Tom was interesting. (Tom에 의해 쓰여진 이야기)

04 다음 괄호 안의 단어들을 바르게 배열하여 문장을 완성하시오. (단, 동사를 어법상 알맞은 형태로 변형할 것.)

(1) The _____ is waiting for her old friends. (the / stand / old lady / street / across)

(2) Who are the _____? (on / perform / boys / stage / that)

(3) Louise is watering _____. (the / an / in / boat / flowers / plant / old)

05 다음 〈보기〉의 각 문장에서 어법상 <u>어색한</u> 부분들을 하나씩 찾아 모두 고치고, 우리말로 해석하시오.

┌─── 보기 ───┐
ⓐ The super player calling Hoop King was really good at playing basketball.
ⓑ We could see many tourists taken pictures in an old square in Austria.
ⓒ The watches producing in Switzerland are enjoying the greatest fame in the world.
ⓓ All the people attending the book concert found the title of the book writing by his little daughter.
ⓔ Groups of migratory birds flown over the sky were making sounds of encouragement.
└─────────┘

➡ ⓐ _____
해석: _____
    _____
ⓑ _____
해석: _____
    _____
ⓒ _____
해석: _____
    _____
ⓓ _____
해석: _____
    _____
ⓔ _____
해석: _____
    _____

06 다음 세 문장을 〈조건〉에 맞게 한 문장으로 다시 쓰시오.

• Peter, Frank's son, brought home his mathematics homework three hours ago.
• As soon as he arrived home, Peter showed Frank his homework, and Frank immediately started to do the homework instead of his son.
• He is still doing it.

┌─── 조건 ───┐
• 완전한 영어 문장으로 쓸 것.
• 접속사, 연결어, since 등은 사용하지 말 것.
• for / son's / Frank를 반드시 포함하되, 총 10 단어를 초과하지 않을 것.
└─────────┘

➡ _____
  _____

07 다음 그림을 보고, 괄호 안의 어휘를 이용하여 우리말에 맞게 빈칸을 채우시오.

As he (A)_____ _____ _____ (suffer) from the toothache, he decides to have his tooth (B)_____(pull) out at the dentist's.

(그는 치통으로 고통을 겪고 있는 중이기 때문에, 치과에서 이를 뽑기로 결심한다.)

08 다음 각 두 문장을 '분사'를 활용하여 한 문장으로 만들 때, 괄호 안의 조건에 맞게 빈칸에 적절한 단어를 넣어 채우시오.

(1) Jaemin wanted to play with the baby. She was crying. (명사 앞에서 수식)
→ Jaemin wanted to play _____ _____ _____ _____.

(2) There was a truck. The truck was illegally parked. (명사 앞에서 수식)
→ There was _____ _____ _____ _____.

(3) We watched the birds. They were flying over the buildings. (명사 뒤에서 수식)
→ We watched _____ _____ _____ _____ _____.

Let's Learn about Cultural Differences
let's+동사원형: ~하자(권유문)

Hi! My name is Kim Minhee. I have been living in America for three
현재완료진행   기간을 이끄는 전치사

years. Since my family moved here, I have experienced many cultural
접속사(~한 이래로)

differences between Korea and America. I would like to share some of

them with you.
cultural differences between Korea and America

Minhee: Look at this shirt. I like it.

Linda: It looks nice. How much is it?

Minhee: It's 19 dollars and 99 cents.

Linda: That's not expensive.

Minhee: Yes, I agree. I want to buy it.

Clerk: That'll be 21 dollars and 20 cents.

Minhee: Really? But the price tag says it's only 19 dollars and 99 cents.
                              says (that): 명사절을 이끄는 접속사 that 생략

Here in America, in most states, people pay a tax when they buy goods.
                                                    시간을 이끄는 접속사(~할 때)

It is called a sales tax. Sales tax rates differ by state. They range from
수동태(~라고 불리다)   range from A to B: A에서 B까지 이르다

less than one percent to more than ten percent. So when you buy goods

in America, you usually need to pay more than the price on the tag.
              빈도부사(일반동사 앞, be동사나 조동사 뒤에 위치)

Jessica: Hi, Mrs. Johnson!

Minhee: Hello, Mrs. Johnson!

Mrs. Johnson: Hi, Jessica! Hi, Minhee! How are you?

Jessica: Fine, thank you. We are here for a burger. Enjoy your meal.

Mrs. Johnson: Thank you. You, too!

Minhee: Jessica, why did you wave to Mrs. Johnson?

---

cultural: 문화와 관련된, 문화의
difference: 차이
experience: 경험하다
would like to V: V하고 싶다
share: 공유하다
expensive: 비싼
tag: 꼬리표
goods: 상품
rate: 비율
range: (범위가 ~에서 …에) 이르다
more than: ~보다 많이, ~ 이상
differ by: ~에 따라 다르다

📎 **확인문제**

● 다음 문장이 본문의 내용과 일치하면 T, 일치하지 않으면 F를 쓰시오.

1 Minhee went to America alone to study English. ☐

2 Minhee hasn't experienced cultural differences since she moved to America. ☐

3 Minhee greeted Mrs. Johnson by waving. ☐

In America, people often greet each other by waving. Waving to an older person is not regarded as rude. When you come to America, you may feel uncomfortable about it at first, but why don't you try it? You can wave to and smile at an elderly man walking on the street. He may wave back.

Andy: Minhee, try this apple pie.
Minhee: No, thanks. I don't want to.
Andy: Why not? Don't you like apple pie?
Minhee: Yes.
Andy: Then, try some. It's delicious.
Minhee: No. I just said I don't like apple pie.
Andy: What?

Americans often ask negative questions, such as "Aren't you coming?" and "Didn't you go to the hospital?" It can be difficult to answer negative questions correctly. Here is some advice. In response to negative questions, such as "Don't you like apple pie?" you should answer "No," if you don't like it. And you should answer "Yes," if you like it. These answers are the same as the answers to positive questions, such as "Do you like apple pie?"

	Like	Don't like
Do you like apple pie?	Yes, I do.	No, I don't.
Don't you like apple pie?	Yes, I do.	No, I don't.

Which cultural difference is most surprising to you? I have been learning about cultural differences since I came to America. Some surprised me at first, but now I am getting used to them.

greet: 인사하다
wave: 손을 흔들다
regard: ~로 여기다
elderly: 연세가 드신
be regarded as: ~로 여겨지다
rude: 무례한
uncomfortable: 불편한
try: 먹어보다
negative: 부정적인
positive: 긍정적인
advice: 충고, 조언
response: 대답, 응답

확인문제

● 다음 문장이 본문의 내용과 일치하면 T, 일치하지 않으면 F를 쓰시오.

1 Waving to an older people is not regarded as impolite. ☐

2 Minhee didn't want to try the apple pie because she was full. ☐

3 Negative questions are hardly used in America. ☐

4 Minhee is not familiar with cultural differences yet. ☐

● 우리말을 참고하여 빈칸에 알맞은 말을 쓰시오.

Let's Learn about Cultural Differences

1 Hi! My name is Kim Minhee. I _____ _____ _____ in America for three years.

2 _____ my family moved here, I _____ _____ many cultural differences _____ Korea _____ America.

3 I _____ _____ _____ _____ some of them with you.

4 Minhee: Look _____ this shirt. I like _____.

5 Linda: It _____ _____. How _____ is it?

6 Minhee: It's 19 _____ and 99 _____.

7 Linda: That's _____ _____.

8 Minhee: Yes, I agree. I want _____ _____ _____.

9 Clerk: That'll _____ 21 _____ and 20 _____.

10 Minhee: Really? But _____ _____ _____ _____ it's only 19 dollars and 99 cents.

11 Here in America, in most states, people _____ _____ _____ when they buy _____.

12 It _____ _____ a sales tax. Sales tax _____ by state.

13 They _____ from _____ _____ one percent to _____ _____ ten percent.

14 So when you _____ _____ in America, you _____ _____ _____ _____ more than the price on the tag.

15 Jessica: Hi, _____ Johnson! Minhee: Hello, _____ Johnson!

16 Mrs. Johnson: Hi, Jessica! Hi, Minhee! _____ are you?

17 Jessica: Fine, thank you. We are here _____ a burger. _____ _____ _____.

18 Mrs. Johnson: Thank you. You, _____!

19 Minhee: Jessica, why _____ you _____ to Mrs. Johnson?

문화적 차이에 대해서 배우자

1 안녕! 내 이름은 김민희야. 나는 미국에 3년 동안 살고 있어.

2 우리 가족이 이곳으로 이민을 온 이후로 나는 한국과 미국의 많은 문화적 차이를 경험하고 있어.

3 나는 그것들 중 몇 가지를 너희들과 공유하고 싶어.

4 민희: 이 셔츠를 봐. 마음에 들어.

5 Linda: 멋져 보인다. 얼마야?

6 민희: 19달러 99센트야.

7 Linda: 비싸지 않네.

8 민희: 응, 나도 그렇게 생각해. 그것을 사고 싶어.

9 점원: 21달러 20센트입니다.

10 민희: 정말이요? 하지만 가격표에는 단지 19달러 99센트라고 쓰여 있는데요.

11 이곳 미국에서는 대부분의 주에서 사람들이 물건을 구입할 때 세금을 내.

12 그것은 판매세라고 불려. 판매세의 비율은 주마다 달라.

13 판매세는 1퍼센트 미만부터 10퍼센트 이상까지 다양해.

14 그래서 미국에서 상품을 살 때, 대개 가격표에 있는 가격보다 더 많은 돈을 지불해야 해.

15 Jessica: 안녕하세요, Johnson 할머니! 민희: 안녕하세요, Johnson 할머니!

16 Mrs. Johnson: 안녕, Jessica! 안녕, 민희! 잘 지내지?

17 Jessica: 잘 지내요, 감사합니다. 저희는 여기 버거 먹으러 왔어요. 식사 맛있게 하세요.

18 Mrs. Johnson: 고맙구나. 너희들도!

19 민희: Jessica, 왜 너는 Johnson 할머니께 손을 흔들었니?

20 In America, people _____ _____ _____ _____ by waving.

21 _____ to an older person _____ not _____ _____ rude.

22 When you come to America, you may _____ _____ about it at first, but why don't you _____ _____?

23 You can _____ _____ and _____ _____ an elderly man walking on the street. He may _____ _____.

24 Andy: Minhee, _____ this apple pie.

25 Minhee: No, thanks. I don't _____ _____.

26 Andy: Why not? _____ you like apple pie?

27 Minhee: _____.

28 Andy: Then, _____ _____. It's _____.

29 Minhee: No. I just said I _____ _____ apple pie.

30 Andy: _____?

31 Americans often ask _____ _____, such as "_____ you coming?" and "_____ you _____ to the hospital?"

32 It can be difficult _____ _____ negative questions correctly. Here _____ some advice.

33 In response to _____ _____, such as "Don't you like apple pie?" you should _____ "_____," if you don't like it.

34 And you should _____ "_____," if you like it.

35 These answers are _____ _____ _____ the answers _____ _____ _____, such as "Do you like apple pie?"

36 _____ _____ _____ is most surprising to you?

37 I _____ _____ _____ about cultural differences _____ I came to America.

38 Some _____ me at first, but now I _____ _____ _____ _____ them.

20 미국에서 사람들은 종종 손을 흔들며 서로에게 인사해.

21 나이가 많은 사람에게 손을 흔드는 것은 무례하다고 여겨지지 않아.

22 네가 미국에 오면 처음에는 그것에 대해 불편하게 느낄 수 있어. 하지만 한번 시도해 보지 않을래?

23 너는 길을 걷고 있는 연세가 많으신 할아버지께 손을 흔들며 미소를 지어도 돼. 그도 너한테 답례로 손을 흔들지도 몰라.

24 Andy: 민희, 이 사과 파이 좀 먹어 봐.

25 민희: 아니야, 고마워. 먹고 싶지 않아.

26 Andy: 왜 안 먹어? 너는 사과 파이를 좋아하지 않니?

27 민희: 응.

28 Andy: 그러면, 좀 먹어 봐. 맛있어.

29 민희: 아니. 내가 사과 파이를 좋아하지 않는다고 방금 말했잖아.

30 Andy: 뭐라고?

31 미국 사람들은 종종 "너 안 오니?", "너 병원 안 갔니?"와 같은 부정의문문으로 질문해.

32 부정의문문에 바르게 대답하는 것은 어려울 수 있어. 여기 약간의 충고 사항이 있어.

33 "너는 사과 파이를 좋아하지 않니?"와 같은 부정의문문의 대답으로 만약 사과 파이를 좋아하지 않는다면 너는 "No."라고 대답해야 해.

34 그리고 만약 그것을 좋아한다면 "Yes."라고 대답해야 해.

35 이 대답들은 "너는 애플파이를 좋아하니?"와 같은 긍정의문문에 대한 대답들과 같아.

36 어떤 문화적인 차이가 너에게 가장 놀랍니?

37 나는 미국에 온 이후로 문화적인 차이에 대해 계속 배우고 있어.

38 어떤 것들은 처음에 나를 놀라게 했지만, 지금은 그것들에 익숙해지고 있어.

• 우리말을 참고하여 본문을 영작하시오.

1 안녕! 내 이름은 김민희야. 나는 미국에 3년 동안 살고 있어.
➡ _____

2 우리 가족이 이곳으로 이민을 온 이후로 나는 한국과 미국의 많은 문화적 차이를 경험하고 있어.
➡ _____

3 나는 그것들 중 몇 가지를 너희들과 공유하고 싶어.
➡ _____

4 민희: 이 셔츠를 봐. 마음에 들어.
➡ _____

5 Linda: 멋져 보인다. 얼마야?
➡ _____

6 민희: 19달러 99센트야.
➡ _____

7 Linda: 비싸지 않네.
➡ _____

8 민희: 응, 나도 그렇게 생각해. 그것을 사고 싶어.
➡ _____

9 점원: 21달러 20센트입니다.
➡ _____

10 민희: 정말이요? 하지만 가격표에는 단지 19달러 99센트라고 쓰여 있는데요.
➡ _____

11 이곳 미국에서는 대부분의 주에서 사람들이 물건을 구입할 때 세금을 내.
➡ _____

12 그것은 판매세라고 불려. 판매세의 비율은 주마다 달라.
➡ _____

13 판매세는 1퍼센트 미만부터 10퍼센트 이상까지 다양해.
➡ _____

14 그래서 미국에서 상품을 살 때, 대개 가격표에 있는 가격보다 더 많은 돈을 지불해야 해.
➡ _____

15 Jessica: 안녕하세요, Johnson 할머니! 민희: 안녕하세요, Johnson 할머니!
➡ _____

16 Mrs. Johnson: 안녕, Jessica! 안녕, 민희! 잘 지내지?
➡ _____

17 Jessica: 잘 지내요, 감사합니다. 저희는 여기 버거 먹으러 왔어요. 식사 맛있게 하세요.
➡ _____

18 Mrs. Johnson: 고맙구나. 너희들도!
➡ _____

19 민희: Jessica, 왜 너는 Johnson 할머니께 손을 흔들었니?
➡ _____

20 미국에서 사람들은 종종 손을 흔들며 서로에게 인사해.
➡ _____

21 나이가 많은 사람에게 손을 흔드는 것은 무례하다고 여겨지지 않아.
➡ _____

22 네가 미국에 오면 처음에는 그것에 대해 불편하게 느낄 수 있어. 하지만 한번 시도해 보지 않을래?
➡ _____

23 너는 길을 걷고 있는 연세가 많으신 할아버지께 손을 흔들며 미소를 지어도 돼. 그도 너한테 답례로 손을 흔들지도 몰라.
➡ _____

24 Andy: 민희, 이 사과 파이 좀 먹어 봐.
➡ _____

25 Minhee: 아니야, 고마워. 먹고 싶지 않아.
➡ _____

26 Andy: 왜 안 먹어? 너는 사과 파이를 좋아하지 않니?
➡ _____

27 Minhee: 응.
➡ _____

28 Andy: 그러면, 좀 먹어 봐. 맛있어.
➡ _____

29 Minhee: 아니. 내가 사과 파이를 좋아하지 않는다고 방금 말했잖아.
➡ _____

30 Andy: 뭐라고?
➡ _____

31 미국 사람들은 종종 "너 안 오니?", "너 병원 안 갔니?"와 같은 부정의문문으로 질문해.
➡ _____

32 부정의문문에 바르게 대답하는 것은 어려울 수 있어. 여기 약간의 충고 사항이 있어.
➡ _____

33 "너는 사과 파이를 좋아하지 않니?"와 같은 부정의문문의 대답으로 만약 사과 파이를 좋아하지 않는다면 너는 "No."라고 대답해야 해.
➡ _____

34 그리고 만약 그것을 좋아한다면 "Yes."라고 대답해야 해.
➡ _____

35 이 대답들은 "너는 애플파이를 좋아하니?"와 같은 긍정의문문에 대한 대답들과 같아.
➡ _____

36 어떤 문화적인 차이가 너에게 가장 놀랍니?
➡ _____

37 나는 미국에 온 이후로 문화적인 차이에 대해 계속 배우고 있어.
➡ _____

38 어떤 것들은 처음에 나를 놀라게 했지만, 지금은 그것들에 익숙해지고 있어.
➡ _____

[01~02] 다음 글을 읽고 물음에 답하시오.

Hi! My name is Kim Minhee. I have been living in America for three years. (A) _____ my family moved here, I have experienced many cultural differences between Korea and America. I would like to share some of them with you.

01 다음 중 빈칸 (A)에 들어갈 말로 가장 적절한 것은?

① Although ② For
③ If ④ Since
⑤ As soon as

02 다음 중 위 글에 이어질 내용으로 가장 적절한 것은?

① Minhee's life in Korea
② common mistakes made by Korean people
③ some cultural differences Minhee experienced
④ the reason why Minhee moved to America
⑤ the reasons why cultural differences exist

[03~05] 다음 글을 읽고 물음에 답하시오.

Minhee: Look at this shirt. I like it.
Linda: It looks nice. How much is it?
Minhee: It's 19 dollars and 99 cents.
Linda: That's not expensive.
Minhee: Yes, I agree. I want to buy it.
Clerk: (A)That'll be 21 dollars and 20 cents.
Minhee: Really? But the price tag says it's only 19 dollars and 99 cents.
Here in America, in most states, people pay a tax when they buy goods. It is called a sales tax. Sales tax rates differ by state. They range from less than one percent to more than ten percent. So when you buy goods in America, you usually need to pay more than the price on the tag.

03 위 글에 따르면, 밑줄 친 (A)와 같이 말한 이유로 가장 적절한 것은?

① Because the clerk didn't like the shirt.
② Because a sales tax was added to the shirt.
③ Because the shirt was not on sale at that time.
④ Because the clerk didn't know the price of the shirt.
⑤ Because the clerk didn't want to sell the shirt to Minhee.

서답형
04 다음 빈칸에 들어갈 알맞은 말을 위 글에서 찾아 쓰시오.

Some large countries such as the USA are divided into smaller areas called _____.

05 다음 중 위 글의 내용을 바르게 이해한 사람은?

① 지유: 판매세는 셔츠에만 부과되는 거야.
② 경효: 원래 가격이 21달러 20센트였던 것을 19달러 99센트로 잘못 보았구나.
③ 유이: 미국에서 물건을 살 땐 가격표에 명시된 금액을 내면 되는 거야.
④ 예지: 물건을 살 때 지불하는 세금이 판매세구나.
⑤ 은별: 모든 주의 판매세가 똑같으니 계산하기 쉽겠어.

[06~08] 다음 글을 읽고 물음에 답하시오.

Jessica: Hi, Mrs. Johnson!

Minhee: Hello, Mrs. Johnson!

Mrs. Johnson: Hi, Jessica! Hi, Minhee! How are you?

Jessica: Fine, thank you. We are here for a burger. Enjoy your meal.

Mrs. Johnson: Thank you. You, too!

Minhee: Jessica, why did you wave to Mrs. Johnson?

  In America, people often greet each other by waving. Waving to an older person is not regarded as (A)_____. When you come to America, you may feel uncomfortable about it at first, but why don't you try it? You can wave to and smile at an elderly man walking on the street. He may wave back.

06 다음 중 빈칸 (A)에 들어갈 말로 가장 적절한 것은?

① polite ② friendly ③ fun
④ rude ⑤ considerate

07 다음 중 위 글의 내용과 일치하는 것은?

① Jessica doesn't know who Mrs. Johnson is.
② Jessica and Minhee are there to meet Mrs. Johnson.
③ Jessica is going to have a burger with Minhee.
④ Minhee waved to Mrs. Johnson.
⑤ Mrs. Johnson wants to meet Jessica.

서답형
08 According to the passage, how do people in America greet each other? Answer in English with a full sentence.

➡ _____

[09~11] 다음 글을 읽고 물음에 답하시오.

Andy: Minhee, (A)try this apple pie.

Minhee: No, thanks. I don't want to.

Andy: Why not? Don't you like apple pie?

Minhee: Yes.

Andy: Then, try some. It's delicious.

Minhee: No. I just said I don't like apple pie.

Andy: What?

  ① Americans often ask negative questions, such as "Aren't you coming?" and "Didn't you go to the hospital?" ② It can be difficult to answer negative questions correctly. ③ In response to negative questions, such as "Don't you like apple pie?" you should answer "No," if you don't like it. ④ And you should answer "Yes," if you like it. ⑤

09 ①~⑤ 중 주어진 문장이 들어가기에 가장 적절한 곳은?

> Here is some advice.

①   ②   ③   ④   ⑤

10 다음 중 밑줄 친 (A)와 쓰임이 같은 것은?

① Please try me for the job.
② Don't try to explain.
③ Let me try a cup of tea.
④ Try whether you can do it or not.
⑤ I will try my best.

서답형
11 위 글을 참고하여 다음 상황에서 Minhee가 할 말을 빈칸에 알맞게 쓰시오.

> Tom brought some chocolate cookies. He said to Minhee, "Don't you want to have some cookies?" But Minhee didn't like cookies. In this situation, what could Minhee say to Tom?
>
> Minhee: _____, _____

[12~15] 다음 글을 읽고 물음에 답하시오.

Hi! My name is Kim Minhee. I have been living in America for three years. Since my family moved here, I have experienced many cultural (A)[similarities / differences] between Korea and America. I would like to share some of them with you.

Minhee: Look at this shirt. I like it.

Linda: It looks nice. How much is it?

Minhee: It's 19 dollars and 99 cents.

Linda: That's not expensive.

Minhee: Yes, I agree. I want to buy it.

Clerk: That'll be 21 dollars and 20 cents.

Minhee: Really? But the price tag says it's only 19 dollars and 99 cents.

Here in America, in most states, people pay a tax when they (B)[sell / buy] goods. It is called a sales tax. Sales tax rates differ by state. They range from less than one percent to more than ten percent. So when you buy goods in America, you usually need to pay (C)[more / less] than the price on the tag.

12 (A)~(C)에서 글의 흐름상 적절한 것끼리 바르게 짝지은 것은?

① similarities – sell – more
② differences – sell – less
③ similarities – buy – more
④ differences – buy – more
⑤ similarities – buy – less

13 다음 중 위 글을 읽고 답할 수 있는 것은?

① How many states in America make people pay a sales tax?
② What is the color of the shirt?
③ Who made the sales tax?
④ What is the range of sales tax rates?
⑤ How did Minhee feel about a sales tax?

서답형

14 According to the passage, what do we need to pay when we buy things in America? Answer in English with a full sentence.

➡ _____

서답형

15 주어진 단어를 활용하여 다음 물음에 완전한 문장의 영어로 답하시오.

Q: When did Minhee move to America?
(ago)

➡ _____

[16~18] 다음 글을 읽고 물음에 답하시오.

Jessica: Hi, Mrs. Johnson!

Minhee: Hello, Mrs. Johnson!

Mrs. Johnson: Hi, Jessica! Hi, Minhee! How are you?

Jessica: Fine, thank you. We are here for a burger. Enjoy your meal.

Mrs. Johnson: Thank you. You, too!

Minhee: Jessica, why did you wave to Mrs. Johnson?

In America, people often greet each other by waving. Waving to an older person is not regarded as rude. When you come to America, you may feel uncomfortable about @it at first, but why don't you try it? You can wave to and smile at an elderly man walking on the street. (A)_____

16 글의 흐름상 빈칸 (A)에 들어갈 말로 가장 적절한 것은?

① He may think that you are rude.
② He may wave flags and cheer.
③ He may wave back.
④ He may be upset and walk away.
⑤ He may wonder who you are.

서답형

17 밑줄 친 ⓐ가 의미하는 것을 위 글에서 찾아 쓰시오.

➡ _____

18 다음 중 위 글의 대화문에서 찾아볼 수 없는 것은?

① Minhee who is with Jessica

② Jessica waving to Mrs. Johnson

③ Mrs. Johnson having her meal

④ Minhee saying hi to Mrs. Johnson

⑤ Mrs. Johnson talking with her friends

[19~24] 다음 글을 읽고 물음에 답하시오.

Americans often ask negative questions, such as "Aren't you coming?" and "Didn't you go to the hospital?"

[A] And you should answer "Yes," if you like it. These answers are the same as the answers to positive questions, such as "Do you like apple pie?"

	Like	Don't like
Do you like apple pie?	Yes, I do.	No, I don't.
Don't you like apple pie?	Yes, I do.	No, I don't.

[B] In response to negative questions, such as "Don't you like apple pie?" you should answer "No," if you don't like it.

[C] It can be difficult to answer negative questions correctly. Here is some advice.

Which cultural difference is most surprising to you? I have been learning about cultural differences since I came to America. Some surprised me at first, but now I am getting used to them.

중요

19 자연스러운 글이 되도록 [A]~[C]를 바르게 배열한 것은?

① [A]–[C]–[B]　　② [B]–[A]–[C]

③ [B]–[C]–[A]　　④ [C]–[B]–[A]

⑤ [C]–[A]–[B]

서답형

20 위 글을 읽고 다음 질문에 바르게 답하시오.

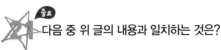

When you are hungry, your friend say to you "Aren't you hungry?" In this situation, what would you say to her?

➡ _____

중요

21 다음 중 위 글의 내용과 일치하는 것은?

① "Do you like to play the violin?" is a negative question.

② Americans hardly use negative questions.

③ The writer learns about cultural differences by reading books.

④ When you are asked "Didn't you come to the party?", you should answer "Yes," if you didn't come to the party.

⑤ The answers to negative questions are the same as the answers to positive questions.

서답형

22 다음과 같이 풀이되는 말을 위 글에서 찾아 쓰시오.

relating to a particular society and its ideas, customs, and art

➡ _____

서답형

23 According to the passage, what has the writer been learning about? Answer in English with a full sentence.

➡ _____

24 문화적 차이에 대한 글쓴이의 현재 반응으로 가장 적절한 것은?

① surprised　　② familiar　　③ scared

④ shocked　　⑤ amused

[01~02] 다음 글을 읽고 물음에 답하시오.

Hi! My name is Kim Minhee. I have been living in America for three years. Since my family moved here, I have experienced many cultural differences between Korea and America. I would like to share some of them with you.

01 How long has Minhee been living in America? Answer in English with a full sentence.

➡ _____

02 What does Minhee want to share with us? Answer with a full sentence and use the words below.

(want / between)

➡ _____

_____

[03~06] 다음 글을 읽고 물음에 답하시오.

Minhee: Look at this shirt. I like it.

Linda: It looks nice. How much is it?

Minhee: It's 19 dollars and 99 cents.

Linda: That's not expensive.

Minhee: Yes, I agree. I want to buy it.

Clerk: That'll be 21 dollars and 20 cents.

Minhee: Really? But the price tag says it's only 19 dollars and 99 cents.

Here in America, in most states, people pay a tax when they buy goods. It is called a sales tax. Sales tax rates differ by state. They range from less than one percent to more than ten percent. So when you buy goods in America, you usually need to pay more than the price on the tag.

03 According to the price tag, how much is the shirt?

➡ _____

04 When do people in America pay a sales tax? Answer in English with a full sentence.

➡ _____

05 다음 중 위 글의 내용과 일치하지 <u>않는</u> 것을 찾아 바르게 고치시오.

I went shopping with my friend. I picked a shirt and tried to pay the price on the tag. However, the clerk wanted me to pay more than the price on the tag, saying I needed to pay a sales tax. He said sales tax rates are equal in most states.

➡ _____

06 다음 질문에 알맞은 답을 주어진 단어를 활용하여 쓰시오.

Q: What doesn't the price on the tag include?
A: (include / it)

➡ _____

[07~09] 다음 글을 읽고 물음에 답하시오.

Jessica: Hi, Mrs. Johnson!

Minhee: Hello, Mrs. Johnson!

Mrs. Johnson: Hi, Jessica! Hi, Minhee! How are you?

Jessica: Fine, thank you. We are here for a burger. Enjoy your meal.

Mrs. Johnson: Thank you. You, too!

Minhee: Jessica, why did you wave to Mrs. Johnson?

In America, people often greet each other by waving. Waving to an older person is not regarded as rude. When you come to America, you may feel uncomfortable about it at first, but why don't you try it? You can (A)_____ to and smile at an elderly man walking on the street. He may wave back.

07 위 글의 흐름상 빈칸 (A)에 들어갈 알맞은 말을 위 글에서 찾아 쓰시오.

➡ _____

08 According to the passage, who waved to Mrs. Johnson? Answer in English with a full sentence.

➡ _____

09 위 글의 내용에 맞게 빈칸에 알맞은 말을 쓰시오.

> _____ is not familiar with the way
> p e o p l e _____ _____ _____
> _____ _____ in America.

[10~13] 다음 글을 읽고 물음에 답하시오.

Andy: Minhee, try this apple pie.
Minhee: No, thanks. I don't want to.
Andy: Why not? Don't you like apple pie?
Minhee: (A)Yes.
Andy: Then, try some. It's delicious.
Minhee: No. I just said I don't like apple pie.
Andy: What?
Americans often ask negative questions, such as "Aren't you coming?" and "Didn't you go to the hospital?" It can be difficult to answer negative questions correctly. Here is some advice.

In response to negative questions, such as "Don't you like apple pie?" you should answer "No," if you don't like it. And you should answer "Yes," if you like it. These answers are the same as the answers to positive questions, such as "Do you like apple pie?"

	Like	Don't like
Do you like apple pie?	Yes, I do.	No, I don't.
Don't you like apple pie?	Yes, I do.	No, I don't.

10 주어진 단어를 바르게 배열하여 위 글의 제목을 완성하시오.

> (correctly / to / negative / how / questions / answer)

➡ _____

11 위 글의 내용을 참고하여 밑줄 친 (A)의 답변을 민희의 의도에 맞게 바르게 표현하시오.

➡ _____

12 위 글의 내용에 맞게 빈칸에 알맞은 대답을 쓰시오.

> I found a book boring. If someone asks me, "Didn't you find the book boring?", I would answer, "_____, _____ _____."

13 위 글의 내용에 맞게 빈칸에 알맞은 말을 쓰시오.

> _____ _____ _____ is not that difficult. When you are in America, just remember this. Response to negative questions is _____ _____ as response to _____ _____.

Project Step 1

A: Can I get your advice on correct English expressions?
~에 대해 조언을 구할 수 있니?

B: Make sure you say window shopping instead of eye shopping.
'반드시 ~해라'라는 의미로 'Make sure (that)+주어+동사' ··· 대신에

C: Make sure you don't say Y-shirt. You should say dress shirt instead.
Make sure (that)+주어+동사   부사: 그 대신에

구문해설 • correct: 옳은 • expression: 표현 • window shopping: 윈도 쇼핑(눈으로만 구경하는 쇼핑)
• instead of: ··· 대신에 • instead: 그 대신에

A: 옳은 영어 표현에 대해 너의 조언을 구할 수 있을까?
B: 반드시 아이 쇼핑 대신 윈도 쇼핑(구경만 하는 쇼핑)이라고 말하도록 해.
C: 절대 와이셔츠라고 말하지 않도록 해. 대신 정장용 셔츠라고 말해야 해.

Project Step 3

Today, I realized I have been using many incorrect English expressions. For
realized 다음에 that 생략   현재완료진행

example, we should say dress shirt instead of Y-shirt. Eye shopping is also an
예를 들어   ~ 대신에

incorrect expression. Make sure you don't use it.
                        Make sure (that)   eye shopping

구문해설 • incorrect: 잘못된, 틀린 • expression: 표현

오늘, 나는 내가 많은 잘못된 영어 표현을 사용해 왔다는 것을 알았습니다. 예를 들어, 우리는 Y-shirt 대신에 dress shirt라는 말을 써야 합니다. 아이 쇼핑도 또한 잘못된 표현입니다. 그것을 사용하지 않도록 명심하세요.

Enjoy Writing

Holi That I Can't Miss

There are many interesting festivals around the world. Among them, I'd like to
흥미로운 : 명사를 꾸며주는 분사   ~중에서   = I want to

attend Holi. People in India have been celebrating this festival for many years.
                현재완료진행형: 축제를 개최해오는 중이다   여러 해 동안

Holi is held in March. I think that if I go, I'll experience a lot of things.
be held 개최되다, 열리다   조건문: 내가 간다면

First, there are people throwing colored powder and water on each other. It
there are+복수명사: ~가 있다   현재분사   서로에게

will be fantastic! Second, I want to dance with other people on the street. I'll

also taste traditional Holi dishes. It's going to be very exciting. I can't wait for
                                                                    ~가 기대된다

the day!

구문해설 • attend: 참여하다 • celebrate: 기념하다, 축하하다 • experience: 경험하다
• throw: 던지다 • taste: 맛보다

놓칠 수 없는 홀리
세계에는 많은 흥미로운 축제들이 있다. 그 중에서, 나는 홀리에 참여하고 싶다. 인도 사람들은 오랫동안 이 축제를 열어오고 있는 중이다. 홀리 축제는 3월에 열린다. 나는 내가 간다면, 많은 것들을 경험할 것이라고 생각한다. 첫째, 서로에게 색색의 가루와 물을 던지는 사람들이 있다. 그것은 환상적일 것이다. 둘째, 나는 거리에서 다른 사람들과 춤을 추고 싶다. 나는 또한 전통적인 홀리 요리를 맛볼 것이다. 그것은 정말 신날 것이다. 나는 그 날이 정말 기대된다!

01 다음 주어진 두 단어의 관계가 같도록 빈칸에 알맞은 단어를 쓰시오.

difference – similarity = negative – _____

02 다음 글의 빈칸 (a)와 (b)에 들어갈 단어로 바르게 짝지어진 것은?

I have been living in America for three years. (a)_____ my family moved here, I have experienced many cultural differences between Korea and America. I would like to (b)_____ some of them with you.

① Because – share ② When – differ
③ Because – differ ④ Since – wrap
⑤ Since – share

[03~04] 다음 영영 풀이에 해당하는 것을 고르시오.

03

the number of the house, name of the road, and name of the town where a person lives or works, and where letters can be sent

① tax ② postal code
③ address ④ sales tax
⑤ entrance fee

04

money paid to the government that is based on your income or the cost of goods or services you have bought

① tax ② expense
③ goods ④ advice
⑤ tag

05 빈칸에 공통으로 들어갈 말을 영어 설명을 읽고 알맞은 형태로 변형해서 쓰시오.

In America, people often greet each other by _____. _____ to an older person is not regarded as rude.
<영어 설명> to raise your hand and move it from side to side as a way of greeting someone

06 다음 밑줄 친 부분의 뜻이 잘못된 것은?

① Americans often ask negative questions, such as "Aren't you coming? (~와 같은)
② It can be difficult to answer negative questions correctly. (올바르게)
③ Which cultural difference is most surprising to you? (문화의)
④ Cultural differences surprised me at first, but now I am getting used to them. (~에 사용되다)
⑤ When we buy goods, we pay the price on the tag. (가격표)

07 다음 대화의 빈칸에 들어갈 말로 적절한 것은?

A: Can I get your _____ on visiting the USA?
B: Sure. You should sit in the back seat in the taxi.

① goods ② advice
③ price ④ hope
⑤ present

08 다음 문장을 읽고, 소녀가 민수에게 경고하는 표현을 사용하여 대화의 빈칸을 완성하시오.

> Minsu asks an American girl how old she is. The girl is unhappy because it's not polite to ask someone's age in Western cultures.

Minsu: How old are you?

Girl: _____ a person's _____ in Western cultures.

[09~11] 다음 대화를 읽고 물음에 답하시오.

Seho: My Chinese friend invited me to his house for dinner this Friday.

Bora: That's good. I hope you enjoy having dinner at his house. (①)

Seho: I want to prepare a small gift for him. You lived in China for several years. (②)

Bora: How about some tea?

Seho: Tea?

Bora: Yes. Most Chinese people like to receive tea as a present. They enjoy drinking tea. Also, they usually serve tea to guests. (③)

Seho: Oh, thanks. Is there anything else that I need to know? (④)

Bora: (A)_____ White and black mean death in China. (⑤)

Seho: Okay. I'll remember that. Thank you for the advice.

09 주어진 문장이 들어갈 위치로 알맞은 것은?

> Can I get your advice on what to bring?

①   ②   ③   ④   ⑤

10 위 대화의 빈칸 (A)에 들어갈 말로 알맞은 것을 고르시오.

① Make sure you use two hands when you hand it to her.
② Make sure you exchange Korean won to Thai baht.
③ Don't wrap the present in white or black paper.
④ Make sure you don't take pictures.
⑤ Don't touch the exhibits.

11 위 대화의 내용과 일치하지 <u>않는</u> 것은?

① Seho was invited by his Chinese friend.
② You can guess Bora knows well about the Chinese culture.
③ Bora suggested some tea as a present.
④ White and black mean death in China.
⑤ Seho will be served tea by Bora.

12 다음 대화의 밑줄 친 (A)와 같은 의미가 되도록 본문에 나오는 단어를 이용하여 8단어로 쓰시오.

> B: I'm going to Japan this summer. Can I get some advice on visiting there?
> G: Make sure you pay when you get off the bus.
> B: Oh, I didn't know that. Are there any other things I should remember?
> G: Pick up the bowl and hold it while eating. Also, when having soup, (A)<u>you should drink it without a spoon.</u>
> B: Okay. Thanks

➡ _____

Grammar

13 다음 중 어법상 올바른 문장은?

① A kitten naming Toto is so cute.

② The teacher recommended the movies directing by Bong-Junho.

③ Those are the jeans produced in Vietnam through OEM.

④ Please show me the device which invented by Professor Sergio Teslar.

⑤ Some of the celebrities inviting to the festival didn't show up.

14 다음 Peter에 대한 정보를 읽고, 〈보기〉에서 알맞은 단어를 선택하여 빈칸에 알맞게 채우시오. (동사는 변형 가능)

> • Peter는 올해 Harvard 대학교에 입학한 이후로, 수학계에서 가장 어려운 문제들 중의 하나를 풀기 위해 지금까지 노력해 오고 있는 중이다.

┌ 보기 ├

for / since / before / by / solve / play / try / be / pass / have / to

---

Peter (A) ＿＿＿＿ ＿＿＿＿ ＿＿＿＿ ＿＿＿＿ ＿＿＿＿ one of the most difficult questions in the world of mathematics (B) ＿＿＿＿ he entered Harvard University this year.

15 다음 빈칸에 알맞은 말이 바르게 짝지어진 것은?

> • The photographer showed me what was ＿＿＿＿ in London.
> • Janet has been picking up the ＿＿＿＿ leaves after the storm passed by.

① taken – fallen　　② taking – falling

③ taking – fell　　④ took – fallen

⑤ took – falling

16 Which of the followings are grammatically incorrect? Choose all.

① The room has been feeling too cold.

② Dorothy has been driving since she got her driver's license.

③ Sam has been running for an hour.

④ My uncle has once played ice hockey.

⑤ I have been being falling in love with the girl group, G-idle.

17 다음 두 문장을 분사를 이용하여 한 문장으로 만드시오.

> • The lady is Ms. Baker.
> • She stays in Kenya to study wild animals.

➡ The lady ＿＿＿＿＿＿＿＿＿＿＿＿

＿＿＿＿＿＿＿＿＿＿＿＿ .

18 다음 그림을 보고 괄호 안의 단어를 활용해서 빈칸에 맞게 채우시오.

(1)

➡ I found a ＿＿＿＿ (move) sentence in *The Old Man and the Sea* by Ernest Hemingway.

(2)

➡ The most famous Egyptian pyramids are those ＿＿＿＿ (find) at Giza in Egypt.

19 다음 밑줄 친 부분의 쓰임이 나머지와 다른 것은?

① The guards <u>protecting</u> the actor were doing their best not to hurt crazy fans.

② John's father was busy <u>doing</u> the laundry that afternoon.

③ Barbara <u>working</u> for the bank fell in love with the police officer.

④ Paul <u>eating</u> pizza every day after midnight got another 5 pounds this week.

⑤ Laura was <u>playing</u> a good character.

20 다음 우리말을 영어로 옮긴 것 중 어법상 어색한 것을 고르시오.

① Paul의 엄마는 팔짱을 낀 채로 그의 아들들에게 얘기를 시작했다.
→ Paul's mom started to tell her sons with her arms folded.

② 우리는 눈을 감은 채로 노래를 불렀다.
→ We sang with our eyes closed.

③ Minsu는 다리를 꼰 상태로 교장 선생님을 보았다.
→ Minsu looked at the principal with his legs crossing.

④ 그녀는 창문을 열어 둔 채로 잠이 들었다.
→ She fell asleep with the window open.

⑤ Tom은 셔츠가 홀딱 젖은 채로 사무실에 왔다.
→ Tom came to the office with his shirts all wet.

21 다음 밑줄 친 부분 중 어법상 옳지 않은 것을 고르시오.

① We <u>have been living</u> here for quite a long time.

② I <u>have been studying</u> Spanish because I'm planning to go to Spain next year.

③ He <u>has been taking</u> care of Peter's little brothers since 3 hours ago.

④ My mom <u>has been owning</u> the bag since I was born.

⑤ Bella <u>has been cooking</u> for her friends until now.

Reading

[22~25] 다음 글을 읽고 물음에 답하시오.

Hi! My name is Kim Minhee. I have been living in America for three years. ⓐSince my family moved here, I have experienced many cultural differences between Korea and America. I would like to share some of them with you.

Minhee: Look at this shirt. I like it.

Linda: It looks nice. How much is it?

Minhee: It's 19 dollars and 99 cents.

Linda: That's not expensive.

Minhee: Yes, I agree. I want to buy it.

Clerk: That'll be 21 dollars and 20 cents.

Minhee: Really? But the price tag says it's only 19 dollars and 99 cents.

Here in America, in most states, people pay a tax when they buy goods.
(A) They range from less than one percent to more than ten percent.
(B) It is called a sales tax. Sales tax rates differ by state.
(C) So when you buy goods in America, you usually need to pay more than the price on the tag.

22 자연스러운 글이 되도록 (A)~(C)를 바르게 배열하시오.

➡ _____

23 다음 중 밑줄 친 ⓐ와 쓰임이 다른 하나는?

① Peter hasn't phoned me since he went to Seoul.

② It has been 5 years since I met her.

③ Since you are alone at home, it is no wonder that you are very scared.

④ She has been ill in bed since the letter arrived.

⑤ I haven't seen her since I moved out of the apartment.

24 According to the passage, what is a sales tax? Answer in English with a full sentence.

➡ _____

_____

25 다음 중 위 글을 읽고 답할 수 있는 것은?

① Why did Minhee move to America?

② What is the most shocking difference between Korea and America?

③ Where was Minhee born?

④ How did Minhee think about the price on the tag?

⑤ How much money did Minhee have when she wanted to buy a shirt?

[26~29] 다음 글을 읽고 물음에 답하시오.

There are many interesting ①festivals around the world. Among ②them, I'd like to attend Holi. People in India have been celebrating this festival ③since many years. Holi is held in March. I think that if I go, I'll experience ④a lot of things. First, there are people throwing colored powder and water on each other. It will be fantastic! Second, I want to dance with other people on the street. I'll also taste traditional Holi ⑤dishes. It's going to be very exciting. I can't wait for the day!

26 다음은 위 글의 제목이다. 빈칸에 알맞은 말을 위 글에서 찾아 어법에 맞게 쓰시오.

Holi, an _____ _____ in India

27 ①~⑤ 중 어법상 바르지 않은 것은?

① ② ③ ④ ⑤

28 In Holi, what do people throw on each other? Answer in English with a full sentence.

➡ _____

29 다음 중 위 글의 내용과 일치하는 것은?

① Holi is held in summer.

② You cannot attend Holi in India.

③ People will celebrate Holi for the first time this year.

④ The writer is looking forward to dancing with people on the street.

⑤ The writer isn't interested in tasting Holi dishes.

단원별 예상문제

출제율 100%

01 다음 짝지어진 단어의 관계가 같도록 빈칸에 알맞은 말을 쓰시오.

> Russia - Russian = Japan - _____

출제율 90%

02 다음 영영 풀이에 해당하는 단어는?

> an opinion that someone offers you about what you should do or how you should act in a particular situation

① thought ② advice
③ praise ④ tag
⑤ tax

출제율 95%

03 다음 대화의 밑줄 친 (A)와 같은 의미의 문장을 주어진 단어를 활용하여 쓰시오.

> A: I'd like to visit Malaysia. Can I get your advice on traveling there?
> B: Sure. (A)You'd better not use your left hand to hand something to someone.
> A: Okay. Thanks.

➡ Make _____

[04~05] 다음 대화를 읽고 물음에 답하시오.

> G: I want to send this to my aunt in the USA.
> B: What is it?
> G: It's her *hanbok*. Can I get your advice on how to write an address in English?
> B: Sure. You should write the street address first.
> G: Like this?
> B: Yes. Then, write the name of the city and the state and then the postal code. Finally, write the country.

출제율 90%

04 To whom does the girl want to send the *hanbok*?

➡ _____

출제율 90%

05 What does the girl need to get advice on?

➡ She needs to get advice on _____

_____ .

출제율 90%

06 다음 그림을 보고 아래 질문에 대해 주어진 단어를 이용하여 조언의 말을 쓰시오.

> Q: Can I get your advice on how to greet each other in Tibet?

➡ _____ in Tibet.

(sure / show / tongue)

[07~08] 다음 대화를 읽고 물음에 답하시오.

> G: (A)모로코 전통 의상을 입고 있는 사람들을 보세요. They are really beautiful. I want to take pictures of them.
> M: Wait. There is an important thing you need to know before taking pictures.
> G: Oh, really? Can I get your advice on it?
> M: Yes. You shouldn't take pictures of Moroccan people without asking.
> G: Why?
> M: They believe (B)_____ when someone takes their picture.

출제율 95%

07 위 대화의 밑줄 친 (A)의 우리말에 맞게 주어진 어구를 알맞게 배열하시오. (필요하면 어형을 바꿀 것)

> (people / traditional / look at / the / wear / Moroccan clothes)

➡ _____

출제율 100%

08 위 대화의 빈칸 (B)에 들어갈 말로 알맞은 것은?

① taking pictures is a popular hobby
② they should pay for it
③ it is similar to making a movie
④ it may have a bad effect on them
⑤ they will sell their pictures

출제율 90%

09 대화의 빈칸 (A)에 들어갈 말로 알맞은 것은?

> B: Sena, I bought a present for Ms. Han. I have stayed at her house here in Korea.
> G: That's great. What did you buy her?
> B: I bought her a hat. Do you think she'll love it?
> G: Yes. (A)_____
> B: Why?
> G: Because giving something to older people with one hand is regarded as rude in Korea.
> B: Okay. I'll remember that.

① Make sure you keep your hands on the table at all times.
② Make sure you use two hands when you hand it to her.
③ Make sure you keep quiet.
④ Make sure you don't fight with your friends.
⑤ Don't wrap the present in white or black paper.

[10~11] 다음 대화를 읽고 물음에 답하시오.

> B: Did you (a)pack everything you need for the trip to Thailand tomorrow?
> G: Not yet. (A)What should I take?
> B: (b)Remember to bring a pair of long pants or a long skirt.
> G: Why? It's very (c)hot in Thailand, isn't it?
> B: Yes, but there are many temples in Thailand. You (d)should wear shorts when you visit a temple.
> G: Okay. Is there anything else?
> B: Make sure you (e)exchange Korean won to Thai baht.

출제율 95%

10 위 대화의 밑줄 친 (a)~(e) 중 문맥상 어색한 것은?

① (a) ② (b) ③ (c) ④ (d) ⑤ (e)

출제율 95%

11 위 대화의 밑줄 친 (A)와 같은 표현을 쓸 때 빈칸에 알맞은 말을 쓰시오.

> What should I take?
> = Can I _____ _____ _____ on what _____ _____ ?

출제율 95%

12 다음 중 어법상 어색한 것을 고르시오.

① What have you been trying to find here?
② Kyle has been walking for 3 hours.
③ Donald's relatives have been playing poker during the last winter party.
④ Everyone has been watching the soccer game on TV since this morning.
⑤ Sarah's parents have been enjoying drawing pictures since last year.

13 다음 각 문장에서 어법상 어색한 부분을 하나씩 골라 고치시오. [출제율 100%]

> ⓐ They have been making some gifts since two months.
> ⓑ The instructor taught us how to swim was almost drowned.
> ⓒ The Spanish language speak in most of Latin American countries is not hard to learn.
> ⓓ Prices have been risen steadily for 5 months.

➡ ⓐ _____ ⓑ _____
  ⓒ _____ ⓓ _____

14 다음 중 밑줄 친 부분의 성격이 나머지 넷과 다른 것은? [출제율 95%]

① All the students in my class came to see the works of Van Gogh <u>displayed</u> in this art museum.
② I know the pretty girl <u>smiling</u> at me in the middle of the field trip.
③ A kettle is used for <u>boiling</u> water.
④ Uncle Brian came home with a huge box <u>filled</u> with tropical fruits.
⑤ Street cleaners are collecting the leaves <u>fallen</u> on the road.

[15~18] 다음 글을 읽고 물음에 답하시오.

> Hi! My name is Kim Minhee. I have been living in America for three years. Since my family moved here, I have experienced many cultural differences between Korea and America. I would like to share some of them with you.

Minhee: Look at this shirt. I like it.
Linda: It looks nice. How much is it?
Minhee: It's 19 dollars and 99 cents.
Linda: That's not expensive.
Minhee: Yes, I agree. I want to buy it.
Clerk: That'll be 21 dollars and 20 cents.
Minhee: Really? But the price tag says it's only 19 dollars and 99 cents.

> Here in America, in most states, people pay a tax when they buy goods. It is called a sales tax. Sales tax rates differ by state. They range from less than one percent to more than ten percent. So when you buy goods in America, you usually need to pay (A)_____.

15 빈칸 (A)에 들어갈 말로 가장 적절한 것은? [출제율 95%]

① more than the sales tax on the tag
② as much as a sales tax on the tag
③ much less than the price on the tag
④ as much as the price on the tag
⑤ more than the price on the tag

16 다음과 같이 풀이되는 말을 위 글에서 찾아 쓰시오. [출제율 90%]

> an amount of money that you have to pay to the government so that it can pay for public services

➡ _____

17 위 글의 내용에 맞게 빈칸에 알맞은 말을 쓰시오. [출제율 90%]

> Sales tax rates differ by state _____ _____ _____ one percent _____ _____ _____ ten percent.

18 다음 중 위 글의 내용과 일치하는 것은?

① Minhee moved to Korea three years ago.
② Minhee got so familiar with American cultures.
③ Minhee went to buy a shirt by herself.
④ People in Korea pay a sales tax like people in America.
⑤ Every state has its own sales tax rate.

[19~22] 다음 글을 읽고 물음에 답하시오.

Andy: Minhee, try this apple pie.
Minhee: No, thanks. I don't want to.
Andy: Why not? Don't you like apple pie?
Minhee: Yes.
Andy: (A)Then, try some. It's delicious.
Minhee: No. I just said I don't like apple pie.
Andy: What?

Americans often ask negative questions, such as "Aren't you coming?" and "Didn't you go to the hospital?" It can be difficult (B)to answer negative questions correctly. Here is some advice.

In response to negative questions, such as "Don't you like apple pie?" you should answer "No," if you don't like it. And you should answer "Yes," if you like it. These answers are the same as the answers to positive questions, such as "Do you like apple pie?"

	Like	Don't like
Do you like apple pie?	Yes, I do.	No, I don't.
Don't you like apple pie?	Yes, I do.	No, I don't.

Which cultural difference is most surprising to you? I have been learning about cultural differences since I came to America. Some surprised me at first, but now I am getting used to (C)them.

19 Andy가 민희에게 밑줄 친 (A)와 같이 말한 이유로 가장 적절한 것은?

① Because he understood Minhee doesn't like apple pie.
② Because he understood Minhee doesn't want to talk with him.
③ Because he understood Minhee likes him.
④ Because he understood Minhee likes apple pie.
⑤ Because he wanted Minhee to try harder.

20 다음 중 밑줄 친 (B)와 쓰임이 같은 것은?

① She ran fast to catch him.
② I am so happy to see you here.
③ It made me nervous to interview him.
④ The bird flew high to reach the top.
⑤ The boys needed something to play with.

21 밑줄 친 (C)가 가리키는 것을 위 글에서 찾아 쓰시오.

➡ _____

22 According to the passage, what has the writer been learning about since she came to America? Answer in English with a full sentence.

➡ _____
_____

01 다음 그림을 보고 아래 〈조건〉에 따라 대화를 완성하시오.

┤ 조건 ├

(A) 'Can I'를 이용하여 대만을 방문하는 것에 대해 조언을 구하는 표현을 쓸 것.

(B) 'eat food or drink water in the subway'를 대답에 활용할 것.

➡ A: _____ Taiwan?

　B: Sure. You should _____

　　_____ .

02 다음 대화를 읽고 아래 질문에 대한 답을 본문에서 찾아 영어로 쓰시오.

> B: Did you pack everything you need for the trip to Thailand tomorrow?
>
> G: Not yet. What should I take?
>
> B: Remember to bring a pair of long pants or a long skirt.
>
> G: Why? It's very hot in Thailand, isn't it?
>
> B: Yes, but there are many temples in Thailand. You shouldn't wear shorts when you visit a temple.
>
> G: Okay. Is there anything else?
>
> B: Make sure you exchange Korean won to Thai baht.

> Q: Why should she pack a pair of long pants or a long skirt?

➡ Because _____

　_____ .

03 다음 대화를 읽고 물음에 영어로 답하시오.

> Seho: My Chinese friend invited me to his house for dinner this Friday.
>
> Bora: That's good. I hope you enjoy having dinner at his house.
>
> Seho: I want to prepare a small gift for him. You lived in China for several years. Can I get your advice on what to bring?
>
> Bora: How about some tea?
>
> Seho: Tea?
>
> Bora: Yes. Most Chinese people like to receive tea as a present. They enjoy drinking tea. Also, they usually serve tea to guests.
>
> Seho: Oh, thanks. (A)내가 알아야 할 또 다른 것이 있을까?
>
> Bora: Make sure you don't wrap the present in white or black paper. White and black mean death in China.

(1) Q: Why did Bora suggest some tea as a gift?

➡ Because _____

　_____ .

(2) 밑줄 친 (A)의 우리말을 보고 주어진 〈조건〉 과 단어를 이용하여 영어로 쓰시오.

┤ 조건 ├

• 관계대명사를 사용할 것.

• there / anything / else / need

➡ _____

04 다음 우리말과 같은 뜻이 되도록 주어진 어휘를 사용하여 글자 수에 맞게 영작하시오. (단어 변형 불가, 숫자는 영어로만 쓸 것.)

나는 한 인도 중학교에서 한국어를 13년 동안 가르치고 있는 중이다. (teaching, for, Indian middle, been, 13 단어)

➡ _____

　_____

05 다음 중 밑줄 친 부분을 어법에 맞게 고치고, 고친 단어의 종류가 다른 하나를 찾아, 그 이유를 설명하시오.

> ⓐ The boy <u>cry</u> at the corner of the street was Jane's youngest brother.
> ⓑ You should wait for the train <u>leave</u> at 5:00 here.
> ⓒ These days, people don't want to buy <u>sleep</u> bags for camping.
> ⓓ My wife saw a beautiful wall of a building <u>cover</u> with ivy.
> ⓔ Robert memorized a poem <u>write</u> by Ralph Waldo Emerson.

➡ ⓐ _____ ⓑ _____ ⓒ _____
　 ⓓ _____ ⓔ _____
　 이유: _____

[06~08] 다음 글을 읽고 물음에 답하시오.

　Americans often ask negative questions, such as "Aren't you coming?" and "Didn't you go to the hospital?" It can be difficult to answer negative questions correctly. Here is some advice.

　In response to negative questions, such as "Don't you like apple pie?" you should answer "No," if you don't like it. And you should answer "Yes," if you like it. These answers are the same as the answers to (A)_____, such as "Do you like apple pie?"

	Like	Don't like
Do you like apple pie?	Yes, I do.	No, I don't.
Don't you like apple pie?	ⓐ _____	ⓑ _____

Which cultural difference is most surprising to you? I have been learning about cultural differences since I came to America. Some surprised me at first, but now I am getting used to them.

06 빈칸 (A)에 알맞은 말을 쓰시오.

➡ _____

07 빈칸 ⓐ와 ⓑ에 적절한 말을 쓰시오.

➡ ⓐ _____　　ⓑ _____

08 다음 상황을 읽고 빈칸에 알맞은 말을 위 글의 내용에 맞게 세 단어로 쓰시오.

> Julian came home late last night. If his mother says this morning, "Didn't you come late last night?", he will answer, "_____."

[09~10] 다음 글을 읽고 물음에 답하시오.

　There are many (A)_____ festivals around the world. Among them, I'd like to attend Holi. People in India have been celebrating this festival for many years. Holi is held in March. I think that if I go, I'll experience a lot of things. First, there are people (B)_____ colored powder and water on each other. It will be fantastic! Second, I want to dance with other people on the street. I'll also taste traditional Holi dishes. It's going to be very exciting. I can't wait for the day!

09 주어진 단어를 어법에 맞게 빈칸 (A)와 (B)에 쓰시오.

> (interest / throw)

➡ (A) _____　(B) _____

10 According to the passage, what have people in India been celebrating for many years? Answer in English with a full sentence.

➡ _____

창의사고력 서술형 문제

01 다음 (A)는 방문할 나라이고, (B)는 그 나라에서 유의해야 할 내용을 경고하는 문장이다. 아래의 대화를 완성하시오.

(A)	(B)
• Russia	• not / give flowers in even numbers
• the USA	• sit in the back seat in the taxi
• Malaysia	• not / use your left hand to hand something to someone
• Thailand	• not / touch someone's head

A: _____

B: Sure. _____ you _____.

02 다음 그림들을 보고, 괄호 안에 주어진 어휘를 모두 활용하여 현재완료진행형 문장을 쓰시오. (인칭과 시제 등에 유의하여 활용할 것.)

(John, eat, sing, since, lunch)　(Susan, clean, towel, table, brother, ten minutes)

(1) _____

(2) _____

03 주어진 단어를 활용하여 세계 축제 홍보 책자를 완성하시오.

Where: in Italy
What: Pizza Festival
When: in June
What you can do is …
① try different kinds of pizza from all around the world
② select the best chef

Pizza Festival that I Can't Miss
There are many interesting festivals around the world. Among them, I'd like to attend _____. People in _____ have been celebrating this festival for many years. Pizza Festival is held _____. I think that if I go, I will experience a lot of things. First, I will _____. Second, I will take part in _____. It's going to be very exciting. I can't wait for the day!

단원별 모의고사

01 다음 단어에 대한 영어 설명이 <u>어색한</u> 것은?

① bump: to hurt part of your body by hitting it against something hard
② rude: not polite
③ goods: things for sale, or the things that you own
④ sales tax: money paid to the government that is based on your income or the cost of goods or services you have bought
⑤ tag: a small piece of paper, cloth, or metal with information on it, tied or stuck onto something larger

02 다음 짝지어진 단어의 관계가 같도록 빈칸에 알맞은 말을 쓰시오.

> elderly : aged = rude : _____

03 다음 빈칸에 알맞은 것으로 짝지어진 것은?

> • Take _____ your shoes here.
> • _____ first I thought he was an Englishman.

① off – For
② off – At
③ on – To
④ on – With
⑤ over – From

04 다음 중 짝지어진 대화가 <u>어색한</u> 것은?

① A: Which country would you like to travel to?
   B: I'd like to visit Singapore.
② A: Is there anything I should know about the country?
   B: Yes. Make sure you don't chew gum on the street.
③ A: Aren't you hungry?
   B: Yes, I'm not.
④ A: Hi, Jessica! Hi, Minhee! How are you?
   B: Fine, thank you. We are here for a burger.
⑤ A: Look at this shirt. I like it.
   B: It looks nice. How much is it?

[05~06] 다음 대화의 빈칸에 들어갈 말로 알맞은 것을 고르시오.

05
> A: _____
> B: Make sure you say window shopping instead of eye shopping.

① Can I get some advice on visiting there?
② Are there any other things I should buy?
③ What is the best thing about shopping?
④ Can I get your advice on correct English expressions?
⑤ What is the name of the shopping mall?

06
> B: I'm going to Japan this summer. Can I get some advice on visiting there?
> G: Make sure you pay when you get off the bus.
> B: Oh, I didn't know that. _____
> G: Pick up the bowl and hold it while eating. Also, when having soup, you should drink it without a spoon.
> B: Okay. Thanks

① What should I take there?
② Can you tell me about your favorite food?
③ What are you going to eat?
④ How about Japanese food?
⑤ Are there any other things I should remember?

[07~08] 다음 대화를 읽고 물음에 답하시오.

Seho: My Chinese friend invited me to his house for dinner this Friday.

Bora: That's good. I hope you enjoy (a)having dinner at his house.

Seho: I want to prepare a small gift for him. You lived in China for several years. Can I get your advice on (b)what to bring?

Bora: How about some tea?

Seho: Tea?

Bora: Yes. Most Chinese people like to receive tea (c)as a present. They enjoy drinking tea. Also, they usually serve tea to guests.

Seho: Oh, thanks. Is there anything else (d)that I need to know?

Bora: (e)Make sure don't wrap the present in white or black paper. White and black mean death in China.

Seho: Okay. I'll remember that. Thank you for the advice.

07 위 대화의 밑줄 친 (a)~(e) 중 어법상 어색한 것은?

① (a) ② (b) ③ (c) ④ (d) ⑤ (e)

08 Why shouldn't Seho wrap the present in white or black paper? (7단어로 쓸 것)

➡ Because _____.

09 다음 대화의 빈칸에 들어갈 알맞은 표현을 쓰시오.

> A: Is there anything I need to remember when I eat in France?
>
> B: Yes. _____ _____ you keep your hands on the table at all times.

[10~11] 다음 대화를 읽고 물음에 답하시오.

G: Look at the people wearing traditional Moroccan clothes. They are really beautiful. I want to take pictures of them.

M: Wait. (A)네가 사진을 찍기 전에 알아야 할 중요한 것이 있어.

G: Oh, really? (B)_____

M: Yes. You shouldn't take pictures of Moroccan people without asking.

G: Why?

M: They believe it may have a bad effect on them when someone takes their picture.

10 위 대화의 밑줄 친 (A)의 우리말 해석에 맞게 주어진 어구를 알맞은 순서로 배열하시오.

> (an / before / important / is / thing / there / need / you / taking pictures / to / know)

➡ _____
_____

11 위 대화의 빈칸 (B)에 들어갈 말로 알맞은 것은?

① Who are you taking pictures of?
② Can I get your advice on it?
③ Is there anything else?
④ Can I get your advice on what to take?
⑤ Can I take pictures of Moroccan people?

12 다음 두 개 이상의 문장들을 주어진 〈조건〉에 맞게 한 문장으로 쓰시오.

> ── 조건 ──
> • 현재완료진행시제를 사용할 것.
> • 분사가 명사의 뒤에서 수식할 것.
> • for를 반드시 사용할 것.
> • 10단어를 넘지 않을 것.

(1) • I started to read the novel last Sunday.
　• Sarah wrote the novel.
　• Today's Tuesday and I'm still reading it.
　= I _____
　_____ days.

(2) • Minsu got a job at a bank last month.
　• Bill founded the bank.
　• Minsu is still working there.
　= Minsu _____
　_____ a month.

13 다음 주어진 문장의 빈칸을 괄호 안의 단어를 사용하여 어법에 맞게 쓸 때, 〈보기〉의 빈칸에 들어갈 말과 쓰임이 같지 않은 것은?

> ── 보기 ──
> • Ethan purchased some drones _____ (make) in Indonesia for his next experiment.

① She has another box _____ (design) to keep fruit fresh.
② We have to put off the meeting _____ (schedule) on Saturday, Oct 26.
③ They decided to help the elderly _____ (live) alone.
④ Don't touch the statue _____ (place) in front of the square.
⑤ Sue gathered the dishes _____ (break) by her mistake.

14 우리말과 일치하도록 괄호 안의 단어를 바르게 배열하시오.

> 오늘 오전부터 나의 영어 선생님이 그 무거운 상자들을 옮기고 있는 중이다.
> (morning, boxes, English, carrying, been, my, the, heavy, since, teacher, this, has).

➡ _____
_____

15 다음 중 밑줄 친 단어의 쓰임이 어법상 옳은 것은?

① We all remember the legendary singer Mr. Shin calling 'Mawang, the Devil King'.
② Can't you see that girl worn a rainbow evening dress.
③ There were a lot of bats hanging upside down from the ceiling.
④ These are old pictures taking 60 years ago.
⑤ I can recite the poem writing by Yoon-Dongju.

[16~18] 다음 글을 읽고 물음에 답하시오.

Hi! My name is Kim Minhee. I have been living in America for three years. Since my family moved here, I have experienced ① many cultural differences between Korea and America. I would like to ②share some of them with you.

Minhee: Look at this shirt. I like it.
Linda: It looks nice. How much is it?
Minhee: It's 19 dollars and 99 cents.
Linda: That's not expensive.
Minhee: Yes, I agree. I want to buy it.
Clerk: That'll be 21 dollars and 20 cents.
Minhee: Really? But the price tag says it's only 19 dollars and 99 cents.

Here in America, in most states, people ③ pay a tax when they buy goods. It is called a sales tax. Sales tax rates ④differ by state. They range from less than one percent to more than ten percent. So when you buy goods ⑤in Korea, you usually need to pay more than the price on the tag.

16 민희가 위 글을 쓴 목적으로 가장 적절한 것은?

① to share some information about how to buy a shirt cheaply
② to introduce some cultural differences she has experienced
③ to complain about how hard it is to live in America
④ to introduce some people she made friends with in America
⑤ to write letters to friends in Korea

17 다음 중 위 글의 내용을 바르게 이해한 사람은?

① Amie: It must be really hard for Minhee to move to Korea.
② Brian: I think it is difficult for Minhee to live alone in America.
③ Clara: Like Minhee, I don't know anything about Korea.
④ David: I think people in Korea pay as much as the price tag says.
⑤ Edward: Korea has also a sales tax, so they always pay more than the price on the tag.

18 ①~⑤ 중 글의 흐름상 어색한 것은?

①   ②   ③   ④   ⑤

[19~21] 다음 글을 읽고 물음에 답하시오.

Jessica: Hi, Mrs. Johnson!
Minhee: Hello, Mrs. Johnson!
Mrs. Johnson: Hi, Jessica! Hi, Minhee! How are you?
Jessica: Fine, thank you. We are here for a burger. Enjoy your meal.
Mrs. Johnson: Thank you. You, too!
Minhee: Jessica, why did you wave to Mrs. Johnson?

In America, people often greet each other ①_____ waving. Waving to an older person is not regarded as (A)[polite / rude]. When you come to America, you may feel (B)[comfortable / uncomfortable] about it ②_____ first, but why don't you try it? You can wave ③_____ and smile ④_____ an elderly man walking ⑤_____ the street. He may (C)[wave / turn] back.

19 다음 중 빈칸 ①~⑤에 들어갈 수 없는 것은?

① by   ② at   ③ to   ④ at   ⑤ for

20 (A)~(C)에서 글의 흐름상 자연스러운 것끼리 바르게 짝지어진 것은?

① polite – comfortable – wave
② rude – comfortable – turn
③ polite – uncomfortable – wave
④ rude – uncomfortable – wave
⑤ polite – uncomfortable – turn

21 According to the passage, how did Jessica greet Mrs. Johnson? Answer in English with six words.

➡ _____

Lesson 3

Future Dreams, Future Jobs

 의사소통 기능

- 확실성 정도 표현하기
  I'm quite sure you could become a great soccer player.
- 의견 표현하기
  It seems to me that you belong to the realistic type.

 언어 형식

- It is[was] ∼ that 강조 구문
  It is the growth ring in a fish **that** interests me.
- have+목적어+과거분사
  It's my responsibility to **have each song played** the same way every time.

Words & Expressions

Key Words

- **among**[əmʎŋ] 전 ~ 중에서
- **analyst**[ǽnəlist] 명 분석가
- **analyze**[ǽnəlàiz] 동 분석하다
- **animator**[ǽnəmèitər] 명 만화 영화 제작자
- **attend**[əténd] 동 출석하다, 참석하다
- **audition**[ɔ:díʃən] 동 오디션을 보다
- **banker**[bǽŋkər] 명 은행가, 은행원
- **bank teller** 은행 창구 직원
- **brush**[brʌʃ] 명 붓, 솔
- **calm**[kɑ:m] 동 진정시키다, 평온하게 하다
- **cast**[kæst] 명 출연자들
- **clear**[kliər] 형 명백한, 투명한
- **conduct**[kəndʎkt] 동 지휘하다, 처신하다
- **create**[kriéit] 동 창조하다
- **creature**[krí:tʃər] 명 생물, 생명체
- **data**[déitə] 명 자료
- **detail**[ditéil] 명 세부, 세목
- **developer**[divéləpər] 명 개발자
- **dish**[diʃ] 명 요리
- **engineer**[èndʒiníər] 명 기술자
- **enough**[inʎf] 부 충분히 형 충분한
- **figure**[fígjər] 명 인물, 형상, 사람 모양의 장난감
- **fix**[fiks] 동 고치다
- **florist**[flɔ́:rist] 명 플로리스트, 화초 연구가
- **gardener**[gɑ́:rdnər] 명 정원사
- **greenery**[grí:nəri] 명 화초, 푸른 잎
- **guide**[gaid] 동 안내하다
- **hairdresser**[hέərdrèsər] 명 미용사
- **handle**[hǽndl] 동 다루다
- **highly**[háili] 부 매우, 대단히
- **historian**[histɔ́:riən] 명 역사가, 역사학자
- **include**[inklú:d] 동 포함하다
- **information**[ìnfərméiʃən] 명 정보
- **lawyer**[lɔ́:jər] 명 변호사
- **lead**[li:d] 동 이끌다, 인도하다
- **machine**[məʃí:n] 명 기계
- **mail carrier** 우편집배원
- **microphone**[máikrəfòun] 명 마이크
- **office worker** 회사원
- **orchestra**[ɔ́:rkəstrə] 명 오케스트라, 관현악단
- **performance**[pərfɔ́:rməns] 명 공연
- **personality**[pə̀:rsənǽləti] 명 성격
- **poet**[póuit] 명 시인
- **police station** 경찰서
- **popular culture** 대중 문화
- **realistic**[rì:əlístik] 형 현실적인
- **recommend**[rèkəménd] 동 추천하다
- **record**[rékə:rd] 명 기록 동 [rikɔ́:rd] 녹화하다, 기록하다
- **reduce**[ridjú:s] 동 줄이다, 완화하다
- **report**[ripɔ́:rt] 명 보고서
- **reporter**[ripɔ́:rtər] 명 기자, 리포터
- **resource**[rí:sɔ:rs] 명 자원
- **responsibility**[rispànsəbíləti] 명 책임
- **run**[rʌn] 동 실행하다
- **seem**[si:m] 동 ~인 것 같다
- **select**[silékt] 동 선택하다, 고르다
- **social worker** 사회복지사
- **someday**[sʎmdei] 부 언젠가
- **specialist**[spéʃəlist] 명 전문가
- **stethoscope**[stéθəskòup] 명 청진기
- **strength**[streŋkθ] 명 힘, 강점
- **tour guide** 관광 가이드
- **traditional**[trədíʃənl] 형 전통의, 전통적인
- **type**[taip] 명 유형
- **veterinarian**[vètərənέəriən] 명 수의사
- **weakness**[wí:knis] 명 약함, 약점

Key Expressions

- **be happy with** ~ ~에 만족하다
- **be interested in** ~ ~에 관심이 있다
- **belong to** (단체, 조직에) 소속하다, 속하다
- **by - ing** ~함으로써
- **care for** ~을 보살피다
- **come true** 실현되다
- **dream of** ~ ~을 꿈꾸다
- **I'm sure that** ~ ~을 확신하다
- **It seems that** ~ ~처럼 보이다, ~일 것 같다
- **make the best use of** ~을 최대한 활용하다

Word Power

※ 서로 비슷한 뜻을 가진 어휘

- □ **run** : **operate** (실행하다, 작동시키다)
- □ **fix** : **repair** (고치다)
- □ **handle** : **deal with** (다루다)
- □ **select** : **choose** (고르다, 선택하다)

- □ **highly** : **greatly** (매우, 대단히)
- □ **include** : **involve** (포함하다)
- □ **guide** : **lead** (안내하다, 이끌다)
- □ **recommend** : **propose** (추천하다)

※ 서로 반대되는 뜻을 가진 어휘

- □ **weakness** (약함, 약점) ↔ **strength** (강함, 강점)
- □ **include** (포함하다) ↔ **exclude** (제외하다)
- □ **clear** (분명한) ↔ **unclear** (불확실한)

- □ **increase** (증가하다) ↔ **decrease** (감소하다)
- □ **construct** (건설하다) ↔ **destroy** (파괴하다)
- □ **lead** (이끌다) ↔ **follow** (따르다)

English Dictionary

- □ **analyst** 분석가
  - → someone whose job is to analyze and examine something
    어떤 것을 분석하고 조사하는 일을 하는 사람

- □ **analyze** 분석하다
  - → to study or examine something in detail, in order to discover more about it
    어떤 것에 대해 더 많은 것을 발견하기 위해 자세히 연구하거나 조사하다

- □ **audition** 오디션을 보다
  - → to give a short performance in order to show that you are suitable for a part in a film, play, show, etc.
    영화, 연극, 쇼 등의 어떤 한 역할에 적합하다는 것을 보여주기 위해 짧은 공연을 하다

- □ **bank teller** 은행 창구 직원
  - → a person whose job is to pay out and take in money in a bank
    은행에서 돈을 지급하고 수납하는 것이 직업인 사람

- □ **belong to** 소속하다, 속하다
  - → to be a member of an organization
    조직의 일원이 되다

- □ **care for** 보살피다
  - → to protect someone or something and provide the things they need, especially someone who is young, old or ill
    누군가나 무언가를 보호하고 특히 어리거나, 늙거나, 병든 사람을 위해서 그들이 필요로 하는 것들을 제공해 주다

- □ **cast** 출연자
  - → the actors in a film, play, or show
    영화, 연극, 또는 쇼에 나오는 배우들

- □ **collect** 모으다
  - → to take things and put them together
    물건을 가져가서 한데 모으다

- □ **data** 자료
  - → facts or information that can be analysed
    분석될 수 있는 사실이나 정보

- □ **developer** 개발자
  - → a person or company that creates new products, especially computer products such as software
    특히 소프트웨어와 같은 컴퓨터 제품을 신제품으로 만드는 사람 또는 회사

- □ **greenery** 푸른 잎, 화초
  - → green plants or branches, especially when cut and used as decoration
    특히 잘려서 장식으로 사용되는 녹색 식물이나 가지

- □ **include** 포함하다
  - → to contain something as a part of something else, or to make something part of something else
    무언가를 다른 것의 일부로 포함하거나 다른 것의 일부로 만들다

- □ **lead** 이끌다
  - → to bring a person or thing to a state or place
    사람이나 사물을 어떤 상태나 장소로 데려오다[가져오다]

- □ **make the best use of** 최대한 활용하다
  - → to use something as much as you can
    당신이 할 수 있는 만큼 많이 무언가를 사용하다

- □ **personality** 성격
  - → the type of person you are, shown by the way you behave, feel, and think
    당신이 어떤 사람인지, 행동하고 느끼고 생각하는 방식으로 보여지는 것

- □ **responsibility** 책임
  - → your job or duty to deal with something or someone
    어떤 것 또는 어떤 사람을 처리해야 할 일이나 의무

- □ **resource** 자원
  - → a useful or valuable possession or quality of a country, organization, or person
    국가, 조직 또는 개인의 유용하거나 가치 있는 소유물 또는 자질

중요

01 다음 문장의 빈칸에 공통으로 들어갈 말로 가장 알맞은 것은?

> • Ted and I _____ the same school.
> • My parents are out of town to _____ the wedding.

① record   ② develop
③ create   ④ attend
⑤ select

서답형

02 다음 글의 빈칸에 들어갈 알맞은 말을 쓰시오.

> A _____ is someone who creates beautiful things with flowers.

[03~04] 다음 설명에 해당하는 단어를 고르시오.

03
> to be a member of an organization

① reduce   ② belong to
③ make up   ④ come true
⑤ make the best use of

중요

04
> a useful or valuable possession or quality of a country, organization, or person

① source   ② personality
③ resource   ④ cast
⑤ developer

서답형

05 다음 우리말에 맞게 빈칸에 알맞은 단어를 쓰시오.

> 나는 내 팀의 강점과 약점을 보여 주기 위해서 그 자료들을 분석합니다.

➡ I _____ the data to show my team's _____s and _____es.

06 다음 빈칸에 공통으로 들어갈 말로 가장 알맞은 것은?

> (A) Children's pictures _____ the walls of the classroom.
> (B) It is a lot of fun to _____ your house with beautiful flowers.

① include   ② increase
③ select   ④ care for
⑤ decorate

서답형

07 다음 짝지어진 단어의 관계가 같도록 빈칸에 알맞은 말을 쓰시오.

> fix : _____ = deal with : handle

중요

08 다음 빈칸에 들어갈 말로 알맞게 짝지어진 것은?

> As a director of a musical theater, I do a lot of things. I _____ the actors and I look for good, strong voices. After selecting the _____, I teach them the songs for each scene. Then, I put the cast and orchestra together for practice.

① lead – gardener   ② conduct – cast
③ record – actor   ④ audition – cast
⑤ analyze – analyst

01 다음 빈칸에 들어갈 말을 〈보기〉에서 찾아 쓰시오.

보기

among　field　reduce　belong to　calm

(1) She helps them _____ stress and _____ themselves.

(2) What are you most interested in _____ the things on this list?

(3) Most people _____ one of six personality types. Realistic is one of the types.

(4) I am an ocean scientist. Ocean science is a big _____ .

02 다음 글의 밑줄 친 우리말에 해당하는 말을 쓰시오. (주어진 단어를 활용하여 쓰시오.)

I am happy when I create (A)다채로운 무언가를 with fresh flowers and greenery. If you like plants and the arts, I (B)강력히 추천합니다(high) you become a florist.

➡ (A) _____

(B) _____

03 다음 우리말과 같은 표현이 되도록 문장의 빈칸을 채우시오.

(1) 나는 스포츠 데이터 분석가입니다.

➡ I am a sport data _____.

(2) 나의 일은 녹화된 경기를 보고 자료를 수집하기 위해 컴퓨터 프로그램을 실행하는 것입니다.

➡ My job is to watch _____ games and run a computer program to collect data.

(3) 공연 동안에, 나는 오케스트라 석에 있고 지휘를 합니다.

➡ _____ the _____, I am in the orchestra area and conduct.

04 영영풀이에 해당하는 단어를 〈보기〉에서 찾아 첫 번째 빈칸에 쓰고, 두 번째 빈칸에는 우리말 뜻을 쓰시오.

보기

greenery　collect　personality

(1) _____: to take things and put them together: _____

(2) _____: the type of person you are, shown by the way you behave, feel, and think: _____

(3) _____: green plants or branches, especially when cut and used as decoration: _____

05 빈칸에 공통으로 들어갈 단어를 쓰시오.

• To _____ an orchestra, you have to be able to hear the music in your head.

• The police officers _____ a school violence prevention campaign in Incheon four times a year.

Conversation

교과서

1 확실성 정도 표현하기

> **I'm quite sure you could become a great soccer player.**
> 나는 네가 훌륭한 축구선수가 될 수 있을 거라고 꽤 확신한다.

- 'I'm sure (that) ~.'은 '나는 ~을 확신해.'라는 의미로 that절의 내용에 대해 자신의 확신을 나타내며, 'I'm (quite/fairly/absolutely) sure[certain] ~.'으로 표현할 수 있다.

- 확실성 정도 표현하기(긍정)
  - I was quite sure (that) you would be a successful fashion designer.
    나는 네가 성공적인 디자이너가 될 거라고 꽤 확신했다.
  - I have no doubt that you will become a great soccer player.
    나는 네가 훌륭한 축구선수가 될 것이라고 의심하지 않는다.

- 확실성 정도 표현하기(부정)
  - I'm not sure you will become a great soccer player.
    나는 네가 훌륭한 축구선수가 될 수 있을 거라고 확신하지 않는다.

- 상대방에게 확신 여부를 물을 때는 '확실해?'를 의미하는 'Are you sure?'를 쓴다.
  - **A:** Where is Kevin? Kevin은 어디에 있니?
  - **B:** He's on the left. 그는 왼쪽에 있어.
  - **A:** Are you sure? 확실해?
  - **B:** Yes, I am. 응, 그래.

핵심 Check

1. 다음 대화의 빈칸에 들어갈 말로 알맞은 것을 <u>모두</u> 고르시오.

   A: I'm interested in art. Which job would be right for me?

   A: _____ a designer could be a good job for you.

   ① I'm fairly certain that
   ② I have no doubt that
   ③ I wonder whether
   ④ I'm quite sure that
   ⑤ Make sure that

2 의견 표현하기

> It seems to me that you belong to the realistic type. 너는 현실적인 타입에 속하는 것 같다.

■ 'It seems to me that ~.'은 '~인 것 같다'라는 의미로 자신의 의견이나 생각을 나타내는 표현이다. 'It seems to me ~'와 유사한 표현으로 'In my opinion, ~', 'I think ~', 'I believe ~', 'In my view, ~', 'For me, ~' 등이 있다.

■ 의견을 표현하는 방법
내 생각에, 너는 현실적인 타입에 속하는 것 같다.
= I think that you belong to the realistic type.
= In my view, you belong to the realistic type.
= In my opinion, you belong to the realistic type.

- **A:** What do you think about bringing cell phones to school? 너는 휴대전화를 학교에 가져오는 것에 대해 어떻게 생각하니?
  B: In my opinion, it is helpful in case of an emergency. 내 생각에, 그것은 응급상황인 경우에 도움이 돼.

- **A:** What do you think about a water saving movement? 물 절약 운동에 대해서 어떻게 생각해?
  B: It seems to me that it is important to save water. 물을 절약하는 것은 중요한 것 같아.

핵심 Check

2. 다음 대화의 빈칸에 들어갈 말로 <u>어색한</u> 것은?

A: I want to be a fashion designer. What would help me become one?
B: _____ going to fashion shows would be helpful.

① In my opinion,
② It seems to me that
③ In my view,
④ For me,
⑤ You have to believe that

Listen & Speak 1 A-1

B: Anne, ❶I'm planning to visit the police station to see my uncle. He is a police officer.

G: Oh, I want to become a police officer someday.

B: ❷You do? Me, too. ❸I have dreamed of becoming a police officer since I was ten.

G: Can I come with you, Matt? I want to meet your uncle and ask him something.

B: Sure. What are you going to ask?

G: I want to ask him ❹what I need to do to become a police officer.

B: I see. ❺I'm sure he would like to meet you.

B: Anne, 나는 우리 삼촌을 보러 경찰서에 갈 예정이야. 그는 경찰관이거든.

G: 오, 나는 언젠가 경찰관이 되고 싶어.

B: 그래? 나도야. 나는 10살 때부터 경찰관이 되는 것을 꿈꿔 왔어.

G: 내가 너와 함께 갈 수 있을까, Matt? 나 너희 삼촌을 만나서 몇 가지 물어보고 싶어.

B: 물론이지. 무엇을 물어볼 거니?

G: 나는 경찰관이 되기 위해 내가 무엇을 해야 하는지 물어보고 싶어.

B: 알겠어. 나는 그가 널 만나고 싶어할 거라고 확신해.

❶ 'be planning to+동사원형'은 미래의 계획을 말할 때 사용하는 표현으로 '~할 예정이다'로 해석한다. to see는 부사적 용법의 목적으로 '~하기 위해'라는 뜻이다.

❷ do는 want to become a police officer를 대신하는 대동사다.

❸ 'since+주어+과거동사'는 '~한 이후로'의 의미로 현재완료와 주로 사용된다. 'dreamed of(전치사)+동명사(V-ing)' 형태를 사용한다.

❹ ask의 직접목적어 자리에 사용된 간접의문문으로 '의문사+주어+동사'의 어순을 취한다.

❺ 'I'm sure (that) ~.'은 '나는 ~을 확신해.'라는 의미로 확실성의 정도를 표현하는 말이다.

Check(√) True or False

(1) Anne wants to be a police officer.   T ☐ F ☐

(2) Matt has dreamed of becoming a police officer since he was ten.   T ☐ F ☐

 Listen & Speak 2 A-1

G: I'm glad to meet you, Mr. Han. Could you please tell me what you do?

M: Okay. I guide travelers to different places in China and give them information about ❶where they should visit.

G: What else do you do?

M: I tell them about popular culture and traditional food in China.

G: ❷It seems to me knowing a lot about China is very important. Are you happy with your job?

M: Yes. I really love my job.

G: 만나 뵙게 되어 반갑습니다, Mr. Han. 당신이 어떤 일을 하시는지 말해 주실 수 있나요?

M: 그래. 나는 중국에 있는 다양한 장소로 여행객들을 안내하고 그들이 방문해야 할 곳에 대한 정보를 제공해.

G: 그 외에 또 어떤 일을 하시나요?

M: 나는 그들에게 중국의 대중문화와 전통 음식에 대해 말해 줘.

G: 중국에 대해 많이 아는 것이 매우 중요한 것 같네요. 당신의 직업에 만족하시나요?

M: 응. 나는 내 직업을 정말 사랑해.

❶ 전치사 about의 목적어 자리에 사용된 간접의문문이다.

❷ 'It seems to me that ~.'은 '~인 것 같다'라는 의미로 자신의 의견이나 생각을 나타내는 표현이다.

Check(√) True or False

(3) Mr. Han must be a tour guide.   T ☐ F ☐

(4) The girl isn't interested in Han's occupation.   T ☐ F ☐

Listen & Speak 1 A-2

M: What's wrong, Jisu?

G: I want to be an animator, but my drawing skill is not ❶good enough.

M: Hmm... ❷Being an animator is not just about being a good artist.

G: What should I do to become an animator?

M: Read a lot of books to make good stories and practice drawing every day.

G: Okay, I'll do so.

M: ❸I'm quite sure that you can be a good animator if you try hard.

G: Thank you very much.

M: 무슨 문제 있니, 지수야?
G: 저는 만화 영화 제작자가 되고 싶은데, 그리기 실력이 좋은 편이 아니에요.
M: 음... 만화 영화 제작자가 되는 것은 단순히 그림을 잘 그린다고 되는 것만은 아니란다.
G: 만화 영화 제작자가 되기 위해서 제가 무엇을 해야 하나요?
M: 좋은 이야기를 만들기 위해 책을 많이 읽고, 그림 그리는 것을 매일 연습하렴.
G: 알겠어요. 그렇게 할게요.
M: 나는 네가 열심히 노력하면 훌륭한 만화 영화 제작자가 될 수 있다고 아주 확신해.
G: 정말 감사해요.

❶ enough는 부사로 형용사 뒤에서 수식을 한다.
❷ Being은 동명사 주어로 단수 취급하고, 전치사 about 뒤에도 동명사 being을 사용한다.
❸ '나는 ~을 아주 확신해.'라는 의미로 that절의 내용에 대한 자신의 확신을 나타내는 표현이다.

Check(√) True or False

(5) Jisu is very good at drawing.　　　　　　　　　　　　　　　T ☐ F ☐

(6) The man advised Jisu to read lots of books and practice drawing every day.　　T ☐ F ☐

Listen & Speak 2 A-2

B: Did you finish the report about your role model?

G: Yes, I did. I wrote about my role model, Ms. Shin. ❶I want to be like her.

B: ❷What does she do?

G: ❸She teaches people how to stretch. She also ❹helps them reduce stress and calm themselves.

B: Good. ❺It seems that she helps to keep both their mind and body healthy.

G: Yes, and I think it's great.

B: 네 롤 모델에 관한 기사 다 썼니?
G: 응. 다 썼어. 나는 나의 롤 모델인 신 씨에 관해 썼어. 나는 그녀처럼 되고 싶어.
B: 그녀는 무슨 일을 하니?
G: 그녀는 사람들에게 스트레칭하는 방법을 가르쳐. 그녀는 또한 그들이 스트레스를 완화하여 평온해지도록 도와 줘.
B: 좋구나. 그녀가 사람들의 몸과 마음을 둘 다 건강하게 유지하도록 돕는 것 같아.
G: 맞아. 그리고 나는 그것이 훌륭하다고 생각해.

❶ want는 to부정사를 목적어로 취하는 동사이고, 'be like'는 '~처럼 되다'는 의미로 이때의 like는 전치사이다.
❷ 직업을 묻는 표현이다.
❸ 'teach+간접목적어+직접목적어(how to stretch)' 구문이다.
❹ 'help+목적어+목적보어(동사원형/to부정사)' 구문으로 '…가 ~하도록 돕다'라는 뜻이다.
❺ 'It seems that+주어+동사 ~'는 '~처럼 보이다, ~인 것 같다'는 의미로 '주어+seem(s) to부정사'로 문장을 전환할 수 있다. help는 to부정사와 동사원형을 목적어로 가질 수 있다.

Check(√) True or False

(7) The girl wants to be like Ms. Shin.　　　　　　　　　　　　T ☐ F ☐

(8) Ms. Shin helps people cure their disease.　　　　　　　　　T ☐ F ☐

Listen & Speak 1 B

- **A:** I'm interested in technology. ❶Which job would be right for me?
- **B:** ❷I'm quite sure that an app developer could be a good job for you.
- **A:** I'm interested in writing. Which job would be right for me?
- **B:** I'm quite sure that a writer could be a good job for you.

❶ which는 명사를 수식하는 의문형용사로 '어느, 어떤'의 의미다.
❷ an app developer: 앱 개발자

Listen & Speak 2 B

- **A:** I want to be a radio program writer. What would ❶help me become one?
- **B:** ❷It seems to me writing your own stories would be helpful.
- **A:** I want to be a social worker. What would help me become one?
- **B:** It seems to me reading books to kids at a hospital would be helpful.

❶ help+목적어+동사원형: 목적어가 ~하는 것을 돕다 one=a writer
❷ It seems to me (that) ... 구문이다. writing은 동명사로 would be의 주어이다.

Real Life Talk

Bora: ❶What are you most interested in among the things on this list?

Jessie: I'm most interested in ❷working outside and playing sports.

Bora: Well, ❸it seems to me that you belong to the realistic type.

Jessie: What do you mean?

Bora: Most people belong to ❹one of six personality types. Realistic is one of the types.

Jessie: Oh, that's interesting. ❺What kind of jobs do they recommend for realistic types?

Bora: A farmer, a police officer, a soccer player, and so on.

Jessie: Oh, I have always wanted to be a soccer player.

Bora: That's good. ❻I'm quite sure you could become a great soccer player.

❶ be interested in ~: ~에 관심이 있다. most는 최상급으로 '가장'의 의미다.
❷ 전치사 in 다음에 동명사 'working ~ and playing ~'이 온다.
❸ belong to는 '~에 속하다'는 의미로 수동태를 사용하지 않는다.
❹ 'one of+복수명사'는 '~ 중 하나'라는 의미이다.
❺ 'What kind of 명사 ~?'는 '어떤 종류의 ~?라는 의미이다.
❻ 확실성의 정도를 표현하는 말이다.

Wrap Up 1

B: Hello, what are you doing, Sumi?

G: I'm looking for a good recipe on the Internet. I need it for my family dinner today.

B: That is nice. Do you cook often?

G: Yes, ❶I try to cook every weekend. I want to be a chef someday.

B: What are you doing ❷to make your dream come true?

G: I'm ❸taking a cooking class. I try to think of new and creative dishes.

B: ❹I'm quite sure you could be a good chef.

❶ try+to부정사: ~하려고 애쓰다[노력하다], try+V-ing: 시험 삼아 ~해 보다
❷ to make는 부사적 용법의 목적으로 '~하기 위해서'라는 뜻이다. 여기서 make는 사역동사로 '목적어(your dream)+동사원형(come)' 형태를 취한다.
❸ 'take a class'는 '수업을 듣다'는 뜻이다.
❹ 'I'm quite sure ~'는 확실성의 정도를 표현하는 말이다.

● 다음 우리말과 일치하도록 빈칸에 알맞은 말을 쓰시오.

Listen & Speak 1 A

1. **B:** Anne, I'm _____ to visit the _____ _____ to see my uncle. He is a police _____.

   G: Oh, I want _____ _____ a police officer _____.

   B: You _____? Me, too. I have _____ of _____ a police officer _____ I was ten.

   G: Can I come _____ you, Matt? I want to meet your uncle and _____ him _____.

   B: Sure. What are you _____ to ask?

   G: I want to ask him _____ I need _____ _____ to become a police officer.

   B: I see. I'm _____ he _____ _____ _____ meet you.

2. **M:** What's _____, Jisu?

   G: I want to be an _____, but my _____ skill is not good _____.

   M: Hmm... _____ an animator is not just about _____ good _____.

   G: What should I do to become an _____?

   M: Read _____ _____ _____ books to make good stories and _____ _____ every day.

   G: Okay, I'll do so.

   M: I'm _____ _____ _____ you can be a good animator _____ you try hard.

   G: Thank you very much.

Listen & Speak 1 B

● **A:** I'm _____ in _____. _____ job would be _____ for me?

   B: I'm quite _____ that an app _____ could be a good job for you.

● **A:** I'm interested _____ _____. _____ _____ would _____ _____ me?

   B: I'm _____ _____ that a writer could _____ _____ _____ _____ _____ you.

Listen & Speak 2 A

1. **G:** I'm _____ to meet you, Mr. Han. Could you please tell me _____ _____ _____?

   M: Okay. I _____ travelers to different places in China and give them _____ about where they should _____.

   G: What _____ do you do?

   M: I tell them about _____ _____ and _____ food in China.

   G: _____ _____ to me _____ a lot about China is very important. Are you _____ _____ your job?

   M: Yes. I really love my job.

2. **B:** Did you finish the report about your _____ _____?

   G: Yes, I did. I wrote about my role model, Ms. Shin. I want to _____ _____ her.

   B: What _____ she _____?

   G: She teaches people _____ _____ _____. She also helps them _____ stress and _____ _____.

   B: Good. _____ _____ _____ she helps _____ _____ _____ their mind _____ body healthy.

   G: Yes, and I think it's great.

Listen & Speak 2 B

- **A:** I want to be a radio _____ _____. What would help me _____ one?

  B: It seems to me _____ your own stories would be _____.

- **A:** I want to be a _____ _____. What would _____ _____ _____ one?

  B: It _____ to me _____ _____ _____ _____ at a hospital would _____ _____.

Real Life Talk

Bora: What are you _____ _____ in _____ the things on this list?

Jessie: I'm most interested in _____ outside and playing sports.

Bora: Well, _____ _____ _____ _____ _____ y o u
_____ _____ the _____ type.

Jessie: What do you _____?

Bora: Most people _____ _____ one of six _____ _____.
_____ is one of the _____.

Jessie: Oh, that's _____. _____ _____ _____ jobs do they
_____ for realistic types?

Bora: A farmer, a police officer, a soccer player, _____ _____
_____.

Jessie: Oh, I have always wanted _____ _____ a soccer player.

Bora: That's good. _____ _____ _____ you could become a
great soccer player.

Communication Task Step 2

A: I have _____ _____, _____ _____, 1 I, and _____
_____.

B: It _____ me that you _____ _____ Type S.

C: Yes. _____ _____ are _____ for Type S are teacher, nurse,
librarian or counselor.

A: Cool. I _____ _____ _____ to be a teacher.

D: That _____ great. I'm _____ _____ _____ _____
_____ be a good teacher.

Wrap Up 1

B: Hello, what are you _____, Sumi?

G: I'm looking for a good _____ on the Internet. I need it for my
family dinner today.

B: That is nice. Do you _____ often?

G: Yes, I try _____ _____ every weekend. I want to be a _____
someday.

B: What are you doing to _____ your dream come true?

G: I'm _____ a cooking class. I try _____ _____ _____ new
and _____ dishes.

B: _____ _____ _____ you could be a good chef.

해석

보라: 음, 내 생각에 너는 현실적인 타입에 속하는 것 같아.

Jessie: 무슨 의미야?

보라: 대부분의 사람들은 여섯 가지 성격 유형 중 한 가지에 속해. 현실적인 타입도 그중 하나야.

Jessie: 오, 재미있다. 현실적인 타입의 사람들에게 그들이 추천하는 직업은 뭐야?

보라: 농부, 경찰관, 축구 선수 같은 거야.

Jessie: 오, 나는 항상 축구 선수가 되고 싶어 해 왔어.

보라: 멋지다. 나는 네가 훌륭한 축구 선수가 될 수 있을 거라고 아주 확신해.

A: 나는 S가 3개, A가 2개, I가 1개, E가 1개 있어.

B: 너는 S 타입에 속해 있는 것 같아.

C: 응. S 타입에게 추천되는 직업은 선생님, 간호사, 사서, 상담사야.

A: 멋지다. 나는 항상 선생님이 되고 싶었어.

D: 그거 멋지네. 나는 네가 좋은 선생님이 될 수 있다고 아주 확신해.

B: 안녕, 뭐 하고 있니, 수미야?

G: 나는 인터넷으로 좋은 요리법을 찾아보고 있어. 나는 오늘 우리 가족의 저녁 식사를 위해 그것이 필요해.

B: 그거 멋지네. 너는 요리를 자주 하니?

G: 응, 나는 매주 주말에 요리를 하려고 노력해. 나는 언젠가 요리사가 되고 싶어.

B: 네 꿈을 이루기 위해서 무엇을 하고 있니?

G: 나는 요리 수업을 듣고 있어. 새롭고 창의적인 요리를 생각해 내기 위해 노력해.

B: 나는 네가 좋은 요리사가 될 것이라고 아주 확신해.

01 우리말 해석에 맞도록 문장의 빈칸에 알맞은 말을 쓰시오.

> • 너는 현실적인 타입에 속하는 것 같다.

➡ _____ _____ to me _____ you belong to the realistic type.

02 다음 대화의 빈칸에 들어갈 말로 알맞은 것은?

> A: I'm interested in art. Which job would be right for me?
> B: _____ a designer could be a good job for you.

① I question whether
② You may think that
③ I'm quite sure that
④ I'm very annoyed that
⑤ You should think

03 다음 대화의 빈칸에 들어갈 말로 가장 알맞은 것은?

> A: I want to be a radio program writer. What would help me become one?
> B: _____

① It seems to me going to fashion shows would be helpful.
② It seems that she helps to keep both their mind and body healthy.
③ I'm quite sure that you could be a radio program writer.
④ It seems to me you are a cook.
⑤ It seems to me writing your own stories would be helpful.

04 다음 대화의 밑줄 친 말의 의도로 알맞은 것은?

> A: Jihun is good at painting.
> B: Yes, he is. <u>I'm sure he will be a great painter.</u>

① 관심 표현하기   ② 확실성 정도 표현하기
③ 의견 표현하기   ④ 동의 표현하기
⑤ 반복 요청하기

[01~02] 다음 대화를 읽고 물음에 답하시오.

B: Anne, I'm (a)planning to visit the police station to see my uncle. He is a police officer.

G: Oh, I want (b)to become a police officer someday.

B: You do? Me, too. I have dreamed of (c)become a police officer since I was ten.

G: Can I come with you, Matt? I want to meet your uncle and ask him something.

B: Sure. What are you going to ask?

G: I want to ask him (d)what I need to do to become a police officer.

B: I see. (e)I'm sure he would like to meet you.

01 위 대화의 밑줄 친 (a)~(e) 중, 어법상 어색한 것은?

① (a) ② (b) ③ (c) ④ (d) ⑤ (e)

02 위 대화의 내용으로 알 수 없는 것은?

① Matt is going to meet his uncle this weekend.

② Anne wants to become a police officer.

③ Matt has wanted to be a police officer since he was ten.

④ Anne wants to ask Matt's uncle something.

⑤ Anne and Matt are going to go to the police station.

03 주어진 문장에 이어질 대화의 순서로 알맞은 것은?

A: I'm interested in animals. Which job is right for me?

(A) That's a person who works at a pet hair salon. He or she designs different hairstyles for pets.

(B) What is a pet hairdresser?

(C) I think a pet hairdresser can be a good job for you.

(D) That sounds nice.

① (B)–(A)–(C)–(D)   ② (B)–(C)–(A)–(D)
③ (C)–(A)–(D)–(B)   ④ (C)–(B)–(A)–(D)
⑤ (D)–(B)–(C)–(A)

04 다음 대화의 빈칸에 들어갈 말로 알맞은 것을 고르시오.

A: I want to be a fashion designer.
_____
B: It seems to me going to fashion shows would be helpful.

① Can I get your advice on fashion shows?

② Do you think I could be a fashion designer?

③ What would help me become one?

④ What would you like to do at fashion shows?

⑤ What do I like to be?

서답형
05 다음 대화의 밑줄 친 문장과 같은 의미가 되도록 주어진 단어를 이용하여 세 단어로 쓰시오.

A: It seems to me he is a cook.
B: That's right.

➡ _____, he is a cook. (opinion)

06 다음 두 사람의 대화가 <u>어색한</u> 것은?

① A: Can you imagine what jobs there will be in the future?
　 B: It seems to me that there will be space travel planners.

② A: Why are you applying to be a self-driving car mechanic?
　 B: I am interested in new technologies and cars.

③ A: Hello, what are you doing, Sumi?
　 B: I'm looking for a good recipe on the Internet.

④ A: What are you doing to make your dream come true?
　 B: I'm taking a cooking class.

⑤ A: I'm interested in technology. Which job would be right for me?
　 B: I'm quite sure that you could become a great soccer player.

서답형

07 다음 대화의 밑줄 친 우리말에 맞게 주어진 어구를 이용하여 영어로 쓰시오. (단어 2개를 추가하고, 어형 변화 필수)

> M: What's wrong, Jisu?
> G: I want to be an animator, but my drawing skill is not good enough.
> M: Hmm... <u>만화 영화 제작자가 되는 것은 단순히 그림을 잘 그린다고 되는 것만은 아니란다.</u>

> be / an animator / not just / about / a good artist.

➡ _____

08 다음 대화의 밑줄 친 부분의 의도로 알맞은 것은?

> A: I want to be a radio program writer. What would help me become one?
> B: <u>It seems to me writing your own stories would be helpful.</u>

① 조언 구하기　　② 의견 표현하기
③ 확신 표현하기　　④ 궁금증 표현하기
⑤ 가능성 묻기

[09~10] 다음 대화를 읽고 물음에 답하시오.

> Bora: What are you most interested in among the things on this list?
> Jessie: I'm most interested in working (a)<u>outside</u> and playing sports.
> Bora: Well, it seems to me that you (b)<u>belong to</u> the realistic type.
> Jessie: What do you mean?
> Bora: Most people belong to one of six personality types. (c)<u>Realistic</u> is one of the types.
> Jessie: Oh, that's interesting. What kind of jobs do they (d)<u>recommend</u> for realistic types?
> Bora: A farmer, a police officer, a soccer player, and so on.
> Jessie: Oh, I have always wanted to be a soccer player.
> Bora: That's good. (e)<u>I'm not sure</u> you could become a great soccer player.

09 위 대화의 밑줄 (a)~(e) 중 <u>어색한</u> 것은?

① (a)　② (b)　③ (c)　④ (d)　⑤ (e)

10 위 대화를 읽고 답할 수 <u>없는</u> 것은?

① What is Jessie most interested in among the things on the list?
② What personality type does Jessie belong to?
③ What kind of job did Bora suggest to Jessie?
④ What has Jessie always wanted to be?
⑤ What jobs do they recommend for the realistic type?

[01~02] 다음 대화를 읽고 물음에 답하시오.

> B: Anne, I'm planning to visit the police station to see my uncle. He is a police officer.
>
> G: Oh, I want to become a police officer someday.
>
> B: You do? Me, too. (A)나는 10살 때부터 경찰관이 되는 것을 꿈꿔왔어.
>
> G: Can I come with you, Matt? I want to meet your uncle and ask him something.
>
> B: Sure. What are you going to ask?
>
> G: I want to ask him what I need to do to become a police officer.
>
> B: I see. (B)_____

01 위 대화의 우리말 (A)에 맞게 주어진 어구를 알맞은 순서로 배열하시오. (부사절을 문장 뒤에 쓸 것.)

> I / have / ten / becoming / a police officer / of / since / was / dreamed / I

➡ _____

_____

02 위 대화의 빈칸 (B)에 들어갈 말을 주어진 〈조건〉에 맞게 쓰시오.

┌─ 조건 ─┐
- 삼촌이 Anne을 만나길 바라실 거라는 확실성 정도를 표현하는 말을 쓸 것.
- 대명사와 would like to를 사용할 것.

➡ _____

03 다음 대화의 빈칸에 들어갈 말로 자연스러운 것을 〈보기〉에서 찾아 문장을 쓰시오.

> G: I'm glad to meet you, Mr. Han.
> (A)_____
>
> M: Okay. I guide travelers to different places in China and give them information about where they should visit.
>
> G: (B)_____
>
> M: I tell them about popular culture and traditional food in China.
>
> G: (C)_____
> Are you happy with your job?
>
> M: Yes. I really love my job.

┌─ 보기 ─┐
- What else do you do?
- It seems to me knowing a lot about China is very important.
- Could you please tell me what you do?

04 다음 대화의 빈칸에 주어진 〈조건〉에 맞게 영어로 쓰시오.

┌─ 조건 ─┐
- (A) 동사 'do'를 사용하여 직업을 묻는 말을 쓸 것.
- (B) 'seem'을 사용하여 의견을 표현하는 말을 쓸 것.

> B: Did you finish the report about your role model?
>
> G: Yes, I did. I wrote about my role model, Ms. Shin. I want to be like her.
>
> B: (A)_____
>
> G: She teaches people how to stretch. She also helps them reduce stress and calm themselves.
>
> B: Good. (B)_____ she helps to keep both their mind and body healthy.
>
> G: Yes, and I think it's great.

Grammar

교과서

① It is[was] ~ that 강조구문

> • **It** is a puppy **that** I want to get for my birthday gift.
> 내가 생일 선물로 받고 싶은 것은 바로 강아지이다.
> • **It** was at the concert **that** Jane met Sean for the first time.
> Jane이 처음으로 Sean을 만난 것은 바로 콘서트에서였다.

■ It+be동사+[명사]+that+불완전한 문장: 주어나 목적어인 명사를 강조한다.
  • **Steve** invented **the machine**.
    → It was **Steve** that invented the machine. 그 기계를 발명한 것은 바로 Steve였다.
    → It was **the machine** that Steve invented. Steve가 발명한 것은 바로 그 기계였다.

■ It+be동사+[부사(구/절)]+that+완전한 문장: 부사(구/절)를 강조한다.
  • I met her at the party.
    → It was **at the party** that I met her.
      내가 그녀를 만난 것은 바로 파티에서였다.

■ 'It is[was] ~ that' 강조구문에서 강조하는 대상이 명사일 경우, that을 관계대명사 who 또는 which 등으로 대체할 수 있다.
  • Dr. King took care of my ants.
    → **It was** Dr. King **that[who]** took care of my ants. 나의 개미들을 돌봤던 이는 바로 King 박사였다.
    → **It was** my ants **that[which]** Dr. King took care of. King 박사가 돌봤던 것은 바로 나의 개미들이었다.

핵심 Check

1. 괄호 안에서 알맞은 것을 고르시오.
   (1) It was Susan's car (who / which) Rooney bought last week.
   (2) It was at the theater (that / which) Mom met Daddy for the first time.

② have+목적어+목적보어

> The orchestra practices hard to **have** each song **played** the same way every time.
> 그 오케스트라는 각각의 곡이 항상 같은 방식으로 연주되도록 하기 위해 열심히 연습한다.
>
> Brian **had** his electric scooter **repaired** at the shop. Brian은 가게에서 그의 전기 스쿠터를 수리시켰다.

- have/has/had+목적어+목적보어: have는 '~하게 시키다, ~하게 하다'는 의미의 사역동사로 목적어의 능동/수동 여부에 따라 목적보어 자리에 원형동사 또는 과거분사가 온다.

  - The researchers **had** students **fill** the questionnaire.
    연구진들은 학생들이 그 질문지에 답하도록 시켰다. (능동: 동사원형)
  - The researchers **had** the questionnaire **filled** by students.
    연구진들은 그 질문지가 학생들에 의해 답변되도록 시켰다. (수동: 과거분사)
  - Please **have** Mr. Trump **come** in. Trump씨가 들어오게 해주세요. (능동)
  - Get out of my place, or I'll **have** you **arrested**.
    내 집에서 나가시오. 그렇지 않으면 당신이 체포되도록 하겠소. (수동)

- have/has/had+목적어+목적보어(과거분사): 좋지 않은 일의 경우, '~ 당하다'의 뜻으로 해석한다.

  - He **had** his bag **stolen** by a thief. 그는 도둑에게 가방을 도난당했다.
  - Karl **had** his hat **blown** off by the wind. 바람에 Karl의 모자가 날아갔다.
  - Sally **had** her ankle **broken** in a car accident. Sally는 자동차 사고로 발목이 부러졌다.

- 그 밖의 5형식 표현 동사들

  - Her teacher **made** her **read** that book. 그녀의 선생님은 그녀에게 그 책을 읽게 했다.
    → She **was made to read** that book by her teacher.
  - I could not **make** people **understand** me in Spanish. 나는 스페인어로 사람들에게 내 말을 이해시킬 수 없었다.
    → I could not **make** myself **understood** in Spanish (by people).
  - Jane **heard** the chairman **call** her name. Jane은 의장이 그녀의 이름을 부르는 것을 들었다.
    → Jane **heard** her name **called** by the chairman.
    → The chairman **was heard to call** Jane's name. 의장이 Jane의 이름을 부르는 것이 들렸다.
  - She **got** her son **to fix** the door. 그녀는 그녀의 아들이 문을 고치도록 시켰다.
    → She **got** the door **fixed** by her son.

핵심 Check

2. 다음 우리말에 맞게 괄호 안의 단어를 바르게 배열하시오.

(1) Peter는 여러 번 다리가 부러졌다. (legs, had, times, Peter, several, broken, his)

➡ _____

(2) 나는 이번 토요일에 머리를 깎을 것이다. (hair, will, have, this, cut, I, Saturday, my)

➡ _____

01 다음 문장에서 어법상 <u>어색한</u> 부분을 바르게 고쳐 쓰시오.

(1) The researchers had the girl watched the other student.

　　＿＿＿＿＿＿＿＿＿ ➡ ＿＿＿＿＿＿＿＿＿

(2) I got my knee injure in a soccer game.

　　＿＿＿＿＿＿＿＿＿ ➡ ＿＿＿＿＿＿＿＿＿

(3) It was last Friday which they lost their puppy.

　　＿＿＿＿＿＿＿＿＿ ➡ ＿＿＿＿＿＿＿＿＿

(4) It is my uncle that encourage me to study.

　　＿＿＿＿＿＿＿＿＿ ➡ ＿＿＿＿＿＿＿＿＿

02 다음 중 어법상 바르지 <u>않은</u> 것은?

① It was two years ago that Christine wrote that novel.
② It was in May that the baby saw the fireworks for the first time.
③ It was James who broke window yesterday.
④ It was the taxi that Frank proposed to Nancy.
⑤ It is when people praise her talent that the actress feels happy.

03 다음 빈칸에 들어갈 말로 알맞은 것은?

Mom ＿＿＿＿＿ me take out the garbage.

① told　　　　　② set　　　　　③ asked
④ had　　　　　⑤ got

04 다음 문장의 밑줄 친 부분을 강조하여 문장을 다시 쓰시오.

Grarbara has always wanted to buy <u>those books</u>.

➡ ＿＿＿＿＿＿＿＿＿＿＿＿＿＿＿＿＿＿＿＿＿＿

⭐ 중요
01 다음 문장의 밑줄 친 단어들 중 'It is[was] ~ that' 구문으로 강조할 수 <u>없는</u> 단어는?

> <u>Jonathan</u> <u>wrote</u> the touching <u>story</u> <u>yesterday</u>
> ①   ②   ③   ④
> <u>afternoon</u> at the cafe.
> ⑤

02 다음 중 밑줄 친 부분의 쓰임이 나머지와 <u>다른</u> 것은?

① It was the lamp <u>that</u> Shelly broke this morning.
② It is my youngest sister <u>that</u> I always take care of.
③ It is his idea <u>that</u> you should join his soccer club.
④ It was at the mall <u>that</u> Lisa bought the stationery.
⑤ It was Minsu <u>that</u> met the mayor at the park last week.

⭐ 중요
03 다음 중 어법상 어색한 문장은?

① The woman had her house paint.
② Will you let her go like this?
③ Tom had his hair cut by a barber last Saturday.
④ She'll make my dream come true.
⑤ Aunt Mary always helped me to do my homework when I lived with her.

04 다음 중 어법상 어색한 문장은?

① Tylor's daddy had him drive his truck yesterday.
② My mother allowed me to buy the smartphone yesterday.
③ Sarah Conner had her car fix by the mechanic.
④ The crowd let the little girl play the piano on the street.
⑤ Walking a little fast helps you to relieve some stress from your daily lives.

서답형
05 다음 대화의 문맥에 맞게, 괄호 안에 주어진 단어를 강조하는 'It is[was] ~ that' 구문의 문장을 영작하시오. (7 단어)

> Mom: Did you tear the letter in two?
> Jinwoo: No, _____.
> (Poppy)

서답형
06 다음 〈보기〉의 문장 중 어법상 <u>어색한</u> 것들을 <u>모두</u> 골라 기호를 쓰고, 고치시오.

> ─┤ 보기 ├─
> ⓐ Those pictures behind you make me think of my golden days.
> ⓑ The director of the film ordered the actress gain 10 kilograms.
> ⓒ Let his son to take your laptop to his school for just a few days.
> ⓓ Mariah helped the new singer performing on the debut stage.
> ⓔ The teacher of Korean literature had Abdullah memorize the poems written by Yun Dongju.
> ⓕ No one could get the addict stops using drugs.

➡ _____

_____

[07~08] 다음 중 'It ~ that'의 쓰임이 나머지 넷과 <u>다른</u> 것은?

07 ① It is my twin sister that you see in this picture.

② It was 30 years ago that Mr. Miles came to govern the region.

③ It is certain that she fell in love with the stranger at first sight.

④ It was in the street that Laura bought the fruit which made them sick.

⑤ It was the skirt that Christine's aunt made on her birthday.

08 ① It is the trumpet that Michelle usually enjoys playing in her free time.

② It was no wonder that Frank got accepted to Harvard University.

③ It was in the warehouse that the secret meeting was held.

④ It was Comet Halley that we happened to see last night.

⑤ It was only a minute ago that the train carrying her family left for LA.

09 다음 중 어법상 <u>어색한</u> 문장은?

① He would not have his mind change by his son's accident.

② The storm made all the items on the shelves fall onto the floor.

③ My grandfather had my daddy take care of the old pine trees in his garden.

④ The fire fighters let everyone inside the building leave at once.

⑤ The Highclass Academy makes its students practice English so hard.

10 다음 문장의 빈칸 (A)~(D)에 들어갈 말로 가장 적절한 것은?

- The guards at the front gate had the guest (A)_____ the mansion. (enter)
- The general ordered our soldiers (B)_____ back a few meters. (step)
- The webtoons Sarah watches every day make her (C)_____. (smile)
- All of my classmates are expecting Haon (D)_____ Highschool Rapper. (win)

	(A)	(B)	(C)	(D)
①	to enter	to step	smile	win
②	to enter	step	to smile	win
③	enter	step	smile	to win
④	enter	to step	to smile	win
⑤	enter	to step	smile	to win

11 다음 중 어법상 옳은 문장은?

① The manager of the hotel had the cleaning crew to wash the floor.

② Dayna's teacher always tells her eat vegetables.

③ The principal let the students to use the computers to prepare for the game.

④ Father always allows me to take pictures with his high-end camera.

⑤ I asked the P.E. teacher help me with the basketball practice.

서답형

12 다음 우리말을 괄호 안의 조건에 맞게 영작하시오.

- Laura는 Tom에게 그녀의 남편이 세탁기를 수리하는 것을 돕도록 시켰다.
(to, had, husband, the washing machine, repair 사용, 총 11단어로 할 것.)

➡ _____

_____

서답형

13 다음 대화가 자연스럽도록 주어진 단어를 모두 활용하여 문장을 완성하시오. (단어들 중 1 단어만 변형할 것.)

> **Father:** Has anyone done something to my plants? I think someone must have watered them too much.
>
> **Daughter:** _____
>
> _____ .
>
> (James / responsible / care / for / it / plants / take / is / is / of / who)

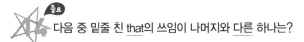 **14** 다음 중 밑줄 친 that의 쓰임이 나머지와 다른 하나는?

① It was in this cake <u>that</u> Michael hid the ring for his proposal.

② It was his bike <u>that</u> Julie's little brothers broke yesterday.

③ It was in 2015 <u>that</u> Leo won the Academy Award of Best Actor.

④ It was her pet kitty <u>that</u> woke Jessy up this morning.

⑤ It was her belief <u>that</u> ghosts were following her anywhere she went.

15 다음 중 밑줄 친 that을 다른 단어로 대체하여 바꿔 쓸 수 없는 문장은?

① It was the robot arm <u>that</u> carried out the difficult task.

② It is true <u>that</u> the team eventually reached the top of the mountain.

③ It was the suspect <u>that</u> met the police officer the other night.

④ It is he <u>that</u> solved the problem.

⑤ It was Mike <u>that</u> found this book in her room.

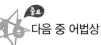 **16** 다음 중 어법상 올바른 문장의 개수는?

> ⓐ The famous actor living next door had the refrigerator fix by a repairman.
> ⓑ Bill's sisters asked him clean their desks.
> ⓒ A lot of crowd watched the boys dancing on the street to the sound of K-pop music.
> ⓓ It was soft that Susan bought a scarf.
> ⓔ The police officer helped an old lady to cross the street with no traffic signal.
> ⓕ Lisa got her son pick up the delivery box.
> ⓖ It was my dog that bit her leg.
> ⓗ Sean must get this work do on time.

① 1개   ② 2개   ③ 3개   ④ 4개   ⑤ 5개

17 다음 우리말을 바르게 영작한 것을 모두 고르시오.

> • 그 가수는 콘서트에서 팬들에게 자신의 사진을 찍도록 했다.

① The singer ordered her fans to take pictures of themselves at the concert.

② The singer let her pictures be taken her fans at the concert.

③ The singer had her fans take pictures of her at the concert.

④ The singer had her fans to take pictures of her at the concert.

⑤ The singer had her pictures taken by her fans at the concert.

서답형

18 다음 문장에서 어법상 어색한 부분을 하나만 찾아서 고치시오.

> • The soccer player had his leg break and got a scar on his forehead during the match.

➡ _____

01 다음 문장을 밑줄 친 부분을 강조하여, 각각 It으로 시작하는 문장으로 바꾸어 쓰시오.

> • <u>John</u> is going to buy <u>the masks</u> <u>at a</u>
>   (A)   (B)
> <u>party</u> <u>this Friday</u>.
>   (C)   (D)

➡ (A) _____
  _____

  (B) _____
  _____

  (C) _____
  _____

  (D) _____
  _____

02 다음 그림을 보고, 우리말에 맞게 괄호 안의 단어를 배열하여 빈칸을 채우시오.

> • As my daddy _____
> pancakes, I was standing with a ladle.
> (help, make, to, him, have, me, 변형 가능)
> 아빠가 내게 아빠를 도와 팬케이크를 만들도록
> 시키셔서, 나는 국자를 들고 서 있었다.

03 다음 각 문장에서 어법상 어색한 부분을 모두 찾아 바르게 고치시오. 단, 강조 구문 자체가 어색할 경우, 전체를 다시 쓰시오.

(1) It is the Hongdae street that the band gives a street performance.

➡ _____

(2) It was carefully that he rescued the injured.

➡ _____

(3) It was chairman of the council who Bush was.

➡ _____

(4) It was the playground that the boy was injured severely.

➡ _____

(5) It is her mistake who she doesn't recognize.

➡ _____

04 〈보기〉의 단어들 중 가장 적절한 것을 골라 다음 문장의 빈칸에 써 넣으시오. (어형 변화 가능하며, 각 단어는 1회만 사용할 것)

> ┤ 보기 ├
> look / cry / come / clean / go

(1) Mom had Karl _____ his room.
(2) They felt some smoke _____ out of the conference hall.
(3) Shelly heard a baby _____ out loud.
(4) Her boss let Joen _____ scuba diving.
(5) That diet will allow you _____ slim.

05 다음 주어진 문장과 뜻이 같도록 빈칸을 알맞게 채우되, it을 반드시 사용하시오.

> • March 14, 1879 is the day Einstein was born on.

➡ It was _____ born.

06 다음 각 문장에서 어법상 어색한 단어를 한 개씩 찾아 올바르게 고치시오.

(1) The customs officers at the airport had the baggage check while a passenger was passing through.

➡ _____

(2) The host of the show got the singer sing that song again.

➡ _____

(3) Her father allowed Gabrielle meet the young boy to find out who he was.

➡ _____

(4) Will you let the boys playing here?

➡ _____

(5) Susan was broke her legs during the practice of the ballet movement.

➡ _____

(6) Those make-ups made you looks more healthy and alive.

➡ _____

07 다음 〈보기〉와 같이 두 문장이 같은 의미가 되도록 주어진 단어를 활용하여 제시된 글자 수에 맞게 쓰시오. (어형 변화 가능)

> ┤ 보기 ├
>
> Please tell the kids not to make noise here. (make, quiet / 5 단어)
> → Make them be quiet here.

(1) The teacher said to Susan, "Clear all the mess on your desk." (have, clean, Susan / 7 단어)

➡ _____

(2) His father looked a lot younger when he put the tie on. (make, much / 8 단어)

➡ _____

(3) Please don't stop the girl from watching the film. (allow, enjoy / 6 단어)

➡ _____

08 다음 문장을 읽고, 각 질문에 'It is[was] ~ that' 강조 구문을 사용하여 답하시오. 답할 수 없는 질문은 '답변 불가'라고 쓰시오.

> • Alicia had John's phone repaired at the repair shop two weeks ago.

(1) Who repaired John's phone?

➡ _____

(2) Who got John's phone repaired?

➡ _____

(3) When did Alicia have John's phone repaired?

➡ _____
_____

(4) How many weeks did it take to repair John's phone?

➡ _____

(5) Where was John's phone repaired two weeks ago?

➡ _____
_____

The World of Wonderful Jobs

Florist

Hi, I am Tom. A florist is someone who creates beautiful things with
<u>주격 관계대명사</u>

flowers. To become a florist, you need to know many things about
<u>to부정사의 부사적 용법 중 목적(~하기 위해서)</u>

flowers. I attended a high school for florists and gardeners. It was at
<u>attended at(×)</u>

this school that I learned how to grow and care for different types of
<u>It was ~ that 강조 구문(at this school 강조)</u>   <u>~하는 방법</u>   <u>=look after</u>

flowers. These days, florists can do a lot of different things. I design
<u>=many</u>

movie sets sometimes and I decorate shops with flowers. I am happy

when I create something colorful with fresh flowers and greenery. If
<u>부정대명사는 형용사의 수식을 뒤에서 받음</u>

you like plants and the arts, I highly recommend you become a florist.
<u>recommend (that) you (should) become a florist</u>

Sport Data Analyst

I am Emma. I am a sport data analyst. It sounds like a difficult job,
<u>~처럼 들리다(sound like+명사)</u>

doesn't it? In fact, it is a lot of fun. I work for a baseball team.
<u>부가의문문</u>   <u>=great</u>

My job is to watch recorded games and run a computer program to
<u>보어</u>   <u>to watch와 병렬 (to) run</u>

collect data. Then, I analyze the data to show my team's strengths and
<u>to부정사의 부사적 용법 중 목적(~하기 위해서)</u>

weaknesses. If the team understands their strengths and weaknesses,

they can do better next time. Since I was young, I have been a big fan
<u>다음번에는</u>   <u>~이었을 때부터</u>   <u>현재완료: 계속</u>

of baseball. Now, in my work, I watch baseball games all the time.
<u>항상</u>

This is a perfect job for me because watching baseball games is my
<u>이유를 이끄는 접속사(~이기 때문에)</u>   <u>동명사 주어 단수 취급</u>

hobby!

wonderful: 놀라운, 경이로운
attend: 참석하다, (~에) 다니다
care for: ~을 보살피다
these days: 요즈음
movie set: 영화 촬영장
decorate: 장식하다, 꾸미다
greenery: 화초
recorded: 녹화된
in fact: 사실
analyze: 분석하다
strength: 강점
weakness: 약점

확인문제

● 다음 문장이 본문의 내용과 일치하면 T, 일치하지 <u>않으면</u> F를 쓰시오.

1 Florists create something beautiful with flowers. ☐

2 Tom's high school taught him how to grow flowers. ☐

3 There's nothing florists can do except growing and caring for different types of

   flowers. ☐

4 Emma is fond of watching basketball. ☐

Director of a Musical Theater

Hi, I am Chris. As a director of a musical theater, I do a lot of things. I
audition the actors and I look for good, strong voices. After selecting
the cast, I teach them the songs for each scene.

Then, I put the cast and orchestra together for practice. During
the performance, I am in the orchestra area and conduct. It's my
responsibility to have each song played the same way every time. I
direct the musicians and the singers to keep the show together.

Conducting and directing is not just about waving my arms around!

Ocean Scientist

My name is Yeji. I am an ocean scientist. Ocean science is a big field.
It includes studies of the oceans and the creatures living in them.
Among other things, I have studied many kinds of fish living in the
seas near Korea. It is the growth ring in a fish that interests me. By
looking at it, I can find out when and where the fish was born. All the
information I get from fish is used to understand sea resources and
manage the oceans better. My job is important because it makes the
best use of nature possible.

audition: 오디션을 보다
select: 선택하다, 선발하다
cast: (영화나 연극의) 출연자들
scene: 장면
orchestra: 오케스트라
performance: 공연, 연주
conduct: 지휘하다
ocean science: 해양 과학
field: 분야
interest: 흥미를 끌다
make the best use of: ~을 최대한 활용하다

 확인문제

● 다음 문장이 본문의 내용과 일치하면 T, 일치하지 않으면 F를 쓰시오.

1 Chris directs a musical performance as a job. ☐

2 Chris became a director of a musical theater by audition. ☐

3 Chris do nothing during the performance. ☐

4 Yeji studies not only fish but also oceans. ☐

5 Yeji is interested in the growth ring in a fish. ☐

● 우리말을 참고하여 빈칸에 알맞은 말을 쓰시오.

The World of Wonderful Jobs

Florist

1 Hi, I am Tom. A florist is someone _____ _____ beautiful things _____ flowers.

2 _____ _____ a florist, you _____ _____ _____ many things about flowers.

3 I _____ a high school _____ florists and gardeners.

4 It was _____ _____ _____ that I learned _____ _____ _____ and care _____ different types of flowers.

5 These days, florists can do _____ things.

6 I design _____ _____ sometimes and I _____ shops with flowers.

7 I am happy when I create _____ _____ with fresh flowers and _____.

8 If you like plants and the arts, I _____ _____ you become a florist.

Sport Data Analyst

9 I am Emma. I am a _____ _____ _____.

10 It sounds like a difficult job, _____ _____?

11 In fact, it is _____ _____ _____ _____. I work for a baseball team.

12 My job is _____ _____ _____ _____ and _____ a computer program _____ _____ data.

13 Then, I _____ the data _____ my team's strengths and weaknesses.

14 If the team _____ their strengths and weaknesses, they can _____ _____ next time.

15 _____ I was young, I _____ _____ a big fan of baseball.

16 Now, in my work, I watch _____ _____ _____ _____ _____.

17 This is a perfect job for me _____ _____ _____ _____ is my hobby!

Director of a Musical Theater

18 Hi, I am Chris. _____ a director of _____ _____ _____, I do a lot of things.

19 I _____ the actors and I _____ _____ good, strong voices.

20 After _____ _____ _____, I teach them the songs _____ _____ _____ _____.

21 Then, I _____ the cast and orchestra _____ for practice.

22 _____ the performance, I am in the orchestra area and _____.

23 It's _____ _____ to have _____ song played the same way every time.

24 I _____ the musicians and the singers _____ _____ the show _____.

25 _____ and _____ is not just about _____ my arms around!

Ocean Scientist

26 My name is Yeji. I am an ocean scientist. Ocean science is _____ _____ _____.

27 It _____ studies of the oceans and the creatures _____ _____ _____.

28 Among other things, I _____ _____ many kinds of fish _____ in the seas near Korea.

29 It is _____ _____ _____ in a fish _____ interests me.

30 _____ _____ at it, I can find out when and where the fish was born.

31 All the information _____ _____ fish _____ _____ _____ sea resources and _____ the oceans better.

32 My job is important _____ it makes _____ _____ _____ of nature possible.

16 지금, 나는 일하는 중에 내내 야구를 봅니다.

17 야구 경기를 보는 것은 나의 취미이기 때문에 이것은 나에게 완벽한 직업입니다!

뮤지컬 극장 감독

18 안녕하세요. 나는 Chris입니다. 뮤지컬 극장 감독으로서 나는 많은 것들을 합니다.

19 나는 배우들을 대상으로 오디션을 실시하고, 훌륭하고 강한 목소리를 찾아냅니다.

20 배역에 맞는 배우를 고른 뒤에, 나는 그들에게 각 장면을 위한 노래를 가르칩니다.

21 그러고 나서, 나는 배우와 오케스트라를 함께 연습시킵니다.

22 공연 동안에, 나는 오케스트라석에 있고 지휘를 합니다.

23 각각의 노래가 매번 동일하게 연주되도록 만드는 것은 나의 책임입니다.

24 나는 공연을 제대로 진행하기 위해 연주자들과 가수들을 감독합니다.

25 지휘하고 감독하는 것은 단지 내 팔을 흔드는 것만이 아닙니다!

해양 과학자

26 나는 예지입니다. 나는 해양 과학자입니다. 해양 과학은 거대한 분야입니다.

27 그것은 바다와 그 안에 살고 있는 생물에 관한 연구를 포함합니다.

28 여러 가지 중에서 나는 한국 주변의 바다에 살고 있는 많은 종류의 물고기를 연구해 왔습니다.

29 나의 흥미를 끄는 것은 바로 물고기 안에 있는 나이테입니다.

30 나이테를 살펴봄으로써, 나는 언제 어디서 그 물고기가 태어났는지 알아낼 수 있습니다.

31 내가 물고기에서 얻은 모든 정보는 바다의 자원을 이해하고 바다를 더 잘 관리하기 위해 사용됩니다.

32 내 직업은 자연을 가장 잘 활용할 수 있게 한다는 점에서 중요합니다.

● 우리말을 참고하여 본문을 영작하시오.

The World of Wonderful Jobs
Florist

1 안녕하세요. 저는 Tom입니다. 플로리스트란 꽃으로 아름다운 것들을 창조하는 사람입니다.
➡ _____

2 플로리스트가 되기 위해서 여러분은 꽃에 관해 많은 것을 알 필요가 있습니다.
➡ _____

3 나는 플로리스트와 정원사를 양성하는 고등학교에 다녔습니다.
➡ _____

4 제가 다양한 종류의 꽃을 기르고 다루는 방법을 배운 곳이 바로 이 학교에서였습니다.
➡ _____

5 오늘날, 플로리스트는 많은 다양한 일을 할 수 있습니다.
➡ _____

6 나는 때때로 영화 세트장을 디자인하고 꽃으로 상점을 꾸밉니다.
➡ _____

7 나는 싱싱한 꽃과 화초로 다채로운 무언가를 창조해 낼 때 행복합니다.
➡ _____

8 만약 당신이 식물과 예술을 좋아한다면, 나는 당신에게 플로리스트가 될 것을 강력히 추천합니다.
➡ _____

Sport Data Analyst

9 나는 Emma입니다. 나는 스포츠 데이터 분석가입니다.
➡ _____

10 어려운 직업처럼 들리죠, 그렇지 않나요?
➡ _____

11 사실, 그것은 매우 재미있습니다. 나는 야구팀을 위해서 일합니다.
➡ _____

12 나의 일은 녹화된 경기를 보고 자료를 수집하기 위해 컴퓨터 프로그램을 실행하는 것입니다.
➡ _____

13 그러고 나서, 나는 내 팀의 강점과 약점을 보여 주기 위해서 그 자료들을 분석합니다.
➡ _____

14 만약 팀이 자신들의 강점과 약점을 이해하면, 그들은 다음번에 더 잘할 수 있습니다.
➡ _____

15 어렸을 때부터, 나는 야구의 열혈 팬이었습니다.
➡ _____

16 지금, 나는 일하는 중에 내내 야구를 봅니다.

➡ _____

17 야구 경기를 보는 것은 나의 취미이기 때문에 이것은 나에게 완벽한 직업입니다!

➡ _____

Director of a Musical Theater

18 안녕하세요. 나는 Chris입니다. 뮤지컬 극장 감독으로서 나는 많은 것들을 합니다.

➡ _____

19 나는 배우들을 대상으로 오디션을 실시하고, 훌륭하고 강한 목소리를 찾아냅니다.

➡ _____

20 배역에 맞는 배우를 고른 뒤에, 나는 그들에게 각 장면을 위한 노래를 가르칩니다.

➡ _____

21 그러고 나서, 나는 배우와 오케스트라를 함께 연습시킵니다.

➡ _____

22 공연 동안에, 나는 오케스트라 석에 있고 지휘를 합니다.

➡ _____

23 각각의 노래가 매번 동일하게 연주되도록 만드는 것은 나의 책임입니다.

➡ _____

24 나는 공연을 제대로 진행하기 위해 연주자들과 가수들을 감독합니다.

➡ _____

25 지휘하고 감독하는 것은 단지 내 팔을 흔드는 것만이 아닙니다!

➡ _____

Ocean Scientist

26 나는 예지입니다. 나는 해양 과학자입니다. 해양 과학은 거대한 분야입니다.

➡ _____

27 그것은 바다와 그 안에 살고 있는 생물에 관한 연구를 포함합니다.

➡ _____

28 여러 가지 중에서 나는 한국 주변의 바다에 살고 있는 많은 종류의 물고기를 연구해 왔습니다.

➡ _____

29 나의 흥미를 끄는 것은 바로 물고기 안에 있는 나이테입니다.

➡ _____

30 나이테를 살펴봄으로써, 나는 언제 어디서 그 물고기가 태어났는지 알아낼 수 있습니다.

➡ _____

31 내가 물고기에서 얻은 모든 정보는 바다의 자원을 이해하고 바다를 더 잘 관리하기 위해 사용됩니다.

➡ _____

32 내 직업은 자연을 가장 잘 활용할 수 있게 한다는 점에서 중요합니다.

➡ _____

[01~03] 다음 글을 읽고 물음에 답하시오.

Hi, I am Tom. A florist is someone who creates beautiful things with flowers. To become a florist, you need to know many things about flowers. I attended a high school for florists and gardeners. It was at this school that I learned how to grow and care for different types of flowers. (A)These days, florists can do a lot of different things. I design movie sets sometimes and I decorate shops with flowers. I am happy when I create something colorful with fresh flowers and greenery. If you like plants and the arts, I highly recommend you become a florist.

01 다음 중 밑줄 친 (A)를 대신하여 쓸 수 있는 것은?

① From time to time ② Nowadays
③ Once in a while ④ Hardly
⑤ Now and then

02 다음 중 위 글의 내용과 일치하는 것은?

① Tom didn't have to know many things about flowers to become a florist.
② Florists care for only flowers.
③ Tom is not satisfied with his job.
④ Tom doesn't recommend his job.
⑤ There is a school for students who want to be florists and gardeners.

서답형
03 According to the passage, who is a florist? Answer in English with a full sentence.

➡ _____

_____

[04~06] 다음 글을 읽고 물음에 답하시오.

I am Emma. I am a sport data analyst. It sounds like a difficult job, doesn't it? In fact, it is a lot of fun. I work for a baseball team. My job is to watch recorded games and run a computer program to collect data. Then, I analyze the data to show my team's strengths and weaknesses. If the team understands their strengths and weaknesses, they can do better next time. Since I was young, I have been a big fan of baseball. Now, in my work, I watch baseball games all the time. This is a perfect job for me (A)_____ watching baseball games is my hobby!

04 다음 중 빈칸 (A)에 들어갈 말로 가장 적절한 것은?

① although ② if ③ because
④ when ⑤ until

05 다음 중 위 글을 읽고 답할 수 있는 것은?

① When did Emma get the job?
② How many games does Emma watch a week?
③ What does Emma do after collecting data?
④ How old is Emma?
⑤ Is Emma good at baseball?

서답형
06 According to the passage, how can the team do better next time? Answer in English with a full sentence.

➡ _____

_____

[07~10] 다음 글을 읽고 물음에 답하시오.

Hi, I am Chris. As a director of a musical theater, I do a lot of things. I audition the actors and I look for good, strong voices. After selecting the cast, I teach them the songs for each scene. Then, I put the cast and orchestra together for practice. During the performance, I am in the orchestra area and conduct. It's my responsibility to have each song (A)_____ the same way every time. I direct the musicians and the singers to keep the show together. Conducting and directing is not just about waving my arms around!

서답형

07 단어 play를 어법에 맞게 빈칸 (A)에 쓰시오.

➡ _____

중요

08 다음 중 뮤지컬 공연 감독이 하는 일이 <u>아닌</u> 것은?

① looking for good, strong voices
② teaching the cast the songs for each scene
③ conducting after the performance
④ directing the musicians and the singers
⑤ choosing actors for a musical performance

서답형

09 What does Chris do after he selects the cast? Answer in English.

➡ _____
_____

서답형

10 다음 빈칸에 들어갈 말을 위 글에서 찾아 쓰시오.

The _____ of a play or film is all the people who act in it.

[11~14] 다음 글을 읽고 물음에 답하시오.

My name is Yeji. I am an ocean scientist. Ocean science is a big field. ①It includes studies of the oceans and the creatures ② living in them. Among other things, I ③have studied many kinds of fish living in the seas near Korea. It is the growth ring in a fish ④ that interests me. (A)_____ looking at it, I can find out when and where the fish was born. All the information I get from fish is used to understand sea resources and ⑤manages the oceans better. My job is important because it makes the best use of nature possible.

11 밑줄 친 ①~⑤ 중 어법상 바르지 <u>않은</u> 것은?

①　　②　　③　　④　　⑤

12 다음 중 빈칸 (A)에 들어갈 말과 같은 말이 들어가는 것은? (대・소문자 무시)

① Can you pay attention _____ my speech?
② She is looking forward _____ seeing him.
③ It depends _____ you and your son.
④ Things will get better as time goes _____.
⑤ This medicine will take _____ your pain.

서답형

13 위 글의 내용에 맞게 빈칸에 알맞은 말을 쓰시오.

Ocean scientists study not only _____
_____ but also _____.

서답형

14 What can the growth ring in a fish tell Yeji? Answer in English with a full sentence.

➡ _____

[15~17] 다음 글을 읽고 물음에 답하시오.

Hi, I am Tom. A florist is someone (A)_____ creates beautiful things with flowers. To become a florist, you need to know many things about flowers. I attended a high school for florists and gardeners. It was at this school that I learned how to grow and care for different types of flowers. These days, florists can do a lot of different things. I design movie sets sometimes and I decorate shops with flowers. I am happy when I create something colorful with fresh flowers and greenery. If you like plants and the arts, I highly recommend you become a florist.

15 다음 중 빈칸 (A)에 들어갈 말로 적절한 것을 <u>모두</u> 고르시오.

① which   ② who   ③ that

④ what   ⑤ whose

16 다음 중 위 글의 내용과 일치하지 <u>않는</u> 것은?

① Tom is a florist.

② It is necessary to know many things about flowers to become a florist.

③ Florists always do the same things.

④ Tom creates something with flowers and greenery.

⑤ Tom feels happy when he does his job.

서답형

17 Where did Tom learn how to grow and care for different types of flowers? Answer in English with a full sentence.

➡ _____

_____

[18~21] 다음 글을 읽고 물음에 답하시오.

I am Emma. I am a sport data analyst. It sounds like a difficult job, ⓐ_____?

[A] Then, I analyze the data to show my team's strengths and weaknesses. If the team understands their strengths and weaknesses, they can do better next time. Since I was young, I have been a big fan of baseball.

[B] In fact, it is a lot of fun. I work for a baseball team. My job is to watch recorded games and run a computer program to collect data.

[C] Now, in my work, I watch baseball games all the time. This is a perfect job for me because watching baseball games is my hobby!

서답형

18 빈칸 ⓐ에 알맞은 말을 쓰시오.

➡ _____

19 위 글의 흐름상 [A]~[C]를 바르게 배열한 것은?

① [A]–[C]–[B]   ② [B]–[A]–[C]

③ [B]–[C]–[A]   ④ [C]–[A]–[B]

⑤ [C]–[B]–[A]

20 According to Emma, what does she feel about her job?

① bored   ② tired   ③ annoyed

④ satisfied   ⑤ uninterested

서답형

21 Write the reason why Emma runs a computer program. Use the phrase 'in order to.'

➡ _____

[22~24] 다음 글을 읽고 물음에 답하시오.

Hi, I am Chris. As a director of a musical theater, I do a lot of things. I audition the actors and I look for good, strong voices. After selecting the cast, I teach them the songs for each scene. Then, I put the cast and orchestra together for practice. During the performance, I am in the orchestra area and conduct. It's my responsibility to have each song played the same way every time. I direct the musicians and the singers to keep the show together. Conducting and directing is not just about waving my arms around!

서답형
22 다음 빈칸에 들어갈 말을 위 글에서 찾아 어법에 맞게 쓰시오.

> If someone _____ an orchestra or choir, they stand in front of it and direct its performance.

중요
23 다음 중 위 글의 내용과 일치하는 것은?

① Chris acts on the stage of a musical theater.

② Chris has a good and strong voice for the musical.

③ The cast is selected and taught some songs by Chris.

④ Chris writes many songs for the musical and has them played.

⑤ The orchestra doesn't need a conductor.

서답형
24 According to the passage, what is Chris's responsibility? Answer in English with a full sentence.

➡ _____

_____

[25~27] 다음 글을 읽고 물음에 답하시오.

My name is Yeji. I am an ocean scientist. Ocean science is a big field. (①) It includes studies of the oceans and the creatures living in them. (②) Among other things, I have studied many kinds of fish living in the seas near Korea. (③) It is the growth ring in a fish that interests me. (④) All the information I get from fish is used to understand sea resources and manage the oceans better. (⑤) My job is important because it makes the best use of nature possible.

중요
25 ①~⑤ 중 주어진 문장이 들어가기에 가장 적절한 곳은?

> By looking at it, I can find out when and where the fish was born.

①   ②   ③   ④   ⑤

26 다음 중 위 글을 읽고 답할 수 있는 것은?

① What did Yeji want to be when she was young?

② How long has Yeji studied ocean science?

③ Why does Yeji study many kinds of fish living in the seas near Korea?

④ Why is Yeji's job important?

⑤ What college did Yeji graduate from?

27 다음 빈칸에 들어갈 말을 위 글에서 찾을 수 없는 것은?

① The price tag ____ tax.

② Damage to the environment affects all wild ____.

③ The country has a lot of energy ____.

④ You pay too much ____ to the news.

⑤ I want to ____ my life better.

[01~04] 다음 글을 읽고 물음에 답하시오.

Hi, I am Tom. A florist is someone who (A) create beautiful things with flowers. To become a florist, you need to know many things about flowers. I attended a high school for florists and gardeners. It was at this school that I learned how to grow and care for different types of flowers. These days, florists can do a lot of different things. I design movie sets sometimes and I decorate shops with flowers. I am happy when I create something colorful with fresh flowers and greenery. If you like plants and the arts, I highly recommend you become a florist.

01 밑줄 친 (A)를 어법에 맞게 고쳐 쓰시오.

➡ _____

02 What kind of high school did Tom attend? Answer in English.

➡ _____

03 What do we need to know in order to become a florist? Answer in English with a full sentence.

➡ _____

04 According to the passage, when does Tom feel happy? Answer in English.

➡ _____

[05~08] 다음 글을 읽고 물음에 답하시오.

I am Emma. I am a sport data analyst. It sounds like a difficult job, doesn't it? In fact, it is a lot of fun. I work for a baseball team. My job is to watch recorded games and run a computer program to collect data. Then, I analyze the data to show my team's strengths and weaknesses. If the team understands their (A)_____, they can do better next time. Since I was young, I have been a big fan of baseball. Now, in my work, I watch baseball games all the time. This is a perfect job for me because watching baseball games is my hobby!

05 빈칸 (A)에 들어갈 말을 위 글에서 찾아 세 단어로 쓰시오.

➡ _____

06 What does Emma do as a sport data analyst? Answer in English.

➡ _____

07 According to Emma, what is her hobby? Answer in English.

➡ _____

08 다음과 같이 풀이되는 말을 위 글에서 찾아 쓰시오.

a person whose job is to analyse a subject and give opinions about it

➡ _____

[09~12] 다음 글을 읽고 물음에 답하시오.

Hi, I am Chris. As a director of a musical theater, I do a lot of things. I audition the actors and I look for good, strong voices. After selecting the cast, I teach them the songs for each scene. Then, I put the cast and orchestra together for practice. During the performance, I am in the orchestra area and conduct. It's my responsibility to have each song played the same way every time. I direct the musicians and the singers to keep the show together. (A) Conducting and directing is not just about waving my arms around!

09 다음은 밑줄 친 (A)와 같은 의미이다. 빈칸에 알맞은 말을 쓰시오.

> According to Chris, conducting and directing means much more than just _____ _____ _____ _____.

10 Where is Chris during the performance?

➡ _____

11 What does Chris do to keep the show together? Answer in English with seven words.

➡ _____

12 It is ~ that 강조 구문을 활용하여 다음 대화에 알맞은 답을 쓰시오.

> A: Chris, who do you audition?
> B: _____

[13~16] 다음 글을 읽고 물음에 답하시오.

My name is Yeji. I am an ocean scientist. Ocean science is a big field. It includes studies of the oceans and the creatures living in them. Among other things, I have studied many kinds of fish living in the seas near Korea. It is the growth ring in a fish that interests me. By looking at it, I can find out when and where the fish was born. All the information I get from fish is used to understand sea resources and manage the oceans better. My job is important because it makes the best use of nature possible.

13 According to the passage, what interests Yeji? Answer in English with a full sentence.

➡ _____

14 Write the reason why Yeji says her job is important. Use the phrase 'It's because.'

➡ _____
_____

15 What has Yeji studied as an ocean scientist? Answer in English with a full sentence.

➡ _____
_____

16 According to the passage, what should we look at if we want to know when and where a fish was born?

➡ _____

Enjoy Writing C

My Dream Job

I like food from around the world and I am good at cooking.
전치사의 목적어

I can also make food look tasty and beautiful. For these reasons, it is a chef
사역동사+목적어+동사원형 look+형용사: ~하게 보이다   it is ~ that … 강조구문: ~한 것은 바로 …다

that I want to be when I grow up. To achieve my dream, I will read magazines
~할 때   부사적 용법(목적)(= In order to[So as to] achieve)

about cooking. Also, I will go to France to learn various cooking skills. My

role model is my dad. He always thinks of new recipes and then cooks these

new dishes for us. I want to have my name remembered by people who enjoy
to us(×)   사역동사+목적어+과거분사(목적어의 수동 의미): 내 이름이 기억되도록 하다

my food.
주격 관계대명사절로 선행사 people을 수식

구문해설 ・be good at: ~을 잘하다 ・tasty: 맛있는 ・reason: 이유 ・chef: 요리사 ・achieve: 이루다
・various: 다양한 ・recipe: 요리법

내 꿈의 직업
나는 전 세계 음식을 좋아하고 요리를 잘한다. 나는 또한 음식을 맛있고 아름다워 보이게 만들 수 있다. 이러한 이유로 내가 자라서 되고 싶은 것은 요리사이다. 내 꿈을 이루기 위해, 나는 요리에 관한 잡지를 읽을 것이다. 또한 나는 프랑스에 가서 다양한 요리 기술을 익힐 것이다. 내 롤 모델은 나의 아빠이다. 그는 항상 새로운 요리법을 생각해 내시고 우리를 위해 이러한 요리를 만들어 주신다. 나는 내 이름이 내 음식을 좋아하는 사람들에게 기억되도록 하고 싶다.

Project

HELP WANTED!!
사람 구함

Do you like robots?

If your answer is yes, it is you that we are looking for.
'It is~ that' 강조 구문: you 강조

Please join us to train and fix robots.
to부정사의 부사적 용법(목적 또는 결과를 나타냄)

For more information, visit our website at www.robots.com.

구문해설 ・wanted: ~을 구하는 ・look for: ~을 찾다

사람 구합니다!
로봇을 좋아하시나요? 당신의 답이 예스라면, 당신이 바로 우리가 찾는 사람입니다. 우리와 함께 로봇을 훈련시키고, 고쳐 보세요. 더 자세한 사항은 우리 웹사이트 www.robots.com을 방문해 주세요.

Project Step 3

Are you good at training and fixing robots? If so, we're sure that you'll be a
동명사로 전치사 at의 목적어

good robot specialist. For more information, visit our websites.
셀 수 없는 명사

구문해설 ・train: 훈련시키다 ・fix: 고치다 ・be sure that ~: ~을 확신하다 ・specialist: 전문가

당신은 로봇을 훈련시키고 수리하는 것을 잘하나요? 만약 그렇다면, 우리는 당신이 좋은 로봇 전문가가 될 것이라고 확신합니다. 더 많은 정보를 위해서, 우리 웹사이트를 방문하세요.

영역별 핵심문제

01 다음 주어진 두 단어의 관계가 같도록 빈칸에 알맞은 단어를 쓰시오.

> highly : greatly = choose : _____

02 다음 글의 빈칸 (A)와 (B)에 들어갈 단어로 바르게 짝지어진 것은?

> I like food from around the world and I am good at cooking. I can also make food look tasty and beautiful. For these (A)_____, it is a chef that I want to be when I grow up. To (B)_____ my dream, I will read magazines about cooking. Also, I will go to France to learn various cooking skills.

① efforts – report ② efforts – achieve
③ reasons – conduct ④ reasons – fix
⑤ reasons – achieve

[03~04] 다음 영영 풀이에 해당하는 것을 고르시오.

03

> your job or duty to deal with something or someone

① resource   ② greenery
③ responsibility ④ historian
⑤ reporter

04

> to contain something as a part of something else, or to make something part of something else

① include ② advise
③ lead   ④ collect
⑤ create

05 빈칸에 들어갈 말을 영어 설명을 읽고 주어진 철자로 시작하여 쓰시오. (복수형을 쓸 것)

> Ocean science includes studies of the oceans and the c_____ living in them. Among other things, I have studied many kinds of fish living in the seas near Korea.
> <영어설명> any large or small living thing that can move independently

06 다음 밑줄 친 부분의 뜻이 잘못된 것은?

① It is the growth ring in a fish that interests me. (나이테)
② Giving up smoking reduces the risk of heart disease. (줄이다)
③ I direct the musicians and the singers to keep the show together. (감독하다)
④ Since I was young, I have been a big fan of baseball. (~이기 때문에)
⑤ This is a perfect job for me because watching baseball games is my hobby! (완벽한)

07 다음 대화의 빈칸에 들어갈 말로 적절한 것은?

> A: I want to be a radio program writer. What would help me become one?
> B: It _____ to me that writing your own stories would be helpful.

① leads   ② seems   ③ is
④ hopes   ⑤ happens

[08~10] 다음 대화를 읽고 물음에 답하시오.

Bora: What are you most interested in among the things on this list?

Jessie: I'm most interested in working outside and playing sports.

Bora: Well, (A)내 생각에 너는 현실적인 타입에 속하는 것 같아.

Jessie: What do you mean?

Bora: Most people belong to one of six personality types. Realistic is one of the types.

Jessie: Oh, that's interesting. What kind of jobs do they recommend for realistic types?

Bora: A farmer, a police officer, a soccer player, and so on.

Jessie: Oh, I have always wanted to be a soccer player.

Bora: That's good. I'm quite sure you could become a great soccer player.

08 밑줄 친 (A)의 우리말에 맞게 주어진 단어를 이용하여 영어로 쓰시오. (어형 변화 필수)

(seem / me / belong / the realistic type)

➡ _____

09 위 대화를 읽고 다음 물음에 영어로 답하시오.

Q: What is Jessie most interested in among the things on the list?

➡ _____

_____

10 위 대화의 내용과 일치하지 <u>않는</u> 것은?

① They are talking about personality types.
② Jessie belongs to the realistic type.
③ Bora recommends a soccer player for Jessie.
④ A farmer belongs to the realistic type.
⑤ Jessie wants to be a soccer player.

11 다음 대화의 빈칸에 들어갈 말을 주어진 단어를 알맞은 순서로 배열하여 완성하시오.

B: Do you cook often?
G: Yes, I try to cook every weekend. I want to be a chef someday.
B: What are you doing to make your dream come true?
G: I'm taking a cooking class. I try to think of new and creative dishes.
B: I'm _____.
(chef / good / quite / you / could / sure / be / a)

Grammar

[12~14] 다음 우리말에 맞게 영작한 것을 고르시오.

12

Tom의 아버지는 Tom에게 세차를 시켰다.

① Tom's father had him wash the car.
② Tom's father told him wash the car.
③ Tom's father had the car wash by him.
④ Tom's father let him washing the car.
⑤ Tom's father said him to wash the car.

13

내게 기운을 북돋아 주는 것은 내 아내이다.

① My wife who cheer me up counts.
② It is my wife that cheer me up.
③ My wife encourages me cheer up.
④ It cheers me up that my wife is.
⑤ It is my wife that cheers me up.

14

Marco는 펜스에 충돌하고 나서 다리가 부러졌다.

① Marco had his leg breaking the fence after hitting.
② Marco had him break his leg after hitting the fence.
③ Marco had got his leg breaking after being hit the fence.
④ Marco had his leg broken after hitting the fence.
⑤ Marco broke his leg after the fence hitting him.

15 다음 중 아래 그림의 내용을 설명하되, 어법상 성격이 다른 한 문장을 고르시오.

① It was a clown that was juggling with red balls.
② It was we that saw a clown juggling.
③ It was on the platform that a clown was performing.
④ It was exciting that my daddy and I were in the amusement park.
⑤ It was my daddy that was holding me up to watch the clown.

16 다음 중 어법상 올바른 문장은?

① David had the repairman fixed the fax machine.
② The police won't let the suspect leaving the country.

③ Her bright smile made Thompson feels so happy.
④ Mom finally allowed me to stay up all night with my friends.
⑤ Amy had her finger break while practicing kick boxing.

17 다음 중 우리말을 영작한 것이 <u>어색한</u> 것을 고르면?

① 어제 오후에 PC방에서 그를 만난 사람은 바로 나였다.
　→ It was I that met him at the Internet cafe yesterday afternoon.
② 아빠가 엄마를 처음 만난 것은 바로 아빠가 대학 신입생 때였다.
　→ It was when he was a freshman that my daddy first met my mom.
③ Bill이 MS를 만든 해는 1975년이었다.
　→ It was 1975 that Bill made MS.
④ 그 트럭을 고장낸 것은 Douglas였다.
　→ It was Douglas that broke the truck.
⑤ 오늘 아침에 그녀가 사장에게 받은 것은 바로 해고 통지서였다.
　→ It was a notice of dismissal that she received from the boss this morning.

18 다음 중 밑줄 친 부분의 쓰임이 〈보기〉와 같은 것은?

> 보기
>
> John <u>had</u> the windows replaced an hour ago.

① The food that I <u>had</u> was fantastic.
② The sports complex building <u>has</u> gas-fired central heating.
③ He <u>had</u> his head in his hands.
④ Sarah was <u>having</u> difficulty in staying awake.
⑤ We're <u>having</u> our car painted blue.

19 다음 중 밑줄 친 that의 쓰임이 나머지와 다른 하나는?

① It was on the snow that my dogs left their footprints.

② It is important that the actor should recover from despair.

③ It is this year that you will graduate from Balsan middle school.

④ It is the skill that makes me money.

⑤ It was those pancakes that my daddy sometimes made for me.

20 다음 중 어법상 어색한 문장은?

① The news made Christina cry a lot against her will.

② The designer had the dress to change from green color to orange.

③ Don't let the errors of the past destroy your present.

④ Yewon noticed a boy trying to get on the bus on her way to school.

⑤ Meditation helps you to escape from your grief.

21 다음 주어진 상황을 읽고, Peter가 여동생에게 할 말을 〈조건〉에 맞게 영작하시오.

• Peter's sister just broke her computer.
• Peter doesn't know how to fix the computer.
• He wants to make her relieved today.
→ Peter: I _____ .

┌─ 조건 ─
fix, have, today, 소유격, 미래시제 등을 활용할 것. 6단어로 빈칸을 채울 것.

Reading

[22~24] 다음 글을 읽고 물음에 답하시오.

Hi, I am Tom. A florist is someone who creates beautiful things with ①flowers. To become a florist, you need to know many things about flowers. I attended a high school for ②florists and gardeners. It was at this school that I learned how to grow and care for different types of flowers. These days, florists can do a lot of ③ different things. I design movie sets sometimes and I decorate shops with flowers. I am happy when I create something ④colorful with fresh flowers and greenery. If you like plants and the arts, I ⑤high recommend you become a florist.

22 위 글의 밑줄 친 ①~⑤ 중 글의 흐름상 어색한 것은?

①   ②   ③   ④   ⑤

23 위 글의 내용에 맞게 빈칸에 알맞은 말을 쓰시오.

The high school that Tom attended taught Tom _____

_____ .

24 다음 중 위 글을 읽고 답할 수 없는 것은?

① What does Tom do for a living?

② What do we need to know if we want to become a florist?

③ Where did Tom learn about growing and caring for different types of flowers?

④ Who recommended Tom to become a florist?

⑤ What does Tom do with flowers?

[25~27] 다음 글을 읽고 물음에 답하시오.

I like food from around the world and I am good at cooking. I can also make food look tasty and beautiful.

[A] He always thinks of new recipes and then cooks these new dishes for us. I want to have my name remembered by people who enjoy my food.

[B] Also, I will go to France to learn various cooking skills. My role model is my dad.

[C] For these reasons, it is a chef that I want to be when I grow up. To achieve my dream, I will read magazines about cooking.

25 자연스러운 글이 되도록 [A]~[C]를 바르게 배열한 것은?

① [A]–[C]–[B]　　② [B]–[A]–[C]
③ [B]–[C]–[A]　　④ [C]–[A]–[B]
⑤ [C]–[B]–[A]

26 위 글의 제목으로 가장 적절한 것은?

① France, the Dream Country
② My Dream Job, A Chef
③ My Mentor, My Father
④ Magazines That Will Help You
⑤ A World Famous Restaurant

27 위 글을 읽고 유추할 수 있는 것은?

① The writer wants to look beautiful.
② The writer is reading many books to become a writer.
③ The writer's father is a chef.
④ The writer travels all around the world.
⑤ The writer wants to remember people's name.

[28~30] 다음 글을 읽고 물음에 답하시오.

I am Emma. I am (A)_____. It sounds like a difficult job, doesn't it? In fact, it is a lot of fun. I work for a baseball team. My job is to watch recorded games and run a computer program to collect data. Then, I analyze the data to show my team's strengths and weaknesses. If the team understands their strengths and weaknesses, they can do better next time. Since I was young, I have been a big fan of baseball. Now, in my work, I watch baseball games all the time. This is a perfect job for me because watching baseball games is my hobby!

28 빈칸 (A)에 들어갈 말로 가장 적절한 것은?

① a cartoonist　　② a sport data analyst
③ a florist　　④ a director of musical
⑤ a baseball player

29 다음 중 위 글의 내용과 일치하는 것은?

① Emma thinks her job is very difficult.
② Emma doesn't want to know her team's weaknesses.
③ Emma didn't like baseball when she was young.
④ Emma likes baseball very much.
⑤ Emma always watches basketball games in her work.

30 According to the passage, what does Emma work for? Answer in English with a full sentence.

➡ _____

01 출제율 95%

다음 짝지어진 단어의 관계가 같도록 빈칸에 알맞은 말을 쓰시오.

weakness : strength = follow : _____

02 출제율 90%

다음 영영 풀이에 해당하는 단어는?

to give a short performance in order to show that you are suitable for a part in a film, play, show, etc.

① analyze   ② direct
③ audition   ④ display
⑤ exhibit

[03~04] 다음 대화를 읽고 물음에 답하시오.

Girl: I'm glad to meet you, Mr. Han. Could you please tell me what you do?

Mr. Han: Okay. I guide travelers to different places in China and give them information about where they should visit.

Girl: What else do you do?

Mr. Han: I tell them about popular culture and traditional food in China.

Girl: (A)In my opinion, knowing a lot about China is very important. Are you happy with your job?

Mr. Han: Yes. I really love my job.

03 출제율 90%

위 글의 밑줄 친 (A)와 같은 의미의 문장을 주어진 단어를 활용하여 쓰시오. (12 words)

(seem / me)

➡ _____

04 출제율 100%

위 대화의 내용으로 보아 알 수 없는 것은?

① Mr. Han guides travelers to many places in China.
② The girl wants to know what Mr. Han does.
③ Mr. Han gives travelers information about where they should visit.
④ It seems to me that Mr. Han is a tour guide.
⑤ Mr. Han really loves popular culture and traditional food in China.

[05~06] 다음 대화를 읽고 물음에 답하시오.

Mr. Kang: What's wrong, Jisu?

Jisu: I want to be an animator, but my drawing skill is not (a)enough good.

Mr. Kang: Hmm... Being an animator is not just about (b)being a good artist.

Jisu: What should I do (c)to become an animator?

Mr. Kang: Read a lot of books to make good stories and (d)practice drawing every day.

Jisu: Okay, I'll do so.

Mr. Kang: I'm quite sure that you can be a good animator (e)if you try hard.

Jisu: Thank you very much.

05 출제율 90%

What does Mr. Kang advise Jisu to do? (대화에서 찾아 2가지를 쓰시오.)

➡ _____

06 출제율 96%

위 대화의 밑줄 (a)~(e) 중 어법상 어색한 것은?

① (a)   ② (b)   ③ (c)   ④ (d)   ⑤ (e)

[07~08] 다음 대화를 읽고 물음에 답하시오.

Bora: What are you most interested in among the things on this list?

Jessie: I'm most interested in working outside and playing sports.

Bora: Well, (A)_____.

Jessie: What do you mean?

Bora: Most people belong to one of six personality types. Realistic is one of the types.

Jessie: Oh, that's interesting. What kind of jobs do they recommend for realistic types?

Bora: A farmer, a police officer, a soccer player, and so on.

Jessie: Oh, I have always wanted to be a soccer player.

Bora: That's good. (B)_____

07 위 글의 빈칸 (A)에 들어갈 말로 알맞은 것은?

① it seems to me that you belong to the artistic type

② I'm quite sure you'll achieve your dream

③ I'm quite sure that people doing those jobs will be in need

④ it seems to me that you belong to the realistic type

⑤ I think that you belong to the soccer team

08 위 대화의 빈칸 (B)에 들어갈 말을 주어진 〈조건〉에 맞게 영어로 쓰시오.

┌─ 조건 ┐
• 확실성 정도를 나타내는 표현을 쓸 것.
• 'quite sure', 'could become'을 사용할 것.
└──────┘

➡ _____

09 다음 대화의 밑줄 친 (A)를 do의 구체적인 의미가 나타나도록 바꾸어 쓰시오.

B: Anne, I'm planning to visit the police station to see my uncle. He is a police officer.

G: Oh, I want to become a police officer someday.

B: (A)You do? Me, too. I have dreamed of becoming a police officer since I was ten.

G: Can I come with you, Matt? I want to meet your uncle and ask him something.

B: Sure. What are you going to ask?

G: I want to ask him what I need to do to become a police officer.

B: I see. I'm sure he would like to meet you.

➡ _____

10 다음 각 문장에 사용된 어법 사항을 〈보기〉에서 기호를 골라 괄호 안에 쓰시오.

┌─ 보기 ┐
ⓐ It ~ that 강조 구문 문장
ⓑ It(가주어) ~ that(진주어) 구문 문장
└──────┘

(1) It is only through practice that you will achieve your goal. (　　)

(2) It is wonderful that the whole family gets together on Chuseok. (　　)

(3) It is when my kids smile at me that I feel the happiest. (　　)

(4) It is Susan's idea that all the club members must gather here. (　　)

(5) What was it that motivated Joe to learn engineering? (　　)

11 다음 대화의 밑줄 친 우리말 해석과 같은 표현을 쓸 때 문장의 빈칸에 알맞은 말을 쓰시오.

> B: Did you finish the report about your role model?
> G: Yes, I did. I wrote about my role model, Ms. Shin. I want to be like her.
> B: What does she do?
> G: She teaches people how to stretch. She also helps them reduce stress and calm themselves.
> B: Good. 그녀가 그들의 몸과 마음을 둘 다 건강하게 유지하도록 돕는 것 같아.
> G: Yes, and I think it's great.

➡ _____ _____ that she helps to keep _____ their mind _____ body _____.

12 아래의 내용을 'It ~ that' 강조 구문으로 다시 설명한 문장 중 내용과 일치하지 <u>않는</u> 것을 고르시오.

> • One day, my uncle Steve accidentally spilled a glass of wine, so my computer broke down. He gave me his credit card and I had the computer repaired at the shop.

① It was my uncle Steve that broke my computer.
② It was by accident that my uncle spilled a glass of wine.
③ It was his credit card that my uncle gave to me.
④ It was my uncle Steve that fixed my computer at the shop.
⑤ It was at the shop that my computer was repaired.

13 다음 중 어법상 <u>어색한</u> 문장은?

① Laura had her umbrella stolen while she was texting her boyfriend.
② Wasn't it hard to have your son transferred?
③ As her husband was looking away, Gloria had her shoes shone.
④ The VIP customer ordered the clerk to have all her purchases packaged.
⑤ The robber forced her to have the money withdrawn from the ATM.

14 다음 중 어법상 옳은 것을 고르시오.

① The movie made me moving.
② The principal of my school had us to wait for the mayor to give a speech.
③ Her parents are so strict that they won't let Peggy going out tonight.
④ All the relatives at camping helped my daddy washed the dishes.
⑤ My wife had me stay still during the wedding.

15 다음 문장의 밑줄 친 ⓐ~ⓓ를 각각 순서대로 'It ~ that' 강조 구문으로 전환하시오.

> The newlyweds bought a table at the mall
>   ⓐ   ⓑ   ⓒ
> 2 weeks ago.
>   ⓓ

➡ (1) ⓐ _____
_____
(2) ⓑ _____
_____
(3) ⓒ _____
_____
(4) ⓓ _____
_____

[16~19] 다음 글을 읽고 물음에 답하시오.

Hi, I am Chris. (A)As a director of a musical theater, I do a lot of things. ① I audition the actors and I look for good, strong voices. ② Then, I put the cast and orchestra together for practice. ③ During the performance, I am in the orchestra area and conduct. ④ It's my responsibility to have each song played the same way every time. ⑤ I direct the musicians and the singers to keep the show together. Conducting and directing is not just about waving my arms around!

출제율 95%

16 다음 중 밑줄 친 (A)와 쓰임이 같은 것은?

① As you are here, you need to vote for us.

② This is as light as a feather.

③ He sat watching TV as she got ready.

④ He worked as a doctor for ten years.

⑤ As you were out, I left a message.

출제율 100%

17 ①~⑤ 중 다음 주어진 문장이 들어가기에 적절한 곳은?

After selecting the cast, I teach them the songs for each scene.

①　　　②　　　③　　　④　　　⑤

출제율 90%

18 When Chris auditions the actors, what does he look for? Answer in English with a full sentence.

➡ _____

출제율 90%

19 Write the reason why Chris directs the musicians and the singers. Answer in English.

➡ _____

_____

[20~23] 다음 글을 읽고 물음에 답하시오.

My name is Yeji. I am an ocean scientist. Ocean science is a big field. It includes studies of the oceans and the creatures living in ⓐ them. Among other things, I have studied many kinds of fish (A)[living / live] in the seas near Korea. It is the growth ring in a fish that interests me. (B)[On / By] looking at it, I can find out when and where the fish was born. All the information I get from fish (C)[is / are] used to understand sea resources and manage the oceans better. My job is important because it makes the best use of nature possible.

출제율 95%

20 (A)~(C)에서 어법상 옳은 것끼리 바르게 짝지어진 것은?

① living – On – is　　② live – On – is

③ living – By – is　　④ live – By – are

⑤ living – By – are

출제율 100%

21 다음 중 위 글의 내용과 일치하는 것은?

① Yeji doesn't know anything about ocean science.

② What Yeji studies is a big field in Korea.

③ Fish that Yeji has studied live far from Korea.

④ What interests Yeji is the growth ring in a tree.

⑤ The information Yeji gathered about fish helps manage the oceans better.

출제율 90%

22 밑줄 친 ⓐ가 가리키는 것을 위 글에서 찾아 쓰시오.

➡ _____

출제율 90%

23 위 글의 내용과 일치하도록 빈칸에 알맞은 말을 쓰시오.

Yeji gets _____ _____ _____ so that she can use it to understand sea resources.

01 다음 그림은 Bora가 관심을 가지고 있는 분야이다. 다음 〈조건〉에 따라 대화를 완성하시오.

technology

┤ 조건 ├

(A) 'interest'를 어형 변화하여 '기술에 관심이 있다'는 표현을 쓸 것.

(B) 확실성 정도를 나타내는 표현을 쓸 것. 'quite'를 사용할 것.

➡ A: _____. Which job would be right for me?

B: _____ an app developer could be a good job for you.

02 다음 대화를 읽고 아래 요약문의 빈칸을 완성하시오.

B: Hello, what are you doing, Sumi?

G: I'm looking for a good recipe on the Internet. I need it for my family dinner today.

B: That is nice. Do you cook often?

G: Yes, I try to cook every weekend. I want to be a chef someday.

B: What are you doing to make your dream come true?

G: I'm taking a cooking class. I try to think of new and creative dishes.

B: I'm quite sure you could be a good chef.

➡ Sumi's _____ is to be a chef. _____ to me _____ class and _____ are important to _____ her dream.

03 다음 대화의 밑줄 친 (A)와 같은 의미가 되도록 주어진 단어를 이용하여 문장의 빈칸을 완성하시오.

M: What's wrong, Jisu?

G: I want to be an animator, but my drawing skill is not good enough.

M: Hmm... Being an animator is not just about being a good artist.

G: What should I do to become an animator?

M: Read a lot of books to make good stories and practice drawing every day.

G: Okay, I'll do so.

M: (A)I'm quite sure that you can be a good animator if you try hard.

G: Thank you very much.

➡ _____

_____ (doubt)

04 다음 그림을 보고, 주어진 어구를 알맞게 배열하여 문맥에 맞게 대화를 완성하시오. (단, 부사구를 강조하는 문장으로 쓰시오.)

Reporter: What is the biggest contribution to your winning this award today?

Winner: It _____

_____.

(award / that / because / received / was / of / my parents / I / this)

05 다음 우리말과 같은 뜻이 되도록 괄호 안에 있는 단어들을 활용하여, 글자 수에 맞게 영작하시오. (동사 형태 변화 가능)

(1) 그녀의 아버지는 Sally에게 Toto를 씻기라고 시켰다. (6 단어)

➡ _____

(2) 그녀의 아버지는 Toto가 Sally에 의해 씻겨지도록 시켰다. (7 단어)
(Sally, Toto, have, wash, father, by, her)

➡ _____

[06~08] 다음 글을 읽고 물음에 답하시오.

I like food from around the world and I am good at cooking. I can also make food look tasty and beautiful. For these reasons, it is a chef that I want to be when I grow up. To achieve my dream, I will read magazines about cooking. Also, I will go to France to learn various cooking skills. My role model is my dad. He always thinks of new recipes and then cooks these new dishes for us. I want to have my name remembered by people who enjoy my food.

06 What does the writer want to be when she grows up? Answer in English with a full sentence.

➡ _____

07 Write the two things that the writer will do in order to achieve her dream. Use the words 'first, second.'

➡ _____
_____
_____

08 What does the writer's father always do?

➡ _____
_____

[09~11] 다음 글을 읽고 물음에 답하시오.

I am Emma. I am a sport data analyst. It sounds like a difficult job, doesn't it? In fact, it is a lot of fun. I work for a baseball team. My job is to watch (A)_____ games and run a computer program to collect data. Then, I analyze the data to show my team's strengths and weaknesses. If the team understands their strengths and weaknesses, they can do better next time. Since I was young, I have been a big fan of baseball. Now, in my work, I watch baseball games all the time. This is a perfect job for me because watching baseball games is my hobby!

09 주어진 단어를 빈칸 (A)에 어법에 맞게 쓰시오.

(record)

➡ _____

10 According to the passage, what is Emma's hobby? Answer in English with a full sentence.

➡ _____

11 What does Emma do all the time in her work? Answer in English with a full sentence.

➡ _____

창의사고력 서술형 문제

01 다음 (A)는 관심 있는 분야이고 (B)는 장래 희망이다. 〈보기〉의 문장처럼 대화를 완성하시오.

(A)	(B)
• art	• a designer
• writing	• a poet
• sports	• a soccer player
• nature	• farmer

A: _____. Which job would be right for me?

B: _____ could be a good job for you.

02 다음 그림들을 보고, 괄호 안에 주어진 어휘를 모두 활용하여, 'have+목적어+과거분사'의 표현이 들어간 문장을 만드시오. (원하는 단어를 추가하되, 어법에 유의할 것.)

(phone / repair / yesterday)　(Sophia / check / a mechanic / tomorrow)

(1) _____

(2) _____

03 다음 내용을 바탕으로 Jina의 장래 희망을 써 봅시다.

Q: What things do you like?

Jina: I like bags from around the world.

Q: What are you good at?

Jina: I am good at making things. I can also make what I made look beautiful.

Q: What do you want to be when you grow up?

Jina: It is a bag designer that I want to be when I grow up.

Q: What will you do to achieve your dream?

Jina: I will read fashion magazines. Also I will go to France to learn to design bags.

I like _____ the world and I am good at _____. I can also make _____. For these reasons, _____ I want to be when I grow up. To achieve my dream, I will _____. Also, I will _____.

단원별 모의고사

01 다음 단어에 대한 영어 설명이 <u>어색한</u> 것은?

① analyzsis: someone whose job is to analyze and examine something

② bank teller: a person whose job is to pay out and take in money in a bank

③ care for: to protect someone or something and provide the things they need, especially someone who is young, old or ill

④ developer: a person or company that creates new products, especially computer products such as software

⑤ make the best use of: to use something as much as you can

02 다음 중 짝지어진 대화가 <u>어색한</u> 것은?

① A: Did you finish the report about your role model?
   B: Yes, I did. I wrote about my role model, Mr. Kang.

② A: What does she do?
   B: She teaches people how to stretch.

③ A: What are you good at?
   B: I am good at writing stories.

④ A: What are you doing to make your dream come true?
   B: I'm taking a cooking class.

⑤ A: Are you happy with your job?
   B: In my opinion, going to fashion shows would be helpful.

03 다음 짝지어진 단어의 관계가 같도록 빈칸에 알맞은 말을 쓰시오.

fix : repair = operate : _____

04 다음 영영풀이에 해당하는 단어를 고르시오.

to bring a person or thing to a state or place

① handle   ② select

③ lead   ④ create

⑤ fetch

[05~06] 다음 대화를 읽고 물음에 답하시오.

A: I'm interested in animals. (A)_____
B: I think a pet hairdresser can be a good job for you.
A: What is a pet hairdresser?
B: (B)_____ He/She designs different hairstyles for pets.
A: That sounds nice. Why do you think it can be a good job for me?
B: You are interested in animals. And I know you are good at designing and making things.

05 위 대화의 빈칸 (A)에 들어갈 말로 알맞은 것은?

① Are you interested in animals?

② What do you do at a pet hair salon?

③ What is the best thing about a pet hairdresser?

④ Which job is right for me?

⑤ What do you think of a pet hairdresser?

06 위 대화의 A의 물음에 맞게, 주어진 어구를 알맞은 순서로 배열하여 빈칸 (B)를 완성하시오.

(works / that's / a pet / who / at / hair salon / a person)

➡ _____

[07~08] 다음 대화를 읽고 물음에 답하시오.

Bora: What are you most interested in among the things on this list?

Jessie: I'm most interested in working outside and (a)playing sports.

Bora: Well, it (b)seems to me that you belong to the realistic type.

Jessie: What do you mean?

Bora: Most people (c)are belonged to one of six personality types. Realistic is one of the types.

Jessie: Oh, that's (d)interesting. What kind of jobs do they recommend for realistic types?

Bora: A farmer, a police officer, a soccer player, and so on.

Jessie: Oh, I have always (e)wanted to be a soccer player.

Bora: That's good. I'm quite sure you could become a great soccer player.

07 위 대화의 밑줄 친 (a)~(e) 중 어법상 어색한 것은?

① (a)   ② (b)   ③ (c)   ④ (d)   ⑤ (e)

08 What jobs do they recommend for the realistic type?

➡ They recommend _____

_____ .

[09~10] 다음 대화를 읽고 물음에 답하시오.

M: What's wrong, Jisu?

G: I want to be an animator, but my drawing skill is not good enough.

M: Hmm... Being an animator is not just about being a good artist.

G: _____

M: Read a lot of books to make good stories and practice drawing every day.

G: Okay, I'll do so.

M: (A)나는 네가 열심히 노력하면 훌륭한 만화 영화 제작자가 될 수 있다고 꽤 확신해.

G: Thank you very much.

09 위 대화의 빈칸에 들어갈 말로 알맞은 것은?

① How many books are you going to read?

② What should I do to become an animator?

③ I think that you can be a good novelist.

④ Can I get your advice on what to read?

⑤ What books do I have to read?

10 위 대화의 (A)의 우리말 해석에 맞게 주어진 어구를 알맞은 순서로 배열하시오.

(I'm / you / quite / if / that / can be / a good / you / animator / try hard / sure)

➡ _____

_____

11 다음을 읽고, 각 질문에 대한 답을 'It ~ that' 강조 구문으로 조건에 맞게 영작하시오.

• Lucy started to read the novel last Sunday.
• Austin wrote the novel two months ago.
• Today's Tuesday and Lucy is still reading it.

(1) For how many days has Lucy been reading the novel? (for, 현재완료진행형을 쓸 것, 총 12단어)

➡ _____

(2) What is the name of the author of the novel that Lucy is reading? (who, novel, write를 이용할 것. 형태 변화 가능하며, 총 7단어)

➡ _____

12 다음 그림을 보고, 우리말에 맞게 주어진 어구를 배열하시오.

(1) 엄마는 나에게 쓰지 않는 물건들을 상자에 모으라고 시키셨다.

(me / the unused things / mom / in / had / put / the boxes).

➡ _____

(2) 나는 그 상자들을 자선단체에 기부하게 할 것이다.

(have / charity / will / donated / the boxes / I / to).

➡ _____

13 다음 각각의 그림을 보고, 우리말과 조건에 맞게 영작하시오. (어형 변화 가능)

(1) 엄마는 내가 혼자 힘으로 이를 닦도록 시켰다. (me, have, brush, myself 활용, 총 8단어).

➡ _____

(2) 그렇게 많은 그릇을 닦고 있는 것은 바로 나의 개 Angel이다.

(dish, wash, so, 'It ~ that' 강조 구문을 활용할 것, 총 11단어)

➡ _____

14 다음 밑줄 친 부분과 어법상 쓰임이 같은 것은?

> The history teacher <u>had</u> all the students go on a field trip to Gyeongju.

① Elizabeth <u>had</u> every reason to get annoyed with that situation.
② Maya <u>had</u> an eye for both modern and ancient paintings.
③ We <u>had</u> him come here earlier.
④ Henry <u>had</u> coffee and cake for dessert.
⑤ Mike <u>had</u> a car accident two years ago.

[15~18] 다음 글을 읽고 물음에 답하시오.

Hi, I am Tom. A florist is someone who creates beautiful things with flowers. ① To become a florist, you need to know many things about flowers. ② It was at this school that I learned how to grow and care for different types of flowers. ③ These days, florists can do a lot of different things. ④ I design movie sets sometimes and I decorate shops with flowers. ⑤ I am happy when I create something colorful with fresh flowers and greenery. If you like (A)_____, I highly recommend you become a florist.

15 ①~⑤ 중 주어진 문장이 들어가기에 가장 적절한 곳은?

> I attended a high school for florists and gardeners.

①　　　②　　　③　　　④　　　⑤

16 빈칸 (A)에 들어갈 말로 가장 적절한 것은?

① drawing and writing
② thinking and doing
③ plants and the arts
④ the arts and the artist
⑤ planting and growing

17 다음 중 플로리스트의 일과 관련이 <u>없는</u> 것은?

① making beautiful things with flowers
② knowing many things about flowers
③ growing and caring for different types of flowers
④ decorating flowers with colored paper
⑤ designing movie sets

18 다음 중 위 글을 읽고 답할 수 <u>없는</u> 것은?

① What is a florist?
② What did Tom learn at his high school?
③ When does Tom feel happy?
④ Where does Tom work?
⑤ How does Tom decorate shops?

[19~21] 다음 글을 읽고 물음에 답하시오.

Hi, I am Chris. As a director of a musical theater, I do a lot of things. I audition the actors and I look for good, strong voices. After selecting the cast, I teach them the songs for each scene. Then, I put the cast and orchestra together for practice. During the performance, I am in the orchestra area and conduct. (A)각각의 노래가 매번 동일하게 연주되도록 만드는 것은 나의 책임입니다. I direct the musicians and the singers to keep the show together. Conducting and directing is not just about (B)<u>waving</u> my arms around!

19 According to the passage, when does Chris conduct? Answer in English with a full sentence.

➡ _____

20 다음 주어진 단어를 활용하여 밑줄 친 (A)를 영어로 쓸 때 빈칸에 알맞은 말을 쓰시오. 필요하다면 어형을 바꾸시오.

(responsibility / play / each / have / to / my / song)

➡ It's _____
the same way every time.

21 다음 중 밑줄 친 (B)와 쓰임이 같은 것은?

① Do you hear a baby <u>crying</u> in the room?
② The <u>rising</u> sun is very bright.
③ <u>Making</u> noises here is not helpful.
④ Jason is <u>playing</u> soccer outside.
⑤ We saw a boy <u>dancing</u> on the street.

22 다음 중 글의 흐름상 <u>어색한</u> 것은?

I like food from around the world and I am good at cooking. ①I can also make food look tasty and beautiful. ②For these reasons, it is a chef that I want to be when I grow up. ③To achieve my dream, I will read magazines about cooking. ④ Also, I will go to France to learn various cooking skills. ⑤My dad always thinks of new recipes and then cooks these new dishes for us. I want to have my name remembered by people who enjoy my food.

①   ②   ③   ④   ⑤

Lesson

4

Are You a Digital Citizen?

 의사소통 기능

- 충고하기
  If I were you, I would change my password.

- 불허하기
  You're not supposed to use your personal information.

언어 형식

- to부정사의 의미상의 주어 'for+목적격'
  It is necessary **for you** to set some rules for using your smartphone.

- 가정법 과거: 'If+주어+동사의 과거형 ~, 주어+would/could+동사원형 …'
  If we had no smartphones, **our lives would be** difficult.

Words & Expressions

Key Words

- **addiction** [ədíkʃən] 명 중독
- **advantage** [ædvǽntidʒ] 명 장점, 유리함
- **alert** [ələ́:rt] 명 알람소리, 경보
- **birth** [bə:rθ] 명 출생, 탄생
- **block** [blɑk] 동 차단하다, 막다
- **cause** [kɔ:z] 동 야기하다, 원인이 되다
- **citizen** [sítəzən] 명 시민
- **comment** [kάment] 명 발언, 논평, 비평
- **contact** [kάntækt] 동 연락하다
- **conversation** [kὰnvərséiʃən] 명 대화
- **copyright** [kάpirait] 명 저작권
- **create** [kriéit] 동 창조하다, 만들다
- **creative** [kriéitiv] 형 창의적인
- **dangerous** [déindʒərəs] 형 위험한
- **detox** [di:tάks] 명 해독
- **device** [diváis] 명 기기, 장치
- **digital** [dídʒətl] 형 디지털의, 디지털 방식을 쓰는
- **disadvantage** [dìsədvǽntidʒ] 명 단점, 약점, 불리한 점
- **enjoyable** [indʒɔ́iəbl] 형 즐거운
- **focus** [fóukəs] 동 집중하다
- **form** [fɔ:rm] 동 만들다, 형성시키다
- **guess** [ges] 동 추측하다
- **half** [hæf] 명 반, 절반
- **imagine** [imǽdʒin] 동 상상하다
- **instead** [instéd] 부 대신에

- **intend** [inténd] 동 ~할 작정이다
- **limit** [límit] 동 제한하다
- **message** [mésidʒ] 명 알림, 메시지
- **mistake** [mistéik] 명 실수
- **necessary** [nésəsèri] 형 필요한
- **noisy** [nɔ́izi] 형 시끄러운
- **outdoor** [άutdɔ:r] 형 옥외의, 야외의
- **pain** [pein] 명 고통
- **password** [pǽswərd] 명 비밀번호
- **personal information** 개인 정보
- **post** [poust] 동 게시하다
- **posting** [póustiŋ] 명 인터넷이나 SNS에 올리는 글
- **reduce** [ridjú:s] 동 줄이다
- **refreshed** [rifréʃt] 형 상쾌한
- **respect** [rispékt] 동 존중하다, 존경하다
- **right** [rait] 명 권리 부 바로
- **score** [skɔ:r] 명 점수
- **share** [ʃɛər] 동 공유하다
- **spend** [spend] 동 (시간을) 보내다
- **suggest** [səgdʒést] 동 제안하다
- **symbol** [símbəl] 명 상징
- **tired** [taiərd] 형 피곤한, 지친
- **uncomfortable** [ənkʌ́mfərtəbəl] 형 불편한
- **until** [əntíl] 전 ~까지
- **wise** [waiz] 형 현명한

Key Expressions

- **be addicted to** ~에 중독되다
- **be good for** ~에 좋다
- **be supposed to+동사원형** ~해야 한다
- **can't help it** 어쩔 수 없다
- **figure out** 알아내다, 계산하다
- **for a while** 잠시 동안
- **for free** 무료로
- **in fact** 사실
- **It seems that+주어+동사** ~인 것 같다

- **on the other hand** 반면에
- **put aside** 치우다
- **right away** 당장
- **set up** 설정하다
- **share A with B** A를 B와 공유하다
- **stay away from** ~에서 떨어져 있다, ~을 멀리하다
- **such as** ~와 같은
- **take A into B** A를 B로 가져가다

Word Power

※ 서로 비슷한 뜻을 가진 어휘

□ **limit** : **restrict** (제한하다)
□ **focus** : **concentrate** (집중하다)
□ **conversation** : **dialogue** (대화)

□ **uncomfortable** : **uneasy** (불편한)
□ **enjoyable** : **pleasurable** (즐거운)
□ **suggest** : **propose** (제안하다)

※ 서로 반대되는 뜻을 가진 어휘

□ **advantage** (장점) ↔ **disadvantage** (단점)
□ **reduce** (줄이다) ↔ **increase** (늘리다, 증가하다)
□ **dangerous** (위험한) ↔ **safe** (안전한)

□ **birth** (출생) ↔ **death** (죽음)
□ **create** (창조하다) ↔ **destroy** (파괴하다)
□ **respect** (존중하다) ↔ **disregard** (무시하다)

English Dictionary

□ **addiction** 중독
→ an inability to stop doing or using something, especially something harmful
무언가, 특히 해로운 것을 하는 것이나 사용하는 것을 중단하지 못하는 것

□ **advantage** 장점
→ something that may help one to gain favorable result
유리한 결과를 얻는 데 도움이 될 만한 것

□ **alert** 경고, 알림
→ a warning to people to be prepared to deal with something dangerous.
위험한 것을 처리할 대비가 되도록 사람들에게 하는 경고

□ **be addicted to** ~에 중독되다
→ to be physically and mentally dependent on an particular substance
특정한 물질에 신체적으로, 정신적으로 의존하다

□ **birth** 출생
→ an act of being born
태어나는 행위

□ **comment** 논평, 해설, 비평
→ something that you say about someone or something
누군가나 무엇에 관해 당신이 말하는 것

□ **contact** 연락하다
→ to communicate with someone by calling or sending them a letter, email, etc.
전화를 걸거나 편지나 이메일 등을 보냄으로써 누군가와 연락하다

□ **conversation** 대화
→ talk between two or more people in which thoughts, feelings, and ideas are expressed, or questions are asked and answered
생각, 감정, 아이디어가 표현되거나, 질문과 답변이 되는 두 명 또는 그 이상의 사람들 사이의 이야기

□ **copyright** 저작권
→ a right to sell a book, music, film, etc.
책, 음악, 영화 등을 판매하는 권리

□ **device** 기기, 장치
→ a mechanical object that is made for a particular purpose
특정한 목적을 위해 만들어진 기계적인 물체

□ **digital** 디지털 방식을 쓰는
→ storing pictures, sound, etc. in a number of small signals or showing them in numbers
다수의 작은 신호로 사진, 소리 등을 저장하거나 그것을 숫자로 보여주는

□ **figure out** 알아내다, 이해하다
→ to understand or solve something
무언가를 이해하거나 해결하다

□ **half** 반, 절반
→ one of two equal parts of something
어떤 것의 두 개의 동일한 부분 중 하나

□ **intend** ~할 작정이다
→ to plan to do something; to have an action planned in your mind
어떤 일을 할 계획을 세우다; 마음 속에 계획된 행동을 가지다

□ **message** 메시지
→ a spoken or written piece of information that you send to someone
당신이 누군가에게 보내는 말이나 서면 정보

□ **mistake** 실수
→ an action, decision, or judgment that produces an unwanted or unintentional result
원하지 않거나 의도하지 않은 결과를 생성하는 행동, 결정 또는 판단

□ **symbol** 상징
→ a thing that is regarded as representing for another
또 다른 것을 대표하는 것으로 여겨지는 것

01 다음 문장의 빈칸에 공통으로 들어갈 말로 가장 알맞은 것은?

> • The number of students is _____ this year.
> • My weight was _____ when I stopped eating sugar.

① increased ② developed
③ created ④ reduced
⑤ selected

02 서답형 다음 문장의 빈칸에 주어진 철자로 시작하는 단어를 쓰시오.

> Be careful that your playing video games doesn't lead to a_____.

03 서답형 다음 우리말에 맞게 빈칸에 세 단어를 쓰시오.

> 나는 고칼로리 음식을 멀리하려고 노력한다.

➡ I try to _____ _____ _____ high-calorie foods.

[04~05] 다음 설명에 해당하는 단어를 고르시오.

04

> to communicate with someone by calling or sending them a letter, email, etc.

① reduce ② contact
③ conversation ④ guess
⑤ post

05

> a thing that is regarded as representing for another

① gift ② score
③ citizen ④ pain
⑤ symbol

06 다음 문장의 빈칸에 들어갈 말이 바르게 짝지어진 것은?

> (A) I sat on a bench and read a book _____.
> (B) I have to _____ the number of guests because my house is too small.

	(A)	(B)
①	instead	guess
②	instead	increase
③	for a while	limit
④	right away	create
⑤	for a while	guess

07 서답형 다음 짝지어진 단어의 관계가 같도록 빈칸에 알맞은 말을 쓰시오.

> advantage – disadvantage : _____ – birth

08 다음 빈칸에 공통으로 들어갈 말은?

> • To fight the addiction, China's Internet _____ Camps are growing rapidly.
> • _____ diets have increasingly become popular as fast and easy ways to get rid of toxins in your body and to lose weight.

① Game ② Drug
③ Vegetable ④ Detox
⑤ Digital

01 다음 빈칸에 들어갈 말을 〈보기〉에서 찾아 쓰시오.

> ┤ 보기 ├
>
> necessary   such as   form   refreshed

(1) Please rearrange the letters to _____ a new word.

(2) I love Korean foods _____ Bibimbap or Bulgogi.

(3) After a sound sleep, I felt _____.

(4) It is _____ for us to drink lots of water every day.

02 다음 문장은 '스마트폰 중독 증상'에 관한 내용이다. 빈칸에 들어갈 단어를 주어진 〈영영풀이〉를 보고 쓰시오.

> I would feel _____ without constant access to information through my smartphone.

> <영영풀이>
>
> not feeling comfortable and pleasant, or not making you feel comfortable and pleasant

03 다음 우리말과 같은 표현이 되도록 문장의 빈칸을 채우시오.

(1) Frank는 게임에 중독되어 있다.

➡ Frank is _____ to games.

(2) 너는 여기에 6시에 오기로 되어 있었다.

➡ You were _____ to be here at six o'clock.

(3) 나의 부모님은 선생님의 논평을 읽었다.

➡ My parents read the teacher's _____.

(4) 내 친구는 내가 방문했을 때 나에게 집 비밀번호를 알려 주었다.

➡ My friend told me the _____ to her house when I visited there.

04 영영풀이에 해당하는 단어를 〈보기〉에서 찾아 첫 번째 빈칸에 쓰고, 두 번째 빈칸에는 우리말 뜻을 쓰시오.

> ┤ 보기 ├
>
> detox   digital   conversation   mistake

(1) _____ : storing pictures, sound, etc. in a number of small signals or showing them in numbers: _____

(2) _____ : an action, decision, or judgment that produces an unwanted or unintentional result: _____

(3) _____ : a period when you stop taking unhealthy or harmful foods, drinks, or drugs into your body for a period: _____

(4) _____ : talk between two or more people in which thoughts, feelings, and ideas are expressed, or questions are asked and answered: _____

05 빈칸에 공통으로 들어갈 단어를 쓰시오.

> • Various Korean food recipes will be _____ed on the Seoul tourism website.
>
> • I took many pictures and _____ed them on Instagram.

교과서
Conversation

> • **If I were you, I would change my password.**
> 만약 내가 너라면, 비밀번호를 바꿀 것이다.

■ 'If I were you, I would ~.'는 충고할 때 사용하는 표현으로 '내가 너라면 ~할 것이다[~할 텐데].'로 해석한다.

A: I want to exercise every day, but I don't have enough time. 매일 운동하고 싶은데, 시간이 별로 없어.

B: If I were you, I'd ride a bicycle to school. 내가 너라면 자전거를 타고 등교하겠어.

■ 충고할 때 사용하는 다양한 표현
 • 'You'd better ~.'는 주로 부모님이나 선생님처럼 더 권위가 있는 사람이 긴급한 상황이나 충고가 필요한 상황에서 쓴다. 친구 사이에 충고를 하는 경우에는 'You should ~.'를 더 많이 쓴다. 충고하는 말 앞에 I think나 Maybe를 써서 좀 더 부드럽게 말할 수 있다.

A: I have a cold. 저는 감기에 걸렸어요.

B: You'd better go home and get some rest. 너는 집에 가서 좀 쉬는 게 낫겠구나.

■ 충고에 답할 때
 상대방의 충고에는 'I see. / Okay, thanks. / All right. / That's a good idea.' 등으로 답하며, 'I'll keep that in mind.'와 같은 다짐을 함께 말할 수도 있다.

핵심 Check

1. 다음 대화의 빈칸에 들어갈 말로 알맞지 <u>않은</u> 것은?

   A: I have a cold.

   B: _____ go home and get some rest.

   ① You should
   ② You had better
   ③ Maybe you should
   ④ I'm quite sure that I
   ⑤ I think you should

2 불허하기

· **You're not supposed to use your personal information.**

너는 너의 개인 정보를 사용하면 안 된다.

■ 'You're not supposed to ~.'는 '~해서는 안 된다.'라는 의미로 불허를 나타내는 표현이다. 이때 'be not supposed to+동사원형'은 'must not', 'should not', 'cannot' 또는 'had better not' 등으로 바꾸어 사용할 수 있다. 또는 부정명령문 'Don't+동사원형 ~.'을 사용하여 '~하지 마!'라는 불허(금지)의 의미를 나타낼 수 있다. 불허하는 또 다른 표현으로 'be not allowed to+동사원형'을 사용하여 '~하도록 허가되지 않다'는 의미를 나타낼 수 있다.

· **A:** Excuse me. You shouldn't use your cell phone here.
실례합니다. 당신은 여기서 휴대전화를 사용하시면 안 됩니다.

B: Oh, I'm sorry. 오, 미안합니다.

· You can't play with Dad's shoe. 아빠 신발을 가지고 놀면 안 돼.

· **A:** Is it okay if I take a picture? 내가 사진을 찍어도 괜찮을까요?

B: No, you're not allowed to do that. 아니요, 사진을 찍으면 안 됩니다.

불허하기 여러 가지 표현

· You are not supposed to ~. 너는 ~해서는 안 된다.

· You are not allowed to ~. 너는 ~해서는 안 된다.

· You should not ~. 너는 ~하지 말아야 한다.

· You must not ~. 너는 ~하지 말아야 한다.

핵심 Check

2. 다음 대화의 빈칸에 들어갈 말로 성격이 <u>다른</u> 하나는?

A: Do you talk to strangers online?

B: Yes.

A: You _____ talk to strangers online.

① should not

② must not

③ are not supposed to

④ had better not

⑤ are allowed to

Listen & Speak 1 A-1

G: You ❶look tired, Peter.

B: I played computer games until late, so last night I slept for less than four hours.

G: ❷Playing computer games too much is not good for your health.

B: I know, Jenny, but I can't stop it. I think ❸I'm addicted to it.

G: ❹If I were you, I would set a daily plan to limit game time.

B: ❺That's a good idea. Thanks.

G: 너 피곤해 보인다, Peter.
B: 나 늦게까지 게임을 해서, 어젯밤에 4시간도 못 잤어.
G: 컴퓨터 게임을 너무 많이 하는 건 네 건강에 좋지 않아.
B: 나도 알아, Jenny, 그런데 멈출 수가 없어. 난 그것에 중독된 것 같아.
G: 만약 내가 너라면, 게임 시간을 제한하기 위해 일일 계획을 짤 거야.
B: 그거 좋은 생각이네. 고마워.

❶ 'look+형용사'로 '~처럼 보이다'라는 뜻이다.
❷ 동명사(Playing) 주어로 동사는 단수 취급한다.
❸ 'be addicted to ~'는 '~에 중독되다'는 의미다.
❹ 가정법과거형(If+주어+과거동사[were] ~, 주어+would[could/should/might]+동사원형)으로 충고할 때 사용하는 표현이다. '내가 너라면 ~할 것이다[~할 텐데]'로 해석한다.
❺ 상대방이 해 준 충고에 대한 답으로 I see. / Okay, thanks. / All right. 등으로 바꾸어 말할 수 있다.

Check(√) True or False

(1) Peter may be addicted to the computer games. T ☐ F ☐

(2) Jenny sets a daily plan to limit game time. T ☐ F ☐

Listen & Speak 2 A-1

G: James, what are you doing?

B: I'm posting some of the pictures ❶that I took with Sarah today.

G: Did you ask Sarah ❷if you could post them online?

B: No, but I think it's okay because she looks good in the pictures.

G: ❸You're not supposed to post someone's pictures without asking.

B: Oh, maybe you're right. I'll call Sarah and ask her right away.

G: James, 뭐 하고 있니?
B: 나 오늘 Sarah와 함께 찍은 사진들 중 몇 장을 올리고 있어.
G: 네가 그걸 온라인에 올려도 될지 Sarah에게 물어봤니?
B: 아니, 그렇지만 그녀가 잘 나왔으니까 괜찮을 것 같아.
G: 너는 다른 사람들의 사진을 물어보지 않고 올리면 안 돼.
B: 오, 네 말이 맞을지 몰라. 내가 지금 당장 Sarah에게 전화해서 물어볼게.

❶ 목적격 관계대명사절로 선행사 the pictures를 수식하는 역할을 한다.
❷ ask의 직접목적어로 '~인지 아닌지'로 해석한다.
❸ '~해서는 안 된다'라는 의미로 불허를 나타내는 표현이다. 이때 'be not supposed to+동사원형'은 'must not', 'should not' 등으로 바꾸어 쓸 수 있다.

Check(√) True or False

(3) James is posting some pictures without asking Sarah. T ☐ F ☐

(4) Sarah looks good in the pictures. T ☐ F ☐

Listen & Speak 1 A-2

W: Tony, you ❶spend too much time on your smartphone.

B: My friends get together on SNS almost every day, so ❷I can't help it, Mom.

W: ❸If I were you, I would suggest doing outdoor activities to your friends.

B: Outdoor activities?

W: Yes. You can do a lot of great activities such as soccer or skating.

B: All right. I will suggest them today.

❶ spend+시간+on+명사: ~에 시간을 보내다
❷ 'can't[cannot] help it'에서 'help'는 '피하다, 그만두다'라는 의미를 가진다.
❸ 가정법과거형으로 be동사는 were를 사용하고, 주절에는 조동사 과거형을 사용한다. suggest는 목적어로 동명사(doing)를 취한다.

 Listen & Speak 2 A-2

G: David, let's watch this new movie on the computer.

B: On the computer?

G: Yes. ❶I have a website we can download it from for free.

B: You're not supposed to download movies from that website, Catherine. It's against the law.

G: Really? I didn't know ❷that.

B: ❸Why don't we go to the movie theater, instead?

G: Okay. Let's go.

❶ I have a website (which/that) we can download it from for free. 전치사 from의 목적어 대신 사용된 목적격 관계대명사가 생략되어 있다. 'for free'는 '무료로'의 뜻이다.
❷ 'that'은 앞 문장의 'It's against the law'를 가리키는 인칭대명사이다.
❸ 'Why don't we+동사원형 ~?'은 '~하는 게 어때?'라고 제안할 때 사용하는 표현이다.

 Real Life Talk

Bora: Seho, look! Somebody posted strange things on your SNS. I don't think you posted ❶them.

Seho: Really? Who did this?

Bora: I think someone figured out your password.

Seho: What should I do?

Bora: If I were you, I would change my password.

Seho: I think ❷I should.

Bora: Is your password easy to guess?

Seho: I used my birth date.

Bora: That is not good. In fact, it is a big mistake. ❸You're not supposed to use your personal information when you make a password.

Seho: Okay, I see. I will change it to a stronger ❹one.

❶ 'them'은 'strange things'를 가리키는 인칭대명사다.
❷ I should change my password.를 줄여 사용한 표현이다.
❸ '~해서는 안 된다'는 의미로 불허를 나타내는 말이다.
❹ 'one'은 'password'를 가리키는 부정대명사다.

 Wrap Up

B: What are you doing, Sohee?

G: I'm writing a posting about the restaurant I visited today.

B: Those are great pictures. Did you take all of them?

G: No. I took the pictures from someone's blog.

B: Then ❶you're not supposed to post them on your blog.

G: Why not?

B: Because only the blog owner has the right ❷to use them.

G: Oh, I see.

❶ 불허를 표현하는 말로, 'be not supposed to'는 'should not'이나 'must not'으로 바꾸어 쓸 수 있다.
❷ 명사 the right를 수식하는 형용사적 용법이다.

● 다음 우리말과 일치하도록 빈칸에 알맞은 말을 쓰시오.

Listen & Speak 1 A

1. G: You look _____, Peter.

   B: I played computer games _____ late, so last night I slept for _____ _____ four hours.

   G: _____ computer games too much is not _____ _____ your health.

   B: I know, Jenny, but I _____ _____ it. I think I'm _____ to it.

   G: If I _____ you, I _____ _____ a daily plan to _____ game time.

   B: That's a good idea. Thanks.

2. W: Tony, you _____ too much time _____ your smartphone.

   B: My friends get together on SNS _____ every day, so I _____ _____ _____, Mom.

   W: _____ _____ _____ _____, I would _____ _____ outdoor activities to your friends.

   B: _____ activities?

   W: Yes. You can do _____ _____ _____ great activities _____ _____ soccer or skating.

   B: All right. I will _____ them today.

Listen & Speak 2 A

1. G: James, what are you doing?

   B: I'm _____ some of the pictures _____ I _____ with Sarah today.

   G: Did you ask Sarah _____ you could _____ them online?

   B: No, but I think it's okay because she _____ _____ in the pictures.

   G: You're _____ _____ _____ post someone's pictures _____ _____.

   B: Oh, maybe you're right. I'll call Sarah and ask her _____ _____.

1. G: 너 피곤해 보인다, Peter.
   B: 나 늦게까지 게임을 해서, 어젯밤에 4시간도 못 잤어.
   G: 컴퓨터 게임을 너무 많이 하는 건 네 건강에 좋지 않아.
   B: 나도 알아, Jenny, 그런데 멈출 수가 없어. 난 그것에 중독된 것 같아.
   G: 만약 내가 너라면, 게임 시간을 제한하기 위해 일일 계획을 짤 거야.
   B: 그거 좋은 생각이네. 고마워.

2. W: Tony, 너 스마트 폰에 너무 많은 시간을 보내는구나.
   B: 제 친구들은 거의 매일 SNS에서 만나기 때문에, 저도 어쩔 수 없어요, 엄마.
   W: 만약 내가 너라면, 친구들에게 야외 활동을 하자고 제안할 거야.
   B: 야외 활동이요?
   W: 응. 너는 축구나 스케이트 타기 등과 같은 많은 멋진 활동을 할 수 있어.
   B: 알겠어요. 오늘 제안해 볼게요.

1. G: James, 뭐 하고 있니?
   B: 나 오늘 Sarah와 함께 찍은 사진들 중 몇 장을 올리고 있어.
   G: 네가 그걸 온라인에 올려도 될지 Sarah에게 물어봤니?
   B: 아니, 그렇지만 그녀가 사진들 속에서 멋져 보이기 때문에 괜찮을 것 같아.
   G: 너는 다른 사람들의 사진을 물어보지 않고 올리면 안 돼.
   B: 오, 네 말이 맞을지 몰라. 내가 지금 당장 Sarah에게 전화해서 물어볼게.

2. G: David, _____ watch this new movie on the computer.

   B: _____ the computer?

   G: Yes. I have a website we can _____ it from _____ _____.

   B: You're not _____ _____ _____ movies from that website, Catherine. It's _____ the law.

   G: Really? I didn't know that.

   B: _____ _____ _____ go to the movie theater, _____?

   G: Okay. Let's go.

2. G: David, 컴퓨터로 이 신작 영화 보
자.
   B: 컴퓨터로?
   G: 응. 우리가 그것을 무료로 내려
받을 수 있는 웹 사이트가 있어.
   B: 너는 그런 웹 사이트에서 영화를
내려 받으면 안 돼, Catherine. 그
건 법에 어긋나.
   G: 정말? 그런지 몰랐어.
   B: 대신, 우리 영화관에 가는 건 어
떨까?
   G: 좋아. 가자.

Real Life Talk

Bora: Seho, look! Somebody _____ strange things _____ your SNS. I don't think you _____ them.

Seho: Really? Who did this?

Bora: I think someone _____ _____ your _____.

Seho: _____ _____ I do?

Bora: If I _____ you, I would _____ my password.

Seho: I think I _____.

Bora: Is your password _____ _____ _____?

Seho: I used my _____ _____.

Bora: That is not good. _____ _____, it is a big mistake. You'_____ _____ _____ _____ _____ your _____ _____ when you make a password.

Seho: Okay, I see. I will _____ it to a _____ _____.

보라: 세호야, 봐! 누군가 네 SNS에 이상한 것을 올렸어. 나는 네가 그것들을 올렸다고 생각하지 않아.
세호: 정말? 누가 그랬지?
보라: 내 생각에 누군가 네 비밀번호를 알아낸 것 같아.
세호: 어떻게 해야 하지?
보라: 내가 너라면 비밀번호를 바꾸겠어.
세호: 내 생각에도 그래야 할 것 같아.
보라: 네 비밀번호는 추측하기 쉽니?
세호: 내 생일 날짜를 사용했어.
보라: 그것은 좋지 않아. 사실 그건 큰 실수야. 비밀번호를 만들 때 개인 정보를 사용하지 말아야 해.
세호: 그래, 알았어. 그걸 더 강한 것으로 바꿀 거야.

Wrap Up

B: What are you doing, Sohee?

G: I'm writing a _____ about the restaurant I visited today.

B: Those are great pictures. Did you _____ all of them?

G: No. I _____ the pictures from someone's _____.

B: Then you'_____ _____ _____ _____ _____ them on your blog.

G: _____ _____?

B: Because only the blog _____ has the _____ to use them.

G: Oh, I see.

B: 뭐 하고 있니, 소희야?
G: 나는 오늘 방문했던 식당에 관한 게시 글을 쓰고 있어.
B: 멋진 사진들이네. 그것들을 네가 다 찍었니?
G: 아니. 누군가의 블로그에서 사진들을 가져왔어.
B: 그럼 너는 그것들을 네 블로그에 게시하면 안 돼.
G: 왜 안 돼?
B: 왜냐하면 그 블로그 주인만이 그것들을 사용할 권리가 있거든.
G: 오, 알겠어.

01 우리말 해석에 맞도록 문장의 빈칸에 알맞은 말을 쓰시오.

> 만약 내가 너라면, 화면 잠금을 설정할 거야.

➡ _____ _____ _____ _____ , I would set up screen lock.

02 다음 대화의 빈칸에 들어갈 말로 알맞은 것은?

> A: Do you use the same password for a long time?
> B: Yes.
> A: _____ the same password for a long time.

① I question whether you should not use
② You have to use
③ I'm not quite sure that you're not supposed to use
④ You're not supposed to use
⑤ You should use

03 다음 대화의 빈칸에 들어갈 말로 적절하지 <u>않은</u> 것은?

> A: It seems that someone checks my smartphone. What should I do?
> B: _____

① If I were you, I would set up screen lock.
② You'd better set up screen lock.
③ You're not supposed to set up screen lock.
④ You have to set up screen lock.
⑤ You should set up screen lock.

04 다음 대화의 밑줄 친 말의 의도로 알맞은 것은?

> A: Have you posted bad comments online?
> B: Yes.
> A: <u>You're not supposed to post bad comments online.</u>

① 용서하기　　　　② 확실성 정도 표현하기
③ 관심 표현하기　　④ 화남 표현하기
⑤ 불허하기

01 다음 대화의 (A)~(D)를 알맞은 순서로 배열한 것은?

> W: Tony, you spend too much time on your smartphone.
> (A) Outdoor activities?
> (B) If I were you, I would suggest doing outdoor activities to your friends.
> (C) Yes. You can do a lot of great activities such as soccer or skating.
> (D) My friends get together on SNS almost every day, so I can't help it, Mom.
> B: All right. I will suggest them today.

① (A)–(C)–(B)–(D)　② (B)–(A)–(C)–(D)
③ (C)–(B)–(A)–(D)　④ (D)–(B)–(A)–(C)
⑤ (D)–(C)–(A)–(B)

 다음 대화의 빈칸에 들어갈 말로 알맞은 것을 고르시오.

> A: A stranger keeps texting me. What should I do?
> B: _____

① If I were you, I would play outside more often.
② If I were you, I would change my password.
③ If I were you, I would block the number.
④ If I were you, I would not eat sweet things.
⑤ If I were you, I would not use my smartphone.

서답형
03 다음 대화의 밑줄 친 우리말에 맞게 주어진 단어를 이용하여 영어로 쓰시오. (단어 하나를 추가하시오.)

> G: David, let's watch this new movie on the computer.
> B: On the computer?
> G: Yes. I have a website we can download it from for free.
> B: You're not supposed to download movies from that website, Catherine. 그건 법에 어긋나.

> it's / the / law

➡ _____

중요
04 다음 중 짝지어진 대화가 <u>어색한</u> 것은?

① A: How often do you change your password?
　B: I change it every month.
② A: It seems that I spend too much time on the Internet. What should I do?
　B: If I were you, I would play outside more often.
③ A: It seems that someone checks my smartphone. What should I do?
　B: If I were you, I would set up screen lock.
④ A: What are you doing, Sohee?
　B: I'm writing a posting about the restaurant I visited today.
⑤ A: Somebody posted strange things on your SNS.
　B: What should you do?

서답형

05 다음 대화의 밑줄 친 문장과 같은 의미가 되도록 바꿔 쓸 때, 주어진 단어를 이용하여 빈칸을 채우시오.

> A: Do you use the same password for a long time?
> B: Yes.
> A: You should not use the same password for a long time.

➡ You _____ use the same password for a long time. (suppose)

[06~08] 다음 대화를 읽고 물음에 답하시오.

> G: You ⓐlook tired, Peter.
> B: I played computer games ⓑuntil late, so last night I slept for less than four hours.
> G: Playing computer games too much ⓒis not good for your health.
> B: I know, Jenny, but I ⓓcan't stop it. I think I'm ⓔaddict to it.
> G: (A)If I were you, I would set a daily plan to limit game time.
> B: That's a good idea. Thanks.

06 위 대화의 밑줄 친 (A)의 의도로 알맞은 것은?

① 조언 구하기   ② 충고하기
③ 확신 표현하기   ④ 궁금증 표현하기
⑤ 가능성 묻기

07 위 대화를 읽고 답할 수 없는 것은?

① Why is Peter tired?
② What problem does Peter have and what is Jenny's advice?
③ What kind of game does Jenny suggest to Peter?
④ Does Peter know playing computer games too much is not good for his health?
⑤ What is Peter planning to do?

08 위 대화의 밑줄 친 ⓐ~ⓔ 중 어법상 어색한 것은?

① ⓐ   ② ⓑ   ③ ⓒ   ④ ⓓ   ⑤ ⓔ

[09~10] 다음 대화를 읽고 물음에 답하시오.

> B: What are you doing, Sohee?
> G: I'm writing a ⓐposting about the restaurant I visited today.
> B: Those are great pictures. Did you ⓑtake all of them?
> G: No. I took the pictures from ⓒsomeone's blog.
> B: Then you're ⓓsupposed to post them on your blog.
> G: Why not?
> B: Because only the blog owner has ⓔthe right to use them.
> G: Oh, I see.

09 위 대화의 흐름상 밑줄 친 ⓐ~ⓔ 중, 어휘의 쓰임이 어색한 것은?

① ⓐ   ② ⓑ   ③ ⓒ   ④ ⓓ   ⑤ ⓔ

10 위 대화의 내용과 일치하지 않는 것은?

① Sohee visited the restaurant that had great pictures.
② Sohee didn't take the pictures of the restaurant.
③ Sohee took the pictures from someone's blog.
④ Sohee didn't know the reason why she shouldn't post the pictures that she took from someone's blog.
⑤ Sohee's friend is talking about the copyright.

[01~02] 다음 대화를 읽고 물음에 답하시오.

Bora: Seho, look! Somebody posted strange things on your SNS. I don't think you posted them.

Seho: Really? Who did this?

Bora: I think someone figured out your password.

Seho: What should I do?

Bora: (A)_____

Seho: I think I should.

Bora: Is your password easy to guess?

Seho: I used my birth date.

Bora: That is not good. In fact, it is a big mistake. You're not supposed to use your personal information when you make a password.

Seho: Okay, I see. I will change it to a stronger one.

 01 위 대화의 빈칸 (A)에 들어갈 말을 〈조건〉에 맞게 쓰시오.

┤ 조건 ├
- If와 조동사 would를 사용할 것.
- 비밀번호를 바꾸라는 충고의 표현을 사용할 것.

➡ _____

02 위 대화를 읽고 다음 물음에 영어로 답하시오. (다섯 단어로 답할 것.)

Q: What did Seho use when he made his password?

➡ _____

03 다음 대화의 빈칸에 들어갈 말로 자연스러운 것을 〈보기〉에서 찾아 쓰시오.

G: James, what are you doing?

B: I'm posting some of the pictures that I took with Sarah today.

G: (A)_____

B: No, but I think it's okay because she looks good in the pictures.

G: (B)_____
_____

B: Oh, maybe you're right. (C)_____
_____

┤ 보기 ├
- Did you ask Sarah if you could post them online?
- I'll call Sarah and ask her right away.
- You're not supposed to post someone's pictures without asking.

04 대화의 내용상 빈칸에 알맞은 말을 주어진 〈조건〉에 맞게 영어로 쓰시오.

┤ 조건 ├
- 'supposed'를 사용하여 불허의 표현을 쓸 것.
- 'download', 'that website'를 사용할 것.

G: David, let's watch this new movie on the computer.

B: On the computer?

G: Yes. I have a website we can download it from for free.

B: (A)_____
_____, Catherine. It's against the law.

G: Really? I didn't know that.

B: Why don't we go to the movie theater, instead?

G: Okay. Let's go.

Grammar

① to부정사의 의미상의 주어: 'for+목적격'

> • It is necessary **for you** to keep it secret. 당신이 그것을 비밀로 유지하는 것이 필요하다.
> • It will be impossible **for Billy** to get an A. Billy가 A를 받는 것은 불가능할 것이다.

■ 동작의 행위자(agent): 동사가 행하는 동작을 '누가' 하는지 나타내는 말을 동사의 행위자라고 한다. 주어가 대부분 행위자이지만 그렇지 않은 경우, '의미상의 주어'라고 한다.

  • I want to buy the car. 나는 그 차를 사기를 원한다.
    : 문장의 주어 I가, 동사 want와 to부정사 to buy의 행위자

  → I want Sam to buy the car. 나는 Sam이 그 차를 사기를 원한다.
    : Sam이 to buy의 행위자 = 의미상의 주어

■ 'It' 가주어, 'to' 진주어 문장에서 to부정사의 '의미상의 주어'는 'for+목적격' 형태로 표현한다.

  • It is important **for me** to learn another language. 내가 다른 언어를 배우는 것은 중요하다.
  • It was easy **for her** to solve the math problem. 그녀가 그 수학 문제를 푸는 것은 쉬웠다.
  • It is necessary **for Brian** to tell the truth to his friends. Brian이 그의 친구들에게 진실을 말하는 것이 필요하다.

■ to부정사의 의미상의 주어가 일반 사람을 가리킬 때는 생략할 수 있다.

  • It is necessary (**for us**) to drink enough water. (우리가) 충분한 물을 마시는 것이 필요하다.
  • It is not difficult (**for people**) to follow the rules. 규칙을 지키는 것은 어렵지 않다.
  • It is easy to make spaghetti. 스파게티를 만드는 것은 쉽다. (일반 사람)
    → It is easy **for me** to make spaghetti. 내가 스파게티를 만드는 것은 쉽다. (특정인)

■ 사람의 성격, 태도 등을 나타내는 형용사는 'of+목적격' 형태로 의미상의 주어를 표현한다.

  • It was kind **of you** to help the kids. 그 아이들을 당신이 도운 것은 친절했다.
  • It was foolish **of him** to stay up all night playing cards. 그가 카드 게임을 하느라 밤을 새운 것은 어리석은 짓이었다.

핵심 Check

1. 다음 괄호 안에서 알맞은 단어를 고르시오.

   (1) It is wise (for / of) Jane to save money for her future.
   (2) It was hard (for / of) me to believe her promise.

2 가정법 과거: 'If+주어+동사 과거형 ~, 주어+would/could+동사원형 …'

- **If I had** more money, **I could buy** a new computer. 내가 돈이 더 많다면, 새 컴퓨터를 살 수 있을 텐데.
- **If** Sally **lived** in Tokyo, she **would have** sushi every morning. Sally가 Tokyo에 산다면, 그녀는 매일 아침 초밥을 먹을 텐데.

■ 가정법 과거: '만약 ~라면 …할 텐데'의 뜻으로, 현재 사실을 반대로 가정하거나 실현 가능성이 없는 일에 대해서 가정할 때 쓰며, 'If+주어+동사 과거형 ~, 주어+would/could+동사원형 …'의 형태로 나타낸다.

- **If he knows** Lisa's phone number, **he will call** her. 그가 Lisa의 전화번호를 안다면, 그녀에게 전화할 것이다. (조건문, 알고 있을지도 모름)
- **If he knew** Lisa's phone number, **he would call** her. 그가 Lisa의 전화번호를 안다면, 그녀에게 전화할 텐데. (가정법 과거, 현재 사실의 반대 가정)
  = **As** he **doesn't know** Lisa's phone number, **he won't call** her. 그가 Lisa의 전화번호를 모르기 때문에, 그는 그녀에게 전화하지 않을 것이다.
- **If I were** Amy, **I would not meet** him. 내가 Amy라면, 나는 그를 만나지 않을 텐데.

■ 'be' 동사는 주어의 인칭 및 수와 관계 없이 'were'를 쓴다. 단, 현대 영어에서는 주어가 1, 3인칭 단수일 때 'was'를 쓰기도 한다.

- **If he were not[wasn't]** blind, **he could see** them. 그가 눈이 보인다면, 그들을 볼 수 있을 텐데.

■ 가정법 과거완료는 이미 일어난 과거 사실을 반대로 가정하는 데 사용하며, 'If+주어+had+과거분사 ~, 주어+would/could+have+과거분사 …'의 형태로 나타낸다.

- If Irene **had seen** that, she **would have helped** us. Irene이 그것을 보았다면, 그녀는 우리를 도와주었을 텐데.

■ 가정법의 다양한 표현들로 직설법의 의미를 나타낼 수 있다.

- **As** she **is** poor, she **cannot** buy the necklace. 그녀가 가난하기 때문에, 목걸이를 살 수 없다. (직설법)
  → **If** she **were not** poor, she **could buy** the necklace. 그녀가 가난하지 않으면, 목걸이를 살 수 있을 텐데. (가정법)
  → **Were** she not poor, she **could buy** the necklace. (If 생략 가능, 도치문으로 가정)

■ without이나 but for는 '~이 없다면'의 뜻으로 가정법 구문에 쓰인다. without이나 but for는 If it were not for(=Were it not for)로 바꿔 쓸 수 있다.

→ **Without** music, the world **would** be a dull place. 음악이 없다면 세계는 따분한 곳이 될 텐데.
→ **If it were not for** music, the world **would** be a dull place.
→ **Were it not for** music, the world **would** be a dull place. (If 생략 후 도치)

핵심 Check

2. 다음 우리말에 맞게 괄호 안의 어구를 바르게 배열하시오.

Paul이 그것을 알면, 비밀번호를 바꿀 텐데. (Paul, the password, knew, he, change, would, it, if)

➡ _____

01 다음 각 가정법 문장에서 어법상 <u>어색한</u> 단어를 한 개씩만 찾아 고치시오.

(1) If we have no smartphones, our lives would be difficult.

_____ ➡ _____

(2) If he had a flying car, he will go to Paris.

_____ ➡ _____

(3) If she has a million dollars, she would travel around the world.

_____ ➡ _____

(4) I will set a daily plan to limit game time if I were you.

_____ ➡ _____

02 다음 중 어법상 바르지 <u>않은</u> 것은?

① Is your password easy to guess?
② It is interesting for David to draw beautiful mountains.
③ It was not easy of him to swim at the beach.
④ It's necessary for you to respect others.
⑤ It will be possible for me to learn yoga next month.

03 다음 빈칸에 들어갈 말로 알맞은 것은?

> If there _____ no televisions, it would not be easy to watch dramas.

① had   ② are   ③ have been
④ were   ⑤ is

04 다음 문장을 가주어 It과 to부정사를 이용하여 다시 쓰시오.

> Living without a smartphone is not easy for you.

➡ _____

 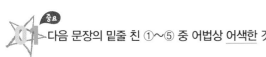

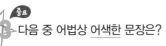 다음 문장의 밑줄 친 ①~⑤ 중 어법상 어색한 것은?

> It was <u>very</u> honest <u>for</u> you to tell the truth,
>   ①   ②
> <u>though</u> it was <u>not</u> easy to do <u>that</u>.
>   ③   ④   ⑤

02 다음 중 빈칸에 들어갈 말이 나머지와 다른 것은?

① It's not safe _____ the babies to play on the swings.

② It is necessary _____ Minju to gain weight.

③ It seems hard _____ the team to win the game.

④ It was rude _____ Charles to ask his teacher such questions.

⑤ Is it okay _____ me to get in?

다음 중 어법상 어색한 문장은?

① If I were in Sydney, I couldn't attend my friend's wedding.

② If Andy knew the solution, he could tell me right now.

③ If Paul pushed him hard, Jay could be hurt.

④ If he had an island, he won't build any houses on it.

⑤ If it were not for the help by the mechanic, we would not able to drive.

04 다음 중 같은 뜻을 가진 문장끼리 짝지어진 것은?

① I didn't have a car, so I couldn't drive.
= If I had a car, I couldn't drive.

② Minsu doesn't have a computer, so he wants to have one.
= Minsu wants if he had a computer.

③ I don't study hard, so I can't succeed.
= If I studied hard, I could succeed.

④ She can't write a letter to Sam, so she knows his address.
= She could write a letter to Sam, if she knew his address.

⑤ It is raining, so Sarah stays home.
= If it rains, Sarah would stay home.

다음 중 빈칸 ⓐ~ⓕ에 같은 단어가 들어가는 것끼리 바르게 짝지어진 것은?

> • It was kind ⓐ_____ her to look after the babies in the orphanage.
> • It wasn't hard ⓑ_____ the students to understand the professor's lecture.
> • It is impossible ⓒ_____ me to exercise for an hour at 6 every morning.
> • It was stupid ⓓ_____ the young lady to reject the offer.
> • It is dangerous ⓔ_____ her to cut the rope with that plastic knife.
> • It is careless ⓕ_____ him to tell her my secret plans.

① ⓐ, ⓒ   ② ⓑ, ⓓ, ⓔ

③ ⓒ, ⓔ, ⓕ   ④ ⓐ, ⓓ, ⓕ

⑤ ⓑ, ⓓ, ⓔ

[06~08] 다음 우리말과 일치하도록 괄호 안에 주어진 어구를 바르게 배열하시오.

06
내가 너라면, 나는 너의 친구들에게 야외 활동을 하자고 제안할 텐데.
(suggest, outdoor activities, were, to, you, I, I, if, doing, your friends, would)

➡ _____
_____

07
Smith가 자전거를 타는 것은 쉽다.
(a bike, for, easy, is, to, Smith, ride, it)

➡ _____

08
텔레비전이 없다면, 우리가 뉴스를 시청하는 것이 쉽지 않을 텐데.
(there, to, it, not, be, the news, easy, if, for, no, us, watch, would, were, televisions)

➡ _____
_____

09 다음 중 밑줄 친 부분의 쓰임이 나머지 넷과 다른 것은?

① It will be fun for us to learn how to play basketball.
② It's good for her to walk for half an hour every day.
③ Isn't it easy to understand the rules of the game?
④ It is too dark to play outside.
⑤ I think that it is necessary for you to finish the homework.

10 다음 문장의 빈칸 (A)~(C)에 들어갈 말로 가장 적절한 것은?

- If my school (A)_____ early, I would go see a movie.
- Were it not for the water, the living things in earth (B)_____ be dead.
- If I (C)_____ a car, I could go on a picnic more often.

	(A)	(B)	(C)
①	finishes	will	have
②	finishes	could	have
③	will finish	could	had had
④	finished	would	had
⑤	finished	will	had

11 다음 중 어법상 옳은 문장은?

① It is difficult of us to move those heavy chairs into the classroom.
② It is very nice for Angela to invite me to her wedding party.
③ It is not hard of me to speak French as well as English.
④ Is it okay for my to leave work a little earlier than usual today?
⑤ It was very cruel of you to mention his poor childhood experience.

12 다음 우리말을 조건에 맞게 영작하시오.

Laura가 충분한 시간이 있으면, 서울에 더 오래 머무를 수 있을 텐데.
(stay, long, can, enough 활용. If로 시작, 총 11 단어로 할 것, 단어 변형 가능)

➡ _____
_____

서답형

13 다음 대화가 자연스럽게 이뤄지도록 주어진 단어를 모두 활용하여 문장을 완성하시오. (1 단어는 어법에 맞게 바꿀 것.)

> Grandma: On this cold day, who opened the window? Somebody left the window open and all the plants froze to death.
>
> Suho: My younger sister Sujin did.
>
> Grandma: _____
>
> _____
>
> (open, for, it, the window, to, her, was, careless, leave)

중요

14 다음 중 어법상 <u>어색한</u> 것은?

① If you told this to him, he would be mad at me.

② If Abe got up early, he wouldn't be late for school.

③ If Sally had worn the jacket, she wouldn't have got a cold.

④ If Chris hadn't missed the subway, he would not be late for school.

⑤ If I were the President, my family would be proud of me.

15 다음 우리말을 영작할 때, 옳지 <u>않은</u> 문장을 고르시오.

> 공기가 없다면, 우리는 살 수 없을 텐데.

① If there were no air, we couldn't live.

② If it were not for air, we couldn't live.

③ If there is no air, we couldn't live.

④ Were it not for air, we couldn't live.

⑤ Without air, we couldn't live.

중요

16 다음 중 어법상 올바른 문장의 개수는?

> ⓐ It is clever of him using the tools.
>
> ⓑ It is very stupid for Mark to do such a thing in public.
>
> ⓒ It was impossible for Janet to arrive at the party on time.
>
> ⓓ It's important of their mothers to watch the kids play together happily.
>
> ⓔ It is generous of Susan to help the old lady to find the way to the city hall.
>
> ⓕ It was quite importantly for the teachers to make the subject easy to understand.
>
> ⓖ It is not easy for the girls to pass by their favorite snack bar.
>
> ⓗ It was wise of Dahyun not to spend her money on such a thing.

① 1개   ② 2개   ③ 3개   ④ 4개   ⑤ 5개

17 다음 중 밑줄 친 부분의 쓰임이 나머지 넷과 <u>다른</u> 것은?

① <u>It</u> is fun for her to speak in Chinese.

② <u>It</u> will soon be the lunch time.

③ <u>It</u> is not hard to search for much information on the Internet.

④ <u>It</u> was natural for you to bring the books here.

⑤ <u>It</u> was my pleasure to meet the beautiful person like you.

서답형

18 다음 문장에서 어법상 <u>어색한</u> 부분을 한 단어만 찾아서 고치시오. (고친 단어는 2개 이상이어도 상관없다.)

> If you took the subway instead of the taxi, you would have saved much time.

➡ _____

Grammar **187**

⭐1 다음 우리말과 일치하도록 괄호 안에 주어진 단어들을 바르게 배열하여 문장을 완성하시오.

(1) 우리가 스마트폰을 갖고 있지 않으면, 우리는 더 자주 밖에서 놀 텐데.

➡ If we _____

_____ often. (play, smartphones, outside, didn't, we, more, would, have)

(2) 텔레비전이 없다면, 우리가 뉴스를 확인하는 것이 더 어려워질 텐데.

➡ If there were no televisions, _____

_____ the news.

(for, it, to, difficult, would, check, us, more, be)

(3) 당신이 디지털 발자국(디지털 정보 기록)을 관리하는 것이 정말로 필요하다.

➡ It's really _____

_____. (footprint, to, for, your, manage, you, necessary, digital

(4) 우리가 디지털 장비를 효과적으로 사용하는 것은 매우 지혜로운 것이다.

➡ It is _____

_____. (wise, efficiently, to, of, use, digital, us, very, devices)

02 다음 〈보기〉의 문장과 같은 뜻이 되도록 괄호 안에 주어진 조건에 맞게 빈칸을 채우시오.

┌─ 보기 ├─
Without money, we could not trade things easily.

(1) _____ money, we could not trade things easily. (it, be동사 활용, 5단어)

(2) _____ money, we could not trade things easily. (there, no 활용, 4 단어)

(3) _____ money, we could not trade things easily. (it, be동사 활용, 4 단어)

(4) _____ money, we can trade things easily. (직설법, 접속사 as 활용, 3 단어)

03 다음 그림을 보고, 우리말에 맞게 괄호 안의 단어를 배열하여 빈칸을 채우시오.

비가 오지 않으면, 나의 개와 산책을 할 수 있을 텐데.

→ If _____.

(dog, walk, I, with, it, do, a, rain, for, can, my, go) 총 12 단어, 어형 변화 가능)

04 다음 주어진 문장과 뜻이 같도록 빈칸을 알맞게 채우시오.

Since David doesn't exercise regularly, he can't be in good shape.

➡ If David _____

in good shape.

5 다음 우리말을 괄호 안에 주어진 어구를 사용하여 영작하시오. (필요시 단어를 추가하거나 변형할 것)

(1) 어른들조차 바다에서 수영하는 것은 매우 위험하다.

➡ It is _____

_____.

(dangerous, very, even, in the sea)

(2) 당신이 그 계곡을 건너려고 노력하는 것은 어리석은 일이다.

➡ It is _____.

(try, the valley, foolish, cross)

(3) 민서가 어제 가족들과 카드 게임을 한 것은 재미있었다.

➡ It was _____

_____.

(Minseo, yesterday, play cards, fun)

06 다음 각 가정법 문장에서 어법상 <u>어색한</u> 부분을 <u>모두</u> 찾아 바르게 고치시오.

(1) If I have a girlfriend, I would see the movie with her.
(2) Sandra couldn't be late for the meeting yesterday if she had caught the bus.
(3) If you was the girl, you would understand her situation.
(4) If I am the superhero, I could save the world and defeat the monsters.
(5) If it not for your help, she could not survive the disease.

(1) _____
(2) _____
(3) _____
(4) _____
(5) _____

07 다음 각 문장에서 어법상 <u>어색한</u> 단어를 한 개씩만 찾아 <u>모두</u> 고치시오.

(1) It was fun for Amy and her family to sitting around the campfire.
(2) It is good for your to make a smile all the time.
(3) It was interesting of Grace to meet the young boy who could play chess well.
(4) It was cruel for the host of the show to make the singer sing that song again.
(5) It is necessary for customs officers checked all the baggage at the airport.

(1) _____ (2) _____
(3) _____ (4) _____
(5) _____

08 다음 〈보기〉와 같이 직설법 문장을 가정법으로 고치시오.

┌ 보기 ┐

As I am not a bird, I won't fly to her.
→ If I were a bird, I would fly to her.

(1) As there isn't another me, I can't make him share my work.

➡ _____

(2) As I am not you, I won't reduce my time on smartphone by half.

➡ _____

_____

(3) As we have televisions, it is easy for us to watch the music shows.

➡ _____

_____

(4) As Sally isn't in Hawaii, she isn't happy.

➡ _____

Reading

교과서

Time for Digital Detox

Hi, students! When you wake up in the morning, what is the first thing
시간을 나타내는 접속사 (~할 때)
you do? Do you read SNS postings on your smartphone? Imagine your
Social Networking Service의 앞 글자를 딴 약자   Imagine (that): ~을 상상해 보아라
smartphone is not near you. How do you feel?

Students, please check items on the list that are true for you.
주격 관계대명사(선행사: items)
Are you addicted to your smartphone?

□ Without my smartphone, I feel uncomfortable.
2형식 동사(+형용사 보어)
□ I take my smartphone into the bathroom.
take A into B: A를 B로 가져가다
□ It is more enjoyable to spend time on my smartphone than with
가주어 it ~ 진주어 to부정사
friends.

□ I often check SNS postings while studying.
= while I am studying
□ I try to reduce the time I spend on my smartphone, but I fail.

□ I check my smartphone right after I hear the sound of an alert.
~한 후에 바로
□ I have my smartphone next to me while I'm eating.
~ 옆에   = while eating
What is your score? Did you check more than half?

If so, you may have a problem with smartphone addiction.
= If you checked more than half
Smartphone addiction causes you to spend too much time on your
cause A to ~ : A가 ~하게 하다
smartphone. Also, you cannot focus on your studies and may have
추측의 조동사
a pain in your neck. Then now is the time for you to start digital
to부정사의 의미상 주어(for+목적격)
detox. Digital detox means staying away from digital devices, such as
동명사(means의 목적어)   = like(~와 같은)
smartphones and computers, for a while.

---

digital: 디지털의
posting: 인터넷이나 SNS에 올리는 글
be addicted to: ~에 중독되다
enjoyable: 즐거운
alert: 경보, 알림 소리
half: 절반
addiction: 중독
detox: (인체 유해물질의) 해독
stay away from: ~에서 떨어져 있다
device: 장치
such as: ~와 같은

확인문제

● 다음 문장이 본문의 내용과 일치하면 T, 일치하지 않으면 F를 쓰시오.

1 Students must check items on the list that are not true for them. ☐

2 The items are about whether or not you are addicted to your computer. ☐

3 Smartphone addiction can make your neck painful. ☐

Digital detox will help you a lot. You can enjoy freedom from the noisy digital world. You can focus more on your work.

Sometimes you can feel refreshed and <u>have new, creative ideas</u>.
(you can) have new, creative ideas

Digital detox will also <u>help you spend</u> more time with <u>others</u>.
help+목적어+(to) V   = other people

<u>Living without a smartphone</u>, however, <u>is</u> not easy. So, <u>it</u> is
동명사 주어(스마트폰 없이 사는 것)   동명사 주어 (단수 취급)   가주어 it

necessary <u>for you</u> to set some rules for <u>using</u> your smartphone.
to부정사의 의미상 주어(for+목적격)   동명사(전치사의 목적어)

You then need to follow the rules. Now, please form groups and, in

your group, <u>create</u> rules for using your smartphones.
form and create 병렬 연결

By Yerim, Yongmin, and Hojin

We will turn off our smartphones <u>while studying</u>.
= while we are studying

We will not take our smartphones into the bathroom.

We will keep our smartphones out of the bedroom and <u>not use</u> <u>them</u> at
(we will) not use = smartphones

night.

By Jina, Hosung, and Minsu

• More Time for Outside Activities – We will <u>spend</u> more time
spend+시간+Ving: V하느라 시간을 보내다

<u>playing</u> outside without our smartphones.

• Fewer SNS Messages – We will post <u>fewer</u> SNS messages on our
셀 수 있는 명사 수식

smartphones.

By Jiho, Sohee, and Yumin

<u>If I were you, I would reduce</u> my time on my smartphone by half.
If+주어+동사의 과거형 ~, 주어+would/could+동사원형 …: 만약 ~라면 …할 텐데 (가정법 과거)

If I were you, I would turn off all alerts.

You did a good job, students! <u>If we had no smartphones</u>, our lives
'스마트폰이 없다면'이라고 현재 사실을 반대로 가정하는 가정법 과거

would be more difficult, but too much use of a smartphone is

dangerous. With digital detox, you can become a wise smartphone user.

freedom: 자유
noisy: 시끄러운, 소란한
refreshed: 상쾌한
necessary: 필요한
form: 만들다, 형성하다
create: 창조하다, 만들다
message: 알림, 메시지
dangerous: 위험한
wise: 현명한

확인문제

● 다음 문장이 본문의 내용과 일치하면 T, 일치하지 <u>않으면</u> F를 쓰시오.

1 Digital detox is recommended to someone who is addicted to his or her smartphone.

2 It is easy to live without smartphones.

3 Our lives are easier because there are smartphones.

• 우리말을 참고하여 빈칸에 알맞은 말을 쓰시오.

Time for Digital Detox

1 Hi, students! _____ you wake up _____ _____ _____, _____ is the first thing you do?

2 Do you _____ SNS postings _____ your smartphone?

3 _____ your smartphone _____ not _____ you. _____ do you feel?

4 Students, please _____ _____ on the list _____ _____ true for you.

5 _____ you _____ to your smartphone?

6 _____ my smartphone, I _____ _____.

7 I _____ my smartphone _____ the bathroom.

8 It is more _____ _____ spend time on my smartphone than with friends.

9 I often check SNS postings _____ _____.

10 I try to _____ the time _____ _____ on my smartphone, but I fail.

11 I check my smartphone _____ _____ I hear the sound of _____ _____.

12 I have my smartphone _____ _____ me _____ I'm eating.

13 _____ is your _____? Did you _____ more than _____?

14 If so, you may _____ a problem _____ smartphone addiction.

15 Smartphone addiction _____ _____ _____ _____ too much time _____ your smartphone.

16 Also, you cannot _____ _____ your studies and may _____ _____ _____ in your neck.

17 Then now is the time _____ _____ _____ _____ digital detox.

디지털 디톡스를 할 시간

1 안녕하세요, 학생 여러분! 여러분은 아침에 일어났을 때, 가장 먼저 하는 일이 무엇인가요?

2 스마트폰으로 SNS 게시물을 읽나요?

3 스마트폰이 여러분 근처에 있지 않다고 상상해 보세요. 기분이 어떤가요?

4 학생 여러분, 이 목록에서 여러분에게 맞는 항목들을 표시해 보세요.

5 너는 스마트폰에 중독되었는가?

6 나는 스마트폰이 없으면, 불편함을 느낀다.

7 나는 스마트폰을 화장실에 가져간다.

8 나는 친구들과 함께 시간을 보내는 것보다 스마트폰을 하면서 보내는 시간이 더 즐겁다.

9 나는 공부하면서 SNS 게시물을 종종 확인한다.

10 나는 스마트폰을 사용하는 시간을 줄이려고 노력하지만, 실패한다.

11 나는 알림음을 듣자마자 스마트폰을 확인한다.

12 나는 식사 중에 스마트폰을 옆에 둔다.

13 여러분의 점수는 어떤가요? 절반보다 더 많이 표시했나요?

14 만약 그렇다면, 여러분은 스마트폰 중독의 문제를 가지고 있을지도 모릅니다.

15 스마트폰 중독은 여러분이 스마트폰에 너무 많은 시간을 보내게 만듭니다.

16 또한 여러분은 학업에 집중할 수 없고 목에 통증이 있을지도 모릅니다.

17 그렇다면 지금 여러분은 디지털 디톡스를 시작할 시간입니다.

18 Digital detox _____ _____ _____ _____ digital devices, such as smartphones and computers, _____ a while.

19 Digital detox will _____ you a lot. You can enjoy _____ _____ the _____ digital world.

20 You can _____ more _____ your work. Sometimes you can _____ _____ and have new, _____ _____.

21 Digital detox will also _____ you _____ more time with others.

22 _____ without a smartphone, _____ _____ not easy.

23 So, it is _____ _____ _____ to set some rules _____ using your smartphone.

24 You then _____ _____ _____ the rules.

25 Now, please _____ groups and, in your group, _____ _____ for _____ your smartphone.

<By Yerim, Yongmin, and Hojin>

26 We will _____ _____ our smartphones _____ studying.

27 We will not _____ our smartphones _____ the bathroom.

28 We will _____ our smartphones _____ _____ _____ and not use _____ at night.

<By Jina, Hosung, and Minsu>

29 _____ _____ _____ Outside Activities – We will _____ _____ _____ _____ outside without our smartphones.

30 _____ SNS Messages – We will post _____ SNS messages _____ our smartphones.

<By Jiho, Sohee, and Yumin>

31 If _____ _____ you, I _____ reduce my time on my smartphone _____ _____.

32 If _____ _____ you, I _____ turn _____ all alerts.

33 You did a good job, students! If we _____ no smartphones, our lives _____ _____ more difficult, but _____ _____ use of a smartphone is dangerous.

34 _____ digital detox, you can become a _____ smartphone user.

18 디지털 디톡스는 스마트폰과 컴퓨터 같은 디지털 기기들로부터 잠시 동안 떨어져 있는 것을 의미합니다.

19 디지털 디톡스는 여러분을 많이 도와줄 것입니다. 여러분은 시끄러운 디지털 세계로부터 자유를 즐길 수 있습니다.

20 여러분은 하는 일에 더욱 집중할 수 있습니다. 종종 여러분은 상쾌함을 느끼고 새롭고 창의적인 아이디어를 얻을 수 있습니다.

21 디지털 디톡스는 또한 여러분이 다른 사람들과 더 많은 시간을 보내도록 도와줄 것입니다.

22 하지만 스마트폰 없이 사는 것은 쉽지 않습니다.

23 그러므로 여러분은 스마트폰을 사용하기 위한 몇 가지 규칙을 정할 필요가 있습니다.

24 그리고 나서 여러분은 그 규칙들을 따라야 합니다.

25 자, 조를 형성하고, 여러분의 조에서, 스마트폰을 사용하기 위한 규칙을 만들어 보세요.

〈예림, 용민, 호진으로부터〉

26 우리는 공부하는 동안 스마트폰을 끌 것이다.

27 우리는 화장실에 스마트폰을 가져가지 않을 것이다.

28 우리는 밤에 스마트폰을 침실 밖에 두고 사용하지 않을 것이다.

〈지나, 호성, 민수로부터〉

29 야외 활동을 위한 더 많은 시간 – 우리는 스마트폰 없이 밖에서 노는 데 더 많은 시간을 보낼 것이다.

30 SNS는 더 적게 – 우리는 스마트폰에 SNS 메시지를 더 적게 올릴 것이다.

〈지호, 소희, 유민〉

31 만약 내가 너라면, 나는 스마트폰에 쓰는 시간을 절반으로 줄일 것이다.

32 만약 내가 너라면, 모든 알림을 끌 것이다.

33 잘했어요, 학생 여러분! 만약 스마트폰이 없다면 우리의 삶이 더 힘들겠지만, 스마트폰을 너무 많이 사용하는 것은 위험합니다.

34 디지털 디톡스와 함께, 여러분은 현명한 스마트폰 사용자가 될 수 있습니다.

● 우리말을 참고하여 본문을 영작하시오.

1 안녕하세요, 학생 여러분! 여러분은 아침에 일어났을 때, 가장 먼저 하는 일이 무엇인가요?

➡ _____

2 스마트폰으로 SNS 게시물을 읽나요?

➡ _____

3 스마트폰이 여러분 근처에 있지 않다고 상상해 보세요. 기분이 어떤가요?

➡ _____

4 학생 여러분, 이 목록에서 여러분에게 맞는 항목들을 표시해 보세요.

➡ _____

5 너는 스마트폰에 중독되었는가?

➡ _____

6 나는 스마트폰이 없으면, 불편함을 느낀다.

➡ _____

7 나는 스마트폰을 화장실에 가져간다.

➡ _____

8 나는 친구들과 함께 시간을 보내는 것보다 스마트폰을 하면서 보내는 시간이 더 즐겁다.

➡ _____

9 나는 공부하면서 SNS 게시물을 종종 확인한다.

➡ _____

10 나는 스마트폰을 사용하는 시간을 줄이려고 노력하지만, 실패한다.

➡ _____

11 나는 알림음을 듣자마자 스마트폰을 확인한다.

➡ _____

12 나는 식사 중에 스마트폰을 옆에 둔다.

➡ _____

13 여러분의 점수는 어떤가요? 절반보다 더 많이 표시했나요?

➡ _____

14 만약 그렇다면, 여러분은 스마트폰 중독의 문제를 가지고 있을지도 모릅니다.

➡ _____

15 스마트폰 중독은 여러분이 스마트폰에 너무 많은 시간을 보내게 만듭니다.

➡ _____

16 또한 여러분은 학업에 집중할 수 없고 목에 통증이 있을지도 모릅니다.

➡ _____

17 그렇다면 지금 여러분은 디지털 디톡스를 시작할 시간입니다.

➡ _____

18 디지털 디톡스는 스마트폰과 컴퓨터 같은 디지털 기기들로부터 잠시 동안 떨어져 있는 것을 의미합니다.

➡ _____

19 디지털 디톡스는 여러분을 많이 도와줄 것입니다. 여러분은 시끄러운 디지털 세계로부터 자유를 즐길 수 있습니다.

➡ _____

20 여러분은 하는 일에 더욱 집중할 수 있습니다. 종종 여러분은 상쾌함을 느끼고 새롭고 창의적인 아이디어를 얻을 수 있습니다.

➡ _____

21 디지털 디톡스는 또한 여려분이 다른 사람들과 더 많은 시간을 보내도록 도와줄 것입니다.

➡ _____

22 하지만 스마트폰 없이 사는 것은 쉽지 않습니다.

➡ _____

23 그러므로 여러분은 스마트폰을 사용하기 위한 몇 가지 규칙을 정할 필요가 있습니다.

➡ _____

24 그리고 나서 여러분은 그 규칙들을 따라야 합니다.

➡ _____

25 자, 조를 형성하고, 여러분의 조에서, 스마트폰을 사용하기 위한 규칙을 만들어 보세요.

➡ _____

By Yerim, Yongmin, and Hojin

26 우리는 공부하는 동안 스마트폰을 끌 것이다.

➡ _____

27 우리는 화장실에 스마트폰을 가져가지 않을 것이다.

➡ _____

28 우리는 밤에 스마트폰을 침실 밖에 두고 사용하지 않을 것이다.

➡ _____

By Jina, Hosung, and Minsu

29 야외 활동을 위한 더 많은 시간 – 우리는 스마트폰 없이 밖에서 노는 데 더 많은 시간을 보낼 것이다.

➡ _____

30 SNS는 더 적게 – 우리는 스마트폰에 SNS 메시지를 더 적게 올릴 것이다.

➡ _____

By Jiho, Sohee, and Yumin

31 만약 내가 너라면, 나는 스마트폰에 쓰는 시간을 절반으로 줄일 것이다.

➡ _____

32 만약 내가 너라면, 모든 알림을 끌 것이다.

➡ _____

33 잘했어요, 학생 여러분! 만약 스마트폰이 없다면 우리의 삶이 더 힘들겠지만, 스마트폰을 너무 많이 사용하는 것은 위험합니다.

➡ _____
_____

34 디지털 디톡스와 함께, 여러분은 현명한 스마트폰 사용자가 될 수 있습니다.

➡ _____

[01~03] 다음 글을 읽고 물음에 답하시오.

Hi, students! When you wake up in the morning, what is the first thing you do? Do you read SNS postings on your smartphone? Imagine your smartphone is not near you. How do you feel?

Students, please check items on the list that are true for you.

Are you addicted to your smartphone?
□ Without my smartphone, I feel uncomfortable.
□ I take my smartphone into the bathroom.
□ It is more enjoyable to spend time on my smartphone than with friends.
□ I often check SNS postings (A)_____ studying.
□ I try to reduce the time I spend on my smartphone, but I fail.
□ I check my smartphone right after I hear the sound of an alert.
□ I have my smartphone next to me (B)_____ I'm eating.

01 빈칸 (A)와 (B)에 공통으로 들어갈 말로 가장 적절한 것은?

① for   ② though   ③ since
④ while   ⑤ during

서답형

02 주어진 어구를 바르게 배열하여 다음 물음의 대답을 완성하시오.

> Q: According to the passage, what is the list about?
> A: It is _____
> _____.
> (your smartphone / about / addicted / whether or not / are / to / you)

03 다음 중 위 글에서 유의어를 찾을 수 있는 것을 <u>모두</u> 고르시오.

① cut down   ② comfortable   ③ false
④ beside   ⑤ save

[04~06] 다음 글을 읽고 물음에 답하시오.

What is your score? Did you check more than half?

If so, you may have a problem with smartphone addiction. Smartphone addiction causes you (A)_____ too much time on your smartphone. Also, you cannot focus on your studies and may have a pain in your neck. Then now is the time for you to start digital detox. Digital detox means staying away from digital devices, such as smartphones and computers, for a while.

서답형

04 빈칸 (A)에 동사 'spend'를 어법에 맞게 쓰시오.

➡ _____

05 **중요** Which is TRUE according to the passage?

① Smartphone addiction is related to too little use of digital devices.
② Smartphone addiction helps people to focus on their studies.
③ Too much use of smartphone causes you to have a pain on your wrist.
④ People who are addicted to smartphone need to start to use their smartphones more often.
⑤ There is a solution for people who are addicted to their smartphones.

서답형

06 다음과 같이 풀이되는 말을 위 글에서 찾아 쓰시오.

> treatment given to people who are addicted to something in order to stop them from being addicted

➡ _____

[07~09] 다음 글을 읽고 물음에 답하시오.

Digital detox will help you a lot. You can enjoy freedom from the noisy digital world. You can focus more on your work. Sometimes you can feel refreshed and have new, creative ideas. Digital detox will also help you spend more time with others. Living without a smartphone, (A)_____, is not easy. So, it is necessary (B)_____ you to set some rules for using your smartphone. You then need to follow the rules.

07 다음 중 빈칸 (A)에 들어갈 말로 가장 적절한 것은?

① for example   ② therefore
③ that's why   ④ in other words
⑤ however

08 다음 중 빈칸 (B)에 들어갈 말로 가장 적절한 것은?

① at   ② in   ③ on   ④ for   ⑤ of

중요

09 Which one is the benefit of digital detox?

① to enjoy the noisy digital world
② to focus on your smartphone
③ to have creative ideas
④ to spend more time with your smartphone
⑤ to make your life easy

[10~12] 다음 글을 읽고 물음에 답하시오.

Now, please form groups and, in your group, create rules for using your smartphone.

By Yerim, Yongmin, and Hojin
We will ①turn off our smartphones while studying.
We will not take our smartphones into the bathroom.
We will keep our smartphones ②out of the bedroom and not use them at night.

By Jina, Hosung, and Minsu
• More Time for Outside Activities – We will spend more time ③playing outside ④with our smartphones.
• Fewer SNS Messages – We will post fewer SNS messages on our smartphones.

By Jiho, Sohee, and Yumin
If I were you, I would ⑤reduce my time on my smartphone by half.
If I were you, I would turn off all alerts.

서답형

10 다음은 위 글의 제목이다. 빈칸에 들어갈 말을 위 글에서 찾아 쓰시오.

> _____ _____ _____ Our Smartphones

중요

11 ①~⑤ 중 글의 흐름상 어색한 것은?

①   ②   ③   ④   ⑤

서답형

12 According to Yerim, Yongmin, and Hojin, where will they not take their smartphones? Answer in English with a full sentence.

➡ _____

_____

[13~16] 다음 글을 읽고 물음에 답하시오.

Hi, students! When you wake up in the morning, ⓐ처음으로 하는 게 무엇인가요? Do you read SNS postings on your smartphone? Imagine your smartphone is not near you. How do you feel?

Students, please check items on the list that are true for you.

Are you addicted to your smartphone?

☐ Without my smartphone, I feel uncomfortable.
☐ I take my smartphone into the bathroom.
☐ It is more enjoyable to spend time on my smartphone than with friends.
☐ I often check SNS postings while studying.
☐ I try to reduce the time I spend (A)_____ my smartphone, but I fail.
☐ I check my smartphone right after I hear the sound of an alert.
☐ I have my smartphone next to me while I'm eating.

What is your score? Did you check more than half? If so, you may have a problem with smartphone addiction.

13 다음 중 빈칸 (A)에 들어갈 말과 같은 말이 들어가는 것은?

① Are you interested _____ the subject?
② She will get _____ the station on time.
③ Can you stay _____ me?
④ He used to take pictures _____ us.
⑤ It depends _____ your ability.

서답형

14 주어진 단어를 바르게 배열하여 밑줄 친 우리말 ⓐ를 영어로 쓰시오.

(do / is / thing / what / first / the / you)

➡ _____

15 다음 중 위 글의 내용과 일치하는 것은?

① The passage is about how to use smartphones wisely.
② There are eight items on the list.
③ The writer recommends that we should never use our smartphone.
④ You may have a problem with smartphone addiction if you checked more than half.
⑤ You should check the items that aren't true to you.

16 다음 중 스마트폰 중독 사항에 해당하지 않는 사람은?

① Amie: I don't feel comfortable when my smartphone is not near me.
② Bryan: I want my smartphone to be with me when I eat my meal.
③ Chris: As soon as I hear the sound of an alert, I check my smartphone.
④ David: I prefer playing with my friends to spending time on my smartphone.
⑤ Eden: I always check SNS postings with my smartphone.

[17~20] 다음 글을 읽고 물음에 답하시오.

Smartphone addiction causes you to spend too much time on your smartphone.
[A] Digital detox will help you a lot. You can enjoy freedom from the noisy digital world. You can focus more on your work. Sometimes you can feel refreshed and have new, creative ideas. Digital detox will also help you spend more time with others.
[B] Also, you cannot focus on your studies and may have a pain in your neck. Then now is the time for you to start digital detox. Digital detox means staying away from digital devices, such as smartphones and computers, for a while.

[C] Living without a smartphone, however, is not easy. ⓐ_____, it is necessary for you to set some rules for using your smartphone. You then need to follow the rules.

17 다음 중 빈칸 ⓐ에 들어갈 말로 가장 적절한 것은?

① On the contrary ② That is
③ So ④ Otherwise
⑤ Unless

18 자연스러운 글이 되도록 [A]~[C]를 바르게 배열하시오.

① [A]–[C]–[B] ② [B]–[A]–[C]
③ [B]–[C]–[A] ④ [C]–[A]–[B]
⑤ [C]–[B]–[A]

19 다음 중 위 글을 읽고 답할 수 있는 것은?

① Who invented smartphones?
② How much time is needed to do digital detox?
③ What does digital detox mean?
④ Who did digital detox for the first time?
⑤ How many rules do we have to follow?

서답형
20 What does smartphone addiction cause you to do? Answer in English with a full sentence.

➡ _____

[21~23] 다음 글을 읽고 물음에 답하시오.

Now, please form groups and, in your group, create rules for using your smartphone.

By Yerim, Yongmin, and Hojin

We will turn off our smartphones while studying.

We will not take our smartphones into the bathroom.

We will keep our smartphones out of the bedroom and not use them at night.

By Jina, Hosung, and Minsu

• More Time for Outside Activities – We will spend more time playing outside without our smartphones.

• Fewer SNS Messages – We will post fewer SNS messages on our smartphones.

By Jiho, Sohee, and Yumin

If I were you, I would reduce my time on my smartphone by half.

If I were you, I would turn off all alerts.

You did a good job, students! If we (A)_____ no smartphones, our lives would be more difficult, but too much use of a smartphone is dangerous. With digital detox, you can become a wise smartphone user.

서답형
21 동사 'have'를 어법에 맞게 빈칸 (A)에 쓰시오.

➡ _____

22 학생들의 규칙에 해당하지 않는 것은?

① to turn off smartphones while studying
② to reduce their time on smartphone by half
③ not to use their smartphones at night
④ to do digital detox every day
⑤ to post fewer SNS messages on their smartphones

서답형
23 What do Jiho, Sohee, and Yumin want to turn off?

➡ _____

[01~04] 다음 글을 읽고 물음에 답하시오.

Students, please check items on the list that are true for you.

Are you addicted to your smartphone?

▫ Without my smartphone, I feel uncomfortable.

▫ I take my smartphone into the bathroom.

▫ It is more enjoyable to spend time on my smartphone than with friends.

▫ I often check SNS postings while studying.

▫ (A)I try to reduce the time I spend on my smartphone, but I succeed.

▫ I check my smartphone right after I hear the sound of an alert.

▫ I have my smartphone next to me while I'm eating.

What is your score? Did you check more than half? (B)If so, you may have a problem with smartphone addiction.

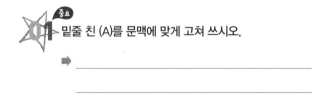

01 밑줄 친 (A)를 문맥에 맞게 고쳐 쓰시오.

➡ _____

_____

02 다음 중 위 글의 내용과 일치하지 <u>않는</u> 것을 두 군데 찾아 바르게 고쳐 쓰시오.

Hi, my name is Norman. Recently, I have noticed that I am addicted to my smartphone. I take my smartphone into the bathroom and I feel comfortable without my smartphone. Besides, I have my smartphone far from me while eating. And I am busy checking SNS postings while studying.

➡ _____

03 밑줄 친 (B)가 의미하는 것을 구체적으로 쓰시오.

➡ _____

04 위 글의 내용에 맞게 빈칸에 알맞은 말을 쓰시오.

When I hear the sound of an alert, _____ _____ _____ _____ immediately.

[05~09] 다음 글을 읽고 물음에 답하시오.

Smartphone addiction causes you to spend too much time on your smartphone. Also, you cannot focus on your studies and may have a pain in your neck. Then now is the time for you to start digital detox. Digital detox means staying away from digital devices, such as smartphones and computers, for a while.

Digital detox will help you a lot. You can enjoy freedom from the noisy digital world. You can focus more on your work. Sometimes you can feel refreshed and have new, creative ideas. Digital detox will also help you spend more time with others.

Living without a smartphone, however, is not easy. So, it is necessary for you to set some rules for using your smartphone. You then need to follow the rules. Now, please form groups and, in your group, create rules for using your smartphone.

05 In addition to spending too much time on smartphones, what are the problems of smartphone addiction? Answer in English with a full sentence.

➡ _____

_____

06 According to the passage, what do we need to do to spend more time with others?

➡ _____

07 With digital detox, what can we enjoy from the noisy digital world? Answer in English with a full sentence.

➡ _____

08 What do we need to do after setting some rules for using smartphones? Answer in English with six words.

➡ _____

09 According to the passage, what is necessary for us to do for using our smartphone?

➡ _____

_____

[10~14] 다음 글을 읽고 물음에 답하시오.

By Yerim, Yongmin, and Hojin

We will turn off our smartphones while studying.

We will not take our smartphones into the bathroom.

We will keep our smartphones out of the bedroom and not use (A)them at night.

By Jina, Hosung, and Minsu

• More Time for Outside Activities – We will spend more time playing outside without our smartphones.

• Fewer SNS Messages – We will post fewer SNS messages on our smartphones.

By Jiho, Sohee, and Yumin

If I were you, I would reduce my time on my smartphone by half.

If I were you, I would turn off all alerts.

You did a good job, students! If we had no smartphones, our lives would be more difficult, but too much use of a smartphone is dangerous. With digital detox, you can become a wise smartphone user.

10 밑줄 친 (A)가 가리키는 것을 위 글에서 찾아 쓰시오.

➡ _____

11 According to Yerim, Yongmin, and Hojin, what will they do while studying?

➡ _____

_____

12 위 글의 내용에 맞게 빈칸에 알맞은 말을 쓰시오.

Jina will _____ _____ _____
_____ _____ instead of playing with her smartphone.

13 How does the writer think about too much use of a smartphone? Answer in English with a full sentence.

➡ _____

14 다음 호진이의 일기의 빈칸에 알맞은 말을 쓰시오.

When I was addicted to my smartphone, I used to _____ _____ _____
_____ the bathroom, but I don't do it anymore after I started digital detox.

교과서

구석구석

Enjoy Writing C

If There Were No Smartphones

There would be some advantages and some disadvantages if there were no
가정법 과거형으로 주절에는 '조동사 과거형+동사원형'을 사용한다.　　　　*'If+주어+과거동사'로 be동사는 were를 사용한다.*
smartphones. First, let's talk about some advantages.

If we didn't have smartphones, we would play outside more often. Plus,
가정법 과거형으로 'If+주어+과거동사 ~　　*주어+would+동사원형'을 사용한다.*　　*게다가(첨가의 의미)*
we would be safe from neck pain. On the other hand, there would be some
　　　　　　　　　　　　　　　　반면에
disadvantages. If there were no smartphones, it would not be easy for us to
→ 직설법: As there are smartphones. it is easy for us to contact people.　*가주어*　　　*의미상 주어*　*진주어*
contact people. Also, it would take so long for us to find information.
　　　　　　　　it takes+시간+for+목적격+to부정사: ~가 ~하는 데 시간이 걸리다

구문해설 • advantage 장점 • disadvantage 단점 • plus 게다가 • pain 고통 • contact 연락하다
• information 정보

Project 2

It is necessary for us to be digital citizens!
가주어　　　*의미상의 주어*　*진주어*
If there were no Internet or SNS, our lives would be more difficult. So, it is
　가정법 과거　　　　　　　　　　　*조동사 과거+원형*　　　　*가주어*
very important for us to use digital devices wisely as a digital citizen.
　　　　의미상의 주어　*진주어*　　　　　　*전치사(~로서)*
I respect myself and others on SNS.
　　　재귀대명사(주어 = 목적어)
I never share my password with anyone.
　　　　　　　　부정문에서 사용된 anyone
I use kind words.

I never use bad words.

I don't spend too much time online.

구문해설 • device: 기기 • citizen: 시민 • password: 비밀번호

Project 3

It's very important for everyone to become a digital citizen. Our group will
　　　　　　　to부정사의 의미상 주어　*진주어*
show you what digital citizens do. Please enjoy.
4형식 동사　*간접의문문(의문사+주어+동사)*

구문해설 • important: 중요한 • citizen: 시민

해석

만약 스마트폰이 없다면
만약 스마트폰이 없다면 몇몇 장점과 단점이 있을 것이다. 첫째로 몇 가지 장점을 이야기해 보자. 만약 우리가 스마트폰을 가지고 있지 않다면, 우리는 밖에서 더 자주 놀 것이다. 게다가, 우리는 목통증의 위험이 없을 것이다. 반면에 몇 가지 단점도 있을 것이다. 만약 스마트폰이 없다면, 우리는 사람들에게 연락하는 것이 쉽지 않을 것이다. 또한 우리가 정보를 찾는 데 시간이 많이 걸릴 것이다.

우리는 디지털 시민이 될 필요가 있다!
만약 인터넷이나 SNS가 없다면, 우리의 삶은 더 힘들 것이다. 그래서 우리는 디지털 시민으로서 디지털 기기들을 현명하게 사용하는 것이 중요하다.
나는 SNS에서 내 자신과 다른 사람들을 존중한다.
나는 절대 내 비밀번호를 누구와도 공유하지 않는다.
나는 친절한 말을 쓴다.
나는 나쁜 말을 절대 쓰지 않는다.
나는 온라인에서 너무 많은 시간을 보내지 않는다.

모두가 디지털 시민이 되는 것은 매우 중요해. 우리 모둠이 디지털 시민이 무엇을 하는지 보여줄게. 재미있게 봐.

영역별 핵심문제

01 다음 주어진 두 단어의 관계가 같도록 빈칸에 알맞은 단어를 쓰시오.

> limit : restrict = dialogue : _____

02 다음 문장의 빈칸 (A)와 (B)에 들어갈 단어가 바르게 짝지어진 것은?

> • The President wants to (A)_____ more jobs for young people.
> • He spent an (B)_____ afternoon at the park with his lovely daughter.

① imagine – easy
② reduce – uncomfortable
③ post – enjoyable
④ create – unhappy
⑤ create – enjoyable

[03~04] 다음 영영풀이에 해당하는 것을 고르시오.

03
> an inability to stop doing or using something, especially something harmful

① advantage　　② danger
③ addiction　　④ posting
⑤ alert

04
> something that may help someone to gain a favorable result

① advantage　　② detox
③ comfort　　④ alert
⑤ disadvantage

05 다음 문장의 빈칸에 들어갈 말을 쓰시오.

> A _____ is the right a creator has over his or her literary and artistic works.

06 다음 대화의 밑줄 친 부분을 같은 말로 바꾸어 쓸 때 문장의 빈칸을 채우시오.

> A: Have you posted bad comments online?
> B: Yes.
> A: <u>You're not supposed to post bad comments online.</u>

➡ If I _____ you, I _____ _____ _____ bad comments online.

07 아래 그림의 여학생의 문제점을 읽고, 남학생이 해 줄 충고의 말을 〈조건〉에 맞게 완성하시오.

I can't focus on my studies.

┤ 조건 ├
• If를 사용할 것.
• 'put aside', 'the smartphone'을 사용할 것.

➡ Boy: _____

_____

08 대화의 빈칸에 들어갈 말을 주어진 어구를 알맞은 순서로 배열하여 완성하시오.

> B: What are you doing, Sohee?
>
> G: I'm writing a posting about the restaurant I visited today.
>
> B: Those are great pictures. Did you take all of them?
>
> G: No. I took the pictures from someone's blog.
>
> B: Then you're not supposed to post them on your blog.
>
> G: Why not?
>
> B: _____
>
> _____ (the right / only / because / to use / the blog owner / has / them)
>
> G: Oh, I see.

[09~11] 다음 대화를 읽고 물음에 답하시오.

> Bora: Seho, look! Somebody posted strange things on your SNS. I don't think you posted them.
>
> Seho: Really? Who did this?
>
> Bora: I think someone figured out your password.
>
> Seho: What should I do?
>
> Bora: (A)_____
>
> Seho: I think I should.
>
> Bora: Is your password easy to guess?
>
> Seho: I used my birth date.
>
> Bora: That is not good. In fact, it is a big mistake. You're not supposed to use your personal information when you make a password.
>
> Seho: Okay, I see. I will change it to a stronger one.

09 What is Seho not supposed to use when he makes a password? Answer in English.

➡ _____

_____

10 빈칸 (A)에 들어갈 말로 알맞은 것은?

① If I were you, I would not use my cellphone.

② If I were you, I would set up screen lock.

③ If I were you, I would sell my smartphone and buy a cellphone which I couldn't play games on.

④ If I were you, I would set a daily plan to limit game time.

⑤ If I were you, I would change my password.

11 위 대화의 내용과 일치하지 <u>않는</u> 것은?

① Somebody posted strange things on Seho's SNS.

② Seho used his birth date when he made a password.

③ Bora suggested to Seho that his password should be easy to guess.

④ Seho is not supposed to use his personal information when he makes a password.

⑤ Seho will change his password to a stronger one.

Grammar

[12~14] 다음 우리말에 맞게 영작한 것은?

12

> Peter가 그의 아버지를 돕다니 착하다.

① It is nice of Peter to help his father.

② It will be nice for Peter to help his father.

③ It is nice for Peter to help his father.

④ Peter is nice of to help to his father.

⑤ Peter is nice for to help to his father.

13

만일 눈이 충분히 온다면 우리가 눈사람을 만들 수 있을 텐데.

① If we have enough snow, we could make a snowman.

② Had we snow enough, we can make a snowman.

③ If it didn't snow much, we wouldn't make a snowman.

④ If it snows enough, we would make a snowman.

⑤ If it snowed enough, we could make a snowman.

14

당신이 긍정적인 마음으로 사는 것이 훨씬 더 건강에 좋을 것이다.

① It is quite healthier for yours to live with a positive mind.

② It will be much healthier of you to live with a positive mind.

③ To live with a positive mind will be very healthier for you.

④ It will be much healthier for you to live with a positive mind.

⑤ It would be quite healthier for you to live with a positive mind.

15 다음 주어진 문장을 가정법으로 바르게 고친 것은?

As John didn't return the car to his girlfriend, she hated him.

① If John returns the car to his girlfriend, she won't hate John.

② If John returned the car to his girlfriend, she would hate John.

③ If John didn't return the car to his girlfriend, she wouldn't hate John.

④ If John had returned the car to his girlfriend, she wouldn't have hated John.

⑤ If John hadn't returned the car to his girlfriend, she would have hated John.

16 다음 중 어법상 올바른 문장의 개수는 <u>모두</u> 몇 개인가?

ⓐ It is difficult for the young kids to diligent all the time.

ⓑ It is possibly for Tom to paint the fences.

ⓒ It won't be easy of the researchers to find out the solution to the problem.

ⓓ Is it interesting for they to watch the pingpong games?

ⓔ It was necessary for me to going abroad to make my dreams come true.

ⓕ It is very polite of her to say hello to every adult she meets.

ⓖ It's important for the students not be late for school.

① 1개 ② 2개 ③ 3개 ④ 4개 ⑤ 5개

17 다음 중 밑줄 친 부분의 쓰임이 〈보기〉와 같은 것은?

┤ 보기 ├

Did you ask Sarah <u>if</u> you could post them online?

① James could call Seohyun <u>if</u> he knew her phone number.

② I would build a beautiful house on the beach <u>if</u> I had an island.

③ Our lives would be difficult <u>if</u> there were no computers.

④ Sarah would wonder <u>if</u> she could succeed in the future when young.

⑤ It would be hard to take pictures <u>if</u> we didn't have smartphones.

18 다음 〈보기〉에 주어진 어구를 활용하여, 우리말과 일치하도록 그림을 참고하여 어법상 알맞은 형태로 바꿔 배열하시오. (사용하지 않는 단어는 없어야 한다.)

> **보기**
>
> the house, the race, play, win, work hard on it, now, at that time, stand strong, be lazy, be hungry

- 그 때 놀지 않았더라면, 지금 배고프지 않을 텐데.
- 내가 열심히 만들었다면, 그 집이 튼튼하게 서 있었을 텐데.
- 내가 게으르지 않았더라면, 경주를 이길 수 있었을 텐데.

(A)　　　　(B)　　　　(C)

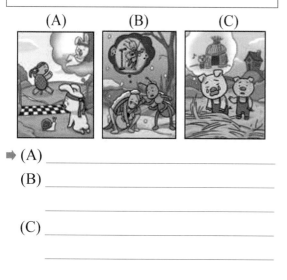

➡ (A) _____

　(B) _____

　　 _____

　(C) _____

　　 _____

19 다음 중 밑줄 친 It[it]의 쓰임이 나머지와 다른 하나는?

① It was difficult for the students in the hall to answer the professor's question.

② It is a ten minutes' walk from here to the museum.

③ Is it so important for us to learn the grammar in foreign languages?

④ It isn't easy for the politician to solve the problem of the city.

⑤ It is good for the old people to take a walk for half an hour every day.

[20~23] 다음 글을 읽고 물음에 답하시오.

　Smartphone addiction causes you to spend too much time on your smartphone. ① Also, you cannot focus on your studies and may have a pain in your neck. ② Then now is the time for you to start digital detox. Digital detox means staying away from digital devices, such as smartphones and computers, for a while. ③ You can enjoy freedom from the noisy digital world. ④ You can focus more on your work. ⑤ Sometimes you can feel refreshed and have new, creative ideas. Digital detox will also help you spend more time with others.

20 ①~⑤ 중 주어진 문장이 들어가기에 가장 적절한 곳은?

> Digital detox will help you a lot.

①　　②　　③　　④　　⑤

21 다음 중 스마트폰 중독에 해당하는 증상으로 적절한 것은?

① hardly spending time on your smartphone

② doing your homework

③ focusing on your studies

④ having a pain in your neck

⑤ having new, creative ideas

22 다음 빈칸에 알맞은 말을 위 글의 내용에 맞게 쓰시오.

> A: Somi, you look really good.
> B: Thanks. Actually I feel refreshed.
> A: How come?
> B: I started _____ _____ in order to enjoy freedom from the noisy digital world.
> A: That sounds great.

23 What does digital detox mean? Answer in English with a full sentence.

➡ _____

_____

_____

[24~26] 다음 글을 읽고 물음에 답하시오.

Living without a smartphone, however, is not ①easy. So, it is necessary for you (A)to set some rules for using your smartphone. You then need to ②follow the rules. Now, please form groups and, in your group, create rules for using your smartphone.

By Yerim, Yongmin, and Hojin

We will turn off our smartphones while ③ studying.

We will not take our smartphones into the bathroom.

We will keep our smartphones out of the bedroom and not use them at night.

By Jina, Hosung, and Minsu

• More Time for Outside Activities – We will spend ④less time playing outside without our smartphones.

• ⑤Fewer SNS Messages – We will post fewer SNS messages on our smartphones.

24 다음 중 밑줄 친 (A)와 쓰임이 같은 것은?

① You should do your best to be a winner.

② The insect is climbing to get to the top.

③ You need something to read.

④ It is essential to listen to your parents.

⑤ The game is dangerous to watch.

25 ①~⑤ 중 글의 흐름상 어색한 것은?

①　　　②　　　③　　　④　　　⑤

26 위 글의 내용에 맞게 빈칸에 알맞은 말을 쓰시오.

According to Yerim's group, they won't take their smartphones into the bedroom and won't _____ _____ _____

_____ .

[27~29] 다음 글을 읽고 물음에 답하시오.

①There would be some advantages and some disadvantages if there were no smartphones. First, let's talk about some (A)_____ . ②If we didn't have smartphones, we would play outside more often. ③Plus, we would be safe from neck pain. ④And it is convenient for us to find the place we don't know how to get to. On the other hand, there would be some (B)_____ . If there were no smartphones, it would not be easy for us to contact people. ⑤Also, it would take so long for us to find information.

27 빈칸 (A)와 (B)에 알맞은 말을 위 글에서 찾아 쓰시오.

➡ (A) _____ (B) _____

28 다음 중 위 글을 읽고 답할 수 있는 것은?

① For what was a smartphone invented?

② How can we use smartphones wisely?

③ What makes it easy for us to contact people?

④ How long does it take for people to find information with smartphones?

⑤ Why do people like to play outside?

29 ①~⑤ 중 글의 흐름상 어색한 문장은?

①　　　②　　　③　　　④　　　⑤

출제율 95%

01 다음 짝지어진 단어의 관계가 같도록 빈칸에 알맞은 말을 쓰시오. (주어진 철자로 시작할 것)

reduce – increase : destroy – c_____

출제율 90%

02 다음 영영풀이에 해당하는 단어는?

a warning to people to be prepared to deal with something dangerous

① device   ② half
③ alert   ④ pain
⑤ message

[03~04] 다음 대화를 읽고 물음에 답하시오.

G: David, let's watch this new movie on the computer.
B: On the computer?
G: Yes. (A)우리가 그것을 무료로 내려 받을 수 있는 웹 사이트가 있어. (I / free / we / have / it / can / a / website / from / for / download)
B: You're not supposed to download movies from that website, Catherine. It's against the law.
G: Really? I didn't know that.
B: Why don't we go to the movie theater, instead?
G: Okay. Let's go.

출제율 90%

03 위 대화의 밑줄 친 (A)의 우리말에 맞게 주어진 단어를 알맞은 순서로 배열하시오.

➡ _____

출제율 100%

04 위 대화의 내용과 일치하지 않는 것은?

① Catherine suggested that they should watch the new movie at the theater.

② David advised Catherine not to download the new movie.
③ Downloading movies from that website for free is against the law.
④ Catherine didn't know downloading movies from that website for free is against the law.
⑤ Catherine will go to the movie theater with David.

[05~06] 다음 대화를 읽고 물음에 답하시오.

G: You look tired, Peter.
B: (a)I played computer games until late, so last night I slept for more than four hours.
G: Playing computer games too much is not good for your health.
B: I know, Jenny, but I can't stop it. I think I'm addicted to it.
G: (A)_____
B: That's a good idea. Thanks.

출제율 100%

05 위 대화의 빈칸 (A)에 들어갈 말로 알맞은 것은?

① You're not supposed to use the same password for a long time.
② If I were you, I would set a daily plan to limit game time.
③ You're not supposed to talk to strangers online.
④ If I were you, I would not post bad comments online.
⑤ If I were you, I would respect copyright.

출제율 96%

06 위 대화의 밑줄 친 (a)에서 의미상 어색한 부분을 찾아 바르게 고치시오.

➡ _____

[07~08] 다음 대화를 읽고 물음에 답하시오.

Bora: Seho, look! Somebody (a)posted strange things on your SNS. I don't think you posted them.

Seho: Really? Who did this?

Bora: I think someone (b)figured out your password.

Seho: What should I do?

Bora: If I were you, I would (c)change my password.

Seho: I think I should.

Bora: Is your password (d)difficult to guess?

Seho: I used my birth date.

Bora: That is not good. In fact, it is a big mistake. You're not supposed to use your (A)_____ when you make a password.

Seho: Okay, I see. I will change it to a (e)stronger one.

✎ 출제율 95%

07 위 대화의 빈칸 (A)에 들어갈 말로 알맞은 것은?

① copyright　　　② bank account

③ complicated number　　④ past

⑤ personal information

✎ 출제율 100%

08 위 글의 흐름상 밑줄 (a)~(e) 중 어휘의 쓰임이 어색한 것은?

① (a)　② (b)　③ (c)　④ (d)　⑤ (e)

✎ 출제율 90%

09 대화의 밑줄 친 우리말에 맞게 주어진 단어를 활용하여 영어로 쓰시오.

W: Tony, you spend too much time on your smartphone.

B: My friends get together on SNS almost every day, so I can't help it, Mom.

W: 만약 내가 너라면, 친구들에게 야외 활동을 하자고 제안할 거야. (if / be / you / suggest / do / outdoor activities / to your friends)

B: Outdoor activities?

W: Yes. You can do a lot of great activities such as soccer or skating.

B: All right. I will suggest them today.

➡ _____
_____

[10~11] 다음 대화를 읽고 물음에 답하시오.

G: James, what are you doing?

B: I'm posting some of the pictures that I took with Sarah today.

G: Did you ask Sarah (a)if you could post them online?

B: No, but I think it's okay because she looks good in the pictures.

G: You're not supposed to post someone's pictures (A)_____ (ask).

B: Oh, maybe you're right. I'll call Sarah and ask her right away.

✎ 출제율 90%

10 위 대화의 흐름상 빈칸 (A)에 들어갈 말을 주어진 단어를 활용하여 쓰시오. (two words)

➡ _____

✎ 출제율 100%

11 밑줄 친 (a)와 같은 의미로 사용된 것은?

① If you see him, give him this note.

② He's a good driver, if he is a little over-confident.

③ Do you know if he's married?

④ I am sorry if I disturbed you.

⑤ If you sit down for a few moments, I'll tell the manager you're here.

12 다음 각 문장에 밑줄 친 It[it]이 어떤 용법으로 쓰였는지 〈보기〉에서 기호를 골라 괄호 안에 쓰시오.

출제율 95%

보기
ⓐ 가주어-진주어 구문의 It[it]
ⓑ It ~ that 강조 구문의 It[it]
ⓒ 비인칭 주어 It

(1) It is 20 kilometers from here to the hotel. (　)

(2) It was her birthday present that her father bought at the mall. (　)

(3) It is clever of the students to recycle the waste material. (　)

(4) It is for my family that I have worked so hard day and night. (　)

(5) It is not true that we will hold a graduation party. (　)

13 다음 중 어법상 올바른 문장은?

출제율 95%

① Her father would feel happy if she makes it to the finals.

② There were no smartphone, if they would be hard to communicate.

③ What would Kelly do if it rained on her wedding day?

④ If she were not so hungry, she will share her meal with me.

⑤ Paul will be really sad if you left him.

14 다음 중 어법상 올바른 문장은?

출제율 95%

① It was kind for Nelly to show him the way to the station.

② It is difficult for Yuna to skating on the ice.

③ It is necessary for those people inside the cave to get some fresh air.

④ It was dangerous of Cindy to jump out of a moving train.

⑤ It is impossible for he to mastering the Latin grammar in a week.

15 괄호 안의 조건과 가정법을 이용하여 다음 대화의 빈칸을 알맞게 채우시오.

출제율 90%

(1) A: Does Sophie know my phone number?
　B: No, but if she ＿＿＿＿＿＿＿＿＿, she ＿＿＿＿＿ you. (know, will, call 활용)

(2) A: Is William a police officer?
　B: No, but if he ＿＿＿＿＿＿＿＿＿, he ＿＿＿＿＿ the evidence. (be, will, find out 활용)

(3) A: Did Lucy see the accident?
　B: No, but if she ＿＿＿＿＿＿＿＿＿, she ＿＿＿＿＿ frightened. (see, will, be 활용)

(4) A: Didn't Alfredo join your club?
　B: Yes, but if he ＿＿＿＿＿＿＿＿＿, he ＿＿＿＿＿＿＿＿＿. (not, join, can, succeed 활용)

[16~18] 다음 글을 읽고 물음에 답하시오.

Hi, students! When you wake up in the morning, what is the first thing you do? Do you read SNS postings on your smartphone? Imagine your smartphone is not near you. How do you feel?
Students, please check items on the list that are true for you.
(A)＿＿＿＿＿＿＿＿＿＿＿＿＿＿＿
▢ Without my smartphone, I feel uncomfortable.
▢ I take my smartphone into the bathroom.

□ It is more enjoyable to spend time on my smartphone than with friends.

□ I often check SNS postings while studying.

□ I try to reduce the time I spend on my smartphone, but I fail.

□ I check my smartphone right after I hear the sound of an alert.

□ I have my smartphone next to me while I'm eating.

What is your (B)score? Did you check more than half? If so, you may have a problem with smartphone addiction.

출제율 95%

16 주어진 단어를 바르게 나열하여 빈칸 (A)에 들어갈 말을 쓰시오. 필요하다면 어형을 바꾸시오.

> (smartphone / are / your / addict / to / you)?

➡ _____

출제율 100%

17 다음 중 위 항목에 해당하는 사항이 <u>아닌</u> 것은?

① to feel uncomfortable without smartphones

② to spend more time with smartphones rather than with friends

③ to bring one's smartphone anywhere he or she goes

④ to fail to decrease the time to be spent on smartphones

⑤ to turn off all the alerts in order to focus on his or her study

출제율 90%

18 다음 중 밑줄 친 (B)와 쓰임이 같은 것을 <u>모두</u> 고르시오.

① This is an orchestral <u>score</u>.

② You have to <u>score</u> the test.

③ I got a perfect <u>score</u> on the test.

④ She thought the film <u>score</u> was beautiful.

⑤ The player wanted to <u>score</u> a goal.

[19~21] 다음 글을 읽고 물음에 답하시오.

Smartphone addiction causes you to spend too much time on your smartphone. ① Also, you cannot focus on your studies and may have a pain in your neck. ② Digital detox means staying away from digital devices, such as smartphones and computers, for a while. ③ Digital detox will help you a lot. You can enjoy freedom from the noisy digital world. ④ You can focus more on your work. Sometimes you can feel refreshed and have new, creative ideas. Digital detox will also help you spend more time with others. ⑤

출제율 100%

19 ①~⑤ 중 다음 문장이 들어가기에 가장 적절한 곳은?

> Then now is the time for you to start digital detox.

①   ②   ③   ④   ⑤

출제율 100%

20 Which is TRUE about digital detox?

① It doesn't make students focus on their studies.

② It makes students feel comfortable with their necks.

③ It results in smartphone addiction.

④ It makes students be familiar with their smartphones.

⑤ It makes students free from the digital world.

출제율 90%

21 According to the passage, what makes you have a pain in your neck? Answer in English with a full sentence.

➡ _____

_____

01 다음 대화를 읽고 질문에 대한 대답을 완성하시오.

G: David, let's watch this new movie on the computer.

B: On the computer?

G: Yes. I have a website we can download it from for free.

B: You're not supposed to download movies from that website, Catherine. It's against the law.

G: Really? I didn't know that.

B: Why don't we go to the movie theater, instead?

G: Okay. Let's go.

Q: Why shouldn't Catherine download movies from the website for free?

➡ Because _____ .

02 다음 대화를 읽고 아래 요약문의 빈칸을 완성하시오.

W: Tony, you spend too much time on your smartphone.

B: My friends get together on SNS almost every day, so I can't help it, Mom.

W: If I were you, I would suggest doing outdoor activities to your friends.

B: Outdoor activities?

W: Yes. You can do a lot of great activities such as soccer or skating.

B: All right. I will suggest them today.

➡ My son, Tony, _____ too much time on his _____ . He and his friends _____ _____ on _____ almost every day. I told him _____ _____ doing _____ with his friends.

03 다음 대화의 밑줄 친 (A)와 같은 의미가 되도록 주어진 단어를 사용하여 영작하시오.

G: James, what are you doing?

B: I'm posting some of the pictures that I took with Sarah today.

G: Did you ask Sarah if you could post them online?

B: No, but I think it's okay because she looks good in the pictures.

G: (A)You must not post someone's pictures without asking.

B: Oh, maybe you're right. I'll call Sarah and ask her right away.

➡ _____

_____ (supposed)

04 다음 사진을 보고, 주어진 어구를 알맞게 배열하여 대화를 완성하시오.

Liz: Olly, have you had a good trip to Busan?

Olly: I'm sorry to tell you that I wasn't able to go there.

Liz: Why? You wanted to see the fireworks festival there, right?

Olly: Yeah. If _____

_____ .

(in Busan, I, seen, have, been, I, the fireworks festival, had, could)

05 다음 우리말과 같은 뜻이 되도록 주어진 단어들을 활용하여, 글자 수에 맞게 영작하시오. (필요한 단어 보충 및 동사 형태 변화 가능)

> (Sally, you, really, too, for, of, boring, careless, stay home, reach out, on, to, a big dog, a sunny day)

(1) Sally는 맑은 날 집안에만 있는 것이 너무 지루했다. (과거시제, 13 단어)

➡ _____

_____

(2) 당신이 커다란 개에게 손을 내미는 것은 정말 부주의하다. (현재시제, 13 단어)

➡ _____

[06~10] 다음 글을 읽고 물음에 답하시오.

(A)_____ without a smartphone, however, is not easy. So, it is necessary for you (B)_____ some rules for using your smartphone. You then need (C)_____ the rules. Now, please form groups and, in your group, create rules for using your smartphone.

By Yerim, Yongmin, and Hojin

We will turn off our smartphones while studying. We will not take our smartphones into the bathroom.

(D)We will keep our smartphones out of the bedroom and use them at night.

By Jina, Hosung, and Minsu

• More Time for Outside Activities – We will spend more time playing outside without our smartphones.

• Fewer SNS Messages – We will post fewer SNS messages on our smartphones.

By Jiho, Sohee, and Yumin

If I were you, I would reduce my time on my smartphone by half.

(E)내가 너라면, 나는 모든 알림을 끌 거야.

You did a good job, students! If we had no smartphones, our lives would be more difficult, but too much use of a smartphone is dangerous. With digital detox, you can become a wise smartphone user.

06 주어진 단어를 내용과 어법에 맞게 빈칸 (A)~(C)에 쓰시오.

> (follow / set / live)

➡ (A)_____ (B)_____ (C)_____

07 글의 흐름에 맞게 밑줄 친 (D)를 올바른 문장으로 고쳐 쓰시오.

➡ _____

_____

08 주어진 어구를 활용하여 밑줄 친 우리말 (E)를 영어로 쓰시오.

> (be / turn / all alerts / if)

➡ _____

09 According to the passage, what is dangerous? Answer in English with a full sentence.

➡ _____

10 What are Jina, Hosung, and Minsu going to do? Use the phrase 'be going to.'

➡ _____

_____

01 온라인에서 해서는 안 되는 일에 대해, 〈보기〉의 문장처럼 불허를 표현하는 대화를 만드시오.

> • post bad comments online
> • talk to strangers online
> • use the same password for a long time

보기

A: Do you talk to strangers online?
B: Yes.
A: You're not supposed to talk to strangers online.

(1) A: _____
    B: _____
    A: _____

(2) A: _____
    B: _____
    A: _____

02 텔레비전이 없을 때의 장점과 단점을 참고하여 다음 글의 빈칸에 알맞은 말을 쓰시오.

> <advantages>
> 1. We will spend more time with our family.
> 2. We will be healthier because we will have more time to exercise.
> <disadvantages>
> 1. It will not be easy for us to watch movies.
> 2. It will be more difficult for us to check the news.

If There Were No _____
There would be some advantages and some disadvantages if there were no _____.
First, let's talk about some advantages. If we didn't have televisions, _____
_____. Plus, _____ because we would have more time to
exercise. On the other hand, there would be some disadvantages. If there were no
televisions, _____. Also, _____
_____.

단원별 모의고사

01 다음 단어에 대한 영어 설명이 <u>어색한</u> 것은?

① copyright: a right to sell a book, music, film, etc.

② comment: something that you say about someone or something

③ half: one of two equal parts of something

④ create: to plan to do something or to have an action planned in your mind

⑤ be addicted to: to be physically and mentally dependent on an particular substance

02 다음 짝지어진 단어의 관계가 같도록 빈칸에 알맞은 말을 쓰시오.

safe – dangerous : advantage – _____

03 다음 영영풀이에 해당하는 단어를 고르시오.

a mechanical object that is made for a particular purpose

① password   ② detox

③ device   ④ addiction

⑤ material

04 다음 중 짝지어진 대화가 <u>어색한</u> 것은?

① A: What should I do to be a digital citizen?

    B: You should protect your private information.

② A: I was wondering if we could get a pet.

    B: You'd better talk to your dad about it.

③ A: I talked to strangers online yesterday.

    B: I think you must not talk to strangers online.

④ A: Can I bring my dog here with me?

    B: You're not supposed to bring your dog here.

⑤ A: Do you use the same password for a long time?

    B: You should not use your personal information.

[05~06] 다음 대화를 읽고 물음에 답하시오.

G: James, what are you doing?

B: I'm posting some of the pictures that I took with Sarah today.

G: (A)_____

B: No, but I think it's okay because she looks good in the pictures.

G: (B)You're not supposed to post someone's pictures without asking.

B: Oh, maybe you're right. I'll call Sarah and ask her right away.

05 위 대화의 빈칸 (A)에 들어갈 말로 알맞은 것은?

① Are you interested in taking pictures?

② Did Sarah like your pictures?

③ Have you ever received text messages from strangers?

④ Did you ask Sarah if you could post them online?

⑤ Did you change your password every month?

06 위 대화의 밑줄 친 (B)와 같은 의미가 되도록 'If I were you' 를 이용하여 충고의 표현을 쓰시오.

➡ If I were you, _____

_____.

[07~08] 다음 대화를 읽고 물음에 답하시오.

Bora: Seho, look! Somebody posted strange things on your SNS. I don't think you posted (a)them. (①)

Seho: Really? Who did this?

Bora: I think someone figured out your password. (②)

Seho: What should I do?

Bora: If I (b)am you, I would change my password.

Seho: I think I should. (③)

Bora: Is your password (c)easy to guess?

Seho: I used my birth date.

Bora: That is not good. (④) You're not supposed (d)to use your personal information when you make a password.

Seho: Okay, I see. (⑤) I will change it to a stronger (e)one.

07 위 대화의 밑줄 친 (a)~(e) 중 어법상 어색한 것은?

① (a) ② (b) ③ (c) ④ (d) ⑤ (e)

08 위 대화의 (①)~(⑤) 중 주어진 문장이 들어갈 위치로 알맞은 것은?

In fact, it is a big mistake.

①   ②   ③   ④   ⑤

09 다음 대화의 빈칸 (A)에 들어갈 말로 알맞은 것은?

G: David, let's watch this new movie on the computer.

B: On the computer?

G: Yes. I have a website we can download it from for free.

B: You're not supposed to download movies from that website, Catherine. It's against the law.

G: Really? I didn't know that.

B: Why don't we go to the movie theater, (A)_____?

G: Okay. Let's go.

① instead   ② however
③ though   ④ therefore
⑤ moreover

10 다음 대화의 빈칸에 들어갈 알맞은 단어를 쓰시오.

G: You look tired, Peter.

B: I played computer games until late, so last night I slept for less than four hours.

G: Playing computer games too much is not good for your health.

B: I know, Jenny, but I can't stop it. I think I'm _____ to it.

G: If I were you, I would set a daily plan to limit game time.

B: That's a good idea. Thanks.

[11~12] 다음 대화를 읽고 물음에 답하시오.

B: What are you doing, Sohee?

G: I'm writing a posting about the restaurant I visited today.

B: Those are great pictures. Did you (a)take all of them?

G: No. I (b)took the pictures from someone's blog.

B: Then (A)너는 그것들을 네 블로그에 게시하면 안 돼 (post / you're / your / not / them / to / supposed / on / blog)

G: Why not?

B: Because only the blog owner has the right to use them.

G: Oh, I see.

11 위 대화의 (A)의 우리말에 맞게 주어진 단어를 알맞은 순서로 배열하시오.

➡ _____

12 위 대화의 밑줄 친 (a)와 (b)의 뜻을 각각 쓰시오.

➡ (a)_____ (b)_____

13 다음 중 밑줄 친 부분의 쓰임이 다른 것은?

① I'd go out to see the movie if it stopped raining.

② I had no idea if the rumor would turn out true.

③ If Angella studied harder, she would get a scholarship.

④ If he were a flim director, he could get me in one of his movies.

⑤ She could call her supervisor anytime if she needed help in doing research.

14 다음 문장을 〈보기〉와 같이 바꿔 쓰시오.

┤ 보기 ├
To find the living things on Mars is impossible. (we)
➡ It is impossible for us to find the living things on Mars.

(1) To build the castle in a month was not possible. (the villagers)

➡ _____
_____

(2) Not to show respect for the old man is rude. (Thomas)

➡ _____

(3) Taking drugs on an airplane is impossible. (the Chinese girl)

➡ _____
_____

15 다음 표를 보고 we를 의미상의 주어로 하여, 찬반의 빈칸에 알맞게 쓰시오.

OK	Not OK
easy to spend more time with our family	not easy to watch shows and dramas
possible to have more time to exercise	difficult to check the news

(1) It's OK.

If there were no televisions,

it _____
_____.

it _____
_____.

(2) It's not OK.

If there were no televisions,

it _____
_____.

it _____.

16 다음 중 〈보기〉 문장의 밑줄 친 <u>would</u>와 쓰임이 같은 것은?

┌─ 보기 ─┐

Brian <u>would</u> attend the meeting if his professor recommended him to.

① I <u>would</u> like to be a superhero.
② I <u>would</u> not choose that car if I were you.
③ Samantha's family <u>would</u> go on a picnic to the lake park when she was young.
④ Ariel said that she <u>would</u> visit the land of human beings beyond the sea.
⑤ <u>Would</u> you do me a favor?

17 다음 주어진 〈보기〉의 문장과 같은 뜻이 되도록 빈칸에 알맞은 말을 쓰시오.

┌─ 보기 ─┐

If Susie were not poor, she could go abroad to study arts.

➡ As Susie _____ poor, she _____ go abroad to study arts.

[18~22] 다음 글을 읽고 물음에 답하시오.

Smartphone addiction causes you to spend too much time on your smartphone. Also, you cannot focus on your studies and may have a pain in your neck. ⓐ그렇다면 지금 여러분은 디지털 디톡스를 시작할 시간입니다. ① Digital detox means staying away from digital devices, such as smartphones and computers, for a while. ② Digital detox will help you a lot. You can enjoy freedom from the noisy digital world. You can focus more on your work. Sometimes you can feel refreshed and have new, creative ideas. ③ Digital detox will also help you spend more time with others.

Living without a smartphone, however, is not easy. ④ So, it is necessary (A)_____ you to set some rules for using your smartphone. ⑤ Now, please form groups and, in your group, create rules for using your smartphone.

18 다음 중 빈칸 (A)에 들어갈 말과 <u>다른</u> 말이 들어가는 것은?

① It is important _____ her to get the message.
② It is dangerous _____ him to cross the road alone.
③ It is hard _____ you to do the job all by yourself.
④ It is possible _____ them to read the book out loud.
⑤ It is polite _____ her to say such nice words.

19 ①~⑤ 중 다음 문장이 들어가기에 가장 적절한 곳은?

You then need to follow the rules.

①   ②   ③   ④   ⑤

20 주어진 단어를 활용하여 밑줄 친 우리말 ⓐ를 영어로 쓰시오.

(then / now / the time / you / start)

➡ _____

21 다음 중 디지털 디톡스의 효과에 해당하지 <u>않는</u> 것은?

① to enjoy freedom from noisy digital world

② to feel refreshed

③ to come up with creative ideas

④ to spend more time all alone

⑤ to focus more on your work

22 다음 중 위 글을 읽고 답할 수 있는 것은?

① How painful is the neck pain?

② How long does it take to do digital detox successfully?

③ How noisy is the digital world?

④ How many rules are there for using smartphones?

⑤ What problems does smarthpone addiction cause?

23 자연스러운 글이 되도록 (A)~(C)를 바르게 나열하시오.

There would be some advantages and some disadvantages if there were no smartphones. First, let's talk about some advantages.

(A) If there were no smartphones, it would not be easy for us to contact people. Also, it would take so long for us to find information.

(B) Plus, we would be safe from neck pain. On the other hand, there would be some disadvantages.

(C) If we didn't have smartphones, we would play outside more often.

➡ _____

[24~25] 다음 글을 읽고 물음에 답하시오.

By Yerim, Yongmin, and Hojin

We will turn off our smartphones while studying.

We will not take our smartphones into the bathroom.

We will keep our smartphones out of the bedroom and not use them at night.

By Jina, Hosung, and Minsu

• More Time for Outside Activities – We will spend more time playing outside without our smartphones.

• Fewer SNS Messages – We will post fewer SNS messages on our smartphones.

By Jiho, Sohee, and Yumin

If I were you, I would reduce my time on my smartphone by half.

If I were you, I would turn off all alerts.

24 주어진 어구를 바르게 나열하여 위 글의 제목을 쓰시오.

(digital detox / the rules / can / what / be / of)

➡ _____

25 다음 중 글의 내용과 일치하지 <u>않는</u> 것은?

① Yongmin won't take his smartphone into the bathroom.

② Jina will have more time for outside activities.

③ Jiho will reduce her time on her smartphone by half.

④ Yumin will post fewer SNS messages on her smartphone.

⑤ Hojin will not use his smartphone at night.

MEMO

Lesson 5

Love for My Country

🎙 의사소통 기능

- 알고 있는지 묻기
  You know about Yun Dongju, don't you?
- 희망 · 기대 표현하기
  I'm looking forward to the visit.

🎙 언어 형식

- '과거완료' had + 과거분사
  I was hungry because I **had not eaten** breakfast.
- '목적'을 나타내는 so that 구문
  I waved at my sister **so that** she could find me.

Words & Expressions

Key Words

- **amusement park** 놀이동산
- **burial** [bériəl] 명 매장, 장례식
- **bury** [béri] 동 묻다, 매장하다
- **circle** [sə́:rkl] 명 원
- **clearly** [klíərli] 부 분명하게
- **complete** [kəmplí:t] 동 끝내다 형 완전한
- **corner** [kɔ́:rnər] 명 구석, 모퉁이
- **crown** [kraun] 명 왕관
- **deep** [di:p] 형 깊은
- **desire** [dizáiər] 명 바람, 갈망
- **direct** [dirékt] 동 감독하다, 지휘[총괄]하다
- **during** [djúəriŋ] 전 ~ 동안
- **educate** [édʒukèit] 동 교육시키다
- **entrance** [éntrəns] 명 입구
- **exhibition** [èksəbíʃən] 명 전시회
- **feed** [fi:d] 동 먹이를 주다, 먹이다
- **flag** [flæg] 명 깃발
- **foggy** [fɔ́:gi] 형 안개 낀
- **general** [dʒénərəl] 명 장군 형 일반적인
- **god** [gɑd] 명 신
- **government** [gʌ́vərmmənt] 명 정부
- **hall** [hɔ:l] 명 홀, 현관
- **Hallyu** 명 한류, 한국 문화 열풍
- **harmony** [hɑ́:rməni] 명 조화
- **independence** [ìndipéndəns] 명 독립
- **Japanese** [dʒæpəní:z] 명 일본인, 일본어 형 일본의
- **kill** [kil] 동 죽이다
- **leader** [lí:dər] 명 지도자, 리더
- **main** [mein] 형 주된, 주요한
- **mean** [mi:n] 동 의미하다
- **member** [mémbər] 명 구성원, 회원
- **mission** [míʃən] 명 임무
- **model** [mɑ́dl] 명 모형
- **movement** [mú:vmənt] 명 (정치적, 사회적) 운동
- **museum** [mju:zí:əm] 명 박물관
- **organization** [ɔ̀rgənizéiʃən] 명 조직, 기구
- **palace** [pǽlis] 명 궁전
- **patriotic** [pèitriɑ́tik] 형 애국적인
- **peace** [pi:s] 명 평화
- **poem** [póuəm] 명 시
- **president** [prézədənt] 명 대통령, 의장, 회장
- **process** [prɑ́ses] 명 과정
- **protect** [prətékt] 동 보호하다
- **republic** [ripʌ́blik] 명 공화국
- **respect** [rispékt] 명 존경, 경의
- **rule** [ru:l] 명 통치, 지배
- **sacrifice** [sǽkrəfàis] 명 희생 동 희생하다
- **secret** [sí:krit] 명 비밀 형 비밀의
- **specialist** [spéʃəlist] 명 전문가
- **spread** [spred] 동 퍼지다, 퍼뜨리다
- **statue** [stǽtʃu:] 명 조각상
- **teen** [ti:n] 명 십대
- **throughout** [θru:áut] 전 ~의 도처에, ~ 내내
- **tomb** [tu:m] 명 묘, 무덤
- **treasure** [tréʒər] 명 보물
- **volunteer work** 자원봉사 활동
- **water** [wɔ́:tər] 동 (화초 등에) 물을 주다
- **war** [wɔ:r] 명 전쟁, 싸움
- **wish** [wiʃ] 명 소원, 바람
- **zip code** 우편 번호

Key Expressions

- **be in need** ~가 필요하다
- **belong to** ~에 속하다
- **carry out** ~을 수행하다
- **hear of** ~에 관해 듣다
- **look forward to+명사/동명사** ~을 기대하다
- **look like+명사** ~처럼 보이다
- **put on** ~을 입다
- **so that+주어+동사** ~하기 위해서

Word Power

※ 서로 비슷한 뜻을 가진 어휘

- □ **desire** : **wish** (바람, 소원)
- □ **bury** : **inter** (매장하다, 묻다)
- □ **protect** : **defend** (보호하다)
- □ **statue** : **figure** (조각상)

- □ **harmony** : **accord** (조화)
- □ **rule** : **reign** (통치)
- □ **specialist** : **expert** (전문가)
- □ **educate** : **teach** (교육하다, 가르치다)

※ 서로 반대되는 뜻을 가진 어휘

- □ **dependence** (의존) ↔ **independence** (독립)
- □ **complete** (완전한) ↔ **incomplete** (불완전한)

- □ **entrance** (입구) ↔ **exit** (출구)
- □ **deep** (깊은) ↔ **shallow** (얕은)

English Dictionary

□ **amusement park** 놀이공원
→ a large outdoor area with fairground rides, shows, and other entertainments
박람회장 놀이기구, 쇼, 그리고 다른 오락거리가 있는 넓은 야외 공간

□ **burial** 매장, 장례식
→ the act of putting a dead body into the ground, or the ceremony connected with this
사체를 땅에 묻는 행위, 또는 이와 관련된 의식

□ **bury** 묻다
→ to place a dead body in the ground, or to put something in the ground and cover it
사체를 땅에 묻거나 어떤 것을 땅에 묻고 그것을 덮다

□ **carry out** 수행하다
→ to do or complete something, especially that you have said you would do or that you have been told
특히 당신이 하겠다고 말해 왔거나 들어 온 일을 하거나 끝내다

□ **crown** 왕관
→ a circular ornament made of gold and decorated head with jewels that is worn by a king or queen on their head
왕이나 여왕이 머리에 쓰는 금으로 만들어지고 보석으로 장식된 원형 장식물

□ **exhibition** 전시회
→ a public display of art works, pictures or other interesting things
예술 작품, 그림 또는 기타 흥미로운 것들의 공개 전시

□ **flag** 깃발
→ a piece of cloth that is usually attached at the end of a pole and represents a country or association
보통 기둥 끝에 붙어 있고 국가나 협회를 대표하는 천 조각

□ **look forward to** 기대하다
→ to feel pleased and excited about something that is going to happen
앞으로 일어날 일에 대해 기쁘고 흥분하다

□ **mission** 임무
→ any work that someone believes it is their duty to do
누군가가 자신이 할 의무라고 믿는 일

□ **organization** 조직
→ a group of people working together for a purpose of being organized
조직화될 목적으로 함께 일하는 사람들의 집단

□ **palace** 궁전
→ a large house that is the official home of a king and queen
왕과 왕비의 공식적인 주택인 큰 집

□ **poem** 시
→ a piece of writing that uses beautiful words that imply deep meanings and sounds rhythmical when you read
깊은 의미를 암시하고 읽을 때 리드미컬하게 들리는 아름다운 단어를 사용하는 한 편의 글

□ **process** 과정
→ a series of things that happen one after another for a particular result
특정한 결과를 위해 차례로 일어나는 일련의 일들

□ **republic** 공화국
→ a country governed by elected representatives
선출직 대표들에 의해 통치되는 나라

□ **sacrifice** 희생
→ giving up something valuable for a specific purpose
특정한 목적을 위해 귀중한 어떤 것을 포기하는 것

□ **statue** 조각상
→ a sculptured figure of a person, animal, etc. in bronze, stone, wood, etc.
청동, 돌, 나무 등에 조각된 사람이나 동물 등의 형상

□ **tomb** 무덤
→ a large stone structure or underground room where someone, especially an important person, is buried
누군가, 특히 중요한 사람이 묻혀 있는 큰 돌 구조물이나 지하 공간

□ **treasure** 보물
→ what is highly valued
매우 귀중한 것

01 다음 문장의 빈칸에 들어갈 말로 가장 알맞은 것은?

> Churchill's _____ stands outside the parliament building.

① exhibition   ② entrance
③ statue   ④ poem
⑤ specialist

서답형
02 빈칸에 주어진 〈영영풀이〉에 해당하는 단어를 쓰시오.

> Nigeria gained _____ from Britain in 1960.

┤영영풀이├
> freedom from being governed or ruled by another country

서답형
03 다음 우리말에 맞게 빈칸에 세 단어를 쓰시오.

> 너한테 멋진 생일 선물 받기를 기대할게!

➡ I will _____ _____ _____ receiving a nice birthday present from you!

[04~05] 다음 설명에 해당하는 단어를 고르시오.

04

> a public display of art works, pictures or other interesting things

① flag   ② exhibition
③ comment   ④ mission
⑤ treasure

05

> a large stone structure or underground room where someone, especially an important person, is buried

① palace   ② statue
③ burial   ④ crown
⑤ tomb

06 다음 빈칸에 들어갈 말로 가장 알맞은 것끼리 짝지어진 것은?

> (A) Fire quickly _____ throughout the building.
> (B) Voting is part of your _____ duty.

	(A)	(B)
①	sacrifice	patriotic
②	water	general
③	spread	patriotic
④	feed	creative
⑤	spread	secret

서답형
07 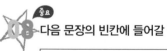 다음 짝지어진 단어의 관계가 같도록 빈칸에 알맞은 말을 쓰시오.

> desire – wish : expert – _____

08 다음 문장의 빈칸에 들어갈 말은?

> I want to let many people know that Dokdo _____ Korea.

① puts on   ② carries on
③ consists of   ④ belongs to
⑤ turns down

224   Lesson 5. Love for My Country

01 다음 빈칸에 들어갈 말을 〈보기〉에서 찾아 쓰시오.

> ┤ 보기 ├
>
> kill   movement   harmony   poem

(1) Many religious leaders work hard to bring peace and _____ to the world.

(2) She was a renowned scientist and pioneer of the global environmental _____.

(3) Lack of rain could _____ the crops.

(4) Her _____s tell us to be strong and live bravely.

02 다음 글은 빈칸에 들어갈 단어에 대한 설명이다. 알맞은 단어를 쓰시오.

> A _____ is a country where power is held by the people or the representatives that they elect.

03 다음 우리말과 같은 표현이 되도록 문장의 빈칸을 채우시오.

(1) 그녀는 병원 정문 근처에 주차 공간을 발견했다.
➡ She found a parking space close to the hospital's main _____.

(2) 만델라는 대통령이 되었을 때 이미 70대였다.
➡ Mandela was already in his seventies when he became _____.

(3) 영국 정부는 원조를 보내겠다고 제안했다.
➡ The UK _____ has offered to send aid.

(4) 나는 여행 갔을 때 많은 일본 음식을 먹었다.
➡ I ate a lot of _____ food when I went on my trip.

04 영영풀이에 해당하는 단어를 〈보기〉에서 찾아 첫 번째 빈칸에 쓰고, 두 번째 빈칸에는 우리말 뜻을 쓰시오.

> ┤ 보기 ├
>
> poem   organization   sacrifice   amusement park

(1) _____: a large outdoor area with fairground rides, shows, and other entertainments: _____

(2) _____: a group of people working together for a purpose of being organized: _____

(3) _____: a piece of writing that uses beautiful words that imply deep meanings and sounds rhythmical when you read: _____

(4) _____: giving up something valuable for a specific purpose: _____

05 다음 빈칸에 공통으로 들어갈 단어를 쓰시오.

> • Some people think physical education and art classes are a _____ waste of time.
> • Sometimes he spends 20 hours to _____ just one piece of artwork.

Conversation

① 알고 있는지 묻기

> ### You know about Yun Dongju, don't you?
> 너는 윤동주에 대해 알고 있지, 그렇지 않니?

■ 'You know ~, don't you?'는 알고 있는지 물어보는 표현이다.
또한 'Do you know about ~? / Did you know that ~? / Are you aware of ~? / Are you aware that ~?' 등을 이용하여 알고 있는지 물을 수 있다.

무언가에 대해 들어서 알고 있는지 물을 때는 'Did you hear about ~?'(너는 ~에 대해 들었니?)라고 말한다. 현재완료를 사용해 'Have you heard about ~?'이라고 들어 본 적이 있는지 물을 수도 있다.

■ 알고 있는지 물어보는 다양한 표현들
- **A:** You know Samgyetang, don't you? 너는 삼계탕을 알고 있지, 그렇지 않니?
 B: Yes, it's a Korean food. People eat it for their health.
  그래, 그것은 한국 음식이야. 사람들은 건강을 위해 삼계탕을 먹어.

- **A:** Have you heard that Ms. Lee is coming to our school? 이 선생님이 우리 학교에 오신다는 것 들었어?
 B: No, I haven't. 아니, 못 들었어.

- Do you know (that) ice cream is from China? 아이스크림이 중국에서 유래했다는 것을 아니?
- Have you heard about the project? 그 프로젝트에 관해 들어봤니?
- Are you aware that gold medals are made mostly of silver? 금메달이 주로 은으로 만들어진다는 것을 아니?
- Did you hear about the accident? 그 사고에 대해 들었니?

핵심 Check

1. 다음 대화의 밑줄 친 문장과 바꾸어 쓸 수 있는 것을 <u>모두</u> 고르시오.

 A: <u>You know about Yun Dongju, don't you?</u>
 B: Sure.

 ① Do you know about Yun Dongju?
 ② I'm sure I know about Yun Dongju.
 ③ Did you hear from Yun Dongju?
 ④ Have you ever heard about Yun Dongju?
 ⑤ Why don't we know about Yun Dongju?

2 희망 · 기대 표현하기

I'm looking forward to the visit.
나는 그 방문을 기대하고 있어.

■ 앞으로 하고 싶은 일에 대한 기대를 표현할 때 'I'm looking forward to ~.'나 'I look forward to ~.'의 표현을 사용한다. 여기서 to는 전치사이므로 뒤에 명사나 동명사가 와야 한다.
- I'm looking forward to traveling to Korea.
- I look forward to my birthday party this weekend.
- **G:** Yubin, I hear you're taking a family trip to Thailand this winter.
  유빈아, 너 이번 겨울에 태국으로 가족 여행을 간다고 들었어.

  B: Yes. I'm looking forward to riding an elephant. 응. 코끼리를 타 보기를 기대하고 있어.
■ 'I can't wait to ~'는 원하던 일이 다가오고 있어 빨리하고 싶은 기대감을 나타내는 표현이며, 직역의 의미대로 '~하는 것을 기다릴 수 없다' 또는 '당장 ~하고 싶다, 빨리 ~했으면 좋겠다' 정도로 해석한다. to 뒤에는 동사원형의 형태가 오는데, 뒤에 명사구가 올 경우에는 'I can't wait for+명사(명사구)'의 형태로 쓰기도 한다.
- I can't wait for my graduation. 내 졸업이 기대된다.

기대를 나타내는 다른 표현들

- I am expecting to 동사원형 ~.
- I am longing to 동사원형 ~.
- I am eager to 동사원형 ~.
- I'm dying to 동사원형 ~.

핵심 Check

2. 다음 대화의 빈칸에 들어갈 말로 <u>어색한</u> 것은?

   A: Do you want to watch *Harry Potter* with me this weekend?
   B: Sure, I'd love to. _____

   ① I can't wait to watch it.
   ② I am longing to watch it.
   ③ I'm dying to watching it.
   ④ I'm looking forward to watching it.
   ⑤ I am eager to watch it.

Listen & Speak 1 A-1

B: Look at Suwon Hawseong. It's huge.

G: It also ❶looks strong.

B: Because ❷it was built to protect the people ❸during wars.

G: Wow. ❹Do you know who built it?

B: Yes. King Jeongjo ❺ordered Jeong Yakyong to direct the building process. ❻You know about Jeong Yakyong, don't you?

G: Yes, I've heard of him. He was a great scientist in Joseon.

B: 수원 화성을 봐. 그것은 거대해.
G: 그것은 또한 튼튼해 보여.
B: 왜냐하면 그것은 전쟁 중에 사람들을 보호하기 위해 지어졌기 때문이야.
G: 우와. 너는 누가 그것을 지었는지 아니?
B: 응. 정조가 정약용에게 건설 과정을 감독할 것을 지시했어. 너는 정약용에 대해 알고 있지, 그렇지 않니?
G: 응. 그에 대해 들어봤어. 그는 조선의 훌륭한 과학자였어.

❶ 'look+형용사'로 '~하게 보이다'라는 뜻이다.
❷ it은 'Suwon Hawseong'을 가리키고, '지어졌다'는 수동태(was built)를 사용한다.
❸ 'during'은 '~ 동안'의 의미로 '특정한 기간'과 함께 사용된다. 반면 'for'는 '숫자로 된 기간'과 함께 사용된다.
❹ 동사 'know'의 목적어 자리에 사용된 간접의문문으로 '의문사 주어(who)+동사(built)' 어순을 취한다.
❺ 'order+목적어+목적보어(to부정사)'로 '~에게 …하라고 명령[지시]하다'로 해석하는 5형식 문장이다.
❻ You know ~, don't you?는 알고 있는지 물어보는 표현이다.

Check(√) True or False

(1) Suwon Hawseong was built to protect the people during wars.   T ☐ F ☐

(2) The girl has heard of King Jeongjo.   T ☐ F ☐

Listen & Speak 2 A-1

G: ❶I'm planning to go to the Gansong Museum.

B: What is the Gansong Museum?

G: It's a museum ❷built by Gansong Jeon Hyeongpil.

B: I heard that he did great things for the country.

G: Yes. He bought many Korean treasures ❸that some Japanese had taken to Japan.

B: Wow. The museum ❹must be interesting.

G: Yes. ❺I'm looking forward to it!

G: 나는 간송 미술관에 갈 예정이야.
B: 간송 미술관이 뭐야?
G: 간송 전형필에 의해 지어진 미술관이야.
B: 나는 그가 나라를 위해 훌륭한 일들을 했다고 들어어.
G: 응. 그는 몇몇 일본사람들이 일본으로 가져갔었던 한국의 많은 문화재들을 샀어.
B: 우와. 그 미술관은 틀림없이 흥미로울 거야.
G: 응. 나는 그곳을 기대하고 있어!

❶ 'be planning to+동사원형'은 앞으로 할 일에 대한 계획을 나타낼 때 사용하는 표현으로 '~할 예정이다'라는 뜻이다.
❷ 명사 a museum을 수식하는 과거분사로 '지어진'의 의미다.
❸ 목적격 관계대명사절로 선행사 'many Korean treasures'를 수식하는 역할을 한다.
❹ 추측의 조동사로 '~임에 틀림없다'라는 뜻이다.
❺ 앞으로 하고 싶은 일에 대한 기대를 표현할 때 사용하는 표현으로 'to'는 전치사이기 때문에 뒤에 '명사나 동명사'를 사용한다.

Check(√) True or False

(3) The Gansong Museum was built by Jeon Hyeongpil.   T ☐ F ☐

(4) Gansong sold Korean treasures to other countries.   T ☐ F ☐

Listen & Speak 1 A-2

G: Brian, you know Taegeukgi, ❶don't you?

B: Sure. It's the national flag of Korea, ❷isn't it?

G: That's right. Do you know ❸what the symbols in Taegeukgi mean?

B: No, I don't. Tell me about ❹them.

G: The circle in the middle means harmony and peace.

B: What do the black lines on the four corners mean?

G: They mean four things: sky, fire, water, and earth.

❶ 부가의문문으로 상대방이 알고 있는지 물어보는 표현이다.
❷ be동사의 부가의문문이다.
❸ know의 목적어 자리에 사용된 간접의문문으로 '의문사(what)+주어(the symbols)+동사(mean)' 어순이다.
❹ 앞 문장의 'the symbols in Taegeukgi'를 나타낸다.

 Real Life Talk

Andy: Bora, what are you reading?

Bora: I'm reading *Sky*, *Wind*, *Star*, *and Poetry* by Yun Dongju. ❶You know about Yun Dongju, don't you?

Andy: I've heard his name, but I don't know much about him.

Bora: He wrote many beautiful poems ❷when Korea was under Japanese rule. ❸His love for the country and his desire for independence can be felt in his poems.

Andy: Really? I didn't know that. I want ❹to read his poems and learn more about him.

Bora: Great. In fact, ❺I'm planning to visit the Yun Dongju Museum soon. Do you want to come with me?

Andy: Yes, when are you going?

Bora: Next Saturday. It's near Gyeongbok Palace. Can you meet me at the palace at 2 p.m.?

Andy: Sure. Let's meet there.

Bora: Great. ❻I'm really looking forward to the visit.

❶ 'You know ~, don't you?'는 알고 있는지 물어보는 표현이다.
❷ 시간의 부사절 접속사로 '~할 때'로 해석한다.
❸ 문장의 주어는 'His love'와 'his desire'이다. 'can be felt'는 조동사가 있는 수동태로 '느껴질 수 있다'로 해석한다.
❹ want의 목적어로 'to read'와 '(to) learn'이 병렬구조로 연결되어 있다.
❺ '~할 계획이다'라는 의미로 미래의 일에 대한 계획을 말하는 표현이다.
❻ 기대를 나타내는 표현으로 'look forward to+명사/동명사'를 사용한다.

 Wrap Up

B: Tomorrow ❶let's put on traditional Korean clothes, *hanbok*, and go to Insadong.

G: Good, but I want to buy gifts for my friends in Germany tomorrow.

B: In Insadong, ❷there are many gift shops.

G: Great. ❸After shopping, what should we eat for lunch?

B: Hmm. ❹You know Samgyetang, don't you?

G: No. What is it?

B: It's a traditional Korean soup. It's delicious and will ❺make you healthy.

G: Sounds good. ❻I'm looking forward to trying it.

❶ 'let's+동사원형'으로 '~하자'라고 제안을 할 때 사용한다.
❷ 'there are+복수명사'로 '~들이 있다'라는 의미다.
❸ 전치사 'After' 뒤에 동명사 'shopping'을 사용한다.
❹ 'You know ~, don't you?'는 알고 있는지 물어보는 표현이다.
❺ 'make+목적어+목적보어(형용사)' 형태로 '…을 ~하게 만들다'라는 의미이다.
❻ 'look forward to+동명사'로 '~하기를 기대하다'라는 뜻이다.

● 다음 우리말과 일치하도록 빈칸에 알맞은 말을 쓰시오.

Listen & Speak 1 A

1. B: Look _____ Suwon Hawseong. It's _____.

   G: It also _____ _____.

   B: _____ it _____ _____ to _____ the people _____ wars.

   G: Wow. Do you know _____ _____ it?

   B: Yes. King Jeongjo _____ Jeong Yakyong _____ _____ the building _____. You know about Jeong Yakyong, _____ _____?

   G: Yes, I've _____ _____ him. He was a great _____ in Joseon.

2. G: Brian, you know Taegeukgi, _____ _____?

   B: Sure. It's the _____ _____ of Korea, _____ it?

   G: That's right. Do you know _____ the _____ in Taegeukgi _____?

   B: No, I don't. Tell me about them.

   G: The _____ in the middle means _____ and _____.

   B: What do the black _____ on the four _____ mean?

   G: They _____ four things: sky, fire, water, and _____.

Listen & Speak 2 A

1. G: I'm _____ _____ _____ to the Gansong Museum.

   B: What is the Gansong Museum?

   G: It's a museum _____ by Gansong Jeon Hyeongpil.

   B: I _____ that he did _____ things for the country.

   G: Yes. He bought many Korean _____ _____ some Japanese _____ _____ to Japan.

   B: Wow. The museum _____ _____ _____ _____.

   G: Yes. I'm _____ _____ _____ it!

2. B: Soyeon, _____ _____ _____ _____ _____ last weekend?

   G: I went to Hyeonchungwon to do _____ _____.

   B: _____ _____ of volunteer work did you do there?

해석

1. B: 수원 화성을 봐, 그것은 거대해.
   G: 그것은 또한 튼튼해 보여.
   B: 왜냐하면 그것은 전쟁 중에 사람들을 보호하기 위해 지어졌기 때문이야.
   G: 우와. 너는 누가 그것을 지었는지 아니?
   B: 응. 정조가 정약용에게 건설 과정을 감독할 것을 지시했어. 너는 정약용에 대해 알고 있지, 그렇지 않니?
   G: 응, 그에 대해 들어봤어. 그는 조선의 훌륭한 과학자였어.

2. G: Brian, 너 태극기를 알고 있지, 그렇지 않니?
   B: 물론이지. 그것은 한국의 국기잖아, 그렇지 않니?
   G: 맞아. 너는 태극기에 있는 상징들이 무엇을 의미하는지 알고 있니?
   B: 아니, 몰라. 그것에 대해 말해 줘.
   G: 가운데 원은 조화와 평화를 의미해.
   B: 네 모서리의 검은 선들은 무엇을 의미하니?
   G: 그것은 하늘, 불, 물 그리고 땅을 의미해.

1. G: 나는 간송 미술관에 갈 예정이야.
   B: 간송 미술관이 뭐야?
   G: 간송 전형필에 의해 지어진 미술관이야.
   B: 나는 그가 나라를 위해 훌륭한 일들을 했다고 들었어.
   G: 응. 그는 몇몇 일본 사람들이 일본으로 가져갔었던 한국의 많은 문화재들을 샀어.
   B: 우와. 그 미술관은 틀림없이 흥미로울 거야.
   G: 응. 나는 그곳을 기대하고 있어!

2. B: 소연아, 지난 주말에 무엇을 했니?
   G: 나는 봉사 활동을 하러 현충원에 갔어.
   B: 그곳에서 어떤 종류의 봉사 활동을 했어?

G: I _____ around the _____. I felt great _____ for the people _____ died for the country.

B: _____ great. Can I do it, too?

G: Sure. I'm _____ _____ _____ there again next Wednesday. Will you _____ me?

B: Sure. _____ _____ _____ _____ it.

Real Life Talk

Andy: Bora, what are you _____?

Bora: I'm reading *Sky, Wind, Star, and* _____ by Yun Dongju. You _____ about Yun Dongju, _____ _____?

Andy: I've _____ his name, but I don't know much about him.

Bora: He wrote many beautiful _____ _____ Korea was _____ Japanese _____. His love for the country and his _____ for _____ can _____ _____ in his _____.

Andy: Really? I didn't know that. I want _____ _____ his _____ and _____ more about him.

Bora: Great. _____ _____, I'm planning _____ _____ the Yun Dongju Museum soon. Do you want to come with me?

Andy: Yes, _____ are you going?

Bora: Next Saturday. It's _____ Gyeongbok _____. Can you meet me at the _____ at 2 p.m.?

Andy: Sure. _____ meet there.

Bora: Great. I'm really _____ _____ _____ the _____.

Wrap Up

B: Tomorrow let's _____ _____ _____ Korean clothes, *hanbok*, and go to Insadong.

G: Good, but I want to buy gifts _____ my friends in _____ tomorrow.

B: In Insadong, _____ _____ many gift shops.

G: Great. After _____, what should we eat for lunch?

B: Hmm. You _____ Samgyetang, _____ _____?

G: No. What is it?

B: It's a _____ Korean _____. It's _____ and will make you _____.

G: Sounds good. I'm looking forward _____ _____ it.

G: 나는 묘 주변을 청소했어. 나는 나라를 위해 돌아가신 분들에게 깊은 경의를 느꼈어.

B: 대단하게 들린다. 나도 그것을 할 수 있을까?

G: 물론이지. 나는 다음 주 수요일에 그곳에 다시 갈 계획이야. 너도 나와 함께 갈래?

B: 물론이지. 나는 그것을 기대하고 있어.

Andy: 보라, 너 무엇을 읽고 있니?

보라: 윤동주 시인의 「하늘과 바람과 별과 시」를 읽고 있어. 너는 윤동주에 대해 알고 있지, 그렇지 않니?

Andy: 나는 그의 이름을 들어 본 적 있지만 그에 대해 잘 알지는 못해.

보라: 그는 한국이 일본의 통치하에 있을 때 아름다운 시를 많이 썼어. 나라에 대한 그의 사랑과 독립에 대한 염원이 그의 시에서 느껴질 수 있어.

Andy: 정말? 나는 그걸 몰랐어. 나는 그의 시를 읽고 그에 대해 더 많이 배우고 싶어.

보라: 아주 좋아. 사실 나는 곧 윤동주 박물관을 방문할 계획이야. 너도 나와 함께 가길 원하니?

Andy: 응, 언제 갈 거니?

보라: 다음 주 토요일에. 그곳은 경복궁 근처에 있어. 오후 2시에 궁에서 만날 수 있니?

Andy: 물론이지. 거기서 만나자.

보라: 좋아. 나는 그 방문을 정말 기대하고 있어.

B: 내일 우리 한국 전통 의상인 한복을 입고 인사동에 가자.

G: 좋아, 그런데 나 내일 독일에 있는 내 친구들을 위한 선물을 사고 싶어.

B: 인사동에 선물 가게가 많아.

G: 잘됐네. 쇼핑하고 나서 점심으로 뭘 먹을까?

B: 흠. 너는 삼계탕에 대해 알고 있지, 그렇지 않니?

G: 아니. 그게 뭐야?

B: 전통적인 한국의 국물 음식이야. 그것은 맛이 좋고 너를 건강하게 만들어 줄 거야.

G: 멋지네. 나는 그것을 먹어보는 것을 기대하고 있어.

01 우리말을 영어로 옮길 때 빈칸에 알맞은 말을 쓰시오.

> 나는 그 방문이 정말 기대돼.

➡ I'm really _____ _____ _____ the visit.

02 다음 대화의 빈칸에 들어갈 말로 알맞은 것은?

> A: _____, don't you?
> B: Yes, I heard about it.

① I hope I will visit Dokdo
② You cannot know about Dokdo
③ I'm not quite sure if you know about Dokdo
④ Look at the island in the picture
⑤ You know Dokdo is windy and foggy

03 다음 대화의 빈칸에 들어갈 말로 <u>어색한</u> 표현은?

> A: Do you remember our plan to visit the Hanok Village in July?
> B: Sure. _____

① I'm looking forward to visiting there.
② I can't wait to visit there.
③ I'm dying to visiting there.
④ I'm expecting to visit there.
⑤ I am longing to visit there.

04 다음 대화의 밑줄 친 말의 의도로 알맞은 것은?

> A: <u>You know that Dokdo has two main islands and 89 small islands, don't you?</u>
> B: No, I didn't know that.

① 확신 표현하기   ② 알고 있는지 묻기
③ 관심 표현하기   ④ 염려 묻기
⑤ 기대 표현하기

[01~02] 다음 대화를 읽고 물음에 답하시오.

Seho: Tomorrow (a)let's put on traditional Korean clothes, *hanbok*, and go to Insadong.

Judy: Good, but I want to buy gifts for my friends in Germany tomorrow.

Seho: In Insadong, (b)there are many gift shops.

Judy: Great. (c)After shopping, what should we eat for lunch?

Seho: Hmm. You know Samgyetang, (d)don't you?

Judy: No. What is it?

Seho: It's a traditional Korean soup. It's delicious and will make you healthy.

Judy: Sounds good. I'm looking forward to (e)try it.

01 위 대화의 밑줄 친 (a)~(e) 중, 어법상 어색한 것은?

① (a) ② (b) ③ (c) ④ (d) ⑤ (e)

 02 위 대화의 내용과 일치하지 <u>않는</u> 것은?

① They are talking about their plans for tomorrow.

② Judy didn't know there are many gift shops in Insadong.

③ Both Seho and Judy are going to put on *hanbok*.

④ They will eat Samgyetang for dinner.

⑤ Judy can't wait to eat Samgyetang.

03 다음 대화의 (A)~(D)를 알맞은 순서로 배열한 것은?

B: Soyeon, what did you do last weekend?

G: I went to Hyeonchungwon to do volunteer work.

(A) Sounds great. Can I do it, too?

(B) I cleaned around the tombs. I felt great respect for the people who died for the country.

(C) Sure. I'm planning to go there again next Wednesday. Will you join me?

(D) What kind of volunteer work did you do there?

B: Sure. I'm looking forward to it.

① (A)–(C)–(B)–(D) ② (B)–(A)–(C)–(D)
③ (C)–(B)–(A)–(D) ④ (D)–(B)–(A)–(C)
⑤ (D)–(C)–(A)–(B)

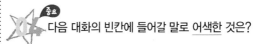 **04** 다음 대화의 빈칸에 들어갈 말로 <u>어색한</u> 것은?

A: You know about An Junggeun, don't you?

B: _____

① No. I don't know much about him.

② Sure. He made a great effort for Korea's independence.

③ You can go to the An Junggeun Museum and get more information about him.

④ No. I want to learn more about him.

⑤ No, I don't. But I'm looking forward to learning more about him.

05 다음 대화의 밑줄 친 문장과 같은 의미가 되도록 주어진 단어를 이용하여 쓰시오.

A: Do you remember our plan to make Gimchi in November?

B: Sure. <u>I'm dying to make it.</u>

➡ _____

(look forward)

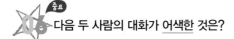 다음 두 사람의 대화가 <u>어색한</u> 것은?

① A: Do you remember our plan to visit the Hanok Village in July?
　B: Sure. I'm looking forward to visiting there.

② A: You know Seho, don't you?
　B: Yes. Isn't he the fastest boy in our school?

③ A: Do you remember our plan to learn the Korean traditional fan dance?
　B: Yes. I'm looking forward to learning it.

④ A: I'm planning to go to the Gansong Museum.
　B: I'd love to, but I'm looking forward to visiting there.

⑤ A: You know Ryu Gwansun, don't you?
　B: Of course. She was an independence activist.

[07~08] 다음 대화를 읽고 물음에 답하시오.

B: Look at Suwon Hawseong. It's huge.
G: It also looks strong.
B: Because it was built to protect the people during wars.
G: Wow. Do you know who built it?
B: Yes. (A)정조가 정약용에게 건설 과정을 감독할 것을 지시했어. You know about Jeong Yakyong, don't you?
G: (B)_____ He was a great scientist in Joseon.

서답형

07 위 대화의 밑줄 친 (A)의 우리말에 맞게 주어진 어구를 이용하여 영어로 쓰시오. (단어 하나를 추가하시오.)

> ordered / direct / Jeong Yakyong / King Jeongjo / the building process

➡ _____

_____

08 위 대화의 빈칸 (B)에 들어갈 말로 알맞은 것을 <u>모두</u> 고르시오.

① I'm looking forward to seeing him.
② Yes, I've heard of him.
③ No. I can't wait to know about him.
④ No, I don't know about him.
⑤ Yes, I saw a program about him on TV.

[09~10] 다음 대화를 읽고 물음에 답하시오.

G: Brian, (a)<u>you know Taegeukgi, don't you?</u>
B: Sure. It's the national flag of Korea, (b)<u>isn't it?</u>
G: That's right. Do you know (c)<u>what do the symbols in Taegeukgi mean?</u>
B: No, I don't. Tell me about them.
G: The circle in the middle (d)<u>means</u> harmony and peace.
B: What do the black lines on the four corners (e)<u>mean?</u>
G: They mean four things: sky, fire, water, and earth.

09 위 대화의 밑줄 친 (a)~(e) 중 어법상 <u>어색한</u> 것은?

① (a)　② (b)　③ (c)　④ (d)　⑤ (e)

10 위 대화의 내용과 일치하지 <u>않는</u> 것은?

① Brian knows what Taegeukgi is.
② The symbols in Taegeukgi have different meanings.
③ Brian wants to know about the meanings of the symbols in Taegeukgi.
④ Taegeukgi has four lines on each corner.
⑤ The black lines mean sky, fire, water and earth.

[01~02] 다음 대화를 읽고 물음에 답하시오.

Andy: Bora, what are you reading?

Bora: I'm reading *Sky, Wind, Star, and Poetry* by Yun Dongju. You know about Yun Dongju, don't you?

Andy: I've heard his name, but I don't know much about him.

Bora: He wrote many beautiful poems when Korea was under Japanese rule. His love for the country and his desire for independence can be felt in his poems.

Andy: Really? I didn't know that. I want to read his poems and learn more about him.

Bora: Great. In fact, I'm planning to visit the Yun Dongju Museum soon. Do you want to come with me?

Andy: Yes, when are you going?

Bora: Next Saturday. It's near Gyeongbok Palace. Can you meet me at the palace at 2 p.m.?

Andy: Sure. Let's meet there.

Bora: Great. (A)_____

01 위 대화를 읽고 다음 질문에 대한 답을 본문에서 찾아 쓰시오.

> Q: What can be felt through Yun Dongju's poems?

➡ _____

_____

02 위 대화의 빈칸 (A)에 들어갈 말을 〈조건〉에 맞게 쓰시오.

┤ 조건 ├
- 'look'을 이용하여 기대나 희망을 나타내는 표현을 쓸 것.
- 현재진행형을 사용하고, 'the visit'을 쓸 것.

➡ _____

03 다음 대화의 빈칸에 들어갈 말로 자연스러운 것을 〈보기〉에서 찾아 문장을 쓰시오.

G: Brian, (A)_____

B: Sure. It's the national flag of Korea, isn't it?

G: That's right. (B)_____
_____

B: No, I don't. Tell me about them.

G: The circle in the middle means harmony and peace.

B: What do the black lines on the four corners mean?

G: (C)_____

┤ 보기 ├
- Do you know what the symbols in Taegeukgi mean?
- you know Taegeukgi, don't you?
- They mean four things: sky, fire, water, and earth.

04 대화의 내용상 빈칸에 주어진 〈조건〉에 맞게 영어로 쓰시오.

┤ 조건 ├
- 정약용에 대해 아는지 묻는 표현을 쓸 것.
- 'know'와 '부가의문문'을 사용할 것.

B: Look at Suwon Hawseong. It's huge.

G: It also looks strong.

B: Because it was built to protect the people during wars.

G: Wow. Do you know who built it?

B: Yes. King Jeongjo ordered Jeong Yakyong to direct the building process.

_____

G: Yes, I've heard of him. He was a great scientist in Joseon.

Grammar

① '과거완료' had + 과거분사

> • I thought about Kim Koo's words in My Wish that I **had read** in the exhibition hall. 나는 전시관에서 읽었던 '나의 소원'에 나오는 김구의 말에 대해 생각했다.
>
> • When my mom came back home, she found Judy **had watered** the plant. 나의 엄마가 집에 돌아왔을 때, 엄마는 Judy가 화분에 물을 주었던 것을 발견했다.

- 과거완료시제는 'had + 과거분사' 형태로 표현하며, 과거의 어느 시점을 기준으로, 그 이전에 일어난 동작이나 상태를 나타낸다.

  • I lost the cellphone that he **had bought** for me. (나는 그가 사 준 핸드폰을 잃어버렸다.)

- 과거의 특정 시점을 기준으로 그 이전에 일어난 동작의 완료, 경험, 계속, 결과를 나타낸다.

  (1) 완료: '막 ~했었다'는 의미로 과거 이전에 시작된 동작이 과거의 어느 시점에 완료된 일을 나타낸다. 보통 already, yet 등의 부사와 함께 쓰인다.

  • They **had arrived** at the base camp before the snow storm began. (그들은 눈보라가 시작되기 전에 베이스 캠프에 도착했다.)

  (2) 경험: '~한 적이 있었다'는 의미로 과거 이전부터 과거의 어느 시점까지의 경험을 나타낸다. 보통 never, ever, once, twice, before 등의 부사(구)와 함께 쓰인다.

  • She realized David at once, for she **had seen** him before. (그녀는 David을 즉시 알아봤는데, 전에 그를 만난 적이 있었기 때문이었다.)

  (3) 결과: '(과거 이전에) ~해서, 그 결과 …했다'는 의미로 과거 이전의 동작이 과거의 어느 시점의 결과에 영향을 미치는 것을 나타낸다.

  • Her son **had gone** to the army by the time Emma was well again. (Emma가 다시 건강해질 무렵 그의 아들은 군에 입대했다.)

  (4) 계속: '계속 ~하고 있었다'는 의미로 과거 이전부터 과거의 어느 시점까지 계속되는 동작이나 상태를 나타낸다. 보통 since, for 등과 함께 쓰인다.

  • Walter **had lived** there for 16 years when he was elected mayor. (Walter는 시장으로 당선되었을 때, 그곳에서 16년간을 살았다.)

- 부정문은 'had+not+과거분사', 의문문은 'Had+주어+과거분사 ~?', 과거 어느 시점을 기준으로 전부터 진행 중인 동작을 강조할 때, 과거완료진행형 'had+been+V-ing'을 쓴다.

  • I was hungry because I **had not eaten** breakfast. (나는 아침을 먹지 않았기 때문에 배가 고팠다.)

  • **Had** James **seen** the actor before? (James가 그 배우를 전에 본 적이 있었나요?)

  • He **had been preparing** dinner when I saw him. (내가 그를 봤을 때, 그는 저녁식사를 준비하고 있던 중이었다.)

핵심 Check

1. 괄호 안에서 알맞은 단어를 고르시오.

   (1) Sally (has / had) lived in Singapore before she moved to Canada.

   (2) Judy had never eaten sushi until she (visits / visited) Japan.

② '목적', '의도'를 나타내는 so that

> • Kim Koo always carried Yun's watch in his jacket **so that** he **would** not forget Yun's sacrifice. 김구는 윤의 희생을 잊지 않기 위해서 그의 시계를 항상 재킷에 넣고 다녔다.
>
> • I waved at my sister **so that** she **could** find me. 나는 내 여동생이 나를 찾을 수 있게 그녀에게 손을 흔들었다.

■ so that은 '~하기 위해', '~하고자', '~하도록'의 의미로 '목적'이나 '의도'를 나타낸다. 일반적으로 '주절 +so that+주어+can/will(조동사)+동사원형 ~'의 구조로 쓰인다.

  • Jinsu got up early **so that** he **could** catch the first train to Barcelona. (진수는 Barcelona로 가는 첫 기차를 타기 위해 일찍 일어났다.)

  • Clara tried her best **so that** she **would** not disappoint her fans. (Clara는 자신의 팬들을 실망시키지 않기 위해서 최선을 다했다.)

■ so that은 다양한 표현들로 같은 의미를 나타낼 수 있다.

  • She went to Mexico **so that** she **could** learn Spanish. (그녀는 스페인어를 배우러 멕시코에 갔다.)
    = She went to Mexico **in order that** she **could** learn Spanish.
    = She went to Mexico **to learn** Spanish. ⟨to부정사의 부사적 용법 – 목적⟩
    = She went to Mexico **so as to learn** Spanish.
    = She went to Mexico **in order to learn** Spanish.

  • He worked hard **so that he wouldn't** be fired. (그는 해고되지 않으려고 열심히 일했다.)
    = He worked hard **in order that he wouldn't** be fired.
    = He worked hard **(in order) not to** be fired.
    = He worked hard **so as not to** be fired.

■ so that을 기준으로 앞과 뒤 동사의 시제를 일치시킨다.

  • Sam **works** hard **so that** he **can** support his family. (Sam은 가족을 부양하기 위해 열심히 일한다.)

  • Sam **worked** hard **so that** he **could** support his family.

■ 목적이 '그래서'의 의미를 갖는 접속사로 쓰이기도 한다. 대개 so that 앞에 쉼표가 온다.

  • Bolt ran every day, **so that** he became a great athlete. (Bolt는 매일 달렸고, 그래서 그는 훌륭한 육상선수가 되었다.)

■ so ~ that 사이에 형용사[부사]가 오면, '너무 ~해서 결국 …하다'라는 뜻이 된다.

  • The girl was **so** happy **that** she cried. 그 소녀는 너무 행복해서 울었다.

  • The room was **so** dark **that** I couldn't see anything. 방이 너무 어두워서 나는 아무것도 볼 수 없었다.

핵심 Check

2. 괄호 안에서 알맞은 말을 고르시오.

  (1) Miranda went to London so (that / where) she could study fashion.

  (2) Please turn the volume down (for that / so that) my daughter can sleep.

01 다음 빈칸에 들어갈 말로 알맞은 것은?

> He came back to Sudan in 2001 as he _____ .

① promise ② promises ③ has promised
④ to promise ⑤ had promised

02 다음 각 문장의 빈칸에 공통으로 들어갈 말로 알맞은 것은? (대·소문자 구분 없음.)

> • Andrew saved much money _____ as to travel around the world.
> • Turn the volume up _____ that we can dance to the music.
> • These are _____ tough that we can't tear them.

① enough ② too ③ so
④ such ⑤ quite

03 다음 밑줄 친 부분 중 어법상 옳은 것을 고르시오.

① Paul <u>has gone</u> to Tokyo before his wife came back.
② I ate the tuna can that I <u>had bought</u> a month before.
③ I <u>had found</u> her purse that she had left in my office.
④ They <u>had lived</u> here for two years until now.
⑤ When <u>had</u> Betty <u>married</u> Chris?

04 다음 두 문장의 의미가 같도록 빈칸에 알맞은 말을 쓰시오.

(1) Mina saved much money to buy the car.
➡ Mina saved much money so _____ she _____ buy the car.

(2) Because it was very hot, Julie turned the air conditioner on.
➡ It was _____ _____ _____ Julie turned the air conditioner on.

(3) Mike will walk fast in order to get there on time.
➡ Mike will walk fast so _____ _____ _____ get there on time.

(4) Judy can't solve the problem because it is very hard.
➡ The problem is _____ _____ _____ Judy _____ solve it.

01 밑줄 친 부분이 어법상 어색한 것은?

① The suspect had already left the room when the police arrived.
② John had broken his arm, so he couldn't play tennis last weekend.
③ Susan asked her friend how to repair the machine which has broken down.
④ I had met him many times before then.
⑤ Amy lost the key that her aunt had given to her.

[02~03] 다음 우리말을 어법상 알맞게 영작한 것을 고르시오.

02

> 김구는 그의 희생을 잊지 않기 위해서 그의 시계를 항상 가지고 다녔다.

① Kim Koo always carried his watch so that he won't forget his sacrifice.
② Kim Koo carried his watch so always that he could not forget his sacrifice.
③ Kim Koo carried his watch always so what he should not forget his sacrifice.
④ Kim Koo always carried his watch so that he would not forget his sacrifice.
⑤ Kim Koo often carried his watch so he would not forget his sacrifice always.

03

> 더위를 잊으려고 우리는 얼음을 먹었다.

① We ate the ice not to forget the heat.
② We ate the ice so that we can forget the heat.
③ We ate the ice in order that forget the heat.
④ We ate the ice so cold that we would forget the heat.
⑤ We ate the ice so that we would forget the heat.

[04~05] 다음 밑줄 친 부분 중 어법상 옳은 것을 고르시오.

04 ① Yujin is hungry because she had not eaten anything so far.
② The crow lived in the jungle before it had moved to the city.
③ Their bodies had been in Japan, but Kim Koo brought them to Korea.
④ Mom required that Jane had finished the dishes.
⑤ For the past five years, I had read your books about the origin of space.

05 ① Billy took his umbrella in order for his wife could use it.
② Justin got up early so that he not being late for the contest.
③ The dolphins were so joy that they could jump above the water.
④ Martha has been saving money for 6 months so to buy a new software.
⑤ Lucy exercised regularly in order that she could reduce stress.

06 다음 두 문장의 의미가 같도록 바꿔 쓸 때 적절하지 <u>않은</u> 것은?

① Kate stood up so that her business partner could find her.
= Kate stood up in order for her business partner to find her.

② Ahn left for America so that he would get a better education.
= Ahn left for America so as to get a better education.

③ Bob made cakes so that he would feel happy.
= Bob made cakes to feel happy.

④ Elizabeth exercises regularly in order for her mom not to get worried.
= Elizabeth exercises regularly so that her mom would not get worried.

⑤ Ted left the meeting quite early not to see his rivals.
= Ted left the meeting quite early, so he could not see his rivals.

07 다음 중 밑줄 친 부분의 쓰임이 〈보기〉와 같은 것은?

> ┤ 보기 ├
> I <u>had</u> already <u>solved</u> the quiz when the teacher called my name.

① Kim Koo <u>had</u> not <u>arrived</u> at the airport when the planes landed.

② Sophia <u>had known</u> him for 10 years when she first found him attractive.

③ The Smiths <u>had lived</u> in Seoul for ten years before they moved to Incheon.

④ Grace <u>had</u> never <u>been</u> ill until last year after the accident.

⑤ Koby <u>had played</u> basketball in America for thirty years since then.

08 서답형 다음 문장에서 어법상 어색한 단어 한 개를 찾아서 고치시오.

> My cousin has been sick in bed for a week when I visited him.

➡ _____

09 다음 중 주어진 문장과 의미가 <u>다른</u> 것은?

> The soldiers trained hard so that they would defeat Japan.

① The soldiers trained hard in order that they would defeat Japan.

② The soldiers trained hard to defeat Japan.

③ The soldiers trained hard so as to defeat Japan.

④ The soldiers trained so hard that they defeated Japan.

⑤ The soldiers trained hard in order to defeat Japan.

10 다음 문장의 밑줄 친 so that의 쓰임이 흐름상 <u>어색한</u> 것은?

① The actor wore sunglasses <u>so that</u> he could hide his face.

② Brian's sisters made some dishes <u>so that</u> they could eat together.

③ Yuna practiced hard <u>so that</u> she could win the piano competition.

④ The boy band performed on the street <u>so that</u> many people could recognize them.

⑤ Irene failed the exam <u>so that</u> she had studied harder than before.

[11~12] 다음 중 어법상 옳은 문장은?

11

① April has never eaten the spice until she visited Vietnam.

② Mom can't see the flower now as my sister had picked it.

③ The students have been sitting for half an hour before the class started.

④ When I met her, Sumin had already completed the assignment.

⑤ My sister found the book that I had been given to her.

12

① My history club went to Hyochang Park so as to visit the Kim Koo Museum.

② Betty practices yoga regularly so as to be stay healthy.

③ John spent most of life in order to that he could be a novelist.

④ I study English so that in order to read many books written in English.

⑤ Mina learned French so that she can watch French movies without subtitles.

13 다음 〈보기〉와 같이 두 문장이 같은 의미가 되도록 주어진 단어를 활용하여 다시 쓰시오.

┌─── 보기 ───┐

I exercise so as to keep in shape. (that, so)

→ I exercise so that I can keep in shape.

└────────────┘

(1) Father Lee Taeseok returned to Sudan to help poor people there. (that, in, could, order)

➡ _____

_____

(2) Amy practices every day to join our sports club. (that, so, can)

➡ _____

_____

(3) Clara left for Paris to study fashion. (that, in, could, order)

➡ _____

_____

(4) Thames ran fast in order not to be late for the meeting. (that, would, so)

➡ _____

_____

14 다음 그림을 보고 자연스러운 문장이 되도록 괄호 안에 주어진 어구를 바르게 배열하여 빈칸을 완성하시오.

(1)

➡ Junsu _____

_____. (the pimples, they, that, disappear, squeezed out, would, so)

(2)

➡ Sudong studied hard _____

_____. (that, in order, a, get, he, college scholarship, could, full)

Grammar 서술형 시험대비

01 다음 우리말과 일치하도록 괄호 안에 주어진 어구를 바르게 배열하여 문장을 완성하시오.

(1) 간송은 몇몇 일본인들이 일본으로 가져갔었던 한국의 많은 문화재들을 샀다.

⇒ Gansong _____

_____.

(Japan, taken, bought, to, that, many, Japanese, Korean treasures, had, some).

(2) 이순신은 사람들을 보호할 수 있게 거북선을 만들었다.

⇒ Yi Sunsin _____

_____. (the Turtle Ship, could, the people, that, he, protect, made, so).

(3) 그 도둑은 아무도 들을 수 없도록 천천히 걸었다.

⇒ The thief _____

_____. (hear, slowly, one, so, walked, could, him, no, that).

02 다음 그림은 학생들이 문화 유산을 조사하고 만든 미니북과 활동 감상문이다. 빈칸에 들어갈 알맞은 말을 괄호 안의 단어와 완료시제를 활용하여 쓰시오.

Before we made this cultural heritage mini book, we _____ (search) for information about the golden crowns of Silla, Bulguksa, *samullori*, and the Nanjungilgi. After we _____ (make) the book, we learned a lesson that it is important to keep our cultural treasures.

03 다음 문장에서 어법상 어색한 것을 바르게 고쳐 다시 쓰시오.

(1) Could you remind me of the time so order that I won't be late for the party?

⇒ _____

_____

(2) Whenever Jane was ill, her mom used to make her a bowl of porridge in order of her to get well.

⇒ _____

(3) They are saving money so which they can buy a big house.

⇒ _____

_____

(4) Remember my number in order for you can contact me.

⇒ _____

_____

_____

(5) The foreigners from Italy went to Gyeongju so that they can see Bulguksa.

⇒ _____

_____

(6) Many people joined the New Korean Society so order to support the Independence movement.

⇒ _____

_____

04 괄호 안에 주어진 어구와 글자 수 및 조건을 활용하여, 다음 우리말을 영작하시오.

(1) 우리가 팥빙수를 만들 수 있기 위해서는 얼음과 설탕이 필요하다. (that, so, ice, can, patbingsu, sugar, need, 11 단어)

➡ _____

(2) 그녀가 물고기 몇 마리를 잡도록 해주기 위해서 우리는 강으로 갔다. (could, that, catch, go, so, fish, the river, some, 12 단어)

➡ _____

_____

(3) 그 코알라들을 구조하기 위해 한 소방대원이 숲 속으로 뛰어들었다. (she, rescue, firefighter, the woods, that, so, run, could, into, the koalas, 13 단어)

➡ _____

_____

(4) 나의 할머니는 건강을 유지하도록 매일 운동을 합니다. (can, grandma, every day, exercise, healthy, keep, order that, 12 단어)

➡ _____

_____

05 다음 우리말을 주어진 〈조건〉에 맞게 영작하시오.

┤ 조건 ├
1. The old man을 포함, 총 19 단어로 쓸 것.
2. 숫자도 영어로 쓸 것.
3. the official, live alone, in, for, until 등을 활용할 것.

그 공무원이 작년에 방문할 때까지 그 노인은 그 집에서 33년간 혼자 살았었다.

→ The old man _____

_____

_____ .

06 다음 각 문장의 밑줄 친 부분이 과거완료시제의 용법 중 어떤 것에 해당하는지 〈보기〉에서 찾아 기호를 쓰고 우리말로 해석하시오.

┤ 보기 ├
ⓐ 완료 ⓑ 경험 ⓒ 결과 ⓓ 계속

(1) Peter had already left for New York when I got there. (   )

➡ _____

(2) William had lived in Busan for 14 years until last year. (   )

➡ _____

(3) They had waited for the singer for almost a day before the concert started. (   )

➡ _____

(4) Maria had never seen the snow until she came to Korea this winter. (   )

➡ _____

(5) By the time I arrived at the airport, the check-in had already been completed. (   )

➡ _____

(6) When we came home, we found somebody had broken the window. (   )

➡ _____

(7) I didn't recognize the person because I had never met him before. (   )

➡ _____

(8) When the couple woke up, someone had finished making shoes. (   )

➡ _____

Reading

My Wish

Last week my history club went to Hyochang Park. We visited the Kim Koo Museum inside the park. At the entrance of the museum, we saw a white statue of Kim Koo. Kim Koo is a great national hero who spent most of his life fighting for the independence of Korea from Japanese rule. In the 1900s, he helped educate young people by building schools. In 1919, when the independence movement had spread throughout the country, he moved to Shanghai, China. There he joined the Government of the Republic of Korea and later became its president.

The exhibition hall in the museum shows a lot of things about Kim Koo's life. While looking around the hall, we stopped at a photo of the Korean Patriotic Organization's members. Kim Koo formed the secret organization in 1931 to fight against Japan. Lee Bongchang and Yun Bonggil belonged to the group. At one place in the hall, we saw two watches under a photo of Kim Koo and Yun Bonggil. In 1932, Kim Koo made a plan to kill Japanese generals in a park in Shanghai.

entrance: 입구
statue: 동상
independence: 독립
Japanese: 일본의
spread: 퍼지다
throughout: ~의 전체에 걸쳐
government: 정부
republic: 공화국
president: 대통령, 의장
exhibition: 전시
hall: 큰 방, 홀, 현관

 확인문제

● 다음 문장이 본문의 내용과 일치하면 T, 일치하지 <u>않으면</u> F를 쓰시오.

1 The history club went to Hyochang Park last month. ☐

2 There is the statue of Kim Koo at the entrance of the park. ☐

3 Kim Koo fought for the independence of Korea from Japanese rule. ☐

4 Yun Bonggil was one of the members of the Korean Patriotic Organization. ☐

As the leader of the Korean Patriotic Organization, he directed Yun to
자격을 나타내는 전치사(~로서)
carry out the mission.
direct+목적어+toV: 목적어가 V할 것을 지시하다

When Yun left for the mission, he told Kim, "Sir, you are wearing a
상해에 있는 한 공원에서 일본 장군들을 암살하는 것
very old watch. Mine is new, but I won't need it anymore. Please take
= My watch
my watch, and let me have yours." Kim Koo always carried Yun's
사역동사+목적어+동사원형(목적어가 V하게 시키다)
watch in his jacket so that he would not forget Yun's sacrifice.
~하기 위해서(목적을 나타내는 구문)

After completing the tour of the museum, we moved to the tombs
동명사(전치사 After의 목적어)
of the three heroes, Lee Bongchang, Yun Bonggil, and Baek Jeonggi.
the three heroes와 동격
Their bodies had been in Japan, but after Korea's independence Kim
김구가 그들의 시신을 가지고 온 것은 과거이며 그 전부터 일본에 있었으므로 과거완료
Koo brought them to Hyochang Park. By doing so, he showed his
일본에 있던 시신들을 한국으로 모셔온 것
deep love and respect for the sacrifice of the three heroes.

As I left Hyochang Park, I thought about Kim Koo's words in

My Wish that I had read in the exhibition hall. It was written in
목적격 관계대명사   My Wish
Baekbeomilji.

If God asks me what my wish is, I would say clearly, "It is Korea's
조건의 부사절을 이끄는 접속사(~라면)
Independence." If he asks me what my second wish is, I would say,
간접의문문(의문사+주어+동사)
"It is the independence of my country." If he asks me what my third
wish is, I would say loudly, "It is the complete independence of my
country." That is my answer.

확인문제

● 다음 문장이 본문의 내용과 일치하면 T, 일치하지 않으면 F를 쓰시오.

1 Kim Koo wanted Yun to give his watch to him. ☐

2 Yun thought he wouldn't need his watch anymore. ☐

3 Kim Koo brought the bodies of the three heroes to Hyochang Park before Korea's independence. ☐

4 The writer read Kim Koo's words in a newspaper. ☐

5 Kim Koo's one and only wish was the complete independence of the country. ☐

direct: 지시하다
carry out: 수행하다
patriotic: 애국적인
organization: 조직
member: 구성원, 회원
general: 장군
leader: 지도자
mission: 임무
belong to: ~에 속하다
sacrifice: 희생; 희생하다
tomb: 무덤
god: 하느님, 신
wish: 소원, 소망
clearly: 분명하게, 확실히

● 우리말을 참고하여 빈칸에 알맞은 말을 쓰시오.

My Wish

1 Last week _____ _____ _____ went to Hyochang Park.

2 We _____ the Kim Koo Museum _____ _____ _____.

3 _____ the _____ of the museum, we saw a white statue of Kim Koo.

4 Kim Koo is _____ _____ _____ _____ who _____ most of his life fighting for the independence of Korea _____ Japanese rule.

5 In the 1900s, he _____ _____ young people _____ _____ schools.

6 _____ 1919, _____ _____ _____ had spread throughout the country, he _____ _____ Shanghai, China.

7 There he _____ the Government of the Republic of Korea and later _____ _____ _____ .

8 _____ _____ _____ in the museum _____ a lot of things about Kim Koo's life.

9 While _____ _____ the hall, we _____ _____ a photo of the Korean _____ _____ members.

10 Kim Koo _____ the secret _____ in 1931 _____ _____ _____ Japan.

11 Lee Bongchang and Yun Bonggil _____ _____ the group.

12 _____ one place in the hall, we _____ _____ _____ under a photo of Kim Koo and Yun Bonggil.

나의 소원

1 지난주에 우리 역사 동아리는 효창 공원에 갔다.

2 우리는 공원 안에 있는 김구 기념관을 방문했다.

3 기념관 입구에서 우리는 하얀색의 김구 조각상을 보았다.

4 김구는 일본 통치로부터 대한의 독립을 위해 싸우는 데 그의 삶 대부분을 보낸 위대한 국민 영웅이다.

5 1900년대에 그는 학교를 설립함으로써 젊은이들을 교육시키는 것을 도왔다.

6 1919년에 3.1 운동이 나라 전체에 걸쳐 퍼져나갔을 때, 그는 중국 상하이로 이동했다.

7 그곳에서 그는 대한민국 임시정부에 합류했고 나중에는 그것의 대표자가 되었다.

8 기념관 안에 있는 전시관은 김구의 삶에 관한 많은 것들을 보여준다.

9 우리는 전시관을 둘러보면서 한인 애국단의 단원들 사진 앞에 섰다.

10 김구는 일본에 맞서 싸우기 위해 1931년에 비밀 조직을 형성했다.

11 이봉창과 윤봉길이 그 집단에 속해 있었다.

12 전시관의 한 곳에서, 우리는 김구와 윤봉길의 사진 아래에 있는 시계 두 개를 보았다.

13 _____ 1932, Kim Koo _____ _____ _____
_____ kill Japanese generals in a park in Shanghai.

14 As the leader of the Korean _____ _____, he _____
Yun _____ _____ out the mission.

15 When Yun _____ _____ the mission, he told Kim,
"Sir, you are _____ _____ _____ _____ _____.
_____ is new, but I won't need _____ anymore. Please
_____ my watch, and _____ me _____ yours."

16 Kim Koo _____ _____ Yun's watch in his jacket
_____ _____ he would not _____ Yun's _____.

17 After _____ the tour of the museum, we _____ _____
the _____ of the three heroes, Lee Bongchang, Yun
Bonggil, and Baek Jeonggi.

18 Their bodies _____ _____ in Japan, but after Korea's
_____ Kim Koo brought _____ to Hyochang Park.

19 _____ _____ _____, he showed his deep love and
respect _____ _____ _____ of the three heroes.

20 _____ I _____ Hyochang Park, I thought about Kim
Koo's _____ in My Wish _____ I _____ _____ in
the exhibition hall.

21 _____ was _____ _____ *Baekbeomilji*.

22 If God asks me _____ _____ _____ _____, I would
say clearly, "It is _____ _____."

23 If he asks me _____ _____ _____ _____ is, I
would say, "It is the _____ of my country."

24 If he _____ _____ _____ _____ _____ _____
_____, I would say loudly, "It is the _____ _____ of
my country." That is my answer.

13 1932년에 김구는 상해에 있는 한 공원에서 일본 장군들을 암살하기 위한 계획을 세웠다.

14 한인 애국단의 지도자로서 그는 윤봉길이 임무를 수행하도록 지시했다.

15 윤봉길이 임무를 위해 떠날 때, 그는 김구에게 말했다. "선생님, 당신은 매우 낡은 시계를 차고 계시는군요. 제 것은 새것이나, 저는 그것이 더 이상 필요하지 않을 것입니다. 부디 제 시계를 가져가시고, 제가 선생님 것을 가지도록 해주십시오."

16 김구는 윤봉길의 희생을 잊지 않기 위해서 윤봉길의 시계를 항상 상의에 넣고 다녔다.

17 기념관 관람을 마치고, 우리는 이봉창, 윤봉길, 그리고 백정기 의사들이 묻힌 삼의사의 묘로 이동했다.

18 그들의 시신은 일본에 있다가 독립이 되고 나서 김구가 그들의 시신을 효창 공원으로 가져왔다.

19 그는 그렇게 함으로써 삼의사들의 희생에 대한 그의 깊은 사랑과 경의를 보여 주었다.

20 내가 효창 공원을 떠날 때, 나는 전시관에서 읽었던 「나의 소원」에 있는 김구의 말을 생각했다.

21 그것은 「백범일지」에 쓰여 있었다.

22 만약 신이 나의 소원이 무엇이냐고 묻는다면, "그것은 대한 독립이오."라고 명확하게 말할 것이다.

23 만약에 그가 나의 두 번째 소원이 무엇이냐고 묻는다면, 나는 "그것은 내 나라의 독립이오."라고 말할 것이다.

24 만약 그가 나의 세 번째 소원이 무엇이냐고 묻는다면, "그것은 내 나라의 완전한 독립이오."라고 큰 소리로 말할 것이다. 그것이 나의 대답이다.

● 우리말을 참고하여 본문을 영작하시오.

1 지난주에 우리 역사 동아리는 효창 공원에 갔다.
➡ _____

2 우리는 공원 안에 있는 김구 기념관을 방문했다.
➡ _____

3 기념관 입구에서 우리는 하얀색의 김구 조각상을 보았다.
➡ _____

4 김구는 일본 통치로부터 대한의 독립을 위해 싸우는 데 그의 삶 대부분을 보낸 위대한 국민 영웅이다.
➡ _____

5 1900년대에 그는 학교를 설립함으로써 젊은이들을 교육시키는 것을 도왔다.
➡ _____

6 1919년에 3.1 운동이 나라 전체에 걸쳐 퍼져나갔을 때, 그는 중국 상하이로 이동했다.
➡ _____
_____

7 그곳에서 그는 대한민국 임시정부에 합류했고 나중에는 그것의 대표자가 되었다.
➡ _____

8 기념관 안에 있는 전시관은 김구의 삶에 관한 많은 것들을 보여 준다.
➡ _____

9 우리는 전시관을 둘러보면서 한인 애국단의 단원들 사진 앞에 섰다.
➡ _____

10 김구는 일본에 맞서 싸우기 위해 1931년에 비밀 조직을 형성했다.
➡ _____

11 이봉창과 윤봉길이 그 집단에 속해 있었다.
➡ _____

12 전시관의 한 곳에서, 우리는 김구와 윤봉길의 사진 아래에 있는 시계 두 개를 보았다.
➡ _____

13 1932년에 김구는 상해에 있는 한 공원에서 일본 장군들을 암살하기 위한 계획을 세웠다.
➡ _____

14 한인 애국단의 지도자로서 그는 윤봉길이 임무를 수행하도록 지시했다.

➡ _____

15 윤봉길이 임무를 위해 떠날 때, 그는 김구에게 말했다. "선생님, 당신은 매우 낡은 시계를 차고 계시는군요. 제 것은 새것이나, 저는 그것이 더 이상 필요하지 않을 것입니다. 부디 제 시계를 가져가시고, 제가 선생님 것을 가지도록 해주십시오."

➡ _____

_____

16 김구는 윤봉길의 희생을 잊지 않기 위해서 윤봉길의 시계를 항상 상의에 넣고 다녔다.

➡ _____

17 기념관 관람을 마치고, 우리는 이봉창, 윤봉길, 그리고 백정기 의사들이 묻힌 삼의사의 묘로 이동했다.

➡ _____

_____

18 그들의 시신은 일본에 있다가 독립이 되고 나서 김구가 그들의 시신을 효창 공원으로 가져왔다.

➡ _____

_____

19 그는 그렇게 함으로써 삼의사들의 희생에 대한 그의 깊은 사랑과 경의를 보여 주었다.

➡ _____

20 내가 효창 공원을 떠날 때, 나는 전시관에서 읽었던 「나의 소원」에 있는 김구의 말을 생각했다.

➡ _____

21 그것은 『백범일지』에 쓰여 있었다.

➡ _____

22 만약 신이 나의 소원이 무엇이냐고 묻는다면, "그것은 대한 독립이오."라고 명확하게 말할 것이다.

➡ _____

23 만약에 그가 나의 두 번째 소원이 무엇이냐고 묻는다면, 나는 "그것은 내 나라의 독립이오."라고 말할 것이다.

➡ _____

24 만약 그가 나의 세 번째 소원이 무엇이냐고 묻는다면, "그것은 내 나라의 완전한 독립이오."라고 큰 소리로 말할 것이다. 그것이 나의 대답이다.

➡ _____

_____

[01~04] 다음 글을 읽고 물음에 답하시오.

Last week my history club went to Hyochang Park. We visited the Kim Koo Museum inside the park. At the entrance of the museum, we saw a white statue of Kim Koo. Kim Koo is a great national hero who spent most of his life fighting for the independence of Korea from Japanese rule. In the 1900s, he helped educate young people (A)_____ building schools. In 1919, when the independence movement had spread throughout the country, he moved to Shanghai, China. There he joined the Government of the Republic of Korea and later became its president.

01 다음 중 빈칸 (A)에 들어갈 말로 가장 적절한 것은?

① about   ② by   ③ at

④ on   ⑤ to

02 Choose the one that is CORRECT about Kim Koo.

① He used to live near Hyochang Park.

② He built a museum for independence of Korea.

③ He spent most of his life fighting for Japan.

④ He built schools to educate young people.

⑤ He lived in Korea all his life.

03 Where is the statue of Kim Koo? Answer in English with eight words.

➡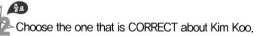

04 When did Kim Koo move to Shanghai? Answer in English with six words.

➡ _____

[05~08] 다음 글을 읽고 물음에 답하시오.

The exhibition hall in the museum shows a lot of things about Kim Koo's life. While looking around the hall, we stopped at a photo of the Korean Patriotic Organization's members. Kim Koo formed the secret organization in 1931 to fight against Japan. Lee Bongchang and Yun Bonggil belonged to the group. At one place in the hall, we saw two watches under a photo of Kim Koo and Yun Bonggil. In 1932, Kim Koo made a plan to kill Japanese generals in a park in Shanghai. As the leader of the Korean Patriotic Organization, he directed Yun to carry out the mission.

When Yun left for the mission, he told Kim, "Sir, you are wearing a very old watch. Mine is new, but I won't need it anymore. Please take my watch, and let me have yours." Kim Koo always carried Yun's watch in his jacket so that he would not forget Yun's sacrifice.

05 다음 중 기념관 내 전시관에서 찾아볼 수 있는 것을 <u>모두</u> 고르시오.

① many books about Kim Koo's life

② a photo of the Korean Patriotic Organization's members

③ the statues of Lee Bongchang and Yun Bonggil

④ two watches which belonged to Yun Bonggil and Kim Koo

⑤ a photo of Kim Koo with his family

06 Where did Kim Koo plan to kill Japanese generals? Answer in English with twelve words.

➡ _____

_____

07 다음 중 위 글을 읽고 답할 수 있는 것은?

① Where was Kim Koo born?
② How many exhibition halls are there in the museum?
③ How many members were there in the Korean Patriotic Organization?
④ What did Kim Koo form in 1931?
⑤ When did Kim Koo and Yun Bonggil take the picture?

08 다음 중 위 글의 내용을 바르게 이해한 사람은?

① Amelia: It is hard to know many things about Kim Koo at the exhibition hall.
② Brian: It is surprising that Kim Koo didn't join the Korean Patriotic Organization.
③ Claire: I'm so sorry Yun didn't leave for the mission.
④ David: Yun was the leader of the Korean Patriotic Organization.
⑤ Ethon: It's so touching that Kim Koo always carried Yun's watch.

[09~11] 다음 글을 읽고 물음에 답하시오.

(A) By doing so, he showed his deep love and respect for the sacrifice of the three heroes.

(B) Their bodies had been in Japan, but after Korea's independence Kim Koo brought them to Hyochang Park.

(C) After completing the tour of the museum, we moved to the tombs of the three heroes, Lee Bongchang, Yun Bonggil, and Baek Jeonggi.

As I left Hyochang Park, I thought about Kim Koo's words in My Wish ⓐ_____ I had read in the exhibition hall. It was written in *Baekbeomilji*.

If God asks me what my wish is, I would say clearly, "It is Korea's Independence." If he asks me what my second wish is, I would say, "It is the independence of my country." If he asks me what my third wish is, I would say loudly, "It is the complete independence of my country." That is my answer.

09 다음 중 빈칸 ⓐ에 들어갈 말로 적절한 것을 모두 고르시오.

① which ② whose ③ that
④ what ⑤ who

10 자연스러운 글이 되도록 (A)~(C)를 바르게 나열한 것은?

① (A)–(C)–(B) ② (B)–(A)–(C)
③ (B)–(C)–(A) ④ (C)–(A)–(B)
⑤ (C)–(B)–(A)

11 주어진 어구를 바르게 나열하여 다음 물음에 대한 답을 완성하시오.

Q: What was written in *Baekbeomilji*?
A: (*Baekbeomilji* / Korea / written / of / independence / in / for / the / Kim Koo's / complete / firm wish / was)

➡ _____

_____

[12~15] 다음 글을 읽고 물음에 답하시오.

Last week my history club went to Hyochang Park. We visited the Kim Koo Museum inside the park. At the entrance of the museum, we saw a white statue of Kim Koo. Kim Koo is a great national hero who spent most of his life fighting for the independence of Korea from Japanese rule. In the 1900s, he helped educate young people by building schools. In 1919, when the independence movement had spread throughout the country, he moved to Shanghai, China. There he joined the Government of the Republic of Korea and later became its president.

서답형
12 위 글의 내용에 맞게 빈칸에 알맞은 말을 쓰시오.

The history club went to Hyochang Park in order to _____ _____ _____
_____ _____ _____ _____
_____.

13 다음 중 효창 공원에서 찾아볼 수 있는 것은?

① the school Kim Koo built for young people
② the pictures of young people taught by Kim Koo
③ a picture of independence movement
④ a large white sculpture of Kim Koo
⑤ a museum Kim Koo built

서답형
14 According to the passage, what did Kim Koo fight for? Answer in English with a full sentence.

➡ _____
_____

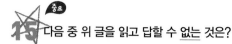

15 다음 중 위 글을 읽고 답할 수 없는 것은?

① Where is the Kim Koo Museum?
② What did the writer's history club do last week?
③ How did Kim Koo help educate young people?
④ How did the club go to Hyochang Park?
⑤ When did the independence movement spread throughout the country?

[16~18] 다음 글을 읽고 물음에 답하시오.

The exhibition hall in the museum shows ① a lot of things about Kim Koo's life. While looking ②after the hall, we stopped ③at a photo of the Korean Patriotic Organization's members. Kim Koo ④formed the secret organization in 1931 to fight against Japan. Lee Bongchang and Yun Bonggil ⑤belonged to the group. At one place in the hall, we saw two watches under a photo of Kim Koo and Yun Bonggil.

16 다음과 같이 풀이되는 말을 위 글에서 찾아 쓰시오.

a public event at which pictures, sculptures, or other objects of interest are displayed

➡ _____

17 밑줄 친 ①~⑤ 중 글의 흐름상 어색한 것은?

①   ②   ③   ④   ⑤

서답형
18 What were there under a photo of Kim Koo and Yun Bonggil?

➡ _____

[19~21] 다음 글을 읽고 물음에 답하시오.

In 1932, ①Kim Koo made a plan to kill Japanese generals in a park in Shanghai. (A)As the leader of the Korean Patriotic Organization, ②he directed Yun to carry out the mission. When ③he left for the mission, Yun told Kim, "Sir, ④you are wearing a very old watch. Mine is new, but I won't need (B)it anymore. Please take my watch, and let me have yours." Kim Koo always carried Yun's watch in ⑤his jacket so that he would not forget Yun's sacrifice.

19 밑줄 친 ①~⑤ 중 가리키는 것이 다른 하나는?

①   ②   ③   ④   ⑤

20 중요   다음 중 밑줄 친 (A)와 쓰임이 같은 것은?

① They were all dressed as clowns.

② You are as kind as your father.

③ As they were out, I left a message.

④ As you know, Susan is leaving soon.

⑤ We look up to him as a doctor.

서답형
21 밑줄 친 (B)가 의미하는 것을 두 단어의 영어로 쓰시오.

➡ _____

[22~25] 다음 글을 읽고 물음에 답하시오.

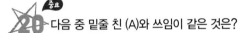

After completing the tour of the museum, we moved to the tombs of the three heroes, Lee Bongchang, Yun Bonggil, and Baek Jeonggi. ①Their bodies had been in Japan, but after Korea's ②independence Kim Koo brought them to Hyochang Park. By doing so, he showed his deep love and respect for the ③sacrifice of the three heroes.

As I left Hyochang Park, I thought about Kim Koo's words in My Wish that I had read in the exhibition hall. It was written in *Baekbeomilji*.

If God asks me what my wish is, I would say clearly, "It is Korea's Independence." If he asks me what my second wish is, I would say, "It is the independence of my country." If he asks me what my third wish is, I would say loudly, "It is the ④complement independence of my country." That is my ⑤answer.

22 중요   밑줄 친 ①~⑤ 중 글의 흐름상 어색한 것은?

①   ②   ③   ④   ⑤

23 According to the passage, what did Kim Koo wish most?

① respect from people

② reliance on Japan

③ achieving independence of Korea

④ making Korea a rich country

⑤ making Korea dependent

24 Choose the sentence that is TRUE according to the passage.

① They have just started touring the museum.

② It is uncertain who were buried in the tombs.

③ Kim Koo brought the bodies before Korea's independence.

④ Kim Koo hardly loved the three heroes.

⑤ It was Kim Koo who brought three heroes' bodies into Korea from Japan.

서답형
25 Where are Kim Koo's words written? Answer in English with a full sentence.

➡ _____

[01~05] 다음 글을 읽고 물음에 답하시오.

Last week my history club went to Hyochang Park. We visited the Kim Koo Museum inside the park. At the entrance of the museum, we saw a white statue of Kim Koo. Kim Koo is a great national hero who spent most of his life fighting for the independence of Korea from Japanese rule. In the 1900s, he helped educate young people by building schools. In 1919, when the independence movement had spread throughout the country, he moved to Shanghai, China. (A) There he joined the Government of the Republic of Korea and later became its president.

01 밑줄 친 (A)가 가리키는 것을 위 글에서 찾아 쓰시오.

➡ _____

02 Where did the writer's history club go last week? Answer in English and use the word 'they.'

➡ _____

03 What was there at the entrance of the museum?

➡ _____
_____

04 Where was the Government of the Republic of Korea? Answer in English with a full sentence.

➡ _____

05 위 글의 내용에 맞게 빈칸에 알맞은 말을 쓰시오.

Kim Koo(1876~1949)
He is a great _____ who fought for _____ from Japanese rule.

[06~08] 다음 글을 읽고 물음에 답하시오.

The exhibition hall in the museum shows a lot of things about Kim Koo's life. While looking around the hall, we stopped at a photo of the Korean Patriotic Organization's members. Kim Koo formed the secret organization in 1931 to fight against Japan. Lee Bongchang and Yun Bonggil belonged to the group. At one place in the hall, we saw two watches under a photo of Kim Koo and Yun Bonggil.

06 Whose photo did the writer see?

➡ _____
_____

07 Write the reason why Kim Koo formed the secret organization in 1931. Use the phrase 'It was because' and 'try to.'

➡ _____

08 위 글의 내용에 맞게 빈칸에 알맞은 말을 쓰시오.

A: Do you know who _____ _____ _____ that Kim Koo formed?
B: Yes, I do. Lee Bongchang and Yun Bonggil did.

[09~11] 다음 글을 읽고 물음에 답하시오.

In 1932, Kim Koo made a plan to kill Japanese generals in a park in Shanghai. As the leader of the Korean Patriotic Organization, he directed Yun to carry out the mission.

When Yun left for the mission, he told Kim, "Sir, you are wearing a very old watch. Mine is new, but I won't need it anymore. Please take my watch, and let me have yours." Kim Koo always carried Yun's watch in his jacket so that he would not forget Yun's sacrifice.

09 What was Kim Koo's plan? Answer in English with a full sentence.

➡ _____

_____

10 위 글의 내용에 맞게 빈칸에 들어갈 알맞은 말을 쓰시오.

> In 1932, Yun _____ _____ with Kim Koo before he left to carry out the mission Kim Koo directed.

11 Write the reason why Kim Koo always carried Yun's watch in his jacket. Use the phrase 'It was because.'

➡ _____

[12~15] 다음 글을 읽고 물음에 답하시오.

After completing the tour of the museum, we moved to the tombs of the three heroes, Lee Bongchang, Yun Bonggil, and Baek Jeonggi. Their bodies had been in Japan, but after Korea's independence Kim Koo brought them to Hyochang Park. By (A)doing so, he showed his deep love and respect for the sacrifice of the three heroes.

As I left Hyochang Park, I thought about Kim Koo's words in My Wish that I had read in the exhibition hall. It was written in *Baekbeomilji*.

If God asks me what my wish is, I would say clearly, "It is Korea's Independence." If he asks me what my second wish is, I would say, "It is the independence of my country." If he asks me what my third wish is, I would say loudly, "It is the complete independence of my country." That is my answer.

12 After they completed the tour of the museum, what did they do? Answer in English with a full sentence.

➡ _____

_____

13 밑줄 친 (A)가 의미하는 것을 우리말로 쓰시오.

➡ _____

14 Where did the writer read My Wish? Answer in English with seven words.

➡ _____

15 According to the passage, what was Kim Koo's third wish? Answer in English with a full sentence.

➡ _____

_____

교과서

구석구석

Real Life Talk Step 3

My group members chose An Junggeun because we were impressed by his
choose의 과거형(choose–chose–chosen)   ~에 깊은 인상을 받았다
sacrifice for the country. You can learn more about him by visiting the An
                   by+Ving: V함으로써
Junggeun Museum or An Junggeun Park.

구문해설 · choose: 선택하다 · sacrifice: ~을 희생하다

해석

우리 그룹은 안중근을 선택했는데, 우리 나라를 위한 희생에 깊은 인상을 받았기 때문입니다. 여러분은 안중근 기념관이나 안중근 공원을 방문함으로써 그에 관하여 더 많은 것을 알 수 있습니다.

Enjoy Writing

Dosan An Changho

An Changho was born in 1878. When he was in his teens, he moved to Seoul
and went to school there. In 1902, he left for America so that he could get
              = in Seoul   '목적' ~하기 위해서 = in order that he could
a better education. In America, An helped improve the lives of the Korean
                        = helped to improve   life의 복수형
people there and became a respected leader. After he had returned to Korea, he
people there = people (who were) there   과거완료시제
founded the New Korean Society in 1907 to fight for Korea's independence.

He also joined the Government of the Republic of Korea in Shanghai in 1919.
        타동사(전치사 불필요)
After that, he built a lot of schools to educate people until he died in 1938.
                  부사적 용법(목적) = so that he could educate   접속사('~할 때까지')

구문해설 · in one's teens: 10대 시절에 · respected: 존경받는 · the New Korean Society: 신민회
· republic: 공화국

도산 안창호

안창호는 1878년에 태어났다. 그가 십 대였을 때, 그는 서울로 이사를 하고 그곳에서 학교를 다녔다. 1902년에 그는 더 나은 교육을 받기 위해서 미국으로 떠났다. 안창호는 미국에서 한국인들의 삶을 개선하는 것을 도왔고, 존경받는 지도자가 되었다. 그가 한국으로 돌아오고 나서, 그는 대한의 독립을 위해 싸우고자 1907년에 신민회를 설립했다. 그는 또한 1919년에 상해의 대한민국 임시정부에 합류했다. 그 후에, 그는 1938년에 죽을 때까지 사람들을 교육하기 위해 많은 학교들을 세웠다.

Project Step 1

A: I want to introduce Bulguksa to foreigners. You know Bulguksa, don't you?
                                       일반동사 긍정문의 부가의문문

B: Yes, I do. It's a temple in Gyeongju.
           = Bulguksa

C: Yes. It's one of the most beautiful temples in Korea.
            one of the 최상급+복수명사: 가장 ~한 것들 중 하나

D: It also has many treasures like the Dabotop.
             many+복수명사   전치사: ~와 같은

구문해설 · introduce: 소개하다 · foreigner: 외국인 · temple: 사원, 절 · treasure: 보물

A: 나는 외국인에게 불국사를 소개하고 싶어. 너는 불국사를 알고 있지, 그렇지 않니?

B: 응, 알고 있어. 그것은 경주에 있는 절이야.

C: 응. 그것은 한국에서 가장 아름다운 절 중 하나야.

D: 그것은 또한 다보탑과 같은 많은 문화재들을 보유하고 있어.

Words & Expressions

01 다음 주어진 두 단어의 관계가 같도록 빈칸에 알맞은 단어를 쓰시오.

> independence - dependence : exit - _____

02 다음 문장의 빈칸 (A)와 (B)에 들어갈 단어가 바르게 짝지어진 것은?

> • I want to work for international (A) _____ such as the UN.
> • There is no love without (B) _____.

① harmony – rule
② statue – dependence
③ specialist – desire
④ leader – member
⑤ organization – sacrifice

[03~04] 다음 영영풀이에 해당하는 것을 고르시오.

03

> a piece of cloth that is usually attached at the end of a pole and represents a country or association

① hall   ② exhibition
③ flag   ④ tomb
⑤ god

04

> a series of things that happen one after another for a particular result

① process   ② republic
③ wish   ④ president
⑤ poem

05 다음 빈칸에 주어진 철자를 이용하여 한 단어를 쓰시오.

> The museum is staging an e_____ of Picasso's works.

06 다음 밑줄 친 부분의 뜻이 잘못된 것은?

① The main part of the building is crowded with people. (주요한)
② Koreans celebrate Independence Day on August 15th. (독립)
③ The government made a new policy. (정부)
④ He had no desire to discuss the matter further. (안건)
⑤ The queen wears a crown only on certain official events. (왕관)

Conversation

07 다음 대화의 빈칸에 들어갈 말을 주어진 어구를 알맞은 순서로 배열하여 완성하시오.

> G: I'm planning to go to the Gansong Museum.
> B: What is the Gansong Museum?
> G: It's a museum built by Gansong Jeon Hyeongpil.
> B: I heard that he did great things for the country.
> G: Yes. _____
> _____
> B: Wow. The museum must be interesting.
> G: Yes. I'm looking forward to it!

> some Japanese / many Korean treasures / he / had taken / bought / that / to Japan

08 그림을 보고 다음 대화의 빈칸을 완성하시오.

G: I'm making a model of the Turtle Ship. _____ _____ about it, _____ you?

B: Yes, I know about it.

[09~11] 다음 대화를 읽고 물음에 답하시오.

Andy: Bora, what are you reading?

Bora: I'm reading *Sky, Wind, Star, and Poetry* by Yun Dongju. You know about Yun Dongju, don't you?

Andy: I've heard his name, but I don't know much about him. (①)

Bora: He wrote many beautiful poems when Korea was under Japanese rule. His love for the country and his desire for independence can be felt in his poems.

Andy: (②) I want to read his poems and learn more about him.

Bora: Great. (③) In fact, I'm planning to visit the Yun Dongju Museum soon. Do you want to come with me?

Andy: Yes, when are you going?

Bora: Next Saturday. It's near Gyeongbok Palace. (④) Can you meet me at the palace at 2 p.m.?

Andy: Sure. Let's meet there. (⑤)

Bora: Great. I'm really looking forward to the visit.

09 위 대화의 (①)~(⑤) 중 주어진 문장이 들어갈 위치로 알맞은 것은?

> Really? I didn't know that.

① ② ③ ④ ⑤

10 위 대화를 읽고 다음 물음에 영어로 답하시오.

> Q: What are they planning to do next Saturday?

➡ _____

11 위 대화의 내용과 일치하지 <u>않는</u> 것은?

① Bora is reading a poem by Yun Dongju.

② Andy doesn't know much about Yun Dongju.

③ Bora suggested to Andy that he should read many poems by Yun Dongju.

④ Bora may have felt Yun Dongju's love for the country and his desire for independence.

⑤ Bora is looking forward to visiting the Yun Dongju Museum.

Grammar

[12~13] 다음 중 어법상 <u>어색한</u> 문장을 고르시오.

12 ① Would you share your recipe so that we can make a good dish like yours?

② Sam learned the computer science so as to develop much better devices.

③ Prepare rice and water so that you can make Juk, the Korean porridge.

④ Tim got up early so as not to miss the bus.

⑤ Isabelle practiced hard so that for her to get a scholarship.

13
① All my family were really full because we had had lunch.
② Betty had read comic books before she went to bed.
③ Yesterday, my wife lost the necklace that my son had bought for her two days before.
④ When the singer arrived at the show, the opening part had just began.
⑤ Susan wasn't able to recognize him, because she had never seen him before.

14 다음 두 문장의 의미가 같도록 바꿔 쓸 때 적절하지 않은 것은?

① Jenny cleaned the house so that the guests could feel comfortable.
   = Jenny cleaned the house for the guests to feel comfortable.
② Robert makes pancakes in order that his five kids can eat.
   = Robert makes pancakes so that his five kids can eat.
③ The young college students held the thief tight so that he could not run away.
   = The young college students held the thief tight in order not for him to run away.
④ Nancy practiced her movement really hard in order to pass the audition.
   = Nancy practiced her movement really hard so that she might pass the audition.
⑤ Daeho went to Tokyo so that he could learn Japanese.
   = Daeho went to Tokyo in order to learn Japanese.

15 다음 그림을 보고 괄호 안의 단어를 배열하여 빈칸을 알맞게 채우시오.

(1)

➡ The students are practicing hard _____ _____ _____ _____ _____ a good performance. (show, so, can, they, that)

(2)

➡ Many tourists gathered at the Louvre Museum _____ _____ _____ _____ _____ _____ _____. (the *Mona Lisa*, they, that, so, could, see)

16 다음 괄호 안에서 어법상 알맞은 것을 고르시오.

(1) An Junggeun was sentenced to death after he (had killed / has killed) Ito Hirobumi.
(2) Some of the K-pop fans around the world said that they (have been / had been) learning Korean to understand the lyrics of the songs clearly.
(3) Yesterday I learned that Kim Koo (had made / made) a plan to kill Japanese generals in Shanghai in 1932.
(4) The queen (has gone / had gone) to London before the prince got injured at the car accident.
(5) Sven dropped the carrot that Olaf (had pulled / has pulled) out of the field in the snow.

17 다음 그림을 참고하여 〈보기〉에 주어진 어구를 우리말과 일치하도록 어법상 알맞은 형태로 바꿔 배열하시오. (모든 단어를 한 번 이상 사용할 것.)

┌─── 보기 ───┐

the rabbit, the ant, the grasshopper, she, he, regretted, reminded, play, sleep, in, that, the middle of, the summer, the race

(1) 토끼는 경주 도중에 잤던 것을 후회했다.
(2) 개미는 베짱이가 여름에 놀았던 것을 일깨워 줬다.

(1)

➡ _____

_____

(2)

➡ _____

_____

Reading

[18~20] 다음 글을 읽고 물음에 답하시오.

Last week my history club went to Hyochang Park. ① At the entrance of the museum, we saw a white statue of Kim Koo. ② Kim Koo is a great national hero who spent most of his life fighting for the independence of Korea from Japanese rule. ③ In the 1900s, he helped educate young people by building schools. ④ In 1919,

when the independence movement had spread throughout the country, he moved to Shanghai, China. ⑤ There he joined the Government of the Republic of Korea and later became its president.

18 ①~⑤ 중 주어진 문장이 들어가기에 가장 적절한 곳은?

┌──────────────────────────┐
│ We visited the Kim Koo Museum inside │
│ the park.   │
└──────────────────────────┘

①   ②   ③   ④   ⑤

19 Write the reason why Kim Koo built schools. Use the phrase 'in order to.'

➡ _____

_____

20 다음 중 위 글의 내용과 일치하는 것은?

① The history club went to Hyochang Park a couple of weeks ago.
② The statue of Kim Koo is at the entrance of the park.
③ Kim Koo spent most of his life educating young people.
④ The independence movement spread throughout the country until 1900s.
⑤ Kim Koo joined the Government of the Republic of Korea in China.

[21~23] 다음 글을 읽고 물음에 답하시오.

An Changho was born in 1878. When he was in his teens, he moved to Seoul and went to school there. In 1902, he left for America ①so that he could get a better education. In America,

An helped ②improve the lives of the Korean people there and became a ③respecting leader. After he ④had returned to Korea, he founded the New Korean Society in 1907 to fight for Korea's independence. He also joined the Government of the Republic of Korea in Shanghai in 1919. After that, he built a lot of schools ⑤to educate people until he died in 1938.

21 ①~⑤ 중 문맥상 바르지 않은 것은?

①   ②   ③   ④   ⑤

22 다음 중 위 글의 내용과 일치하지 않는 곳을 찾아 바르게 고쳐 쓰시오.

> An Changho was born in Korea and left for America in his twenties. After spending some time in America, he returned to Korea and found the New Korean Society in 1907 in order to fight for Korea's independence.

➡ _____

23 다음 중 위 글을 읽고 답할 수 없는 것은?

① When was An Changho born?
② When did An Changho leave for America?
③ What did An Chanho do in America?
④ How many schools did An Changho build?
⑤ What did An Changho do until he died?

[24~26] 다음 글을 읽고 물음에 답하시오.

The exhibition hall in the museum shows (A) a lot of things about Kim Koo's life. While looking around the hall, we stopped at a photo of the Korean Patriotic Organization's members. Kim Koo formed the secret organization in 1931 to fight against Japan. Lee Bongchang and Yun Bonggil belonged to the group. At one place in the hall, we saw two watches under a photo of Kim Koo and Yun Bonggil. In 1932, Kim Koo made a plan to kill Japanese generals in a park in Shanghai. As the leader of the Korean Patriotic Organization, he directed Yun to carry out the mission.

24 다음 중 밑줄 친 (A)를 대신하여 쓰일 수 없는 것은?

① lots of   ② many
③ a number of   ④ the number of
⑤ plenty of

25 According to the passage, when did Kim Koo form the Korean Patriotic Organization?

➡ _____
_____

26 According to the passage, choose the sentence that is TRUE.

① The Korean Patriotic Organization was a public organization.
② Kim Koo formed an organization to fight for Japan.
③ Lee Bongchang was the only member of the Korean Patriotic Organization.
④ Kim Koo planned to kill Japanese generals in a park in Korea.
⑤ Kim Koo directed Yun Bonggil to kill Japanese generals.

출제율 95%

01 다음 짝지어진 단어의 관계가 같도록 빈칸에 알맞은 말을 쓰시오.

complete – incomplete : deep – _____

출제율 90%

02 다음 영영풀이에 해당하는 단어는?

a circular ornament made of gold and decorated with jewels that is worn by a king or queen on their head

① device　　　② clown

③ crown　　　④ couch

⑤ hall

[03~04] 다음 대화를 읽고 물음에 답하시오.

B: Soyeon, what did you do last weekend?

G: I went to Hyeonchungwon to do volunteer work.

B: What kind of volunteer work did you do there?

G: I cleaned around the tombs. (A)나는 나라를 위해 돌아가신 분들에게 대단한 경의를 느꼈어.

B: Sounds great. Can I do it, too?

G: Sure. I'm planning to go there again next Wednesday. Will you join me?

B: Sure. I'm looking forward to it.

출제율 90%

03 위 대화의 밑줄 친 (A)의 우리말에 맞게 주어진 어구를 알맞은 순서로 배열하시오.

I / for the country / who / felt / for the people / died / great respect

➡ _____

_____

출제율 100%

04 위 대화의 내용과 일치하지 <u>않는</u> 것은?

① Soyeon did volunteer work in the museum.

② Soyeon felt respect while doing volunteer work.

③ Soyeon cleaned around the tombs.

④ Soyeon is planning to go there again next Wednesday.

⑤ Both Soyeon and the boy will go to Hyeonchungwon together.

[05~06] 다음 대화를 읽고 물음에 답하시오.

G: Brian, you know Taegeukgi, don't you?

B: Sure. It's the national flag of Korea, isn't it?

G: That's right. (A)_____

B: No, I don't. Tell me about them.

G: The circle in the middle means (B) _____ and peace.

B: What do the black lines on the four corners mean?

G: They mean four things: sky, fire, water, and earth.

출제율 95%

05 위 대화의 빈칸 (A)에 들어갈 말로 알맞은 것은?

① What do you know about Taegeukgi?

② Can you draw Taegeukgi?

③ Do you know the origin of Taegeukgi?

④ Do you know what the symbols in Taegeukgi mean?

⑤ Do you know who made Taegeukgi?

06 위 대화의 빈칸 (B)에 들어갈 단어를 <영영풀이>를 참고하여 쓰시오.

<영영풀이>

a situation in which people are peaceful and agree with each other, or when things seem right or suitable together

➡ _____

[07~08] 다음 대화를 읽고 물음에 답하시오.

Andy: Bora, what are you reading?

Bora: I'm reading *Sky, Wind, Star, and Poetry* by Yun Dongju. (A)<u>너는 윤동주에 대해 알고 있지, 그렇지 않니?</u>

Andy: I've heard his name, but I don't know much about him.

Bora: He wrote many beautiful poems when Korea was under Japanese rule. His love for the country and his desire for independence (B)<u>can feel</u> in his poems.

Andy: Really? I didn't know that. I want to read his poems and learn more about him.

Bora: Great. In fact, I'm planning to visit the Yun Dongju Museum soon. Do you want to come with me?

Andy: Yes, when are you going?

Bora: Next Saturday. It's near Gyeongbok Palace. Can you meet me at the palace at 2 p.m.?

Andy: Sure. Let's meet there.

Bora: Great. I'm really looking forward to the visit.

07 위 대화의 밑줄 친 (A)에 맞게 주어진 단어를 활용하여 영작하시오.

about, Yun Dongju

➡ _____

08 위 대화의 밑줄 친 (B)를 알맞은 형태로 고친 것은?

① can feel
② can to be felt
③ can felt
④ can be feeling
⑤ can be felt

09 대화의 밑줄 친 (A)를 문법적으로 맞게 고쳐 쓰시오.

G: I'm planning to go to the Gansong Museum.

B: What is the Gansong Museum?

G: (A)<u>It's a museum was built by Gansong Jeon Hyeongpil.</u>

B: I heard that he did great things for the country.

G: Yes. He bought many Korean treasures that some Japanese had taken to Japan.

B: Wow. The museum must be interesting.

G: Yes. I'm looking forward to it!

➡ _____
_____
_____

10 다음 각 빈칸에 공통으로 들어갈 단어 중 나머지 넷과 성격이 다른 하나는?

① Please turn the light on _____ that we can find the way out.
② Eddy hurried _____ that he wouldn't miss the plane Susan was in.
③ The police officer talked louder _____ that the old lady could understand.
④ Will and Ben woke up early _____ that they could see their daddy off.
⑤ Jacob was _____ busy that he couldn't join our party.

11 다음 〈보기〉의 문장과 같은 뜻이 되도록 각 괄호 안의 주어진 조건에 맞게 빈칸을 채우시오.

> ─ 보기 ─
>
> Paula had to read the textbook many times so that she would not forget the contents.

(1) Paula had to read the textbook many times ＿＿＿＿＿＿＿ the contents. (to부정사의 부사적 용법 활용, 3 단어)

(2) Paula had to read the textbook many times ＿＿＿＿＿＿＿ the contents. (so as 활용, 5 단어)

(3) Paula had to read the textbook many times ＿＿＿＿＿＿＿ she would not forget the contents. (in 활용, 3 단어)

12 다음 중 어법상 올바른 문장을 모두 고르면?

① The grass looked greener than before because it had rained last week.

② Sandy heard that the manager has overworked the day before.

③ Yuna's husband was surprised that she has been elected as a chairwoman.

④ The first period began when I had arrived at the court.

⑤ Jonathan returned the book which he had borrowed from the library.

13 다음 문장의 빈칸 (a)~(d)에 들어갈 말을 〈보기〉에서 골라 순서대로 나열한 것은?

> • Vicky plays classical music to her son every day (a)＿＿＿＿.
> • Kate has been practicing 500 shots a day for the past 4 years (b)＿＿＿＿.
> • Taylor returned all of the overdue books to the library (c)＿＿＿＿.
> • Clara stopped eating junk food (d) ＿＿＿＿.

> ─ 보기 ─
>
> (A) so that he wouldn't be fined
> (B) so that she could become healthier
> (C) so that he can be a great musician
> (D) so that she can win the gold medal

① (A)-(B)-(C)-(D) ② (A)-(C)-(D)-(B)
③ (B)-(D)-(A)-(C) ④ (C)-(D)-(A)-(B)
⑤ (C)-(A)-(B)-(D)

[14~16] 다음 글을 읽고 물음에 답하시오.

Last week my history club went to Hyochang Park. We visited the Kim Koo Museum inside the park. At the entrance of the museum, we saw a white statue of Kim Koo. Kim Koo is a great national hero ①who spent most of his life ②fight for the independence of Korea from Japanese rule. In the 1900s, he helped ③educate young people by building schools. In 1919, when the independence movement ④had spread throughout the country, he moved to Shanghai, China. There he ⑤joined the Government of the Republic of Korea and later became its president.

14 ①~⑤ 중 어법상 바르지 않은 것은?

① ② ③ ④ ⑤

15 주어진 단어를 활용하여 다음 물음에 답하시오. 필요하다면 어휘를 변형하시오.

> Q: What did Kim Koo do in the 1900s?
> (build / to / help)

➡ ＿＿＿＿＿＿＿＿＿＿＿＿＿＿＿＿

16 다음 중 위 글을 읽고 답할 수 있는 것은?

① Where is Hyochang Park?
② How did they get to Hyochang Park?
③ What is there inside Hyochang Park?
④ Who made the statue of Kim Koo?
⑤ How did Kim Koo build schools?

[17~19] 다음 글을 읽고 물음에 답하시오.

An Changho was born in 1878. ① When he was in his teens, he moved to Seoul and went to school there. ② In America, An helped improve the lives of the Korean people there and became a respected leader. ③ After he had returned to Korea, he founded the New Korean Society in 1907 to fight for Korea's independence. ④ He also joined the Government of the Republic of Korea in Shanghai in 1919. ⑤ After that, he built a lot of schools to educate people until he died in 1938.

17 ①~⑤ 중 주어진 문장이 들어가기에 가장 적절한 곳은?

In 1902, he left for America so that he could get a better education.

①　　②　　③　　④　　⑤

18 According to the passage, what did An Changho do until he died in 1938? Answer in English with a full sentence.

➡ _____

19 다음 중 위 글의 내용과 일치하지 않는 것은?

① An Changho was born in the late 1800s.
② An Changho went to school in Seoul.
③ People in America respected An Changho.
④ An Changho didn't return to Korea again.
⑤ It was An Changho who founded the New Korean Society in 1907.

[20~21] 다음 글을 읽고 물음에 답하시오.

At one place in the hall, we saw two watches under a photo of Kim Koo and Yun Bonggil. In 1932, Kim Koo made a plan (A)to kill Japanese generals in a park in Shanghai. As the leader of the Korean Patriotic Organization, he directed Yun to carry out (B) the mission.

20 다음 중 밑줄 친 (A)와 쓰임이 같은 것은?

① We went into the building to meet them.
② Is there any chance to see you again?
③ It was impossible to get there on time.
④ To make it delicious, I added some sugar.
⑤ He must be generous to give you his watch.

21 밑줄 친 (B)가 의미하는 것을 위 글에서 찾아 우리말로 쓰시오.

➡ _____

01 다음 대화를 읽고 '수원 화성'에 대한 요약문을 완성하시오.

> B: Look at Suwon Hawseong. It's huge.
>
> G: It also looks strong.
>
> B: Because it was built to protect the people during wars.
>
> G: Wow. Do you know who built it?
>
> B: Yes. King Jeongjo ordered Jeong Yakyong to direct the building process. You know about Jeong Yakyong, don't you?
>
> G: Yes, I've heard of him. He was a great scientist in Joseon.

➡ Suwon Hwaseong _____
the people during wars. Jeong Yakyong _____ its _____.

02 다음 그림을 보고, 내용에 맞게 〈보기〉에서 알맞은 단어를 하나씩 선택하여 ⓐ~ⓕ의 빈칸에 어법상 알맞은 형태로 써 넣으시오. (A)의 빈칸에는 〈보기〉에 없는 단어 두 개를 이용하여, 내용과 어법에 맞게 써 넣으시오.

┌─── 보기 ───┐
like   allow   complete   burn
use   disappoint
└──────────────┘

The principal ⓐ_____ us ⓑ_____ the cooking studio in our school when the exam was over. Half an hour ago, before Annie and I ⓒ_____ the chocolate pie, it ⓓ_____ up. I was so ⓔ_____. I just wanted to give David delicious food (A)_____ he could ⓕ _____ me.

03 다음 중에서 틀린 문장을 찾아 기호를 쓰고, 바르게 고쳐 문장을 다시 쓰시오.

① The secretary said she had already finished her work before noon.

② The young politician was tired because he had played soccer the day before.

③ Shane refused to go to the theater as he had already watched the movie.

④ I had found out that she lost her bag.

⑤ The repairman said that someone had broken the toilet cover.

➡ _____

04 다음 우리말로 제시한 세 문장을 영작할 때, 〈보기〉의 어구를 사용하여 빈칸에 알맞게 써 넣으시오. (중복 사용 불가)

┌─── 보기 ───┐
could / my uncle / in order to / had / it / so that / warm / bought / show / my body / which
└──────────────┘

(1) 나는 내 몸을 덥힐 수 있도록 뜨거운 커피를 주문했다.

➡ I ordered hot coffee _____
_____.

(2) 우리집 반려동물 토토가 삼촌이 나를 위해 사줬던 스커트를 물어뜯었다.

➡ My pet Toto bit off the skirt _____
_____ for me.

(3) 세호는 어머니에게 보여드리기 위해서 춤 동작들을 연습했다.

➡ Seho practiced the dance movements _____ them to his mom.

[05~07] 다음 글을 읽고 물음에 답하시오.

An Changho was born in 1878. When he was in his teens, he moved to Seoul and went to school there. (A)In 1902, he left for America so that he could get a better education. In America, An helped improve the lives of the Korean people there and became a respected leader. After he had returned to Korea, he founded the New Korean Society in 1907 to fight for Korea's independence. He also joined the Government of the Republic of Korea in Shanghai in 1919. After that, he built a lot of schools to educate people until he died in 1938.

05 빈칸에 알맞은 말을 써서 밑줄 친 (A)와 같은 의미의 문장을 완성하시오.

= In 1902, he left for America _____ _____ _____ get a better education.
= In 1902, he left for America _____ get a better education.

06 Write the reason why An Changho founded the New Korean Society in 1907. Answer in English with eight words.

➡ _____

_____

07 What did An Changho do in America? Answer in Korean.

➡ _____

[08~10] 다음 글을 읽고 물음에 답하시오.

After completing the tour of the museum, we moved to the tombs of the three heroes, Lee Bongchang, Yun Bonggil, and Baek Jeonggi. Their bodies had been in Japan, but after Korea's independence Kim Koo brought them to Hyochang Park. By doing so, he showed his deep love and respect for the sacrifice of the three heroes.

As I left Hyochang Park, I thought about Kim Koo's words in My Wish that I had read in the exhibition hall. (A)It was written in *Baekbeomilji*.

If God asks me what my wish is, I would say clearly, "It is Korea's Independence." If he asks me what my second wish is, I would say, "It is the independence of my country." If he asks me what my third wish is, I would say loudly, "It is the complete independence of my country." That is my answer.

08 밑줄 친 (A)가 가리키는 것을 위 글에서 찾아 쓰시오.

➡ _____

09 Where are the tombs of the three heroes now? Answer in English with five words.

➡ _____

10 위 글의 내용에 맞도록 주어진 단어 중에서 골라 빈칸에 알맞게 쓰시오.

(inspire / desire / love / crisis)

Kim Koo's words in My Wish make us feel his _____ for the independence of Korea and his _____ for the country.

창의사고력 서술형 문제

01 다음은 독도에 관한 사실이다. 이 사실을 아는지 묻는 표현을 〈보기〉처럼 쓰시오.

> • Dokdo has two main islands and 89 small islands.
> • Dokdo is windy and foggy.
> • There is a rock on Dokdo that looks like Korea.

---보기---

> A: You know that Dokdo has two main islands and 89 small islands, don't you?
> B: Yes, I heard about it.

02 다음 그림과 각 그림에 주어진 단어들을 활용하여, so that을 사용한 문장을 어법에 맞게 자유롭게 영작하시오.

(passing, rescue, shout, cry,   (birds, look, watch, observe,
boat, ship, yell, help)   telescope, tool)

(1) _____

(2) _____

03 김좌진 장군에 대한 대화문을 참고하여 다음 글을 완성하시오.

> Q: When was he born?
> A: He was born in 1889.
> Q: Who was he?
> A: He was a Korean general who fought against Japanese rule.
> Q: What did he do to defeat Japan?
> A: He gathered and trained soldiers.
> Q: How did his efforts turn out to be?
> A: His efforts paid off at Cheongsanri, where his soldiers earned one of their greatest victories against Japan.

> Kim Jwajin was born in Hong Seong _____. He was a Korean general _____. When Korea was under Japanese rule, he _____ _____ to defeat Japan. His efforts paid off at Cheongsanri, _____ _____.

단원별 모의고사

01 다음 단어에 대한 영어 설명이 <u>어색한</u> 것은?

① desire: a strong wish or feeling

② treasure: what is highly valued

③ look forward to: to feel pleased and excited about something that is going to happen

④ mission: any work that someone believes it is their duty to do

⑤ state: a sculptured figure of a person, animal, etc. in bronze, stone, wood, etc.

02 다음 짝지어진 단어의 관계가 같도록 빈칸에 알맞은 말을 쓰시오.

> educate – teach : reign – _____

03 다음 영영풀이에 해당하는 단어를 고르시오.

> to place a dead body in the ground, to put something in the ground and cover it

① bury ② spread ③ kill
④ mean ⑤ direct

04 다음 중 짝지어진 대화가 <u>어색한</u> 것은?

① A: Do you remember our plan to go to the War Memorial?
   B: Sure. I'm looking forward to going there.

② A: What kind of volunteer work did you do there?
   B: I cleaned around the tombs.

③ A: I'm planning to go to the Gansong Museum.
   B: What is the Gansong Museum?

④ A: Have you ever heard about An Junggeun?
   B: No, I haven't. He was an independence activist.

⑤ A: I'm planning to visit the Hangeul Museum next week. Do you want to join me?
   B: I'd love to. I'm looking forward to visiting there.

[05~06] 다음 대화를 읽고 물음에 답하시오.

B: Tomorrow let's put on traditional Korean clothes, hanbok, and go to Insadong.

G: Good, but I want to buy gifts for my friends in Germany tomorrow.

B: In Insadong, there are many gift shops.

G: Great. After shopping, what should we eat for lunch?

B: Hmm. (A)_____

G: No. What is it?

B: It's a traditional Korean soup. It's delicious and will make you healthy.

G: Sounds good. (B)<u>I'm looking forward to trying it.</u>

05 위 대화의 빈칸 (A)에 들어갈 말로 알맞지 <u>않은</u> 것은? (2개)

① Have you ever heard about Samgyetang?
② Do you know how to cook Samgyetang?
③ You know Samgyetang, don't you?
④ Why don't you eat Samgyetang?
⑤ Did you hear about Samgyetang?

06 위 대화의 밑줄 친 (B)와 같은 의미가 되도록 'die'를 이용하여 기대의 표현을 쓰시오.

➡ _____

[07~08] 다음 대화를 읽고 물음에 답하시오.

Andy: Bora, what are you reading?

Bora: I'm reading *Sky, Wind, Star, and Poetry* by Yun Dongju. (a)You know about Yun Dongju, don't you?

Andy: I've heard his name, but I don't know much about him.

Bora: He wrote many beautiful poems (b)when Korea was under Japanese rule. His love for the country and his desire for independence can be felt in his poems.

Andy: Really? I didn't know (c)that. I want to read his poems and learn more about him.

Bora: Great. In fact, (d)I'm planning to visit the Yun Dongju Museum soon. Do you want to come with me?

Andy: Yes, when are you going?

Bora: Next Saturday. It's near Gyeongbok Palace. Can you meet me at the palace at 2 p.m.?

Andy: Sure. Let's meet there.

Bora: Great. (e)I'm really looking forward to the visit.

07 위 대화의 밑줄 친 (a)~(e)에 대한 설명 중 잘못된 것은?

① (a): 상대방이 알고 있는지 물어보는 표현이다.

② (b): '한국이 일본의 통치하에 있을 때'의 뜻으로 'when'은 부사절 접속사다.

③ (c): 지시대명사로 앞 문장의 '나라에 대한 그의 사랑과 독립에 대한 염원이 그의 시에서 느껴진다'는 문장을 대신한다.

④ (d): 미래의 계획을 말하는 표현으로 'be going to+동사원형' 구문을 이용하여 바꿔 쓸 수 있다.

⑤ (e): 앞으로 하고 싶은 일에 대한 기대를 표현하는 것으로 'to' 다음에는 명사나 동사원형이 와야 한다.

08 위 대화를 읽고 답할 수 없는 질문은?

① What is Bora reading?

② Who wrote the poem *Sky, Wind, Star, and Poetry*?

③ What can be felt through Yun Dongju's poems?

④ How many poems does Bora want to read?

⑤ What are they planning to do next Saturday?

09 다음 대화의 빈칸 (A)와 (B)에 공통으로 들어갈 말로 알맞은 것은?

G: I'm planning to go to the Gansong Museum.

B: What is the Gansong Museum?

G: It's a museum built by Gansong Jeon Hyeongpil.

B: I heard (A)_____ he did great things for the country.

G: Yes. He bought many Korean treasures (B)_____ some Japanese had taken to Japan.

B: Wow. The museum must be interesting.

G: Yes. I'm looking forward to it!

① that
② what
③ which
④ who
⑤ when

10 다음 대화의 (A)와 (B)가 가리키는 것을 제시된 단어 수에 맞게 찾아 쓰시오.

G: Brian, you know Taegeukgi, don't you?

B: Sure. It's the national flag of Korea, isn't it?

G: That's right. Do you know what the symbols in Taegeukgi mean?

B: No, I don't. Tell me about (A)them.

G: The circle in the middle means harmony and peace.

B: What do the black lines on the four corners mean?

G: (B)They mean four things: sky, fire, water, and earth.

➡ (A) _____ (4 단어)

(B) _____ (3 단어)

[11~12] 다음 대화를 읽고 물음에 답하시오.

(A)

B: Look at Suwon Hawseong. It's huge.

G: It also looks strong.

B: Because it (1)_____ to protect the people during wars.

G: Wow. Do you know who (2)_____ it?

B: Yes. King Jeongjo ordered Jeong Yakyong to direct the building process. (a)_____ Jeong Yakyong, don't you?

G: Yes, I've heard of him. He was a great scientist in Joseon.

(B)

G: I'm planning to go to the Gansong Museum.

B: What is the Gansong Museum?

G: It's a museum (3)_____ by Gansong Jeon Hyeongpil.

B: I heard that he did great things for the country.

G: Yes. He bought many Korean treasures that some Japanese had taken to Japan.

B: Wow. The museum must be interesting.

G: Yes. (b)_____ to it!

11 위 대화의 빈칸 (1)~(3)에 'build'를 활용하여 알맞게 써 넣으시오.

➡ (1)_____ (2)_____ (3)_____

12 위 대화 (A)의 빈칸 (a)는 '알고 있는지 묻는 표현'을, (B)의 빈칸 (b)는 '기대, 희망'을 나타내는 표현을 각각 쓰시오.

➡ (a)_____ (b)_____

13 다음 주어진 우리말을 영작한 것으로 옳지 <u>않은</u> 것은?

Bradley는 부자가 되기 위해 밤낮으로 일했다.

① Bradley worked day and night so as to become rich.

② Bradley worked day and night in order that he became rich.

③ Bradley worked day and night so that he could become rich.

④ Bradley worked day and night to be rich.

⑤ Bradley worked day and night in order to be rich.

14 다음 두 문장을 한 문장으로 만들 때 빈칸에 들어갈 말로 가장 알맞은 것은?

- There was a yellow dust storm all day long.
- The cars were covered with thick dust.

→ The cars were covered with thick dust because _____.

① there is a yellow dust storm all day long

② there has come a yellow dust storm all day long

③ there has been a yellow dust storm all day long

④ there had been a yellow dust storm all day long

⑤ there had been being a yellow dust storm all day long

15 다음 중 밑줄 친 부분의 쓰임이 나머지 넷과 <u>다른</u> 것은?

① Smith will send you his phone number <u>so that</u> you can contact him anytime.

② Frank hurried to the radio station <u>so that</u> he wouldn't be late for the program.

③ Minju did her best <u>so that</u> her research team could find another galaxy.

④ Dave answered loudly, <u>so that</u> the teacher heard him clearly.

⑤ John turned off the radio <u>so that</u> his wife could focus on the book better.

16 다음 각 그림을 보고, 주어진 어구를 알맞게 배열하여 영작하되, 과거완료시제를 반드시 포함하시오. (동사는 변형 가능)

(1) Pinocchio, the goddess, say, lie, that

➡ _____

(2) Pooh, the hive, after, touch, by bees, be stung, he

➡ _____

[17~18] 다음 글을 읽고 물음에 답하시오.

Last week my history club went to Hyochang Park. We visited the Kim Koo Museum inside the park. At the entrance of the museum, we saw a white statue of Kim Koo. Kim Koo is ① <u>a great national hero</u> who spent most of his life ②<u>fighting for</u> the independence of Korea from Japanese rule. In the 1900s, he helped ③<u>educate young people</u> by building schools. In 1919, when the independence movement had spread throughout the country, he ④<u>moved</u> to Shanghai, China. There he ⑤<u>left</u> the Government of the Republic of Korea and later became its president.

17 위 글의 내용과 일치하지 <u>않는</u> 것은?

① The writer is a member of the history club.

② The Kim Koo Museum is located in Hyochang Park.

③ There was a time when Korea was ruled by Japan.

④ Kim Koo lived in Korea all his life.

⑤ The Government of the Republic of Korea was in Shanghai.

18 ①~⑤ 중 글의 흐름상 <u>어색한</u> 것은?

①   ②   ③   ④   ⑤

[19~22] 다음 글을 읽고 물음에 답하시오.

The exhibition hall in the museum shows a lot of things about Kim Koo's life. While looking around the hall, we stopped at a photo of the Korean Patriotic Organization's members. Kim Koo formed the secret organization in 1931 to fight against Japan.

Lee Bongchang and Yun Bonggil belonged to the group. At one place in the hall, we saw two watches under a photo of Kim Koo and Yun Bonggil. In 1932, Kim Koo made a plan to kill Japanese generals in a park in Shanghai. As the leader of the Korean Patriotic Organization, he directed Yun to (A) carry out the mission.

When Yun left for the mission, he told Kim, "(B)Sir, you are wearing a very old watch. Mine is new, but I won't need it anymore. Please take my watch, and let me have yours." Kim Koo always carried Yun's watch in his jacket so that he would not forget Yun's sacrifice.

19 Choose the sentence that is TRUE about the Korean Patriotic Organization.

① It was founded by Lee Bongchang.

② It was an open organization.

③ It was formed in 1932.

④ Its purpose was to fight against Japan.

⑤ Yun Bonggil didn't know about the organization.

20 다음 중 밑줄 친 (A)를 대신하여 쓰일 수 있는 것은?

① ignore ② perform

③ introduce ④ practice

⑤ threat

21 다음 중 윤봉길이 밑줄 친 (B)와 같이 말한 이유로 가장 적절한 것은?

① his interest in Kim Koo's old watch

② his firm opinion to buy a new watch

③ his strong will to devote his life to the mission

④ his deep respect fot Kim Koo

⑤ his natural spirit of helping other people

22 According to the passage, what does the exhibition hall show?

➡ _____

[23~24] 다음 글을 읽고 물음에 답하시오.

An Changho was born in 1878. When he was in his teens, he moved to Seoul and went to school there. In 1902, he left for America so that he could get a better education. In America, An helped improve the lives of the Korean people there and became a respected leader. After he had returned to Korea, he founded the New Korean Society in 1907 to fight for Korea's independence. He also joined the Government of the Republic of Korea in Shanghai in 1919. After that, he built a lot of schools to educate people until he died in 1938.

23 위 글의 내용에 맞게 주어진 문장을 바르게 나열하시오.

ⓐ He returned to Korea.

ⓑ He joined the Government of the Republic of Korea.

ⓒ He went to America to get a better education.

ⓓ He founded the New Korean Society.

ⓔ He studied in Seoul.

ⓕ He became a respected leader by helping people in America.

➡ _____

24 What did An Changho do in order to fight for Korea's independence? Answer in English with a full sentence.

➡ _____
_____

MEMO

MEMO

중간 + 기말

plus⁺

적중100

영어 기출문제집

영어 중 **3**

시사 | 박준언

Best Collection

내용문의 중등영어발전소 적중100 편집부 TEL 070-7707-0457

INSIGHT
on the textbook

교과서 파헤치기

영어 기출 문제집

적중 100 plus
1학기 전과정

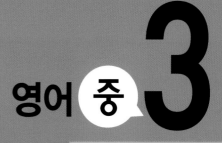

영어 중 3

시사 | 박준언

INSIGHT
on the textbook
교과서 파헤치기

※ 다음 영어를 우리말로 쓰시오.

01 fantastic _____

02 automatically _____

03 forward _____

04 goal _____

05 recognize _____

06 different _____

07 nature _____

08 scene _____

09 basement _____

10 countryside _____

11 advise _____

12 early adopter _____

13 technology _____

14 free _____

15 pretty _____

16 forest _____

17 product _____

18 comfortable _____

19 among _____

20 interest _____

21 choice _____

22 save _____

23 furniture _____

24 guest _____

25 create _____

26 skill _____

27 designed _____

28 floor _____

29 imagine _____

30 humorous _____

31 motto _____

32 refreshed _____

33 photo-taking _____

34 subject _____

35 get along with _____

36 stop -ing _____

37 be full of ~ _____

38 would like to+동사원형 _____

39 be interested in _____

40 be good at _____

41 here are+복수명사 _____

42 look like+명사 _____

43 wake up _____

※ 다음 우리말을 영어로 쓰시오.

01 제품

02 그려진, 디자인된

03 사진촬영

04 자동으로

05 선택

06 진짜의

07 편안한

08 가구

09 조언하다, 충고하다

10 매우, 꽤

11 ~ 중에서

12 환상적인, 매우 멋진

13 연습하다

14 과목, 주제

15 앞으로

16 목표

17 구하다

18 관심, 흥미

19 인식하다

20 시골(지역)

21 재미있는, 유머러스한

22 만들다

23 언어

24 (건물의) 층

25 손님

26 상상하다

27 지하층[실]

28 장면

29 한가한, 다른 계획이 없는

30 숲

31 자연

32 기술

33 영웅

34 (기분이) 상쾌한

35 ~을 잘하다

36 ~하고 싶다

37 단지 ~가 아닌

38 (잠에서) 깨다, 일어나다

39 ~로 가득 차다

40 ~하는 것을 그만두다

41 ~와 잘 지내다

42 ~처럼 보이다

43 여기에 ~가 있다

※ 다음 영영풀이에 알맞은 단어를 <보기>에서 골라 쓴 후, 우리말 뜻을 쓰시오.

1 _____ : to go into a place:: _____

2 _____ : in the middle of a group: _____

3 _____ : to make something happen or exist: _____

4 _____ : a large area of land that is covered with trees: _____

5 _____ : to tell someone that they should do something: _____

6 _____ : extremely good, attractive, enjoyable: _____

7 _____ : part of a building that is under the level of the ground: _____

8 _____ : to form or have a mental picture or idea of something: _____

9 _____ : land that is not in towns or cities and may have farms, fields, etc.:

_____

10 _____ : a short sentence or phrase that expresses a belief or purpose: _____

11 _____ : a very brave person, often a man, that a lot of people admire: _____

12 _____ : the possibility of choosing between two or more things: _____

13 _____ : a person who takes photographs, either as a job or hobby: _____

14 _____ : things such as chairs, tables, and beds that you put into a room or building:

_____

15 _____ : an animal that is kept in the home as a companion and treated kindly:

_____

16 _____ : to know someone or something because you have seen or heard him or

her or experienced it before: _____

※ 다음 우리말과 일치하도록 빈칸에 알맞은 말을 쓰시오.

Warm Up

B1: Hello, my name is Kim Chanho. I _____ _____ _____ you about _____. I'm _____ _____ music. I_____ _____ _____ _____ the drums.

G1: Hi! I am Teri. I _____ _____ in the evening. I feel _____ _____ I exercise.

B2: Hello, my name is Jack. I'_____ _____ in the stars. I _____ _____ _____ _____ _____ stars at night.

G2: I am Lee Bora. I want to be a _____ in the future, so I _____ _____ when I have _____ _____.

B3: I am Mark. I like dancing. I want to _____ _____ _____ in the dance _____.

Listen & Speak 1 A

1. **G:** Jiho, _____ was your first day of _____ _____?

   B: It was _____ good. The teachers and my new classmates are all good.

   G: That _____ _____. Who is your _____ _____?

   B: My homeroom teacher is Mr. Kim. He _____ math.

   G: _____ _____ _____ _____ more _____ him?

   B: Yes. He is _____ and _____ us some _____ _____ about math. It was _____.

   G: Cool! I hope you _____ _____ math.

2. **G:** Ted, _____ _____ this movie poster. I want _____ _____ this movie.

   B: It _____ interesting. Can you _____ me about it, Amy?

   G: Yes. It is _____ a hero _____ the Earth.

   B: It _____ _____ an SF movie.

   G: Yes, it is. Actually, SF is my _____ _____ _____ movie. I like the _____ _____ _____ computer _____. They are _____ and look _____.

   B: That's _____. I am free this weekend. _____ _____ to see it together.

   G: _____ good.

B1: 안녕, 내 이름은 김찬호야. 너에게 나에 대해 말해주고 싶어. 나는 음악에 관심이 있어. 나는 드럼을 잘 쳐.

G1: 안녕, 나는 Teri야. 나는 저녁에 달리는 것을 좋아해. 나는 달릴 때 상쾌함을 느껴.

B2: 안녕, 내 이름은 Jack이야. 나는 별들에 관심이 있어. 나는 보통 밤에 별을 보러 나가.

G2: 나는 이보라야. 나는 미래에 디자이너가 되고 싶어서, 시간이 날 때 그림 그리는 연습을 해.

B3: 나는 Mark야. 나는 춤추는 걸 좋아해. 나는 춤 대회에서 1등을 하고 싶어.

1. **G:** 지호야, 너의 3학년 첫 날은 어땠어?

   B: 꽤 좋았어. 선생님들과 새로운 반 친구들 모두 좋아.

   G: 그거 좋네. 담임 선생님은 누구셔?

   B: 내 담임 선생님은 김 선생님이셔. 그는 수학을 가르치셔.

   G: 나에게 그에 대해 더 말해 줄 수 있니?

   B: 응. 그는 유머가 있으시고 우리에게 수학에 대한 재미있는 몇 가지 이야기를 해 주셨어. 그것은 흥미로웠어.

   G: 멋지네! 네가 수학 공부를 즐기기 바라.

2. **G:** Ted, 이 영화 포스터 좀 봐. 이 영화 보고 싶어.

   B: 그거 재미있어 보이네. 나에게 그것에 관해 말해 줄 수 있니, Amy?

   G: 응. 그것은 지구를 구하는 영웅에 대한 거야.

   B: 공상 과학 영화 같네.

   G: 응, 맞아. 사실 공상 과학은 내가 가장 좋아하는 영화 장르야. 나는 컴퓨터 기술로 제작된 장면들을 좋아해. 그 장면들은 환상적이고 진짜 같아 보여.

   B: 그거 멋지네. 나 이번 주말에 시간 있어. 같이 그거 보러 가자.

   G: 좋아.

A: _____ you _____ me _____ your plan for this weekend?

B: Yes. I _____ _____ _____ _____ a birthday party.

A: Can you tell me about your _____ _____ _____ _____ ?

B: Yes. I want _____ _____ _____ fast food.

A: 나에게 너의 이번 주말 계획에 대해 말해 줄 수 있니?
B: 응. 나는 생일 파티를 할 거야.
A: 나에게 너의 올해 목표에 대해 말해 줄 수 있니?
B: 응. 나는 패스트푸드를 그만 먹고 싶어.

Listen & Speak 2 A

1. **G:** I often _____ _____ _____ my family. _____ I like _____ about traveling is _____ new foods.

2. **B:** My _____ _____ is music. I can _____ _____ _____ and guitar. _____ them, _____ the guitar is _____ I _____ _____ .

3. **G:** This is a picture of Dora. She is my best friend, _____ _____ a pet. _____ _____ her in my free time is _____ I like most.

1. G: 나는 가끔 나의 가족들과 여행을 가. 여행에 관해 내가 가장 좋아하는 것은 새로운 음식들을 먹어보는 거야.
2. B: 내가 가장 좋아하는 과목은 음악이야. 나는 드럼과 기타를 연주할 수 있어. 그것들 중에서, 기타를 연주하는 것이 내가 가장 좋아하는 거야.
3. G: 이것은 Dora 사진이야. 그녀는 단순히 애완동물이 아니라, 나의 가장 친한 친구야. 여가시간에 그녀와 함께 노는 것이 내가 가장 좋아하는 거야.

Real Life Talk

Seho: Nice to meet you. I'_____ _____ _____ _____ your photo club.

Bora: Thank you _____ _____ _____ in the club. Can you tell me _____ _____ ?

Seho: Yes. My name is Kim Seho. I am _____ the _____ _____ , class 8.

Andy: Tell me _____ . _____ do you like to do _____ in your _____ _____ ?

Seho: Well, _____ I like most is _____ _____ pictures.

Bora: That's great. What is your dream _____ _____ _____ ?

Seho: I want _____ _____ _____ .

Andy: Then you made the right _____ . You can learn a lot of _____ _____ here. _____ _____ our club.

Seho: Thank you. I'm so _____ !

세호: 만나서 반가워. 나는 너희의 사진 동아리에 가입하고 싶어.
보라: 동아리에 관심을 가져 줘서 고마워. 너에 대해 말해 줄래?
세호: 응. 내 이름은 김세호야. 나는 3학년 8반이야.
Andy: 좀 더 말해 줘. 너는 여가 시간에 무엇을 하는 걸 가장 좋아하니?
세호: 음, 내가 가장 좋아하는 건 사진 찍는 거야.
보라: 멋지다. 너의 장래 희망은 뭐니?
세호: 나는 사진 작가가 되고 싶어.
Andy: 그러면 너는 정말 좋은 선택을 했구나. 너는 여기서 사진 찍는 기술을 많이 배울 수 있어. 우리 동아리에 온 걸 환영해.
세호: 고마워. 나도 기뻐!

Communication Task Step 2

A: What is your _____?

B: My nickname is Speedy _____ I can _____ _____.

C: What do you _____ _____?

B: _____ _____ _____ _____ is to play baseball.

D: _____ _____ _____ _____ _____ your dream job?

B: I _____ _____ _____ a baseball player.

A: What is your _____?

B: My _____ is "You can go _____ _____, but _____ _____
_____."

Wrap Up

W: Today, we have a _____ _____ Hojun. Hojun, can you please
_____ _____ to the class?

B: Yes. Hi, my name is Kim Hojun. I am _____ Busan. _____
_____ _____ you.

W: _____ _____ _____ _____ _____ about yourself?

B: Yes. I like sports, _____ soccer. I want _____ _____ a sports
club.

W: Is there _____ _____ you want _____ _____ your new
friends?

B: I want to _____ _____ _____ everyone. Please help me
_____ I'm _____ _____.

W: Thanks, Hojun. _____ _____ _____ _____.

※ 다음 우리말에 맞도록 대화를 영어로 쓰시오.

Warm Up

B1: _____

_____

G1: _____

B2: _____

G2: _____

B3: _____

B1: 안녕, 내 이름은 김찬호야. 너에게 나에 대해 말해주고 싶어. 나는 음악에 관심이 있어. 나는 드럼을 잘 쳐.

G1: 안녕. 나는 Teri야. 나는 저녁에 달리는 것을 좋아해. 나는 달릴 때 상쾌함을 느껴.

B2: 안녕, 내 이름은 Jack이야. 나는 별들에 관심이 있어. 나는 보통 밤에 별을 보러 나가.

G2: 나는 이보라야. 나는 미래에 디자이너가 되고 싶어서, 시간이 날 때 그림 그리는 연습을 해.

B3: 나는 Mark야. 나는 춤추는 걸 좋아해. 나는 춤 대회에서 1등을 하고 싶어.

Listen & Speak 1 A

1. G: _____

B: _____

G: _____

B: _____

G: _____

B: _____

_____

G: _____

2. G: _____

B: _____

G: _____

B: _____

G: _____

B: _____

G: _____

1. G: 지호야, 너의 3학년 첫 날은 어땠어?

B: 꽤 좋았어. 선생님들과 새로운 반 친구들 모두 좋아.

G: 그거 좋네. 담임 선생님은 누구셔?

B: 내 담임 선생님은 김 선생님이셔. 그는 수학을 가르치셔.

G: 나에게 그에 대해 더 말해 줄 수 있니?

B: 응. 그는 유머가 있으시고 우리에게 수학에 대한 재미있는 몇 가지 이야기를 해 주셨어. 그것은 흥미로웠어.

G: 멋지네! 네가 수학 공부를 즐기기 바라.

2. G: Ted, 이 영화 포스터 좀 봐. 이 영화 보고 싶어.

B: 그거 재미있어 보이네. 나에게 그것에 관해 말해 줄 수 있니, Amy?

G: 응. 그것은 지구를 구하는 영웅에 대한 거야.

B: 공상 과학 영화 같네.

G: 응, 맞아. 사실 공상 과학은 내가 가장 좋아하는 영화 장르야. 나는 컴퓨터 기술로 제작된 장면들을 좋아해. 그 장면들은 환상적이고 진짜 같아 보여.

B: 그거 멋지네. 나 이번 주말에 시간 있어. 같이 그거 보러 가자.

G: 좋아.

Listen & Speak 1 B

A: _____

B: _____

A: _____

B: _____

A: 나에게 너의 이번 주말 계획에 대해 말해 줄 수 있니?

B: 응. 나는 생일 파티를 할 거야.

A: 나에게 너의 올해 목표에 대해 말해 줄 수 있니?

B: 응. 나는 패스트푸드를 그만 먹고 싶어.

Listen & Speak 2 A

1. G: _____

   _____

2. B: _____

3. G: _____

   _____

1. G: 나는 가끔 나의 가족들과 여행을 가. 여행에 관해 내가 가장 좋아하는 것은 새로운 음식들을 먹어보는 거야.

2. B: 내가 가장 좋아하는 과목은 음악이야. 나는 드럼과 기타를 연주할 수 있어. 그것들 중에서, 기타를 연주하는 것이 내가 가장 좋아하는 거야.

3. G: 이것은 Dora 사진이야. 그녀는 단순히 애완동물이 아니라, 나의 가장 친한 친구야. 여가시간에 그녀와 함께 노는 것이 내가 가장 좋아하는 거야.

Real Life Talk

Seho: _____

Bora: _____

Seho: _____

Andy: _____

Seho: _____

Bora: _____

Seho: _____

Andy: _____

Seho: _____

세호: 만나서 반가워. 나는 너희의 사진 동아리에 가입하고 싶어.

보라: 동아리에 관심을 가져 줘서 고마워. 너에 대해 말해 줄래?

세호: 응. 내 이름은 김세호야. 나는 3학년 8반이야.

Andy: 좀 더 말해 줘. 너는 여가 시간에 무엇을 하는 걸 가장 좋아하니?

세호: 음, 내가 가장 좋아하는 건 사진 찍는 거야.

보라: 멋지다. 너의 장래 희망은 뭐니?

세호: 나는 사진 작가가 되고 싶어.

Andy: 그러면 너는 정말 좋은 선택을 했구나. 너는 여기서 사진 찍는 기술을 많이 배울 수 있어. 우리 동아리에 온 걸 환영해.

세호: 고마워. 나도 기뻐!

Communication Task Step 2

A: _____

B: _____

C: _____

B: _____

D: _____

B: _____

A: _____

B: _____

A: 너의 별명이 뭐니?

B: 내 별명은 스피디인데 나는 빨리 달릴 수 있기 때문이야.

C: 너는 무엇을 가장 좋아하니?

B: 내가 가장 좋아하는 것은 야구를 하는 거야.

D: 나에게 네가 꿈꾸는 직업에 대해 말해 줄 수 있니?

B: 나는 야구 선수가 되고 싶어.

A: 너의 좌우명은 뭐니?

B: 나의 좌우명은 "앞으로 천천히 나아갈 수 있지만, 절대 물러설 수는 없다"야.

Wrap Up

W: _____
_____

B: _____

W: _____

B: _____

W: _____

B: _____

W: _____

W: 오늘, 새로 온 학생 호준이가 있어요. 호준아, 반 친구들에게 너를 소개해 주겠니?

B: 네. 안녕, 내 이름은 김호준이야. 나는 부산에서 왔어. 만나서 반가워.

W: 너에 대해 더 말해 줄 수 있니?

B: 네. 나는 스포츠, 특히 축구를 좋아해. 나는 스포츠 동아리에 가입하고 싶어.

W: 너의 새로운 친구들에게 더 말하고 싶은 게 있니?

B: 모두와 함께 잘 지내고 싶어. 나는 이곳에 새로 왔으니 도와주길 바라.

W: 고마워, 호준아. 우리 반에 온 것을 환영한단다.

※ 다음 우리말과 일치하도록 빈칸에 알맞은 것을 골라 쓰시오.

My Dream House

1 _____ you _____ _____ about your dream house?

    A. ever   B. have   C. thought

2 Today, _____ _____, we _____ our dream house.

    A. class   B. in   C. created

3 _____ _____ some of the dream houses _____ we _____.

    A. are   B. made   C. that   D. here

A House in Nature - Minho

4 _____ is _____ _____ friend.

    A. my   B. good   C. nature

5 I do _____ _____ when I _____ in the _____.

    A. feel   B. forest   C. good   D. walk

6 I'd _____ _____ _____ a dream house _____ the countryside.

    A. in   B. to   C. have   D. like

7 It _____ _____ a big garden _____ many _____ and trees.

    A. with   B. have   C. flowers   D. should

8 I _____ always _____ the _____ of birds.

    A. excited   B. am   C. sound   D. by

9 It will be _____ to _____ _____ in the morning and listen _____ the songs of the birds.

    A. up   B. wonderful   C. to   D. wake

10 Also, I'd _____ to _____ many pets. It will be fun _____ _____ with them!

    A. play   B. like   C. to   D. have

A Fun Place - Julie

11 _____ _____ my _____ house!

    A. to   B. welcome   C. dream

12 _____ fun is _____ I want most, _____ my dream house is _____ of exciting things.

    A. what   B. full   C. so   D. having

13 It _____ a _____ _____ the _____.

    A. basement   B. in   C. has   D. theater

14 There, I _____ _____ cookies and _____ my _____ movies.

    A. enjoy   B. eat   C. favorite   D. can

15 My dream house _____ a game room _____ the _____.

    A. on   B. has   C. floor   D. second

내가 꿈꾸는 집

1 여러분은 꿈의 집에 대해 생각해 본 적이 있나요?

2 오늘. 우리는 수업 시간에 우리가 꿈꾸는 집을 만들었습니다.

3 여기 우리가 만든 몇몇 꿈의 집이 있습니다.

자연 속의 집 – 민호

4 자연은 나의 좋은 친구입니다.

5 나는 숲속에서 걸을 때 기분이 정말 좋습니다.

6 나는 시골에 꿈의 집을 갖고 싶습니다.

7 집에는 많은 꽃과 나무가 있는 큰 정원이 있을 것입니다.

8 나는 항상 새소리에 신이 납니다.

9 아침에 깨어나서 새들의 노래 소리를 듣는 것은 멋질 것입니다.

10 또한 나는 많은 애완동물을 갖고 싶습니다. 그들과 노는 것은 매우 재미있을 것입니다!

재미있는 장소 – Julie

11 나의 꿈의 집에 온 것을 환영합니다!

12 즐겁게 지내는 것은 내가 가장 원하는 것입니다. 그래서 내 꿈의 집은 흥미로운 것들로 가득 합니다.

13 집에는 지하에 영화관이 있습니다.

14 그곳에서 나는 쿠키를 먹을 수 있고 내가 좋아하는 영화들을 즐길 수 있습니다.

15 내 꿈의 집에는 2층에 게임방이 있습니다.

16 I can _____ many different _____ _____ _____ there.
    A. kinds   B. play   C. of   D. games

17 My house _____ has a _____ _____.
    A. swimming   B. also   C. pool

18 I want to do _____ _____ _____ my friends in my house. You can be my _____!
    A. guest   B. things   C. fun   D. with

A Place for Family - Misun

19 My family is _____ _____ _____ _____ to me.
    A. important   B. the   C. thing   D. most

20 In my dream house, my family _____ _____ and _____.
    A. safe   B. feels   C. comfortable

21 _____ the gate, you can find a _____ _____ sign with my family's picture _____ it.
    A. on   B. beautifully   C. at   D. designed

22 _____ you _____ the house, you will _____ a _____ living room.
    A. enter   B. see   C. when   D. large

23 My family _____ _____ board games and _____ there.
    A. plays   B. sings   C. sometimes

24 It will _____ a garden _____ a large _____ for family picnics.
    A. with   B. picnic   C. have   D. table

25 There, we _____ _____ barbecues. _____ you _____ my dream house?
    A. like   B. enjoy   C. do   D. will

A House with New Technology - Bryan

26 I am an _____ _____ of new _____.
    A. adopter   B. early   C. technology

27 I do _____ to use new _____ and technology _____ _____.
    A. before   B. products   C. others   D. like

28 When I _____ _____ my house, the front door _____ my face and _____ automatically.
    A. recognizes   B. near   C. opens   D. get

29 The furniture _____ the weather _____ and _____ me _____ what to wear.
    A. conditions   B. on   C. advises   D. checks

30 The bathroom mirror _____ me my _____ and the _____ of my _____.
    A. weight   B. health   C. tells   D. condition

31 A robot _____ the house and _____ me.
    A. for   B. cooks   C. cleans

32 This is _____ _____ _____ _____ about my dream house.
    A. can   B. what   C. imagine   D. I

16 나는 그곳에서 많은 다양한 종류의 게임을 할 수 있습니다.

17 나의 집에는 또한 수영장이 있습니다.

18 나는 나의 집에서 친구들과 함께 즐거운 일들을 하고 싶습니다. 여러분도 나의 손님이 될 수 있습니다!

가족을 위한 장소 – 미선

19 나의 가족은 나에게 가장 중요한 것입니다.

20 내 꿈의 집에서 가족은 안전하고 편안함을 느낍니다.

21 현관에서 여러분은 가족 사진이 있는 아름답게 디자인된 문패를 발견할 수 있습니다.

22 여러분이 집에 들어서면 여러분은 큰 거실을 보게 될 것입니다.

23 나의 가족은 때때로 그곳에서 보드 게임도 하고 노래를 부르기도 합니다.

24 가족 소풍을 위한 커다란 피크닉 테이블이 있는 큰 정원을 갖게 될 것입니다.

25 그곳에서 우리는 바비큐를 즐길 것입니다. 내 꿈의 집이 마음에 드나요?

신기술이 있는 집 – Bryan

26 나는 남들보다 먼저 신기술을 써 보는 것을 좋아하는 사람입니다.

27 나는 새로운 제품이나 기술을 다른 사람보다 먼저 사용하는 것을 정말 좋아합니다.

28 내가 집 근처에 도착할 때, 현관문은 내 얼굴을 인식하고 자동으로 문을 엽니다.

29 가구는 날씨 상태를 확인하여 내게 무엇을 입을지 조언해 줍니다.

30 욕실 거울은 나에게 체중과 건강 상태를 알려 줍니다.

31 로봇은 집을 청소하고 나를 위해 요리합니다.

32 이것이 내가 나의 꿈의 집에 대해 상상할 수 있는 것입니다.

※ 다음 우리말과 일치하도록 빈칸에 알맞은 말을 쓰시오.

My Dream House

1 _____ you _____ _____ _____ your dream house?

2 Today, _____ _____, we _____ our dream house.

3 Here _____ some of the dream houses _____ we _____.

A House in Nature - Minho

4 _____ is my _____ _____.

5 I _____ _____ _____ when I walk in the _____.

6 I'd _____ _____ _____ a dream house _____ the _____.

7 It _____ _____ a big garden _____ _____ _____ and trees.

8 I _____ _____ _____ _____ the sound of birds.

9 It will be _____ _____ _____ _____ in the morning and _____ _____ the songs of the birds.

10 Also, I'd _____ _____ many pets. It will _____ _____ _____ them!

A Fun Place - Julie

11 _____ _____ my dream house!

12 _____ _____ is _____ I want most, so my dream house _____ _____ _____ _____ _____.

13 It has a theater _____ _____ _____.

14 There, I can eat cookies and _____ my _____.

15 My dream house _____ a game room _____ the _____ _____.

내가 꿈꾸는 집

1 여러분은 꿈의 집에 대해 생각해 본 적이 있나요?

2 오늘, 우리는 수업 시간에 우리가 꿈꾸는 집을 만들었습니다.

3 여기 우리가 만든 몇몇 꿈의 집이 있습니다.

자연 속의 집 – 민호

4 자연은 나의 좋은 친구입니다.

5 나는 숲속에서 걸을 때 기분이 정말 좋습니다.

6 나는 시골에 꿈의 집을 갖고 싶습니다.

7 집에는 많은 꽃과 나무가 있는 큰 정원이 있을 것입니다.

8 나는 항상 새소리에 신이 납니다.

9 아침에 깨어나서 새들의 노래 소리를 듣는 것은 멋질 것입니다.

10 또한 나는 많은 애완동물을 갖고 싶습니다. 그들과 노는 것은 매우 재미있을 것입니다!

재미있는 장소 – Julie

11 나의 꿈의 집에 온 것을 환영합니다!

12 즐겁게 지내는 것은 내가 가장 원하는 것입니다. 그래서 내 꿈의 집은 흥미로운 것들로 가득합니다.

13 집에는 지하에 영화관이 있습니다.

14 그곳에서 나는 쿠키를 먹을 수 있고 내가 좋아하는 영화들을 즐길 수 있습니다.

15 내 꿈의 집에는 2층에 게임방이 있습니다.

16 I can play many different _____ _____ _____ there.

17 My house _____ has _____ _____ _____.

18 I want to _____ _____ _____ my friends in my house. You can be _____ _____!

A Place for Family - Misun

19 My family is _____ _____ _____ _____ to me.

20 In my dream house, my family _____ _____ and _____.

21 _____ _____ _____, you can find a _____ _____ _____ with my family's picture _____ it.

22 _____ you _____ the house, you will _____ _____ _____ _____ _____.

23 My family sometimes plays _____ _____ and sings there.

24 It will _____ a garden _____ _____ for family picnics.

25 There, we will _____ barbecues. _____ my dream house?

A House with New Technology - Bryan

26 I am _____ _____ _____ of new _____.

27 I _____ _____ to use new products and technology _____ _____.

28 When I _____ _____ my house, the front door _____ my face and _____ _____.

29 The furniture _____ the weather _____ and _____ me _____ _____ _____ _____.

30 The bathroom mirror _____ _____ _____ _____ _____ and the _____ of my health.

31 A robot _____ the house and _____ _____ me.

32 This is _____ _____ _____ _____ about my dream house.

(Korean sidebar 16–32)

16 나는 그곳에서 많은 다양한 종류의 게임을 할 수 있습니다.
17 나의 집에는 또한 수영장이 있습니다.
18 나는 나의 집에서 친구들과 함께 즐거운 일들을 하고 싶습니다. 여러분도 나의 손님이 될 수 있습니다!
가족을 위한 장소 – 미선
19 나의 가족은 나에게 가장 중요한 것입니다.
20 내 꿈의 집에서 가족은 안전하고 편안함을 느낍니다.
21 현관에서 여러분은 가족 사진이 있는 아름답게 디자인된 문패를 발견할 수 있습니다.
22 여러분이 집에 들어서면 여러분은 큰 거실을 보게 될 것입니다.
23 나의 가족은 때때로 그곳에서 보드 게임도 하고 노래를 부르기도 합니다.
24 가족 소풍을 위한 커다란 피크닉 테이블이 있는 큰 정원을 갖게 될 것입니다.
25 그곳에서 우리는 바비큐를 즐길 것입니다. 내 꿈의 집이 마음에 드나요?
신기술이 있는 집 – Bryan
26 나는 남들보다 먼저 신기술을 써 보는 것을 좋아하는 사람입니다.
27 나는 새로운 제품이나 기술을 다른 사람보다 먼저 사용하는 것을 정말 좋아합니다.
28 내가 집 근처에 도착할 때, 현관문은 내 얼굴을 인식하고 자동으로 문을 엽니다.
29 가구는 날씨 상태를 확인하여 내게 무엇을 입을지 조언해 줍니다.
30 욕실 거울은 나에게 체중과 건강 상태를 알려 줍니다.
31 로봇은 집을 청소하고 나를 위해 요리합니다.
32 이것이 내가 나의 꿈의 집에 대해 상상할 수 있는 것입니다.

※ 다음 문장을 우리말로 쓰시오.

My Dream House

1 Have you ever thought about your dream house?

➡ _____

2 Today, in class, we created our dream house.

➡ _____

3 Here are some of the dream houses that we made.

➡ _____

A House in Nature - Minho

4 Nature is my good friend.

➡ _____

5 I do feel good when I walk in the forest.

➡ _____

6 I'd like to have a dream house in the countryside.

➡ _____

7 It should have a big garden with many flowers and trees.

➡ _____

8 I am always excited by the sound of birds.

➡ _____

9 It will be wonderful to wake up in the morning and listen to the songs of the birds.

➡ _____

10 Also, I'd like to have many pets. It will be fun to play with them!

➡ _____

A Fun Place - Julie

11 Welcome to my dream house!

➡ _____

12 Having fun is what I want most, so my dream house is full of exciting things.

➡ _____

13 It has a theater in the basement.

➡ _____

14 There, I can eat cookies and enjoy my favorite movies.

➡ _____

15 My dream house has a game room on the second floor.

➡ _____

16 ▸ I can play many different kinds of games there.

➡ _____

17 ▸ My house also has a swimming pool.

➡ _____

18 ▸ I want to do fun things with my friends in my house. You can be my guest!

➡ _____

A Place for Family - Misun

19 ▸ My family is the most important thing to me.

➡ _____

20 ▸ In my dream house, my family feels safe and comfortable.

➡ _____

21 ▸ At the gate, you can find a beautifully designed sign with my family's picture on it.

➡ _____

22 ▸ When you enter the house, you will see a large living room.

➡ _____

23 ▸ My family sometimes plays board games and sings there.

➡ _____

24 ▸ It will have a garden with a large picnic table for family picnics.

➡ _____

25 ▸ There, we will enjoy barbecues. Do you like my dream house?

➡ _____

A House with New Technology - Bryan

26 ▸ I am an early adopter of new technology.

➡ _____

27 ▸ I do like to use new products and technology before others.

➡ _____

28 ▸ When I get near my house, the front door recognizes my face and opens automatically.

➡ _____

29 ▸ The furniture checks the weather conditions and advises me on what to wear.

➡ _____

30 ▸ The bathroom mirror tells me my weight and the condition of my health.

➡ _____

31 ▸ A robot cleans the house and cooks for me.

➡ _____

32 ▸ This is what I can imagine about my dream house.

➡ _____

※ 다음 괄호 안의 단어들을 우리말에 맞도록 바르게 배열하시오.

My Dream House

1 (you / have / thought / ever / your / about / house? / dream)
➡ _____

2 (in / today, / class, / created / we / dream / our / house.)
➡ _____

3 (are / here / of / some / dream / the / that / houses / made. / we)
➡ _____

A House in Nature - Minho

4 (is / nature / good / my / friend.)
➡ _____

5 (do / I / feel / when / good / walk / I / the / forest. / in)
➡ _____

6 (like / I'd / have / to / house / a / dream / in / countryside. / the)
➡ _____

7 (should / it / a / have / big / garden / many / with / trees. / and / flowers)
➡ _____

8 (am / I / always / by / excited / the / sound / birds. / of)
➡ _____

9 (will / it / be / to / wonderful / up / wake / the / in / morning / and / to / listen / songs / the / of / birds. / the)
➡ _____

10 (I'd / also, / like / have / to / pets. / many // will / it / be / to / play / fun / them! / with)
➡ _____

A Fun Place - Julie

11 (to / welcome / dream / my / house!)
➡ _____

12 (fun / having / what / is / want / I / most, / my / so / house / dream / full / is / of / things. / exciting)
➡ _____

13 (has / it / theater / a / the / in / basement.)
➡ _____

14 (I / there, / eat / can / cookies / and / my / enjoy / movies. / favorite)
➡ _____

15 (dream / my / house / a / has / game / room / the / on / floor. / second)
➡ _____

내가 꿈꾸는 집

1 여러분은 꿈의 집에 대해 생각해 본 적이 있나요?

2 오늘, 우리는 수업 시간에 우리가 꿈꾸는 집을 만들었습니다.

3 여기 우리가 만든 몇몇 꿈의 집이 있습니다.

자연 속의 집 – 민호

4 자연은 나의 좋은 친구입니다.

5 나는 숲속에서 걸을 때 기분이 정말 좋습니다.

6 나는 시골에 꿈의 집을 갖고 싶습니다.

7 집에는 많은 꽃과 나무가 있는 큰 정원이 있을 것입니다.

8 나는 항상 새소리에 신이 납니다.

9 아침에 깨어나서 새들의 노래 소리를 듣는 것은 멋질 것입니다.

10 또한 나는 많은 애완동물을 갖고 싶습니다. 그들과 노는 것은 매우 재미있을 것입니다!

재미있는 장소 – Julie

11 나의 꿈의 집에 온 것을 환영합니다!

12 즐겁게 지내는 것은 내가 가장 원하는 것입니다. 그래서 내 꿈의 집은 흥미로운 것들로 가득합니다.

13 집에는 지하에 영화관이 있습니다.

14 그곳에서 나는 쿠키를 먹을 수 있고 내가 좋아하는 영화들을 즐길 수 있습니다.

15 내 꿈의 집에는 2층에 게임방이 있습니다.

16 (can / I / play / different / many / of / kinds / games / there.)
➡ _____

17 (house / my / has / also / a / pool. / swimming)
➡ _____

18 (want / I / to / fun / do / things / with / friends / my / in / house. / my // can / you / my / be / guest!)
➡ _____

A Place for Family - Misun

19 (family / my / the / is / important / most / to / me. / thing)
➡ _____

20 (my / in / dream / house, / family / my / safe / feels / comfortable. / and)
➡ _____

21 (the / at / gate, / can / you / a / find / beautifully / sign / designed / my / family's / with / on / it. / picture)
➡ _____

22 (you / when / enter / house, / the / will / you / see / large / a / room. / living)
➡ _____

23 (family / my / plays / sometimes / games / board / and / there. / sings)
➡ _____

24 (will / it / have / garden / a / with / large / a / table / picnic / for / picnics. / family)
➡ _____

25 (we / there, / will / barbecues. / enjoy // you / do / my / like / house? / dream)
➡ _____

A House with New Technology - Bryan

26 (am / I / early / an / of / adopter / technology. / new)
➡ _____

27 (do / I / like / use / to / products / new / and / before / technology / others.)
➡ _____

28 (I / when / get / my / near / house, / front / the / recognizes / door / face / my / and / automatically. / opens)
➡ _____

29 (furniture / the / checks / weather / the / conditions / and / me / advises / what / on / wear. / to)
➡ _____

30 (bathroom / the / tells / mirror / my / me / weight / and / condition / the / my / of / health.)
➡ _____

31 (robot / a / cleans / house / the / and / for / me. / cooks)
➡ _____

32 (is / this / I / what / can / about / imagine / my / house. / dream)
➡ _____

16 나는 그곳에서 많은 다양한 종류의 게임을 할 수 있습니다.

17 나의 집에는 또한 수영장이 있습니다.

18 나는 나의 집에서 친구들과 함께 즐거운 일들을 하고 싶습니다. 여러분도 나의 손님이 될 수 있습니다!

가족을 위한 장소 – 미선

19 나의 가족은 나에게 가장 중요한 것입니다.

20 내 꿈의 집에서 가족은 안전하고 편안함을 느낍니다.

21 현관에서 여러분은 가족 사진이 있는 아름답게 디자인된 문패를 발견할 수 있습니다.

22 여러분이 집에 들어서면 여러분은 큰 거실을 보게 될 것입니다.

23 나의 가족은 때때로 그곳에서 보드 게임도 하고 노래를 부르기도 합니다.

24 가족 소풍을 위한 커다란 피크닉 테이블이 있는 큰 정원을 갖게 될 것입니다.

25 그곳에서 우리는 바비큐를 즐길 것입니다. 내 꿈의 집이 마음에 드나요?

신기술이 있는 집 – Bryan

26 나는 남들보다 먼저 신기술을 써 보는 것을 좋아하는 사람입니다.

27 나는 새로운 제품이나 기술을 다른 사람보다 먼저 사용하는 것을 정말 좋아합니다.

28 내가 집 근처에 도착할 때, 현관문은 내 얼굴을 인식하고 자동으로 문을 엽니다.

29 가구는 날씨 상태를 확인하여 내게 무엇을 입을지 조언해 줍니다.

30 욕실 거울은 나에게 체중과 건강 상태를 알려 줍니다.

31 로봇은 집을 청소하고 나를 위해 요리합니다.

32 이것이 내가 나의 꿈의 집에 대해 상상할 수 있는 것입니다.

※ 다음 우리말을 영어로 쓰시오.

My Dream House

1 ▶ 여러분은 꿈의 집에 대해 생각해 본 적이 있나요?

➡ _____

2 ▶ 오늘, 우리는 수업 시간에 우리가 꿈꾸는 집을 만들었습니다.

➡ _____

3 ▶ 여기 우리가 만든 몇몇 꿈의 집이 있습니다.

➡ _____

A House in Nature - Minho

4 ▶ 자연은 나의 좋은 친구입니다.

➡ _____

5 ▶ 나는 숲속에서 걸을 때 기분이 정말 좋습니다.

➡ _____

6 ▶ 나는 시골에 꿈의 집을 갖고 싶습니다.

➡ _____

7 ▶ 집에는 많은 꽃과 나무가 있는 큰 정원이 있을 것입니다.

➡ _____

8 ▶ 나는 항상 새소리에 신이 납니다.

➡ _____

9 ▶ 아침에 깨어나서 새들의 노래 소리를 듣는 것은 멋질 것입니다.

➡ _____

10 ▶ 또한 나는 많은 애완동물을 갖고 싶습니다. 그들과 노는 것은 매우 재미있을 것입니다!

➡ _____

A Fun Place - Julie

11 ▶ 나의 꿈의 집에 온 것을 환영합니다!

➡ _____

12 ▶ 즐겁게 지내는 것은 내가 가장 원하는 것입니다. 그래서 내 꿈의 집은 흥미로운 것들로 가득합니다.

➡ _____

13 ▶ 집에는 지하에 영화관이 있습니다.

➡ _____

14 ▶ 그곳에서 나는 쿠키를 먹을 수 있고 내가 좋아하는 영화들을 즐길 수 있습니다.

➡ _____

15 ▶ 내 꿈의 집에는 2층에 게임방이 있습니다.

➡ _____

16 나는 그곳에서 많은 다양한 종류의 게임을 할 수 있습니다.

➡ _____

17 나의 집에는 또한 수영장이 있습니다.

➡ _____

18 나는 나의 집에서 친구들과 함께 즐거운 일들을 하고 싶습니다. 여러분도 나의 손님이 될 수 있습니다!

➡ _____

A Place for Family - Misun

19 나의 가족은 나에게 가장 중요한 것입니다.

➡ _____

20 내 꿈의 집에서 가족은 안전하고 편안함을 느낍니다.

➡ _____

21 현관에서 여러분은 가족 사진이 있는 아름답게 디자인된 문패를 발견할 수 있습니다.

➡ _____

22 여러분이 집에 들어서면 여러분은 큰 거실을 보게 될 것입니다.

➡ _____

23 나의 가족은 때때로 그곳에서 보드 게임도 하고 노래를 부르기도 합니다.

➡ _____

24 가족 소풍을 위한 커다란 피크닉 테이블이 있는 큰 정원을 갖게 될 것입니다.

➡ _____

25 그곳에서 우리는 바비큐를 즐길 것입니다. 내 꿈의 집이 마음에 드나요?

➡ _____

A House with New Technology - Bryan

26 나는 남들보다 먼저 신기술을 써 보는 것을 좋아하는 사람입니다.

➡ _____

27 나는 새로운 제품이나 기술을 다른 사람보다 먼저 사용하는 것을 정말 좋아합니다.

➡ _____

28 내가 집 근처에 도착할 때, 현관문은 내 얼굴을 인식하고 자동으로 문을 엽니다.

➡ _____

29 가구는 날씨 상태를 확인하여 내게 무엇을 입을지 조언해 줍니다.

➡ _____

30 욕실 거울은 나에게 체중과 건강 상태를 알려 줍니다.

➡ _____

31 로봇은 집을 청소하고 나를 위해 요리합니다.

➡ _____

32 이것이 내가 나의 꿈의 집에 대해 상상할 수 있는 것입니다.

➡ _____

※ 다음 우리말과 일치하도록 빈칸에 알맞은 말을 쓰시오.

After You Read - Read and Match

1. I like _____ _____ new _____ and _____.

2. _____ _____ m a n y   i t e m s _____ _____ _____
   _____ in my dream house.

3. _____ _____ my furniture _____ the weather and tells me
   _____ _____ _____.

4. A robot _____ _____ _____.

1. 나는 새로운 제품과 기술을 이용하는 것이 좋다.
2. 내가 꿈꾸는 집에는 새로운 기술을 이용하는 물건들이 많이 있다.
3. 매일 내 가구들은 날씨를 확인해서 내가 무엇을 입을지 말해 준다.
4. 로봇은 나에게 요리를 해 준다.

Project Step 1

1. A: We _____ _____ _____ know more about you, Minho.
   What is your _____ _____?

2. B: I _____ pizza _____.

3. C: _____ you _____ _____ your favorite _____?

4. B: A r t   i s _____ I _____ _____. I _____ _____
   _____ an art teacher _____ Mr. Kim.

5. D: _____ do you _____ _____ _____ after school?

6. B: I _____ _____ _____ taegwondo and _____ songs.

1. A: 우리는 너에 대해서 더 많이 알고 싶어, 민호야. 네가 가장 좋아하는 음식은 뭐니?
2. B: 나는 피자를 가장 좋아해.
3. C: 나에게 네가 가장 좋아하는 과목에 대해 말해 줄 수 있니?
4. B: 미술이 내가 가장 좋아하는 거야. 나는 김 선생님과 같은 미술 선생님이 되고 싶어.
5. D: 너는 방과 후에 무엇을 하는 것을 좋아하니?
6. B: 나는 태권도를 연습하고, 노래 부르는 것을 좋아해.

Project Step 3

1. We _____ an M and an H _____ _____ Minho _____.

2. Minho likes art and pizza, _____ we made an M _____ a
   _____ _____, _____ p e n c i l s, a n d _____ _____
   _____ pizza.

3. We _____ an H _____ a _____ _____ and taegwondo.

1. 우리는 민호가 좋아하는 것으로 M과 H를 만들었습니다.
2. 민호는 예술과 피자를 좋아합니다. 그래서 우리는 붓, 색연필, 그리고 피자 조각으로 M을 만들었습니다.
3. 우리는 태권도와 음표로 H를 만들었습니다.

※ 다음 우리말을 영어로 쓰시오.

After You Read - Read and Match

1. 나는 새로운 제품과 기술을 이용하는 것이 좋다.

   ➡ _____

2. 내가 꿈꾸는 집에는 새로운 기술을 이용하는 물건들이 많이 있다.

   ➡ _____

3. 매일 내 가구들은 날씨를 확인해서 내가 무엇을 입을지 말해 준다.

   ➡ _____

4. 로봇은 나에게 요리를 해 준다.

   ➡ _____

Project Step 1

1. A: 우리는 너에 대해서 더 많이 알고 싶어, 민호야. 네가 가장 좋아하는 음식은 뭐니?

   ➡ _____

2. B: 나는 피자를 가장 좋아해.

   ➡ _____

3. C: 나에게 네가 가장 좋아하는 과목에 대해 말해 줄 수 있니?

   ➡ _____

4. B: 미술이 내가 가장 좋아하는 거야. 나는 김 선생님과 같은 미술 선생님이 되고 싶어.

   ➡ _____

5. D: 너는 방과 후에 무엇을 하는 것을 좋아하니?

   ➡ _____

6. B: 나는 태권도를 연습하고, 노래 부르는 것을 좋아해.

   ➡ _____

Project Step 3

1. 우리는 민호가 좋아하는 것으로 M과 H를 만들었습니다.

   ➡ _____

2. 민호는 예술과 피자를 좋아합니다. 그래서 우리는 붓, 색연필, 그리고 피자 조각으로 M을 만들었습니다.

   ➡ _____

3. 우리는 태권도와 음표로 H를 만들었습니다.

   ➡ _____

※ 다음 영어를 우리말로 쓰시오.

01 greet

02 bowl

03 place

04 correctly

05 since

06 differ

07 elderly

08 temple

09 experience

10 finally

11 address

12 state

13 goods

14 rate

15 serve

16 present

17 prepare

18 difference

19 hand

20 negative question

21 pack

22 tongue

23 pay

24 exchange

25 uncomfortable

26 wave

27 bump

28 postal code

29 tax

30 entrance fee

31 price tag

32 sales tax

33 death

34 wrap

35 get used to ~

36 between A and B

37 in response to

38 have a bad effect on

39 be regarded as

40 the same as ~

41 remember to V

42 range from A to B

43 place 목적어 together

※ 다음 우리말을 영어로 쓰시오.

01 그릇		
02 긍정의문문		
03 죽음		
04 율, 비율		
05 입장료		
06 준비하다		
07 상품, 제품		
08 차이		
09 놓다		
10 주소		
11 지불하다		
12 선물		
13 나이 든		
14 가격표		
15 부딪치다		
16 교환하다, 환전하다		
17 정확하게, 올바르게		
18 손님		
19 마지막으로		
20 포장하다, 싸다		
21 혀		

22 판매세		
23 우편 번호		
24 세금		
25 주		
26 다르다		
27 (손을) 흔들다		
28 ~에게 인사하다		
29 사원		
30 경험하다		
31 전통적인		
32 제공하다, 대접하다		
33 문화의, 문화적인		
34 불편한		
35 서로		
36 ~의 대답으로		
37 ~로 여겨지다		
38 ~에 익숙해지다		
39 반드시 ~하다		
40 (범위가) A에서 B에 이르다		
41 A와 B 사이에		
42 ~할 것을 기억하다		
43 ~에 나쁜 영향을 미치다		

※ 다음 영영풀이에 알맞은 단어를 <보기>에서 골라 쓴 후, 우리말 뜻을 쓰시오.

1 _____ : not polite: _____

2 _____ : things for sale, or the things that you own: _____

3 _____ : a tax paid by people when they buy goods or services: _____

4 _____ : to cover or surround something with paper, cloth, or other material: _____

5 _____ : to raise your hand and move it from side to side as a way of greeting someone: _____

6 _____ : to hurt part of your body by hitting it against something hard: _____

7 _____ : to give something to someone and receive something from that person: _____

8 _____ : not feeling comfortable and pleasant, or not making you feel comfortable and pleasant: _____

9 _____ : the number of the house, name of the road, and name of the town where a person lives or works, and where letters can be sent: _____

10 _____ : in a way that is in agreement with the true facts or with what is generally accepted: _____

11 _____ : an amount of money that you pay in order to be allowed into a cinema, theater, etc.: _____

12 _____ : an opinion that someone offers you about what you should do or how you should act in a particular situation: _____

13 _____ : a short series of letters and numbers that is part of an address, and shows exactly where a place is: _____

14 _____ : a small piece of paper, cloth, or metal with information on it, tied or stuck onto something larger: _____

15 _____ : money paid to the government that is based on your income or the cost of goods or services you have bought: _____

16 _____ : following or belonging to the customs or ways of behaving that have continued in a group of people or society for a long time without changing: _____

보기

uncomfortable	traditional	bump	wave
rude	address	sales tax	postal code
exchange	tax	entrance fee	tag
goods	correctly	wrap	advice

※ 다음 우리말과 일치하도록 빈칸에 알맞은 말을 쓰시오.

Warm Up

1. People _____ _____ _____ in _____.
2. People _____ their hands _____ and say "Namaste" in _____.
3. Men _____ _____ _____ in the United Arab Emirates.

해석

1. 티베트 사람들은 그들의 혀를 보여준다.
2. 인도 사람들은 손을 모으고 "나마스테"라고 말한다.
3. 아랍에미리트에서 남자들은 코를 부딪친다.

Listen & Speak 1 A

1. G: I want _____ _____ this to my _____ in the USA.
   B: _____ is it?
   G: It's her *hanbok*. Can I _____ your _____ on _____ _____ _____ an _____ _____ _____?
   B: Sure. You _____ _____ the _____ _____ first.
   G: _____ this?
   B: Yes. Then, write the name of the city and the _____ and then the _____ _____. _____, write the _____.
   G: Thanks _____ your _____.

2. G: _____ _____ the people _____ Moroccan clothes. They are really beautiful. I want _____ _____ _____ them.
   M: Wait. _____ _____ an important thing you _____ _____ know _____ _____ pictures.
   G: Oh, really? Can I _____ your _____ _____ it?
   M: Yes. You _____ _____ _____ _____ _____ _____ _____ people _____ _____.
   G: Why?
   M: They _____ it may have _____ _____ _____ _____ them _____ someone takes their picture.

1. G: 나는 이것을 미국에 계신 이모에게 보내고 싶어.
   B: 그게 뭔데?
   G: 이모의 한복이야. 영어로 주소를 어떻게 쓰는지에 대해 내가 너의 조언을 구할 수 있을까?
   B: 물론이지. 먼저 거리 주소부터 적어야 해.
   G: 이렇게?
   B: 응. 그러고 나서, 도시 이름과 주 그리고 그 다음에 우편 번호를 적어. 마지막으로 국가를 적어.
   G: 도와줘서 고마워.

2. G: 모로코 전통 의상을 입고 있는 사람들을 보세요. 그들은 매우 아름다워요. 그들의 사진을 찍고 싶어요.
   M: 잠깐. 네가 사진을 찍기 전에 알아야 할 중요한 것이 있어.
   G: 오, 정말요? 그것에 대해 조언을 구할 수 있을까요?
   M: 응. 너는 물어보지 않고 모로코 사람들의 사진을 찍으면 안 돼.
   G: 왜요?
   M: 그들은 누군가가 자신의 사진을 찍으면 그것이 그들에게 나쁜 영향을 끼칠 것이라고 믿어.

Listen & Speak 1 B

A: _____ _____ _____ your _____ on _____ the Netherlands?
B: Sure. You _____ _____ on a bike _____.
A: Can I _____ _____ _____ _____ _____ _____ the USA?
B: Sure. You _____ _____ in the _____ _____ in the taxi.

A: 네덜란드를 방문하는 것에 대해 너의 조언을 구할 수 있을까?
B: 물론이지. 너는 자전거 도로에 서 있으면 안 돼.

A: 미국을 방문하는 것에 대해 너의 조언을 구할 수 있을까?
B: 물론이지. 택시에서는 뒷좌석에 앉아야 해.

Listen & Speak 2 A

1. **B:** Sena, I _____ a _____ for Ms. Han. I _____ _____ at her house here in Korea.

   G: That's great. _____ did you _____ her?

   B: I _____ her a hat. Do you _____ she'll love it?

   G: Yes. _____ _____ you use two hands _____ you _____ it _____ her.

   B: Why?

   G: Because _____ something to _____ people _____ one hand _____ _____ _____ _____ in Korea.

   B: Okay. I'll _____ that.

2. **B:** Did you _____ _____ you _____ for the trip _____ Thailand tomorrow?

   G: Not _____. What _____ I _____?

   B: _____ _____ _____ a pair of long _____ or a long _____.

   G: Why? It's very hot in Thailand, _____ it?

   B: Yes, but _____ _____ many _____ in Thailand. You _____ _____ _____ when you visit a _____.

   G: Okay. Is there _____ _____?

   B: _____ _____ you _____ Korean won _____ Thai baht.

Listen & Speak 2 B

A: Is there _____ I need to _____ when I eat in _____?

B: Yes. _____ _____ you _____ your hands _____ the table _____ _____ _____.

A: Is there _____ I _____ _____ remember _____ I eat in Uzbekistan?

B: Yes. _____ _____ you _____ _____ _____ your hat or shoes _____ _____ a meal.

Real Life Talk

Seho: My _____ friend _____ me _____ his house for dinner this Friday.

Bora: That's good. I hope you _____ _____ dinner at his house.

1. B: 세나야, 나 한 씨 아주머니께 드릴 선물을 샀어. 이곳 한국에서 그녀의 집에 머물고 있거든.
G: 그거 잘 됐네. 그녀를 위해 무엇을 샀니?
B: 모자를 샀어. 그녀가 그것을 좋아할 거라고 생각하니?
G: 응. 그녀에게 그것을 건넬 때 반드시 두 손으로 건네도록 해.
B: 왜?
G: 연장자에게 한 손으로 무언가를 주는 것은 한국에서 무례한 것으로 여겨지거든.
B: 알겠어. 그걸 기억할게.

2. B: 너는 내일 태국 여행에 필요한 모든 것을 챙겼니?
G: 아니 아직. 무엇을 가져가야 할까?
B: 긴 바지나 긴 치마를 한 벌 가져가는 것을 기억해.
G: 왜? 태국은 매우 덥잖아, 그렇지 않니?
B: 응, 하지만 태국에는 절이 많아. 너는 절을 방문할 때 반바지를 입으면 안 돼.
G: 알겠어. 다른 것이 또 있니?
B: 반드시 한국 원화를 태국 바트로 환전하도록 해.

A: 내가 프랑스에서 식사할 때 기억해야 할 것이 있니?
B: 응. 반드시 항상 손을 식탁 위에 올려 두도록 해.

A: 내가 우즈베키스탄에서 식사할 때 기억해야 할 것이 있니?
B: 응. 식사할 때 모자나 신발을 절대 벗지 않도록 해.

세호: 나의 중국인 친구가 이번 주 금요일 저녁 식사에 나를 집으로 초대했어.
보라: 좋네. 그 친구 집에서 네가 즐거운 저녁 식사하기를 바라.

Seho: I want to _____ a small _____ for him. You lived in China _____ _____ years. Can I get your _____ on _____ _____ _____?

Bora: _____ _____ some tea?

Seho: Tea?

Bora: Yes. _____ Chinese people like to _____ tea _____ a _____. They _____ _____ tea. Also, they _____ _____ tea to _____.

Seho: Oh, thanks. Is there _____ else _____ I _____ _____ know?

Bora: _____ _____ _____ _____ _____ _____ the present in white or black paper. White and black _____ _____ in China.

Seho: Okay. I'll _____ that. Thank you for the _____.

Communication Task Step 2

A: _____ _____ would you _____ _____ _____?

B: I'd like to visit Malaysia. Can I _____ your _____ on _____ there?

C: Sure. _____ _____ you _____ _____ your _____ _____ _____ something to someone.

B: Okay. Thanks.

Wrap Up

1. **B:** I'm _____ to Japan this summer. Can I _____ some _____ on _____ there?

   G: Make sure you _____ when you _____ _____ the bus.

   B: Oh, I didn't know that. Are there any _____ _____ I should _____?

   G: _____ _____ the bowl and _____ it _____ _____. Also, _____ _____ soup, you _____ drink it _____ a spoon.

   B: Okay. Thanks.

2. **M:** I want _____ _____ flowers to my friend _____ Russia. Is there _____ I _____ _____?

   W: _____ _____ you don't give flowers in even numbers.

세호: 그에게 줄 작은 선물을 준비하고 싶어. 너는 몇 년 동안 중국에 살았지. 무엇을 가져가야 할지 조언을 구해도 될까?

보라: 차를 가져가는 게 어때?

세호: 차?

보라: 응. 중국 사람들 대부분은 선물로 차를 받는 것을 좋아해. 그들은 차 마시는 것을 즐기거든. 또 그들은 대개 손님들에게 차를 대접해.

세호: 오, 고마워. 내가 알아야 할 또 다른 것이 있을까?

보라: 선물을 흰색이나 검은색 종이로 포장하지 않도록 해. 흰색과 검은색은 중국에서 죽음을 의미해.

세호: 알겠어. 기억할게. 조언해 줘서 고마워.

A: 너는 어떤 나라를 방문하고 싶니?

B: 나는 말레이시아를 방문하고 싶어. 그곳을 여행하는 것에 대해 너의 조언을 구할 수 있을까?

C: 물론이지. 누군가에게 무엇을 건넬 때 절대 왼손을 사용하지 않도록 해.

B: 알겠어. 고마워.

1. B: 나는 이번 여름에 일본에 갈 거야. 그곳을 방문하는 것에 대해 몇 가지 조언을 구할 수 있을까?

   G: 반드시 버스에서 내릴 때 돈을 내도록 해.

   B: 오, 그걸 몰랐어. 내가 기억해야 할 다른 것들이 또 있니?

   G: 먹는 동안에는 그릇을 들어올리고 그것을 잡고 있어. 또한 국을 먹을 때, 숟가락 없이 그것을 마셔야 해.

   B: 알겠어. 고마워.

2. M: 나는 러시아에서 온 내 친구에게 꽃을 주고 싶어. 내가 기억해야 하는 것이 있니?

   W: 짝수로 꽃을 주지 않도록 해라.

※ 다음 우리말에 맞도록 대화를 영어로 쓰시오.

Warm Up

1. _____

2. _____

3. _____

1. 티베트 사람들은 그들의 혀를 보여준다.
2. 인도 사람들은 손을 모으고 "나마스테"라고 말한다.
3. 아랍에미리트에서 남자들은 코를 부딪친다.

Listen & Speak 1 A

1. G: _____

   B: _____

   G: _____

   B: _____

   G: _____

   B: _____

   G: _____

2. G: _____

   M: _____

   G: _____

   M: _____

   G: _____

   M: _____

1. G: 나는 이것을 미국에 계신 이모에게 보내고 싶어.
   B: 그게 뭔데?
   G: 이모의 한복이야. 영어로 주소를 어떻게 쓰는지에 대해 내가 너의 조언을 구할 수 있을까?
   B: 물론이지. 먼저 거리 주소부터 적어야 해.
   G: 이렇게?
   B: 응. 그리고 나서, 도시 이름과 주 그리고 그 다음에 우편 번호를 적어. 마지막으로 국가를 적어.
   G: 도와줘서 고마워.

2. G: 모로코 전통 의상을 입고 있는 사람들을 보세요. 그들은 매우 아름다워요. 그들의 사진을 찍고 싶어요.
   M: 잠깐. 네가 사진을 찍기 전에 알아야 할 중요한 것이 있어.
   G: 오, 정말요? 그것에 대해 조언을 구할 수 있을까요?
   M: 응. 너는 물어보지 않고 모로코 사람들의 사진을 찍으면 안 돼.
   G: 왜요?
   M: 그들은 누군가가 자신의 사진을 찍으면 그것이 그들에게 나쁜 영향을 끼칠 것이라고 믿어.

Listen & Speak 1 B

A: _____

B: _____

A: _____

B: _____

A: 네덜란드를 방문하는 것에 대해 너의 조언을 구할 수 있을까?
B: 물론이지. 너는 자전거 도로에 서 있으면 안 돼.

A: 미국을 방문하는 것에 대해 너의 조언을 구할 수 있을까?
B: 물론이지. 택시에서는 뒷좌석에 앉아야 해.

Listen & Speak 2 A

1. B: _____
   _____
   G: _____
   B: _____
   G: _____
   B: _____
   G: _____
   _____
   B: _____

2. B: _____
   G: _____
   B: _____
   G: _____
   B: _____
   _____
   G: _____
   B: _____

Listen & Speak 2 B

A: _____
B: _____
A: _____
B: _____

Real Life Talk

Seho: _____
Bora: _____

Seho: _____

_____

Bora: _____

Seho: _____

Bora: _____

_____

Seho: _____

Bora: _____

_____

Seho: _____

세호: 그에게 줄 작은 선물을 준비하고 싶어. 너는 몇 년 동안 중국에 살았지. 무엇을 가져가야 할지 조언을 구해도 될까?

보라: 차를 가져가는 게 어때?

세호: 차?

보라: 응. 중국 사람들 대부분은 선물로 차를 받는 것을 좋아해. 그들은 차 마시는 것을 즐기거든. 또 그들은 대개 손님들에게 차를 대접해.

세호: 오, 고마워. 내가 알아야 할 또 다른 것이 있을까?

보라: 선물을 흰색이나 검은색 종이로 포장하지 않도록 해. 흰색과 검은색은 중국에서 죽음을 의미해.

세호: 알겠어. 기억할게. 조언해 줘서 고마워.

Communication Task Step 2

A: _____

B: _____

C: _____

B: _____

A: 너는 어떤 나라를 방문하고 싶니?

B: 나는 말레이시아를 방문하고 싶어. 그곳을 여행하는 것에 대해 너의 조언을 구할 수 있을까?

C: 물론이지. 누군가에게 무엇을 건넬 때 절대 왼손을 사용하지 않도록 해.

B: 알겠어. 고마워.

Wrap Up

1. B: _____

G: _____

B: _____

G: _____

B: _____

1. B: 나는 이번 여름에 일본에 갈 거야. 그곳을 방문하는 것에 대해 몇 가지 조언을 구할 수 있을까?

G: 반드시 버스에서 내릴 때 돈을 내도록 해.

B: 오, 그걸 몰랐어. 내가 기억해야 할 다른 것들이 또 있니?

G: 먹는 동안에는 그릇을 들어올리고 그것을 잡고 있어. 또한 국을 먹을 때, 숟가락 없이 그것을 마셔야 해.

B: 알겠어. 고마워.

2. M: _____

W: _____

2. M: 나는 러시아에서 온 내 친구에게 꽃을 주고 싶어. 내가 기억해야 하는 것이 있니?

W: 짝수로 꽃을 주지 않도록 해라.

※ 다음 우리말과 일치하도록 빈칸에 알맞은 것을 골라 쓰시오.

Let's Learn about Cultural Differences

1 Hi! My name is Kim Minhee. I _____ _____ _____ in America _____ three years.
   A. living   B. for   C. have   D. been

2 _____ my family moved here, I have _____ many cultural differences _____ Korea _____ America.
   A. between   B. since   C. and   D. experienced

3 I _____ _____ to _____ some of them _____ you.
   A. like   B. with   C. would   D. share

4 Minhee: Look _____ this shirt. I like _____.
   A. it   B. at

5 Linda: It _____ _____. How _____ is it?
   A. nice   B. much   C. looks

6 Minhee: It's 19 _____ and 99 _____.
   A. cents   B. dollars

7 Linda: That's _____ _____.
   A. expensive   B. not

8 Minhee: Yes, I _____. I want to _____ _____.
   A. buy   B. agree   C. it

9 Clerk: That'll _____ 21 _____ and 20 _____.
   A. dollars   B. be   C. cents

10 Minhee: Really? But the _____ _____ says it's _____ 19 dollars and 99 cents.
    A. only   B. tag   C. price

11 Here in America, in most _____, people _____ a _____ when they buy _____.
    A. goods   B. tax   C. states   D. pay

12 It is _____ a _____ tax. Sales tax _____ _____ by state.
    A. differ   B. called   C. rates   D. sales

13 They _____ from _____ _____ one percent to _____ than ten percent.
    A. more   B. less   C. range   D. than

14 So when you buy _____ in America, you usually need to _____ more than the _____ on the _____.
    A. price   B. goods   C. tag   D. pay

문화적 차이에 대해서 배우자

1 안녕! 내 이름은 김민희야. 나는 미국에 3년 동안 살고 있어.

2 우리 가족이 이곳으로 이민을 온 이후로 나는 한국과 미국의 많은 문화적 차이를 경험하고 있어.

3 나는 그것들 중 몇 가지를 너희 들과 공유하고 싶어.

4 민희: 이 셔츠를 봐. 마음에 들어.

5 Linda: 멋져 보인다. 얼마야?

6 민희: 19달러 99센트야.

7 Linda: 비싸지 않네.

8 민희: 응. 나도 그렇게 생각해. 그것을 사고 싶어.

9 점원: 21달러 20센트입니다.

10 민희: 정말이요? 하지만 가격표 에는 단지 19달러 99센트라고 쓰여 있는데요.

11 이곳 미국에서는 대부분의 주에 서 사람들이 물건을 구입할 때 세금을 내.

12 그것은 판매세라고 불려. 판매 세의 비율은 주마다 달라.

13 판매세는 1퍼센트 미만부터 10 퍼센트 이상까지 다양해.

14 그래서 미국에서 상품을 살 때, 대개 가격표에 있는 가격보다 더 많은 돈을 지불해야 해.

15 Jessica: Hi, _____ Johnson! Minhee: _____, Mrs. Johnson!
A. hello　　　B. Mrs.

16 Mrs. Johnson: _____, Jessica! Hi, Minhee! _____ are you?
A. how　　　B. hi

17 Jessica: Fine, thank you. We are here _____ a burger. _____ your _____.
A. enjoy　　　B. for　　　C. meal

18 Mrs. Johnson: _____ you. You, _____!
A. too　　　B. thank

19 Minhee: Jessica, _____ did you _____ _____ Mrs. Johnson?
A. wave　　　B. why　　　C. to

20 In America, people often _____ each _____ by _____.
A. waving　　　B. other　　　C. greet

21 _____ to an older person is not _____ _____ rude.
A. regarded　　　B. waving　　　C. as

22 When you come to America, you may _____ _____ about it at first, but why _____ you _____ it?
A. uncomfortable　　B. don't　　C. feel　　D. try

23 You can _____ to and smile _____ an _____ man walking on the street. He may wave _____.
A. back　　　B. at　　　C. wave　　　D. elderly

24 Andy: Minhee, _____ this apple _____.
A. pie　　　B. try

25 Minhee: No, _____. I don't _____ _____.
A. to　　　B. thanks　　　C. want

26 Andy: Why _____? _____ you _____ apple pie?
A. don't　　　B. like　　　C. not

27 _____: _____.
A. yes　　　B. Minhee

28 Andy: Then, _____. It's _____.
A. some　　　B. delicious　　　C. try

본문 Test **33**

29 Minhee: No. I _____ _____ I _____ like apple pie.

    A. said   B. just   C. don't

30 _____ : _____ ?

    A. what   B. Andy

31 Americans often ask _____ questions, such _____ " _____ you coming?" and " _____ you go to the hospital?"

    A. aren't   B. as   C. negative   D. didn't

32 It can be _____ to answer _____ questions _____ . Here is some _____ .

    A. correctly   B. difficult   C. advice   D. negative

33 In _____ to negative questions, _____ _____ "Don't you like apple pie?" you should answer "No," _____ you don't like it.

    A. as   B. if   C. response   D. such

34 And you _____ _____ "Yes," if you _____ it.

    A. answer   B. like   C. should

35 These answers are the _____ _____ the answers to _____ , such as "Do you like apple pie?"

    A. positive   B. as   C. questions   D. same

36 Which _____ _____ is most _____ to you?

    A. surprising   B. difference   C. cultural

37 I have _____ _____ about cultural _____ _____ I came to America.

    A. learning   B. since   C. been   D. differences

38 Some _____ me at first, but now I am _____ _____ _____ them.

    A. to   B. used   C. surprised   D. getting

29 민희: 아니. 내가 사과 파이를 좋아하지 않는다고 방금 말했잖아.

30 Andy: 뭐라고?

31 미국 사람들은 종종 "너 안 오니?", "너 병원 안 갔니?"와 같은 부정의문문으로 질문해.

32 부정의문문에 바르게 대답하는 것은 어려울 수 있어. 여기 약간의 충고 사항이 있어.

33 "너는 사과 파이를 좋아하지 않니?"와 같은 부정의문문의 대답으로 만약 사과 파이를 좋아하지 않는다면 너는 "No."라고 대답해야 해.

34 그리고 만약 그것을 좋아한다면 "Yes."라고 대답해야 해.

35 이 대답들은 "너는 애플파이를 좋아하니?"와 같은 긍정의문문에 대한 대답들과 같아.

36 어떤 문화적인 차이가 너에게 가장 놀랍니?

37 나는 미국에 온 이후로 문화적인 차이에 대해 계속 배우고 있어.

38 어떤 것들은 처음에 나를 놀라게 했지만, 지금은 그것들에 익숙해지고 있어.

※ 다음 우리말과 일치하도록 빈칸에 알맞은 말을 쓰시오.

Let's Learn about Cultural Differences

1　Hi! My name is Kim Minhee. I _____ _____ _____ in America _____ _____ _____ .

2　_____ my family moved here, I _____ _____ many cultural _____ _____ Korea _____ America.

3　I _____ _____ _____ _____ some of them with you.

4　Minhee: _____ _____ this shirt. I like _____ .

5　Linda: It _____ _____ . _____ _____ is it?

6　Minhee: It's 19 _____ and 99 _____ .

7　Linda: That's _____ _____ .

8　Minhee: Yes, I _____ . I want _____ _____ _____ .

9　Clerk: That'll _____ 21 _____ and 20 _____ .

10　Minhee: Really? But _____ _____ _____ _____ it's _____ 19 dollars and 99 cents.

11　Here in America, in _____ _____ , people _____ _____ _____ when they buy _____ .

12　It _____ _____ a _____ _____ . Sales tax _____ _____ _____ _____ .

13　They _____ from _____ one percent to _____ _____ ten percent.

14　So when you _____ _____ in America, you _____ _____ _____ _____ more than the price on the tag.

1　안녕! 내 이름은 김민희야. 나는 미국에 3년 동안 살고 있어.

2　우리 가족이 이곳으로 이민을 온 이후로 나는 한국과 미국의 많은 문화적 차이를 경험하고 있어.

3　나는 그것들 중 몇 가지를 너희들과 공유하고 싶어.

4　민희: 이 셔츠를 봐. 마음에 들어.

5　Linda: 멋져 보인다. 얼마야?

6　민희: 19달러 99센트야.

7　Linda: 비싸지 않네.

8　민희: 응, 나도 그렇게 생각해. 그것을 사고 싶어.

9　점원: 21달러 20센트입니다.

10　민희: 정말이요? 하지만 가격표에는 단지 19달러 99센트라고 쓰여 있는데요.

11　이곳 미국에서는 대부분의 주에서 사람들이 물건을 구입할 때 세금을 내.

12　그것은 판매세라고 불려. 판매세의 비율은 주마다 달라.

13　판매세는 1퍼센트 미만부터 10퍼센트 이상까지 다양해.

14　그래서 미국에서 상품을 살 때, 대개 가격표에 있는 가격보다 더 많은 돈을 지불해야 해.

15 Jessica: Hi, _____ Johnson! Minhee: Hello, _____ Johnson!

16 Mrs. Johnson: Hi, Jessica! Hi, Minhee! _____ are you?

17 Jessica: Fine, thank you. We are here _____ a burger. _____ _____ _____.

18 Mrs. Johnson: Thank you. You, _____!

19 Minhee: Jessica, _____ _____ you _____ _____ Mrs. Johnson?

20 In America, people _____ _____ _____ _____ by _____.

21 _____ to an older person _____ not _____ _____ _____.

22 When you come to America, you may _____ _____ about it at first, but _____ _____ you _____ _____?

23 You can _____ _____ and _____ _____ an _____ man _____ on the street. He may _____ _____.

24 Andy: Minhee, _____ this _____ _____.

25 Minhee: No, _____. I don't _____ _____.

26 Andy: Why _____? _____ you like apple pie?

27 Minhee: _____.

28 Andy: Then, _____ _____. It's _____.

---

15 Jessica: 안녕하세요, Johnson 할머니! 민희: 안녕하세요, Johnson 할머니!

16 Mrs. Johnson: 안녕, Jessica! 안녕, 민희! 잘 지내지?

17 Jessica: 잘 지내요, 감사합니다. 저희는 여기 버거 먹으러 왔어요. 식사 맛있게 하세요.

18 Mrs. Johnson: 고맙구나. 너희들도!

19 민희: Jessica, 왜 너는 Johnson 할머니께 손을 흔들었니?

20 미국에서 사람들은 종종 손을 흔들며 서로에게 인사해.

21 나이가 많은 사람에게 손을 흔드는 것은 무례하다고 여겨지지 않아.

22 네가 미국에 오면 처음에는 그것에 대해 불편하게 느낄 수 있어. 하지만 한번 시도해 보지 않을래?

23 너는 길을 걷고 있는 연세가 많으신 할아버지께 손을 흔들며 미소를 지어도 돼. 그도 너한테 답례로 손을 흔들지도 몰라.

24 Andy: 민희, 이 사과 파이 좀 먹어 봐.

25 민희: 아니야, 고마워. 먹고 싶지 않아.

26 Andy: 왜 안 먹어? 너는 사과 파이를 좋아하지 않니?

27 민희: 응.

28 Andy: 그러면, 좀 먹어 봐. 맛있어.

29 Minhee: No. I _____ said I _____ _____ apple pie.

30 Andy: _____?

31 Americans _____ _____ _____ _____, such as "_____ you coming?" and "_____ you _____ to the hospital?"

32 _____ can be difficult _____ _____ negative questions _____. Here _____ some advice.

33 In response to _____ _____, _____ _____ "Don't you like apple pie?" you should _____ "_____," if you don't like it.

34 And you _____ _____ "_____," _____ you like it.

35 These answers are _____ _____ _____ the answers _____ _____ _____, such as "Do you like apple pie?"

36 _____ _____ _____ is most _____ to you?

37 I _____ _____ _____ about _____ _____ _____ I came to America.

38 Some _____ me _____ _____, but now I _____ _____ _____ _____ them.

29 민희: 아니. 내가 사과 파이를 좋아하지 않는다고 방금 말했잖아.

30 Andy: 뭐라고?

31 미국 사람들은 종종 "너 안 오니?", "너 병원 안 갔니?"와 같은 부정의문문으로 질문해.

32 부정의문문에 바르게 대답하는 것은 어려울 수 있어. 여기 약간의 충고 사항이 있어.

33 "너는 사과 파이를 좋아하지 않니?"와 같은 부정의문문의 대답으로 만약 사과 파이를 좋아하지 않는다면 너는 "No."라고 대답해야 해.

34 그리고 만약 그것을 좋아한다면 "Yes."라고 대답해야 해.

35 이 대답들은 "너는 애플파이를 좋아하니?"와 같은 긍정의문문에 대한 대답들과 같아.

36 어떤 문화적인 차이가 너에게 가장 놀랍니?

37 나는 미국에 온 이후로 문화적인 차이에 대해 계속 배우고 있어.

38 어떤 것들은 처음에 나를 놀라게 했지만, 지금은 그것들에 익숙해지고 있어.

※ 다음 문장을 우리말로 쓰시오.

1 Hi! My name is Kim Minhee. I have been living in America for three years.

➡ _____

2 Since my family moved here, I have experienced many cultural differences between Korea and America.

➡ _____

3 I would like to share some of them with you.

➡ _____.

4 Minhee: Look at this shirt. I like it.

➡ _____

5 Lynda: It looks nice. How much is it?

➡ _____

6 Minhee: It's 19 dollars and 99 cents.

➡ _____

7 Linda: That's not expensive.

➡ _____

8 Minhee: Yes, I agree. I want to buy it.

➡ _____

9 Clerk: That'll be 21 dollars and 20 cents.

➡ _____

10 Minhee: Really? But the price tag says it's only 19 dollars and 99 cents.

➡ _____

11 Here in America, in most states, people pay a tax when they buy goods.

➡ _____

12 It is called a sales tax. Sales tax rates differ by state.

➡ _____

13 They range from less than one percent to more than ten percent.

➡ _____

14 So when you buy goods in America, you usually need to pay more than the price on the tag.

➡ _____

15 Jessica: Hi, Mrs. Johnson! Minhee: Hello, Mrs. Johnson!

➡ _____

16 Mrs. Johnson: Hi, Jessica! Hi, Minhee! How are you?

➡ _____

17 Jessica: Fine, thank you. We are here for a burger. Enjoy your meal.

➡ _____

18 Mrs. Johnson: Thank you. You, too!

➡ _____

19 Minhee: Jessica, why did you wave to Mrs. Johnson?

➡ _____

20 In America, people often greet each other by waving.

➡ _____

21 Waving to an older person is not regarded as rude.

➡ _____

22 When you come to America, you may feel uncomfortable about it at first, but why don't you try it?

➡ _____

23 You can wave to and smile at an elderly man walking on the street. He may wave back.

➡ _____

24 Andy: Minhee, try this apple pie.

➡ _____

25 Minhee: No, thanks. I don't want to.

➡ _____

26 Andy: Why not? Don't you like apple pie?

➡ _____

27 Minhee: Yes.

➡ _____

28 Andy: Then, try some. It's delicious.

➡ _____

29 Minhee: No. I just said I don't like apple pie.

➡ _____

30 Andy: What?

➡ _____

31 Americans often ask negative questions, such as "Aren't you coming?" and "Didn't you go to the hospital?"

➡ _____

32 It can be difficult to answer negative questions correctly. Here is some advice.

➡ _____

33 In response to negative questions, such as "Don't you like apple pie?" you should answer "No," if you don't like it.

➡ _____

➡ _____

34 And you should answer "Yes," if you like it.

➡ _____

35 These answers are the same as the answers to positive questions, such as "Do you like apple pie?"

➡ _____

36 Which cultural difference is most surprising to you?

➡ _____

37 I have been learning about cultural differences since I came to America.

➡ _____

38 Some surprised me at first, but now I am getting used to them.

➡ _____

※ 다음 괄호 안의 단어들을 우리말에 맞도록 바르게 배열하시오.

Let's Learn about Cultural Differences

1 (hi! // name / my / is / Minhee. / Kim // living / have / I / been / America / in / three / years. / for)
➡ _____

2 (my / since / family / here, / moved / have / I / many / experienced / cultural / between / differences / Korea / America. / and)
➡ _____
_____

3 (would / I / like / share / to / of / some / them / you. / with)
➡ _____

4 (Minhee: / at / look / shirt. / this // like / it. / I)
➡ _____

5 (Linda: / looks / it / nice. // much / how / it? / is)
➡ _____

6 (Minhee: / 19 / it's / dollars / 99 / and / cents.)
➡ _____

7 (Linda: / not / that's / expensive.)
➡ _____

8 (Minhee: / I / yes, / agree. // want / I / to / it. / buy)
➡ _____

9 (Clerk: / be / that'll / dollars / 21 / and / cents. / 20)
➡ _____

10 (Minhee: / really? // the / but / tag / price / it's / says / 19 / only / dollars / and / cents. / 99)
➡ _____

11 (in / here / America, / most / in / states, / pay / people / tax / a / when / they / goods. / buy)
➡ _____

12 (is / it / called / sales / a / tax. // tax / sales / differ / rates / state. / by)
➡ _____

13 (range / they / less / from / than / percent / one / more / to / ten / than / percent.)
➡ _____

14 (when / so / buy / you / in / goods / America, / usually / you / to / need / pay / than / more / price / the / the / on / tag.)
➡ _____

문화적 차이에 대해서 배우자

1 안녕! 내 이름은 김민희야. 나는 미국에 3년 동안 살고 있어.

2 우리 가족이 이곳으로 이민을 온 이후로 나는 한국과 미국의 많은 문화적 차이를 경험하고 있어.

3 나는 그것들 중 몇 가지를 너희 들과 공유하고 싶어.

4 민희: 이 셔츠를 봐. 마음에 들어.

5 Linda: 멋져 보인다. 얼마야?

6 민희: 19달러 99센트야.

7 Linda: 비싸지 않네.

8 민희: 응, 나도 그렇게 생각해. 그것을 사고 싶어.

9 점원: 21달러 20센트입니다.

10 민희: 정말이요? 하지만 가격표 에는 단지 19달러 99센트라고 쓰여 있는데요.

11 이곳 미국에서는 대부분의 주에 서 사람들이 물건을 구입할 때 세금을 내.

12 그것은 판매세라고 불려. 판매 세의 비율은 주마다 달라.

13 판매세는 1퍼센트 미만부터 10 퍼센트 이상까지 다양해.

14 그래서 미국에서 상품을 살 때, 대개 가격표에 있는 가격보다 더 많은 돈을 지불해야 해.

15 (Jessica: / Mrs. / hi, / Johnson! // Minhee: / Mrs. / hello, / Johnson!)

➡ _____

16 (Mrs. Johnson: / Jessica! / hi, // Minhee! / hi, // are / you? / how)

➡ _____

17 (Jessica: / thank / fine, / you. // are / we / for / here / burger. / a // your / enjoy / meal.)

➡ _____

18 (Mrs. Johnson: / you. / thank // too! / you,)

➡ _____

19 (Minhee: / why / Jessica, / you / did / to / wave / Johnson? / Mrs.)

➡ _____

20 (America, / in / often / people / each / greet / other / waving. / by)

➡ _____

21 (to / waving / an / person / older / not / is / as / rude. / regarded)

➡ _____

22 (you / when / to / come / America, / may / you / uncomfortable / feel / it / about / first, / at / why / but / you / don't / it? / try)

➡ _____

➡ _____

23 (can / you / to / wave / and / at / smile / elderly / an / walking / man / the / on / street. // may / he / back. / wave)

➡ _____

➡ _____

24 (Andy: / try / Minhee, / apple / this / pie.)

➡ _____

25 (Minhee: / thanks. / no, // don't / I / to. / want)

➡ _____

26 (Andy: / not? / why // you / don't / apple / like / pie?)

➡ _____

27 (Minhee: / yes.)

➡ _____

28 (Andy: / try / then, / some. // delicious. / it's)

➡ _____

15 Jessica: 안녕하세요, Johnson 할머니! 민희: 안녕하세요, Johnson 할머니!

16 Mrs. Johnson: 안녕, Jessica! 안녕, 민희! 잘 지내지?

17 Jessica: 잘 지내요, 감사합니다. 저희는 여기 버거 먹으러 왔어요. 식사 맛있게 하세요.

18 Mrs. Johnson: 고맙구나. 너희들도!

19 민희: Jessica, 왜 너는 Johnson 할머니께 손을 흔들었니?

20 미국에서 사람들은 종종 손을 흔들며 서로에게 인사해.

21 나이가 많은 사람에게 손을 흔드는 것은 무례하다고 여겨지지 않아.

22 네가 미국에 오면 처음에는 그것에 대해 불편하게 느낄 수 있어. 하지만 한번 시도해 보지 않을래?

23 너는 길을 걷고 있는 연세가 많으신 할아버지께 손을 흔들며 미소를 지어도 돼. 그도 너한테 답례로 손을 흔들지도 몰라.

24 Andy: 민희, 이 사과 파이 좀 먹어 봐.

25 민희: 아니야. 고마워. 먹고 싶지 않아.

26 Andy: 왜 안 먹어? 너는 사과 파이를 좋아하지 않니?

27 민희: 응.

28 Andy: 그러면, 좀 먹어 봐. 맛있어.

29 (Minhee: / no. // just / I / said / don't / I / apple / like / pie.)

➡ _____

30 (what? / Andy:)

➡ _____

31 (often / Americans / negative / ask / questions, / as / such / you / coming?" / "aren't / and / "didn't / go / you / the / hospital?" / to)

➡ _____

_____

32 (can / it / difficult / be / answer / to / questions / negative / correctly. // is / here / advice. / some)

➡ _____

_____

33 (response / in / negative / to / questions, / as / such / "don't / like / you / pie?" / apple / should / you / answer / "no," / you / if / like / don't / it.)

➡ _____

_____

34 (you / and / answer / should / "yes," / you / if / it. / like)

➡ _____

35 (answers / these / the / are / same / the / as / to / answers / questions, / positive / as / such / "do / like / you / pie?" / apple)

➡ _____

_____

36 (cultural / which / is / difference / most / to / surprising / you?)

➡ _____

37 (have / I / learning / been / cultural / about / since / differences / I / came / America. / to)

➡ _____

_____

38 (surprised / some / at / me / first, / now / but / am / I / used / getting / them. / to)

➡ _____

_____

29 민희: 아니. 내가 사과 파이를 좋아하지 않는다고 방금 말했잖아.

30 Andy: 뭐라고?

31 미국 사람들은 종종 "너 안 오니?", "너 병원 안 갔니?"와 같은 부정의문문으로 질문해.

32 부정의문문에 바르게 대답하는 것은 어려울 수 있어. 여기 약간의 충고 사항이 있어.

33 "너는 사과 파이를 좋아하지 않니?"와 같은 부정의문문의 대답으로 만약 사과 파이를 좋아하지 않는다면 너는 "No."라고 대답해야 해.

34 그리고 만약 그것을 좋아한다면 "Yes."라고 대답해야 해.

35 이 대답들은 "너는 애플파이를 좋아하니?"와 같은 긍정의문문에 대한 대답들과 같아.

36 어떤 문화적인 차이가 너에게 가장 놀랍니?

37 나는 미국에 온 이후로 문화적인 차이에 대해 계속 배우고 있어.

38 어떤 것들은 처음에 나를 놀라게 했지만, 지금은 그것들에 익숙해지고 있어.

※ 다음 우리말을 영어로 쓰시오.

1 안녕! 내 이름은 김민희야. 나는 미국에 3년 동안 살고 있어.

➡ _____

2 우리 가족이 이곳으로 이민을 온 이후로 나는 한국과 미국의 많은 문화적 차이를 경험하고 있어.

➡ _____

3 나는 그것들 중 몇 가지를 너희들과 공유하고 싶어.

➡ _____

4 민희: 이 셔츠를 봐. 마음에 들어.

➡ _____

5 Linda: 멋져 보인다. 얼마야?

➡ _____

6 민희: 19달러 99센트야.

➡ _____

7 Linda: 비싸지 않네.

➡ _____

8 민희: 응, 나도 그렇게 생각해. 그것을 사고 싶어.

➡ _____

9 점원: 21달러 20센트입니다.

➡ _____

10 민희: 정말이요? 하지만 가격표에는 단지 19달러 99센트라고 쓰여 있는데요.

➡ _____

11 이곳 미국에서는 대부분의 주에서 사람들이 물건을 구입할 때 세금을 내.

➡ _____

12 그것은 판매세라고 불려. 판매세의 비율은 주마다 달라.

➡ _____

13 판매세는 1퍼센트 미만부터 10퍼센트 이상까지 다양해.

➡ _____

14 그래서 미국에서 상품을 살 때, 대개 가격표에 있는 가격보다 더 많은 돈을 지불해야 해.

➡ _____

15 Jessica: 안녕하세요, Johnson 할머니! 민희: 안녕하세요, Johnson 할머니!

➡ _____

16 Mrs. Johnson: 안녕, Jessica! 안녕, 민희! 잘 지내지?

➡ _____

17 Jessica: 잘 지내요, 감사합니다. 저희는 여기 버거 먹으러 왔어요. 식사 맛있게 하세요.

➡ _____

18 Mrs. Johnson: 고맙구나. 너희들도!

➡ _____

19 민희: Jessica, 왜 너는 Johnson 할머니께 손을 흔들었니?

➡ _____

20 미국에서 사람들은 종종 손을 흔들며 서로에게 인사해.

➡ _____

21 나이가 많은 사람에게 손을 흔드는 것은 무례하다고 여겨지지 않아.

➡ _____

22 네가 미국에 오면 처음에는 그것에 대해 불편하게 느낄 수 있어. 하지만 한번 시도해 보지 않을래?

➡ _____

23 너는 길을 걷고 있는 연세가 많으신 할아버지께 손을 흔들며 미소를 지어도 돼. 그도 너한테 답례로 손을 흔들지도 몰라.

➡ _____

24 Andy: 민희, 이 사과 파이 좀 먹어 봐.

➡ _____

25 Minhee: 아니야, 고마워. 먹고 싶지 않아.

➡ _____

26 Andy: 왜 안 먹어? 너는 사과 파이를 좋아하지 않니?

➡ _____

27 Minhee: 응.

➡ _____

28 Andy: 그러면, 좀 먹어 봐. 맛있어.

➡ _____

29 Minhee: 아니. 내가 사과 파이를 좋아하지 않는다고 방금 말했잖아.
➡ _____

30 Andy: 뭐라고?
➡ _____

31 미국 사람들은 종종 "너 안 오니?", "너 병원 안 갔니?"와 같은 부정의문문으로 질문해.
➡ _____

32 부정의문문에 바르게 대답하는 것은 어려울 수 있어. 여기 약간의 충고 사항이 있어.
➡ _____

33 "너는 사과 파이를 좋아하지 않니?"와 같은 부정의문문의 대답으로 만약 사과 파이를 좋아하지 않는다면 너는 "No."라고 대답해야 해.
➡ _____

34 그리고 만약 그것을 좋아한다면 "Yes."라고 대답해야 해.
➡ _____

35 이 대답들은 "너는 애플파이를 좋아하니?"와 같은 긍정의문문에 대한 대답들과 같아.
➡ _____

36 어떤 문화적인 차이가 너에게 가장 놀랍니?
➡ _____

37 나는 미국에 온 이후로 문화적인 차이에 대해 계속 배우고 있어.
➡ _____

38 어떤 것들은 처음에 나를 놀라게 했지만, 지금은 그것들에 익숙해지고 있어.
➡ _____

※ 다음 우리말과 일치하도록 빈칸에 알맞은 말을 쓰시오.

Project Step 1

1. A: Can I get your advice _____ _____ _____ _____?
2. B: _____ _____ you say window shopping _____ _____ _____ _____.
3. C: _____ _____ _____ _____ _____ Y-shirt. You _____ _____ dress shirt _____.

Project Step 3

1. Today, I _____ I _____ _____ _____ many _____ English expressions.
2. _____ _____, we _____ _____ dress shirt _____ _____ Y-shirt.
3. Eye shopping is also _____ _____ _____. _____ _____ _____ _____ it.

Enjoy Writing

1. Holi That I _____ _____.
2. _____ _____ many interesting festivals _____ _____ _____.
3. _____ them, I'd _____ _____ _____ Holi.
4. People in India _____ _____ _____ this festival _____ _____.
5. Holi _____ _____ _____ March.
6. I think that _____ _____ _____, I'll experience _____ _____ _____ _____.
7. First, there are _____ _____ colored powder and water _____ _____.
8. It _____ _____ _____!
9. Second, I want _____ _____ _____ _____ _____ on the street.
10. I'll also _____ _____ Holi _____.
11. It's _____ be very _____.
12. I _____ _____ _____ the day!

1. A: 옳은 영어 표현에 대해 너의 조언을 구할 수 있을까?
2. B: 반드시 아이 쇼핑 대신 윈도 쇼핑(구경만 하는 쇼핑)이라고 말하도록 해.
3. C: 절대 와이셔츠라고 말하지 않도록 해. 대신 정장용 셔츠라고 말해야 해.

1. 오늘, 나는 내가 많은 잘못된 영어 표현을 사용해 왔다는 것을 알았습니다.
2. 예를 들어, 우리는 Y-shirt 대신에 dress shirt라는 말을 써야 합니다.
3. 아이 쇼핑도 또한 잘못된 표현입니다. 그것을 사용하지 않도록 명심하세요.

1. 놓칠 수 없는 홀리
2. 세계에는 많은 흥미로운 축제들이 있다.
3 그 중에서, 나는 홀리에 참여하고 싶다.
4 인도 사람들은 오랫동안 이 축제를 열어오고 있는 중이다.
5 홀리 축제는 3월에 열린다.
6 나는 내가 간다면, 많은 것들을 경험할 것이라고 생각한다.
7 첫째, 서로에게 색색의 가루와 물을 던지는 사람들이 있다.
8 그것은 환상적일 것이다.
9 둘째, 나는 거리에서 다른 사람들과 춤을 추고 싶다.
10 나는 또한 전통적인 홀리 요리를 맛볼 것이다.
11 그것은 정말 신날 것이다.
12 나는 그 날이 정말 기대된다!

※ 다음 우리말을 영어로 쓰시오.

Project Step 1

1. A: 옳은 영어 표현에 대해 너의 조언을 구할 수 있을까?
➡ _____

2. B: 반드시 아이 쇼핑 대신 윈도 쇼핑(구경만 하는 쇼핑)이라고 말하도록 해.
➡ _____

3. C: 절대 와이셔츠라고 말하지 않도록 해. 대신 정장용 셔츠라고 말해야 해.
➡ _____

Project Step 3

1. 오늘, 나는 내가 많은 잘못된 영어 표현을 사용해 왔다는 것을 알았습니다.
➡ _____

2. 예를 들어, 우리는 Y-shirt 대신에 dress shirt라는 말을 써야 합니다.
➡ _____

3. 아이 쇼핑도 또한 잘못된 표현입니다. 그것을 사용하지 않도록 명심하세요.
➡ _____

Project

1. 놓칠 수 없는 홀리
➡ _____

2. 세계에는 많은 흥미로운 축제들이 있다.
➡ _____

3. 그 중에서, 나는 홀리에 참여하고 싶다.
➡ _____

4. 인도 사람들은 오랫동안 이 축제를 열어오고 있는 중이다.
➡ _____

5. 홀리 축제는 3월에 열린다.
➡ _____

6. 나는 내가 간다면, 많은 것들을 경험할 것이라고 생각한다.
➡ _____

7. 첫째, 서로에게 색색의 가루와 물을 던지는 사람들이 있다.
➡ _____

8. 그것은 환상적일 것이다.
➡ _____

9. 둘째, 나는 거리에서 다른 사람들과 춤을 추고 싶다.
➡ _____

10. 나는 또한 전통적인 홀리 요리를 맛볼 것이다.
➡ _____

11. 그것은 정말 신날 것이다.
➡ _____

12. 나는 그 날이 정말 기대된다!
➡ _____

※ 다음 영어를 우리말로 쓰시오.

01 enough _____

02 analyze _____

03 attend _____

04 figure _____

05 calm _____

06 cast _____

07 personality _____

08 detail _____

09 developer _____

10 highly _____

11 florist _____

12 analyst _____

13 weakness _____

14 include _____

15 among _____

16 resource _____

17 conduct _____

18 reduce _____

19 specialist _____

20 handle _____

21 creature _____

22 recommend _____

23 poet _____

24 veterinarian _____

25 mail carrier _____

26 select _____

27 greenery _____

28 strength _____

29 microphone _____

30 audition _____

31 stethoscope _____

32 performance _____

33 gardener _____

34 realistic _____

35 by -ing _____

36 come true _____

37 care for _____

38 be happy with ~ _____

39 belong to _____

40 make the best use of _____

41 It seems that ~ _____

42 I'm sure that ~ _____

43 dream of ~ _____

※ 다음 우리말을 영어로 쓰시오.

01	성격
02	분석하다
03	출연자들
04	힘, 강점
05	청진기
06	지휘하다, 처신하다
07	수의사
08	약함, 약점
09	세부, 세목
10	선택하다, 고르다
11	정원사
12	전문가
13	개발자
14	마이크
15	매우, 대단히
16	~ 중에서
17	플로리스트, 화초 연구가
18	오디션을 보다
19	화초, 푸른 잎
20	분석가
21	다루다

22	포함하다
23	진정시키다, 평온하게 하다
24	책임
25	현실적인
26	전통의, 전통적인
27	추천하다
28	공연
29	생물, 생명체
30	자원
31	줄이다, 완화하다
32	언젠가
33	기술자
34	충분히; 충분한
35	~을 보살피다
36	(단체, 조직에) 소속하다, 속하다
37	~을 꿈꾸다
38	~에 만족하다
39	실현되다
40	~함으로써
41	~처럼 보이다, ~일 것 같다
42	~을 확신하다
43	~을 최대한 활용하다

※ 다음 영영풀이에 알맞은 단어를 <보기>에서 골라 쓴 후, 우리말 뜻을 쓰시오.

1 _____: the actors in a film, play, or show: _____

2 _____: facts or information that can be analysed: _____

3 _____: to take things and put them together: _____

4 _____: to bring a person or thing to a state or place: _____

5 _____: to be a member of an organization: _____

6 _____: your job or duty to deal with something or someone: _____

7 _____: someone whose job is to analyze and examine something: _____

8 _____: a person whose job is to pay out and take in money in a bank: _____

9 _____: green plants or branches, especially when cut and used as decoration: _____

10 _____: the type of person you are, shown by the way you behave, feel, and think: _____

11 _____: a useful or valuable possession or quality of a country, organization, or person: _____

12 _____: to study or examine something in detail, in order to discover more about it: _____

13 _____: to contain something as a part of something else, or to make something part of something else: _____

14 _____: to give a short performance in order to show that you are suitable for a part in a film, play, show, etc.: _____

15 _____: a person or company that creates new products, especially computer products such as software: _____

16 _____: to protect someone or something and provide the things they need, especially someone who is young, old or ill: _____

보기			
resource	data	belong to	greenery
include	analyst	responsibility	analyze
care for	lead	collect	bank teller
personality	cast	developer	audition

※ 다음 우리말과 일치하도록 빈칸에 알맞은 말을 쓰시오.

Listen & Speak 1 A

1. **B:** Anne, I'm _____ to visit the _____ _____ to see my uncle. He is a _____ _____.

   G: Oh, I want _____ _____ a police officer _____.

   B: You _____? Me, _____. I have _____ _____ _____ a police officer _____ I was ten.

   G: Can I come _____ you, Matt? I want to meet your uncle and _____ him _____.

   B: Sure. What _____ you _____ _____ _____?

   G: I want to ask him _____ I need _____ _____ _____ _____ a police officer.

   B: I see. I'm _____ he _____ _____ _____ meet you.

2. **M:** What's _____, Jisu?

   G: I want to be an _____, but my _____ _____ is not good _____.

   M: Hmm... _____ _____ _____ is not just about _____ good _____.

   G: What should I _____ _____ _____ an _____?

   M: Read _____ _____ _____ books _____ _____ good stories and _____ _____ every day.

   G: Okay, I'll do so.

   M: I'm _____ _____ _____ you can be a good animator _____ you _____ _____.

   G: Thank you very much.

Listen & Speak 1 B

• **A:** I'm _____ in _____. _____ job would be _____ for me?

   B: I'm quite _____ that an app _____ could be a good job for you.

• **A:** I'm _____ _____ _____. _____ _____ would _____ _____ _____ me?

   B: I'm _____ _____ that a writer could _____ _____ _____ _____ you.

해석

1. **B:** Anne, 나는 우리 삼촌을 보러 경찰서에 갈 예정이야. 그는 경찰관이거든.

   G: 오, 나는 언젠가 경찰관이 되고 싶어.

   B: 그래? 나도야. 나는 10살 때부터 경찰관이 되는 것을 꿈꿔왔어.

   G: 내가 너와 함께 갈 수 있을까, Matt? 나 너희 삼촌을 만나서 몇 가지 물어보고 싶어.

   B: 물론이지. 무엇을 물어볼 거니?

   G: 나는 경찰관이 되기 위해 내가 무엇을 해야 하는지 물어보고 싶어.

   B: 알겠어. 나는 그가 널 만나고 싶어 할 거라고 확신해.

2. **M:** 무슨 문제 있니, 지수야?

   G: 저는 만화 영화 제작자가 되고 싶은데, 그리기 실력이 좋은 편이 아니에요.

   M: 음... 만화 영화 제작자가 되는 것은 단순히 그림을 잘 그린다고 되는 것만은 아니란다.

   G: 만화 영화 제작자가 되기 위해서 제가 무엇을 해야 하나요?

   M: 좋은 이야기를 만들기 위해 책을 많이 읽고, 그림 그리는 것을 매일 연습하렴.

   G: 알겠어요. 그렇게 할게요.

   M: 나는 네가 열심히 노력하면 훌륭한 만화 영화 제작자가 될 수 있다고 아주 확신해.

   G: 정말 감사해요.

• **A:** 나는 기술에 관심이 있어. 어떤 직업이 나에게 맞을까?

   B: 나는 앱 개발자가 너에게 좋은 직업이 될 수 있을 거라고 아주 확신해.

• **A:** 나는 쓰기에 관심이 있어. 어떤 직업이 나에게 맞을까?

   B: 나는 작가가 너에게 좋은 직업이 될 수 있을 거라고 아주 확신해.

Listen & Speak 2 A

1. **G:** I'm _____ _____ _____ you, Mr. Han. Could you please tell me _____ _____ _____?

   M: Okay. I _____ travelers to _____ _____ in China and give them _____ about where they should _____.

   G: What _____ do you do?

   M: I tell them about _____ _____ and _____ food in China.

   G: _____ _____ to me _____ _____ _____ about China is very important. Are you _____ _____ your job?

   M: Yes. I really love _____ _____.

2. **B:** Did you _____ the report about your _____ _____?

   G: Yes, I did. I _____ about my role model, Ms. Shin. I want to _____ _____ her.

   B: What _____ she _____?

   G: She teaches people _____ _____ _____. She _____ _____ them _____ stress and _____ _____.

   B: Good. _____ _____ _____ she helps _____ _____ _____ their mind _____ body healthy.

   G: Yes, and I think it's great.

Listen & Speak 2 B

- **A:** I want to be a radio _____ _____. What would help me _____ one?

  B: It _____ _____ me _____ your own stories would be _____.

- **A:** I want to be a _____ _____. What would _____ _____ _____ one?

  B: It _____ to me _____ _____ _____ _____ at a hospital would _____ _____.

Real Life Talk

Bora: What are you _____ _____ in _____ the things on this list?

Jessie: I'm most _____ _____ _____ outside and playing sports.

---

1. **G:** 만나 뵙게 되어 반갑습니다, Mr. Han. 당신이 어떤 일을 하시는지 말해 주실 수 있나요?
   M: 그래. 나는 중국에 있는 다양한 장소로 여행객들을 안내하고 그들이 방문해야 할 곳에 대한 정보를 제공해.
   G: 그 외에 또 어떤 일을 하시나요?
   M: 나는 그들에게 중국의 대중문화와 전통 음식에 대해 말해 줘.
   G: 중국에 대해 많이 아는 것이 매우 중요한 것 같네요. 당신의 직업에 만족하시나요?
   M: 응. 나는 내 직업을 정말 사랑해.

2. **B:** 네 롤 모델에 관한 기사 다 썼니?
   G: 응, 다 썼어. 나는 나의 롤 모델인 신 씨에 관해 썼어. 나는 그녀처럼 되고 싶어.
   B: 그녀는 무슨 일을 하니?
   G: 그녀는 사람들에게 스트레칭하는 방법을 가르쳐. 그녀는 또한 그들이 스트레스를 완화하여 평온해지도록 도와 줘.
   B: 좋구나. 그녀가 사람들의 몸과 마음을 둘 다 건강하게 유지하도록 돕는 것 같아.
   G: 맞아, 그리고 나는 그것이 훌륭하다고 생각해.

- **A:** 나는 라디오 방송 작가가 되고 싶어. 내가 그것이 되는 데 뭐가 도움이 될까?
  B: 너 자신만의 이야기를 쓰는 것이 도움이 될 것 같아.
- **A:** 나는 사회복지사가 되고 싶어. 내가 그것이 되는 데 뭐가 도움이 될까?
  B: 병원에서 아이들에게 책을 읽어 주는 것이 도움이 될 것 같아.

보라: 너는 이 목록에 있는 것들 중에서 무엇에 가장 관심이 있니?
Jessie: 나는 밖에서 일하는 것과 스포츠 하는 것에 가장 관심이 있어.

Bora: What are you _____ _____ in _____ the things on this list?

Jessie: I'm most interested in _____ outside and _____ sports.

Bora: Well, _____ _____ _____ _____ _____ you _____ _____ the _____ type.

Jessie: What do you _____?

Bora: Most people _____ _____ one of six _____ _____. _____ is _____ _____ the _____.

Jessie: Oh, that's _____. _____ _____ _____ jobs do they _____ for realistic types?

Bora: A farmer, a _____ _____, a soccer player, _____ _____ _____.

Jessie: Oh, I have always wanted _____ _____ a soccer player.

Bora: That's good. _____ _____ _____ you could become a great _____ _____.

Communication Task Step 2

A: I have _____ _____, _____ _____, 1 I, and _____ _____.

B: It _____ _____ me that you _____ _____ Type S.

C: Yes. _____ _____ are _____ for Type S are teacher, nurse, _____ or _____.

A: Cool. I _____ _____ _____ to be a teacher.

D: That _____ great. I'm _____ _____ _____ _____ _____ be a good teacher.

Wrap Up 1

B: Hello, what _____ you _____, Sumi?

G: I'm _____ _____ a good _____ on the Internet. I need it for my family dinner today.

B: That is nice. Do you _____ _____?

G: Yes, I try _____ _____ every weekend. I want to be a _____ _____.

B: What are you doing to _____ your dream _____ _____?

G: I'm _____ a cooking class. I try _____ _____ _____ new and _____ dishes.

B: _____ _____ _____ you could be a _____ _____.

보라: 음, 내 생각에 너는 현실적인 타입에 속하는 것 같아.
Jessie: 무슨 의미야?
보라: 대부분의 사람들은 여섯 가지 성격 유형 중 한 가지에 속해. 현실적인 타입도 그중 하나야.
Jessie: 오, 재미있다. 현실적인 타입의 사람들에게 그들이 추천하는 직업은 뭐야?
보라: 농부, 경찰관, 축구 선수 같은 거야.
Jessie: 오, 나는 항상 축구 선수가 되고 싶어 해 왔어.
보라: 멋지다. 나는 네가 훌륭한 축구 선수가 될 수 있을 거라고 아주 확신해.

A: 나는 S가 3개, A가 2개, I가 1개, E가 1개 있어.
B: 너는 S 타입에 속해 있는 것 같아.
C: 응. S 타입에게 추천되는 직업은 선생님, 간호사, 사서, 상담사야.
A: 멋지다. 나는 항상 선생님이 되고 싶었어.
D: 그거 멋지네. 나는 네가 좋은 선생님이 될 수 있다고 아주 확신해.

B: 안녕, 뭐 하고 있니, 수미야?
G: 나는 인터넷으로 좋은 요리법을 찾아보고 있어. 나는 오늘 우리 가족의 저녁 식사를 위해 그것이 필요해.
B: 그거 멋지네. 너는 요리를 자주 하니?
G: 응, 나는 매주 주말에 요리를 하려고 노력해. 나는 언젠가 요리사가 되고 싶어.
B: 네 꿈을 이루기 위해서 무엇을 하고 있니?
G: 나는 요리 수업을 듣고 있어. 새롭고 창의적인 요리를 생각해 내기 위해 노력해.
B: 나는 네가 좋은 요리사가 될 것이라고 아주 확신해.

※ 다음 우리말에 맞도록 대화를 영어로 쓰시오.

Listen & Speak 1 A

1. B: _____

   _____

   G: _____

   B: _____

   _____

   G: _____

   _____

   B: _____

   G: _____

   B: _____

2. M: _____

   G: _____

   M: _____

   G: _____

   M: _____

   G: _____

   M: _____

   G: _____

Listen & Speak 1 B

• A: _____

  B: _____

• A: _____

  B: _____

해석

1. B: Anne, 나는 우리 삼촌을 보러 경찰서에 갈 예정이야. 그는 경찰관이거든.
   G: 오, 나는 언젠가 경찰관이 되고 싶어.
   B: 그래? 나도야. 나는 10살 때부터 경찰관이 되는 것을 꿈꿔왔어.
   G: 내가 너와 함께 갈 수 있을까, Matt? 나 너희 삼촌을 만나서 몇 가지 물어보고 싶어.
   B: 물론이지. 무엇을 물어볼 거니?
   G: 나는 경찰관이 되기 위해 내가 무엇을 해야 하는지 물어보고 싶어.
   B: 알겠어. 나는 그가 널 만나고 싶어 할 거라고 확신해.

2. M: 무슨 문제 있니, 지수야?
   G: 저는 만화 영화 제작자가 되고 싶은데, 그리기 실력이 좋은 편이 아니에요.
   M: 음... 만화 영화 제작자가 되는 것은 단순히 그림을 잘 그린다고 되는 것만은 아니란다.
   G: 만화 영화 제작자가 되기 위해서 제가 무엇을 해야 하나요?
   M: 좋은 이야기를 만들기 위해 책을 많이 읽고, 그림 그리는 것을 매일 연습하렴.
   G: 알겠어요. 그렇게 할게요.
   M: 나는 네가 열심히 노력하면 훌륭한 만화 영화 제작자가 될 수 있다고 아주 확신해.
   G: 정말 감사해요.

• A: 나는 기술에 관심이 있어. 어떤 직업이 나에게 맞을까?
  B: 나는 앱 개발자가 너에게 좋은 직업이 될 수 있을 거라고 아주 확신해.
• A: 나는 쓰기에 관심이 있어. 어떤 직업이 나에게 맞을까?
  B: 나는 작가가 너에게 좋은 직업이 될 수 있을 거라고 아주 확신해.

Listen & Speak 2 A

1. **G:** _____

   M: _____

   _____

   G: _____

   M: _____

   G: _____

   _____

   M: _____

2. **B:** _____

   G: _____

   B: _____

   G: _____

   _____

   B: _____

   G: _____

Listen & Speak 2 B

- **A:** _____

  B: _____

- **A:** _____

  B: _____

Real Life Talk

Bora: _____

Jessie: _____

1. G: 만나 뵙게 되어 반갑습니다, Mr. Han. 당신이 어떤 일을 하시는지 말해 주실 수 있나요?
   M: 그래. 나는 중국에 있는 다양한 장소로 여행객들을 안내하고 그들이 방문해야 할 곳에 대한 정보를 제공해.
   G: 그 외에 또 어떤 일을 하시나요?
   M: 나는 그들에게 중국의 대중문화와 전통 음식에 대해 말해 줘.
   G: 중국에 대해 많이 아는 것이 매우 중요한 것 같네요. 당신의 직업에 만족하시나요?
   M: 응. 나는 내 직업을 정말 사랑해.

2. B: 네 롤 모델에 관한 기사 다 썼니?
   G: 응, 다 썼어. 나는 나의 롤 모델인 신 씨에 관해 썼어. 나는 그녀처럼 되고 싶어.
   B: 그녀는 무슨 일을 하니?
   G: 그녀는 사람들에게 스트레칭하는 방법을 가르쳐. 그녀는 또한 그들이 스트레스를 완화하여 평온해지도록 도와 줘.
   B: 좋구나. 그녀가 사람들의 몸과 마음을 둘 다 건강하게 유지하도록 돕는 것 같아.
   G: 맞아, 그리고 나는 그것이 훌륭하다고 생각해.

- A: 나는 라디오 방송 작가가 되고 싶어. 내가 그것이 되는 데 뭐가 도움이 될까?
  B: 너 자신만의 이야기를 쓰는 것이 도움이 될 것 같아.
- A: 나는 사회복지사가 되고 싶어. 내가 그것이 되는 데 뭐가 도움이 될까?
  B: 병원에서 아이들에게 책을 읽어 주는 것이 도움이 될 것 같아.

보라: 너는 이 목록에 있는 것들 중에서 무엇에 가장 관심이 있니?
Jessie: 나는 밖에서 일하는 것과 스포츠 하는 것에 가장 관심이 있어.

Bora: _____

Jessie: _____

Bora: _____

_____

Jessie: _____

_____

Bora: _____

Jessie: _____

Bora: _____

보라: 음, 내 생각에 너는 현실적인 타입에 속하는 것 같아.

Jessie: 무슨 의미야?

보라: 대부분의 사람들은 여섯 가지 성격 유형 중 한 가지에 속해. 현실적인 타입도 그중 하나야.

Jessie: 오, 재미있다. 현실적인 타입의 사람들에게 그들이 추천하는 직업은 뭐야?

보라: 농부, 경찰관, 축구 선수 같은 거야.

Jessie: 오, 나는 항상 축구 선수가 되고 싶어 해 왔어.

보라: 멋지다. 나는 네가 훌륭한 축구 선수가 될 수 있을 거라고 아주 확신해.

Communication Task Step 2

A: _____

B: _____

C: _____

_____

A: _____

D: _____

A: 나는 S가 3개, A가 2개, I가 1개, E가 1개 있어.

B: 너는 S 타입에 속해 있는 것 같아.

C: 응. S 타입에게 추천되는 직업은 선생님, 간호사, 사서, 상담사야.

A: 멋지다. 나는 항상 선생님이 되고 싶었어.

D: 그거 멋지네. 나는 네가 좋은 선생님이 될 수 있다고 아주 확신해.

Wrap Up 1

B: _____

G: _____

_____

B: _____

G: _____

B: _____

G: _____

B: _____

B: 안녕, 뭐 하고 있니, 수미야?

G: 나는 인터넷으로 좋은 요리법을 찾아보고 있어. 나는 오늘 우리 가족의 저녁 식사를 위해 그것이 필요해.

B: 그거 멋지네. 너는 요리를 자주 하니?

G: 응, 나는 매주 주말에 요리를 하려고 노력해. 나는 언젠가 요리사가 되고 싶어.

B: 네 꿈을 이루기 위해서 무엇을 하고 있니?

G: 나는 요리 수업을 듣고 있어. 새롭고 창의적인 요리를 생각해 내기 위해 노력해.

B: 나는 네가 좋은 요리사가 될 것이라고 아주 확신해.

※ 다음 우리말과 일치하도록 빈칸에 알맞은 것을 골라 쓰시오.

The World of Wonderful Jobs

Florist

1 Hi, I am Tom. A _____ is someone _____ _____ beautiful things _____ flowers.

    A. with   B. who   C. florist   D. creates

2 _____ _____ a florist, you _____ to know many _____ about flowers.

    A. need   B. to   C. things   D. become

3 I _____ a high school _____ florists and _____.

    A. for   B. attended   C. gardeners

4 It was at this school that I learned _____ _____ grow and _____ _____ different types of flowers.

    A. how   B. for   C. to   D. care

5 These _____, florists can do a _____ _____ _____ things.

    A. lot   B. days   C. different   D. of

6 I design _____ _____ sometimes and I _____ shops _____ flowers.

    A. sets   B. decorate   C. movie   D. with

7 I am happy when I create _____ _____ with _____ flowers and _____.

    A. fresh   B. something   C. greenery   D. colorful

8 _____ you like plants and the arts, I _____ _____ you _____ a florist.

    A. recommend   B. highly   C. become   D. if

Sport Data Analyst

9 I am Emma. I am a _____ _____ _____.

    A. data   B. sport   C. analyst

10 It _____ _____ a difficult job, _____ _____?

    A. like   B. doesn't   C. sounds   D. it

11 _____ _____, it is a lot of fun. I _____ _____ a baseball team.

    A. fact   B. for   C. in   D. work

12 My job is to _____ _____ games and _____ a computer program to _____ data.

    A. recorded   B. collect   C. run   D. watch

플로리스트

1 안녕하세요. 저는 Tom입니다. 플로리스트란 꽃으로 아름다운 것들을 창조하는 사람입니다.

2 플로리스트가 되기 위해서 여러분은 꽃에 관해 많은 것을 알 필요가 있습니다.

3 나는 플로리스트와 정원사를 양성하는 고등학교에 다녔습니다.

4 제가 다양한 종류의 꽃을 기르고 다루는 방법을 배운 곳이 바로 이 학교에서였습니다.

5 오늘날, 플로리스트는 많은 다양한 일을 할 수 있습니다.

6 나는 때때로 영화 세트장을 디자인하고 꽃으로 상점을 꾸밉니다.

7 나는 싱싱한 꽃과 화초로 다채로운 무언가를 창조해 낼 때 행복합니다.

8 만약 당신이 식물과 예술을 좋아한다면, 나는 당신에게 플로리스트가 될 것을 강력히 추천합니다.

스포츠 데이터 분석가

9 나는 Emma입니다. 나는 스포츠 데이터 분석가입니다.

10 어려운 직업처럼 들리죠, 그렇지 않나요?

11 사실, 그것은 매우 재미있습니다. 나는 야구팀을 위해서 일합니다.

12 나의 일은 녹화된 경기를 보고 자료를 수집하기 위해 컴퓨터 프로그램을 실행하는 것입니다.

13 Then, I _____ the data to _____ my team's _____ and _____ .

   A. weaknesses   B. strengths   C. analyze   D. show

14 _____ the team _____ their strengths and weaknesses, they can _____ _____ next time.

   A. better   B. understands C. do   D. if

15 _____ I was young, I _____ _____ a _____ fan of baseball.

   A. big   B. since   C. been   D. have

16 Now, in my _____ , I _____ baseball games _____ the _____ .

   A. time   B. work   C. all   D. watch

17 This is a _____ job for me _____ _____ baseball games is my _____ !

   A. watching   B. perfect   C. hobby   D. because

Director of a Musical Theater

18 Hi, I am Chris. _____ a _____ of a musical _____ , I do a _____ of things.

   A. theater   B. as   C. director   D. lot

19 I _____ the actors and I _____ _____ good, strong _____ .

   A. for   B. audition   C. look

20 After _____ the _____ , I teach them the songs for _____ .

   A. scene   B. selecting   C. each   D. cast

21 Then, I _____ the _____ and orchestra _____ for _____ .

   A. together   B. put   C. practice   D. cast

22 _____ the _____ , I am in the orchestra _____ and _____ .

   A. conduct   B. during   C. performance D. area

23 It's my _____ to have _____ song _____ the same _____ every time.

   A. played   B. responsibility C. way   D. each

13 그리고 나서, 나는 내 팀의 강점과 약점을 보여 주기 위해서 그 자료들을 분석합니다.

14 만약 팀이 자신들의 강점과 약점을 이해하면, 그들은 다음번에 더 잘할 수 있습니다.

15 어렸을 때부터, 나는 야구의 열혈 팬이었습니다.

16 지금, 나는 일하는 중에 내내 야구를 봅니다.

17 야구 경기를 보는 것은 나의 취미이기 때문에 이것은 나에게 완벽한 직업입니다!

뮤지컬 극장 감독

18 안녕하세요. 나는 Chris입니다. 뮤지컬 극장 감독으로서 나는 많은 것들을 합니다.

19 나는 배우들을 대상으로 오디션을 실시하고, 훌륭하고 강한 목소리를 찾아냅니다.

20 배역에 맞는 배우를 고른 뒤에, 나는 그들에게 각 장면을 위한 노래를 가르칩니다.

21 그리고 나서, 나는 배우와 오케스트라를 함께 연습시킵니다.

22 공연 동안에, 나는 오케스트라 석에 있고 지휘를 합니다.

23 각각의 노래가 매번 동일하게 연주되도록 만드는 것은 나의 책임입니다.

24 I _____ the musicians and the singers _____ _____ the show _____.

A. keep　　　　B. direct　　　　C. together　　　　D. to

25 _____ and _____ is not just about _____ my arms _____!

A. waving　　　　B. directing　　　　C. around　　　　D. conducting

Ocean Scientist

26 My name is Yeji. I am an ocean _____. Ocean science is a _____ _____.

A. big　　　　B. scientist　　　　C. field

27 It _____ _____ of the oceans and the _____ _____ in them.

A. creatures　　　　B. studies　　　　C. includes　　　　D. living

28 _____ other things, I _____ _____ many kinds of fish _____ in the seas near Korea.

A. have　　　　B. living　　　　C. among　　　　D. studied

29 It is the _____ _____ in a fish _____ _____ me.

A. interests　　　　B. growth　　　　C. ring　　　　D. that

30 _____ _____ at it, I can find _____ when and where the fish was _____.

A. born　　　　B. looking　　　　C. by　　　　D. out

31 All the information I get from fish is _____ _____ understand sea _____ and _____ the oceans better.

A. to　　　　B. manage　　　　C. used　　　　D. resources

32 My job is important _____ it makes _____ _____ _____ of nature possible.

A. best　　　　B. because　　　　C. use　　　　D. the

24 나는 공연을 제대로 진행하기 위해 연주자들과 가수들을 감독합니다.

25 지휘하고 감독하는 것은 단지 내 팔을 흔드는 것만이 아닙니다!

해양 과학자

26 나는 예지입니다. 나는 해양 과학자입니다. 해양 과학은 거대한 분야입니다.

27 그것은 바다와 그 안에 살고 있는 생물에 관한 연구를 포함합니다.

28 여러 가지 중에서 나는 한국 주변의 바다에 살고 있는 많은 종류의 물고기를 연구해 왔습니다.

29 나의 흥미를 끄는 것은 바로 물고기 안에 있는 나이테입니다.

30 나이테를 살펴봄으로써, 나는 언제 어디서 그 물고기가 태어났는지 알아낼 수 있습니다.

31 내가 물고기에서 얻은 모든 정보는 바다의 자원을 이해하고 바다를 더 잘 관리하기 위해 사용됩니다.

32 내 직업은 자연을 가장 잘 활용할 수 있게 한다는 점에서 중요합니다.

※ 다음 우리말과 일치하도록 빈칸에 알맞은 말을 쓰시오.

The World of Wonderful Jobs

Florist

1 Hi, I am Tom. A _____ is someone _____ _____ beautiful things _____ flowers.

2 _____ _____ a florist, you _____ _____ _____ _____ about flowers.

3 I _____ a high school _____ florists and _____.

4 It was _____ _____ _____ that I learned _____ _____ _____ and _____ _____ different types of flowers.

5 _____ _____, florists can do _____ _____ things.

6 I design _____ _____ sometimes and I _____ shops _____ _____.

7 I am happy when I create _____ _____ _____ fresh flowers and _____.

8 If you like _____ and the arts, I _____ _____ you become a florist.

Sport Data Analyst

9 I am Emma. I am a _____ _____ _____.

10 It _____ _____ a difficult job, _____ _____?

11 _____ _____, it is _____. I work for a baseball team.

12 My job is _____ _____ and _____ a computer program _____ _____ data.

플로리스트

1 안녕하세요. 저는 Tom입니다. 플로리스트란 꽃으로 아름다운 것들을 창조하는 사람입니다.

2 플로리스트가 되기 위해서 여러분은 꽃에 관해 많은 것을 알 필요가 있습니다.

3 나는 플로리스트와 정원사를 양성하는 고등학교에 다녔습니다.

4 제가 다양한 종류의 꽃을 기르고 다루는 방법을 배운 곳이 바로 이 학교에서였습니다.

5 오늘날, 플로리스트는 많은 다양한 일을 할 수 있습니다.

6 나는 때때로 영화 세트장을 디자인하고 꽃으로 상점을 꾸밉니다.

7 나는 싱싱한 꽃과 화초로 다채로운 무언가를 창조해 낼 때 행복합니다.

8 만약 당신이 식물과 예술을 좋아한다면, 나는 당신에게 플로리스트가 될 것을 강력히 추천합니다.

스포츠 데이터 분석가

9 나는 Emma입니다. 나는 스포츠 데이터 분석가입니다.

10 어려운 직업처럼 들리죠, 그렇지 않나요?

11 사실, 그것은 매우 재미있습니다. 나는 야구팀을 위해서 일합니다.

12 나의 일은 녹화된 경기를 보고 자료를 수집하기 위해 컴퓨터 프로그램을 실행하는 것입니다.

13 Then, I _____ the data _____ _____ my team's strengths and _____.

14 If the team _____ their _____ and weaknesses, they can _____ _____ next time.

15 _____ I was young, I _____ _____ a big fan of baseball.

16 Now, in my work, I watch _____ _____ _____ _____ _____.

17 This is a _____ _____ for me _____ _____ _____ _____ is my _____!

Director of a Musical Theater

18 Hi, I am Chris. _____ a director of _____ _____ _____, I do _____ _____ _____ things.

19 I _____ the actors and I _____ _____ good, strong _____.

20 After _____ _____ _____, I teach them the songs _____ _____ _____.

21 Then, I _____ the _____ and orchestra _____ for practice.

22 _____ the _____, I am in the orchestra area and _____.

23 It's _____ _____ to have _____ song _____ the _____ _____ every time.

13 그러고 나서, 나는 내 팀의 강점과 약점을 보여 주기 위해서 그 자료들을 분석합니다.

14 만약 팀이 자신들의 강점과 약점을 이해하면, 그들은 다음번에 더 잘할 수 있습니다.

15 어렸을 때부터, 나는 야구의 열혈 팬이었습니다.

16 지금, 나는 일하는 중에 내내 야구를 봅니다.

17 야구 경기를 보는 것은 나의 취미이기 때문에 이것은 나에게 완벽한 직업입니다!

뮤지컬 극장 감독

18 안녕하세요. 나는 Chris입니다. 뮤지컬 극장 감독으로서 나는 많은 것들을 합니다.

19 나는 배우들을 대상으로 오디션을 실시하고, 훌륭하고 강한 목소리를 찾아냅니다.

20 배역에 맞는 배우를 고른 뒤에, 나는 그들에게 각 장면을 위한 노래를 가르칩니다.

21 그러고 나서, 나는 배우와 오케스트라를 함께 연습시킵니다.

22 공연 동안에, 나는 오케스트라 석에 있고 지휘를 합니다.

23 각각의 노래가 매번 동일하게 연주되도록 만드는 것은 나의 책임입니다.

62 Lesson 3. Future Dreams, Future Jobs

24 I _____ the musicians and the singers _____ _____ the show _____.

25 _____ and _____ is not just about _____ my arms around!

Ocean Scientist

26 My name is Yeji. I am an _____ _____. Ocean science is _____ _____ _____.

27 It _____ studies of the _____ and the _____ _____ _____ _____.

28 _____ other things, I _____ _____ many kinds of fish _____ in the seas near Korea.

29 It is _____ _____ _____ in a fish _____ _____ me.

30 _____ _____ at it, I can _____ _____ when and where the fish _____ _____.

31 All the information _____ _____ _____ fish _____ _____ _____ _____ sea resources and _____ the _____ _____.

32 My job is important _____ it _____ _____ _____ _____ _____ nature possible.

24 나는 공연을 제대로 진행하기 위해 연주자들과 가수들을 감독합니다.

25 지휘하고 감독하는 것은 단지 내 팔을 흔드는 것만이 아닙니다!

해양 과학자

26 나는 예지입니다. 나는 해양 과학자입니다. 해양 과학은 거대한 분야입니다.

27 그것은 바다와 그 안에 살고 있는 생물에 관한 연구를 포함합니다.

28 여러 가지 중에서 나는 한국 주변의 바다에 살고 있는 많은 종류의 물고기를 연구해 왔습니다.

29 나의 흥미를 끄는 것은 바로 물고기 안에 있는 나이테입니다.

30 나이테를 살펴봄으로써, 나는 언제 어디서 그 물고기가 태어났는지 알아낼 수 있습니다.

31 내가 물고기에서 얻은 모든 정보는 바다의 자원을 이해하고 바다를 더 잘 관리하기 위해 사용됩니다.

32 내 직업은 자연을 가장 잘 활용할 수 있게 한다는 점에서 중요합니다.

※ 다음 문장을 우리말로 쓰시오.

The World of Wonderful Jobs

Florist

1 Hi, I am Tom. A florist is someone who creates beautiful things with flowers.

➡ _____

2 To become a florist, you need to know many things about flowers.

➡ _____

3 I attended a high school for florists and gardeners.

➡ _____

4 It was at this school that I learned how to grow and care for different types of flowers.

➡ _____

5 These days, florists can do a lot of different things.

➡ _____

6 I design movie sets sometimes and I decorate shops with flowers.

➡ _____

7 I am happy when I create something colorful with fresh flowers and greenery.

➡ _____

8 If you like plants and the arts, I highly recommend you become a florist.

➡ _____

Sport Data Analyst

9 I am Emma. I am a sport data analyst.

➡ _____

10 It sounds like a difficult job, doesn't it?

➡ _____

11 In fact, it is a lot of fun. I work for a baseball team.

➡ _____

12 My job is to watch recorded games and run a computer program to collect data.

➡ _____

13 Then, I analyze the data to show my team's strengths and weaknesses.

➡ _____

14 If the team understands their strengths and weaknesses, they can do better next time.

➡ _____

15 Since I was young, I have been a big fan of baseball.

➡ _____

16 Now, in my work, I watch baseball games all the time.

➡ _____

17 This is a perfect job for me because watching baseball games is my hobby!

➡ _____

Director of a Musical Theater

18 Hi, I am Chris. As a director of a musical theater, I do a lot of things.

➡ _____

19 I audition the actors and I look for good, strong voices.

➡ _____

20 After selecting the cast, I teach them the songs for each scene.

➡ _____

21 Then, I put the cast and orchestra together for practice.

➡ _____

22 During the performance, I am in the orchestra area and conduct.

➡ _____

23 It's my responsibility to have each song played the same way every time.

➡ _____

24 I direct the musicians and the singers to keep the show together.

➡ _____

25 Conducting and directing is not just about waving my arms around!

➡ _____

Ocean Scientist

26 My name is Yeji. I am an ocean scientist. Ocean science is a big field.

➡ _____

27 It includes studies of the oceans and the creatures living in them.

➡ _____

28 Among other things, I have studied many kinds of fish living in the seas near Korea.

➡ _____

29 It is the growth ring in a fish that interests me.

➡ _____

30 By looking at it, I can find out when and where the fish was born.

➡ _____

31 All the information I get from fish is used to understand sea resources and manage the oceans better.

➡ _____

32 My job is important because it makes the best use of nature possible.

➡ _____

※ 다음 괄호 안의 단어들을 우리말에 맞도록 바르게 배열하시오.

The World of Wonderful Jobs

Florist

1 (hi, / am / I / Tom. // florist / a / someone / is / creates / who / things / beautiful / flowers. / with)

➡ _____

_____

2 (become / to / florist, / a / need / you / know / to / things / many / flowers. / about)

➡ _____

3 (attended / I / a / school / high / florists / for / gardeners. / and)

➡ _____

4 (was / it / this / at / school / that / learned / I / to / how / grow / and / for / care / types / different / flowers. / of)

➡ _____

5 (days, / these / can / florists / do / lot / a / of / things. / different)

➡ _____

6 (design / I / sets / movie / sometimes / and / decorate / I / with / shops / flowers.)

➡ _____

7 (am / I / when / happy / create / I / something / with / colorful / flowers / fresh / greenery. / and)

➡ _____

8 (you / if / like / and / plants / arts, / the / highly / I / you / recommend / become / florist. / a)

➡ _____

Sport Data Analyst

9 (am / I / Emma. // am / I / sport / a / analyst. / data)

➡ _____

10 (sounds / it / a / like / job, / difficult / it? / doesn't)

➡ _____

11 (fact, / in / is / it / lot / a / fun. / of // I / for / work / baseball / team. / a)

➡ _____

12 (job / my / to / is / recorded / watch / games / and / a / run / computer / program / collect / to / data.)

➡ _____

_____

플로리스트

1 안녕하세요. 저는 Tom입니다. 플로리스트란 꽃으로 아름다운 것들을 창조하는 사람입니다.

2 플로리스트가 되기 위해서 여러분은 꽃에 관해 많은 것을 알 필요가 있습니다.

3 나는 플로리스트와 정원사를 양성하는 고등학교에 다녔습니다.

4 제가 다양한 종류의 꽃을 기르고 다루는 방법을 배운 곳이 바로 이 학교에서였습니다.

5 오늘날, 플로리스트는 많은 다양한 일을 할 수 있습니다.

6 나는 때때로 영화 세트장을 디자인하고 꽃으로 상점을 꾸밉니다.

7 나는 싱싱한 꽃과 화초로 다채로운 무언가를 창조해 낼 때 행복합니다.

8 만약 당신이 식물과 예술을 좋아한다면, 나는 당신에게 플로리스트가 될 것을 강력히 추천합니다.

스포츠 데이터 분석가

9 나는 Emma입니다. 나는 스포츠 데이터 분석가입니다.

10 어려운 직업처럼 들리죠, 그렇지 않나요?

11 사실, 그것은 매우 재미있습니다. 나는 야구팀을 위해서 일합니다.

12 나의 일은 녹화된 경기를 보고 자료를 수집하기 위해 컴퓨터 프로그램을 실행하는 것입니다.

13 (then, / analyze / I / data / the / show / to / team's / my / strengths / weaknesses. / and)

➡ _____

14 (the / if / team / understands / strengths / their / weaknesses, / and / can / they / better / do / time. / next)

➡ _____
_____

15 (I / since / young, / was / have / I / been / big / a / fan / baseball. / of)

➡ _____

16 (now, / my / in / work, / watch / I / games / baseball / the / all / time.)

➡ _____

17 (is / this / a / perfect / for / job / me / watching / because / games / baseball / my / is / hobby!)

➡ _____
_____

Director of a Musical Theater

18 (hi, / am / I / Chris. // a / as / director / a / of / theater, / musical / do / I / lot / a / things. / of)

➡ _____

19 (audition / I / actors / the / and / look / I / good, / for / voices. / strong)

➡ _____

20 (selecting / after / cast, / the / teach / I / them / songs / the / each / for / scene.)

➡ _____

21 (then, / put / I / cast / the / and / together / orchestra / practice. / for)

➡ _____

22 (the / during / performace, / am / I / in / orchestra / the / and / area / conduct.)

➡ _____

---

13 그러고 나서, 나는 내 팀의 강점과 약점을 보여 주기 위해서 그 자료들을 분석합니다.

14 만약 팀이 자신들의 강점과 약점을 이해하면, 그들은 다음번에 더 잘할 수 있습니다.

15 어렸을 때부터, 나는 야구의 열혈 팬이었습니다.

16 지금, 나는 일하는 중에 내내 야구를 봅니다.

17 야구 경기를 보는 것은 나의 취미이기 때문에 이것은 나에게 완벽한 직업입니다!

뮤지컬 극장 감독

18 안녕하세요. 나는 Chris입니다. 뮤지컬 극장 감독으로서 나는 많은 것들을 합니다.

19 나는 배우들을 대상으로 오디션을 실시하고, 훌륭하고 강한 목소리를 찾아냅니다.

20 배역에 맞는 배우를 고른 뒤에, 나는 그들에게 각 장면을 위한 노래를 가르칩니다.

21 그러고 나서, 나는 배우와 오케스트라를 함께 연습시킵니다.

22 공연 동안에, 나는 오케스트라 석에 있고 지휘를 합니다.

23 (my / it's / responsibility / have / to / song / each / played / same / the / every / way / time.)

➡ _____

_____

24 (direct / I / musicians / the / and / singers / the / keep / to / show / the / together.)

➡ _____

25 (directing / and / conducting / is / just / not / waving / about / arms / my / around!)

➡ _____

Ocean Scientist

26 (name / my / Yeji. / is // am / I / ocean / an / scientist. // science / ocean / a / is / field. / big)

➡ _____

27 (includes / it / of / studies / the / oceans / the / and / living / creatures / them. / in)

➡ _____

28 (other / among / things, / have / I / kinds / many / studied / of / living / fish / the / in / seas / Korea. / near)

➡ _____

_____

29 (is / it / growth / the / ring / a / in / fish / interests / that / me.)

➡ _____

30 (looking / by / it, / at / can / I / out / find / where / and / when / fish / the / born. / was)

➡ _____

31 (the / all / information / get / I / fish / from / used / is / to / sea / understand / manage / and / resources / oceans / the / better.)

➡ _____

_____

32 (job / my / is / because / important / makes / it / best / the / use / nature / of / possible.)

➡ _____

23 각각의 노래가 매번 동일하게 연주되도록 만드는 것은 나의 책임입니다.

24 나는 공연을 제대로 진행하기 위해 연주자들과 가수들을 감독합니다.

25 지휘하고 감독하는 것은 단지 내 팔을 흔드는 것만이 아닙니다!

해양 과학자

26 나는 예지입니다. 나는 해양 과학자입니다. 해양 과학은 거대한 분야입니다.

27 그것은 바다와 그 안에 살고 있는 생물에 관한 연구를 포함합니다.

28 여러 가지 중에서 나는 한국 주변의 바다에 살고 있는 많은 종류의 물고기를 연구해 왔습니다.

29 나의 흥미를 끄는 것은 바로 물고기 안에 있는 나이테입니다.

30 나이테를 살펴봄으로써, 나는 언제 어디서 그 물고기가 태어났는지 알아낼 수 있습니다.

31 내가 물고기에서 얻은 모든 정보는 바다의 자원을 이해하고 바다를 더 잘 관리하기 위해 사용됩니다.

32 내 직업은 자연을 가장 잘 활용할 수 있게 한다는 점에서 중요합니다.

※ 다음 우리말을 영어로 쓰시오.

The World of Wonderful Jobs

Florist

1 안녕하세요. 저는 Tom입니다. 플로리스트란 꽃으로 아름다운 것들을 창조하는 사람입니다.

➡ _____

2 플로리스트가 되기 위해서 여러분은 꽃에 관해 많은 것을 알 필요가 있습니다.

➡ _____

3 나는 플로리스트와 정원사를 양성하는 고등학교에 다녔습니다.

➡ _____

4 제가 다양한 종류의 꽃을 기르고 다루는 방법을 배운 곳이 바로 이 학교에서였습니다.

➡ _____

5 오늘날, 플로리스트는 많은 다양한 일을 할 수 있습니다.

➡ _____

6 나는 때때로 영화 세트장을 디자인하고 꽃으로 상점을 꾸밉니다.

➡ _____

7 나는 싱싱한 꽃과 화초로 다채로운 무언가를 창조해 낼 때 행복합니다.

➡ _____

8 만약 당신이 식물과 예술을 좋아한다면, 나는 당신에게 플로리스트가 될 것을 강력히 추천합니다.

➡ _____

Sport Data Analyst

9 나는 Emma입니다. 나는 스포츠 데이터 분석가입니다.

➡ _____

10 어려운 직업처럼 들리죠, 그렇지 않나요?

➡ _____

11 사실, 그것은 매우 재미있습니다. 나는 야구팀을 위해서 일합니다.

➡ _____

12 나의 일은 녹화된 경기를 보고 자료를 수집하기 위해 컴퓨터 프로그램을 실행하는 것입니다.

➡ _____

13 그리고 나서, 나는 내 팀의 강점과 약점을 보여 주기 위해서 그 자료들을 분석합니다.

➡ _____

14 만약 팀이 자신들의 강점과 약점을 이해하면, 그들은 다음번에 더 잘할 수 있습니다.

➡ _____

15 어렸을 때부터, 나는 야구의 열혈 팬이었습니다.

➡ _____

16 지금, 나는 일하는 중에 내내 야구를 봅니다.
➡ _____

17 야구 경기를 보는 것은 나의 취미이기 때문에 이것은 나에게 완벽한 직업입니다!
➡ _____

Director of a Musical Theater

18 안녕하세요. 나는 Chris입니다. 뮤지컬 극장 감독으로서 나는 많은 것들을 합니다.
➡ _____

19 나는 배우들을 대상으로 오디션을 실시하고, 훌륭하고 강한 목소리를 찾아냅니다.
➡ _____

20 배역에 맞는 배우를 고른 뒤에, 나는 그들에게 각 장면을 위한 노래를 가르칩니다.
➡ _____

21 그러고 나서, 나는 배우와 오케스트라를 함께 연습시킵니다.
➡ _____

22 공연 동안에, 나는 오케스트라 석에 있고 지휘를 합니다.
➡ _____

23 각각의 노래가 매번 동일하게 연주되도록 만드는 것은 나의 책임입니다.
➡ _____

24 나는 공연을 제대로 진행하기 위해 연주자들과 가수들을 감독합니다.
➡ _____

25 지휘하고 감독하는 것은 단지 내 팔을 흔드는 것만이 아닙니다!
➡ _____

Ocean Scientist

26 나는 예지입니다. 나는 해양 과학자입니다. 해양 과학은 거대한 분야입니다.
➡ _____

27 그것은 바다와 그 안에 살고 있는 생물에 관한 연구를 포함합니다.
➡ _____

28 여러 가지 중에서 나는 한국 주변의 바다에 살고 있는 많은 종류의 물고기를 연구해 왔습니다.
➡ _____

29 나의 흥미를 끄는 것은 바로 물고기 안에 있는 나이테입니다.
➡ _____

30 나이테를 살펴봄으로써, 나는 언제 어디서 그 물고기가 태어났는지 알아낼 수 있습니다.
➡ _____

31 내가 물고기에서 얻은 모든 정보는 바다의 자원을 이해하고 바다를 더 잘 관리하기 위해 사용됩니다.
➡ _____

32 내 직업은 자연을 가장 잘 활용할 수 있게 한다는 점에서 중요합니다.
➡ _____

※ 다음 우리말과 일치하도록 빈칸에 알맞은 말을 쓰시오.

Enjoy Writing C

1. My _____ _____.

2. I like food from _____ _____ _____ and I _____ _____ _____ _____.

3. I can also _____ _____ _____ _____ and _____.

4. _____ _____ _____, it is a chef _____ I want to be _____ I _____.

5. _____ _____ my dream, I will read magazines _____ _____.

6. Also, I will go to France _____ _____ _____ _____ _____.

7. _____ _____ _____ is my dad.

8. He _____ _____ of new _____ and then cooks these new dishes for us.

9. I want to _____ _____ _____ _____ by people _____ _____ _____ _____.

1. 내 꿈의 직업
2. 나는 전 세계 음식을 좋아하고 요리를 잘한다.
3. 나는 또한 음식을 맛있고 아름다워 보이게 만들 수 있다.
4. 이러한 이유로 내가 자라서 되고 싶은 것은 요리사이다.
5. 내 꿈을 이루기 위해, 나는 요리에 관한 잡지를 읽을 것이다.
6. 또한 나는 프랑스에 가서 다양한 요리 기술을 익힐 것이다.
7. 내 롤 모델은 나의 아빠이다.
8. 그는 항상 새로운 요리법을 생각해 내시고 우리를 위해 이러한 요리를 만들어 주신다.
9. 나는 내 이름이 내 음식을 좋아하는 사람들에게 기억되도록 하고 싶다.

Project

1. HELP _____!!

2. Do you _____ _____?

3. If your answer is yes, _____ is you that we _____ _____ _____.

4. Please join us _____ _____ and _____ _____.

5. _____ more information, _____ _____ _____ at www.robots.com.

1. 사람 구합니다!
2. 로봇을 좋아하시나요?
3. 당신의 답이 예스라면, 당신이 바로 우리가 찾는 사람입니다.
4. 우리와 함께 로봇을 훈련시키고, 고쳐 보세요.
5. 더 자세한 사항은 우리 웹사이트 www.robots.com을 방문해 주세요.

Project Step 3

1. _____ you _____ _____ _____ and _____ robots?

2. If _____, we're sure that you'll be _____ _____ _____.

3. _____ _____ _____, _____ our websites.

1. 당신은 로봇을 훈련시키고 수리하는 것을 잘하나요?
2. 만약 그렇다면, 우리는 당신이 좋은 로봇 전문가가 될 것이라고 확신합니다.
3. 더 많은 정보를 위해서, 우리 웹사이트를 방문하세요.

※ 다음 우리말을 영어로 쓰시오.

Enjoy Writing C

1. 내 꿈의 직업
➡ _____

2. 나는 전 세계 음식을 좋아하고 요리를 잘한다.
➡ _____

3. 나는 또한 음식을 맛있고 아름다워 보이게 만들 수 있다.
➡ _____

4. 이러한 이유로 내가 자라서 되고 싶은 것은 요리사이다.
➡ _____

5. 내 꿈을 이루기 위해, 나는 요리에 관한 잡지를 읽을 것이다.
➡ _____

6. 또한 나는 프랑스에 가서 다양한 요리 기술을 익힐 것이다.
➡ _____

7. 내 롤 모델은 나의 아빠이다.
➡ _____

8. 그는 항상 새로운 요리법을 생각해 내시고 우리를 위해 이러한 요리를 만들어 주신다.
➡ _____

9. 나는 내 이름이 내 음식을 좋아하는 사람들에게 기억되도록 하고 싶다.
➡ _____

Project

1. 사람 구합니다!
➡ _____

2. 로봇을 좋아하시나요?
➡ _____

3. 당신의 답이 예스라면, 당신이 바로 우리가 찾는 사람입니다.
➡ _____

4. 우리와 함께 로봇을 훈련시키고, 고쳐보세요.
➡ _____

5. 더 자세한 사항은 우리 웹사이트 www.robots.com을 방문해 주세요.
➡ _____

Project Step 3

1. 당신은 로봇을 훈련시키고 수리하는 것을 잘하나요?
➡ _____

2. 만약 그렇다면, 우리는 당신이 좋은 로봇 전문가가 될 것이라고 확신합니다.
➡ _____

3. 더 많은 정보를 위해서, 우리 웹사이트를 방문하세요.
➡ _____

※ 다음 영어를 우리말로 쓰시오.

01 score

02 alert

03 birth

04 comment

05 contact

06 advantage

07 detox

08 uncomfortable

09 addiction

10 disadvantage

11 enjoyable

12 form

13 necessary

14 noisy

15 half

16 dangerous

17 reduce

18 citizen

19 post

20 focus

21 instead

22 creative

23 mistake

24 intend

25 guess

26 limit

27 posting

28 refreshed

29 respect

30 copyright

31 outdoor

32 pain

33 suggest

34 cause

35 in fact

36 for free

37 on the other hand

38 put aside

39 right away

40 set up

41 for a while

42 stay away from

43 figure out

※ 다음 우리말을 영어로 쓰시오.

01 중독

02 출생, 탄생

03 불편한

04 야기하다, 원인이 되다

05 제한하다

06 게시하다

07 차단하다, 막다

08 줄이다

09 저작권

10 알람소리, 경보

11 상쾌한

12 장점, 유리함

14 존중하다, 존경하다

15 시끄러운

16 단점, 약점, 불리한 점

17 즐거운

18 실수

19 집중하다

20 발언, 논평, 비평

21 만들다, 형성시키다

22 ~할 작정이다

23 제안하다

24 시민

25 연락하다

26 필요한

27 반, 절반

28 옥외의, 야외의

29 고통

30 창의적인

31 위험한

32 해독

33 비밀번호

34 기기, 장치

35 잠시 동안

36 치우다

37 ~ 와 같은

38 ~에서 떨어져 있다, ~을 멀리하다

39 사실

40 치우다

41 무료로

42 알아내다, 계산하다

43 반면에

※ 다음 영영풀이에 알맞은 단어를 <보기>에서 골라 쓴 후, 우리말 뜻을 쓰시오.

1 _____ : an act of being born: _____

2 _____ : one of two equal parts of something: _____

3 _____ : a right to sell a book, music, film, etc.: _____

4 _____ : a thing that is regarded as representing for another: _____

5 _____ : something that may help one to gain favorable result: _____

6 _____ : something that you say about someone or something: _____

7 _____ : a warning to people to be prepared to deal with something dangerous:
_____

8 _____ : a mechanical object that is made for a particular purpose: _____

9 _____ : to plan to do something, to have an action planned in your mind: _____

10 _____ : an inability to stop doing or using something, especially something
harmful: _____

11 _____ : a spoken or written piece of information that you send to someone: _____

12 _____ : to communicate with someone by calling or sending them a letter, email,
etc.: _____

13 _____ : an action, decision, or judgment that produces an unwanted or unintentional
result: _____

14 _____ : storing pictures, sound, etc. in a number of small signals or showing them
in numbers: _____

15 _____ : a period when you stop taking unhealthy or harmful foods, drinks, or
drugs into your body for a period: _____

16 _____ : talk between two or more people in which thoughts, feelings, and ideas
are expressed, or questions are asked and answered: _____

※ 다음 우리말과 일치하도록 빈칸에 알맞은 말을 쓰시오.

Listen & Speak 1 A

1. G: You _____ _____, Peter.

   B: I played computer games _____ _____, _____ last night I _____ _____ _____ _____ four hours.

   G: _____ computer games too much _____ _____ _____ _____ _____ _____.

   B: I know, Jenny, but I _____ _____ it. I think I'm _____ to it.

   G: If I _____ you, I _____ _____ a daily plan _____ _____ game time.

   B: That's a good idea. Thanks.

2. W: Tony, you _____ too _____ _____ _____ your smartphone.

   B: My friends _____ _____ on SNS _____ every day, so I _____ _____ _____, Mom.

   W: _____ _____ _____ _____, I would _____ _____ _____ to your friends.

   B: _____ activities?

   W: Yes. You can do _____ _____ _____ great activities _____ _____ soccer or skating.

   B: All _____. I will _____ them today.

Listen & Speak 2 A

1. G: James, what _____ you _____?

   B: I'm _____ some of the pictures _____ I _____ _____ Sarah today.

   G: Did you ask Sarah _____ you _____ _____ them online?

   B: No, but I think it's okay _____ she _____ _____ in the pictures.

   G: You're _____ _____ _____ _____ someone's pictures _____ _____.

   B: Oh, maybe you're right. I'll _____ Sarah and ask her _____ _____.

1. G: 너 피곤해 보인다, Peter.
   B: 나 늦게까지 게임을 해서, 어젯밤에 4시간도 못 잤어.
   G: 컴퓨터 게임을 너무 많이 하는 건 네 건강에 좋지 않아.
   B: 나도 알아, Jenny, 그런데 멈출 수 가 없어. 난 그것에 중독된 것 같아.
   G: 만약 내가 너라면, 게임 시간을 제 한하기 위해 일일 계획을 짤 거야.
   B: 그거 좋은 생각이네. 고마워.

2. W: Tony, 너 스마트 폰에 너무 많은 시간을 보내는구나.
   B: 제 친구들은 거의 매일 SNS에서 만 나기 때문에, 저도 어쩔 수 없어요, 엄마.
   W: 만약 내가 너라면, 친구들에게 야 외 활동을 하자고 제안할 거야.
   B: 야외 활동이요?
   W: 응. 너는 축구나 스케이트 타기 등 과 같은 많은 멋진 활동을 할 수 있 어.
   B: 알겠어요. 오늘 제안해 볼게요.

1. G: James, 뭐 하고 있니?
   B: 나 오늘 Sarah와 함께 찍은 사진들 중 몇 장을 올리고 있어.
   G: 네가 그걸 온라인에 올려도 될지 Sarah에게 물어봤니?
   B: 아니, 그렇지만 그녀가 사진들 속에 서 멋져 보이기 때문에 괜찮을 것 같 아.
   G: 너는 다른 사람들의 사진을 물어보 지 않고 올리면 안 돼.
   B: 오, 네 말이 맞을지 몰라. 내가 지금 당장 Sarah에게 전화해서 물어볼게.

2. **G:** David, _____ _____ this new movie on the computer.

   B: _____ the computer?

   G: Yes. I have a website we can _____ it from _____ _____.

   B: You're not _____ _____ _____ movies _____ that website, Catherine. It's _____ the _____.

   G: Really? I didn't know that.

   B: _____ _____ _____ _____ to the movie theater, _____?

   G: Okay. _____ go.

Real Life Talk

Bora: Seho, look! Somebody _____ _____ _____ _____ your SNS. I don't think you _____ _____.

Seho: Really? Who did this?

Bora: I think someone _____ _____ your _____.

Seho: _____ _____ I _____?

Bora: If I _____ you, I would _____ my _____.

Seho: I think I _____.

Bora: Is your password _____ _____ _____ _____?

Seho: I _____ my _____ _____.

Bora: That is not good. _____ _____, it is a big mistake. You'_____ _____ _____ _____ _____ your _____ _____ when you _____ _____ _____.

Seho: Okay, I see. I will _____ it to a _____ _____.

Wrap Up

B: What are you _____, Sohee?

G: I'm _____ a _____ about the restaurant I visited today.

B: Those are great pictures. Did you _____ all of them?

G: No. I _____ the pictures _____ someone's _____.

B: Then you'_____ _____ _____ _____ _____ _____ _____ them on your blog.

G: _____ _____?

B: _____ only the blog _____ has the _____ _____ them.

G: Oh, I see.

2. G: David, 컴퓨터로 이 신작 영화 보자.
B: 컴퓨터로?
G: 응. 우리가 그것을 무료로 내려 받을 수 있는 웹 사이트가 있어.
B: 너는 그런 웹 사이트에서 영화를 내려 받으면 안 돼, Catherine. 그건 법에 어긋나.
G: 정말? 그런지 몰랐어.
B: 대신, 우리 영화관에 가는 건 어떨까?
G: 좋아. 가자.

보라: 세호야, 봐! 누군가 네 SNS에 이상한 것을 올렸어. 나는 네가 그것들을 올렸다고 생각하지 않아.
세호: 정말? 누가 그랬지?
보라: 내 생각에 누군가 네 비밀번호를 알아낸 것 같아.
세호: 어떻게 해야 하지?
보라: 내가 너라면 비밀번호를 바꾸겠어.
세호: 내 생각에도 그래야 할 것 같아.
보라: 네 비밀번호는 추측하기 쉽니?
세호: 내 생일 날짜를 사용했어.
보라: 그것은 좋지 않아. 사실 그건 큰 실수야. 비밀번호를 만들 때 개인 정보를 사용하지 말아야 해.
세호: 그래, 알았어. 그걸 더 강한 것으로 바꿀 거야.

B: 뭐 하고 있니, 소희야?
G: 나는 오늘 방문했던 식당에 관한 게시 글을 쓰고 있어.
B: 멋진 사진들이네. 그것들을 네가 다 찍었니?
G: 아니. 누군가의 블로그에서 사진들을 가져왔어.
B: 그럼 너는 그것들을 네 블로그에 게시하면 안 돼.
G: 왜 안 돼?
B: 왜냐하면 그 블로그 주인만이 그것들을 사용할 권리가 있거든.
G: 오, 알겠어.

※ 다음 우리말에 맞도록 대화를 영어로 쓰시오.

Listen & Speak 1 A

1. G: _____

   B: _____

   _____

   G: _____

   B: _____

   G: _____

   B: _____

2. W: _____

   B: _____

   W: _____

   B: _____

   W: _____

   B: _____

1. G: 너 피곤해 보인다, Peter.
   B: 나 늦게까지 게임을 해서, 어젯밤에 4시간도 못 잤어.
   G: 컴퓨터 게임을 너무 많이 하는 건 네 건강에 좋지 않아.
   B: 나도 알아, Jenny, 그런데 멈출 수가 없어. 난 그것에 중독된 것 같아.
   G: 만약 내가 너라면, 게임 시간을 제한하기 위해 일일 계획을 짤 거야.
   B: 그거 좋은 생각이네. 고마워.

2. W: Tony, 너 스마트 폰에 너무 많은 시간을 보내는구나.
   B: 제 친구들은 거의 매일 SNS에서 만나기 때문에, 저도 어쩔 수 없어요, 엄마.
   W: 만약 내가 너라면, 친구들에게 야외 활동을 하자고 제안할 거야.
   B: 야외 활동이요?
   W: 응. 너는 축구나 스케이트 타기 등과 같은 많은 멋진 활동을 할 수 있어.
   B: 알겠어요. 오늘 제안해 볼게요.

Listen & Speak 2 A

1. G: _____

   B: _____

   G: _____

   B: _____

   G: _____

   B: _____

2. G: _____

   B: _____

   G: _____

   B: _____

   _____

   G: _____

   B: _____

   G: _____

1. G: James, 뭐 하고 있니?
   B: 나 오늘 Sarah와 함께 찍은 사진들 중 몇 장을 올리고 있어.
   G: 네가 그걸 온라인에 올려도 될지 Sarah에게 물어봤니?
   B: 아니, 그렇지만 그녀가 사진들 속에서 멋져 보이기 때문에 괜찮을 것 같아.
   G: 너는 다른 사람들의 사진을 물어보지 않고 올리면 안 돼.
   B: 오, 네 말이 맞을지 몰라. 내가 지금 당장 Sarah에게 전화해서 물어볼게.

2. G: David, 컴퓨터로 이 신작 영화 보자.
   B: 컴퓨터로?
   G: 응. 우리가 그것을 무료로 내려 받을 수 있는 웹 사이트가 있어.
   B: 너는 그런 웹 사이트에서 영화를 내려 받으면 안 돼, Catherine. 그건 법에 어긋나.
   G: 정말? 그런지 몰랐어.
   B: 대신, 우리 영화관에 가는 건 어떨까?
   G: 좋아. 가자.

Real Life Talk

Bora: _____

_____

Seho: _____

Bora: _____

Seho: _____

Bora: _____

Seho: _____

Bora: _____

Seho: _____

Bora: _____

_____

Seho: _____

보라: 세호야, 봐! 누군가 네 SNS에 이상한 것을 올렸어. 나는 네가 그것들을 올렸다고 생각하지 않아.

세호: 정말? 누가 그랬지?

보라: 내 생각에 누군가 네 비밀번호를 알아낸 것 같아.

세호: 어떻게 해야 하지?

보라: 내가 너라면 비밀번호를 바꾸겠어.

세호: 내 생각에도 그래야 할 것 같아.

보라: 네 비밀번호는 추측하기 쉽니?

세호: 내 생일 날짜를 사용했어.

보라: 그것은 좋지 않아. 사실 그건 큰 실수야. 비밀번호를 만들 때 개인 정보를 사용하지 말아야 해.

세호: 그래, 알았어. 그걸 더 강한 것으로 바꿀 거야.

Wrap Up

B: _____

G: _____

B: _____

G: _____

B: _____

G: _____

B: _____

G: _____

B: 뭐 하고 있니, 소희야?

G: 나는 오늘 방문했던 식당에 관한 게시 글을 쓰고 있어.

B: 멋진 사진들이네. 그것들을 네가 다 찍었니?

G: 아니. 누군가의 블로그에서 사진들을 가져왔어.

B: 그럼 너는 그것들을 네 블로그에 게시하면 안 돼.

G: 왜 안 돼?

B: 왜냐하면 그 블로그 주인만이 그것들을 사용할 권리가 있거든.

G: 오, 알겠어.

※ 다음 우리말과 일치하도록 빈칸에 알맞은 것을 골라 쓰시오.

Time for Digital Detox

1 Hi, students! _____ you _____ _____ in the morning, what is the _____ thing you do?
  A. first   B. up   C. when   D. wake

2 Do you _____ SNS _____ _____ your _____?
  A. postings   B. read   C. smartphone   D. on

3 _____ your smartphone is not _____ you. _____ do you _____?
  A. feel   B. imagine   C. near   D. how

4 Students, please _____ _____ _____ the list that are _____ for you.
  A. on   B. check   C. true   D. items

5 _____ you _____ _____ your smartphone?
  A. addicted   B. are   C. to

6 _____ my smartphone, I _____ _____.
  A. feel   B. without   C. uncomfortable

7 I _____ my smartphone _____ the _____.
  A. into   B. take   C. bathroom

8 It is _____ enjoyable to _____ time _____ my smartphone _____ with friends.
  A. than   B. spend   C. more   D. on

9 I often _____ SNS _____ _____ _____.
  A. while   B. check   C. studying   D. postings

10 I _____ to _____ the time I spend _____ my smartphone, but I _____.
  A. fail   B. reduce   C. try   D. on

11 I check my smartphone _____ I hear the _____ of an _____.
  A. alert   B. right   C. sound   D. after

12 I have my smartphone _____ _____ me _____ I'm _____.
  A. while   B. next   C. eating   D. to

13 What is your _____? Did you check _____ _____ _____?
  A. half   B. score   C. than   D. more

14 If _____, you may have a _____ _____ smartphone _____.
  A. with   B. so   C. addiction   D. problem

15 Smartphone _____ _____ you to _____ too much on your smartphone.
  A. causes   B. addiction   C. spend   D. time

16 Also, you cannot _____ on your _____ and may have a _____ in your _____.
  A. pain   B. studies   C. neck   D. focus

17 Then now is the time _____ _____ _____ _____ digital detox.
  A. to   B. for   C. start   D. you

디지털 디톡스를 할 시간

1 안녕하세요, 학생 여러분! 여러분은 아침에 일어났을 때, 가장 먼저 하는 일이 무엇인가요?

2 스마트폰으로 SNS 게시물을 읽나요?

3 스마트폰이 여러분 근처에 있지 않다고 상상해 보세요. 기분이 어떤가요?

4 학생 여러분, 이 목록에서 여러분에게 맞는 항목들을 표시해 보세요.

5 너는 스마트폰에 중독되었는가?

6 나는 스마트폰이 없으면, 불편함을 느낀다.

7 나는 스마트폰을 화장실에 가져간다.

8 나는 친구들과 함께 시간을 보내는 것보다 스마트폰을 하면서 보내는 시간이 더 즐겁다.

9 나는 공부하면서 SNS 게시물을 종종 확인한다.

10 나는 스마트폰을 사용하는 시간을 줄이려고 노력하지만, 실패한다.

11 나는 알림음을 듣자마자 스마트폰을 확인한다.

12 나는 식사 중에 스마트폰을 옆에 둔다.

13 여러분의 점수는 어떤가요? 절반보다 더 많이 표시했나요?

14 만약 그렇다면, 여러분은 스마트폰 중독의 문제를 가지고 있을지도 모릅니다.

15 스마트폰 중독은 여러분이 스마트폰에 너무 많은 시간을 보내게 만듭니다.

16 또한 여러분은 학업에 집중할 수 없고 목에 통증이 있을지도 모릅니다.

17 그렇다면 지금 여러분은 디지털 디톡스를 시작할 시간입니다.

18 Digital detox means _____ _____ from digital devices, _____ as smartphones and computers, for a _____ .
A. while   B. away   C. such   D. staying

19 Digital detox will help you a _____ . You can enjoy _____ _____ the _____ digital world.
A. noisy   B. from   C. freedom   D. lot

20 You can _____ more on your _____ . Sometimes you can feel _____ and have new, _____ ideas.
A. work   B. creative   C. refreshed   D. focus

21 Digital detox will also _____ you _____ more time _____ .
A. others   B. help   C. with   D. spend

22 _____ _____ a smartphone, _____ , is not _____ .
A. however   B. without   C. easy   D. living

23 So, it is _____ for you to _____ some _____ for your smartphone.
A. rules   B. necessary   C. set   D. using

24 You then _____ _____ _____ the rules.
A. to   B. need   C. follow

25 Now, please _____ groups and, in your group, _____ _____ for _____ your smartphone.
A. create   B. form   C. using   D. rules

<By Yerim, Yongmin, and Hojin>

26 We will _____ _____ our smartphones _____ _____ .
A. off   B. studying   C. turn   D. while

27 We will not _____ our _____ the _____ .
A. into   B. take   C. bathroom   D. smarphones

28 We will _____ our smartphones _____ _____ the bedroom and not _____ them at night.
A. of   B. keep   C. out   D. use

<By Jina, Hosung, and Minsu>

29 More Time for Outside Activities – We will _____ more time _____ _____ our smartphones.
A. without   B. spend   C. outside   D. playing

30 Fewer SNS Messages – We will _____ _____ SNS _____ our smartphones.
A. fewer   B. on   C. post   D. messages

<By Jiho, Sohee, and Yumin>

31 If I _____ you, I would _____ my time on my smartphone _____ _____ .
A. reduce   B. half   C. were   D. by

32 If I were you, I _____ _____ _____ all _____ .
A. alerts   B. turn   C. would   D. off

33 You did a good job, students! If we had no smartphones, our _____ would be more _____ , but too much _____ of a smartphone is _____ .
A. dangerous   B. lives   C. use   D. difficult

34 _____ digital detox, you can _____ a _____ smartphone _____ .
A. wise   B. with   C. become   D. user

18 디지털 디톡스는 스마트폰과 컴퓨터 같은 디지털 기기들로부터 잠시 동안 떨어져 있는 것을 의미합니다.

19 디지털 디톡스는 여러분을 많이 도와줄 것입니다. 여러분은 시끄러운 디지털 세계로부터 자유를 즐길 수 있습니다.

20 여러분은 하는 일에 더욱 집중할 수 있습니다. 종종 여러분은 상쾌함을 느끼고 새롭고 창의적인 아이디어를 얻을 수 있습니다.

21 디지털 디톡스는 또한 여러분이 다른 사람들과 더 많은 시간을 보내도록 도와줄 것입니다.

22 하지만 스마트폰 없이 사는 것은 쉽지 않습니다.

23 그러므로 여러분은 스마트폰을 사용하기 위한 몇 가지 규칙을 정할 필요가 있습니다.

24 그러고 나서 여러분은 그 규칙들을 따라야 합니다.

25 자, 조를 형성하고, 여러분의 조에서, 스마트폰을 사용하기 위한 규칙을 만들어 보세요.

〈예림, 용민, 호진으로부터〉

26 우리는 공부하는 동안 스마트폰을 끌 것이다.

27 우리는 화장실에 스마트폰을 가져가지 않을 것이다.

28 우리는 밤에 스마트폰을 침실 밖에 두고 사용하지 않을 것이다.

〈지나, 호성, 민수로부터〉

29 야외 활동을 위한 더 많은 시간 – 우리는 스마트폰 없이 밖에서 노는 데 더 많은 시간을 보낼 것이다.

30 SNS는 더 적게 – 우리는 스마트폰에 SNS 메시지를 더 적게 올릴 것이다.

〈지호, 소희, 유민〉

31 만약 내가 너라면, 나는 스마트폰에 쓰는 시간을 절반으로 줄일 것이다.

32 만약 내가 너라면, 모든 알림을 끌 것이다.

33 잘했어요, 학생 여러분! 만약 스마트폰이 없다면 우리의 삶이 더 힘들겠지만, 스마트폰을 너무 많이 사용하는 것은 위험합니다.

34 디지털 디톡스와 함께, 여러분은 현명한 스마트폰 사용자가 될 수 있습니다.

※ 다음 우리말과 일치하도록 빈칸에 알맞은 말을 쓰시오.

Time for Digital Detox

1 Hi, students! _____ you _____ _____ _____ _____ _____, _____ is the first thing you do?

2 Do you _____ SNS _____ _____ your smartphone?

3 _____ your smartphone _____ not _____ you. _____ do you feel?

4 Students, please _____ _____ on the list _____ _____ true for you.

5 _____ you _____ _____ your smartphone?

6 _____ my smartphone, I _____ _____.

7 I _____ my smartphone _____ the _____.

8 It is _____ _____ _____ spend time _____ my smartphone _____ _____ friends.

9 I often _____ SNS _____ _____ _____.

10 I try to _____ the time _____ _____ _____ my smartphone, but I _____.

11 I check my smartphone _____ _____ I hear the sound of _____ _____.

12 I have my smartphone _____ _____ me _____ I'm eating.

13 _____ is your _____? Did you _____ _____ _____ _____?

14 If so, you may _____ a problem _____ smartphone _____.

15 Smartphone addiction _____ _____ _____ _____ _____ too much time _____ your smartphone.

16 _____, you cannot _____ _____ your _____ and may _____ _____ _____ _____ _____ your _____.

17 Then now is the time _____ _____ _____ _____ _____ _____.

1 안녕하세요, 학생 여러분! 여러분은 아침에 일어났을 때, 가장 먼저 하는 일이 무엇인가요?

2 스마트폰으로 SNS 게시물을 읽나요?

3 스마트폰이 여러분 근처에 있지 않다고 상상해 보세요. 기분이 어떤가요?

4 학생 여러분. 이 목록에서 여러분에게 맞는 항목들을 표시해 보세요.

5 너는 스마트폰에 중독되었는가?

6 나는 스마트폰이 없으면, 불편함을 느낀다.

7 나는 스마트폰을 화장실에 가져간다.

8 나는 친구들과 함께 시간을 보내는 것보다 스마트폰을 하면서 보내는 시간이 더 즐겁다.

9 나는 공부하면서 SNS 게시물을 종종 확인한다.

10 나는 스마트폰을 사용하는 시간을 줄이려고 노력하지만, 실패한다.

11 나는 알림음을 듣자마자 스마트폰을 확인한다.

12 나는 식사 중에 스마트폰을 옆에 둔다.

13 여러분의 점수는 어떤가요? 절반보다 더 많이 표시했나요?

14 만약 그렇다면, 여러분은 스마트폰 중독의 문제를 가지고 있을지도 모릅니다.

15 스마트폰 중독은 여러분이 스마트폰에 너무 많은 시간을 보내게 만듭니다.

16 또한 여러분은 학업에 집중할 수 없고 목에 통증이 있을지도 모릅니다.

17 그렇다면 지금 여러분은 디지털 디톡스를 시작할 시간입니다.

18 Digital detox _____ _____ _____ _____ digital devices, such as smartphones and computers, _____ a while.

19 Digital detox will _____ you _____ _____. You can enjoy _____ _____ the _____ digital world.

20 You can _____ more _____ your work. Sometimes you can _____ _____ and have new, _____ _____.

21 Digital detox will also _____ you _____ more time _____.

22 _____ without a smartphone, _____ _____ _____ not easy.

23 So, it is _____ _____ _____ _____ some rules _____ _____ your smartphone.

24 You then _____ _____ _____ the rules.

25 Now, please _____ groups and, in your group, _____ _____ _____ _____ your smartphone.

<By Yerim, Yongmin, and Hojin>

26 We will _____ _____ our smartphones _____ _____.

27 We will not _____ our smartphones _____ the bathroom.

28 We will _____ our smartphones _____ _____ _____ and not use _____ at night.

<By Jina, Hosung, and Minsu>

29 _____ _____ _____ Outside Activities – We will _____ _____ _____ _____ _____ _____ _____ our smartphones.

30 _____ SNS Messages – We will _____ _____ SNS messages _____ our smartphones.

<By Jiho, Sohee, and Yumin>

31 If _____ _____ you, I _____ _____ my time _____ my smartphone _____ _____.

32 If _____ _____ you, I _____ turn _____ all alerts.

33 You did a good job, students! If we _____ no smartphones, our lives _____ _____ _____ _____ _____, but _____ _____ use of a smartphone is _____.

34 _____ digital detox, you can become a _____ _____ _____.

18 디지털 디톡스는 스마트폰과 컴퓨터 같은 디지털 기기들로부터 잠시 동안 떨어져 있는 것을 의미합니다.

19 디지털 디톡스는 여러분을 많이 도와줄 것입니다. 여러분은 시끄러운 디지털 세계로부터 자유를 즐길 수 있습니다.

20 여러분은 하는 일에 더욱 집중할 수 있습니다. 종종 여러분은 상쾌함을 느끼고 새롭고 창의적인 아이디어를 얻을 수 있습니다.

21 디지털 디톡스는 또한 여러분이 다른 사람들과 더 많은 시간을 보내도록 도와줄 것입니다.

22 하지만 스마트폰 없이 사는 것은 쉽지 않습니다.

23 그러므로 여러분은 스마트폰을 사용하기 위한 몇 가지 규칙을 정할 필요가 있습니다.

24 그리고 나서 여러분은 그 규칙들을 따라야 합니다.

25 자, 조를 형성하고, 여러분의 조에서, 스마트폰을 사용하기 위한 규칙을 만들어 보세요.

〈예림, 용민, 호진으로부터〉

26 우리는 공부하는 동안 스마트폰을 끌 것이다.

27 우리는 화장실에 스마트폰을 가져가지 않을 것이다.

28 우리는 밤에 스마트폰을 침실 밖에 두고 사용하지 않을 것이다.

〈지나, 호성, 민수로부터〉

29 야외 활동을 위한 더 많은 시간 – 우리는 스마트폰 없이 밖에서 노는 데 더 많은 시간을 보낼 것이다.

30 SNS는 더 적게 – 우리는 스마트폰에 SNS 메시지를 더 적게 올릴 것이다.

〈지호, 소희, 유민〉

31 만약 내가 너라면, 나는 스마트폰에 쓰는 시간을 절반으로 줄일 것이다.

32 만약 내가 너라면, 모든 알림을 끌 것이다.

33 잘했어요, 학생 여러분! 만약 스마트폰이 없다면 우리의 삶이 더 힘들겠지만, 스마트폰을 너무 많이 사용하는 것은 위험합니다.

34 디지털 디톡스와 함께, 여러분은 현명한 스마트폰 사용자가 될 수 있습니다.

※ 다음 문장을 우리말로 쓰시오.

1 Hi, students! When you wake up in the morning, what is the first thing you do?
➡ _____

2 Do you read SNS postings on your smartphone?
➡ _____

3 Imagine your smartphone is not near you. How do you feel?
➡ _____

4 Students, please check items on the list that are true for you.
➡ _____

5 Are you addicted to your smartphone?
➡ _____

6 Without my smartphone, I feel uncomfortable.
➡ _____

7 I take my smartphone into the bathroom.
➡ _____

8 It is more enjoyable to spend time on my smartphone than with friends.
➡ _____

9 I often check SNS postings while studying.
➡ _____

10 I try to reduce the time I spend on my smartphone, but I fail.
➡ _____

11 I check my smartphone right after I hear the sound of an alert.
➡ _____

12 I have my smartphone next to me while I'm eating.
➡ _____

13 What is your score? Did you check more than half?
➡ _____

14 If so, you may have a problem with smartphone addiction.
➡ _____

15 Smartphone addiction causes you to spend too much time on your smartphone.
➡ _____

16 Also, you cannot focus on your studies and may have a pain in your neck.
➡ _____

17 Then now is the time for you to start digital detox.
➡ _____

18 Digital detox means staying away from digital devices, such as smartphones and computers, for a while.
➡ _____

19 Digital detox will help you a lot. You can enjoy freedom from the noisy digital world.
➡ _____

20 You can focus more on your work. Sometimes you can feel refreshed and have new, creative ideas.
➡ _____
_____

21 Digital detox will also help you spend more time with others.
➡ _____

22 Living without a smartphone, however, is not easy.
➡ _____

23 So, it is necessary for you to set some rules for using your smartphone.
➡ _____

24 You then need to follow the rules.
➡ _____

25 Now, please form groups and, in your group, create rules for using your smartphone.
➡ _____

By Yerim, Yongmin, and Hojin
26 We will turn off our smartphones while studying.
➡ _____

27 We will not take our smartphones into the bathroom.
➡ _____

28 We will keep our smartphones out of the bedroom and not use them at night.
➡ _____

By Jina, Hosung, and Minsu
29 More Time for Outside Activities – We will spend more time playing outside without our smartphones.
➡ _____

30 Fewer SNS Messages – We will post fewer SNS messages on our smartphones.
➡ _____

By Jiho, Sohee, and Yumin
31 If I were you, I would reduce my time on my smartphone by half.
➡ _____

32 If I were you, I would turn off all alerts.
➡ _____

33 You did a good job, students! If we had no smartphones, our lives would be more difficult, but too much use of a smartphone is dangerous.
➡ _____
_____

34 With digital detox, you can become a wise smartphone user.
➡ _____

※ 다음 괄호 안의 단어들을 우리말에 맞도록 바르게 배열하시오.

Time for Digital Detox

1 (students! / hi, // you / when / up / wake / the / in / morning, / is / what / first / the / thing / do? / you)
➡ _____

2 (you / do / SNS / read / postings / on / smartphone? / your)
➡ _____

3 (your / imagine / smarphone / not / is / you. / near // do / how / feel? / you)
➡ _____

4 (please / students, / items / check / the / on / that / list / true / are / you. / for)
➡ _____

5 (you / are / to / addicted / smartphone? / your)
➡ _____

6 (my / without / smartphone, / feel / I / uncomfortable.)
➡ _____

7 (take / I / smarphone / my / the / bathroom. / into)
➡ _____

8 (is / it / enjoyable / more / spend / to / time / my / on / smartphone / with / friends. / than)
➡ _____

9 (often / I / check / postings / SNS / studying. / while)
➡ _____

10 (try / I / reduce / to / time / the / spend / I / my / on / smartphone, / I / but / fail.)
➡ _____

11 (check / I / smartphone / my / after / right / hear / I / sound / the / of / alert. / an)
➡ _____

12 (have / I / smartphone / my / to / next / while / me / eating. / I'm)
➡ _____

13 (is / what / score? / your // you / did / more / check / half? / than)
➡ _____

14 (so, / if / may / you / have / problem / a / with / addiction. / smartphone)
➡ _____

15 (addiction / smartphone / you / causes / spend / to / much / too / on / time / smartphone. / your)
➡ _____

16 (you / also, / focus / cannot / your / on / studies / may / and / a / have / in / pain / neck. / your)
➡ _____

17 (now / then / the / is / for / time / you / start / to / detox. / digital)
➡ _____

디지털 디톡스를 할 시간

1 안녕하세요, 학생 여러분! 여러분은 아침에 일어났을 때, 가장 먼저 하는 일이 무엇인가요?

2 스마트폰으로 SNS 게시물을 읽나요?

3 스마트폰이 여러분 근처에 있지 않다고 상상해 보세요. 기분이 어떤가요?

4 학생 여러분, 이 목록에서 여러분에게 맞는 항목들을 표시해 보세요.

5 너는 스마트폰에 중독되었는가?

6 나는 스마트폰이 없으면, 불편함을 느낀다.

7 나는 스마트폰을 화장실에 가져간다.

8 나는 친구들과 함께 시간을 보내는 것보다 스마트폰을 하면서 보내는 시간이 더 즐겁다.

9 나는 공부하면서 SNS 게시물을 종종 확인한다.

10 나는 스마트폰을 사용하는 시간을 줄이려고 노력하지만, 실패한다.

11 나는 알림음을 듣자마자 스마트폰을 확인한다.

12 나는 식사 중에 스마트폰을 옆에 둔다.

13 여러분의 점수는 어떤가요? 절반보다 더 많이 표시했나요?

14 만약 그렇다면, 여러분은 스마트폰 중독의 문제를 가지고 있을지도 모릅니다.

15 스마트폰 중독은 여러분이 스마트폰에 너무 많은 시간을 보내게 만듭니다.

16 또한 여러분은 학업에 집중할 수 없고 목에 통증이 있을지도 모릅니다.

17 그렇다면 지금 여러분은 디지털 디톡스를 시작할 시간입니다.

18 (detox / digital / staying / means / from / away / devices, / digital / as / such / and / smartphones / for / computers, / while. / a)
➡ _____

19 (detox / digital / help / will / a / you / lot. // can / you / freedom / enjoy / from / noisy / the / world. / digital)
➡ _____

20 (can / you / more / focus / on / work. / your // you / sometimes / feel / can / and / refreshed / new, / have / ideas. / creative)
➡ _____

21 (detox / digital / also / will / you / help / more / spend / with / time / others.)
➡ _____

22 (without / living / smartphone, / a / is / however, / easy. / not)
➡ _____

23 (it / so, / is / for / necessary / you / set / to / rules / some / using / for / smartphone. / your)
➡ _____

24 (then / you / to / need / follow / rules. / the)
➡ _____

25 (please / now, / groups / form / and, / your / in / group, / rules / create / for / using / smartphone. / your)
➡ _____

By Yerim, Yongmin, and Hojin
26 (will / we / off / turn / smartphones / our / studying. / while)
➡ _____

27 (will / we / take / not / smartphones / our / into / bathroom. / the)
➡ _____

28 (will / we / our / keep / out / smartphones / of / bedroom / the / and / use / not / them / night. / at)
➡ _____

By Jina, Hosung, and Minsu
29 (Time / More / for / Activities / Outside / – / will / we / more / spend / playing / time / without / outside / smartphones. / our)
➡ _____

30 (SNS / Fewer / Messages / – / will / we / fewer / post / messages / SNS / our / on / smartphones.)
➡ _____

By Jiho, Sohee, and Yumin
31 (I / if / you, / were / would / I / my / time / reduce / my / on / by / smartphone / half.)
➡ _____

32 (I / if / you, / were / would / I / off / alerts. / turn / all)
➡ _____

33 (did / you / good / a / students! / job, / we / if / no / had / smartphones, / lives / our / be / would / more / but / difficult, / much / too / of / use / is / smartphone / a / dangerous.)
➡ _____

34 (digital / with / detox, / can / you / a / become / smartphone / wise / user.)
➡ _____

18 디지털 디톡스는 스마트폰과 컴퓨터 같은 디지털 기기들로부터 잠시 동안 떨어져 있는 것을 의미합니다.

19 디지털 디톡스는 여러분을 많이 도와줄 것입니다. 여러분은 시끄러운 디지털 세계로부터 자유를 즐길 수 있습니다.

20 여러분은 하는 일에 더욱 집중할 수 있습니다. 종종 여러분은 상쾌함을 느끼고 새롭고 창의적인 아이디어를 얻을 수 있습니다.

21 디지털 디톡스는 또한 여러분이 다른 사람들과 더 많은 시간을 보내도록 도와줄 것입니다.

22 하지만 스마트폰 없이 사는 것은 쉽지 않습니다.

23 그러므로 여러분은 스마트폰을 사용하기 위한 몇 가지 규칙을 정할 필요가 있습니다.

24 그리고 나서 여러분은 그 규칙들을 따라야 합니다.

25 자, 조를 형성하고, 여러분의 조에서, 스마트폰을 사용하기 위한 규칙을 만들어 보세요.

〈예림, 용민, 호진으로부터〉
26 우리는 공부하는 동안 스마트폰을 끌 것이다.

27 우리는 화장실에 스마트폰을 가져가지 않을 것이다.

28 우리는 밤에 스마트폰을 침실 밖에 두고 사용하지 않을 것이다.

〈지나, 호성, 민수로부터〉
29 야외 활동을 위한 더 많은 시간 – 우리는 스마트폰 없이 밖에서 노는 데 더 많은 시간을 보낼 것이다.

30 SNS는 더 적게 – 우리는 스마트폰에 SNS 메시지를 더 적게 올릴 것이다.

〈지호, 소희, 유민〉
31 만약 내가 너라면, 나는 스마트폰에 쓰는 시간을 절반으로 줄일 것이다.

32 만약 내가 너라면, 모든 알림을 끌 것이다.

33 잘했어요, 학생 여러분! 만약 스마트폰이 없다면 우리의 삶이 더 힘들겠지만, 스마트폰을 너무 많이 사용하는 것은 위험합니다.

34 디지털 디톡스와 함께, 여러분은 현명한 스마트폰 사용자가 될 수 있습니다.

※ 다음 우리말을 영어로 쓰시오.

1 안녕하세요, 학생 여러분! 여러분은 아침에 일어났을 때, 가장 먼저 하는 일이 무엇인가요?
➡ _____

2 스마트폰으로 SNS 게시물을 읽나요?
➡ _____

3 스마트폰이 여러분 근처에 있지 않다고 상상해 보세요. 기분이 어떤가요?
➡ _____

4 학생 여러분, 이 목록에서 여러분에게 맞는 항목들을 표시해 보세요.
➡ _____

5 너는 스마트폰에 중독되었는가?
➡ _____

6 나는 스마트폰이 없으면, 불편함을 느낀다.
➡ _____

7 나는 스마트폰을 화장실에 가져간다.
➡ _____

8 나는 친구들과 함께 시간을 보내는 것보다 스마트폰을 하면서 보내는 시간이 더 즐겁다.
➡ _____

9 나는 공부하면서 SNS 게시물을 종종 확인한다.
➡ _____

10 나는 스마트폰을 사용하는 시간을 줄이려고 노력하지만, 실패한다.
➡ _____

11 나는 알림음을 듣자마자 스마트폰을 확인한다.
➡ _____

12 나는 식사 중에 스마트폰을 옆에 둔다.
➡ _____

13 여러분의 점수는 어떤가요? 절반보다 더 많이 표시했나요?
➡ _____

14 만약 그렇다면, 여러분은 스마트폰 중독의 문제를 가지고 있을지도 모릅니다.
➡ _____

15 스마트폰 중독은 여러분이 스마트폰에 너무 많은 시간을 보내게 만듭니다.
➡ _____

16 또한 여러분은 학업에 집중할 수 없고 목에 통증이 있을지도 모릅니다.
➡ _____

17 그렇다면 지금 여러분은 디지털 디톡스를 시작할 시간입니다.
➡ _____

18 디지털 디톡스는 스마트폰과 컴퓨터 같은 디지털 기기들로부터 잠시 동안 떨어져 있는 것을 의미합니다.
➡ _____

19 디지털 디톡스는 여러분을 많이 도와줄 것입니다. 여러분은 시끄러운 디지털 세계로부터 자유를 즐길 수 있습니다.

➡ _____

20 여러분은 하는 일에 더욱 집중할 수 있습니다. 종종 여러분은 상쾌함을 느끼고 새롭고 창의적인 아이디어를 얻을 수 있습니다.

➡ _____

21 디지털 디톡스는 또한 여려분이 다른 사람들과 더 많은 시간을 보내도록 도와줄 것입니다.

➡ _____

22 하지만 스마트폰 없이 사는 것은 쉽지 않습니다.

➡ _____

23 그러므로 여러분은 스마트폰을 사용하기 위한 몇 가지 규칙을 정할 필요가 있습니다.

➡ _____

24 그리고 나서 여러분은 그 규칙들을 따라야 합니다.

➡ _____

25 자, 조를 형성하고, 여러분의 조에서, 스마트폰을 사용하기 위한 규칙을 만들어 보세요.

➡ _____

By Yerim, Yongmin, and Hojin

26 우리는 공부하는 동안 스마트폰을 끌 것이다.

➡ _____

27 우리는 화장실에 스마트폰을 가져가지 않을 것이다.

➡ _____

28 우리는 밤에 스마트폰을 침실 밖에 두고 사용하지 않을 것이다.

➡ _____

By Jina, Hosung, and Minsu

29 야외 활동을 위한 더 많은 시간 – 우리는 스마트폰 없이 밖에서 노는 데 더 많은 시간을 보낼 것이다.

➡ _____

30 SNS는 더 적게 – 우리는 스마트폰에 SNS 메시지를 더 적게 올릴 것이다.

➡ _____

By Jiho, Sohee, and Yumin

31 만약 내가 너라면, 나는 스마트폰에 쓰는 시간을 절반으로 줄일 것이다.

➡ _____

32 만약 내가 너라면, 모든 알림을 끌 것이다.

➡ _____

33 잘했어요, 학생 여러분! 만약 스마트폰이 없다면 우리의 삶이 더 힘들겠지만, 스마트폰을 너무 많이 사용하는 것은 위험합니다.

➡ _____

34 디지털 디톡스와 함께, 여러분은 현명한 스마트폰 사용자가 될 수 있습니다.

➡ _____

※ 다음 우리말과 일치하도록 빈칸에 알맞은 말을 쓰시오.

Enjoy Writing C

1. _____ _____ _____ No Smartphones
2. There _____ _____ some _____ and some _____ _____ there _____ no smartphones.
3. First, _____ _____ _____ some advantages.
4. _____ we _____ smartphones, we _____ _____ _____ more often.
5. _____, we _____ _____ _____ _____ neck pain.
6. _____ _____ _____ _____, there _____ _____ some _____.
7. _____ there were no smartphones, it _____ _____ be easy _____ _____ _____ _____ people.
8. Also, it _____ _____ so long _____ _____ _____ _____ _____.

1. 만약 스마트폰이 없다면
2. 만약 스마트폰이 없다면 몇몇 장점과 단점이 있을 것이다.
3. 첫째로 몇 가지 장점을 이야기해 보자.
4. 만약 우리가 스마트폰을 가지고 있지 않다면, 우리는 밖에서 더 자주 놀 것이다.
5. 게다가, 우리는 목통증의 위험이 없을 것이다.
6. 반면에 몇 가지 단점도 있을 것이다.
7. 만약 스마트폰이 없다면, 우리는 사람들에게 연락하는 것이 쉽지 않을 것이다.
8. 또한 우리가 정보를 찾는 데 시간이 많이 걸릴 것이다.

Project 2

1. _____ is necessary _____ _____ _____ _____ _____ digital _____!
2. _____ there were no _____ or _____, our lives _____ _____ _____ _____.
3. So, _____ is very important _____ _____ _____ _____ digital devices _____ as a digital citizen.
4. I _____ _____ and _____ on SNS.
5. I never _____ _____ _____ _____ anyone.
6. I _____ _____ _____.
7. I _____ _____ _____ _____.
8. I _____ too _____ _____ _____.

1. 우리는 디지털 시민이 될 필요가 있다!
2. 만약 인터넷이나 SNS가 없다면, 우리의 삶은 더 힘들 것이다.
3. 그래서 우리는 디지털 시민으로서 디지털 기기들을 현명하게 사용하는 것이 중요하다.
4. 나는 SNS에서 내 자신과 다른 사람들을 존중한다.
5. 나는 절대 내 비밀번호를 누구와도 공유하지 않는다.
6. 나는 친절한 말을 쓴다.
7. 나는 나쁜 말을 절대 쓰지 않는다.
8. 나는 온라인에서 너무 많은 시간을 보내지 않는다.

Project 3

1. It's very important _____ _____ _____ _____ a digital citizen.
2. Our group will _____ you _____ _____ _____ _____ _____.
3. Please _____.

1. 모두가 디지털 시민이 되는 것은 매우 중요해.
2. 우리 모두가 디지털 시민이 무엇을 하는지 보여줄게.
3. 재미있게 봐.

※ 다음 우리말을 영어로 쓰시오.

Enjoy Writing C

1. 만약 스마트폰이 없다면
➡ _____

2. 만약 스마트폰이 없다면 몇몇 장점과 단점이 있을 것이다.
➡ _____

3. 첫째로 몇 가지 장점을 이야기해 보자.
➡ _____

4. 만약 우리가 스마트폰을 가지고 있지 않다면, 우리는 밖에서 더 자주 놀 것이다.
➡ _____

5. 게다가, 우리는 목통증의 위험이 없을 것이다.
➡ _____

6. 반면에 몇 가지 단점도 있을 것이다.
➡ _____

7. 만약 스마트폰이 없다면, 우리는 사람들에게 연락하는 것이 쉽지 않을 것이다.
➡ _____

8. 또한 우리가 정보를 찾는 데 시간이 많이 걸릴 것이다.
➡ _____

Project 2

1. 우리는 디지털 시민이 될 필요가 있다!
➡ _____

2. 만약 인터넷이나 SNS가 없다면, 우리의 삶은 더 힘들 것이다.
➡ _____

3. 그래서 우리는 디지털 시민으로서 디지털 기기들을 현명하게 사용하는 것이 중요하다.
➡ _____

4. 나는 SNS에서 내 자신과 다른 사람들을 존중한다.
➡ _____

5. 나는 절대 내 비밀번호를 누구와도 공유하지 않는다.
➡ _____

6. 나는 친절한 말을 쓴다.
➡ _____

7. 나는 나쁜 말을 절대 쓰지 않는다.
➡ _____

8. 나는 온라인에서 너무 많은 시간을 보내지 않는다.
➡ _____

Project 3

1. 모두가 디지털 시민이 되는 것은 매우 중요해.
➡ _____

2. 우리 모둠이 디지털 시민이 무엇을 하는지 보여줄게.
➡ _____

3. 재미있게 봐.
➡ _____

※ 다음 영어를 우리말로 쓰시오.

01 burial

02 respect

03 rule

04 sacrifice

05 desire

06 zip code

07 secret

08 general

09 government

10 harmony

11 educate

12 specialist

13 spread

14 feed

15 movement

16 throughout

17 entrance

18 protect

19 reader

20 main

21 mission

22 tomb

23 organization

24 palace

25 treasure

26 patriotic

27 foggy

28 president

29 independence

30 direct

31 statue

32 bury

33 republic

34 complete

35 exhibition

36 belong to

37 put on

38 hear of

39 be in need

40 carry out

41 look like+명사

42 so that+주어+동사

43 look forward to+명사/동명사

※ 다음 우리말을 영어로 쓰시오.

01 묻다, 매장하다 _____

02 비밀; 비밀의 _____

03 바람, 갈망 _____

04 존경, 경의 _____

05 정부 _____

06 통치, 지배 _____

07 교육시키다 _____

08 매장, 장례식 _____

09 안개 낀 _____

10 장군 _____

11 희생; 희생하다 _____

12 시 _____

13 독립 _____

14 궁전 _____

15 주된, 주요한 _____

16 묘, 무덤 _____

17 감독하다. 지휘[총괄]하다 _____

18 보물 _____

19 먹이를 주다, 먹이다 _____

20 애국적인 _____

21 조각상 _____

22 보호하다 _____

23 퍼지다, 퍼뜨리다 _____

24 우편 번호 _____

25 입구 _____

26 끝내다; 완전한 _____

27 지도자, 리더 _____

28 조직, 기구 _____

29 전문가 _____

30 조화 _____

31 전시회 _____

32 임무 _____

33 공화국 _____

34 ～의 도처에, ～ 내내 _____

35 (정치적, 사회적) 운동 _____

36 ～을 입다 _____

37 ～에 속하다 _____

38 ～을 수행하다 _____

39 ～처럼 보이다 _____

40 ～가 필요하다 _____

41 ～에 관해 듣다 _____

42 ～하기 위해서 _____

43 ～을 기대하다 _____

※ 다음 영영풀이에 알맞은 단어를 <보기>에서 골라 쓴 후, 우리말 뜻을 쓰시오.

1 _____ : what is highly valued: _____

2 _____ : a country governed by elected representatives: _____

3 _____ : a public display of art works, pictures or other interesting things: _____

4 _____ : any work that someone believes it is their duty to do: _____

5 _____ : a large house that is the official home of a king and queen: _____

6 _____ : a group of people working together for a purpose of being organized: _____

7 _____ : to place a dead body in the ground, to put something in the ground and cover it: _____

8 _____ : a series of things that happen one after another for a particular result: _____

9 _____ : giving up of something valuable for a specific purpose: _____

10 _____ : a sculptured figure of a person animal, etc. in bronze, stone, wood, etc.: _____

11 _____ : the act of putting a dead body into the ground, or the ceremony connected with this: _____

12 _____ : a large stone structure or underground room where someone, especially an important person, is buried: _____

13 _____ : a large outdoor area with fairground rides, shows, and other entertainments: _____

14 _____ : a circular ornament made of gold and decorated with jewels that is worn by a king or queen on their head: _____

15 _____ : a piece of writing that uses beautiful words that imply deep meanings and sounds rhythmical when you read: _____

16 _____ : a piece of cloth that is usually attached at the end of a pole and represents a country or association: _____

보기

poem	statue	republic	mission
sacrifice	crown	bury	process
flag	tomb	treasure	exhibition
burial	amusement park	palace	organization

※ 다음 우리말과 일치하도록 빈칸에 알맞은 말을 쓰시오.

Listen & Speak 1 A

1. **B:** _____ _____ Suwon Hawseong. It's _____.

   G: It also _____ _____.

   B: _____ it _____ _____ _____ _____ the people _____ wars.

   G: Wow. Do you know _____ _____ it?

   B: Yes. King Jeongjo _____ Jeong Yakyong _____ _____ the building _____. You know about Jeong Yakyong, _____ _____?

   G: Yes, I've _____ _____ him. He was a _____ _____ in Joseon.

2. **G:** Brian, you know Taegeukgi, _____ _____?

   B: Sure. It's the _____ _____ of Korea, _____ _____?

   G: That's right. Do you know _____ the _____ in Taegeukgi _____?

   B: No, I don't. _____ _____ about _____.

   G: The _____ in the middle _____ _____ and _____.

   B: What do the black _____ on the four _____ _____?

   G: They _____ four things: sky, fire, water, and _____.

Listen & Speak 2 A

1. **G:** I'm _____ _____ _____ to the Gansong Museum.

   B: What is the Gansong Museum?

   G: It's a _____ _____ _____ Gansong Jeon Hyeongpil.

   B: I _____ that he did _____ _____ for the country.

   G: Yes. He _____ many Korean _____ _____ some Japanese _____ _____ to Japan.

   B: Wow. The museum _____ _____ _____.

   G: Yes. I'm _____ _____ _____ it!

2. **B:** Soyeon, _____ _____ _____ _____ last weekend?

   G: I went to Hyeonchungwon _____ _____ _____ _____.

   B: _____ _____ _____ volunteer work did you do there?

1. B: 수원 화성을 봐, 그것은 거대해.
   G: 그것은 또한 튼튼해 보여.
   B: 왜냐하면 그것은 전쟁 중에 사람들을 보호하기 위해 지어졌기 때문이야.
   G: 우와. 너는 누가 그것을 지었는지 아니?
   B: 응. 정조가 정약용에게 건설 과정을 감독할 것을 지시했어. 너는 정약용에 대해 알고 있지, 그렇지 않니?
   G: 응, 그에 대해 들어봤어. 그는 조선의 훌륭한 과학자였어.

2. G: Brian, 너 태극기를 알고 있지, 그렇지 않니?
   B: 물론이지. 그것은 한국의 국기잖아, 그렇지 않니?
   G: 맞아. 너는 태극기에 있는 상징들이 무엇을 의미하는지 알고 있니?
   B: 아니, 몰라. 그것에 대해 말해 줘.
   G: 가운데 원은 조화와 평화를 의미해.
   B: 네 모서리의 검은 선들은 무엇을 의미하니?
   G: 그것은 하늘, 불, 물 그리고 땅을 의미해.

1. G: 나는 간송 미술관에 갈 예정이야.
   B: 간송 미술관이 뭐야?
   G: 간송 전형필에 의해 지어진 미술관이야.
   B: 나는 그가 나라를 위해 훌륭한 일들을 했다고 들었어.
   G: 응. 그는 몇몇 일본 사람들이 일본으로 가져갔던 한국의 많은 문화재들을 샀어.
   B: 우와. 그 미술관은 틀림없이 흥미로울 거야.
   G: 응. 나는 그곳을 기대하고 있어!

2. B: 소연아, 지난 주말에 무엇을 했니?
   G: 나는 봉사 활동을 하러 현충원에 갔어.
   B: 그곳에서 어떤 종류의 봉사 활동을 했어?

G: I _____ _____ the _____. I felt great _____ for the people _____ _____ for the country.

B: _____ great. Can I do it, _____?

G: Sure. I'm _____ _____ _____ there again next Wednesday. Will you _____ me?

B: Sure. _____ _____ _____ _____ it.

Real Life Task

Andy: Bora, what are you _____?

Bora: I'm reading *Sky*, *Wind*, *Star*, *and* _____ by Yun Dongju. You _____ about Yun Dongju, _____ _____?

Andy: I've _____ his name, but I don't know _____ about him.

Bora: He wrote many beautiful _____ _____ Korea was _____ Japanese _____. His love for the country and his _____ for _____ can _____ _____ in his _____.

Andy: Really? I didn't know that. I want _____ _____ his _____ and _____ _____ about him.

Bora: Great. _____ _____, I'm _____ _____ _____ the Yun Dongju Museum soon. Do you want to come with me?

Andy: Yes, _____ are you _____?

Bora: Next Saturday. It's _____ Gyeongbok _____. Can you meet me at the _____ _____ 2 p.m.?

Andy: Sure. _____ _____ there.

Bora: Great. I'm really _____ _____ _____ the _____.

Wrap Up

B: Tomorrow _____ _____ _____ _____ Korean clothes, *hanbok*, and go to Insadong.

G: Good, but I want to buy _____ _____ my friends in _____ tomorrow.

B: In Insadong, _____ _____ many _____ _____.

G: Great. After _____, what should we eat _____ _____?

B: Hmm. You _____ Samgyetang, _____ _____?

G: No. What is it?

B: It's a _____ Korean _____. It's _____ and will _____ _____ _____.

G: Sounds good. I'm _____ _____ _____ _____ it.

G: 나는 묘 주변을 청소했어. 나는 나라를 위해 돌아가신 분들에게 깊은 경의를 느꼈어.

B: 대단하게 들린다. 나도 그것을 할 수 있을까?

G: 물론이지. 나는 다음 주 수요일에 그곳에 다시 갈 계획이야. 너도 나와 함께 갈래?

B: 물론이지. 나는 그것을 기대하고 있어.

Andy: 보라, 너 무엇을 읽고 있니?

보라: 윤동주 시인의 「하늘과 바람과 별과 시」를 읽고 있어. 너는 윤동주에 대해 알고 있지, 그렇지 않니?

Andy: 나는 그의 이름을 들어 본 적 있지만 그에 대해 잘 알지는 못해.

보라: 그는 한국이 일본의 통치하에 있을 때 아름다운 시를 많이 썼어. 나라에 대한 그의 사랑과 독립에 대한 염원이 그의 시에서 느껴질 수 있어.

Andy: 정말? 나는 그걸 몰랐어. 나는 그의 시를 읽고 그에 대해 더 많이 배우고 싶어.

보라: 아주 좋아. 사실 나는 곧 윤동주 박물관을 방문할 계획이야. 너도 나와 함께 가길 원하니?

Andy: 응, 언제 갈 거니?

보라: 다음 주 토요일에. 그곳은 경복궁 근처에 있어. 오후 2시에 궁에서 만날 수 있니?

Andy: 물론이지. 거기서 만나자.

보라: 좋아. 나는 그 방문을 정말 기대하고 있어.

B: 내일 우리 한국 전통 의상인 한복을 입고 인사동에 가자.

G: 좋아, 그런데 나 내일 독일에 있는 내 친구들을 위한 선물을 사고 싶어.

B: 인사동에 선물 가게가 많아.

G: 잘됐네. 쇼핑하고 나서 점심으로 뭘 먹을까?

B: 흠. 너는 삼계탕에 대해 알고 있지, 그렇지 않니?

G: 아니. 그게 뭐야?

B: 전통적인 한국의 국물 음식이야. 그것은 맛이 좋고 너를 건강하게 만들어 줄 거야.

G: 멋지네. 나는 그것을 먹어보는 것을 기대하고 있어.

※ 다음 우리말에 맞도록 대화를 영어로 쓰시오.

Listen & Speak 1 A

1. B: _____

    G: _____

    B: _____

    G: _____

    B: _____

       _____

    G: _____

2. G: _____

    B: _____

    G: _____

    B: _____

    G: _____

    B: _____

    G: _____

1. B: 수원 화성을 봐, 그것은 거대해.
   G: 그것은 또한 튼튼해 보여.
   B: 왜냐하면 그것은 전쟁 중에 사람들을 보호하기 위해 지어졌기 때문이야.
   G: 우와. 너는 누가 그것을 지었는지 아니?
   B: 응. 정조가 정약용에게 건설 과정을 감독할 것을 지시했어. 너는 정약용에 대해 알고 있지, 그렇지 않니?
   G: 응, 그에 대해 들어봤어. 그는 조선의 훌륭한 과학자였어.

2. G: Brian, 너 태극기를 알고 있지, 그렇지 않니?
   B: 물론이지. 그것은 한국의 국기잖아, 그렇지 않니?
   G: 맞아. 너는 태극기에 있는 상징들이 무엇을 의미하는지 알고 있니?
   B: 아니, 몰라. 그것에 대해 말해 줘.
   G: 가운데 원은 조화와 평화를 의미해.
   B: 네 모서리의 검은 선들은 무엇을 의미하니?
   G: 그것은 하늘, 불, 물 그리고 땅을 의미해.

Listen & Speak 2 A

1. G: _____

    B: _____

    G: _____

    B: _____

    G: _____

       _____

    B: _____

    G: _____

2. B: _____

    G: _____

    B: _____

1. G: 나는 간송 미술관에 갈 예정이야.
   B: 간송 미술관이 뭐야?
   G: 간송 전형필에 의해 지어진 미술관이야.
   B: 나는 그가 나라를 위해 훌륭한 일들을 했다고 들었어.
   G: 응. 그는 몇몇 일본 사람들이 일본으로 가져갔었던 한국의 많은 문화재들을 샀어.
   B: 우와. 그 미술관은 틀림없이 흥미로울 거야.
   G: 응. 나는 그곳을 기대하고 있어!

2. B: 소연아, 지난 주말에 무엇을 했니?
   G: 나는 봉사 활동을 하러 현충원에 갔어.
   B: 그곳에서 어떤 종류의 봉사 활동을 했어?

G: _____

B: _____

G: _____

B: _____

G: 나는 묘 주변을 청소했어. 나는 나라를 위해 돌아가신 분들에게 깊은 경의를 느꼈어.
B: 대단하게 들린다. 나도 그것을 할 수 있을까?
G: 물론이지. 나는 다음 주 수요일에 그곳에 다시 갈 계획이야. 너도 나와 함께 갈래?
B: 물론이지. 나는 그것을 기대하고 있어.

Real Life Task

Andy: _____

Bora: _____
_____

Andy: _____

Bora: _____
_____
_____

Andy: _____
_____

Bora: _____
_____

Andy: _____

Bora: _____
_____

Andy: _____

Bora: _____

Andy: 보라, 너 무엇을 읽고 있니?
보라: 윤동주 시인의 「하늘과 바람과 별과 시」를 읽고 있어. 너는 윤동주에 대해 알고 있지, 그렇지 않니?
Andy: 나는 그의 이름을 들어 본 적 있지만 그에 대해 잘 알지는 못해.
보라: 그는 한국이 일본의 통치하에 있을 때 아름다운 시를 많이 썼어. 나라에 대한 그의 사랑과 독립에 대한 염원이 그의 시에서 느껴질 수 있어.
Andy: 정말? 나는 그걸 몰랐어. 나는 그의 시를 읽고 그에 대해 더 많이 배우고 싶어.
보라: 아주 좋아. 사실 나는 곧 윤동주 박물관을 방문할 계획이야. 너도 나와 함께 가길 원하니?
Andy: 응, 언제 갈 거니?
보라: 다음 주 토요일에. 그곳은 경복궁 근처에 있어. 오후 2시에 궁에서 만날 수 있니?
Andy: 물론이지. 거기서 만나자.
보라: 좋아. 나는 그 방문을 정말 기대하고 있어.

Wrap Up

B: _____

G: _____

B: _____

G: _____

B: _____

G: _____

B: _____

G: _____

B: 내일 우리 한국 전통 의상인 한복을 입고 인사동에 가자.
G: 좋아, 그런데 나 내일 독일에 있는 내 친구들을 위한 선물을 사고 싶어.
B: 인사동에 선물 가게가 많아.
G: 잘됐네. 쇼핑하고 나서 점심으로 뭘 먹을까?
B: 흠. 너는 삼계탕에 대해 알고 있지, 그렇지 않니?
G: 아니. 그게 뭐야?
B: 전통적인 한국의 국물 음식이야. 그것은 맛이 좋고 너를 건강하게 만들어 줄 거야.
G: 멋지네. 나는 그것을 먹어보는 것을 기대하고 있어.

※ 다음 우리말과 일치하도록 빈칸에 알맞은 것을 골라 쓰시오.

My Wish

1 _____ _____ my history club _____ _____ Hyochang Park.

A. went　　　　B. last　　　　C. to　　　　D. week

2 We _____ the Kim Koo Museum _____ the _____.

A. inside　　　　B. visited　　　　C. park

3 At the _____ of the _____, we _____ a white _____ of Kim Koo.

A. statue　　　　B. entrance　　　　C. saw　　　　D. museum

4 Kim Koo is a great _____ _____ who spent most of his life _____ for the _____ of Korea from Japanese rule.

A. fighting　　　　B. hero　　　　C. national　　　　D. independence

5 In the 1900s, he _____ _____ young people _____ _____ schools.

A. educate　　　　B. building　　　　C. helped　　　　D. by

6 In 1919, when the independence _____ had _____ _____ the country, he _____ to Shanghai, China.

A. throughout　　　　B. movement　　　　C. moved　　　　D. spread

7 There he _____ the Government of the Republic of Korea and _____ _____ its _____.

A. later　　　　B. joined　　　　C. president　　　　D. became

8 The _____ hall in the museum _____ a _____ of things about Kim Koo's _____.

A. life　　　　B. exhibition　　　　C. lot　　　　D. shows

9 _____ _____ _____ the hall, we _____ at a photo of the Korean Patriotic Organization's members.

A. stopped　　　　B. looking　　　　C. while　　　　D. around

10 Kim Koo _____ the _____ organization in 1931 to _____ _____ Japan.

A. against　　　　B. secret　　　　C. fight　　　　D. formed

11 Lee Bongchang and Yun Bonggil _____ _____ the _____.

A. to　　　　B. group　　　　C. belonged

12 At one _____ in the _____, we saw two _____ a photo of Kim Koo and Yun Bonggil.

A. under　　　　B. place　　　　C. watches　　　　D. hall

나의 소원

1 지난주에 우리 역사 동아리는 효창 공원에 갔다.

2 우리는 공원 안에 있는 김구 기념관을 방문했다.

3 기념관 입구에서 우리는 하얀색의 김구 조각상을 보았다.

4 김구는 일본 통치로부터 대한의 독립을 위해 싸우는 데 그의 삶 대부분을 보낸 위대한 국민 영웅이다.

5 1900년대에 그는 학교를 설립함으로써 젊은이들을 교육시키는 것을 도왔다.

6 1919년에 3.1 운동이 나라 전체에 걸쳐 퍼져나갔을 때, 그는 중국 상하이로 이동했다.

7 그곳에서 그는 대한민국 임시정부에 합류했고 나중에는 그것의 대표자가 되었다.

8 기념관 안에 있는 전시관은 김구의 삶에 관한 많은 것들을 보여준다.

9 우리는 전시관을 둘러보면서 한인 애국단의 단원들 사진 앞에 섰다.

10 김구는 일본에 맞서 싸우기 위해 1931년에 비밀 조직을 형성했다.

11 이봉창과 윤봉길이 그 집단에 속해 있었다.

12 전시관의 한 곳에서, 우리는 김구와 윤봉길의 사진 아래에 있는 시계 두 개를 보았다.

13 In 1932, Kim Koo _____ a _____ to _____ Japanese _____ in a park in Shanghai.

    A. kill   B. generals   C. made   D. plan

14 As the leader of the Korean Patriotic Organization, he _____ Yun to _____ _____ the _____.

    A. carry   B. directed   C. mission   D. out

15 When Yun _____ for the mission, he told Kim, "Sir, you are wearing a very old watch. Mine is new, but I won't _____ it _____. Please take my watch, and _____ me have yours."

    A. anymore   B. left   C. let   D. need

16 Kim Koo always _____ Yun's watch in his jacket _____ that he would not _____ Yun's _____.

    A. forget   B. carried   C. so   D. sacrifice

17 After _____ the _____ of the museum, we moved to the _____ of the three _____, Lee Bongchang, Yun Bonggil, and Baek Jeonggi.

    A. tombs   B. completing   C. heroes   D. tour

18 Their _____ had _____ in Japan, but after Korea's _____ Kim Koo _____ them to Hyochang Park.

    A. independence   B. been   C. brought   D. bodies

19 _____ doing so, he showed his _____ love and _____ for the _____ of the three heroes.

    A. respect   B. deep   C. by   D. sacrifice

20 _____ I left Hyochang Park, I _____ about Kim Koo's _____ in My Wish that I had read in the _____ hall.

    A. exhibition   B. thought   C. as   D. words

21 It _____ _____ _____ *Baekbeomilji*.

    A. written   B. was   C. in

22 If God asks me _____ my _____ is, I would _____ _____, "It is Korea's Independence."

    A. clearly   B. what   C. say   D. wish

23 If he asks me what my _____ wish is, I _____ say, "It is the _____ of my _____."

    A. independence   B. second   C. would   D. country

24 If he asks me _____ my third wish is, I would say _____, "It is the _____ _____ of my country." That is my answer.

    A. complete   B. what   C. loudly   D. independence

13 1932년에 김구는 상해에 있는 한 공원에서 일본 장군들을 암살하기 위한 계획을 세웠다.

14 한인 애국단의 지도자로서 그는 윤봉길이 임무를 수행하도록 지시했다.

15 윤봉길이 임무를 위해 떠날 때, 그는 김구에게 말했다. "선생님, 당신은 매우 낡은 시계를 차고 계시는군요. 제 것은 새것이나, 저는 그것이 더 이상 필요하지 않을 것입니다. 부디 제 시계를 가져가시고, 제가 선생님 것을 가지도록 해주십시오."

16 김구는 윤봉길의 희생을 잊지 않기 위해서 윤봉길의 시계를 항상 상의에 넣고 다녔다.

17 기념관 관람을 마치고, 우리는 이봉창, 윤봉길, 그리고 백정기 의사들이 묻힌 삼의사의 묘로 이동했다.

18 그들의 시신은 일본에 있다가 독립이 되고 나서 김구가 그들의 시신을 효창 공원으로 가져왔다.

19 그는 그렇게 함으로써 삼의사들의 희생에 대한 그의 깊은 사랑과 경의를 보여 주었다.

20 내가 효창 공원을 떠날 때, 나는 전시관에서 읽었던 「나의 소원」에 있는 김구의 말을 생각했다.

21 그것은 「백범일지」에 쓰여 있었다.

22 만약 신이 나의 소원이 무엇이냐고 묻는다면, "그것은 대한 독립이오."라고 명확하게 말할 것이다.

23 만약에 그가 나의 두 번째 소원이 무엇이냐고 묻는다면, 나는 "그것은 내 나라의 독립이오."라고 말할 것이다.

24 만약 그가 나의 세 번째 소원이 무엇이냐고 묻는다면, "그것은 내 나라의 완전한 독립이오."라고 큰 소리로 말할 것이다. 그것이 나의 대답이다.

※ 다음 우리말과 일치하도록 빈칸에 알맞은 말을 쓰시오.

My Wish

1 Last week _____ _____ _____ went to Hyochang Park.

2 We _____ the Kim Koo Museum _____ _____ _____ .

3 _____ the _____ of the museum, we saw a _____ _____ of Kim Koo.

4 Kim Koo is _____ _____ _____ _____ who _____ most of his life _____ for the _____ of Korea _____ _____ _____ .

5 In the 1900s, he _____ _____ young people _____ _____ schools.

6 _____ 1919, _____ _____ _____ had spread _____ the country, he _____ _____ Shanghai, China.

7 There he _____ the Government of the Republic of Korea and _____ _____ _____ _____ .

8 _____ _____ _____ in the museum _____ a lot of things about Kim Koo's life.

9 _____ _____ _____ the hall, we _____ _____ a photo of the Korean _____ _____ members.

10 Kim Koo _____ the _____ _____ in 1931 _____ _____ _____ Japan.

11 Lee Bongchang and Yun Bonggil _____ _____ the group.

12 _____ one place in the hall, we _____ _____ _____ _____ a photo of Kim Koo and Yun Bonggil.

1 지난주에 우리 역사 동아리는 효창 공원에 갔다.

2 우리는 공원 안에 있는 김구 기념관을 방문했다.

3 기념관 입구에서 우리는 하얀색의 김구 조각상을 보았다.

4 김구는 일본 통치로부터 대한의 독립을 위해 싸우는 데 그의 삶 대부분을 보낸 위대한 국민 영웅이다.

5 1900년대에 그는 학교를 설립함으로써 젊은이들을 교육시키는 것을 도왔다.

6 1919년에 3.1 운동이 나라 전체에 걸쳐 퍼져나갔을 때, 그는 중국 상하이로 이동했다.

7 그곳에서 그는 대한민국 임시정부에 합류했고 나중에는 그것의 대표자가 되었다.

8 기념관 안에 있는 전시관은 김구의 삶에 관한 많은 것들을 보여준다.

9 우리는 전시관을 둘러보면서 한인 애국단의 단원들 사진 앞에 섰다.

10 김구는 일본에 맞서 싸우기 위해 1931년에 비밀 조직을 형성했다.

11 이봉창과 윤봉길이 그 집단에 속해 있었다.

12 전시관의 한 곳에서, 우리는 김구와 윤봉길의 사진 아래에 있는 시계 두 개를 보았다.

13 _____ 1932, Kim Koo _____ _____ _____ kill _____ _____ in a park in Shanghai.

14 As the leader of the Korean _____ _____, he _____ Yun _____ _____ _____ the mission.

15 When Yun _____ _____ the mission, he told Kim, "Sir, you are _____ _____ _____ _____ _____. _____ is new, but I _____ need _____ _____. Please _____ my watch, and _____ me _____ yours."

16 Kim Koo _____ _____ Yun's watch in his jacket _____ _____ he _____ _____ _____ Yun's _____.

17 After _____ the tour of the museum, we _____ _____ the _____ of the _____ _____, Lee Bongchang, Yun Bonggil, and Baek Jeonggi.

18 Their bodies _____ _____ in Japan, but _____ Korea's _____ Kim Koo brought _____ to Hyochang Park.

19 _____ _____ _____, he showed his _____ _____ and respect _____ _____ _____ of the three heroes.

20 _____ I _____ Hyochang Park, I _____ about Kim Koo's _____ in My Wish _____ I _____ _____ in the _____ _____.

21 _____ was _____ _____ *Baekbeomilji*.

22 If God asks me _____ _____ _____ _____, I would say _____, "It is _____ _____."

23 If he asks me _____ _____ _____ _____ _____ is, I would say, "It is the _____ of my country."

24 If he _____ _____ _____ _____, I would say _____, "It is the _____ _____ of my country." That is my answer.

13 1932년에 김구는 상해에 있는 한 공원에서 일본 장군들을 암살하기 위한 계획을 세웠다.

14 한인 애국단의 지도자로서 그는 윤봉길이 임무를 수행하도록 지시했다.

15 윤봉길이 임무를 위해 떠날 때, 그는 김구에게 말했다. "선생님, 당신은 매우 낡은 시계를 차고 계시는군요. 제 것은 새것이나, 저는 그것이 더 이상 필요하지 않을 것입니다. 부디 제 시계를 가져가시고, 제가 선생님 것을 가지도록 해주십시오."

16 김구는 윤봉길의 희생을 잊지 않기 위해서 윤봉길의 시계를 항상 상의에 넣고 다녔다.

17 기념관 관람을 마치고, 우리는 이봉창, 윤봉길, 그리고 백정기 의사들이 묻힌 삼의사의 묘로 이동했다.

18 그들의 시신은 일본에 있다가 독립이 되고 나서 김구가 그들의 시신을 효창 공원으로 가져왔다.

19 그는 그렇게 함으로써 삼의사들의 희생에 대한 그의 깊은 사랑과 경의를 보여 주었다.

20 내가 효창 공원을 떠날 때, 나는 전시관에서 읽었던 「나의 소원」에 있는 김구의 말을 생각했다.

21 그것은 「백범일지」에 쓰여 있었다.

22 만약 신이 나의 소원이 무엇이냐고 묻는다면, "그것은 대한 독립이오."라고 명확하게 말할 것이다.

23 만약에 그가 나의 두 번째 소원이 무엇이냐고 묻는다면, 나는 "그것은 내 나라의 독립이오."라고 말할 것이다.

24 만약 그가 나의 세 번째 소원이 무엇이냐고 묻는다면, "그것은 내 나라의 완전한 독립이오."라고 큰 소리로 말할 것이다. 그것이 나의 대답이다.

※ 다음 문장을 우리말로 쓰시오.

1 ▶ Last week my history club went to Hyochang Park.

➡ _____

2 ▶ We visited the Kim Koo Museum inside the park.

➡ _____

3 ▶ At the entrance of the museum, we saw a white statue of Kim Koo.

➡ _____

4 ▶ Kim Koo is a great national hero who spent most of his life fighting for the independence of Korea from Japanese rule.

➡ _____

5 ▶ In the 1900s, he helped educate young people by building schools.

➡ _____

6 ▶ In 1919, when the independence movement had spread throughout the country, he moved to Shanghai, China.

➡ _____

7 ▶ There he joined the Government of the Republic of Korea and later became its president.

➡ _____

8 ▶ The exhibition hall in the museum shows a lot of things about Kim Koo's life.

➡ _____

9 ▶ While looking around the hall, we stopped at a photo of the Korean Patriotic Organization's members.

➡ _____

10 ▶ Kim Koo formed the secret organization in 1931 to fight against Japan.

➡ _____

11 ▶ Lee Bongchang and Yun Bonggil belonged to the group.

➡ _____

12 ▶ At one place in the hall, we saw two watches under a photo of Kim Koo and Yun Bonggil.

➡ _____

13 ▶ In 1932, Kim Koo made a plan to kill Japanese generals in a park in Shanghai.

➡ _____

14 As the leader of the Korean Patriotic Organization, he directed Yun to carry out the mission.

➡ _____

15 When Yun left for the mission, he told Kim, "Sir, you are wearing a very old watch. Mine is new, but I won't need it anymore. Please take my watch, and let me have yours."

➡ _____

_____

_____

16 Kim Koo always carried Yun's watch in his jacket so that he would not forget Yun's sacrifice.

➡ _____

17 After completing the tour of the museum, we moved to the tombs of the three heroes, Lee Bongchang, Yun Bonggil, and Baek Jeonggi.

➡ _____

18 Their bodies had been in Japan, but after Korea's independence Kim Koo brought them to Hyochang Park.

➡ _____

19 By doing so, he showed his deep love and respect for the sacrifice of the three heroes.

➡ _____

20 As I left Hyochang Park, I thought about Kim Koo's words in My Wish that I had read in the exhibition hall.

➡ _____

21 It was written in *Baekbeomilji*.

➡ _____

22 If God asks me what my wish is, I would say clearly, "It is Korea's independence."

➡ _____

23 If he asks me what my second wish is, I would say, "It is the independence of my country."

➡ _____

24 If he asks me what my third wish is, I would say loudly, "It is the complete independence of my country." That is my answer.

➡ _____

_____

※ 다음 괄호 안의 단어들을 우리말에 맞도록 바르게 배열하시오.

My wish

1 (week / last / history / my / went / club / Hyochang / to / Park.)
➡ _____

2 (visited / we / Kim / the / Koo / inside / Museum / park. / the)
➡ _____

3 (the / at / of / entrance / museum, / the / saw / we / white / a / statue / Kim / of / Koo.)
➡ _____

4 (Koo / Kim / a / is / national / great / who / hero / most / spent / his / of / fighting / life / the / for / of / independence / from / Korea / rule. / Japanese)
➡ _____

5 (the / in / 1900s, / helped / he / young / educate / people / by / schools. / building)
➡ _____

6 (1919, / in / the / when / movement / independence / spread / had / the / throughout / contry, / he / to / moved / China. / Shanghai,)
➡ _____
_____

7 (he / there / the / joined / Government / the / of / Republic / Korea / of / and / became / later / president. / its)
➡ _____
_____

8 (exhibition / the / in / hall / museum / the / shows / lot / a / of / things / about / Koo's / life. / Kim)
➡ _____
_____

9 (looking / while / the / around / hall, / the / stopped / we / a / at / photo / of / Korean / the / Patriotic / members. / Organization)
➡ _____
_____

10 (Koo / Kim / the / formed / secret / in / organization / 1931 / fight / to / Japan. / against)
➡ _____

11 (Bongchang / Lee / and / Bonggil / Yun / to / belonged / group. / the)
➡ _____

12 (one / at / in / place / hall, / the / saw / we / watches / two / a / under / photo / Kim / of / Koo / and / Bonggil. / Yun)
➡ _____
_____

나의 소원

1 지난주에 우리 역사 동아리는 효창 공원에 갔다.

2 우리는 공원 안에 있는 김구 기념관을 방문했다.

3 기념관 입구에서 우리는 하얀색의 김구 조각상을 보았다.

4 김구는 일본 통치로부터 대한의 독립을 위해 싸우는 데 그의 삶 대부분을 보낸 위대한 국민 영웅이다.

5 1900년대에 그는 학교를 설립함으로써 젊은이들을 교육시키는 것을 도왔다.

6 1919년에 3.1 운동이 나라 전체에 걸쳐 퍼져나갔을 때, 그는 중국 상하이로 이동했다.

7 그곳에서 그는 대한민국 임시정부에 합류했고 나중에는 그것의 대표자가 되었다.

8 기념관 안에 있는 전시관은 김구의 삶에 관한 많은 것들을 보여준다.

9 우리는 전시관을 둘러보면서 한인애국단의 단원들 사진 앞에 섰다.

10 김구는 일본에 맞서 싸우기 위해 1931년에 비밀 조직을 형성했다.

11 이봉창과 윤봉길이 그 집단에 속해 있었다.

12 전시관의 한 곳에서, 우리는 김구와 윤봉길의 사진 아래에 있는 시계 두 개를 보았다.

13 (1932, / in / Koo / Kim / a / made / plan / kill / to / generals / Japanese / in / park / a / Shanghai. / in)

➡ _____

14 (the / as / of / leader / Korean / the / Organization, / Patriotic / directed / he / to / Yun / out / carry / mission. / the)

➡ _____

15 (Yun / when / for / left / mission, / the / told / he / you / Kim, / "Sir, / wearing / are / very / a / watch. / old // is / mine / new, / I / but / need / it / won't / anymore. // take / please / watch, / my / and / me / let / yours." / have)

➡ _____
_____
_____

16 (Koo / Kim / carried / always / watch / Yun's / in / jacket / his / that / so / would / he / forget / not / sacrifice. / Yun's)

➡ _____
_____

17 (completing / after / tour / the / the / of / museum, / moved / we / the / to / tombs / the / of / heroes, / three / Bongchang, / Lee / Bonggil, / Yun / and / Jeonggi. / Baek)

➡ _____
_____

18 (bodies / their / been / had / Japan, / in / after / but / independence / Korea's / Koo / Kim / them / brought / Hyochang / to / Park.)

➡ _____
_____

19 (doing / by / so, / showed / he / deep / his / and / love / for / respect / sacrifice / the / the / of / heroes. / three)

➡ _____
_____

20 (I / as / left / Park, / Hyochang / thought / I / Kim / about / words / Koo's / in / Wish / My / that / had / I / read / the / in / hall. / exhibition)

➡ _____
_____

21 (was / it / written / *Baekbeomilji.* / in)

➡ _____

22 (God / if / me / asks / my / what / is, / wish / would / I / clearly, / say / is / "it / Independence." / Korea's)

➡ _____

23 (he / if / asks / what / me / my / wish / second / is, / would / I / say, / is / "it / independence / the / of / country." / my)

➡ _____

24 (he / if / me / asks / my / what / wish / third / is, / would / I / loudly, / say / is / "it / complete / the / of / independence / country." / my // is / that / answer. / my)

➡ _____
_____

13 1932년에 김구는 상해에 있는 한 공원에서 일본 장군들을 암살하기 위한 계획을 세웠다.

14 한인 애국단의 지도자로서 그는 윤봉길이 임무를 수행하도록 지시했다.

15 윤봉길이 임무를 위해 떠날 때, 그는 김구에게 말했다. "선생님, 당신은 매우 낡은 시계를 차고 계시는군요. 제 것은 새것이나, 저는 그것이 더 이상 필요하지 않을 것입니다. 부디 제 시계를 가져가시고, 제가 선생님 것을 가지도록 해주십시오."

16 김구는 윤봉길의 희생을 잊지 않기 위해서 윤봉길의 시계를 항상 상의에 넣고 다녔다.

17 기념관 관람을 마치고, 우리는 이봉창, 윤봉길, 그리고 백정기 의사들이 묻힌 삼의사의 묘로 이동했다.

18 그들의 시신은 일본에 있다가 독립이 되고 나서 김구가 그들의 시신을 효창 공원으로 가져왔다.

19 그는 그렇게 함으로써 삼의사들의 희생에 대한 그의 깊은 사랑과 경의를 보여 주었다.

20 내가 효창 공원을 떠날 때, 나는 전시관에서 읽었던 「나의 소원」에 있는 김구의 말을 생각했다.

21 그것은 「백범일지」에 쓰여 있었다.

22 만약 신이 나의 소원이 무엇이냐고 묻는다면, "그것은 대한 독립이오."라고 명확하게 말할 것이다.

23 만약에 그가 나의 두 번째 소원이 무엇이냐고 묻는다면, 나는 "그것은 내 나라의 독립이오."라고 말할 것이다.

24 만약 그가 나의 세 번째 소원이 무엇이냐고 묻는다면, "그것은 내 나라의 완전한 독립이오."라고 큰 소리로 말할 것이다. 그것이 나의 대답이다.

※ 다음 우리말을 영어로 쓰시오.

1 지난주에 우리 역사 동아리는 효창 공원에 갔다.

➡ _____

2 우리는 공원 안에 있는 김구 기념관을 방문했다.

➡ _____

3 기념관 입구에서 우리는 하얀색의 김구 조각상을 보았다.

➡ _____

4 김구는 일본 통치로부터 대한의 독립을 위해 싸우는 데 그의 삶 대부분을 보낸 위대한 국민 영웅이다.

➡ _____

_____

5 1900년대에 그는 학교를 설립함으로써 젊은이들을 교육시키는 것을 도왔다.

➡ _____

6 1919년에 3.1 운동이 나라 전체에 걸쳐 퍼져나갔을 때, 그는 중국 상하이로 이동했다.

➡ _____

_____

7 그곳에서 그는 대한민국 임시정부에 합류했고 나중에는 그것의 대표자가 되었다.

➡ _____

8 기념관 안에 있는 전시관은 김구의 삶에 관한 많은 것들을 보여 준다.

➡ _____

9 우리는 전시관을 둘러보면서 한인 애국단의 단원들 사진 앞에 섰다.

➡ _____

10 김구는 일본에 맞서 싸우기 위해 1931년에 비밀 조직을 형성했다.

➡ _____

11 이봉창과 윤봉길이 그 집단에 속해 있었다.

➡ _____

12 전시관의 한 곳에서, 우리는 김구와 윤봉길의 사진 아래에 있는 시계 두 개를 보았다.

➡ _____

13 1932년에 김구는 상해에 있는 한 공원에서 일본 장군들을 암살하기 위한 계획을 세웠다.

➡ _____

14 한인 애국단의 지도자로서 그는 윤봉길이 임무를 수행하도록 지시했다.

➡ _____

15 윤봉길이 임무를 위해 떠날 때, 그는 김구에게 말했다. "선생님, 당신은 매우 낡은 시계를 차고 계시는군요. 제 것은 새것이나, 저는 그것이 더 이상 필요하지 않을 것입니다. 부디 제 시계를 가져가시고, 제가 선생님 것을 가지도록 해주십시오."

➡ _____

_____

16 김구는 윤봉길의 희생을 잊지 않기 위해서 윤봉길의 시계를 항상 상의에 넣고 다녔다.

➡ _____

17 기념관 관람을 마치고, 우리는 이봉창, 윤봉길, 그리고 백정기 의사들이 묻힌 삼의사의 묘로 이동했다.

➡ _____

_____

18 그들의 시신은 일본에 있다가 독립이 되고 나서 김구가 그들의 시신을 효창 공원으로 가져왔다.

➡ _____

_____

19 그는 그렇게 함으로써 삼의사들의 희생에 대한 그의 깊은 사랑과 경의를 보여 주었다.

➡ _____

20 내가 효창 공원을 떠날 때, 나는 전시관에서 읽었던 「나의 소원」에 있는 김구의 말을 생각했다.

➡ _____

_____

21 그것은 『백범일지』에 쓰여 있었다.

➡ _____

22 만약 신이 나의 소원이 무엇이냐고 묻는다면, "그것은 대한 독립이오."라고 명확하게 말할 것이다.

➡ _____

23 만약에 그가 나의 두 번째 소원이 무엇이냐고 묻는다면, 나는 "그것은 내 나라의 독립이오."라고 말할 것이다.

➡ _____

24 만약 그가 나의 세 번째 소원이 무엇이냐고 묻는다면, "그것은 내 나라의 완전한 독립이오."라고 큰 소리로 말할 것이다. 그것이 나의 대답이다.

➡ _____

_____

※ 다음 우리말과 일치하도록 빈칸에 알맞은 말을 쓰시오.

Real Life Talk Step 3

1. My group members _____ An Junggeun _____ we _____
   _____ _____ his _____ _____ the country.

2. You _____ _____ _____ _____ him _____ _____
   the An Junggeun Museum or An Junggeun Park.

1. 우리 그룹은 안중근을 선택했는데, 우리 나라를 위한 희생에 깊은 인상을 받았기 때문입니다.
2. 여러분은 안중근 기념관이나 안중근 공원을 방문함으로써 그에 관하여 더 많은 것을 알 수 있습니다.

Enjoy Writing

Dosan An Changho

1. An Changho _____ _____ _____ 1878.

2. _____ he was _____ _____ _____, he _____ _____
   Seoul and _____ _____ school _____.

3. In 1902, he _____ _____ America _____ _____ he could
   _____ _____ _____ _____.

4. In America, An _____ _____ _____ _____ of the Korean
   people there and _____ _____ _____ _____.

5. After he _____ _____ _____ Korea, he _____ the New Korean
   Society in 1907 _____ _____ _____ _____.

6. He also joined the _____ _____ _____
   _____ in Shanghai in 1919.

7. After that, he _____ _____ _____ _____ schools _____
   _____ people _____ he _____ _____ 1938.

도산 안창호
1. 안창호는 1878년에 태어났다.
2. 그가 십 대였을 때, 그는 서울로 이사를 하고 그곳에서 학교를 다녔다.
3. 1902년에 그는 더 나은 교육을 받기 위해서 미국으로 떠났다.
4. 안창호는 미국에서 한국인들의 삶을 개선하는 것을 도왔고, 존경받는 지도자가 되었다.
5. 그가 한국으로 돌아오고 나서, 그는 대한의 독립을 위해 싸우고자 1907년에 신민회를 설립했다.
6. 그는 또한 1919년에 상해의 대한민국 임시정부에 합류했다.
7. 그 후에, 그는 1938년에 죽을 때까지 사람들을 교육하기 위해 많은 학교들을 세웠다.

Project Step 1

1. A: I want _____ _____ Bulguksa _____ _____. You
   know Bulguksa, _____ _____?

2. B: Yes, I do. It's _____ _____ _____ Gyeongju.

3. C: Yes. It's _____ _____ _____ _____ _____ _____
   in Korea.

4. D: It also _____ _____ _____ _____ the Dabotop.

1. A: 나는 외국인에게 불국사를 소개하고 싶어. 너는 불국사를 알고 있지, 그렇지 않니?
2. B: 응, 알고 있어. 그것은 경주에 있는 절이야.
3. C: 응. 그것은 한국에서 가장 아름다운 절 중 하나야.
4. D: 그것은 또한 다보탑과 같은 많은 문화재들을 보유하고 있어.

※ 다음 우리말을 영어로 쓰시오.

Real Life Talk Step 3

1. 우리 그룹은 안중근을 선택했는데, 우리 나라를 위한 희생에 깊은 인상을 받았기 때문입니다.
   ➡ _____
   _____

2. 여러분은 안중근 기념관이나 안중근 공원을 방문함으로써 그에 관하여 더 많은 것을 알 수 있습니다.
   ➡ _____

Enjoy Writing

Dosan An Changho

1. 안창호는 1878년에 태어났다.
   ➡ _____

2. 그가 십 대였을 때, 그는 서울로 이사를 하고 그곳에서 학교를 다녔다.
   ➡ _____

3. 1902년에 그는 더 나은 교육을 받기 위해서 미국으로 떠났다.
   ➡ _____

4. 안창호는 미국에서 한국인들의 삶을 개선하는 것을 도왔고, 존경받는 지도자가 되었다.
   ➡ _____

5. 그가 한국으로 돌아오고 나서, 그는 대한의 독립을 위해 싸우고자 1907년에 신민회를 설립했다.
   ➡ _____
   _____

6. 그는 또한 1919년에 상해의 대한민국 임시정부에 합류했다.
   ➡ _____

7. 그 후에, 그는 1938년에 죽을 때까지 사람들을 교육하기 위해 많은 학교들을 세웠다.
   ➡ _____

Project Step 1

1. A: 나는 외국인에게 불국사를 소개하고 싶어. 너는 불국사를 알고 있지, 그렇지 않니?
   ➡ _____

2. B: 응, 알고 있어. 그것은 경주에 있는 절이야.
   ➡ _____

3. C: 응. 그것은 한국에서 가장 아름다운 절 중 하나야.
   ➡ _____

4. D: 그것은 또한 다보탑과 같은 많은 문화재들을 보유하고 있어.
   ➡ _____

MEMO

MEMO

영어 기출 문제집

적중100

1학기

정답 및 해설

시사 | 박준언

중 3

Lesson 1

All about Me

시험대비 실력평가   p.08

01 basement   02 ②   03 ④   04 ①
05 feels, comfortable   06 ③
07 counsel   08 ⑤

01 '지면 아래에 있는 건물의 일부'라는 의미로 '지하실'이 적절하다.

02 자연은 좋은 친구라고 했으므로 숲속을 걸을 때 기분이 좋다는 말이 자연스럽다.

03 '전에 보거나 듣고 경험했기 때문에 사람이나 사물을 알다'는 뜻으로 'recognize(인식하다)'가 적절하다.

04 두 가지 이상의 것 중에서 선택할 가능성

05 'feel+형용사'는 '~하게 느끼다'는 의미로, '주어가 3인칭 단수'이므로 동사는 feels를 쓰고 '편안한'은 'comfortable'이다.

06 (A) 남들보다 먼저 신기술을 사용하는 사람을 일컫는 'an early adopter'가 적절하다. (B) 프랑스는 유럽에서 한국 고아들의 가장 큰 입양인이다.

07 유의어 관계이다.

08 (A) '다른 사람들보다 먼저 새로운 제품과 기술을 사용한다.'는 의미로 before가 적절하다. (B) '정문이 얼굴을 인식해서 자동으로 열린다.'로 recognizes가 적절하다.

서술형 시험대비   p.09

01 (1) technology   (2) furniture   (3) exciting
    (4) advise
02 (1) stop eating   (2) good at   (3) interested in
    (4) get along with
03 (1) language   (2) nickname   (3) (c)reated
04 (1) fantastic, 환상적인   (2) forward, 앞으로
    (3) imagine, 상상하다
05 (1) (k)ind   (2) (g)oal

01 (1) 나는 컴퓨터 기술(technology)로 만들어진 장면을 좋아해. (2) 그 방은 오래된 가구(furniture)로 가득 차 있다. (3) 내 꿈의 집은 흥미로운(exciting) 것들로 가득 차 있다. (4) 제가 무엇을 해야 할지 조언해(advise) 주시겠어요?

02 (1) '올해 나의 목표는 fast food를 먹는 것을 그만두는 것이다'라는 의미가 적절하다. 'stop+-ing' 형태를 쓴다. (2) '나는 드

럼 연주를 잘한다'라는 의미로 'be good at'이 적절하다. (3) 밤에 별을 보러 나간다고 했으므로 별에 관심이 있다는 의미가 적절하다. 'be interested in'이 '~에 관심이 있다'라는 뜻이다. (4) '동아리에 있는 모든 사람들과 잘 지내기를 바란다'라는 의미로 'get along with'가 적절하다.

03 (1) 언어: language (2) 별명: nickname (3) 만들다: create

04 (1) 매우 좋거나 매력적이고 즐길만한 (2) 당신 앞에 있는 장소나 위치를 향하여 (3) 어떤 것에 대한 마음 속의 그림이나 생각을 형성하거나 가지다

05 (1) kind: 종류; 친절한 / 너는 장래에 어떤 종류의 것들을 원하니? / 친절한 남자가 우리를 도와주었다. (2) goal: 목표; 골, 득점 / 우리의 목표는 쓰레기를 10% 줄이는 것이다. / 리버풀이 3대 1로 이겼다.

교과서 Conversation

핵심 Check   p.10~11

1 ⑤   2 ③

교과서 대화문 익히기

Check(√) True or False   p.12~13

1 T   2 F   3 T   4 F   5 T   6 F   7 T   8 T   9 F

교과서 확인학습   p.15~17

Warm Up

want to tell, myself, interested in, 'm good at playing / refreshed when / 'm interested, usually, to see / designer, practice drawing, win, contest

Listen & Speak 1 A

1. how, grade / pretty / good, homeroom teacher / teaches / Can you tell me, about / humorous, told / fun stories, interesting / enjoy studying
2. to see / looks / about, who saves / looks like / favorite, scenes made, fantastic, real / cool / Sounds

Listen & Speak 1 B

about / have / goal / stop eating

명사절을 이용한다. 선행사가 단수 명사 a hero이므로 save는 단수 형태 saves로 쓴다.

04 B가 I like pizza most.라고 답하고 있으므로 좋아하는 음식이 무엇인지 묻는 말이 적절하다.

05 관계대명사 what을 이용하고 '가장 (많이)'의 의미로 most를 쓴다.

06 궁금증을 표현하거나 보다 많은 정보를 알고 싶을 때 사용하는 표현으로 Can you tell me about ...?을 사용한다.

07 '내가 가장 좋아하는 것은'의 의미를 가지며, 주어 자리에 사용되는 관계대명사 what이 적절하다.

08 ③번은 대화에 언급되어 있지 않다.

09 어떤 그룹의 한 가운데에서

10 이번 주말 계획을 묻는 말에 (B) 생일 파티를 할 예정이라는 답을 하고 → (A) 올해 목표를 묻는 말에 → (C) fast food 먹는 것을 그만두겠다는 대답이 오는 것이 적절하다.

11 ②번은 '너에 관해 말해 줄 수 있니?'라는 A의 말에 '내 친구들은 모두 내게 친절해.'라고 말하는 것은 자연스럽지 않다.

12 관계대명사 What으로 문장을 시작하고 뒤에 '주어+동사' 어순이 온다.

Listen & Speak 2 A

1. go traveling / What, most
2. favorite / Among, playing, what
3. not just / Playing, what

Real Life Talk

'd like to / for, about yourself / in, third / more, What, most / what, to take / photographer / choice, photo-taking / glad

Communication Task Step 2

nickname / because / most / What I like most / Can you tell me about / motto / motto / forward / back

Wrap Up

new student, introduce yourself / from / Can you tell us more / especially / anything / get along with, because / Welcome

---

시험대비 기본평가   p.18

01 Can you tell me about   02 ④   03 ⑤
04 refreshed when

01 궁금증을 표현하거나 보다 많은 정보를 알고 싶을 때 사용하는 표현으로 Can you tell me about ...?을 사용한다.

02 B의 대답으로 보아 앞으로의 계획에 관해 물어보는 말이 적절하다.

03 가장 좋아하는 과목이 음악이고, 드럼과 기타를 연주할 수 있다고 말하고 있으므로 빈칸에는 ⑤번이 가장 적절하다.

04 '~하게 느끼다'는 의미로 'feel+형용사' 형태를 사용한다. refreshed는 형용사로 '상쾌한'의 의미고, '~할 때'의 의미를 가진 접속사는 when을 사용한다.

시험대비 실력평가   p.19~20

01 ③, ⑤   02 (a) traveling   (b) Playing[To play]
03 It is about a hero who saves the Earth.
04 ④   05 what I like most   06 ④
07 ③   08 ③   09 (A)mong
10 (B) – (A) – (C)   11 ②
12 What I like most about traveling

01 '내가 가장 좋아하는 것'이라는 의미로 관계대명사 what과 the thing that이 적절하다.

02 (a) 전치사 about 뒤에 동명사 형태가 적절하고, (b) 주어 자리에 동명사나 to부정사 형태가 오는 것이 적절하다.

03 '~에 관한 것이다'는 be about이고, a hero를 수식하는 관계대

서술형 시험대비   p.21

01 Can you tell us more about yourself?
02 I want to get along with everyone.
03 (A) because I can run fast.
   (B) What I like most is to play baseball.
   (C) What is your motto?
04 about a hero who[that] saves the Earth
05 (a) movie   (b) this weekend

01 '~에 관해 더 말해 줄래?'라는 표현은 Can you tell us more about ~?을 이용한다.

02 get along with ~: ~와 잘 지내다

04 '~에 관한 것이다'는 'be about'을 사용하고, 사람을 선행사로 하는 관계대명사 who나 that을 사용한다. 주격 관계대명사의 동사는 단수 동사인 saves를 쓴다.

05 (a) Amy가 보고 싶어 하는 것은 '영화'다. (b) Ted와 영화를 보러 가기로 한 때는 '이번 주말'이다.

3

Grammar
교과서

핵심 Check   p.22~23

1 (1) do (2) does
2 (1) Janet gave me what she had made.
  (2) What are produced in the factory are cars.

시험대비 기본평가   p.24

01 (1) which → what (2) does → do
   (3) felt → feel (4) what → that
02 ②   03 ⑤
04 (1) What he wrote on the paper was interesting.
   (2) She does feel proud of what her mother
       makes.

01 (1) 전치사 by의 목적어와 had의 목적어 두 개의 명사가 필요한
   자리에 관계대명사 what을 쓴다. (2) 동사를 강조하는 do는 주
   어의 인칭과 수 및 시제 등에 맞춘다. They 뒤에는 do를 쓴다.
   (3) 강조의 do[did]를 쓰면, 동사는 원형이 온다. (4) 선행사
   all 뒤에는 관계대명사 that이 온다. 이 문제의 경우, All을 없애
   고, What만 남겨도 어법상 바르게 된다.
02 ② 강조하는 did가 있으므로 동사 원형 build를 써야 한다.
03 강조하는 do 뒤에는 동사 원형을 써야 한다.
04 (1) 시제에 유의하여 write를 wrote로 쓴다. (2) 인칭과 수 및
   시제에 맞춰 does와 makes를 쓴다.

시험대비 실력평가   p.25~27

01 ④	02 that → what	03 ⑤
04 ③	05 ④	06 ①	07 ②
08 ④	09 ①	10 ④, ⑤	11 ②
12 ③	13 ⓓ, ⓕ	14 ④	15 ③
16 what, was	17 ④	18 ③	19 ⑤
20 ④	21 ①		

01 두 문장이 하나가 되었으므로, 앞 문장에서의 보어와 뒤 문장에
   서의 목적어로 명사 두 개가 필요한데, 이 조건을 충족시키는 것
   은 관계대명사 what이다.
02 what was worse는 '설상가상으로'라는 뜻이다.
03 'Arthur 왕이 전설의 검을 정말로 찾아냈다.'라는 문장과 '전설
   의 검을 찾을 수 있었다.'라는 문장은 서로 같지 않다.
04 첫 번째 빈칸 뒤에 동사원형이 있으므로 강조의 does 또는 did
   가능, 두 번째 빈칸은 선행사와 관계대명사를 포함하여 명사절

을 이끄는 What이 들어가야 한다.
05 '접속사와 대명사 역할의 관계대명사가 필요한 자리이다. 선행사
   가 있으므로 that이 들어간다.
06 동사 강조의 do를 현재시제 3인칭 단수형에 맞게 쓴다. do the
   dishes: 설거지를 하다
07 명령문은 Do로 강조 가능하다. did warned → did warn, did
   changed → did change, does believed → does believe, do
   looks → do look
08 관계대명사 what과 의문대명사 what의 문장 구조는 동일할 때
   가 있다. 이때 구분의 기준은 해석으로서 관계대명사는 '~하는
   것'으로, 의문대명사는 '무엇(이/을)로 해석한다. ④ 너는 엄마
   가 무엇을 요리하고 계시는지 모르겠다. (의문대명사)
09 ② a new car와 his wife의 자리를 바꿔야 한다. ③ what
   → that ④ what → which[that] ⑤ said him → said to
   him(또는 told him)
10 ④ what → which[that] ⑤ Which → What
11 6년 전 과거의 일이므로 does를 did로 바꿔야 한다.
12 강조의 did를 쓰면 동사는 원형이 와야 한다.
13 ⓐ which → what ⓑ what → which[that] ⓒ The thing
   → The thing that[which] 또는 What ⓔ that → what ⓖ
   that → what
14 동사를 강조할 때 do, does, did를 시제와 인칭에 맞게 사용한
   다.
15 동사 강조의 do(does/did)를 찾는다.
16 과거의 그: what he was, 과거의 그의 재산: what he had 현
   재의 그: what he is, 현재의 그의 재산: what he has
17 관계대명사 what과 의문대명사 what을 구분하는 문제이다.
18 ① do → does ② made → make ④ what → which[that]
   ⑤ it 삭제
19 동사 강조의 do(does/did)를 찾는다.
20 Pay attention to what she is saying.
21 ① what → which[that]

서술형 시험대비   p.28~29

01 (1) did build (2) do think (3) did write
02 (1) I don't believe what they said to me the other
      day.
   (2) Show her what you put in your mouth.
   (3) She did feel friendly to Mike.
   (4) I did love Susan, but she left me forever.
   (5) That she asked him to help her was not true.
03 (1) What Sarah bought were comic books.
   (2) Robert couldn't believe what the researchers
      explained.
   (3) What was discussed was shocking.

04 (1) What she had found in the cave surprised the world.

    (2) Do be quiet in this room.

    (3) What she bought from the market were all expensive.

05 (1) Charlie did find his missing child.

    (2) He does know many K-pop singers.

    (3) Jeremy did write those essays last year.

06 (1) Carl himself bought the hamster yesterday.

    (2) It was the hamster that Carl bought yesterday.

    (3) Carl did buy the hamster yesterday.

    (4) It was yesterday that Carl bought the hamster.

07 (1) She finally accepted what he offered.

    (2) He did feel satisfied with the result.

    (3) It is quite different from what they have been waiting for.

    (4) That I saw him yesterday is not true.

    (5) What people believed in the past does surprise me.

08 (1) does (2) that 또는 which (3) kill (4) What, are

09 As John did feel a toothache

---

01 수와 시제 등에 유의하여 do를 활용하되 do 뒤에는 동사원형이 와야 한다.

02 (1) believe의 목적어와 said의 목적어 역할을 하는 what이 적절하다. (2) 그녀에게 '네가 입에 넣은 것'을 보여주라는 문장이므로 접속사 that을 관계대명사 what으로 바꾼다. (3) 강조의 조동사 뒤에는 동사원형이 나온다. (4) 과거시제 동사를 강조할 때는 did + 동사원형이 적절하다. (5) What 뒤에는 불완전한 문장 구조가 나와야 한다. 주어 역할을 하는 명사절을 이끄는 접속사 That이 적절하다.

03 관계대명사 what은 문맥에 따라 단/복수 취급에 유의해야 한다. (1) Sarah가 산 것들은 만화책이었다. (2) Robert는 연구자들이 설명하는 것을 믿을 수 없었다. (3) 논의된 것은 충격적이었다.

04 (1) 관계대명사 what을 활용한다. (2) 명령문의 Be를 강조할 때에도 Do를 사용한다. (3) be동사를 were로 사용하는 것에 주의한다. what은 문맥에 따라 복수 취급도 가능하다.

05 수와 시제 등에 유의하여 do/did/does를 활용하되 강조를 위해 사용한 do 뒤에는 동사 원형이 와야 한다.

06 (1) himself를 문미로 보내도 된다. (2) 'It ~ that 강조 구문'으로 목적어를 강조한다. (3) 'did+동사원형'으로 동사를 강조한다. (4) 부사 yesterday를 'It ~ that 강조 구문'으로 강조한다.

07 (1) '그가 제안하는 것'이므로 what이 적절하다. (2) 강조의 did 뒤에는 동사 원형을 쓴다. (3) '그들이 기다려왔던 것'이므로 what이 적절하다. (4) What 뒤에는 완전한 절이 올 수 없다. 내용상 '내가 어제 그를 보았다는 것'이라는 명사절로서 접속

사 That이 적절하다. (5) does로 강조하면 동사 surprise는 원형을 써야 한다.

08 (1) like가 원형이므로, 부사는 쓸 수 없다. does로 강조한다. (2) 선행사가 있으므로 관계대명사 that 또는 which를 쓴다. (3) 강조의 did 뒤에는 원형동사 kill이 적절하다. (4) 중요한 '것'이므로 주어는 What이 적절하며, what절 내의 동사가 are인 것으로 보아, 본동사도 are가 적절하다.

09 동사를 강조하는 'do'를 시제에 맞게 활용한다.

교과서
Reading

확인문제   p.30

1 T 2 T 3 F 4 F 5 T

확인문제   p.31

1 F 2 F 3 T 4 T 5 F

교과서 확인학습 A   p.32~33

01 Have, ever thought   02 created

03 are, that

04 Nature   05 do feel good

06 like to have, in

07 should have, with

08 am, excited by

09 wonderful to wake up, listen to

10 like to have, to play   11 to

12 Having fun, what, is full of

13 in the basement

14 enjoy, movies   15 has, on, floor

16 kinds of games

17 a swimming pool

18 do fun things, my guest

19 the most important thing

20 feels safe, comfortable

21 At, beautifully designed sign, on

22 enter, see a large living room

23 board games

24 a large picnic table

25 enjoy, Do you like

26 an early adopter

27 do like, before

28 get near, recognizes, opens
29 checks, conditions, advises, on
30 tells me, condition
31 cleans, cooks for
32 what I can imagine

1 Have you ever thought about your dream house?
2 Today, in class, we created our dream house.
3 Here are some of the dream houses that we made.
4 Nature is my good friend.
5 I do feel good when I walk in the forest.
6 I'd like to have a dream house in the countryside.
7 It should have a big garden with many flowers and trees.
8 I am always excited by the sound of birds.
9 It will be wonderful to wake up in the morning and listen to the songs of the birds.
10 Also, I'd like to have many pets. It will be fun to play with them!
11 Welcome to my dream house!
12 Having fun is what I want most, so my dream house is full of exciting things.
13 It has a theater in the basement.
14 There, I can eat cookies and enjoy my favorite movies.
15 My dream house has a game room on the second floor.
16 I can play many different kinds of games there.
17 My house also has a swimming pool.
18 I want to do fun things with my friends in my house. You can be my guest!
19 My family is the most important thing to me.
20 In my dream house, my family feels safe and comfortable.
21 At the gate, you can find a beautifully designed sign with my family's picture on it.
22 When you enter the house, you will see a large living room.
23 My family sometimes plays board games and sings there.
24 It will have a garden with a large picnic table for family picnics.
25 There, we will enjoy barbecues. Do you like my dream house?

26 I am an early adopter of new technology.
27 I do like to use new products and technology before others.
28 When I get near my house, the front door recognizes my face and opens automatically.
29 The furniture checks the weather conditions and advises me on what to wear.
30 The bathroom mirror tells me my weight and the condition of my health.
31 A robot cleans the house and cooks for me.
32 This is what I can imagine about my dream house.

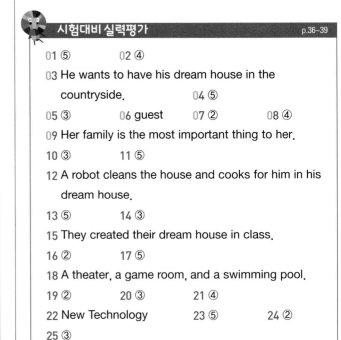

01 ⑤　　　02 ④
03 He wants to have his dream house in the countryside.　　04 ⑤
05 ③　　　06 guest　　07 ②　　08 ④
09 Her family is the most important thing to her.
10 ③　　　11 ⑤
12 A robot cleans the house and cooks for him in his dream house.
13 ⑤　　　14 ③
15 They created their dream house in class.
16 ②　　　17 ⑤
18 A theater, a game room, and a swimming pool.
19 ②　　　20 ③　　　21 ④
22 New Technology　　23 ⑤　　　24 ②
25 ③

01 이어지는 말로 보아 기분이 좋다는 말이 들어가는 것이 적절하다.
02 민호는 자신이 만든 꿈의 집에 대해 말하고 있다.
03 '민호는 시골에 자신의 꿈의 집을 갖기를 원한다고 하였다.
04 주어진 문장의 there가 가리키는 것은 2층에 있는 게임방이라고 보는 것이 적절하다.
05 Julie는 지하실(basement)에 극장을 둔다고 하였다. ground floor: 1층
06 '당신이 초대하여서 당신을 방문한 사람'은 '손님'이다.
07 미선이는 자신의 꿈의 집에 관해 말하고 있으며, 자신에게 가장 중요한 가족을 위한 공간임을 말하고 있다.
08 미선의 가족은 거실에서 보드 게임을 하거나 노래를 부른다고 하였다.
09 미선이는 그녀에게 가족이 가장 중요하다고 하였다.
10 빈칸 ⓐ에 들어갈 말은 관계대명사 what이다. ①, ②, ④에는 관계대명사 that, ⑤에는 명사절 접속사 That이 쓰이며 ③번에

는 what이 쓰인다.

11 adapter: (별개의 전기 기구를 연결하는 데 쓰는) 어댑터, adopter: (신기술) 사용자, get near: 가까워지다, get away: 떠나다, 멀어지다, 날씨 상태를 보고 '무엇을 입을지' 조언한다는 표현이 적절하다.

12 꿈의 집에서 로봇은 Bryan을 위해 청소를 하고 요리를 해준다고 하였다.

13 also는 '또한, 게다가'라는 의미이다. ① 그러나 ② 그럼에도 불구하고 ③ 그러므로 ④ 예를 들어 ⑤ 게다가

14 우리가 만든 꿈의 집 몇 개가 있다'고 말하며 민호의 집을 소개하고 있으므로 이어질 내용으로는 다른 학생이 만든 꿈의 집을 소개하는 내용이 이어진다고 보는 것이 적절하다.

15 수업 시간에 꿈의 집을 만들었다고 하였다.

16 글의 내용으로 미루어 보아 민호는 자연친화적임을 알 수 있다.

17 빈칸 (A)에는 전치사 of가 쓰인다. ① be interested in: ~에 흥미가 있다 ② pay attention to: ~에 주의를 기울이다 ③ depend on: ~에 의존하다 ④ belong to: ~에 속하다 ⑤ get rid of: ~을 없애다

18 Julie가 만든 꿈의 집에는 극장, 게임방, 그리고 수영장이 있다고 하였다.

19 (B)는 '~하는 용도'라는 의미로 쓰인 동명사이다. 모두 현재분사로 명사를 수식하거나 설명하지만 ②번은 동명사이다.

20 각각 ① safe ② large ④ comfortable ⑤ important의 반의어이다.

21 정원에서 바비큐를 즐길 것이라고 하였다. ① 미선은 가족들과 함께 살 것이며, ② 가족들이 집을 안전하고 편안하게 느낄 것이라고 하였다. ③ 꿈의 집에는 거실이 있고, ⑤ 가족들과의 소풍을 위한 피크닉 테이블이 있다.

22 글의 내용으로 보아 'New Technology(새로운 기술)'를 쓰는 것이 적절하다.

23 is의 보어와 imagine의 목적어 역할을 할 수 있는 what을 쓰는 것이 가장 적절하다.

24 새로운 상품이나 기술을 다른 사람들보다 먼저 사용하는 것을 좋아하는 사람이 early adopter이다. 따라서 before라고 쓰는 것이 적절하다.

25 Bryan이 집에 가까워지면 현관이 그의 얼굴을 인식하여 자동으로 문이 열린다고 하였다. story: (건물 등의) 층

서술형 시험대비 p.40~41

01 He feels good when he walks in the forest.
02 They made their dream house in class today.
03 We can find many flowers and trees in the garden of Minho's house.
04 many pets

05 Having fun is what she wants most.
06 We can find a theater in the basement.
07 strange → exciting
08 We can find the game room on the second floor.
09 my family does feel safe and comfortable
10 We can see a beautifully designed sign with her family's picture on it.
11 Misun's dream house
12 like to use new products and technology before others
13 It checks the weather conditions and advises Bryan on what to wear.
14 What
15 It's because she does want to remember what happened in her middle school days.

01 민호는 숲 속을 걸을 때 기분이 좋다고 하였다.

02 학생들은 오늘 수업 시간에 자신들의 꿈의 집을 만들었다고 하였다.

03 많은 꽃과 나무를 가진 큰 정원이 있는 집이라고 하였다.

04 앞 문장의 'many pets'를 지칭하는 말이다.

05 Julie가 가장 원하는 것은 즐거운 시간을 보내는 것이라고 하였다.

06 극장은 지하실에 있다고 하였다.

07 집에는 이상한 것들이 아니라 신나는 것들로 가득 차 있다고 하였다.

08 게임방은 2층에 있다고 하였다.

09 밑줄 친 문장의 동사는 feels이므로 does를 이용하여 강조하는 문장을 만들 수 있다.

10 미선이의 가족 사진이 있는 아름답게 꾸며진 문패를 볼 수 있다.

11 미선이의 꿈의 집을 가리키는 말이다.

12 Early adopter는 신기술 사용자를 의미하며 다른 사람보다 먼저 신제품이나 신기술을 이용하는 것을 좋아하는 사람이다.

13 Bryan의 꿈의 집에서는 가구가 날씨를 확인하고 그에게 무엇을 입을지 조언해 준다고 하였다.

14 put의 목적어와 are의 주어 역할을 할 수 있는 'what'이 적절하다.

15 자신의 중학교 시절에 무슨 일이 일어났는지를 정말로 기억하고 싶어서라고 하였다.

영역별 핵심문제 p.43~47

01 forward 02 ④ 03 ③ 04 ①
05 technology / technology 06 ⑤ 07 ④
08 ⑤ 09 ③ 10 ①, ④ 11 ③

12 What I like most is to play baseball.

13 ⑤

14 (1) Peter that[who] solved the problems

   (2) did solve the problems in the last class

   (3) in the last class that Peter solved the

      problems

15 ①　　　　　16 ④, ⑤　　　　17 what

18 does/did　19 what　　　20 ②　　　21 ⑤

22 ③, ④　　　23 ①, ④

24 The dream house

25 The sound of birds always makes Minho excited.

26 ④　　　　27 ③　　　　28 ③　　　　29 ③

30 It's because it shows what good friends they are.

31 ⑤

32 things Jina wants to put into her memory box

01 반의어 관계다. 넓은 : 좁은 = 뒤로 : 앞으로

02 (a): 우리가 만든 몇 개의 꿈의 집이 여기에 있다는 말로 보아 꿈의 집을 만들었다가 적절하다. (b): 나의 꿈의 집에서 친구들과 재미있는 것을 하고 싶다고 했으므로 너는 내 손님이 될 수 있다는 말이 적절하다.

03 집에서 동반자로 길러지고 친절하게 대접받는 동물

04 믿음이나 목적을 표현하는 짧은 문장이나 문구

05 가구가 날씨를 확인하고 무엇을 입을지 말해 준다고 했기 때문에 새로운 '기술'이 적절하고, 로마인들은 콘크리트를 만드는 데 매우 진보적인 '기술'을 갖고 있었다.

07 (a)는 저녁에 달리는 것을 좋아한다고 했기 때문에 'refreshed'가 적절하고, (b)는 밤에 별을 보러 나간다고 했기 때문에 '~에 관심이 있다'라는 interested가 적절하다.

08 3학년 첫날이 어땠는지 묻는 말에 → (C) 매우 좋았다고 답하고, 담임 선생님이 누군지 묻는 G의 질문에 → (B) 담임 선생님에 대한 설명이 오고, 선생님에 대해 더 말해 달라는 G의 물음에 → (A) 긍정의 답을 하고 선생님에 대한 추가적인 설명을 하는 것이 적절하다.

09 제시문의 여가 시간에 무엇을 하는지 묻는 말은 사진을 찍는 것을 가장 좋아한다는 대답 앞에 오는 것이 적절하다.

10 Seho의 대답이 사진작가가 되고 싶다고 했으므로 (A)에는 미래의 직업이나 꿈을 묻는 말이 적절하다.

11 Seho가 이미 많은 사진촬영 기술을 알고 있는지는 대화에 언급되어 있지 않다.

13 ① Jenny가 3인칭 단수이므로 does look이 적절하다. ② They look handsome on the stage. be동사와 상태를 나타내는 look이 같이 쓰였다. are를 생략하거나 do look으로 강조해야 한다. ③ does believe가 적절하다. ④ 과거동사 met을 강조할 때는 did meet이 적절하다.

14 원래의 문장을 영작하면, Peter solved the problems in the

last class.이다. (1) 주어인 Peter 강조 (2) 동사 solve를 강조하기 위해 did 사용 (3) 부사구인 in the last class를 강조하기 위해 'It ~ that 강조 구문' 사용

15 첫 번째 문장에서는 '백악관 앞에서 찍힌 것들(사진들)'을 가리키는 말이므로 what이 적절하다. 두 번째 문장에서는 동사 원형 start로 보아 did가 적절하다.

16 ④ does like가 적절하다. ⑤ 강조의 did 뒤에는 동사 원형을 써야 한다.

17 the thing(s) that[which] = what

18 '노인과 바다'는 3인칭 단수이고, 동사원형 make가 쓰였으므로, 강조의 조동사 does 또는 did가 적절하다.

19 showed와 believed의 목적어가 들어갈 자리이므로 what이 적절하다.

20 do some laundry '빨래를 하다'라는 뜻의 본동사이다. 다른 문장들의 do[does, did]는 강조를 위해 사용되었다. villain role: 악역

21 ① (A) 본동사 (B) 강조 ② (A) 강조 (B) 본동사 ③ (A) 본동사 (B) 강조 ④ (A) 강조 (B) 의문문을 만드는 조동사 ⑤ (A) 본동사 (B) 본동사

22 ③ said의 목적어와 was의 주어 두 가지 역할을 하는 자리이므로 That을 What으로 고쳐야 한다. ④ 선행사가 있으므로 what이 아닌 관계대명사 which나 that이 적절하다.

23 사물을 선행사로 받아주는 목적격 관계대명사 which나 that이 적절하다.

24 앞 문장에서 제시한 꿈의 집을 가리키는 말이다.

25 민호는 새 소리에 항상 신난다고 하였다.

26 (B)는 가주어 It이다. ①, ② 비인칭 주어 ③, ⑤ 인칭대명사

27 민호의 꿈의 집은 도시 한 가운데가 아닌 시골에 있다고 하였다.

28 spend+시간+Ving: V하느라 시간을 보내다

29 (A)는 '마지막으로'라는 의미이다.

30 세민이로부터 온 편지를 넣으려는 이유는 그들이 얼마나 좋은 친구인지를 보여 주어서이다.

31 지나가 언제 축구를 시작했는지는 위 글을 읽고 알 수 없다.

32 위 글은 지나가 자신의 기억 상자에 넣기를 원하는 것들에 관한 것이다.

단원별 예상문제　　　　　　　p.48~51

01 advise　　　02 ②

03 really curious about your dream job

04 (1) He is from Busan.　(2) He likes soccer.

   (3) He wants to get along with everyone.

05 Is there anything else you want to tell your new friends?

06 (1) What Jiho likes most about traveling is trying new foods.

   (2) What Bora likes most is playing the guitar.

(3) What Jenny likes most is playing with her pet[Dora] in her free time.

07 ④　　　　　08 ③　　　　　09 ②

10 what I like most is to take pictures　　　11 ⑤

12 things which　　　　13 ①, ②, ④　　14 ③, ⑤

15 (1) That is not what Harry has always wanted.
　 (2) My parents already know what happened three weeks ago.
　 (3) Tell her what have been bothering you.

16 ⓐ the soccer ball　ⓑ the school newspaper
　 ⓒ the letter

17 What I hope from you　　18 ④　　　19 ④

20 ③　　　　　21 ③　　　　　22 recognize

23 It tells him his weight and the condition of his health.

01 유의어 관계다. 대답하다 = 조언하다

02 도시에 있지 않고 농장, 밭 등을 가질 수도 있는 땅

03 궁금증을 표현하거나 보다 많은 정보를 알고 싶을 때 'be curious about+명사'를 사용할 수 있다.

04 (1) Hojun의 출신지는 부산이고, (2) 축구를 좋아한다. (3) 모두와 잘 지내기를 원한다.

06 '~가 가장 좋아하는 것'의 의미로 관계대명사 what을 이용하여 'What+주어+likes most is ~'를 쓴다.

07 명사 the scenes를 수식하는 분사 형태로 '컴퓨터 기술로 만들어진 장면'이므로 수동의 의미를 갖는 과거분사 made가 적절하다.

08 영화는 지구를 구하는 영웅에 관한 것이다.

09 Seho의 대답으로 보아 빈칸 (A)에는 '너에 대해 말해 줄래?'라는 표현이 적절하다. ⑤번은 대답이 No로 나와야 하므로 적절하지 않다.

10 '내가 가장 좋아하는 것은'의 의미로 관계대명사 what을 이용하여 'What+주어(I)+동사(like) most is ~'를 쓴다.

11 Seho의 사진작가가 되고 싶다는 말에 대해 '그렇다면 올바른 선택을 했어.'라는 말이 오는 것이 적절하다.

12 본동사가 were이므로 선행사를 복수로 쓴다.

13 ① 선행사 the only one이 있으므로 선행사를 포함하는 관계대명사 what은 불가능하다. who도 좋지만 the only가 선행사 앞에 올 때는 관계대명사 that을 더 자주 쓴다. ② 강조의 did 뒤에 과거형 동사가 있다. 원형동사로 바꿔 줘야 적절하다. ④ 'It ~ that 강조 구문'의 be동사는 is/was 둘 뿐이다.

14 what이 관계대명사인지 의문대명사인지 구분하는 것은 해석으로 판단한다. 때로는 구분이 모호한 경우도 많다. 일반적으로 의문대명사 what은 '무엇'으로, 관계대명사 what은 '~하는 것'으

로 해석한다. ① 의문대명사 ② 의문대명사 ③ 관계대명사 ④ 의문대명사 ⑤ 관계대명사 (과거에 예의바른 것으로 여겨졌던 것이 오늘날 항상 그렇게 여겨지는 것은 아니다.)

15 관계대명사 what은 선행사를 포함하며, 문맥에 따라 단/복수 취급한다. (1) 그것은 Harry가 항상 원해 왔던 것이 아니다. (2) 나의 부모님은 3주 전에 생긴 일들을 이미 알고 있다. (3) 그녀에게 너를 괴롭혀 오고 있는 것들을 말하라.

16 축구를 하며 시간을 많이 보내기 때문에 축구공을, 중학교 시절에 무슨 일이 일어났는지 기억하고 싶으므로 신문을, 진짜 친구임을 보여주는 것이므로 편지를 넣는다고 보는 것이 적절하다.

17 '~하는 것'이므로 what을 써서 문장을 만든다.

18 Jina는 3가지 물건을 추억 상자에 넣으며 자신이 이것을 영원히 간직하기를 원한다.

19 enter는 '~로 들어가다'라는 의미의 타동사로, 전치사 없이 목적어를 취한다. 따라서 into 없이 enter만 쓰는 것이 적절하다.

20 큰 피크닉 테이블은 정원에 있다고 하였다.

21 현관문이 Bryan의 얼굴을 알아보고 자동으로 문을 열어준다고 하였다. identify: (신원 등을) 확인하다, 알아보다

22 사람이나 사물을 알아보는 것은 'recognize'이다.

23 욕실 거울은 그의 체중과 건강 상태에 대해 말해 준다고 하였다.

🦉 서술형 실전문제　　　　　　p.52~53

01 (A) how was your first day of third grade?
　 (B) Can you tell me more about him?

02 I like the scenes made with computer technology.

03 (1) He likes to take pictures most.
　 (2) He can learn a lot of photo-taking skills.

04 (1) I must make the most of what I have.
　 (2) What you do is much more important than what you say.

05 (1) People in Hong Kong do love freedom.
　 (2) Was it yesterday that he broke the door?
　 (3) The wall was painted by Mr. Lee himself.

06 (1) the furniture
　 (2) a robot
　 (3) the bathroom mirror

07 It does open automatically

08 what to do → what to wear /
　 my classroom → the house

09 a beautifully designed sign

10 They will enjoy barbecues in the garden.

02 '주어(I)+동사(like)+목적어(the scenes)' 어순으로 문장을 시작하고, the scenes 뒤에 과거분사 made with computer

9

technology를 써서 명사 the scenes를 수식한다.

03 (1) Seho는 여가 시간에 무엇을 하는 것을 가장 좋아하는가?
   (2) Seho는 사진 동아리에서 무엇을 배울 수 있는가?

04 (1) make the most of: ~을 최대한 이용하다 (2) 관계대명사 what을 이용해야 글자 수에 맞는 영작이 가능하다.

05 (1) 동사의 강조는 do를 사용한다. (2) 부사를 강조할 때는 'It ~ that 강조 구문'을 쓴다. 의문문이므로, 의문문의 형식으로 be동사 was와 it의 위치를 바꿔 준다. (3) 명사의 강조를 위해 재귀대명사를 사용한다. Mr.는 남성이므로 himself가 적절하다.

06 날씨를 확인하는 것은 가구, 요리를 하는 것은 로봇, 건강 상태를 말해 주는 것은 화장실 거울이다.

07 정말로 문이 자동으로 열리는지 묻고 있으므로 동사를 강조하여 '정말로 자동으로 문이 열린다'라고 쓸 수 있다.

08 가구가 날씨를 확인하고 무엇을 입을지 알려준다고 하였고, 로봇은 집을 청소한다고 하였다.

09 아름답게 만들어진 문패를 가리키는 말이다.

10 정원에서 바비큐를 즐길 것이라고 하였다.

창의사고력 서술형 문제   p.54

|모범답안|

01 Can you tell me about / to have a birthday party / Can you tell me about / stop eating fast food

02 (1) |모범답안| I know what Ms. Smith was looking for in the kitchen.
   (2) |모범답안| What Brian bought at the market was the bag.
   (3) |모범답안| This book is what Kathy found at the library.

03 my dancing shoes, the first prize from a dancing performance, some pictures with friends / my dancing shoes, they are related to my future dream / the first prize from a dancing performance, I can remember my happiest moment / put in some pictures with friends, I don't want to forget my friends from middle school

단원별 모의고사   p.55~58

01 ④   02 draw   03 ①   04 ④
05 ③   06 ②, ⑤   07 ③

08 He wants to join a sports club. / He wants to get along with everyone.

09 Can you tell me about your best friend?

10 What do you like most / What I like most / What I

like most, listen to

11 ④   12 ⑤

13 (1) what Sarah wrote in her mail
   (2) what Gloria wants to visit someday

14 ③   15 ③, ⑤

16 (1) This is what she purchased from a Japanese carpenter last year.
   (2) It was the English teacher who moved the heavy box.
   (3) What John fixed in the office was a photocopy machine.

17 pet   18 ⑤

19 He feels good when he walks in the forest.

20 ①, ③   21 It means an elephant.   22 ⑤

23 It's because having fun is what she wants most.

24 She can eat cookies and enjoy her favorite movies.

01 ④번은 create에 대한 설명이다.

02 유의어 관계이다. 들어가다 : 그리다

03 나무로 덮여 있는 넓은 지역의 땅

04 A가 '가장 좋아하는 과목에 관해 말해 줄래?'라는 말에 B가 '미술 교사가 되고 싶어.'라고 말하는 것은 어색하다.

05 B가 '내가 가장 좋아하는 것은 야구를 하는 거야.'라고 대답하고 있으므로 C는 무엇을 가장 좋아하는지 묻는 것이 자연스럽다.

06 B의 대답으로 보아 가장 좋아하는 과목을 묻는 말이 적절하다.

07 빈칸 다음의 말이 '여기 새로 왔기 때문에 나를 도와줘.'라고 했으므로 모두와 잘 지내고 싶다는 ③번이 가장 적절하다.

10 가장 좋아하는 것을 묻는 표현은 'What do you like most?'를 사용하고, 가장 좋아하는 것을 말하는 표현은 'What I like most is ~'를 사용한다.

11 (A)와 (B)에 공통으로 들어갈 수 있는 말은 '내가 가장 좋아하는 것'이다.

12 motto는 자신의 믿음이나 인생의 가치관, 신념을 표현하는 짧은 문장이나 문구를 말하는 것으로 ⑤번은 속담(proverb)으로 '집만한 곳은 없다'는 모토가 되기에 어색하다.

13 (1)과 (2) 각각의 선행사와 관계대명사를 써보면, the words that, the place which가 되는데, 문맥상 what으로 바꾸는 데 무리가 없다.

14 '①, ②, ③은 모두 'It ~ that 강조 구문'의 형식을 취하고 있는데, ③에서 보인 very hungry는 'It ~ that 강조 구문'의 강조 대상이 될 수 없다. ④, ⑤는 동사를 강조하는 형태로 문법적으로 어색한 부분이 없다.

15 ①, ②, ④는 모두 조동사로서 각각 부정문, 의문문, 명령의 조동사로 사용됐다. ③, ⑤는 동사를 강조하는 do/did로 사용되었고, 주어진 문장의 밑줄 친 does와 같은 기능을 한다.

17 우리 곁에 있으면서 즐거움을 주기 위해 집에 데리고 있는 동물은 '애완동물'이다.

18 [B]의 첫 문장에서 It이 가리키는 것은 [C]에 나오는 시골의 꿈의 집이다. [B]에서 새 소리에 신난다고 하였고 [A]에서 새 소리를 들으며 잠에서 깨는 것이 아주 멋질 것이라고 하였다. 따라서 [C]-[B]-[A]가 가장 자연스럽다.

19 숲 속을 걸을 때 기분이 좋다고 하였다.

20 사람들은 Tanabat을 Chang이라고 부른다. Carl의 이름은 부모님이 지어준 것이 아니라 어떤 목록에서 선택된 것이라고 하였다.

21 Chang은 코끼리를 의미한다고 하였다.

22 수영장이 2층에 있다는 말은 나와 있지 않다.

23 Julie의 꿈의 집에 신나는 것들이 가득 차 있는 이유는 그녀가 가장 원하는 것이 즐거움이기 때문이다.

24 Julie는 극장 안에서 쿠키를 먹고 자신이 가장 좋아하는 영화를 볼 수 있다고 하였다.

2
Experience Different Cultures!

01 '민희의 가족이 미국으로 이사 온 이후로, 그들은 한국과 미국의 문화적 차이를 많이 경험했다.

02 대화의 내용상 A가 영어로 주소를 쓰는 방법에 대해 조언(advice)을 해줄 수 있니?라고 묻는 말이 적절하다.

03 '영화관, 극장 등에 들어갈 수 있도록 지불하는 돈'의 의미로 '입장료'가 적절하다.

04 '편안하고 쾌적하지 않거나, 편안하고 쾌적하지 못하도록 하는'의 의미로 '불편한'이 적절하다.

05 '…로 여겨지다'는 'be regarded as …'이다.

06 (A) 미국인들은 "너 오고 있지 않니?"와 같은 부정의문문으로 종종 묻는다. (B) 과학자들은 그 이론에 대해 상당히 부정적인 태도를 취하고 있다.

07 한국-한국인, 한국어의 관계와 같이 중국(China)-중국인 또는 중국어를 나타내는 Chinese가 적절하다.

08 (A) 미국에서는 제품을 구매할 때 판매세라는 세금을 지불한다는 내용이므로 '세금'을 뜻하는 tax가 적절하다. (B) They는 Sales tax rates를 가리키므로 '판매세의 비율'이 '~의 범위에 이르다'라는 range가 적절하다.

서술형 시험대비
p.63

01 (1) stayed (2) Make (3) tag (4) cultural

02 (A) In response to (B) the same as (C) positive

03 (1) rude (2) prepare (3) shorts, temple

04 (1) wave, 흔들다 (2) correctly, 정확하게

　(3) exchange, 교환하다

05 (1) (g)ood (2) (h)and

01 (1) 집에 머물렀다는 과거형 stayed가 적절하다. (2) '반드시 ~해라'라는 의미로 'Make sure+주어+동사'를 사용한다. (3) 가격표에 있는 가격보다 많이 지불한다는 의미로 tag가 적절하다. (4) 명사를 수식하는 형용사 형태로 cultural이 적절하다.

02 (A) ~의 대답으로: in response to (B) ~와 같은: the same as (C) 긍정의: positive

03 (1) 무례한: rude (2) 준비하다: prepare (3) 반바지: shorts, 사원: temple

04 (1) 누군가에게 인사하기 위한 방법으로 손을 들고 좌우로 움직이다 (2) 참된 사실 또는 일반적으로 받아들여지는 것과 일치하는 방식으로 (3) 누군가에게 무언가를 주고 그 사람에게서 무언가를 받다

05 (1) good: (형) 좋은, (명) (-s) 상품 / 그들은 또한 우리들을 잘 돌보아 줍니다. / 그날 그 가게는 있는 상품을 모조리 진열했다. (2) hand: (명) 손, (동) 건네주다 / 그녀에게 그것을 건네줄 때 두 손을 사용해야 해.

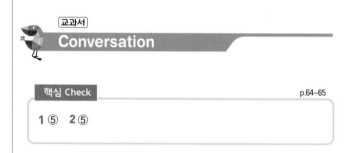

교과서
Conversation

핵심 Check
p.64~65

1 ⑤ 2 ⑤

교과서 대화문 익히기

Check(√) True or False
p.66~67

1 F 2 T 3 F 4 T 5 T 6 F 7 F 8 T

교과서 확인학습
p.69~71

Warm Up

1. show their tongues
2. place, together
3. bump their noses

Listen & Speak 1 A

1. to send, aunt / What / get, advice, how to write, address / street address / Like / state / postal code, Finally

2. Look at, wearing traditional, to take pictures of / There is, before taking / advice on / take pictures of Moroccan, without asking / a bad effect on, when

Listen & Speak 1 B

Can I get, advice, visiting / shouldn't, path / get your

advice on visiting / should sit, back seat

Listen & Speak 2 A

1. present, have stayed / What, buy / bought / Make sure, hand, to / giving, is regarded as rude

2. pack / yet, take / Remember to bring / isn't / there are, temples, shorts, temple / else / Make sure, exchange, to

Listen & Speak 2 B

remember, France / Make sure, keep, on, at all times / anything, when / Make sure, take off, when having

Real Life Talk

Chinese, invited / having / prepare, several, advice, what to bring / How about / Most, receive, as, present, drinking, serve, guests / that / Make sure, wrap, mean death / advice

Communication Task Step 2

Which / get, advice, traveling / Make sure, hand

Wrap Up

1. going, get, visiting / pay, get off / remember / Pick, while eating, when having, without

2. to give, from, remember / Make sure

시험대비 기본평가   p.72

01 Can I get your advice on what to wear?

02 ⑤   03 ③   04 place, together

01 'Can I get your advice on ~?'이 '제가 당신의 조언을 구할 수 있을까요?'라는 의미이다. '무엇을 입을지'는 '의문사+to V'를 이용한다.

02 상대방에게 충고하는 표현으로 'had better+동사원형 ~', 'Don't forget to+동사원형 ~', 'remember to+동사원형 ~'을 사용할 수 있다.

03 B가 '자전거 도로에 서 있으면 안 돼.'라고 말하는 것으로 보아 빈칸에는 주의해야 할 일에 대해 물어보는 말이 자연스럽다.

04 '~을 모으다'는 'place 목적어 together'를 쓴다.

시험대비 실력평가   p.73~74

01 ③   02 ②   03 ③   04 ⑤

05 Make sure   06 ④

07 Remember to bring a pair of long pants or a long skirt.

08 ②   09 ④   10 ⑤

01 B가 'You should write the street address first.'라고 말하고 있으므로 영어로 주소를 쓰는 방법을 물어보는 말이 적절하다.

02 여학생이 한복을 입을지 말지를 결정해야 하는 내용은 대화에 언급되어 있지 않다.

03 어떤 나라를 방문하고 싶은지 묻는 말에 (B) 말레이시아를 방문하고 싶다고 말하고, 여행할 때 조언을 구하고 있다. → (C) 여행할 때 주의해야 할 일에 대해 말해주자 → (A) 고맙다고 답한다.

04 B의 대답이 '거리에서 껌을 씹으면 안 돼.'라고 주의를 주고 있으므로, 싱가포르에서 주의해야 할 조언을 구하는 질문이 적절하다.

05 남자의 질문이 '러시아에서 온 친구에게 꽃을 줄 때 기억해야 할 것이 있니?'라고 묻고 있으므로, 상대방에게 경고하는 표현으로 'Make sure+주어+동사 ~'의 형태를 사용한다.

06 ④번은 '그녀가 그것을 좋아할까?'라는 A의 물음에 '반드시 그것을 줄 때는 두 손을 사용해라.'라고 말하는 것은 자연스럽지 않다.

07 '~할 것을 기억하다'는 'remember to V'를 사용한다. 바지는 항상 복수형을 사용해야 하는 pants를 사용해야 한다.

08 'Make sure+주어+동사 ~'는 상대방에게 주의나 경고를 할 때 사용하는 표현이다.

09 제시문은 '내가 알아야 할 또 다른 것이 있을까?'라는 뜻으로 또 다른 조언을 구한다는 것을 알 수 있다. 두 번째 조언을 구하는 부분으로 ④가 적절하다.

10 어떤 색깔로 선물을 포장해야 하는지는 언급되어 있지 않다.

서술형 시험대비   p.75

01 Can I get your advice on what to bring?

02 Make sure you don't wrap the present in white or black paper.

03 (A) What should I take?

(B) You shouldn't wear shorts when you visit a temple.

(C) Make sure you exchange Korean won to Thai baht.

04 123 Van Ness Street, San Francisco, California 94101, USA

01 조언을 구할 때는 'Can I get your advice on ~?'으로 표현할 수 있다.

02 make sure 다음에 접속사 that을 생략할 수 있고 당부하고자 하는 내용을 주어와 동사를 갖춘 문장으로 쓴다.

04 영어로 주소를 쓸 때는 '거리 주소, 도시, 주, 우편번호, 나라'의 순서로 쓴다.

핵심 Check   p.76~77

1 (1) since (2) for
2 (1) repaired (2) broken

시험대비 기본평가   p.78

01 (1) understanding → understood
   (2) gone → been (3) studied → studying
   (4) writing → written
02 ④   03 ②
04 (1) The picture taken by Peter was interesting.
   (2) Billy's mom has been cooking for five hours.

01 (1) 불어로 자기 자신을 이해받게(남들이 이해하도록) 만드는
    것이므로, 과거분사를 써야 한다. make oneself understood:
    소통하다, 이해시키다 (2) 1, 2인칭의 주어 뒤에 have gone은
    어법상 부적절하다. (3) 작년 이후로 수학을 공부하는 중이라는
    현재완료진행시제이므로, have been+V-ing 형태가 적절하다.
    (4) 스페인어로 쓰여진 편지이므로, written이 적절하다.
02 현재완료진행시제는 '동작'이 아닌 '상태'를 나타내는 know 등
    의 동사는 쓸 수 없다.
03 피곤함을 느끼는 것은 능동이 아니라 수동의 과거분사를 써야 한
    다.
04 (1) take를 과거분사로 써야 함에 유의한다. (2) 수와 시제에 맞
    춰 has been cooking을 쓴다.

시험대비 실력평가   p.79~81

01 ③   02 making → made
03 (1) many people watching
   (2) built by my father is
04 ③   05 has been playing, for   06 ②
07 wearing a yellow T-shirt is sitting under the maple
08 ⑤   09 ①, ④, ⑤   10 ⑤
11 (1) writing → witten (2) making → made
   (3) cried → crying   12 ⑤   13 ①, ④
14 ⑤   15 ⑤
16 (1) has been listening (2) have been painting
   (3) has been teaching (4) has been taking
   (5) have been traveling
17 (A) written (B) known (C) named (D) related
18 ②   19 sitting, nothing

01 '과거+현재진행'은 현재완료진행시제로 표현한다. has been
    writing이 적절하다.
02 필리핀에서 제조된 가방이므로 과거분사가 적절하다.
03 분사가 명사의 뒤에서 꾸며주는 것을 적절히 활용한다. (1)
    은 watching fireworks가 people을 꾸며주고(능동), (2)는
    built by my father가 warehouse를 뒤에서 꾸민다.(수동)
04 (1) 쓰레기를 줍는 소녀(능동) (2) 휴가에 쓰인 돈(수동) (3) 지
    루한 강의(능동) 등에 적절하게 분사를 활용한다.
05 과거에 시작된 일이 현재에도 진행되고 있을 때, 현재완료진행시
    제로 표현한다. 동사는 has been playing이 적절하고, 전치사
    는 기간(~ 동안)을 나타내는 for가 알맞다.
06 ②는 tried의 목적어로 쓰인 동명사이고, 나머지는 모두 명사를
    앞 또는 뒤에서 꾸며주는 현재분사이다.
07 분사가 명사 뒤에서 꾸며주는 것을 활용한다. 능동이므로 wearing
    을 사용하고, 본동사는 'be동사+sitting'을 쓴다.
08 ⓐ 타는 불, ⓑ 지나가는 학생들 모두 '진행'의 의미를 갖고 있으
    며, 명사를 앞, 뒤에서 꾸며주고 있다.
09 ① 이야기책을 읽는 소녀이므로 reads → reading ④ '거짓말
    을 해오고 있다'는 뜻으로 현재완료진행형을 써야 한다. lied →
    lying, ⑤ 내 가족이 만난 사람들이므로, 분사가 아니라 관계사
    절의 동사가 적절하다. meeting → met
10 ① 직업을 잃는 것은 현재완료진행형으로 쓸 수 없다. has been
    losing→ has lost ② 관계대명사 뒤에는 동사를 써야 한다.
    who 뒤에 was를 추가하거나, sitting을 sat으로 바꾼다. ③
    rides→ riding ④ 남겨진 과자가 없는 것이므로 leaving →
    left가 적절하다.
11 (1) 쓰인 책(수동) (2) 만들어진 쿠키(수동) (3) 우는 아기(능동)
12 <보기>는 현재완료시제의 용법 중 '경험'이며, ⑤는 'Emily가
    가족과 하와이로 떠나서 현재 여기 없다'는 내용의 '결과' 용법으
    로 사용되었다.
13 ① 신나는 날 excited→ exciting ④ 감동적인 장면들
    touched → touching
14 현재완료시제의 '계속' 용법, 또는 현재완료진행시제가 적절하다.
15 현재완료진행시제는 과거에 시작한 일이 현재까지 진행되고 있
    음을 의미하며, ⑤를 제외하고 모두 가능하다. ⑤는 명백한 과
    거시제 표현이므로 부적절하다.
16 (1) 라디오 프로그램 청취 (2) 낙후된 마을 벽에 그림 그리기 (3)
    수학 강의 (4) 약 복용 (5) 유럽 여행 등의 내용에 적절하게 동사
    를 선택하고, 주어의 수에 has/have 등을 활용하여 현재완료진
    행시제를 쓴다.
17 (A) 쓰여진 소설 (B) ~로서 알려진 악기를 연주하는 (C) ~라고
    이름 불리는 (D) 관련된 영화
18 <보기>는 현재완료의 용법 중 '계속'이며, 과거에 시작된 일이
    현재에도 지속되고 있음을 나타낸다. ②는 '청소를 끝냈다'는 내
    용으로, '완료' 용법으로 사용되었다.

19 어법에 맞게 배열하면, 'Have you been sitting here calmly and doing nothing to help them?'이 된다.

서술형 시험대비

p.82~83

01 (1) David has been chewing gum after dinner for an hour.

(2) Margaret has been blogging since she first started the Internet.

(3) Our team members have been working out in the gym for over six hours.

02 (1) has been practicing playing the drums for 6 weeks

(2) has been writing letters for 3 hours

03 (1) flying　(2) washing　(3) standing　(4) sitting

(5) closed　(6) sent　(7) written

04 (1) old lady standing across the street

(2) boys performing on that stage

(3) the flowers planted in an old boat

05 ⓐ calling → called

해석: Hoop King이라고 불리는 뛰어난 선수는 정말 농구 경기를 잘했다.

ⓑ taken → taking

해석: 우리는 오스트리아의 한 오래된 광장에서 사진을 찍는 많은 관광객들을 볼 수 있었다.

ⓒ producing → produced

해석: 스위스에서 생산된 시계들이 세계 최고의 명성을 누린다.

ⓓ writing → written

해석: 북 콘서트에 참가한 모든 사람들은 그의 어린 딸에 의해 쓰여진 책 제목을 알게 되었다.

ⓔ flown → flying

해석: 하늘 위로 날아가는 철새 무리들이 격려의 소리를 내고 있었다.

06 Frank has been doing his son's homework for three hours.

07 (A) has been suffering　(B) pulled

08 (1) with the crying baby

(2) an illegally parked truck

(3) the birds flying over the buildings

01 현재완료진행시제에 맞게 각 단어를 적절히 활용한다.

03 (1)~(4)는 현재분사, (5)~(7)은 과거분사를 쓴다.

04 명사의 뒤에서 꾸미는 분사 활용 (1) 서 있는 할머니(능동) (2) 공연하는 소년들(능동) (3) 심어진 꽃들(수동)

05 ⓐ Hoop King이라고 불리는 선수(수동) ⓑ 사진을 찍는 관광객들(능동) ⓒ 생산된 시계(수동) ⓓ 쓰인 제목(수동) ⓔ 날아가는 철새들(능동) 등에 맞게 분사를 적절히 고치고, 분사의 의

미에 맞게 우리말로 해석한다.

06 3시간 전에 집에 도착한 아들이, 집에 도착하자마자 아버지에게 숙제를 보여줬고, 즉시 아들 대신 숙제를 시작한 아버지 Frank가 3시간 동안 숙제를 하고 있는 중이므로, 현재완료진행시제를 활용하여 영작한다.

07 (A) 빈칸이 3개이고, 내용상 현재완료진행형이므로, has been suffering이 적절하다. (B) 이가 뽑히는(수동) 것이므로 과거분사 pulled가 적절하다.

08 (1) 울고 있는 아기 (2) 불법으로 주차된 트럭(부정관사 an에 유의한다.) (3) 건물들 위로 날아가고 있는 새들

교과서 Reading

확인문제
p.84

1 F　2 F　3 F

확인문제
p.85

1 T　2 F　3 F　4 F

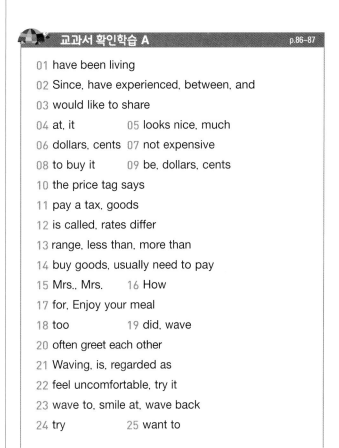

교과서 확인학습 A
p.86~87

01 have been living

02 Since, have experienced, between, and

03 would like to share

04 at, it　　05 looks nice, much

06 dollars, cents　07 not expensive

08 to buy it　　09 be, dollars, cents

10 the price tag says

11 pay a tax, goods

12 is called, rates differ

13 range, less than, more than

14 buy goods, usually need to pay

15 Mrs., Mrs.　16 How

17 for, Enjoy your meal

18 too　　19 did, wave

20 often greet each other

21 Waving, is, regarded as

22 feel uncomfortable, try it

23 wave to, smile at, wave back

24 try　　25 want to

26 Don't 　　　　27 Yes

28 try some, delicious

29 don't like 　　　30 What

31 negative questions, Aren't, Didn't, go

32 to answer, is

33 negative questions, answer, No

34 answer, Yes

35 the same as, to positive questions

36 Which cultural difference

37 have been learning, since

38 surprised, am getting used to

교과서 확인학습 B　　　　　　　　　p.88~89

1 Hi! My name is Kim Minhee. I have been living in America for three years.

2 Since my family moved here, I have experienced many cultural differences between Korea and America.

3 I would like to share some of them with you.

4 Minhee: Look at this shirt. I like it.

5 Linda: It looks nice. How much is it?

6 Minhee: It's 19 dollars and 99 cents.

7 Linda: That's not expensive.

8 Minhee: Yes, I agree. I want to buy it.

9 Clerk: That'll be 21 dollars and 20 cents.

10 Minhee: Really? But the price tag says it's only 19 dollars and 99 cents.

11 Here in America, in most states, people pay a tax when they buy goods.

12 It is called a sales tax. Sales tax rates differ by state.

13 They range from less than one percent to more than ten percent.

14 So when you buy goods in America, you usually need to pay more than the price on the tag.

15 Jessica: Hi, Mrs. Johnson! Minhee: Hello, Mrs. Johnson!

16 Mrs. Johnson: Hi, Jessica! Hi, Minhee! How are you?

17 Jessica: Fine, thank you. We are here for a burger. Enjoy your meal.

18 Mrs. Johnson: Thank you. You, too!

19 Minhee: Jessica, why did you wave to Mrs. Johnson?

20 In America, people often greet each other by waving.

21 Waving to an older person is not regarded as rude.

22 When you come to America, you may feel uncomfortable about it at first, but why don't you try it?

23 You can wave to and smile at an elderly man walking on the street. He may wave back.

24 Andy: Minhee, try this apple pie.

25 Minhee: No, thanks. I don't want to.

26 Andy: Why not? Don't you like apple pie?

27 Minhee: Yes.

28 Andy: Then, try some. It's delicious.

29 Minhee: No. I just said I don't like apple pie.

30 Andy: What?

31 Americans often ask negative questions, such as "Aren't you coming?" and "Didn't you go to the hospital?"

32 It can be difficult to answer negative questions correctly. Here is some advice.

33 In response to negative questions, such as "Don't you like apple pie?" you should answer "No," if you don't like it.

34 And you should answer "Yes," if you like it.

35 These answers are the same as the answers to positive questions, such as "Do you like apple pie?"

36 Which cultural difference is most surprising to you?

37 I have been learning about cultural differences since I came to America.

38 Some surprised me at first, but now I am getting used to them.

시험대비 실력평가　　　　　　　　　p.90~93

01 ④	02 ③	03 ②	04 states
05 ④	06 ④	07 ③	

08 People in America greet each other by waving.

09 ③	10 ③	11 No, I don't like them.
12 ④	13 ④	

14 We need to pay a sales tax.

15 She moved to America three years ago.

16 ③	17 waving to an older person
18 ⑤	19 ④　　　　20 Yes, I am (hungry).
21 ⑤	22 cultural

23 The writer has been learning about cultural differences. 　　　24 ②

01 가족들이 미국으로 이사 온 이래로 많은 문화적 차이를 경험해 왔다는 의미가 적절하다. 따라서 '~한 이래로'라는 의미의 since가 적절하다.

02 민희는 자신이 경험한 문화적 차이를 말하고 싶다고 하였다.

03 미국에서는 물건을 살 때 가격표 금액에 더하여 판매세를 지불해야 한다. 따라서 19달러 99센트에 판매세가 붙어서이다.

04 미국과 같은 큰 나라는 '주'라고 불리는 작은 지역으로 나뉘어져 있다. sate는 '주(州)'라는 의미로 쓰이고 있다.

05 물건을 살 때 지불하는 세금이 판매세이며, 미국 대부분의 주에서 판매세가 붙고 판매세의 비율은 주마다 다르다.

06 미국에 오면 처음에는 나이든 사람에게 손을 흔들며 인사하는 것이 불편하게 느껴질 수도 있다고 하였으므로, 이것이 '무례한' 것으로 여겨지지 않는다고 말하는 것이 가장 적절하다.

07 Jessica는 민희와 함께 버거를 먹기 위해 이곳에 왔다고 하였다.

08 미국 사람들은 손을 흔들면서 서로 인사한다고 하였다.

09 부정의문문에 올바르게 대답하기가 어려울 수 있다고 말하며 조언을 주는 말이 들어간 후 부정의문문에 답변하는 방법을 말해주는 것이 가장 자연스럽다.

10 밑줄 친 (A)는 '먹어보다'라는 의미로 쓰였다. ① ~을 시험 삼아 써보다 ② ~하려고 노력하다 ③ 먹어보다, 마셔보다 ④ ~인지 아닌지 시험해 보다 ⑤ try one's best: 최선을 다하다

11 좋아하지 않을 경우 'No.'라고 답하면 된다고 하였다.

12 (A) 미국과 한국의 문화적 차이에 대해 말하고 있다. similarity: 유사성 (B) 판매세는 물건을 살 때 지불하는 것이다. (C) 가격표에 판매세를 더하여 물건 값을 지불하므로 more가 적절하다.

13 판매세 비율의 범위는 1퍼센트 이하부터 10퍼센트 이상이라고 하였다.

14 미국에서 물건을 살 때 우리는 판매세를 지불해야 한다.

15 미국에 3년 동안 살고 있다고 하였으므로 3년 전에 미국으로 이사를 간 것이다.

16 미국에서 나이든 사람들에게 손을 흔들며 인사하는 것은 무례하다고 여겨지지 않으며 사람들은 서로 손을 흔들며 인사한다고 하였다. 따라서 ③번이 가장 적절하다.

17 나이든 사람에게 손을 흔드는 것을 의미한다.

18 Johnson 할머니가 친구와 함께 대화를 나누는 모습은 찾아볼 수 없다.

19 [C] 부정의문문에 바르게 대답하기 어렵다고 말하며 조언을 줌 [B] 대답하는 방법을 제시하며, 싫으면 'No'라고 답하고 [A] 좋으면 'Yes'라고 답해야 한다고 말함.

20 부정의문문에 대한 대답은 긍정의문문에 대한 대답과 똑같다고 하였다. 배가 고프면 '그렇다'라고 대답하면 된다.

21 부정의문문에 대한 대답은 긍정의문문에 대한 대답과 같다고 하였다.

22 특정한 사회와 그것의 생각, 관습, 그리고 예술과 관련된 것은

'cultural(문화와 관련된, 문화의)'이다.

23 글쓴이는 문화적 차이에 관해 배워오고 있다고 하였다.

24 문화적 차이를 배워 오고 있다고 하였으므로 ②번이 적절하다. ① 놀란 ② 익숙한 ③ 무서운 ④ 충격적인 ⑤ 즐거운

서술형 시험대비
p.94~95

01 She has been living in America for three years.

02 She wants to share some cultural differences between Korea and America.

03 It's 19 dollars and 99 cents.

04 People in America pay a sales tax when they buy goods.

05 are equal in most states → differ by state

06 It doesn't include a sales tax.

07 wave

08 Jessica waved to Mrs. Johnson.

09 Minhee, greet each other by waving

10 How to Answer Negative Questions Correctly

11 No, I don't like it.

12 Yes, I did

13 Answering negative questions, the same, positive questions

01 민희는 3년 동안 미국에서 살고 있다고 하였다.

02 민희는 한국과 미국 사이의 문화적 차이를 공유하고 싶다고 하였다.

03 가격표에 따르면 셔츠 가격은 19달러 99센트이다.

04 미국 사람들은 물건을 살 때 판매세를 낸다고 하였다.

05 주마다 판매세 비율이 다르다고 하였다.

06 가격표에는 판매세가 포함되어 있지 않다.

07 나이가 많은 사람에게 손을 흔들며 인사하라고 제안하고 있으므로 wave가 적절하다.

08 Johnson 할머니에게 손을 흔든 것은 Jessica이다.

09 해석: 민희는 미국에서 사람들이 손을 흔들며 서로 인사하는 방식에 익숙하지 않다.

10 위 글은 부정의문문에 올바르게 대답하는 방법을 제시하고 있다.

11 긍정의문문과 부정의문문의 대답은 같다고 하였다. 민희는 사과 파이를 좋아하지 않는다고 하였으므로 부정의문문에 'No, I don't like it.'이라고 답하는 것이 적절하다.

12 긍정의문문에 대한 대답과 부정의문문에 대한 대답은 같다고 하였다. 책을 지루하게 여겼다고 하였으므로 부정 의문문에 대한 대답은 'Yes, I did.'라고 하는 것이 적절하다.

13 해석: 부정의문문에 답하는 것은 그렇게 어렵지 않다. 당신이 미

국에 있다면, 단지 이것만 기억해라. 부정의문문에 대한 대답은
긍정의문문에 대한 대답과 같다.

p.97~101

영역별 핵심문제

01 positive   02 ⑤   03 ③   04 ①

05 waving, Waving   06 ④   07 ②

08 Make sure you don't ask, age

09 ②   10 ③   11 ⑤

12 Make sure you drink it without a spoon.

13 ③

14 (A) has been trying to solve   (B) since

15 ①   16 ①, ⑤

17 staying in Kenya to study wild animals is Ms.
Baker

18 (1) moving   (2) found   19 ②   20 ③

21 ④   22 (B)–(A)–(C)   23 ③

24 It is a tax that people pay when they buy goods
in America.

25 ④   26 Interesting, Festival   27 ③

28 People throw colored powder and water on each
other.

29 ④

01 반의어 관계이다. 차이 : 닮음 = 부정적인 : 긍정적인

02 (a)는 현재완료(have experienced)를 사용하고 있기 때문에 'since(~한 이후로)'가 적절하고, (b)는 '나는 그것들 중 몇 가지를 너희들과 공유하고 싶어.'라는 말이 적절하다.

03 집의 번호, 도로의 이름, 사람이 살거나 일하는 마을의 이름, 그리고 편지가 발송될 수 있는 곳

04 당신의 수입이나 구입한 상품이나 서비스의 비용에 근거해서 정부에 지불되는 돈

05 영어 설명은 '누군가에게 인사하기 위한 방법으로 손을 들고 좌우로 움직이다'라는 의미로 동사 'wave'에 대한 설명이다. 전치사 by 뒤와, 주어 자리에는 동명사 형태가 와야 하므로 동명사 waving이 적절하다.

06 get used to ...: …에 익숙해지다

07 미국을 방문하는 것에 대해 조언을 구하는 표현이다.

08 서양 문화권에서는 사람의 나이를 물어보는 것이 예의바르지 않다. 이 상황에서 소녀가 경고할 말은 '절대 다른 사람의 나이를 묻지 않도록 해'가 적절하다.

09 무엇을 가져가야 할지에 대한 조언을 구하는 말이므로 Bora의 '차는 어때?'라고 묻는 말 앞에 오는 것이 적절하다.

10 흰색과 검은색은 중국에서 죽음을 의미한다고 했으므로 선물을 흰색이나 검은색 종이로 포장하지 말라는 조언이 적절하다.

11 세호가 보라에게 차를 대접받는다는 내용은 대화에 언급되어 있지 않다.

12 '~해야 한다'라는 의미로 Make sure를 이용할 수 있다.

13 ① Toto라고 '이름이 불리는' 것이므로 named가 적절하다. ② Bong-Junho에 의해 '연출된 영화들'이 되어야 하므로 directed를 써야 한다. ④ which 뒤에 be동사를 써주거나 which를 생략해서 뒤에서 명사를 꾸미는 형태로 쓰는 것이 적절하다. ⑤ 축제에 '초대 받은 유명인사들'이므로 invited가 적절하다.

14 대학에 입학한 이후로 지금까지 문제를 풀기 위해 노력해 오고 있다는 말로 보아 try to solve 표현을 활용하여, 현재완료진행 시제로 쓰도록 한다.

15 첫 번째 문장에서는 '런던에서 찍힌 사진(수동)'을 가리키는 말이므로 taken이 적절하다. 두 번째 문장에서도 '떨어진 잎들(수동)'을 가리키므로 fallen이 적절하다.

16 ① 방이 춥게 느껴지는 '상태'이므로, 진행형은 부적절하다. has felt 또는 feels가 적절하다. ⑤ have been being ~ing 형태는 어색한 구문이다. I have fallen in love with ~ 로 쓰면 적절하다.

17 분사가 명사의 앞, 뒤에서 꾸미는 것을 적절히 활용하여 영작한다.

18 (1) 책에서 발견한 감동적인(감동을 주는) 문장(능동)이므로, moving이 적절하다. (2) Giza에서 발견된 pyramids(수동)이므로, 과거분사 found가 적절하다.

19 ② be busy ~ing는 '~하느라 바쁘다'라는 뜻의 동명사의 관용적 표현이다. 다른 문장들에서는 밑줄 친 부분들 모두가 현재분사로 사용되었다. 단, ①, ③, ④는 명사 뒤에서 수식하는 역할인데 반해, ⑤는 서술적 용법으로 쓰였다.

20 with+A+형용사/분사 형태는 A의 능동/수동 여부에 따라 현재분사 또는 과거분사를 쓴다. ③ with one's legs crossed '다리를 꼰 상태로'인데, crossing은 부적절하다. ① with one's arms folded: 팔짱을 낀 채로 ② with one's eyes closed: 눈을 감은 채로 ④ with the window open: 창문이 열린 채로 ⑤ with one's shirts wet: 셔츠가 젖은 채로

21 현재완료진행시제는 과거에 시작한 일이 현재까지 진행되고 있음을 의미하며, '동작의 진행'을 나타내기 때문에 상태 표현에 사용할 수 없다. ④ own은 '소유하고 있다'는 뜻으로 진행형으로 쓰지 않는다.

22 (B)의 It이 가리키는 것은 a tax이며, (A)의 They가 가리키는 것은 (B) 문장의 sales tax rates이다. 주 별로 판매세가 다르다고 끝맺으며 1퍼센트 이하에서부터 10퍼센트 이상에까지 걸쳐 있다고 설명하고, 그래서 가격표에 있는 가격보다 더 많은 금액을 지불해야 한다고 말하는 것이 적절하다.

23 (A)는 '~한 이래로'라는 의미로 쓰인 접속사이다. 모두 같은 의미로 쓰였지만 ③번은 '~ 때문에'라는 의미로 쓰이고 있다.

24 판매세는 미국에서 사람들이 물건을 살 때 지불하는 세금이라고 하였다.

25 가격표에 있던 가격을 본 민희는 비싸지 않다고 생각했다.

26 전 세계의 흥미로운 축제 중 인도의 Holi에 대해 소개하고 있다.

27 기간을 이끄는 말이 이어지고 있으므로 for를 쓰는 것이 적절하다. since는 특정 시점을 이끈다.

28 사람들은 홀리 축제에서 서로에게 형형색색의 가루와 물을 던진다고 하였다.

29 글쓴이는 사람들과 함께 길거리에서 춤추고 싶다고 하였다. look forward to: ~을 고대하다

단원별 예상문제   p.102~105

01 Japanese   02 ②

03 sure you don't use your left hand

04 She wants to send it[the hanbok] to her aunt in the USA.

05 how to write an address in English

06 Make sure (that) you show your tongue

07 Look at the people wearing traditional Moroccan clothes.

08 ④   09 ②   10 ④

11 get your advice, to take   12 ③

13 ⓐ since → for   ⓑ taught → teaching
    ⓒ speak → spoken ⓓ risen → rising   14 ③

15 ⑤   16 tax

17 from less than, to more than   18 ⑤

19 ④   20 ③   21 cultural differences

22 She has been learning about cultural differences since she came to America.

01 국가 – 국민(언어) 관계이다.

02 어떤 상황에서 무엇을 해야 하는지, 어떻게 행동해야 하는지에 대해 누군가가 여러분에게 제안하는 의견

03 had better not은 '~하지 않는 게 낫다'라는 의미로 '~하지 않도록 확실히 해라'라는 의미로 'Make sure you don't'를 사용하는 것이 적절하다.

04 미국에 계신 이모에게 한복을 보내기를 원한다.

05 영어로 주소를 쓰는 방법에 관한 충고를 얻고자 한다.

06 Tibet에서 인사하는 방법에 대해 조언을 구하고 있다. 'Make sure+주어+동사'를 이용하여 '반드시 혀를 보여주도록 해라'라고 조언한다.

07 동사원형으로 시작하는 명령문 형태로 Look at을 먼저 쓰고, 현재분사 wearing(입고 있는)이 명사 people을 뒤에서 수식한다.

08 모로코 사람들에게 물어보지 않고 사진을 찍으면 안 된다고 했기 때문에 빈칸에는 그 이유로 부정적인 의미가 오는 것이 적절하다.

09 G의 마지막 말에 연장자에게 한 손으로 무언가를 주는 것은 한국

에서 무례한 것으로 여겨진다고 말하고 있으므로 ②가 적절하다.

10 태국에는 절이 많기 때문에 절을 방문할 때 짧은 옷을 입으면 안 된다는 것이 적절하다. should wear를 shouldn't wear로 바꾸어 준다.

11 조언을 구하는 표현으로 바꾸어 말할 수 있다. 'Can I get your advice on ~' 구문과 '의문사+to부정사'를 이용한다.

12 모든 문장들에 현재완료진행시제가 사용되었다. ③번 문장은 시제 자체에는 문제가 없으나, during the last winter party가 '명백한 과거 시점'을 지칭하므로, '과거에 시작된 일이 지금도 진행되고 있다'는 의미의 현재완료진행시제로 표현할 수 없다. during을 since로 바꾸면, '지난 겨울 파티 이후로 Donald의 친지들이 포커 게임을 해오고 있는 중이다'가 된다.

13 ⓐ '2달 동안'이므로 for (단, '2달 전부터 가능하기 때문에 그 경우 months뒤에 ago를 추가하면 된다.) ⓑ '수영을 가르치는 강사'(능동) ⓒ '대부분의 라틴 아메리카 국가들에서 말해지는 스페인어'라는 뜻의 수동이므로 과거분사를 써야 한다. ⓓ 가격이 꾸준히 상승해 오고 있다.(현재완료진행형)

14 ③번은 전치사의 목적어로 쓰인 동명사이다. 그 외에는 모두 명사의 뒤에서 꾸미는 분사로 사용되었다.

15 가격표에 있는 가격에 판매세를 더해서 물건 가격을 지불해야 하므로 ⑤번이 가장 적절하다.

16 정부가 공공 서비스를 위해 쓸 수 있도록 당신이 정부에 지불하는 돈은 '세금'이다.

17 판매세율은 주마다 다른데, 1퍼센트 이하에서부터 10퍼센트 이상에 이른다고 하였다.

18 판매세율은 주마다 다르다고 하였다..

19 민희가 부정의문문에 긍정으로 답하였으므로 Andy는 민희가 사과파이를 좋아한다고 이해하였다. 따라서 한 번 더 사과파이를 권한 것이다.

20 (B)는 진주어로 쓰인 to부정사이다. ①, ④ 부사적 용법 중 목적 ② 부사적 용법 중 감정의 원인 ③ 진주어 ⑤ 형용사적 용법으로 something을 수식

21 문화적 차이를 가리키는 말이다.

22 글쓴이는 미국에 온 이래로 문화적인 차이에 대해 배우고 있다고 하였다.

서술형 실전문제   p.106~107

01 A: Can I get your advice on visiting
    B: not eat food or drink water in the subway

02 she shouldn't wear shorts when she visits a temple

03 (1) most Chinese people like to receive tea as a present
    (2) Is there anything else that I need to know?

04 I have been teaching Korean in an Indian middle school for thirteen years.

05 ⓐ crying ⓑ leaving ⓒ sleeping ⓓ covered ⓔ written

이유: ⓒ만 동명사이고, 나머지는 모두 분사이다.

06 positive questions

07 ⓐ Yes, I do. ⓑ No, I don't.

08 Yes, I did

09 (A) interesting (B) throwing

10 They have been celebrating Holi for many years.

---

01 (A) 조언을 구하는 표현으로 'Can I get your advice on ~?'을 이용하고, 전치사 on 뒤에는 동명사 visiting이 적절하다. (B) 주어진 그림은 음식과 음료 금지를 나타내므로 should not을 이용한다.

02 긴 바지와 치마를 챙겨야 하는 이유는 태국에서 절을 방문할 때 짧은 옷을 입으면 안 되기 때문이다.

03 (1) 대부분의 중국인들은 차를 선물로 받는 것을 좋아하기 때문이다. (2) '~가 있다'라는 there is를 이용한 의문문을 사용하고, 형용사 else는 anything을 뒤에서 수식한다. 목적격 관계대명사 that[which]을 사용하고 need는 to부정사를 사용하므로 need to know를 쓴다.

05 ⓐ '울고 있는 아이'(능동) ⓑ '5시에 출발하는 기차'(능동) ⓒ '침낭'은 '잠을 자고 있는 가방'이 아니라, '잠을 자기 위한 용도의 가방'이므로 동명사 ⓓ '담쟁이로 덮인 건물 벽'(수동) ⓔ '에머슨에 의해 쓰여진 시'(수동)

06 예를 들어 이어지는 의문문의 형태로 보아 '긍정의문문'이라는 말이 들어가는 것이 가장 적절하다.

07 부정의문문에 대한 대답과 긍정의문문에 대한 대답이 같다고 하였으므로 위와 같이 쓰는 것이 적절하다.

08 부정의문문으로 묻는다 하더라도 의문문에 대한 대답이 사실이면 'Yes, I did.'로 답하는 것이 적절하다.

09 (A) 흥미를 유발하는 축제이므로 interesting, (B) '가루와 물을 던지는 사람들'이라는 의미이므로 현재분사 throwing을 쓴다.

10 인도 사람들은 수년 동안 Holi 축제를 기념해 오고 있다고 하였다.

창의사고력 서술형 문제   p.108

|모범답안|

01 A: Can I get your advice on visiting Russia?
   B: Make sure, don't give flowers in even numbers

02 (1) |모범답안| John has been singing since he ate lunch.

   (2) |모범답안| Susan's brother has been cleaning

---

the table with a towel for ten minutes.

03 Pizza Festival, Italy, in June, try different kinds of pizza from all around the world, selecting the best chef

단원별 모의고사   p.109~112

01 ④	02 impolite	03 ②	04 ③
05 ④	06 ⑤	07 ⑤	

08 white and black mean death in China

09 Make sure

10 There is an important thing you need to know before taking pictures.

11 ②

12 (1) have been reading the novel written by Sarah for three

   (2) has been working at a bank founded by Bill for

13 ③

14 My English teacher has been carrying the heavy boxes since this morning.

15 ③	16 ②	17 ④	18 ⑤
19 ⑤	20 ④		

21 She greeted Mrs. Johnson by waving.

01 ④번은 '당신의 수입이나 구입한 상품이나 서비스의 비용에 근거해서 정부에 지불되는 돈'의 의미로 tax에 관한 설명이다.

02 유의어 관계이다. 나이 든 : 무례한

03 take off: 벗다 at first: 처음에

04 A가 부정의문문으로 '배고프지 않니?'라고 물었을 때 B가 'Yes'라고 긍정의 대답을 하고 있으므로 'I am'으로 하는 것이 적절하다.

05 B의 대답으로 보아 올바른 영어 표현에 대한 조언을 구하고 있다는 것을 알 수 있다.

06 G의 대답으로 보아 또 다른 조언을 구하고 있다는 것을 알 수 있다.

07 make sure는 뒤에 '주어+동사'가 와야 한다. Make sure (that) you don't wrap이 되어야 적절하다.

08 Q: 왜 Seho는 선물을 흰색이나 검은색 종이로 포장해서는 안 되는가?

09 A가 '프랑스에서 식사할 때 기억해야 할 것이 있니?'라고 묻고 있으므로 B의 빈칸에는 주의해야 할 일을 경고하는 표현이 적절하다.

10 '~가 있다'는 'There is+단수 명사(an important thing)'로 문장을 시작하고, thing을 수식하는 관계대명사절을 뒤에 사용한다. 마지막으로 'before+동명사'를 사용한다.

11 빈칸 다음에 '너는 물어보지 않고 모로코 사람들의 사진을 찍으면 안 돼.'라고 말하고 있으므로, (B)에는 모로코 사람을 사진 찍는 것에 대한 조언을 구하는 말이 적절하다.

12 조건을 충족시키면서 10단어를 넘지 않도록 하고, 명사를 뒤에서 꾸미는 분사의 능동/수동에 유의한다. (1) 지난 일요일에 읽기 시작해서 오늘이 화요일이므로 기간은 3일 동안이 된다. (2) 글자 수에 유의하여 마지막에 for가 오도록 영작한다.

13 주어진 문장과 ①, ②, ④, ⑤는 모두 수동의 의미로 명사를 뒤에서 꾸미는 과거분사가 적절하다. ③번만 현재분사이다.

15 명사의 뒤에서 꾸며주는 분사의 능동/수동을 적절하게 구분해야 한다. ① called ② wearing ④ taken ⑤ written이 적절하고, ③의 hanging은 자동사로서 '매달려 있다, 늘어져 있다'는 뜻으로 어법상 옳게 쓰였다.

16 민희는 자신이 경험한 문화적 차이를 공유하고 싶다고 하였다. 따라서 ②번이 가장 적절하다.

17 민희는 가족과 함께 미국으로 이사를 가서 한국과 미국의 문화적 차이를 경험하고 있다고 하였다. 미국에서는 가격표에 제시된 금액에 더해서 판매세를 내야 하는 것을 문화적 차이로 소개하고 있으므로 한국에서는 가격표의 금액만큼을 지불한다는 것을 유추할 수 있다.

18 한국이 아닌 미국에서 물건을 살 때 판매세를 내는 것이다.

19 ① by+Ving: V함으로써 ② at first: 처음에 ③ wave to: ~에게 손을 흔들다 ④ smile at: ~을 향해 웃다 ⑤ on the street: 거리에서

20 글의 내용상 나이 든 사람에게 손을 흔들며 인사하는 것은 무례하게 여겨지지 않으므로 한번 시도해 보라고 말하는 것이 자연스럽다. 미소 지으며 손을 흔들며 인사하면 그 사람도 손을 흔들며 인사할 것이라고 말하는 것이 적절하다.

21 Jessica는 Johnson 할머니에게 손을 흔들며 인사를 하였다.

Future Dreams, Future Jobs

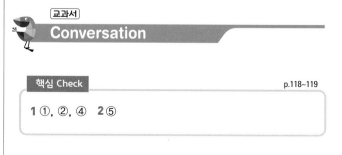

시험대비 실력평가　　　　　　　　p.116

01 ④　　02 florist　　03 ②　　04 ③
05 analyze, strength, weakness　　06 ⑤
07 repair　　08 ④

01 '학교에 다니다'와 '결혼식에 참석하다'는 의미를 가지는 'attend'가 적절하다.

02 꽃으로 아름다운 것들을 창조하는 사람이라는 의미로 florist(플로리스트)가 적절하다.

03 '조직의 일원이 되다'는 의미로 '~에 속하다'는 belong to가 적절하다.

04 '국가, 조직 또는 개인의 유용하거나 가치 있는 소유물 또는 자질'의 의미로 'resource(자원)'가 적절하다.

05 analyze: 분석하다, strength: 강점, weakness: 약점

06 (A) 아이들의 그림이 교실 벽을 장식한다. (B) 아름다운 꽃으로 집을 장식하는 것은 아주 재미있다.

07 유의어 관계다. 고치다 : 다루다

08 (A) 뮤지컬 극장의 감독으로서, '나는 배우들을 대상으로 오디션을 실시하고'가 적절하다. (B) 오디션을 본 다음 '배역에 맞는 배우를 고른 뒤에'라는 말이 적절하므로 'cast'가 와야 한다.

서술형 시험대비　　　　　　　　p.117

01 (1) reduce, calm　(2) among　(3) belong to
　(4) field
02 (A) something colorful　(B) highly recommend
03 (1) analyst　(2) recorded　(3) During, performance
04 (1) collect, 모으다　(2) personality, 성격
　(3) greenery, 화초, 푸른 잎
05 conduct

01 (1) 그녀는 그들이 스트레스를 완화하고 평온해지도록(calm) 도와줘. (2) 너는 이 목록에 있는 것들 중에서(among) 무엇에 가장 관심이 있니? (3) 대부분의 사람들은 여섯 가지 성격 유형 중 한 가지에 속해(belong to). 현실적인 타입도 그 중 하나야. (4) 나는 해양 과학자입니다. 해양 과학은 거대한 분야(field)입니다.

02 (A) something은 형용사가 뒤에서 수식을 한다. 다채로운: colorful (B) '매우, 대단히'의 의미로 부사 highly를 사용한다.

03 (1) analyst: 분석가 (2) record: 녹화하다. 명사 games를 꾸며주며 수동의 의미('녹화된')로 과거분사 recorded가 적절하다. (3) '~ 동안에'의 의미로 'the+명사'가 뒤에 있기 때문에 전치사 during이 적절하다. performance: 공연

04 (1) 물건을 가져가서 함께 모으다 (2) 당신이 어떤 사람인지, 행동하고 느끼고 생각하는 방식으로 보여 지는 것 (3) 특히 잘려서 장식으로 사용되는 녹색 식물이나 가지

05 • 오케스트라를 지휘하려면, 여러분은 머릿속에서 음악을 들을 수 있어야 합니다. • 경찰관들은 1년에 네 번 인천에서 학교 폭력 예방 캠페인을 실시합니다.

교과서
Conversation

핵심 Check　　　　　　　　p.118~119

1 ①, ②, ④　2 ⑤

교과서 대화문 익히기

Check(√) True or False　　　　　　　　p.120~121

1 T　2 T　3 T　4 F　5 F　6 T　7 T　8 F

교과서 확인학습　　　　　　　　p.123~125

Listen & Speak 1 A

1. planning, police station, officer / to become, someday / do, dreamed, becoming, since / with, ask, something / going / what, to do / sure, would like to

2. wrong / animator, drawing, enough / Being, a, artist / animator / a lot of, practice drawing / quite sure that, if

Listen & Speak 1 B

interested, technology, Which, right / sure, developer in writing. Which job, be right for / quite sure, be a good job for

Listen & Speak 2 A

1. glad, what you do / guide, information, visit / else / popular culture, traditional / It seems, knowing, happy with

2. role model / be like / does, do / how to stretch / reduce, calm themselves / It seems that, to keep both, and

Listen & Speak 2 B

program writer, become / writing, helpful
social worker, help me become / seems, reading books to kids, be helpful

Real Life Talk

most interested, among / working / it seems to me that, belong to, realistic / mean / belong to, personality types. Realistic, types / interesting, What kind of, recommend / and so on / to be / I'm quite sure

Communication Task Step 2

3 Ss, 2 As, 1 E / seems to, belong to / Jobs that, recommended / have always wanted / sounds, quite sure that you could

Wrap Up 1

doing / recipe, cook / to cook, chef / make / taking, to think of, creative / I'm quite sure

---

시험대비 기본평가   p.126

01 It seems, that   02 ③   03 ⑤
04 ②

01 'It seems to me that 주어+동사 ~.'는 '~인 것 같다'라는 의미로 자신의 의견이나 생각을 나타내는 표현이다.

02 어떤 직업이 맞는지 묻는 말에 '나는 ~라고 확신해.'라는 의미로 확실성을 표현하는 말이 적절하다.

03 라디오 방송 작가가 되고 싶어 하는 A에게 도움이 되는 말로 ⑤가 적절하다.

04 'I'm sure (that) ~.'은 '나는 ~을 확신해.'라는 의미로 확실성 정도를 표현하는 말이다.

시험대비 실력평가   p.127~128

01 ③   02 ①   03 ④   04 ③
05 In my opinion   06 ⑤
07 Being an animator is not just about being a good artist.
08 ②   09 ⑤   10 ③

01 전치사 of 뒤에 동사가 올 때는 동명사를 사용해야 한다. become을 becoming으로 고쳐야 한다.

---

02 ① Matt가 이번 주말에 삼촌을 만날 것인지는 대화에서 언급되어 있지 않다.

03 동물에 관심이 있어서 어떤 직업이 나에게 맞는지 묻는 말에 → (C) 애완동물 미용사가 적합한 직업이라 말하고 → (B) 애완동물 미용사가 무엇인지 묻고 → (A) 직업을 설명한다. → 마지막으로 (D) 멋지다고 답하는 것이 적절하다.

04 A가 패션 디자이너가 되고 싶다는 말에 B가 패션쇼에 가는 것이 도움이 될 것 같다고 했으므로 빈칸에는 '내가 그것이 되는 데 뭐가 도움이 될까?'라는 말이 적절하다.

05 의견을 말하는 표현으로 'It seems to me ~' 대신 'In my opinion, ~'을 사용할 수 있다.

06 ⑤번은 '나는 기술에 관심이 있어. 어떤 직업이 나에게 맞을까?'라는 물음에 '네가 훌륭한 축구 선수가 될 수 있을 것이라고 꽤 확신한다.'라는 대답은 어색하다.

07 주어 자리에 동사 be를 동명사 Being으로 바꾸고, 동사 is를 추가한다. 전치사 about 뒤에도 동명사 being을 추가하여 문장을 완성한다.

08 'It seems to me that ~.'은 '~처럼 보인다, ~인 것 같다'라는 의미로 자신의 의견이나 생각을 나타내는 표현이다.

09 현실적인 타입이고, 항상 축구선수가 되기를 원하는 Jessie의 말에 '멋지다'라고 말한 다음 훌륭한 축구 선수가 될 수 있을 거라고 확신하지 못한다고 말하는 것은 어색하다.

10 ③ 보라가 Jessie에게 어떤 직업을 제안했는지는 대화에 언급되어 있지 않다.

서술형 시험대비   p.129

01 I have dreamed of becoming a police officer since I was ten.
02 I'm (quite) sure (that) he would like to meet you.
03 (A) Could you please tell me what you do?
   (B) What else do you do?
   (C) It seems to me knowing a lot about China is very important.
04 (A) What does she do?   (B) It seems to me that

01 '10살 때부터'는 'since I was ten'을 쓰고, 주절에는 현재완료 'have dreamed'를 쓴다. '~이 되는 것을 꿈꾸다'는 'dream of'와 동명사 being을 사용한다.

02 확실성의 정도를 나타내는 말은 'I'm (quite) sure (that) 주어+동사'를 이용한다.

Grammar

핵심 Check
p.130~131

1 (1) which (2) that

2 (1) Peter had his legs broken several times.

　　(2) I will have my hair cut this Saturday.

시험대비 기본평가
p.132

01 (1) watched → watch

　　(2) injure → injured　(3) which → that

　　(4) encourage → encourages

02 ④　　　**03** ④

04 It is those books that[which] Barbara has always wanted to buy.

---

01 (1) 소녀가 다른 학생을 관찰하는 것이므로, 수동의 과거분사 watched는 부적절하다. 동사원형 watch를 써야 한다. (2) 다리를 부상당한 것이므로 수동의 과거분사 injured로 고쳐야 한다. (3) 'It ~ that' 강조구문으로 부사구 last Friday를 강조한다. (4) 삼촌이 격려하는 것이므로 현재시제, 3인칭 단수 주어에 맞는 동사형을 써야 한다.

02 the taxi를 강조하면, that 뒤에는 불완전한 문장이 와야 하는데, 구조가 완전하다. 내용상 Frank가 Nancy에게 청혼을 한 장소를 강조하는 문장이 되어야 하기 때문에 It was in the taxi that Frank proposed to Nancy.가 적절하다.

03 목적보어 자리에 동사원형이 왔으므로, 사역동사 had가 적절하다.

04 목적어를 강조하는 것이므로, 'It ~ that' 강조구문을 사용한다. 강조되는 대상이 복수라 하더라도 be동사는 is/was만 가능하며, 주절의 문장이 현재완료 시제이므로, 강조구문의 시제도 is로 하는 것에 유의한다.

시험대비 실력평가
p.133~135

01 ②　　**02** ③　　**03** ①

04 ③　　**05** it was Poppy that tore the letter

06 ⓑ gain → to gain,　ⓒ to take → take,

　　ⓓ performing → (to) perform, ⓕ stops → to stop

07 ③　　**08** ②　　**09** ①　　**10** ⑤

11 ④

12 Laura had Tom help her husband to repair the washing machine.

13 It is James who is responsible for taking care of

---

plants.　**14** ⑤　　**15** ②　　**16** ③

17 ③, ⑤　　**18** break → broken

---

01 'It is[was] ~ that' 강조구문의 강조 대상은 문장 내의 명사(주어, 목적어)와 부사(구/절) 뿐이다.

02 ③의 that은 진주어로 쓰였다. 나머지는 모두 'It ~ that' 강조 구문의 that이다.

03 'have/has/had+목적어+목적보어' 형태에서 목적어의 능동/수동에 따라 목적보어 자리에 동사원형 또는 과거분사를 쓴다. 집이 '칠해지는' 것이므로, 과거분사 painted가 적절하다.

04 자동차가 '수리되는' 것이므로 fixed가 적절하다.

05 과거시제 동사 tore 형태에 유의하여, 'It is[was] ~ that' 강조구문을 글자 수에 맞게 쓴다.

06 ⓑ order+목적어+to부정사 ⓒ let+목적어+원형부정사 ⓓ help+목적어+(to)부정사 ⓕ get+목적어+to부정사 등의 형태로 쓰는 것이 적절하다. the addict: 중독자

07 ③은 가주어 It과 진주어 명사절을 이끄는 접속사 that이 쓰였다. 나머지는 모두 'It ~ that' 강조 구문이다.

08 ②는 가주어 It과 진주어 명사절을 이끄는 접속사 that이 쓰였다. 나머지는 모두 'It ~ that' 강조 구문이다.

09 ①번 문장은 '그는 아들의 사고에 의해서도 마음이 바뀌지 않았다'는 내용이며, 전치사 by와 문맥을 통해 수동임을 알 수 있다. change를 changed로 고치는 것이 적절하다.

10 (A), (C)는 사역동사 have, make 뒤의 목적보어 자리이므로 원형부정사를, (B), (D)는 order, expect이므로 목적보어로 to부정사를 쓰는 것이 적절하다.

11 ④의 allow는 목적보어 자리에 to부정사를 사용한다. ① to wash → wash, ② eat → to eat, ③ to use → use, ⑤ help → to help

12 사역동사 'have+목적어+동사원형'과 'help+목적어+(to) V' 형태를 적절하게 활용하여 영작한다.

13 내용상 아버지가 기르는 화초에 대한 책임을 맡고 있는 사람에 대한 강조 문장이므로 'It ~ who' 강조 구문을 사용한다. 전치사 for 뒤의 동명사 taking의 형태에 주의한다.

14 ⑤번 문장의 that은 접속사로 쓰였다. 나머지는 모두 'It ~ that' 강조 구문의 that이다.

15 'It ~ that' 강조구문에서는 강조되는 명사의 성격에 따라 that을 who 또는 which로 대체할 수 있다. ②는 진주어 명사절을 이끄는 접속사 that이며 다른 단어로 대체 불가하다.

16 옳은 문장은 ⓒ, ⓔ, ⓖ 3개이다. ⓐ fix → fixed, ⓑ clean → to clean, ⓓ 'It ~ that' 강조구문에서는 형용사를 강조할 수 없다. ⓕ pick → to pick ⓗ do → done

17 사역동사 'have+목적어+원형/과거분사' 형태를 적절하게 활용한 문장을 선택한다. ①은 우리말과 일치하지 않으며, ②도 내용뿐 아니라 어법상 be taken 뒤에 by가 와야 한다. ④는 to take

---

24 정답 및 해설

의 to를 삭제하는 것이 적절하다.

18 '시합 중 그 축구 선수의 다리가 부러졌다'라는 의미가 정확하게 표현되려면, 수동의 과거분사가 목적보어 자리에 와야 한다. break를 broken으로 고치는 것이 적절하다.

01 (A) It is John that[who] is going to buy the masks at a party this Friday.
   (B) It is the masks that[which] John is going to buy at a party this Friday.
   (C) It is at a party that John is going to buy the masks this Friday.
   (D) It is this Friday that John is going to buy the masks at a party.

02 had me help him to make

03 (1) the Hongdae street → on(in) the Hongdae street
   (2) He rescued the injured carefully.
   (3) Bush was chairman of the council.
   (4) the playground → on[in] the playground
   (5) who → that[which]

04 (1) clean   (2) come[coming]   (3) cry[crying]
   (4) go   (5) to look

05 on March 14, 1879 that Einstein was

06 (1) check → checked   (2) sing → to sing
   (3) meet → to meet   (4) playing → play
   (5) was → was 삭제   (6) looks → look

07 (1) The teacher had Susan clean her desk.
   (2) The tie made his father look much younger.
   (3) Allow her to enjoy the film.

08 (1) 답변 불가
   (2) It was Alicia that[who] had John's phone repaired.
   (3) It was two weeks ago that Alicia had John's phone repaired.
   (4) 답변 불가
   (5) It was at the repair shop that John's phone was repaired two weeks ago.

01 강조하는 대상에 따라 알맞게 강조하는 대상이 사람일 때는 who, 사물일 때는 which를 써도 좋다. 'It ~ that' 강조 구문'으로 표현한다.

02 '시키다'의 의미를 갖는 사역동사 have를 시제에 맞게 had로 사용하는 것에 유의하여, 단어들을 배열한다.

03 (1) '부사구'로 장소를 강조하는 것이므로 전치사를 써야 한다.
   (2) 태도를 나타내는 '양태 부사'는 'It ~ that' 강조 구문의 강조

대상이 될 수 없다. (3) '주격보어'도 'It ~ that' 강조 구문의 강조 대상이 될 수 없다. (4) '부사구'로서 장소를 강조하는 것이므로 전치사를 써야 한다. (5) 강조 대상이 사람이 아니므로 who는 쓸 수 없다. which 또는 that이 적절하다.

04 (1)~(4)는 사역/지각동사 (5)는 일반 5형식 동사이다. (5)의 목적보어 자리에는 to look의 형태가 적절하다.

05 '1879년 3월 14일이 Einstein이 태어난 날'이라는 문장을 '부사구'를 강조하는 'It ~ that 강조 구문'으로 표현해야 한다. 전치사 on과 함께 쓰는 것에 유의하여 영작한다.

06 (1) '짐 검사를 당하는 것'이니까 수동의 표현이 필요하다. 'have+목적어+과거분사' 형태가 적절하다. (2) get+목적어+to V (3) allow+목적어+to V (4) let+목적어+원형동사 (5) break one's legs 다리가 부러지다 (6) make+목적어+원형동사

07 (1) 사역동사 had + 목적어 + 동사원형. (2) 사역동사 made + 목적어 + 동사원형. (3) 일반 5형식 동사 allow 뒤에 나오는 목적보어 자리에는 to 부정사를 쓰는 것이 적절하다.

08 (1) 사역동사 'have +목적어+ p.p.' 형태에서는 행위자를 파악할 수 없다. 일반적으로 제3자가 행위자이므로, 보기의 문장만으로는 누가 전화기를 수리했는지 답변할 수 없다. (4) 주어진 문장만으로는 수리 시점(2주 전)만을 알 수 있고, 수리 기간은 파악할 수 없으므로 답변 불가임. (2), (3), (5)번은 'It ~ that' 강조 구문에 맞춰 적절히 영작한다.

교과서
Reading

확인문제   p.138
1 T   2 T   3 F   4 F

확인문제   p.139
1 T   2 F   3 F   4 T   5 T

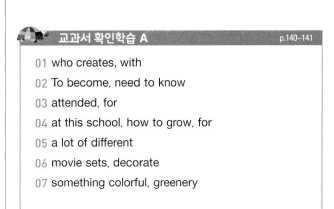

교과서 확인학습 A   p.140~141

01 who creates, with
02 To become, need to know
03 attended, for
04 at this school, how to grow, for
05 a lot of different
06 movie sets, decorate
07 something colorful, greenery

08 highly recommend

09 sport data analyst

10 doesn't it   11 a lot of fun

12 to watch recorded games, run, to collect

13 analyze, to show

14 understands, do better

15 Since, have been

16 baseball games all the time

17 because watching baseball games

18 As, a musical theater

19 audition, look for

20 selecting the cast, for each scene

21 put, together

22 During, conduct

23 my responsibility, each

24 direct, to keep, together

25 Conducting, directing, waving

26 a big field   27 includes, living in them

28 have studied, living

29 the growth ring, that

30 By looking

31 I get from, is used to understand, manage

32 because, the best use

교과서 확인학습 B   p.142~143

1 Hi, I am Tom. A florist is someone who creates beautiful things with flowers.

2 To become a florist, you need to know many things about flowers.

3 I attended a high school for florists and gardeners.

4 It was at this school that I learned how to grow and care for different types of flowers.

5 These days, florists can do a lot of different things.

6 I design movie sets sometimes and I decorate shops with flowers.

7 I am happy when I create something colorful with fresh flowers and greenery.

8 If you like plants and the arts, I highly recommend you become a florist.

9 I am Emma. I am a sport data analyst.

10 It sounds like a difficult job, doesn't it?

11 In fact, it is a lot of fun. I work for a baseball team.

12 My job is to watch recorded games and run a computer program to collect data.

13 Then, I analyze the data to show my team's strengths and weaknesses.

14 If the team understands their strengths and weaknesses, they can do better next time.

15 Since I was young, I have been a big fan of baseball.

16 Now, in my work, I watch baseball games all the time.

17 This is a perfect job for me because watching baseball games is my hobby!

18 Hi, I am Chris. As a director of a musical theater, I do a lot of things.

19 I audition the actors and I look for good, strong voices.

20 After selecting the cast, I teach them the songs for each scene.

21 Then, I put the cast and orchestra together for practic

22 During the performance, I am in the orchestra area and conduct.

23 It's my responsibility to have each song played the same way every time.

24 I direct the musicians and the singers to keep the show together.

25 Conducting and directing is not just about waving my arms around!

26 My name is Yeji. I am an ocean scientist. Ocean science is a big field.

27 It includes studies of the oceans and the creatures living in them.

28 Among other things, I have studied many kinds of fish living in the seas near Korea.

29 It is the growth ring in a fish that interests me.

30 By looking at it, I can find out when and where the fish was born.

31 All the information I get from fish is used to understand sea resources and manage the oceans better."

32 My job is important because it makes the best use of nature possible.

시험대비 실력평가   p.144~147

01 ②   02 ⑤

03 A florist is someone who creates beautiful things with flowers.

04 ③   05 ③

06 They can do better next time if the team understands their strengths and weaknesses.

07 played　　08 ③

09 (After selecting the cast,) He teaches them the songs for each scene.

10 cast　　11 ⑤　　12 ④

13 the oceans, the creatures living in them

14 It can tell Yeji when and where the fish was born.

15 ②, ③　　16 ③

17 He learned how to grow and care for different types of flowers at a school for florists and gardeners.

18 doesn't it　19 ②　　20 ④

21 She does it in order to collect data.

22 conducts　23 ③

24 His responsibility is to have each song played the same way every time.

25 ④　　　26 ④　　　27 ④

01 (A)는 '오늘날'이라는 의미이다. 따라서 ②번이 적절하다. ①, ③, ⑤ 가끔 ④ 거의 ~하지 않는

02 Tom은 플로리스트와 정원사들을 양성하는 학교에 다녔다고 하였으므로 ⑤번이 글의 내용과 일치한다.

03 플로리스트는 꽃으로 아름다운 것들을 창조하는 사람이라고 하였다.

04 야구 경기를 보는 것이 자신의 취미이기 때문에 완벽한 직업이라고 말하는 것이 적절하다.

05 자료를 수집한 후 분석한다고 하였다.

06 팀이 자신들의 강점과 약점을 알면 다음번에 더 잘할 수 있다고 하였다.

07 각각의 노래가 연주되도록 하는 것이므로 과거분사 형태를 쓰는 것이 적절하다.

08 ③ 공연 중에 지휘한다고 하였다.

09 배역에 맞는 배우를 고른 뒤에, Chris는 그들에게 각 장면을 위한 노래를 가르친다고 하였다.

10 어떤 영화나 연극에 출연하는 사람들은 '출연자들(배역진)'이다.

11 to understand와 병렬 관계이므로 manage라고 쓰는 것이 적절하다.

12 빈칸 (A)에는 By가 들어간다. ① pay attention to: ~에 주의를 기울이다 ② look forward to: ~을 기대하다 ③ depend on: ~에 의존하다 ④ go by: 지나가다, 흐르다 ⑤ take away: ~을 없애주다

13 해양 과학자들은 바다뿐만 아니라 바다에 사는 생명체를 연구한다고 하였다.

14 물고기의 나이테로 물고기가 언제 어디에서 태어났는지를 알 수 있다고 하였다.

15 사람을 선행사로 받는 주격 관계대명사 who가 쓰이며, who를 대신하여 that을 써도 무방하다.

16 항상 같은 일을 하는 것이 아니라 여러 가지 일을 한다고 하였다.

17 Tom은 플로리스트와 정원사들을 위한 학교에서 갖가지 종류의 꽃을 키우고 관리하는 방법을 배웠다고 하였다. 'It was at a high school for florists and gardeners that he learned how to grow and care for different types of flowers.'라고 답해도 좋다.

18 일반동사의 부가의문문이고, 주어가 it이므로 doesn't it이라고 쓰는 것이 적절하다.

19 어려운 직업처럼 들리지만 [B] 사실 매우 재미있다고 말하며 녹화된 경기를 보고 자료를 수집한다고 말함 [A] 수집한 자료를 분석하여 팀에게 보여주는 일을 한다고 설명. 어릴 때부터 야구의 열혈 팬이었고 [C] 지금 일하는 내내 야구를 보므로 자신에게 완벽한 직업이라고 함.

20 어렸을 때부터 야구의 열혈 팬이었던 Emma는 자신의 직업에 만족하고 있다는 것을 글을 통해 알 수 있다.

21 Emma는 자료를 수집하기 위하여 컴퓨터 프로그램을 실행한다고 하였다.

22 오케스트라나 합창단 앞에 서서 공연을 지시하는 것은 '지휘하다'이다.

23 Chris는 배역에 맞는 배우를 고르고 그들에게 각 장면을 위한 노래를 가르친다고 하였다. 따라서 ③번이 일치한다.

24 각각의 노래가 매번 동일하게 연주되도록 만드는 것이 Chris의 책임이라고 하였다.

25 주어진 문장의 it이 가리키는 것은 the growth ring in a fish 이다.

26 예지의 작업은 자연을 가장 잘 활용할 수 있게 한다는 점에서 중요하다고 하였다.

27 ① includes ② creatures ③ resources ④ attention ⑤ manage

서술형 시험대비

p.148~149

01 creates

02 He attended a high school for florists and gardeners.

03 We need to know many things about flowers to become a florist.

04 He feels happy when he creates something colorful with fresh flowers and greenery.

05 strengths and weaknesses

06 She watches recorded games and runs a computer program to collect data. Then, she analyzes the data to show her team's strengths and weaknesses.

27

07 Her hobby is watching baseball games.

08 analyst

09 waving his arms around

10 He is in the orchestra area during the performance.

11 He directs the musicians and the singers.

12 It is the actors that I audition.

13 It is the growth ring in a fish that interests Yeji.

14 It's because her job makes the best use of nature possible.

15 As an ocean scientist, she has studied many kinds of fish living in the seas near Korea.

16 We should look at the growth ring in a fish.

---

01 주격 관계대명사의 선행사가 someone이므로 단수 동사를 쓰는 것이 적절하다.

02 Tom은 플로리스트와 정원사들을 위한 학교를 다녔다고 하였다.

03 플로리스트가 되기 위해서 여러분은 꽃에 관해 많은 것을 알 필요가 있다고 하였다.

04 그는 싱싱한 꽃과 화초로 다채로운 무언가를 창조해 낼 때 행복하다고 하였다.

05 팀이 자신들의 강점과 약점을 이해하면 다음번에 더 잘할 수 있다는 의미이다.

06 스포츠 데이터 분석가로서 Emma는 녹화된 경기를 보고 자료를 수집하기 위해 컴퓨터 프로그램을 실행한 후 팀의 강점과 약점을 보여주기 위해서 자료를 분석하는 일을 한다고 하였다.

07 Emma는 자신의 취미가 야구 경기를 보는 것이라고 하였다.

08 어떠한 주제를 분석하여 그것에 관한 의견을 주는 사람은 '분석가'이다.

09 Chris에 따르면 지휘하고 감독하는 것은 단지 그의 팔을 흔드는 것 이상을 의미한다.

10 Chris는 공연 동안에 오케스트라 석에 있다고 하였다.

11 공연을 제대로 진행하기 위해 그는 연주자들과 가수들을 감독한다고 하였다.

12 Chris는 배우들을 대상으로 오디션을 실시한다고 하였다. 따라서 강조하는 대상을 the actors로 하여 답할 수 있다.

13 'The growth ring in a fish interests Yeji.'라고 답해도 좋다.

14 그녀의 직업은 자연을 가장 잘 활용할 수 있게 한다는 점에서 중요하다고 하였다.

15 예지는 해양 과학자로서 한국 주변의 바다에 살고 있는 많은 종류의 물고기를 연구해 왔다고 하였다.

16 물고기가 언제 어디서 태어났는지 알고 싶으면 물고기 안에 있

는 나이테를 보면 된다고 하였다.

01 select   02 ⑤   03 ③   04 ①

05 (c)reatures   06 ④   07 ②

08 it seems to me that you belong to the realistic type.

09 She is most interested in working outside and playing sports.

10 ③

11 quite sure you could be a good chef   12 ①

13 ⑤   14 ④   15 ④   16 ④

17 ③   18 ⑤   19 ②   20 ②

21 will have your computer fixed today   22 ⑤

23 how to grow and care for different types of flowers   24 ④   25 ⑤   26 ②

27 ③   28 ②   29 ④

30 She works for a baseball team.

---

01 유의어 관계다. 매우, 대단히 = 고르다, 선택하다

02 (A)의 앞 문장에 전 세계의 요리를 좋아하고 요리를 잘할 수 있으며 음식을 맛있고 아름답게 만들 수 있다는 말을 하고 있고 그에 대한 결과로 요리사가 되고 싶다고 했기 때문에 의미상 '이러한 이유로'가 적절하다. (B)는 '내 꿈을 이루기 위해'가 의미상 적절하다.

03 어떤 것 또는 어떤 사람을 처리해야 할 일이나 의무

04 무언가를 다른 것의 일부로 포함하거나 다른 것의 일부로 만들다

05 영어 설명은 '독립적으로 움직일 수 있는 크거나 작은 생물'이란 의미로 creature가 적절하다.

06 since가 현재완료와 함께 사용이 될 때는 '~일 때부터'의 의미가 된다.

07 자산의 의견을 나타내는 표현으로 '~처럼 보이다'는 의미로 'It seems to me that ~'을 사용한다.

08 '~인 것 같다'는 의미로 'it seems to me that 주어+동사 ~'를 쓴다.

09 목록에 있는 것 중에서 Jessie가 가장 관심이 있는 것은 무엇인가?

10 Jessie에게 축구 선수를 추천한 것은 보라가 아니라 the things on the list에서 추천한 것이다.

11 확실성 정도를 표현하는 말로 'I'm quite sure+주어+동사' 어순이 적절하고 '나는 네가 좋은 요리사가 될 것이라고 꽤 확신해'라는 의미가 된다.

12 have+목적어+동사원형: ~하게 시키다

13 'It ~ that' 강조 구문으로 표현한다. ②는 cheer 동사의 수의 일치가 부적절하고, ③은 to cheer가 어법상 적절하다.

---

14 'have+목적어+과거분사' 문장이다. ⑤번의 break one's leg 도 '다리가 부러지다'라는 뜻이지만, '펜스가 그를 쳤다'는 내용이 부적절하다.

15 ④는 가주어 It과 진주어 명사절을 이끄는 접속사 that이 쓰인 문장이다. 나머지는 모두 'It ~ that' 강조 구문이 쓰였다.

16 ① fixed → fix ② leaving → leave ③ feels → feel ④ allow의 목적보어 자리에 to부정사는 적절하다. ⑤ break → broken

17 'It ~ that' 강조 구문에서 일어난 해를 가리키는 표현은 연도 앞에 in을 쓰는 것이 적절하다.

18 <보기>의 have는 'have+목적어+p.p.' 형태로 '목적어가 ~되도록 시키다'라는 의미이다. 같은 의미로 쓰인 문장은 ⑤번이다. 다른 문장들의 have는 ① 먹다 ② (특징)으로 ~이 있다 ③ (잡고) 있다 ④ 겪다 등의 의미로 쓰였다.

19 ②는 가주어 It과 진주어 명사절을 이끄는 접속사 that으로 쓰였다. 나머지는 모두 'It ~ that' 강조 구문의 that이다.

20 'have+목적어+과거분사' 형태이다. to change를 changed로 고치는 것이 적절하다. grief: 슬픔

21 주어진 조건대로 영작할 때, '오늘 네 컴퓨터를 고쳐줄게'라고 해야 한다. Peter는 컴퓨터를 고칠 줄 모르기 때문에, 누군가 제3자가 고치도록 해야 하므로, 그에 맞는 표현인 'have+목적어+p.p.'를 활용한다.

22 '매우' 추천한다는 의미이므로 highly라고 쓰는 것이 적절하다.

23 Tom이 다닌 학교는 다양한 종류의 꽃을 기르고 다루는 방법을 그에게 가르쳐 주었다.

24 누가 Tom이 플로리스트가 되도록 권했는지는 위 글을 읽고 알 수 없다.

25 [C]에서 말하는 these reasons는 주어진 문장에서 언급한 '자신이 잘하는 것들'을 가리키는 말이다. [C]에서 꿈을 위해 요리 잡지를 보고 [B]에서 또한 프랑스로 가서 다양한 요리 기술을 배우겠다고 말하며 자신의 롤 모델이 아버지라고 언급한다. [A] 아버지에 대한 이야기가 기술되고 있다.

26 자신의 꿈의 직업인 요리사에 관한 글이다.

27 요리사가 되고 싶은 글쓴이의 롤 모델이 아버지라고 하였고, 아버지는 항상 새로운 조리법에 대해 생각하고 이것을 요리해준다고 하였으므로 ③번을 유추할 수 있다.

28 스포츠 경기를 보고 컴퓨터 프로그램을 돌려 분석하는 직업으로 ②번이 가장 적절하다.

29 Emma는 어렸을 때부터 야구의 열혈 팬이었고 야구 경기를 보는 것이 자신의 취미라고 하였으므로 ④번이 글의 내용과 일치한다.

30 Emma는 야구팀을 위해서 일한다고 하였다.

단원별 예상문제 p.156~159

01 lead 　　　02 ③

03 It seems to me knowing a lot about China is very important. 04 ⑤

05 Read a lot of books and practice drawing every day. 　06 ① 　　　 07 ④

08 I'm quite sure (that) you could become a (great) soccer player.

09 Do you want to become a police officer?

10 (1) ⓐ 　(2) ⓑ 　(3) ⓐ 　(4) ⓑ 　(5) ⓐ

11 It seems, both, and, healthy 　　　　12 ④

13 ③ 　　　　14 ⑤

15 (1) ⓐ It was the newlyweds that bought a table at the mall 2 weeks ago.
　(2) ⓑ It was a table that the newlyweds bought at the mall 2 weeks ago.
　(3) ⓒ It was at the mall that the newlyweds bought a table 2 weeks ago.
　(4) ⓓ It was 2 weeks ago that the newlyweds bought a table at the mall.

16 ④ 　　　　17 ②

18 He looks for good, strong voices.

19 He directs the musicians and the singers to keep the show together. 　20 ③ 　　21 ⑤

22 the oceans 　　　　23 information from fish

01 반의어 관계다. 약함 - 강함 : 따르다 - 이끌다

02 영화, 연극, 쇼 등의 한 부분에 적합하다는 것을 보여주기 위해 짧은 공연을 하다.

03 'In my opinion, 주어+동사 ~'는 의견을 말할 때 사용하는 표현으로 'It seems to me (that)+주어+동사 ~'로 바꾸어 쓸 수 있다.

05 지수에게 많은 책을 읽고, 매일 그리기 연습을 하라고 조언하고 있다.

06 enough는 형용사를 뒤에서 수식하므로 good enough로 바꾸어야 한다.

07 Jessie의 '무슨 의미야?'라는 질문에 대한 보라의 대답으로 보아 '너는 현실적인 타입에 속하는 것 같아.'라는 말이 적절하다.

08 확실성 정도를 나타내는 표현은 'I'm quite sure (that) 주어+동사'를 이용한다.

09 'You do?'의 do는 대동사로 앞 문장의 become a police officer를 대신하는 말이다. 구어체에서 일반동사 의문문의 Do가 생략되어 'You want to ~?' 형태로 사용하기도 한다.

10 (2), (4) 문장들은 접속사 that이 이끄는 진주어 명사절과 형용사 보어(2), 명사보어(4)로 이뤄진 문장이다. (1) 부사구를 강조 (3) 부사절을 강조 (5) 의문사를 강조하는 'It ~ that' 강조 구문이다.

11 '~인 것 같다'는 'It seems that ~'을 이용하고, 'A와 B 둘 다'는 'both A and B' 구문을 사용한다. '건강하게'는 우리말로 부사로 해석되지만 'keep+목적어+목적보어' 구문으로 목적보어 자리에는 형용사 healthy를 사용해야 한다.

12 ④ 글의 내용상 나의 컴퓨터가 shop에서 수리되었으므로, '컴퓨터를 수리한 것은 삼촌이다'라는 내용의 문장은 부적절하다.

13 'have+목적어+p.p.' 형태의 문장들이다. 각각 ① '우산을 도둑맞다' ② '아들을 전학보내다' ④ '구매품들을 포장시키다' ⑤ '돈을 인출하다'를 뜻하며, ③번 '신발을 닦다'라는 의미로 쓰려면, shone을 shined로 쓰는 것이 적절하다.

14 ⑤ 'have+목적어+동사원형'이 쓰였다. ① moving → moved ② to wait → wait ③ going → go ④ washed → (to) wash 로 고치는 것이 적절하다.

16 (A)는 자격을 나타내어 '~로서'라고 해석되는 전치사이다. ① ~ 때문에, ~이므로 ② ~만큼 ③ ~하는 동안에 ④ ~로서 ⑤ ~ 때문에

17 the cast는 Chris가 오디션을 실시하여 고른 배우들을 의미한다. 이들에게 노래를 가르친 후 배우와 오케스트라를 함께 연습시킨다는 흐름이 자연스럽다.

18 Chris는 훌륭하고 강한 목소리를 찾아낸다고 하였다.

19 Chris는 공연을 제대로 진행하기 위해 연주자들과 가수들을 감독한다고 하였다.

20 (A) '한국 주변의 바다에 살고 있는'이 fish를 수식하므로 현재분사 형태, (B) by Ving: V함으로써, on Ving: V하자마자 (C) 핵심 주어가 all the information이므로 단수 동사를 쓰는 것이 적절하다.

21 예지가 물고기에 대해 얻은 정보는 바다의 자원을 이해하고 바다를 더 잘 관리하기 위해 사용된다고 하였다.

22 바다를 가리키는 말이다.

23 예지는 물고기로부터 정보를 얻어서 바다 자원을 이해한다고 하였다.

07 First, she will read magazines about cooking. Second, she will go to France to learn various cooking skills.

08 He always thinks of new recipes and then cooks these new dishes for his family.

09 recorded

10 Her hobby is watching baseball games.

11 She watches baseball games all the time in her work.

01 (A) '~에 관심이 있다'는 'be interested in'을 사용한다. (B) 확실성 정도는 'I'm quite sure that ~'을 사용한다.

02 수미의 꿈은 요리사가 되는 것이다. 요리 수업을 듣고 새롭고 창조적인 요리를 생각해 내기 위해 노력하는 것이 그녀의 꿈을 이루는 데 중요한 것 같다.

03 확실성 정도를 표현하는 말은 'I'm quite sure (that)+주어+동사'나 'I have no doubt that+주어+동사'를 사용할 수 있다.

04 기자의 질문이 '수상에 가장 크게 기여한 것'을 묻는 것이므로, 부모님 때문이라는 내용으로 'because of my parents'를 'it ~ that' 구문으로 강조하는 문장을 쓰는 것이 적절하다.

05 사역동사 'have+목적어+원형[과거분사]' 형태를 적절하게 활용하도록 한다.

06 글쓴이는 자라서 요리사가 되기를 원한다.

07 글쓴이는 꿈을 이루기 위해 요리 잡지를 읽고, 다양한 요리 기술을 배우기 위하여 프랑스로 갈 것이라고 하였다.

08 아버지는 항상 새로운 조리법에 대해 생각하고 그것을 요리해 준다고 하였다.

09 녹화된 경기라는 의미이므로 과거분사를 쓰는 것이 적절하다.

10 그녀의 취미는 야구 경기를 보는 것이라고 하였다.

11 그녀는 일하는 중에 내내 야구를 본다고 하였다.

서술형 실전문제
p.160~161

01 A: I'm interested in technology
   B: I'm quite sure that

02 dream, It seems, taking a cooking, trying to think of new and creative dishes, achieve

03 I have no doubt that you can be a good animator if you try hard.

04 was because of my parents that I received this award

05 (1) Her father had Sally wash Toto.
   (2) Her father had Toto washed by Sally.

06 She wants to be a chef (when she grows up).

창의사고력 서술형 문제
p.162

|모범답안|

01 A: I'm interested in art.
   B: I'm quite sure that a designer

02 (1) |모범답안| I had my phone repaired yesterday.
   (2) |모범답안| Sophia will have her car checked by a mechanic at the repair shop tomorrow.

03 bags from around, making things, what I made look beautiful, it is a bag designer that, read fashion magazines, go to France to learn to design bags

01 ①   02 ⑤   03 run   04 ③

05 ④

06 That's a person who works at a pet hair salon.

07 ③

08 a farmer, a police officer, a soccer player, and so on

09 ②

10 I'm quite sure that you can be a good animator if you try hard.

11 (1) It is for three days that Lucy has been reading the novel.

   (2) It is Austin who wrote the novel.

12 (1) Mom had me put the unused things in the boxes.

   (2) I will have the boxes donated to charity.

13 (1) Mom had me brush my teeth for myself.

   (2) It is my dog Angel that is washing so many dishes.

14 ③   15 ②   16 ③   17 ④

18 ④

19 He conducts during the performance.

20 my responsibility to have each song played

21 ③   22 ⑤

---

01 ①번은 'analyst(분석가)'에 관한 설명이다.

02 '직업에 만족하나요?'라는 A의 말에 B가 '내 생각으로는, 패션 쇼에 가는 것이 도움이 될 거야.'라고 말하는 것은 자연스럽지 못하다.

03 유의어 관계다. 고치다 : 실행하다

04 사람이나 사물을 어떤 상태나 장소로 데려오다[가져오다]

05 '애완동물 미용사가 너에게 좋은 직업이 될 거라고 생각한다.'는 B의 대답으로 보아 (A)에는 자신에게 맞는 직업의 종류를 물어 보는 것이 자연스럽다.

06 '애완동물 미용사는 무엇이니?'라는 A의 질문에 대한 답으로 '그 것은 애완동물 미용실에서 일하는 사람이다'라는 답이 적절하다. 주격 관계대명사 who를 이용하여 선행사 a person을 수식한다.

07 belong to는 자동사이므로 수동태를 사용할 수 없다.

08 Q: 현실적인 타입의 사람들에게 그들이 추천하는 직업은 무엇 인가?

09 빈칸 다음에 좋은 이야기를 만들기 위해 책을 많이 읽고, 그림 그리는 것을 매일 연습하라고 조언하고 있으므로 빈칸에는 만화 영화 제작자가 되기 위해 조언을 구하는 말이 적절하다.

10 '~을 꽤 확신해'는 'I'm quite sure that+주어+동사' 구문을 이 용하고, '노력한다면'은 'if+주어+동사'를 이용한다.

11 내용을 정확히 이해하고, 조건에 맞게 질문에 답하도록 한다. (1) 일요일에 시작해서 화요일이므로 '3일 동안'이다. (2) who 를 쓰는 것이 조건이므로 that을 쓰지 않는 것에 유의한다.

12 시제와 능동/수동에 유의하여, 'have+목적어+원형/과거분사' 형 태로 주어진 단어를 배열한다.

13 (1) 혼자 힘으로: for myself (2) '그릇을 닦고 있는'이라는 우 리말로 보아 현재진행시제로 영작하는 것이 적절하다.

14 주어진 문장과 ③번은 사역동사 have로서 '시키다'라는 의미로 쓰였다. 각 문장에 쓰인 have의 의미는 ①, ② '갖고 있다' ④ '먹다' ⑤ '경험하다' 등이다.

15 ②번 이후의 문장에서 말하는 at this school은 주어진 문장의 a high school for florists and gardeners이다.

16 글의 내용상 '식물과 예술'을 좋아한다면 플로리스트가 될 것을 강력히 추천한다는 말이 가장 적절하다.

17 색종이로 꽃을 장식하는 것은 위 글에 나와 있지 않다.

18 Tom이 어디에서 일하는지는 위 글을 읽고 알 수 없다.

19 Chris는 공연 중에 지휘를 한다고 하였다.

20 노래가 연주되도록 하는 것이므로 사역동사 have의 목적격 보 어로 과거분사 played를 쓰는 것이 적절하다.

21 (B)는 전치사 about의 목적어로 쓰인 동명사이다. 모두 명사를 수식하는 현재분사이지만 ③번은 '~하는 것'으로 해석되는 동명 사이다.

22 자신의 꿈에 관하여 이야기하고 있으므로 아버지가 항상 새로운 요리법에 관해 생각한다는 것은 글의 흐름상 어색하다.

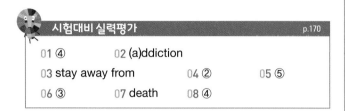

Are You a Digital Citizen?

시험대비 실력평가   p.170

01 ④   02 (a)ddiction

03 stay away from   04 ②   05 ⑤

06 ③   07 death   08 ④

---

01 학생들의 수가 올해 감소되었다. 설탕을 먹는 것을 그만두었을 때 나의 체중이 줄었다.

02 비디오 게임이 중독으로 이어지지 않게 조심해라.

03 stay away from: ~을 멀리하다, ~에서 떨어져 있다

04 전화를 걸거나 편지나 이메일 등을 보냄으로써 누군가와 연락하다: contact(연락하다)

05 또 다른 것을 대표하는 것으로 여겨지는 것: 상징(symbol)

06 (A) 나는 벤치에 앉아 잠시 동안 책을 읽었다. (B) 나의 집이 너무 작기 때문에 손님의 수를 제한해야 한다.

07 반의어 관계다. 장점-단점 : 죽음-출생

08 • 중독과 싸우기 위해, 중국의 인터넷 중독 치료 캠프가 빠르게 성장하고 있다. • 해독 다이어트는 당신의 몸에 있는 독소를 제거하고 살을 빼는 데 빠르고 쉬운 방법으로써 점점 인기가 많아지고 있다.

서술형 시험대비   p.171

01 (1) form   (2) such as   (3) refreshed   (4) necessary

02 uncomfortable

03 (1) addicted   (2) supposed   (3) comment

    (4) password

04 (1) digital, 디지털의   (2) mistake, 실수

    (3) detox, 해독   (4) conversation, 대화

05 post(ed)

---

01 (1) 새로운 단어를 만들기 위해 글자를 재배열하세요. (2) 나는 비빔밥이나 불고기와 같은 한국 음식을 좋아한다. (3) 푹 잔 후에, 나는 상쾌함을 느꼈다. (4) 우리가 매일 많은 물은 마시는 것은 필요하다. colorful (B) '매우, 대단히'의 의미로 부사 highly를 사용한다.

02 '편안하고 쾌적하게 느끼지 않거나, 편안하고 쾌적하지 못하도록 하는'의 의미로 '불편한(uncomfortable)'이 적절하다.

03 (1) be addicted to: ~에 중독되다 (2) be supposed to+동사원형: ~하기로 되어 있다 (3) comment: 논평 (4) password: 비밀번호

04 (1) 다수의 작은 신호로 사진, 소리 등을 저장하거나 그것을 숫자로 보여주는 (2) 원하지 않거나 의도하지 않은 결과를 생성하는 행동, 결정 또는 판단 (3) 건강에 좋지 않거나 해로운 음식, 음료, 약을 일정 기간 동안 몸에 섭취하지 않는 기간 (4) 생각, 감정, 아이디어가 표현되거나, 질문과 답변이 되는 두 명 또는 그 이상의 사람들 사이의 이야기

05 • 다양한 한국 음식에 대한 요리법이 서울 관광 웹 사이트에 게재될 예정이다. • 나는 많은 사진을 찍고 그것을 인스타그램에 게시했어.

Conversation (교과서)

핵심 Check   p.172~173

1 ④   2 ⑤

교과서 대화문 익히기

Check(√) True or False   p.174

1 T   2 F   3 T   4 T

교과서 확인학습   p.176~177

Listen & Speak 1 A

1. tired / until, less than / Playing, good for / can't stop, addicted / were, would set, limit

2. spend, on / almost, can't help it / If I were you, suggest doing / Outdoor / a lot of, such as / suggest

Listen & Speak 2 A

1. posting, that, took / if, post / looks good / not supposed to, without asking / right away

2. let's / On / download, for free / supposed to download, against / Why don't we, instead

Real Life Talk

posted, on, posted / figured out, password / What should / were, change / should / easy to guess / birth date / In fact, (You)'re not supposed to use, personal information / change, stronger one

Wrap Up

posting / take / took, blog / (you)'re not supposed to post / Why not / owner, right

시험대비 기본평가   p.178

01 If I were you   02 ④   03 ③
04 ⑤

01 'If I were you, I would ~.'는 충고할 때 사용하는 표현으로 '내가 너라면 ~할 것이다[~할 텐데]'의 의미다.

02 오랜 기간 동안 동일한 비밀번호를 사용하는 상대방에게 '오랜 기간 동안 동일한 비밀번호를 사용해서는 안 된다'는 말이 적절하다. 'be not supposed to'를 사용하는 것이 옳다.

03 빈칸에는 상대에게 '스마트폰 화면 잠금을 설정하라'는 충고의 표현이 적절하다.

04 'You're not supposed to ~.'는 '~해서는 안 된다'라는 의미로 불허를 나타내는 표현이다.

시험대비 실력평가   p.179~180

01 ④   02 ③   03 It's against the law.
04 ⑤   05 are not supposed to   06 ②
07 ③   08 ⑤   09 ④   10 ①

01 스마트폰에 너무 많은 시간을 보낸다는 엄마의 말에 → (D) 친구들이 SNS에 모여서 어쩔 수 없다는 이유를 말하고 → (B) 야외 활동을 해보라는 엄마의 충고가 나오고 → (A) 되묻는 말에 대해 → 마지막으로 (C) 되묻는 말에 확인해 주는 말이 오는 순서가 자연스럽다.

02 '낯선 사람이 계속 문자를 보낸다.'는 A의 말에 '내가 너라면 그 번호를 차단할 거야.'라는 대답이 적절하다.

03 '~에 반대하여, ~에 거슬러'의 의미를 가지는 'against'를 추가하여 문장을 완성한다.

04 ⑤ '누군가 네 SNS에 이상한 것을 올렸어.'라는 말에 '넌 어떻게 해야 하니?'라는 물음은 어색하다.

05 '~해서는 안 된다'라는 의미로 불허를 나타낼 때 'should not, must not, be not supposed to' 등을 사용한다.

06 'If I were you, I would ~.'는 충고할 때 사용하는 표현이다.

07 Jenny가 Peter에게 어떤 종류의 게임을 제안하는지는 대화에 언급되어 있지 않다.

08 '~에 중독되다'라는 의미로 수동 형태인 'be addicted to'를 사용한다.

09 블로그 주인만이 사진을 사용할 권리가 있다고 말하는 것으로 보아 불허의 표현으로 'you're not supposed to post'가 적절하다.

10 소희는 멋진 사진이 있는 식당을 방문한 것이 아니라 방문한 식당의 사진을 가지고 있다.

서술형 시험대비   p.181

01 If I were you, I would change my password.
02 He used his birth date.
03 (A) Did you ask Sarah if you could post them online?
   (B) You're not supposed to post someone's pictures without asking.
   (C) I'll call Sarah and ask her right away.
04 (A) You're not supposed to download movies from that website

01 'If I were you, I would ~.'는 충고할 때 사용하는 표현으로 '내가 너라면 ~할 것이다[~할 텐데]'로 해석한다.

02 질문: 비밀번호를 만들 때 세호는 무엇을 사용했는가?

[교과서]
Grammar

핵심 Check   p.182~183

1 (1) of   (2) for
2 If Paul knew it, he would change the password.

시험대비 기본평가   p.132

01 (1) have → had   (2) will → would
   (3) has → had   (4) will → would
02 ③   03 ④
04 It is not easy for you to live without a smartphone.

01 문제에서 모든 문장이 가정법 과거 문장이므로, if절의 동사를 과거로, 주절의 조동사도 과거형으로 고치는 것이 적절하다.

02 to부정사가 진주어가 되는 구문에서 to부정사의 의미상의 주어는 전치사 'for 또는 of+목적격'의 형태로 표현한다. of를 쓰는 경우는 to부정사의 '의미상의 주어에 대해 성격이나 태도'를 나타내는 형용사가 있을 때이다.

03 주절에 조동사의 과거형이 나왔으므로, 가정법 문장이다. 내용상 be동사의 과거형이 필요한데, 가정법 과거에서 be동사의 과거형은 주로 were를 쓴다.

04 to부정사의 의미상의 주어를 표현할 때 전치사 for를 쓴다. 일반적으로 '가주어-진주어' 구문에서 동명사 주어는 진주어로 잘 쓰지 않으며, 문제의 조건에서 to부정사를 이용하라고 한 것에 유의한다.

시험대비 실력평가   p.185~187

01 ②   02 ④   03 ④   04 ③

05 ④

06 If I were you, I would suggest doing outdoor
    activities to your friends.

07 It is easy for Smith to ride a bike.

08 If there were no televisions, it would not be easy for
    us to watch the news.

09 ④   10 ④   11 ⑤

12 If Laura had enough time, she could stay longer
    in Seoul.washing machine.

13 It was careless of her to leave the window open.

14 ④   15 ③   16 ④   17 ②

18 took → had taken

01 honest는 사람의 성품에 관한 형용사이다. 이때 의미상의 주어는 for가 아니라 of를 쓴다.

02 to부정사의 의미상의 주어는 전치사 for를 사용하는데, 사람의 성격이나 태도를 나타낼 때는 of를 쓴다. ④ 'Charles가 선생님께 그런 질문들을 한 것은 무례했다.'는 내용이므로 of를 써야 하며, 다른 문장들은 모두 for를 쓴다.

03 ④ 가정법 문장이라면 won't를 wouldn't로, 직설법 문장이라면 had를 has로 쓰는 것이 적절하다.

04 가정법 과거로서 직설법 현재 시제와 적절하게 전환된 문장은 ③번뿐이다. ①은 가정법 과거완료가 필요하고, ②와 ⑤는 가정법 전환이 이상한 문장이며, ④는 직설법의 인과 관계가 어색하게 표현되었다.

05 to부정사의 의미상의 주어를 표현할 때 알맞은 전치사를 고르는 문제이다. ⓐ, ⓓ, ⓕ에는 사람의 성격이나 태도에 관한 형용사가 있으므로 전치사 of를 쓰는 것이 적절하며, 나머지는 모두 for를 쓴다. *orphanage: 고아원

06 가정법 과거 시제의 문장이다. If I were you로 시작하고 주절에 조동사의 과거형 would를 쓰되, suggest 뒤에 동명사가 목적어로 온다는 사실에 유의하여 배열한다.

07 가주어 It과 진주어 to부정사구를 이용할 때, 의미상의 주어 Smith를 전치사 for로 받는 것에 유의하여 배열한다.

08 가정법 과거와 '가주어-진주어'가 혼합된 문장이다. '~가 없다면'이라는 표현은 'If there were no ~'로 나타내는 것이 적절

하고, 가주어 it과 진주어 to watch the news를 활용하여 조동사 과거형 would를 적절하게 배열한다.

09 ④번의 It은 비인칭 주어로서 날씨, 요일, 계절, 명암 등에 사용된다. 나머지는 모두 가주어 it으로 사용되었다.

10 가정법 과거 형태의 문장들이다. If절에는 동사의 과거형을, 주절에는 조동사의 과거형을 쓰는 것이 적절하다.

11 ⑤ 성격을 나타내는 형용사를 받을 때는 to부정사의 의미상의 주어에 of를 사용한다. '당신이 그의 불우한 어린 시절 경험을 언급한 것은 매우 잔인했다' ① of → for, ② for → of, ③ of → for, ④ my → me(전치사 뒤에는 목적격)

12 내용상 가정법의 형태로 문장이 구성된다. have동사의 과거형과 조동사 can의 과거형을 사용하되, long의 비교급을 쓰는 것에 유의하여 영작한다.

13 대화의 내용상 여동생 수진이가 추운 날씨에 창문을 열어놓아서, 화초가 얼어 죽은 것에 대해 '그녀가 창문을 열어 둔 것은 부주의했다'라는 문장을 만드는 것이 적절하다. 단어를 모두 배열할 때, 의미상의 주어 자리의 for는 of로 바꾼다.

14 ④ 가정법 과거완료 문장이다. If절에 'had+p.p' 형태, 주절에는 '조동사 과거+have+p.p' 형태가 온다. 'would not be'를 'would not have been'으로 고치는 것이 적절하다.

15 '~가 없다면'이라는 가정법 표현은 'If there were no ~'로 나타내며, Without 또는 'If it were not for ~'로 대체할 수 있다. 'If it were not for'는 if를 생략해서 'Were it not for ~'로 표현 가능하다.

16 옳은 문장은 ⓒ, ⓔ, ⓖ, ⓗ 4개이다. ⓐ using → to use, ⓑ for → of, ⓓ of → for ⓕ importantly → important

17 ②는 시간, 요일, 날짜, 날씨, 무게, 거리, 금액, 명암 등을 표현할 때 쓰는 '비인칭 주어' it이다. 나머지는 모두 to부정사구를 진주어로 하는 '가주어-진주어' 구문으로 쓰였다.

18 '택시 대신 지하철을 탔더라면 많은 시간을 절약할 수 있었을 텐데.'라는 의미의 가정법 과거완료 문장이다. 가정법 과거로도 고칠 수 있지만, 단어 하나만 찾아 고치는 문제이므로 took을 had taken으로 고치는 것이 적절하다.

서술형 시험대비   p.188~189

01 (1) didn't have smartphones, we would play outside
      more

    (2) it would be more difficult for us to check

    (3) necessary for you to manage your digital footprint

    (4) very wise of us to use digital devices efficiently

02 (1) If it were not for   (2) If there were no

    (3) Were it not for   (4) As there is

03 it didn't rain, I could go for a walk with my dog

04 exercised regularly, he could be

05 (1) very dangerous for even adults to swim in the
sea

   (2) foolish of you to try to cross the valley

   (3) fun for Minseo to play cards with her family
yesterday

06 (1) have → had   (2) be → have been

   (3) was → were   (4) am → were[was]

   (5) it not → it were not

07 (1) sitting → sit   (2) your → you   (3) of → for

   (4) for → of   (5) checked → to check

08 (1) If there were another me, I could make him share
my work.

   (2) If I were you, I would reduce my time on
smartphone by half.

   (3) If we didn't have televisions, it would not be easy
for us to watch the music shows.

   (4) If Sally were[was] in Hawaii, she would be happy.

01 가정법과 '가주어-진주어' 구문, to부정사의 의미상의 주어 등에
유의하여, 주어진 단어들을 적절히 배열한다.

02 '돈이 없으면, 물건을 쉽게 거래할 수 없다'는 내용으로 직설법으
로 표현하면, '돈이 있어서 물건을 쉽게 거래할 수 있다'가 된다.
가정법 과거를 전제로, 'Without = If it were not for = Were
it not for'를 기억해 두는 것이 좋다.

03 직설법으로 표현하면, '비가 오기 때문에 산책을 할 수 없다'는 것
이다. 글자 수와 어법에 맞게 do를 didn't로, can을 could로 변형
하는 것에 유의하여, 단어를 적절히 배열한다.

04 'David이 규칙적으로 운동을 하지 않기 때문에 건강이 좋지 않
다.'라는 직설법 문장을 가정법으로 표현하면, 'David이 규칙적
으로 운동을 하면, 건강이 좋을 것이다.'가 된다. If절에 과거동
사, 주절에 조동사 과거형에 유의하여 영작한다.

05 (1) '어른들조차'를 의미상의 주어로 표현할 때는 for even
adults로 쓰는 것에 유의한다. (2) '어리석다'는 사람의 성질을
나타내므로 전치사 of를 쓴다. (3) 같은 의미로 'Minseo had
fun playing cards with her family yesterday.' 형태로도
표현이 가능하다.

06 문제에서 모든 문장이 가정법이라고 했으므로, (1) if절 동사를
과거시제로 고치는 것이 적절하다. (2) 내용상 시제가 '가정법 과
거완료'이므로, 주절을 '조동사+have+p.p'로 고쳐야 한다. (3)
가정법 과거의 be동사는 were가 일반적이며, 현대 영어에서는
주어가 1, 3인칭 단수일 때는 was도 쓸 수 있다. (4) if절의 be
동사를 과거로 고친다. (5) '~가 없다면'이라는 가정법 표현은 'If
it were not for'로 쓴다.

07 '가주어-진주어' 구문에서 to부정사의 의미상의 주어와 그에 맞

는 전치사의 활용에 유의하여, 어색한 단어를 하나만 찾아서 적
절하게 고치도록 한다.

08 직설법 현재 문장을 가정법으로 바꿀 때, 종속절에는 동사의 과
거형을, 주절에는 '조동사의 과거형+동사원형'을 쓰는 것에 유
의하여, 문장을 전환한다. (3)에서 'it is easy'는 가정법으로
바꾸면 조동사 would를 활용하고, 내용이 반대가 되므로 'it
would not be easy'로 바뀌는 것에 유의한다.

Reading

| 확인문제 | p.190 |

   1 F   2 F   3 T

| 확인문제 | p.191 |

   1 T   2 F   3 T

교과서 확인학습 A
p.192~193

01 When, in the morning, what

02 read, on

03 Imagine, is, near, How

04 check items, that are

05 Are, addicted

06 Without, feel uncomfortable

07 take, into   08 enjoyable to

09 while studying

10 reduce, I spend

11 right after, an alert

12 next to, while   13 What, score, check, half

14 have, with   15 causes you to spend, on

16 focus on, have a pain

17 for you to start

18 means staying away from, for

19 help, freedom from, noisy

20 focus, on, feel refreshed, creative ideas

21 help, spend

22 Living, however, is

23 necessary for you, for

24 need to follow

25 form, create rules, using

26 turn off, while   27 take, into

28 keep, out of the bedroom, them

29 More Time for , spend more time playing

30 Fewer, fewer, on

31 I were, would, by half

32 I were, would, off

33 had, would be, too much

34 With, wise

1 Hi, students! When you wake up in the morning, what is the first thing you do?

2 Do you read SNS postings on your smartphone?

3 Imagine your smartphone is not near you. How do you feel?

4 Students, please check items on the list that are true for you.

5 Are you addicted to your smartphone?

6 Without my smartphone, I feel uncomfortable.

7 I take my smartphone into the bathroom.

8 It is more enjoyable to spend time on my smartphone than with friends.

9 I often check SNS postings while studying.

10 I try to reduce the time I spend on my smartphone, but I fail.

11 I check my smartphone right after I hear the sound of an alert.

12 I have my smartphone next to me while I'm eating.

13 What is your score? Did you check more than half?

14 If so, you may have a problem with smartphone addiction.

15 Smartphone addiction causes you to spend too much time on your smartphone.

16 Also, you cannot focus on your studies and may have a pain in your neck.

17 Then now is the time for you to start digital detox.

18 Digital detox means staying away from digital devices, such as smartphones and computers, for a while.

19 Digital detox will help you a lot. You can enjoy freedom from the noisy digital world.

20 You can focus more on your work. Sometimes you can feel refreshed and have new, creative ideas.

21 Digital detox will also help you spend more time with others.

22 Living without a smartphone, however, is not easy.

23 So, it is necessary for you to set some rules for using your smartphone.

24 You then need to follow the rules.

25 Now, please form groups and, in your group, create rules for using your smartphone.

26 We will turn off our smartphones while studying.

27 We will not take our smartphones into the bathroom.

28 We will keep our smartphones out of the bedroom and not use them at night.

29 More Time for Outside Activities – We will spend more time playing outside without our smartphones.

30 Fewer SNS Messages – We will post fewer SNS messages on our smartphones.

31 If I were you, I would reduce my time on my smartphone by half.

32 If I were you, I would turn off all alerts.

33 You did a good job, students! If we had no smartphones, our lives would be more difficult, but too much use of a smartphone is dangerous.

34 With digital detox, you can become a wise smartphone user.

01 ④

02 about whether or not you are addicted to your smartphone

03 ①, ④   04 to spend   05 ⑤   06 detox

07 ⑤   08 ④   09 ③

10 Rules for Using   11 ④

12 They will not take their smartphones into the bathroom.

13 ⑤

14 what is the first thing you do?

15 ④   16 ④   17 ③   18 ②

19 ③

20 Smartphone addiction causes us to spend too much time on our smartphones.

21 had   22 ④

23 They want to turn off all alerts.

01 (A)와 (B)에는 '~하는 동안에'라는 의미의 접속사 while이 적절하다. 주절의 주어와 종속절의 주어가 같은 경우, 종속절의 주어와 be동사를 생략하여 (A)와 같이 나타낼 수 있다.

02 목록은 스마트폰에 중독되었는지 여부에 관한 것이다.

03 ① reduce의 유의어 ② uncomfortable의 반의어 ③ true의 반의어 ④ next to의 유의어 ⑤ spend의 반의어

04 cause는 to부정사를 목적격 보어로 취하는 동사이다. 따라서 to spend라고 쓰는 것이 적절하다.

05 스마트폰에 중독된 사람들을 위한 해결책으로 디지털 디톡스를 제시하고 있다.

06 '사람들이 무언가에 중독된 것을 멈추게 하기 위하여 그들에게 주어지는 치료'는 'detox(해독)'이다.

07 디지털 디톡스의 장점에 관해 언급하다가 스마트폰 없이 사는 것이 어렵다고 글의 흐름을 전환하고 있으므로 however가 적절하다.

08 빈칸 (B)에는 to부정사의 의미상의 주어가 들어간다. 앞서 나온 형용사가 사람의 성질을 나타내는 형용사가 아니므로 'for+목적격'을 쓴다.

09 디지털 디톡스의 장점은 시끄러운 디지털 세상으로부터 자유를 즐기고, 일에 조금 더 집중하고, 생기를 되찾으며, 새롭고 창의적인 생각을 갖게 하고, 다른 사람들과 더 많은 시간을 보낼 수 있는 것이라고 하였다.

10 위 글은 학생들이 자신의 스마트폰 사용에 대한 몇 가지 규칙에 관한 것이다.

11 글의 흐름상 스마트폰 없이 밖에서 노는 데 더 많은 시간을 쓸 것이라고 말하는 것이 적절하다. with → without

12 예림, 용민, 호진이는 그들의 스마트폰을 화장실로 가져가지 않을 것이라고 하였다.

13 빈칸 (A)에는 전치사 on이 들어가 'spend+시간+on+N: N에 시간을 쓰다'는 의미를 완성한다. ① be interested in: ~에 흥미가 있다 ② get to: ~에 도착하다 ③ stay with: ~와 함께 머물다 ④ take a picture of: ~의 사진을 찍다 ⑤ depend on: ~에 의존하다, ~에 달려 있다

14 'the first thing'과 'you do' 사이에는 목적격 관계대명사 that 혹은 which가 생략되어 있다. '당신이 하는 첫 번째의 것'이라는 의미로 'the first thing you do'라고 쓸 수 있다.

15 반 이상에 체크했다면 스마트폰 중독 문제를 갖고 있을지도 모르는 것이라고 하였다.

16 친구들과 보내는 시간보다 스마트폰을 하면서 보내는 시간이 더 즐거운 것이 스마트폰 중독 사항에 해당한다.

17 스마트폰 없이 사는 것은 쉽지 않으므로 스마트폰 사용에 대한 몇 가지 규칙을 정할 필요가 있다는 연결이 자연스러우므로, 결과를 이끄는 so가 가장 적절하다.

18 스마트폰 중독이 야기할 수 있는 문제 제시 - [B] 또 다른 문제 제시와 디지털 디톡스의 개념 설명 - [A] 디지털 디톡스의 장점 - [C] 하지만 스마트폰 없이 사는 것이 쉬운 것은 아님

19 디지털 디톡스란 스마트폰과 컴퓨터 같은 디지털 장치들로부터 잠시 동안 떨어져 있는 것을 의미한다.

20 스마트폰 중독은 우리가 스마트폰에 너무 많은 시간을 보내게 한다고 하였다.

21 주절로 미루어 보아 가정법 과거 문장임을 알 수 있다. 따라서 had가 적절하다.

22 매일 디지털 디톡스를 하겠다는 계획은 없다.

23 지호, 소희, 유민은 모든 알림을 끄기를 원한다.

서술형 시험대비 p.200~201

01 I try to reduce the time I spend on my smartphone, but I fail.

02 comfortable → uncomfortable, far from → next to

03 If you checked more than half

04 I check my smartphone

05 You cannot focus on your studies and may have a pain in your neck.

06 We need to start digital detox.

07 We can enjoy freedom from the noisy digital world.

08 We need to follow the rules.

09 It is necessary for us to set some rules for using our smartphone.

10 our smartphones

11 They will turn off their smartphones while studying.

12 spend more time playing outside

13 The writer thinks that it is dangerous.

14 take my smartphone into

---

01 스마트폰에 중독되었는지 확인하기 위한 항목이므로, 스마트폰 사용 시간을 줄이려고 노력하지만 실패한다고 말하는 것이 글의 흐름상 적절하다.

02 스마트폰 중독은 스마트폰이 없으면 불안함을 느끼고, 식사 중에 스마트폰을 옆에 가지고 있는 것이다. far from: ~로부터 먼

03 '반 이상에 체크했다면'이란 의미이다.

04 알림소리를 듣자마자 스마트폰을 확인하는 것이 항목에 있었다. immediately: 즉시

05 스마트폰 중독은 스마트폰에 너무 많은 시간을 소비하게 하는 것에 더해서, 공부에 집중할 수 없고 목에 통증을 느낄 수 있다.

06 다른 사람들과 더 많은 시간을 보낼 수 있으려면 디지털 디톡스를 시작해야 한다.

07 시끄러운 디지털 세상으로부터 자유를 즐길 수 있도록 하는 것이 디지털 디톡스라고 하였다.

08 규칙을 정한 후 그것들을 따라야 한다고 하였다.

09 몇 가지 규칙을 정할 필요가 있다고 하였다.

10 '우리의 스마트폰'을 가리키는 말이다.

11 공부하는 동안 스마트폰을 끌 것이라고 하였다.

12 호성, 민수와 함께 지나는 스마트폰 없이 밖에서 노는 데 더 많은 시간을 쓸 것이라고 하였다. 따라서 '스마트폰으로 노는 대신에'로 표현할 수 있다.

13 글쓴이는 지나친 스마트폰 사용이 위험하다고 생각한다.

14 호진이는 디지털 디톡스의 방법으로 화장실에 스마트폰을 가져가지 않겠다고 하였다

영역별 핵심문제 p.203~207

01 conversation 02 ⑤ 03 ③
04 ① 05 copyright 06 were, would not post
07 If I were you, I would put aside the smartphone.
08 Because only the blog owner has the right to use them.
09 He is not supposed to use his personal information.
10 ⑤ 11 ③ 12 ① 13 ⑤
14 ④ 15 ④ 16 ① 17 ④
18 (A) If I hadn't been lazy, I could have won the race.
   (B) If I hadn't played at that time, I wouldn't be hungry now.
   (C) If I had worked hard on it, the house would have stood strong.
19 ② 20 ③ 21 ④
22 digital detox
23 Digital detox means staying away from digital devices, such as smartphones and computers, for a while. 24 ④ 25 ④
26 use them at night
27 (A) advantages (B) disadvantages
28 ③ 29 ④

---

01 유의어 관계다. 제한하다 – 대화

02 (A)는 젊은이를 위해 더 많은 일자리를 만들기(create)를 원한다는 의미가 적절하다. (B)는 그의 사랑스런 딸과 공원에서 즐거운(enjoyable) 오후를 보냈다는 의미가 적절하다.

03 무언가, 특히 해로운 것을 하는 것이나 사용하는 것을 중단하지 못하는 것: 중독(addiction)

04 어떤 사람이 유리한 결과를 얻는 데 도움이 될 만한 것: 장점, 유리함(advantage)

05 저작권은 창작자가 그나 그녀의 문학과 예술 작품에 가지고 있는 권리이다.

06 'be not supposed to+동사원형'은 '~해서는 안 된다'는 불허의 의미로, 'If I were you, I would not+동사원형'을 사용해

서 '내가 너라면 ~하지 않을 텐데.'의 의미로 '~하지 마라'라는 충고의 의미를 나타낼 수 있다.

07 'If I were you, I would ~.'는 충고할 때 사용하는 표현으로 '내가 너라면 ~할 것이다(~할 텐데)'로 해석한다. 'put aside'는 '치우다'라는 의미이다.

08 다른 사람의 블로그에서 가져온 사진을 자신의 블로그에 게시하면 안 되는 이유를 'Because+주어+동사' 어순으로 쓴다.

09 질문: 세호는 비밀번호를 만들 때 무엇을 사용하면 안 되나?

10 '누군가 네 비밀번호를 알아낸 것 같아.'라는 문제에 대해 알맞은 충고는 비밀번호를 바꾸라는 것이 적절하다.

11 보라는 비밀번호를 만들 때 개인 정보를 사용하지 말라고 충고하고 있다.

12 nice(착하다)는 의미상의 주어를 of Peter로 쓴다.

13 가정법 과거에는 동사의 과거형이 온다. 이 경우 비인칭 주어 it과 동사 snowed를 쓸 수 있다는 것에 유의한다.

14 비교급 강조는 much, 의미상의 주어는 for you이다.

15 '과거시제의 직설법 문장'을 가정법으로 고치면 '가정법 과거완료'가 된다. If절에 'had+p.p.', 주절에 '조동사 과거+have+p.p'를 쓰며, 직설법과 반대되도록 not을 활용한다.

16 옳은 문장은 ⓕ, 1개이다. ⓐ to diligent → to be diligent, ⓑ possibly → possible, ⓒ of → for, ⓓ they → them, ⓔ going → go, ⓖ not be → not to be

17 <보기>의 if는 간접의문문의 명사절을 이끄는 접속사로서 '~인지'라는 뜻으로 쓰였다. ④의 if가 보기와 쓰임이 같으며, 이때 쓰인 would도 '과거의 습관'을 의미하는 뜻으로 사용된 것에 유의한다. ④를 제외한 나머지는 모두 가정법 과거시제를 이끄는 종속 접속사로 쓰였다.

18 (B)는 혼합 가정문으로, If절에 'had p.p' 형태가, 주절에 '조동사 과거+동사원형'이 온다. 시간 표현이 동반되는 것에 유의한다. (A)와 (C)는 모두 가정법 과거완료 문장으로, If절의 과거완료와 주절의 표현에 유의하여 영작하도록 한다.

19 ②는 비인칭 주어로서 거리를 나타낸다. 나머지는 모두 '진주어 to부정사구'를 받는 가주어 It이다.

20 주어진 문장은 디지털 디톡스가 여러분을 돕는다는 의미이므로, 구체적으로 어떠한 도움을 주는지 열거하고 있는 ③번이 적절하다.

21 스마트폰 중독 증상으로는 스마트폰에 너무 많은 시간을 소비하고, 공부에 집중할 수 없고, 목에 통증을 느끼는 것이라고 하였다.

22 상쾌함을 느끼는 이유가 시끄러운 디지털 세상으로부터 자유를 즐기기 위해 디지털 디톡스를 시작해서라고 말할 수 있다.

23 디지털 디톡스란 스마트폰과 컴퓨터 같은 디지털 기기들로부터 잠시 동안 떨어져 있는 것을 의미한다고 하였다.

24 (A)는 진주어로 쓰인 to부정사이다. ①, ② 부사적 용법 중 목적 ③ 형용사적 용법 ④ 진주어 ⑤ 부사적 용법 중 형용사 수식

25 스마트폰 사용에 대한 규칙에 관한 글이므로 스마트폰 없이 밖에서 시간을 덜 보내겠다는 것은 어색하며 **more**가 더 적절하다.

26 밤에 스마트폰을 침실 밖에 두고 사용하지 않을 것이라고 하였으므로, 그들의 스마트폰을 침실로 가져가지 않고 밤에 사용하지 않겠다고 말하는 것이 적절하다.

27 빈칸 (A)와 (B) 이후에 나열된 사항들은 각각 스마트폰의 장점과 단점이다. 따라서 advantages, disadvantages 순서로 쓰는 것이 적절하다.

28 스마트폰이 없다면 우리가 사람들과 연락하는 것이 쉽지 않을 것이라고 하였으므로, ③번에 대한 대답으로 '스마트폰'이라고 답할 수 있다.

29 스마트폰이 없을 때의 장점을 말하고 있는데 스마트폰 사용의 장점을 말하는 ④번은 글의 흐름상 어색하다.

단원별 예상문제
p.208~211

01 (c)reate 02 ③

03 I have a website we can download it from for free. 04 ① 05 ②

06 more than → less than 07 ⑤ 08 ④

09 If I were you, I would suggest doing outdoor activities to your friends.

10 without asking 11 ③

12 (1) ⓒ (2) ⓑ (3) ⓐ (4) ⓑ (5) ⓐ

13 ③ 14 ③

15 (1) knew your phone number, would call
(2) were[was] a police officer, would find out
(3) had seen the accident, would have been
(4) hadn't joined my club, couldn't have succeeded

16 Are you addicted to your smartphone?

17 ⑤ 18 ③ 19 ② 20 ⑤

21 Smartphone addiction makes us have a pain in our neck.

---

01 반의어 관계다. 줄이다-늘리다 : 파괴하다-만들다

02 위험한 것을 처리할 대비가 되도록 사람들에게 하는 경고

03 '우리가 그것을 무료로 내려 받을 수 있는'이 '웹 사이트'를 수식하는 구조로 'a website (that/which) we can download it from for free' 어순을 사용한다.

05 컴퓨터 게임에 중독되었다고 말하는 친구에게 해 줄 충고로 게임 시간을 제한하기 위해 일일 계획을 짜라는 말이 적절하다.

06 피곤해 보인다는 말에 4시간 이상 잤다는 말보다는 4시간도 못 잤다는 말이 자연스럽다.

07 생일 날짜를 비밀번호로 사용했다는 말로 보아 개인정보를 사용하지 말라는 충고가 적절하다.

08 SNS의 비밀번호가 누군가에 의해 도용된 것이므로 비밀번호가 추측하기에 쉬웠느냐고 묻는 것이 적절하다. (d)번의 difficult를 easy로 바꾸어야 한다.

09 '내가 너라면'은 가정법 과거형으로 be동사는 'were'를 사용한다. '~할 텐데, ~할 것이다'라는 의미로 주절에는 'would+동사원형'을 사용하고, suggest는 동명사를 목적어로 취하는 동사이다.

11 '~인지 아닌지'의 의미로 동사의 목적어 자리에 사용된 if를 찾는다. ②번은 '~일지라도'의 양보의 의미를 가지는 if이다.

12 (1) 거리를 나타내는 비인칭 주어 (3) 가주어 It, 진주어 to부정사 (2), (4) It ~ that 강조구문 (5) 가주어 It, 진주어 that절

13 가정법 과거 문장들이다. ① makes → made ② 'If there were no smartpones, it would be hard ~'로 고쳐야 한다. ④ will share → would share ⑤ will → would

14 ① for → of ② skating → skate ④ of → for ⑤ he to mastering → him to master

15 (1), (2)는 가정법 과거, (3), (4)는 가정법 과거완료이다. If절 동사의 시제와 주절의 조동사의 과거 뒤의 표현에 유의하여 빈칸에 알맞게 영작한다. (1)의 my를 your로 (4)의 your를 my로 전환하는 것도 주의하고, 특히 (4) B의 대답이 Yes이므로, but 뒤에는 '부정 의미'를 갖는 가정법이 필요하며, 내용상 주절에도 not이 와야 한다.

16 글의 흐름상 '스마트폰에 중독되었나요?'라는 말이 들어가는 것이 자연스럽다.

17 공부에 집중하기 위해서 스마트폰의 알림을 끄는 것은 위 항목에 해당하지 않는다.

18 score는 명사로 쓰여 '(경기, 시합의) 득점, (시험의) 점수, (음악) 악보'라는 의미가 있으며, 동사로 쓰여 '득점하다', '채점하다'라는 의미가 있다. 밑줄 친 (B)는 '점수'라는 의미로 쓰였다. ①, ④ 악보, ② 채점하다, ③ 득점, 점수 ⑤ 득점하다

19 주어진 문장의 now란 스마트폰으로 인한 여러 문제를 가지고 있는 지금을 의미한다. 주어진 문장에서 digital detox를 처음으로 언급하고 이를 설명하는 문장이 뒤이어 나오는 것이 자연스럽다. 따라서 ②번이 적절하다.

20 디지털 티독스는 학생들이 디지털 세계로부터 자유를 즐길 수 있도록 한다.

21 스마트폰 중독은 우리가 스마트폰에 너무 많은 시간을 소비하게 하고, 공부에 집중할 수 없고, 목에 통증을 느낄 수 있게 한다고 하였다.

01 it's against the law
02 spends, smartphone, get together, SNS, to
suggest, outdoor activities
03 You're not supposed to post someone's pictures
without asking.
04 I had been in Busan, I could have seen the
fireworks festival
05 (1) It was too boring for Sally to stay home on a
sunny day.
(2) It is really careless of you to reach out to a big
dog.
06 (A) Living(또는 To live)　(B) to set　(C) to follow
07 We will keep our smartphones out of the
bedroom and not use them at night.
08 If I were you, I would turn off all alerts.
09 Too much use of a smartphone is dangerous.
10 They are going to spend more time for outside
activities, and post fewer SNS messages.

01 왜 Catherine은 웹 사이트에서 무료로 영화를 다운로드하면 안
되는가?

02 내 아들, Tony는 스마트폰에 너무 많은 시간을 보낸다. 그와 그
의 친구들은 거의 매일 SNS에서 만난다. 나는 그에게 친구들과
야외 활동을 하는 것을 제안해 보라고 말했다.

03 'must not, should not'은 '~해서는 안 된다'는 불허, 금지의
표현으로 'be not supposed to'로 바꾸어 쓸 수 있다.

04 내용상 '내가 부산에 있었다면, 불꽃 축제를 볼 수 있었을 텐데'가
빈칸에 적절하다. 가정법 과거완료 시제이므로 'If I had been'
을 종속절에, 주절에는 'could have seen'을 쓴다.

05 의미상의 주어에 알맞은 전치사에 유의한다. '부주의하다'에는 전
치사 of를 쓴다. 가주어 It과 be동사를 시제에 맞게, 주어진 단어
들을 적절히 배열, 글자 수에 맞추어 영작한다.

06 (A) '스마트폰 없이 사는 것'이라는 주어로 to부정사나 동명사를
쓸 수 있다. (B) '규칙을 정하는 것'이라는 의미로 진주어 to부정
사를 쓴다. (C) 규칙을 따르는 것'이라는 의미가 적절하며, 동사
need는 to부정사를 목적어로 취한다.

07 스마트폰을 밤에 침실 밖에 두고 사용하지 않을 것이라고 말하는
것이 적절하다.

08 가정법 과거를 활용하여 쓸 수 있다. 가정법 과거는 'If+주어+동
사의 과거형, 주어+조동사의 과거형+동사원형'으로 표현한다.

09 스마트폰을 너무 많이 사용하는 것은 위험하다고 하였다.

10 지나, 호성, 민수는 스마트폰을 현명하게 사용하기 위하여 밖에서
노는 데 더 많은 시간을 보내고 SNS 메시지를 더 적게 올릴 것이
라고 하였다.

|모범답안|
01 (1) A: Do you use the same password for a long
time?
B: Yes.
A: You're not supposed to use the same
password for a long time.
(2) A: Do yo u post bad comments online?
B: Yes.
A: You're not supposed to post bad comments
online.
02 Televisions, televisions, we should spend more
time with our family, we would be healthier, it
would not be easy for us to watch movies, it
would be more difficult for us to check the news

단원별 모의고사　　　　　　　　　p.215~219

01 ④　　　　　　02 disadvantage　　　　03 ③
04 ⑤　　　　　　05 ④
06 I would not[wouldn't] post someone's pictures
without asking
07 ②　　　　　08 ④　　　　　09 ①
10 addicted
11 you're not supposed to post them on your blog
12 (a) (사진을) 찍다　(b) 가져왔다
13 ②
14 (1) It was not possible for the villagers to build
the castle in a month.
(2) It is rude of Thomas not to show respect for
the old man.
(3) It is impossible for the Chinese girl to take
drugs on an airplane.
15 (1) would be easy for us to spend more time with our
family / would be possible for us to have more time
to exercise
(2) would not be easy for us to watch shows and
dramas / would be difficult for us to check the
news
16 ②　　　　　17 is, cannot　18 ⑤　　　　19 ⑤
20 Then now is the time for you to start digital detox.
21 ④　　　　　22 ⑤
23 (C)—(B)—(A)
24 What can be the rules of digital detox?
25 ④

01 ④번은 'intend(의도하다)'에 관한 설명이다. 'create'에 대한 영어 설명은 'to make something new, or invent something'이 되어야 한다.

02 반의어 관계다. 안전한–위험한 : 장점–단점

03 특정한 목적을 위해 만들어진 기계적인 물체

04 '오랜 기간 동안 같은 비밀번호를 사용하니?'라고 묻는 A의 물음에 개인 정보를 사용하면 안 된다는 B의 말은 자연스럽지 않다.

05 대화의 흐름상 'Sarah에게 사진을 올려도 되는지 물어봤니?'라는 말이 오는 것이 자연스럽다.

06 'be not supposed to+동사원형'은 '~해서는 안 된다'라는 의미로 'If I were you'를 사용하여 '내가 너라면 ~하지 않을 텐데'의 의미로 'If I were you, I would not[wouldn't] ~' 형태로 문장을 완성하면 된다.

07 주절의 동사가 'would+동사원형'이므로 if절의 시제는 가정법 과거형이 적절하다. be동사는 'were'를 사용한다.

08 In fact는 앞 문장의 내용을 강조하면서 덧붙여 말하는 기능을 한다. 그래서 '그것은 좋지 않아. 사실 그것은 큰 실수야.'라는 내용으로 ④가 적절하다. 그리고 내용상 'it'은 '생일 날짜를 사용한 것'을 가리키는 인칭대명사이다.

09 '웹 사이트에서 영화를 내려 받지 말고 극장에 가는 게 어때?'라고 말하고 있으므로 대안을 제시하는 'instead'가 적절하다.

10 컴퓨터 게임을 하는 것을 멈출 수가 없다고 말하고 있으므로 '중독되었다'는 의미가 적절하다.

11 '~해서는 안 된다'는 'be not supposed to+동사원형'을 사용한다.

13 ②의 if는 간접의문문 명사절을 이끄는 접속사이며, 나머지는 모두 가정의 조건절을 이끄는 종속접속사이다.

14 to부정사 또는 동명사가 주어인 문장을 '가주어-진주어' 구조로 표현할 때, 일반적으로 'It ~ for+의미상의 주어+to V' 형태로 쓴다. 사람의 성질이나 태도를 나타내는 형용사가 있을 때는 of를 for 자리에 쓴다. (2)는 무례하다는 뜻이므로, of를 쓰는 것이 적절하며, (1), (3)은 'for+의미상의 주어' 형태로 쓴다.

15 전제 조건 'If there were no televisions'가 가정법 과거 문장이므로 it 뒤의 be동사는 would be이다. we를 의미상 주어로 하면 for us, 나머지는 표에 맞추어 적절히 배열한다.

16 <보기>의 would는 가정법의 주절에서 쓰이는 조동사이다. ① would like to = want to ③ 과거의 습관적 행위 ④ will의 과거시제 ⑤ 공손한 질문

17 가정법과거 문장은 직설법 현재 문장으로 바꿔 쓸 수 있다.

18 앞서 나온 형용사가 사람의 성질을 나타내는 것이 아니므로 to부정사의 의미상의 주어로 'for+목적격'이 쓰인다. 모두 for가 쓰이지만 polite는 사람의 성질을 나타내는 형용사이므로 'of+목적격'으로 의미상의 주어를 표현한다.

19 주어진 문장의 the rules가 가리키는 것은 스마트폰 사용을 위해 만든 규칙인 'to set some rules for using your smartphones'를 의미한다.

20 디지털 디톡스를 시작하는 주체는 '여러분'이므로 to부정사의 의미상 주어로 'for you'를 쓰는 것에 유의한다.

21 다른 사람들과 함께 보낼 시간이 많아진다고 하였다.

22 스마트폰 중독이 야기할 수 있는 문제는 스마트폰에 너무 많은 시간을 보내게 하고, 공부에 집중할 수 없고, 목에 통증을 느끼는 것이라고 하였다.

23 장점에 대해 말하자고 하였으므로 장점을 언급한 (C) → (B) 또 다른 장점을 언급하고 반면 단점도 있다고 말함 → (A) 스마트폰이 없을 경우의 단점에 관해 말함

24 학생들은 디지털 디톡스의 규칙에 관해 이야기하고 있다.

25 스마트폰에 SNS 메시지를 더 적게 올릴 것이라고 말한 그룹은 지나, 호성, 민수의 그룹이다.

Lesson 5

Love for My Country

시험대비 실력평가   p.224

01 ③   02 independence

03 look forward to   04 ②   05 ⑤

06 ③   07 specialist   08 ④

01 처칠의 동상이 의회 건물 밖에 서 있다.

02 다른 나라에 의해 지배되거나 통치되는 것으로부터의 해방[벗어남]: independence(독립)

03 look forward to+동명사: ~하기를 기대하다

04 예술 작품, 그림 또는 기타 흥미로운 것들의 공개적인 전시

05 누군가, 특히 중요한 사람이 묻혀 있는 큰 석조 구조물이나 지하 공간

06 (A) 건물 전체로 불이 빠르게 퍼졌다. (B) 투표는 당신의 애국적인 의무 중 일부다.

07 유의어 관계이다. 바람, 소원 : 전문가

08 나는 독도가 한국에 속한다는 것을 많은 사람들에게 알리고 싶다. '~에 속하다'라는 의미로 'belong to'를 사용한다.

서술형 시험대비   p.225

01 (1) harmony   (2) movement   (3) kill   (4) poem

02 republic

03 (1) entrance   (2) president   (3) government
   (4) Japanese

04 (1) amusement park, 놀이공원
   (2) organization, 조직   (3) poem, 시
   (4) sacrifice, 희생

05 complete

01 (1) 많은 종교 지도자들은 세상에 평화와 화합을 가져오기 위해 열심히 노력한다. (2) 그녀는 저명한 과학자이며 세계 환경 운동의 선구자였다. (3) 가뭄은 작물을 죽일 수도 있다. (4) 그녀의 시는 우리에게 강하고 용감하게 살라고 말합니다.

02 공화국은 국민이나 그들이 선출하는 대표자들에 의해 권력이 유지되는 나라이다.

03 (1) entrance: 입구 (2) president: 대통령 (3) government: 정부 (4) Japanese: 일본의

04 (1) 박람회장 놀이기구, 쇼, 그리고 다른 오락거리가 있는 넓은 야외 공간 (2) 조직될 목적으로 함께 일하는 사람들의 집단

(3) 깊은 의미를 암시하고 읽을 때 리드미컬하게 들리는 아름다운 단어를 사용하는 한 편의 글 (4) 특정한 목적을 위해 귀중한 어떤 것을 포기하는 것

05 • 몇몇 사람들은 예체능 수업이 완전한 시간 낭비라고 생각한다.
   • 때때로, 그는 단지 하나의 작품을 끝내기 위해 20 시간을 보내기도 한다.

교과서 Conversation

핵심 Check   p.226~227

1 ①, ④   2 ③

교과서 대화문 익히기

Check(√) True or False   p.228

1 T   2 F   3 T   4 F

교과서 확인학습   p.230~231

Listen & Speak 1 A

1. at, huge / looks strong / Because, was built, protect, during / who built / ordered, to direct, process, don't you / heard of, scientist

2. don't you / national flag, isn't / what, symbols, mean / circle, harmony, peace / lines, corners / mean, earth

Listen & Speak 2 A

1. planning to go / built / heard, great / treasures that, had taken / must be interesting / looking forward to

2. what did you do / volunteer work / What kind / cleaned, tombs, respect, who / Sounds / planning to go, join / I'm looking forward to

Real Life Talk

reading / Poetry, know, don't you / heard / poems when, under, rule, desire, independence, be felt, poems / to read, poems, learn / In fact, to visit / when / near, Palace, palace / Let's / looking forward to, visit

Wrap Up

put on traditional / for, Germany / there are / shopping / know, don't you / traditional, soup, delicious, healthy, to trying

---

구문을 사용한다. direct를 to direct로 바꾸어 쓴다.

09 'know'의 목적어로 '의문사+주어+동사' 어순의 간접의문문으로 사용해야 한다. 'what the symbols in Taegeukgi mean'이 되어야 한다.

10 각각의 모서리에 4개의 선이 있는 것이 아니라 네 모서리에 검은 선들이 있다.

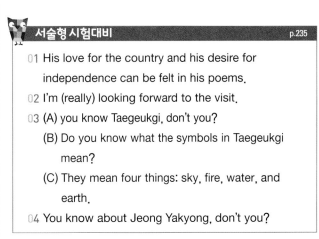

시험대비 기본평가 p.232

01 looking forward to   02 ⑤   03 ③
04 ②

---

01 앞으로 하고 싶은 일에 대한 기대를 표현할 때 'I'm looking forward to ~.'나 'I look forward to ~.'의 표현을 사용한다.

02 빈칸 뒤의 부가의문문 형태가 'don't you?'인 것으로 보아 앞의 평서문은 일반동사 긍정문 형태가 오는 것이 적절하고, B가 대답으로 '그것에 관해 들었어.'라고 말하므로 그것에 관해 아는지 확인하는 말이 적절하다.

03 앞으로 하고 싶은 일에 대한 기대를 표현할 때 'be dying to+동사원형'을 사용한다.

04 'You know ~, don't you?'는 알고 있는지 물어보는 표현이다.

시험대비 실력평가 p.233~234

01 ⑤   02 ④   03 ④   04 ③
05 I'm looking forward to making it.   06 ④
07 King Jeongjo ordered Jeong Yakyong to direct the building process.   08 ②, ⑤   09 ③
10 ④

---

01 'look forward to'에서 to는 전치사이므로 명사나 동명사가 온다. trying이 적절하다.

02 Judy와 Seho는 점심으로 삼계탕을 먹을 것이다.

03 봉사 활동하러 현충원에 갔다는 말에 → (D) 거기(현충원)서 어떤 종류의 봉사 활동을 했는지 묻고 → (B) 묘 주변을 청소했다는 대답을 하고 → (A) 자기도 할 수 있는지 묻는 말에 → 마지막으로 (C) '물론이지.'라고 승낙의 답을 한다.

04 '너는 안중근에 대해 알지, 그렇지 않니?'라는 물음에 '너는 안중근 박물관에 가서 그에 대해 더 많은 정보를 얻을 수 있어.'라고 답하는 것은 어색하다.

05 '~하는 것을 기대하고 있다'라는 의미로 'be dying to+동사원형'은 'look forward to+동명사'로 쓸 수 있다.

06 ④번은 '나는 간송 박물관에 갈 예정이야.'라는 말에 '그러고 싶지만, 그곳을 방문하는 것이 기대가 돼.'라고 말하는 것은 어색하다.

07 '~에게 …하라고 명령[지시]하다'는 'order+목적어+to부정사'

서술형 시험대비 p.235

01 His love for the country and his desire for independence can be felt in his poems.
02 I'm (really) looking forward to the visit.
03 (A) you know Taegeukgi, don't you?
   (B) Do you know what the symbols in Taegeukgi mean?
   (C) They mean four things: sky, fire, water, and earth.
04 You know about Jeong Yakyong, don't you?

---

01 질문: 윤동주의 시를 통해 무엇이 느껴질 수 있나?

02 기대나 희망을 나타낼 때 'look forward to+명사/동명사'를 사용한다.

교과서
Grammar

핵심 Check p.236~237

1 (1) had   (2) visited
2 (1) that   (2) so that

시험대비 기본평가 p.238

01 ⑤   02 ③   03 ②
04 (1) that, could[might]   (2) so hot that
   (3) that, he can[may]   (4) so hard that, can't

---

01 본동사의 시제가 과거이고, 그 이전에 일어난 약속이므로 과거완료시제를 쓴다.

02 'so as to V' 또는 'so that ~ 주어 can'은 '~하기 위해서'라는 뜻이며, 'so 형용사 that 주어 V'는 '너무 ~해서 …하다'라는 의미이다.

03 ① came(과거) 이전에 일어난 일이므로 had gone으로 써야 한다. ③ had found → found, ④ had lived → have lived, ⑤ when은 '시점'을 묻는 의문사이므로 완료시제와 함

께 쓸 수 없다.

04 '목적'을 나타내는 'so that'과 '결과'를 나타내는 'so+수식어+that+can[can't]'를 이해하고, 적용하는 문제이다. that을 기준으로 앞, 뒤 문장에 나타난 동사의 시제를 일치시키는데 유의하여, so that을 활용하도록 한다.

시험대비 실력평가   p.239~241

01 ③	02 ④	03 ⑤	04 ③
05 ⑤	06 ⑤	07 ①	
08 has → had	09 ④	10 ⑤	11 ④
12 ①			

13 (1) Father Lee Taeseok returned to Sudan in order that he could help poor people there.
　(2) Amy practices every day so that she can join our sports club.
　(3) Clara left for Paris in order that she could study fashion.
　(4) Thames ran fast so that he would not be late for the meeting.

14 (1) squeezed out the pimples so that they would disappear
　(2) in order that he could get a full college scholarship

01 과거 시점 이전에 발생한 일이다. has broken → had broken

03 'so that+주어+조동사'가 적절히 사용된 것을 찾는다.

04 ① had not eaten → has not eaten ② 까마귀가 도시로 이주하기 전 정글에 살았다는 문장이므로 The crow had lived in the jungle before it moved to the city.가 옳은 문장이다. ④ 설거지를 끝내야 한다고 요구한 것이므로 had finished → (should) finish ⑤ had read → have read

05 ① in order for → in order that ② not being → would not be ③ so joy that → so joyful that ④ so to → so as to 또는 in order to

06 다른 문장들은 모두 '목적'을 나타내는 표현인데, ⑤의 두 번째 문장은 '결과'를 나타낸다. 보통, '결과'의 so (that)는 앞 문장의 끝에 콤마(쉼표)를 쓴다.

07 <보기>의 had solved는 과거완료시제 중 '완료' 용법으로 쓰였다. ②, ③, ⑤는 '계속' ④는 '경험' 용법이다.

08 과거의 특정 시점 이전에 계속된 일이므로 과거완료시제이다.

09 '일본을 물리치기 위해 군인들은 열심히 훈련했다'라는 문장들로서 모두 '목적'을 나타내는데, ④만 '군인들은 열심히 훈련해서 일본을 물리쳤다'라는 뜻의 '결과'를 나타낸다.

10 ⑤ 'Irene이 전보다 더 열심히 공부했기 위해서 시험에 떨어졌

다'는 이상한 문장이다. (al)though와 같은 '양보'의 접속사로 바꾸는 것이 적절하다.

11 ① has → had ② had picked → has picked 또는 picked ③ have → had ⑤ had been given → had given

12 ② be stay → be 또는 stay로 동사를 하나만 쓴다. ③ in order to that → in order that ④ so that 생략 또는 in order to → I can ⑤ she can → she could *subtitles: 자막

13 '목적'을 나타내는 to부정사 또는 'in order to', 'so as to' 등의 표현은 'so[in order]+that+주어+조동사'로 바꿔 쓸 수 있다.

14 목적'을 나타내는 부사절 'so that', 'in order that' 뒤의 문장 구조에 유의하여, 그림에 맞게 적절히 영작한다. *squeeze out: 짜내다 *pimple: 여드름

서술형 시험대비   p.242~243

01 (1) bought many Korean treasures that some Japanese had taken to Japan
　(2) made the Turtle Ship so that he could protect the people
　(3) walked slowly so that no one could hear him

02 had searched, had made

03 (1) Could you remind me of the time so that I won't be late for the party? 또는 Could you remind me of the time in order that I won't be late for the party?
　(2) Whenever Jane was ill, her mom used to make her a bowl of porridge in order for her to get well.
　(3) They are saving money so that they can buy a big house.
　(4) Remember my number in order that you can contact me. 또는 Remember my number in order for you to contact me.
　(5) The foreigners from Italy went to Gyeongju so that they could see Bulguksa.
　(6) Many people joined the New Korean Society in order to support the Independence movement.

04 (1) We need ice and sugar so that we can make patbingsu.
　(2) We went to the river so that she could catch some fish.
　(3) A firefighter ran into the woods so that she could rescue the koalas.
　(4) My grandma exercises every day in order that she can keep healthy.

05 had lived alone in the house for thirty-three years until the official visited him last year

06 (1) ⓐ, 내가 그곳에 도착했을 때, Peter는 이미 뉴욕으로 떠나 버렸다.

(2) ⓓ, 작년까지 William은 14년간 부산에서 살았다.

(3) ⓓ, 콘서트가 시작되기 전까지 그들은 그 가수를 거의 하루 동안 기다렸다.

(4) ⓑ, Maria는 이번 겨울에 한국에 올 때까지 눈을 본 적이 없었다.

(5) ⓐ, 내가 공항에 도착했을 무렵 탑승 수속이 이미 끝났다.

(6) ⓒ, 우리가 집에 왔을 때, 누군가가 창문을 깬 것을 알게 되었다.

(7) ⓑ, 나는 전에 그 사람을 만난 적이 없어서 그 사람을 알아보지 못했다.

(8) ⓐ, 그 부부가 깨었을 때, 누군가가 구두 만들기를 끝내놓았다.

01 (1) 과거의 특정 시점 이전에 일어난 일은 '과거완료시제'로 사용하는 것에 유의한다. (2), (3) '목적'을 나타내는 부사절에 'so that 주어 could'를 사용한다.

02 과거의 어느 특정 시점을 기준으로 먼저 일어난 일을 과거완료시제로 표현한다. Before, After가 있을 때, 시간의 전후 관계가 명확하므로 과거시제도 쓸 수 있으나, 문제에서 완료시제로 쓸 것을 요구했음에 유의한다.

03 (1) so order that → so that 또는 in order that (2) of her → for her (3) so which → so that (4) in order for you can → in order for you to 또는 in order that you can (5) can → could (6) so order to → in order to

04 주어진 단어들 중 동사의 수와 시제에 유의하여, 'so that' 또는 'in order that'으로 적절한 문장을 영작한다. (3) 소방대원은, 괄호에 주어진 단어가 she이므로 여성임에 유의한다.

05 과거의 어느 특정 시점을 기준으로 그 전부터 시작된 동작이나 상태는 과거완료시제로 표현한다. 작년에 공무원이 방문한 과거의 시점을 기준으로 노인이 혼자 산 것이므로 'had lived alone'을 쓰는 것이 적절하다.

06 과거완료시제는 완료, 경험, 결과, 계속 등의 용법으로 구분할 수 있으며, 해석을 정확하게 하는 것이 중요하다.

[교과서] Reading

확인문제 p.244

1 F 2 F 3 T 4 T

확인문제 p.245

1 F 2 T 3 F 4 F 5 T

교과서 확인학습 A p.246~247

01 my history club

02 visited, inside the park

03 At, entrance

04 a great national hero, spent, from

05 helped educate, by building

06 In, when the independence movement, moved to

07 joined, became its president

08 The exhibition hall, shows

09 looking around, stopped at, Patriotic Organization's

10 formed, organization, to fight against

11 belonged to

12 At, saw two watches

13 In, made a plan to

14 Patriotic Organization, directed, to carry

15 left for, wearing a very old watch, Mine, it, take, let, have

16 always carried, so that, forget, sacrifice

17 completing, moved to, tombs

18 had been, independence, them

19 By doing so, for the sacrifice

20 As, left, words, that, had read

21 It, written in

22 what my wish is, Korea's Independence

23 what my second wish, independence

24 asks me what my third wish is, complete independence

교과서 확인학습 B p.248~249

1 Last week my history club went to Hyochang Park.

2 We visited the Kim Koo Museum inside the park.

3 At the entrance of the museum, we saw a white statue of Kim Koo.

4 Kim Koo is a great national hero who spent most of his life fighting for the independence of Korea from Japanese rule.

5 In the 1900s, he helped educate young people by building schools.

6 In 1919, when the independence movement had spread throughout the country, he moved to Shanghai, China.

7 There he joined the Government of the Republic of Korea and later became its president.

8 The exhibition hall in the museum shows a lot of things about Kim Koo's life.

9 While looking around the hall, we stopped at a photo of the Korean Patriotic Organization's members.

10 Kim Koo formed the secret organization in 1931 to fight against Japan.

11 Lee Bongchang and Yun Bonggil belonged to the group.

12 At one place in the hall, we saw two watches under a photo of Kim Koo and Yun Bonggil.

13 In 1932, Kim Koo made a plan to kill Japanese generals in a park in Shanghai.

14 As the leader of the Korean Patriotic Organization, he directed Yun to carry out the mission.

15 When Yun left for the mission, he told Kim, "Sir, you are wearing a very old watch. Mine is new, but I won't need it anymore. Please take my watch, and let me have yours."

16 Kim Koo always carried Yun's watch in his jacket so that he would not forget Yun's sacrifice.

17 After completing the tour of the museum, we moved to the tombs of the three heroes, Lee Bongchang, Yun Bonggil, and Baek Jeonggi.

18 Their bodies had been in Japan, but after Korea's independence Kim Koo brought them to Hyochang Park.

19 By doing so, he showed his deep love and respect for the sacrifice of the three heroes.

20 As I left Hyochang Park, I thought about Kim Koo's words in My Wish that I had read in the exhibition hall.

21 It was written in *Baekbeomilji*.

22 If God asks me what my wish is, I would say clearly, "It is Korea's Independence."

23 If he asks me what my second wish is, I would say, "It is the independence of my country."

24 If he asks me what my third wish is, I would say loudly, "It is the complete independence of my country." That is my answer.

01 ②   02 ④

03 It is at the entrance of the museum.

04 He moved to Shanghai in 1919.

05 ②, ④

06 He planned to kill the Japanese generals in a park in Shanghai.

07 ④   08 ⑤   09 ①, ③   10 ⑤

11 Kim Koo's firm wish for the complete independence of Korea was written in *Baekbeomilji*.

12 visit the Kim Koo Museum inside the park

13 ④

14 He fought for the independence of Korea from Japanese rule.

15 ④   16 exhibition   17 ②

18 There were two watches.

19 ③   20 ⑤   21 my watch   22 ④

23 ③   24 ⑤

25 They are written in *Baekbeomilji*.

01 동명사와 함께 쓰이면서 '~함으로써'라는 의미를 완성하는 전치사 by가 적절하다.

02 김구 선생은 학교를 설립함으로써 젊은이들을 교육시키는 것을 도왔다. ③ 그는 생의 대부분을 일본을 위해 싸우느라 보낸 것이 아니라 일본에 대항해서 싸우느라 보냈다.

03 기념관 입구에 김구 선생의 동상이 있다고 하였다.

04 김구가 중국 상해로 이동한 때는 1919년이라고 하였다.

05 기념관 안에 있는 전시관에는 한인 애국단 멤버의 사진, 김구와 윤봉길의 사진 아래에 있는 두 개의 시계가 있다고 하였다.

06 김구는 상해에 있는 한 공원에서 일본 장군들을 죽일 계획을 하였다.

07 김구가 일본에 맞서 싸우기 위해 1931년에 만든 것은 비밀 조직이었다.

08 윤봉길의 희생을 잊지 않기 위해서 김구는 그의 시계를 항상 가지고 다녔다.

09 선행사가 Kim Koo's words in My Wish이므로 which나 that을 쓰는 것이 적절하다.

10 (B)의 대명사 Their가 가리키는 것은 (C)의 이봉창, 윤봉길, 백정기이며, 독립 이후 이들의 시신을 일본에서 효창공원으로 모셔왔다. (A)에서 말하는 By doing so는 김구의 이러한 행동을 의미하는 말이다.

11 백범일지에는 한국의 독립에 대한 김구의 단호한 소망이 적혀 있다고 하였다.

12 역사 동아리는 효창 공원 안에 있는 김구 기념관을 방문하기 위하여 그 공원으로 갔다.

13 효창공원 입구에는 하얀색의 김구 조각상이 있다고 하였다.

14 김구는 일본 통치로부터 한국의 독립을 위해 싸웠다고 하였다.

15 역사 동아리가 어떻게 효창 공원으로 갔는지는 위 글을 읽고 답할 수 없다.

16 사진, 조각 혹은 다른 흥미로운 물건들이 전시되는 공개 행사는 '전시회(exhibition)'이다.

17 '전시관을 둘러보던 중'이라는 말이므로 around라고 쓰는 것이 적절하다.

18 김구와 윤봉길 사진 아래에는 두 개의 시계가 있었다고 하였다.

19 모두 김구를 가리키는 말이지만 ③번은 윤봉길을 가리키는 말이다.

20 (A)는 '~로서'라고 해석되는 전치사로 자격을 나타낼 때 쓰인다. ① 전치사(~처럼) ② 부사(~만큼 …한) ③ 접속사(~이기 때문에) ④ 접속사(~이듯이) ⑤ 전치사(~로서)

21 자신의 시계를 가리키는 말이다.

22 글의 흐름상 나라의 완전한 독립을 의미하는 것이므로 'complete'이라고 쓰는 것이 적절하다. *complement: 보충[보족]물

23 나의 소원'에 따르면 김구가 가장 바란 것은 한국의 독립이었다.

24 세 영웅의 시신을 일본에서 한국으로 모셔온 사람은 김구이다.

25 김구의 말이 쓰여 있는 책은 '백범일지'이다.

서술형 시험대비 p.254~255

01 Shanghai, China

02 They went to Hyochang Park last week.

03 A white statue of Kim Koo was (at the entrance of the museum).

04 It was in Shanghai, China.

05 national hero, the independence of Korea

06 The writer saw a photo of the Korean Patriotic Organization's members.

07 It was because he tried to fight against Japan.

08 belonged to the secret group

09 His plan was to kill Japanese generals in a park in Shanghai.

10 exchanged watches

11 It was because he would not forget Yun's sacrifice.

12 They moved to the tombs of the three heroes, Lee Bongchang, Yun Bonggil, and Baek Jeonggi.

13 일본에 있던 삼의사의 시신을 독립 이후에 효창 공원으로 모셔온 것

14 The writer read it in the exhibition hall.

15 It(=His third wish) was the complete independence of his country.

01 중국 상해를 가리키는 말이다.

02 글쓴이의 역사 동아리가 지난주에 간 곳은 효창 공원이다.

03 기념관 입구에는 하얀색의 김구의 조각상이 있다고 하였다.

04 위 글의 내용에 따르면 대한민국 임시 정부는 중국 상하이에 있었다.

05 김구는 일본 통치로부터 한국의 독립을 위해 싸우는 데 그의 삶 대부분을 보낸 위대한 국민 영웅이다.

06 글쓴이는 한인 애국단 단원들의 사진을 보았다고 하였다.

07 김구가 비밀 조직을 만든 이유는 일본에 맞서 싸우기 위해서라고 하였다.

08 대답으로 미루어 보아 김구가 만든 비밀 조직에 누가 속해 있었는지를 묻는 말을 쓰는 것이 적절하다.

09 김구의 계획은 상해에 있는 한 공원에서 일본 장군들을 암살하는 것이었다.

10 윤봉길은 김구가 지시한 임무를 수행하기 위해 떠나기 전 그와 함께 시계를 교환하였다. exchange: 교환하다

11 윤봉길의 희생을 잊지 않기 위하여 그의 시계를 항상 가지고 다녔다.

12 기념관 관람을 마치고 이봉창, 윤봉길, 백정기 의사들이 묻힌 삼의사의 묘로 이동했다.

13 세 사람의 시신은 일본에 있었지만, 독립 이후에 김구가 그들을 효창 공원으로 모셔온 것을 의미한다.

14 글쓴이는 전시관에서 '나의 소원'을 읽었다고 하였다.

15 김구의 세 번째 소원은 나라의 완전한 독립이라고 하였다.

영역별 핵심문제 p.257~261

01 entrance   02 ⑤   03 ③   04 ①

05 (e)xhibition 06 ④

07 He bought many Korean treasures that some Japanese had taken to Japan.

08 You know, don't   09 ②

10 They are planning to visit the Yun Dongju Museum.

11 ③   12 ⑤   13 ④   14 ③

15 (1) so that they can show
   (2) so that they could see the *Mona Lisa*

16 (1) had killed   (2) had been   (3) made
   (4) had gone   (5) had pulled

17 (1) The rabbit regretted that she had slept in the middle of the race.
   (2) The ant reminded the grasshopper that he had played in the summer.

18 ①

19 He built schools in order to help educate young people.

20 ⑤　　21 ③　　　　22 found → founded

23 ④　　24 ④

25 He formed the Korean Patriotic Organization in 1931.

26 ⑤

01 반의어 관계이다. 독립-의존 : 출구-입구

02 (A) 나는 UN과 같은 국제 조직에서 일하고 싶다. (B) 희생 없는 사랑은 없다.

03 보통 기둥 끝에 붙어 있고 국가나 협회를 대표하는 천 조각: flag(깃발)

04 특정한 결과를 위해 차례로 일어나는 일련의 일들: process(과정)

05 박물관은 피카소 작품을 전시하고 있다.

06 'desire'는 '바람, 갈망'의 뜻이다.

07 대화의 내용상 전형필이 한 훌륭한 일에 대한 글로, 주격인 he를 주어로 시작하여 동사는 bought를 사용하고 목적어로는 many Korean treasures가 오는 것이 적절하다. 그 다음 many Korean treasures를 수식하는 목적격 관계대명사절로 '주어+동사' 어순으로 영작한다.

08 상대방이 알고 있는지 확인하는 표현으로 'You know ~, don't you?'를 사용한다.

09 주어진 문장이 '정말? 난 그걸 몰랐어.'라고 말하고 있으므로 'that'은 앞 문장에 언급된 윤동주의 나라에 대한 사랑과 독립에 대한 염원이 시에서 느껴진다는 것을 가리킨다.

10 질문: 그들은 다음 주 토요일에 무엇을 할 예정인가?

11 보라가 Andy에게 윤동주의 시를 많이 읽어 보라고 제안하는 내용은 대화에서 언급되어 있지 않다.

12 so that 뒤에는 절을 써야 한다. for her to get을 she could get으로 고치는 것이 적절하다. 아니면, so that for her를 삭제해도 무방하다.

13 과거완료시제가 사용된 문장들이다. begin의 과거분사형은 began이 아니라 begun이다.

14 not은 to부정사 앞에 위치해야 한다. in order not for him → in order for him not to

15 (1) 학생들이 좋은 공연을 보여줄 수 있도록 열심히 연습 중이다. (2) 많은 관광객들이 모나리자를 보려고 루브르 박물관에 모여들었다.

16 (1), (2), (4), (5) 과거의 어느 특정 시점을 기준으로 그 이전에 시작된 일은 과거완료시제로 표현한다. (3) 역사적 사실은 주절의 동사 시제와 상관없이 과거시제를 쓴다.

17 우리말에 맞게 과거완료시제와 주어진 단어들을 적절히 사용하여 배열한다.

18 주어진 문장의 the park는 효창 공원을 의미한다. 공원 안에 있는 김구 기념관을 방문했다는 말이 나온 후 기념관 입구에서 김구 선생의 동상을 보았다고 말하는 것이 자연스럽다.

19 젊은이들을 교육시키는 데 도우려고 학교를 설립했다고 하였다.

20 김구는 중국 상해에서 대한민국 임시 정부에 가입하였다.

21 '존경받는 지도자'라는 의미가 자연스럽다. 따라서 과거분사 respected를 쓰는 것이 적절하다.

22 안창호는 1907년 신민회(the New Korean Society)를 설립하였다. find-found-found(발견하다), found-founded-founded(설립하다).

23 안창호가 몇 개의 학교를 설립했는지는 위 글을 읽고 답할 수 없다.

24 모두 '많은(= many)'이라는 의미로 쓰일 수 있지만 'the number of'는 '~의 수'라는 의미이다.

25 김구가 한인 애국단을 조직한 때는 1931년이다.

26 김구는 한인 애국단의 지도자로서 윤봉길에게 일본 장군들을 암살하도록 지시하였다.

단원별 예상문제　　　　　　　p.262~265

01 shallow　　02 ③

03 I felt great respect for the people who died for the country.　04 ①　　　05 ④

06 harmony

07 You know about Yun Dongju, don't you?

08 ⑤

09 It's a museum built by Gansong Jeon Hyeongpil. 또는 It's a museum which[that] was built by Gansong Jeon Hyeongpil.

10 ⑤

11 (1) not to forget　(2) so as not to forget
(3) in order that

12 ①, ⑤　　13 ④　　　14 ②

15 He built schools to help educate young people.

16 ③　　　17 ②

18 He built a lot of schools to educate people (until he died in 1938).　　19 ④　　　20 ②

21 상해에 있는 한 공원에서 일본 장군들을 암살하는 것

01 반의어 관계이다. 완전한 - 불완전한 : 깊은 - 얕은

02 왕이나 여왕이 쓰는 금으로 만들어지고 보석으로 장식된 원형 장식물: crown(왕관)

03 '주어(I)+동사(felt)+목적어(respect)'를 먼저 쓰고, 우리말 해석의 '나라를 위해 돌아가신'이 'the people'을 수식하는 구조로

'for the people who died for the country'의 어순을 사용하여 문장을 완성한다.

04 Soyeon이가 봉사활동을 한 곳은 박물관이 아니라 현충원이다.

05 대화의 내용상 태극기의 상징이 무엇을 의미하는지 묻는 말이 적절하다.

06 사람들이 평화롭고 서로 동의하거나 일이 옳거나 적절해 보이는 상황.

07 'You know ~, don't you?'는 알고 있는지 물어보는 표현이다.

08 주어인 '나라에 대한 그의 사랑과 독립에 대한 염원'이 느껴질 수 있는 것이므로 수동태인 'can be felt'가 적절하다.

09 'It is ~'로 문장의 주어, 동사가 있기 때문에 동사 'was built'를 사용할 수 없다. museum을 수식하는 과거분사 built만 남겨두고 was는 생략해야 한다. 또는 관계대명사를 첨가하여 'which[that] was built'로 고칠 수 있다.

10 모든 빈칸에 들어갈 단어는 so이다. ⑤는 '너무 ~해서 …하다'라는 '결과'를 나타내는 상관접속사 'so ~ that'이다. 나머지는 모두 '목적'을 뜻하는 'so that'이다.

11 목적을 나타내는 'so that'과 같은 의미의 표현들로 'in order that', 'so as to', 'in order to' 등을 활용하도록 한다.

12 과거 이전에 발생한 일은 과거완료시제로 표현한다. ② has overworked → had overworked ③ has been → had been ④번 문장은 내용의 인과관계상 사건의 발생 순서를 바로잡아야 한다. '내가 경기장에 도착했을 때, 1피리어드가 시작되었다.'는 내용이므로 The first period had begun when I arrived at the court.로 하는 것이 적절하다.

13 (a)+(C): Vicky는 그의 아들이 위대한 음악가가 될 수 있게 매일 그에게 클래식 음악을 들려준다. (b)+(D): Kate는 금메달을 따기 위해 지난 4년간 하루 500개씩 슛 연습을 해왔다. (c)+(A): Taylor는 벌금을 물지 않기 위해 연체된 모든 책들을 도서관에 반납했다. (d)+(B): Clara는 건강해지기 위해 정크푸드 섭취를 중단했다.

14 spend+시간+Ving: V하느라 시간을 쓰다

15 1900년대에 김구는 젊은 사람들을 교육하는 데 도움이 되기 위하여 학교를 설립하였다.

16 효창 공원 안에는 김구 기념관이 있다고 하였다.

17 ②번 앞 문장에서는 안창호가 10대 때 서울로 갔다고 하였고, ②번 뒤 문장에서는 안창호의 미국 활동에 대해 이야기하고 있으므로, 안창호가 미국으로 이주했다는 내용은 ②번에 들어가는 것이 적절하다.

18 안창호는 1938년 그가 죽을 때까지 사람들을 교육시키기 위하여 많은 학교를 설립하였다.

19 안창호는 한국으로 돌아와 1907년에 신민회를 설립하였다.

20 (A)는 a plan을 수식하는 형용사로 쓰인 to부정사이다. ①, ④ 부사적 용법 중 목적(~하기 위해서) ② any chance를 수식하는 형용사 ③ 명사적 용법으로 쓰인 진주어 ⑤ 부사적 용법 중 판단의 이유

21 'to kill Japanese generals in a park in Shanghai'를 의미한다.

서술형 실전문제
p.266~267

01 was built to protect, directed, building process

02 ⓐ allowed, ⓑ to use, ⓒ completed, ⓓ had burnt, ⓔ disappointed, (A) so that, ⓕ like

03 ④ I found out that she had lost her bag.

04 (1) so that it could warm my body
   (2) which my uncle had bought
   (3) in order to show

05 in order to / to

06 He founded it to fight for Korea's independence.

07 **미국에 있는 한국인들의 삶을 향상시키는 것을 도왔다.**

08 My Wish

09 They are in Hyochang Park.

10 desire, love

---

01 수원 화성은 전쟁 동안 사람들을 보호하기 위해 지어졌다. 정약용이 건설 과정을 감독했다.

02 ⓐ when이 이끄는 부사절이 과거시제이므로 과거동사 allowed, ⓑ 'allow+목적어+목적격보어(to부정사)', ⓒ 30분 전이 과거 시점이므로 과거동사 completed, ⓓ 과거 이전의 시점이므로 had burnt, ⓔ 실망하게 된 것이므로 disappointed ⓕ 조동사 뒤에 동사원형이 나와야 하므로 like, (A)에는 '그가 나를 좋아하도록'의 뜻이 되어야 하므로 2 단어는 'so that'이 적절하다.

03 내가 알아낸 것과 그녀가 가방을 잃어버린 것의 전후 관계를 정리하면, '나는 그녀가 가방을 잃어버린 것을 알아냈다'가 된다. 그에 적절하게 과거완료시제를 사용한다.

04 (1), (3) <보기>의 단어들을 사용하고, 중복 없이 문맥에 맞게 영작해야 하므로, '목적'의 의미를 표현할 때, 'so that 부사절'과 'in order to 부사구'를 어디에 쓰는 것이 좋을지 결정하는 것에 유의한다. (2) 과거완료시제를 적절히 사용한다.

05 so that은 목적을 이끄는 부사절 접속사이다. 따라서 '~하기 위해서'라고 해석되는 in order to 혹은 to부정사 구문으로 대체할 수 있으며, in order to를 대신하여 so as to를 써도 무방하다.

06 안창호가 신민회를 설립한 이유는 한국의 독립을 위해 싸우기 위함이었다.

07 미국으로 간 안창호는 미국에 거주하는 한국인들의 삶을 향상시키는 것을 도왔다고 하였다.

08 백범일지에 쓰여 있는 '나의 소원'을 가리키는 말이다.

09 이봉창, 윤봉길, 백정기 삼의사의 묘는 효창 공원에 있음을 알 수 있다.

10 '나의 소원'에 있는 김구의 말은 한국의 독립에 대한 그의 열망과 조국에 대한 그의 사랑을 느끼게 한다.

창의사고력 서술형 문제
p.268

|모범답안|

01 (1) A: You know Dokdo is windy and foggy, don't you?
　　　B: Yes, I heard about it.
　　(2) A: You know that there is a rock on Dokdo that looks like Korea, don't you?
　　　B: Yes, I heard about it.

02 (1) He shouted so that a passing ship could rescue him.
　　(2) He used a telescope so that he could look at the birds.

03 in 1889, who fought against Japanese rule. gathered and trained soldiers, where his soldiers earned one of their greatest victories against Japan

02 어법과 그림에 어울리는 내용으로 적절하게 영작한다.

단원별 모의고사
p.269~273

01 ⑤　　　　02 rule[govern]　　　03 ①
04 ④　　　　05 ②, ④
06 I'm dying to try it.
07 ⑤　　　　08 ④　　　　09 ①
10 (A) the symbols in Taegeukgi
　　(B) the black lines
11 (1) was built　(2) built　(3) built
12 (a) You know about　(b) I'm looking forward
13 ②　　　　14 ④　　　　15 ④
16 (1) The goddess said that Pinocchio had lied.
　　(2) Pooh was stung by bees after he had touched the hive.　　　17 ④　　　18 ⑤
19 ④　　　　20 ②　　　　21 ③
22 It shows a lot of things about Kim Koo's life.
23 ⓔ–ⓒ–ⓕ–ⓐ–ⓓ–ⓑ
24 He founded the New Korean Society in 1907 (to fight for Korea's independence).

01 ⑤번은 'statue(조각상)'에 관한 설명이다. 'state(상태)'에 대한 영어 설명은 'a condition or way of being that exists at a particular time'이다.

02 유의어 관계이다. 교육하다 : 통치하다

03 사체를 땅에 묻거나 어떤 것을 땅에 묻고 그것을 덮다

04 안중근에 대해 들어본 적이 있는지 묻는 말에 '아니, 없어. 그는 독립 운동가였어.'라고 답하는 것은 자연스럽지 못하다.

05 대화의 흐름상 '삼계탕을 요리하는 법을 아니?'라고 묻는 말은 어색하다.

06 'be dying to+동사원형'을 이용하여 '몹시 ~하고 싶다'는 기대를 나타낼 수 있다.

07 ⑤번의 'to'는 전치사로 명사나 동명사가 와야 한다.

08 보라가 얼마나 많은 시를 읽기를 원하는지는 대화에서 언급되어 있지 않다.

09 (A)는 'heard'의 목적어를 이끄는 명사절 접속사 'that'이 들어가고, (B)는 선행사 'treasures'를 수식하는 관계대명사절을 이끄는 'that'이 적절하다.

11 (1) 수원 화성이 지어졌다는 수동의 의미를 나타내므로 'be+과거분사'가 적절하다. (2) '누가 그것을 지었니?'라는 능동형 과거동사 'built'가 적절하고, (3)은 'a museum'을 수식하는 과거분사 'built'가 적절하다.

12 (a) You know ~, don't you?는 알고 있는지 물어보는 표현이고, (b) 앞으로 하고 싶은 일에 대한 기대를 표현할 때 'be looking forward to ~.'를 사용한다.

13 ② '~하기 위해서'라는 목적의 부사절을 만들 때, so that 또는 in order that 절 뒤에 can[may] 또는 could[might] 등의 조동사를 쓴다. became을 could[might] become으로 고치는 것이 적절하다.

14 자동차가 짙은 모래먼지로 뒤덮인 것은 하루 종일 황사가 온 탓이고, 과거보다 더 앞선 시점의 일이다. 과거완료시제로 쓰는 것이 적절하다.

15 모두 '목적'을 나타내는 부사절 접속사 'so that'인데, ④번만 '결과'의 의미로 쓰였다.

16 (1) 여신은 피노키오가 거짓말을 했다고 말했다. (2) 푸우는 벌집을 건드린 후에 벌들에게 쏘였다. hive: 벌집

17 김구는 1919년에 중국 상하이로 이동했다고 하였으므로 평생을 한국에서 살았다는 것은 위 글의 내용과 맞지 않다.

18 훗날 임시 정부의 주석이 되었다고 하였으므로 임시 정부를 떠난 것(left)이 아니라 가입한 것(joined)이라고 말하는 것이 적절하다.

19 한인 애국단은 김구가 일본에 맞서 싸우기 위해 1931년에 만든 비밀 조직으로, 이봉창과 윤봉길은 이 조직 소속이었다.

20 carry out은 '수행하다'라는 의미이므로 ②번이 적절하다.

21 밑줄 친 (B)는 목숨을 걸고 임무를 수행하려는 윤봉길의 의지를 나타낸다.

22 전시관은 김구의 삶에 관한 많은 것들을 보여 준다고 하였다.

23 안창호는 10대 때 서울에서 공부하였고(ⓔ) 더 나은 교육을 받기 위하여 미국으로 건너갔다(ⓒ). 미국에 거주하는 한국인들의 삶을 향상시켰고 그는 존경받는 지도자가 되었다(ⓕ). 다시 한국으로 돌아온 안창호는(ⓐ), 신민회를 설립하고(ⓓ) 임시 정부에도 가입하였다(ⓑ).

24 안창호는 한국의 독립을 위해 신민회를 설립하였다.

교과서 파헤치기

Lesson **1**

01 환상적인, 매우 멋진	02 자동으로
03 앞으로 04 목표	05 인식하다
06 다른, 다양한 07 자연	08 장면
09 지하층[실] 10 시골(지역)	11 조언하다, 충고하다
12 (남들보다 먼저 신기술을 사서 써 보는 사람) 얼리 어답터	
13 기술 14 한가한, 다른 계획이 없는	
15 매우, 꽤 16 숲	17 제품
18 편안한 19 ~ 중에서	20 관심, 흥미
21 선택 22 구하다	23 가구
24 손님 25 만들다	26 기술
27 그려진, 디자인된 28 (건물의) 층	29 상상하다
30 재미있는, 유머러스한	31 좌우명, 모토
32 (기분이) 상쾌한 33 사진촬영	34 과목, 주제
35 ~와 잘 지내다 36 ~하는 것을 그만두다	
37 ~로 가득 차다 38 ~하고 싶다	39 ~에 관심이 있다
40 ~을 잘하다 41 여기에 ~가 있다	42 ~처럼 보이다
43 (잠에서) 깨다, 일어나다	

01 product	02 designed	03 photo-taking
04 automatically	05 choice	06 real
07 comfortable	08 furniture	09 advise
10 pretty	11 among	12 fantastic
13 practice	14 subject	15 forward
16 goal	17 save	18 interest
19 recognize	20 countryside	21 humorous
22 create	23 language	24 floor
25 guest	26 imagine	27 basement
28 scene	29 free	30 forest
31 nature	32 technology	33 hero
34 refreshed	35 be good at	
36 would like to+동사원형		37 not just ~
38 wake up	39 be full of[be filled with]	
40 stop -ing	41 get along with	42 look like+명사
43 here are+복수명사		

1 enter, 들어가다   **2** among, ~ 중에서
3 create, 만들다, 창출하다   **4** forest, 숲
5 advise, 충고하다   **6** fantastic, 환상적인
7 basement, 지하실[층]   **8** imagine, 상상하다
9 countryside, 시골   **10** motto, 좌우명, 모토
11 hero, 영웅   **12** choice, 선택
13 photographer, 사진사   **14** furniture, 가구
15 pet, 애완동물   **16** recognize, 인식하다, 알아차리다

Warm Up

want to tell, myself, interested in, 'm good at playing / like running, refreshed when / 'm interested, usually go out to see / designer, practice drawing, free time / win first prize, contest

Listen & Speak 1 A

1 how, third grade / pretty / sounds good, homeroom teacher / teaches / Can you tell me, about / humorous, told, fun stories, interesting / enjoy studying

2 look at, to see / looks, tell / about, who saves / looks like / favorite kind of, scenes made with, technology, fantastic, real / cool, Let's go / Sounds

Listen & Speak 1 B

Can, tell, about / am going to have / goal for the year / to stop eating

Listen & Speak 2 A

1 go traveling with, What, most, trying

2 favorite subject, play the drums, Among, playing, what, like most

3 not just / Playing with, what

Real Life Talk

'd like to join / for your interest, about yourself / in, third grade / more, What, most, free time / what, to take / for the future / to be a photographer / choice, photo-taking, skills, Welcome to / glad

Communication Task Step 2

nickname / because, run fast / like most / What I like most / Can you tell me about / want to be / motto / motto, forward slowly, never go back

Wrap Up

new student, introduce yourself / from, Nice to meet / Can you tell us more / especially, to join / anything else, to tell / get along with, because, new here / Welcome to our class

Warm Up

B1: Hello, my name is Kim Chanho. I want to tell you about myself. I'm interested in music. I'm good at playing the drums.

G1: Hi! I am Teri. I like running in the evening. I feel refreshed when I exercise.

B2: Hello, my name is Jack. I'm interested in the stars. I usually go out to seestars at night.

G2: I am Lee Bora. I want to be a designer in the future, so I practice drawing when I have free time.

B3: I am Mark. I like dancing. I want to win first prize in the dance contest.

Listen & Speak 1 A

1 G: Jiho, how was your first day of third grade?

  B: It was pretty good. The teachers and my new classmates are all good.

  G: That sounds good. Who is your homeroom teacher?

  B: My homeroom teacher is Mr. Kim. He teaches math.

  G: Can you tell me more about him?

  B: Yes. He is humorous and told us some fun stories about math. It was interesting.

  G: Cool! I hope you enjoy studying math.

2 G: Ted, look at this movie poster. I want to see this movie.

  B: It looks interesting. Can you tell me about it, Amy?

  G: Yes. It is about a hero who saves the Earth.

  B: It looks like an SF movie.

  G: Yes, it is. Actually, SF is my favorite kind of movie. I like the scenes made with computer technology. They are fantastic and look real.

  B: That's cool. I am free this weekend. Let's go to see it together.

  G: Sounds good.

Listen & Speak 1 B

A: Can you tell me about your plan for this weekend?

B: Yes. I am going to have a birthday party.

A: Can you tell me about your goal for the year?

B: Yes. I want to stop eating fast food.

Listen & Speak 2 A

1 G: I often go traveling with my family. What I like most about traveling is trying new foods.

2 B: My favorite subject is music. I can play the drums and guitar. Among them, playing the guitar is what I like most.

3 G: This is a picture of Dora. She is my best friend, not just a pet. Playing with her in my free time is what I like most.

Real Life Talk

Seho: Nice to meet you. I'd like to join your photo club.

Bora: Thank you for your interest in the club. Can you tell me about yourself?

Seho: Yes. My name is Kim Seho. I am in the third grade, class 8.

Andy: Tell me more. What do you like to do most in your free time?

Seho: Well, what I like most is to take pictures.

Bora: That's great. What is your dream for the future?

Seho: I want to be a photographer.

Andy: Then you made the right choice. You can learn a lot of photo-taking skills here. Welcome to our club.

Seho: Thank you. I'm so glad!

Communication Task Step 2

A: What is your nickname?

B: My nickname is Speedy because I can run fast.

C: What do you like most?

B: What I like most is to play baseball.

D: Can you tell me about your dream job?

B: I want to be a baseball player.

A: What is your motto?

B: My motto is "You can go forward slowly, but never go back."

Wrap Up

W: Today, we have a new student Hojun. Hojun, can you please introduce yourself to the class?

B: Yes. Hi, my name is Kim Hojun. I am from Busan. Nice to meet you.

W: Can you tell us more about yourself?

B: Yes. I like sports, especially soccer. I want to join a sports club.

W: Is there anything else you want to tell your new friends?

B: I want to get along with everyone. Please help me because I'm new here.

W: Thanks, Hojun. Welcome to our class.

01 Have, ever thought
02 in class, created
03 Here are, that, made
04 Nature, my good
05 feel good, walk, forest
06 like to have, in
07 should have, with, flowers
08 am, excited by, sound
09 wonderful, wake up
10 like, have, to play
11 Welcome to, dream
12 Having, what, so, full
13 has, theater in, basement
14 can eat, enjoy, favorite
15 has, on, second floor
16 play, kinds of games
17 also, swimming pool
18 fun things with, guest
19 the most important thing
20 feels safe, comfortable
21 At, beautifully designed, on
22 When, enter, see, large
23 sometimes plays, signs
24 have, with, picnic table
25 will enjoy, Do, like
26 early adopter, technology
27 like, products, before others
28 get near, recognizes, opens
29 checks, conditions, advises, on
30 tells, weight, condition, health
31 cleans, cooks for
32 what I can imagine

01 Have, ever thought about
02 in class, created
03 are, that, made
04 Nature, good friend
05 do feel good, forest
06 like to have, in, countryside
07 should have, with many flowers
08 am always excited by
09 wonderful to wake up, listen to
10 like to have, be fun to play with
11 Welcome to

12 Having fun, what, is full of exciting things
13 in the basement
14 enjoy, favorite movies
15 has, on, second floor
16 kinds of games
17 also, a swimming pool
18 do fun things with, my guest
19 the most important thing
20 feels safe, comfortable
21 At the gate, beautifully designed sign, on
22 When, enter, see a large living room
23 board games
24 have, with a large picnic table
25 enjoy, Do you like
26 an early adopter, technology
27 do like, before others
28 get near, recognizes, opens automatically
29 checks, conditions, advises, on what to wear
30 tells me my weight, condition
31 cleans, cooks for
32 what I can imagine

1 여러분은 꿈의 집에 대해 생각해 본 적이 있나요?
2 오늘, 우리는 수업 시간에 우리가 꿈꾸는 집을 만들었습니다.
3 여기 우리가 만든 몇몇 꿈의 집이 있습니다.
4 자연은 나의 좋은 친구입니다.
5 나는 숲속에서 걸을 때 기분이 정말 좋습니다.
6 나는 시골에 꿈의 집을 갖고 싶습니다.
7 집에는 많은 꽃과 나무가 있는 큰 정원이 있을 것입니다.
8 나는 항상 새소리에 신이 납니다.
9 아침에 깨어나서 새들의 노래 소리를 듣는 것은 멋질 것입니다.
10 또한 나는 많은 애완동물을 갖고 싶습니다. 그들과 노는 것은 매우 재미있을 것입니다!
11 나의 꿈의 집에 온 것을 환영합니다!
12 즐겁게 지내는 것은 내가 가장 원하는 것입니다. 그래서 내 꿈의 집은 흥미로운 것들로 가득합니다.
13 집에는 지하에 영화관이 있습니다.
14 그곳에서 나는 쿠키를 먹을 수 있고 내가 좋아하는 영화들을 즐길 수 있습니다.
15 내 꿈의 집에는 2층에 게임방이 있습니다.
16 나는 그곳에서 많은 다양한 종류의 게임을 할 수 있습니다.
17 나의 집에는 또한 수영장이 있습니다.
18 나는 나의 집에서 친구들과 함께 즐거운 일들을 하고 싶습니다. 여러분도 나의 손님이 될 수 있습니다!
19 나의 가족은 나에게 가장 중요한 것입니다.
20 내 꿈의 집에서 가족은 안전하고 편안함을 느낍니다.

21 여러분은 가족 사진이 있는 아름답게 디자인된 문패를 발견할 수 있습니다.

22 여러분이 집에 들어서면 여러분은 큰 거실을 보게 될 것입니다.

23 나의 가족은 때때로 그곳에서 보드 게임도 하고 노래를 부르기도 합니다.

24 가족 소풍을 위한 커다란 피크닉 테이블이 있는 큰 정원을 갖게 될 것입니다.

25 그곳에서 우리는 바비큐를 즐길 것입니다. 내 꿈의 집이 마음에 드나요?

26 나는 남들보다 먼저 신기술을 써 보는 것을 좋아하는 사람입니다.

27 나는 새로운 제품이나 기술을 다른 사람보다 먼저 사용하는 것을 정말 좋아합니다.

28 내가 집 근처에 도착할 때, 현관문은 내 얼굴을 인식하고 자동으로 문을 엽니다.

29 가구는 날씨 상태를 확인하여 내게 무엇을 입을지 조언해 줍니다.

30 욕실 거울은 나에게 체중과 건강 상태를 알려 줍니다.

31 로봇은 집을 청소하고 나를 위해 요리합니다.

32 이것이 내가 나의 꿈의 집에 대해 상상할 수 있는 것입니다.

본문 TEST Step 4~Step 5   p.17~20

1 Have you ever thought about your dream house?

2 Today, in class, we created our dream house.

3 Here are some of the dream houses that we made.

4 Nature is my good friend.

5 I do feel good when I walk in the forest.

6 I'd like to have a dream house in the countryside.

7 It should have a big garden with many flowers and trees.

8 I am always excited by the sound of birds.

9 It will be wonderful to wake up in the morning and listen to the songs of the birds.

10 Also, I'd like to have many pets. It will be fun to play with them!

11 Welcome to my dream house!

12 Having fun is what I want most, so my dream house is full of exciting things.

13 It has a theater in the basement.

14 There, I can eat cookies and enjoy my favorite movies.

15 My dream house has a game room on the second floor.

16 I can play many different kinds of games there.

17 My house also has a swimming pool.

18 I want to do fun things with my friends in my

house. You can be my guest!

19 My family is the most important thing to me.

20 In my dream house, my family feels safe and comfortable.

21 At the gate, you can find a beautifully designed sign with my family's picture on it.

22 When you enter the house, you will see a large living room.

23 My family sometimes plays board games and sings there.

24 It will have a garden with a large picnic table for family picnics.

25 There, we will enjoy barbecues. Do you like my dream house?

26 I am an early adopter of new technology.

27 I do like to use new products and technology before others.

28 When I get near my house, the front door recognizes my face and opens automatically.

29 The furniture checks the weather conditions and advises me on what to wear.

30 The bathroom mirror tells me my weight and the condition of my health.

31 A robot cleans the house and cooks for me.

32 This is what I can imagine about my dream house.

구석구석지문 TEST Step 1   p.21

After You Read - Read and Match

1. to use, products, technology

2. There are, that use new technology

3. Every day, checks, what to wear

4. cooks for me

Project Step 1

1. would like to, favorite food

2. like, most

3. Can, tell me about, subject

4. what, like most, want to become, like

5. What, like to do

6. like to practice, sing

Project Step 3

1. made, with what, likes

2. so, with, paint brush, colored, a piece of

3. made, with, musical note

After You Read - Read and Match

1. I like to use new products and technology.
2. There are many items that use new technology in my dream house.
3. Every day my furniture checks the weather and tells me what to wear.
4. A robot cooks for me.

Project Step 1

1. A: We would like to know more about you, Minho. What is your favorite food?
2. B: I like pizza most.
3. C: Can you tell me about your favorite subject?
4. B: Art is what I like most. I want to become an art teacher like Mr. Kim.
5. D: What do you like to do after school?
6. B: I like to practice taegwondo and sing songs.

Project Step 3

1. We made an M and an H with what Minho likes.
2. Minho likes art and pizza, so we made an M with a paint brush, colored pencils, and a piece of pizza.
3. We made an H with a musical note and taegwondo.

Lesson **2**

01 ~에게 인사하다	02 그릇	03 놓다
04 정확하게, 올바르게		05 ~한 이후로
06 다르다	07 나이 든	08 사원
09 경험하다	10 마지막으로	11 주소
12 주	13 상품, 제품	14 율, 비율
15 제공하다, 대접하다		16 선물
17 준비하다	18 차이	19 건네주다
20 부정의문문	21 (짐을) 싸다, 꾸리다	
22 혀	23 지불하다	
24 교환하다, 환전하다		25 불편한
26 (손을) 흔들다	27 부딪치다	28 우편 번호
29 세금	30 입장료	31 가격표
32 판매세	33 죽음	34 포장하다, 싸다
35 ~에 익숙해지다	36 A와 B 사이에	37 ~의 대답으로
38 ~에 나쁜 영향을 미치다		39 ~로 여겨지다
40 ~와 똑같은	41 ~할 것을 기억하다	
42 (범위가) A에서 B에 이르다		43 ~을 모으다

01 bowl	02 positive question	
03 death	04 rate	05 entrance fee
06 prepare	07 goods	08 difference
09 place	10 address	11 pay
12 present	13 elderly	14 price tag
15 bump	16 exchange	17 correctly
18 guest	19 finally	20 wrap
21 tongue	22 sales tax	23 postal code
24 tax	25 state	26 differ
27 wave	28 greet	29 temple
30 experience	31 traditional	32 serve
33 cultural	34 uncomfortable	35 each other
36 in response to	37 be regarded as	
38 get used to ~	39 make sure (that)+주어 ~	
40 range from A to B		
41 between A and B		42 remember to V
43 have a bad effect on		

1 rude, 무례한   2 goods, 상품, 제품   3 sales tax, 판매세

4 wrap, 포장하다   5 wave, 흔들다   6 bump, 부딪히다

7 exchange, 교환하다   8 uncomfortable, 불편한

9 address, 주소   10 correctly, 올바르게, 맞게

11 entrance fee, 입장료   12 advice, 충고, 조언

13 postal code, 우편번호   14 tag, 꼬리표

15 tax, 세금   16 traditional, 전통적인

Warm Up

1 show their tongues, Tibet

2 place, together, India

3 bump their noses

Listen & Speak 1 A

1 to send, aunt / What / get, advice, how to write, address in English / should write, street address / Like / state, postal code, Finally, country / for, help

2 Look at, wearing traditional, to take pictures of / There is, need to, before taking / get, advice on / shouldn't take pictures of Moroccan, without asking / believe, a bad effect on, when

Listen & Speak 1 B

Can I get, advice, visiting / shouldn't stand, path / get your advice on visiting / should sit, back seat

Listen & Speak 2 A

1 bought, present, have stayed / What, buy / bought, think / Make sure, when, hand, to / giving, older, with, is regarded as rude / remember

2 pack everything, need, to / yet, should, take / Remember to bring, pants, skirt / isn't / there are, temples, shouldn't wear shorts, temple / anything else / Make sure, exchange, to

Listen & Speak 2 B

anything, remember, France / Make sure, Keep, on, at all times / anything, need to, when / Make sure, don't take off / when having

Real Life Talk

Chinese, invited, to / enjoy having / prepare, gift, for several, advice, what to bring / How about / Most, receive, as, present, enjoy drinking, usually serve, guests / Make sure you don't wrap / mean death / remember, advice

Communication Task Step 2

Which country, like to visit / get, advice, traveling / Make sure, don't use, left hand to hand

Wrap Up

1 going, get, advice, visiting / pay, get off / other things, remember / Pick up, hold, while eating, when having, should, without

2 to give, from, anything, should remember / Make sure

Warm Up

1 People show their tongues in Tibet.

2 People place their hands together and say "Namaste" in India.

3 Men bump their noses in the United Arab Emirates.

Listen & Speak 1 A

1 G: I want to send this to my aunt in the USA.

   B: What is it?

   G: It's her hanbok. Can I get your advice on how to write an address in English?

   B: Sure. You should write the street address first.

   G: Like this?

   B: Yes. Then, write the name of the city and the state and then the postal code. Finally, write the country.

   G: Thanks for your help.

2 G: Look at the people wearing traditional Moroccan clothes. They are really beautiful. I want to take pictures of them.

   M: Wait. There is an important thing you need to know before taking pictures.

   G: Oh, really? Can I get your advice on it?

   M: Yes. You shouldn't take pictures of Moroccan people without asking.

   G: Why?

   M: They believe it may have a bad effect on them when someone takes their pictures.

Listen & Speak 1 B

A: Can I get your advice on visiting the Netherlands?

B: Sure. You shouldn't stand on a bike path.

A: Can I get your advice on visiting the USA?

B: Sure. You should sit in the back seat in the taxi.

Listen & Speak 2 A

1 B: Sena, I bought a present for Ms. Han. I have stayed at her house here in Korea.

   G: That's great. What did you buy her?

   B: I bought her a hat. Do you think she'll love it?

   G: Yes. Make sure you use two hands when you

hand it to her.

B: Why?

G: Because giving something to older people with one hand is regarded as rude in Korea.

B: Okay. I'll remember that.

2 B: Did you pack everything you need for the trip to Thailand tomorrow?

G: Not yet. What should I take?

B: Remember to bring a pair of long pants or a long skirt.

G: Why? It's very hot in Thailand, isn't it?

B: Yes, but there are many temples in Thailand. You shouldn't wear shorts when you visit a temple.

G: Okay. Is there anything else?

B: Make sure you exchange Korean won to Thai baht.

Listen & Speak 2 B

A: Is there anything I need to remember when I eat in France?

B: Yes. Make sure you keep your hands on the table at all times.

A: Is there anything I need to remember when I eat in Uzbekistan?

B: Yes. Make sure you don't take off your hat or shoes when having a meal.

Real Life Talk

Seho: My Chinese friend invited me to his house for dinner this Friday.

Bora: That's good. I hope you enjoy having dinner at his house.

Seho: I want to prepare a small gift for him. You lived in China for several years. Can I get your advice on what to bring?

Bora: How about some tea?

Seho: Tea?

Bora: Yes. Most Chinese people like to receive tea as a present. They enjoy drinking tea. Also, they usually serve tea to guests.

Seho: Oh, thanks. Is there anything else that I need to know?

Bora: Make sure you don't wrap the present in white or black paper. White and black mean death in China.

Seho: Okay. I'll remember that. Thank you for the advice.

Communication Task Step 2

A: Which country would you like to visit?

B: I'd like to visit Malaysia. Can I get your advice on

traveling there?

C: Sure. Make sure you don't use your left hand to hand something to someone.

B: Okay. Thanks.

Wrap Up

1 B: I'm going to Japan this summer. Can I get some advice on visiting there?

G: Make sure you pay when you get off the bus.

B: Oh, I didn't know that. Are there any other things I should remember?

G: Pick up the bowl and hold it while eating. Also, when having soup, you should drink it without a spoon.

B: Okay. Thanks.

2 M: I want to give flowers to my friend from Russia. Is there anything I should remember?

W: Make sure you don't give flowers in even numbers.

본문 TEST Step 1   p.32~34

01 have been living, for

02 Since, experienced, between, and

03 would like, share, with

04 at, it   05 looks nice, much

06 dollars, cents 07 not expensive

08 agree, buy it   09 be, dollars, cents

10 price tag, only 11 states, pay, tax, goods

12 called, sales, rates differ

13 range, less than, more

14 goods, pay, price, tag   15 Mrs., Hello

16 Hi, How   17 for, Enjoy, meal

18 Thank, too   19 why, wave to

20 greet, other, waving

21 Waving, regarded as

22 feel uncomfortable, don't, try

23 wave, at, elderly, back   24 try, pie

25 thanks, want to   26 not, Don't, like

27 Minhee, Yes   28 try some, delicious

29 just said, don't   30 Andy, What

31 negative as, Aren't, Didn't

32 difficult, negative, correctly, advice

33 response, such as, if

34 should answer, like

35 same as, positive questions

36 cultural difference, surprising

37 been learning, differences since

38 surprised, getting used to

01 have been living, for three years
02 Since, have experienced, differences between, and
03 would like to share
04 Look at, it　05 looks nice, How much
06 dollars, cents　07 not expensive
08 agree, to buy it
09 be, dollars, cents
10 the price tag says, only
11 most states, pay a tax, goods
12 is called, sales tax, rates differ by state
13 range, less than, more than
14 buy goods, usually need to pay
15 Mrs., Mrs.　16 How
17 for, Enjoy your meal
18 too　　19 why did, wave to
20 often greet each other, waving
21 Waving, is, regarded as rude
22 feel uncomfortable, why don't, try it
23 wave to, smile at, elderly, walking, wave back
24 try, apple pie　25 thanks, want to
26 not, Don't　27 Yes
28 try some, delicious
29 just, don't like　30 What
31 often ask negative questions, Aren't, Didn't, go
32 It, to answer, correctly, is
33 negative questions, such as, answer, No
34 should nswer, Yes, if
35 the same as, to positive questions
36 Which cultural difference, surprising
37 have been learning, cultural differences since
38 surprised, at first, am getting used to

1 안녕! 내 이름은 김민희야. 나는 미국에 3년 동안 살고 있어.
2 우리 가족이 이곳으로 이민을 온 이후로 나는 한국과 미국의 많은 문화적 차이를 경험하고 있어.
3 나는 그것들 중 몇 가지를 너희들과 공유하고 싶어.
4 민희: 이 셔츠를 봐. 마음에 들어.
5 Linda: 멋져 보인다. 얼마야?
6 민희: 19달러 99센트야.
7 Linda: 비싸지 않네.
8 민희: 응, 나도 그렇게 생각해. 그것을 사고 싶어.
9 점원: 21달러 20센트입니다.
10 민희: 정말이요? 하지만 가격표에는 단지 19달러 99센트라고 쓰여 있는데요.

11 이곳 미국에서는 대부분의 주에서 사람들이 물건을 구입할 때 세금을 내.
12 그것은 판매세라고 불려. 판매세의 비율은 주마다 달라.
13 판매세는 1퍼센트 미만부터 10퍼센트 이상까지 다양해.
14 그래서 미국에서 상품을 살 때, 대개 가격표에 있는 가격보다 더 많은 돈을 지불해야 해.
15 Jessica: 안녕하세요, Johnson 할머니! 민희: 안녕하세요, Johnson 할머니!
16 Mrs. Johnson: 안녕, Jessica! 안녕, 민희! 잘 지내지?
17 Jessica: 잘 지내요, 감사합니다. 저희는 여기 버거 먹으러 왔어요. 식사 맛있게 하세요.
18 Mrs. Johnson: 고맙구나. 너희들도!
19 민희: Jessica, 왜 너는 Johnson 할머니께 손을 흔들었니?
20 미국에서 사람들은 종종 손을 흔들며 서로에게 인사해.
21 나이가 많은 사람에게 손을 흔드는 것은 무례하다고 여겨지지 않아.
22 네가 미국에 오면 처음에는 그것에 대해 불편하게 느낄 수 있어. 하지만 한번 시도해 보지 않을래?
23 너는 길을 걷고 있는 연세가 많으신 할아버지께 손을 흔들며 미소를 지어도 돼. 그도 너한테 답례로 손을 흔들지도 몰라.
24 Andy: 민희, 이 사과 파이 좀 먹어 봐.
25 Minhee: 아니야, 고마워. 먹고 싶지 않아.
26 Andy: 왜 안 먹어? 너는 사과 파이를 좋아하지 않니?
27 Minhee: 응.
28 Andy: 그러면, 좀 먹어 봐. 맛있어.
29 Minhee: 아니. 내가 사과 파이를 좋아하지 않는다고 방금 말했잖아.
30 Andy: 뭐라고?
31 미국 사람들은 종종 "너 안 오니?", "너 병원 안 갔니?"와 같은 부정의문문으로 질문해.
32 부정의문문에 바르게 대답하는 것은 어려울 수 있어. 여기 약간의 충고 사항이 있어.
33 "너는 사과 파이를 좋아하지 않니?"와 같은 부정의문문의 대답으로 만약 사과 파이를 좋아하지 않는다면 너는 "No."라고 대답해야 해.
34 그리고 만약 그것을 좋아한다면 "Yes."라고 대답해야 해.
35 이 대답들은 "너는 애플파이를 좋아하니?"와 같은 긍정의문문에 대한 대답들과 같아.
36 어떤 문화적인 차이가 너에게 가장 놀랍니?
37 나는 미국에 온 이후로 문화적인 차이에 대해 계속 배우고 있어.
38 어떤 것들은 처음에 나를 놀라게 했지만, 지금은 그것들에 익숙해지고 있어.

1 Hi! My name is Kim Minhee. I have been living in America for three years.

2 Since my family moved here, I have experienced many cultural differences between Korea and America.

3 I would like to share some of them with you.

4 Minhee: Look at this shirt. I like it.

5 Linda: It looks nice. How much is it?

6 Minhee: It's 19 dollars and 99 cents.

7 Linda: That's not expensive.

8 Minhee: Yes, I agree. I want to buy it.

9 Clerk: That'll be 21 dollars and 20 cents.

10 Minhee: Really? But the price tag says it's only 19 dollars and 99 cents.

11 Here in America, in most states, people pay a tax when they buy goods.

12 It is called a sales tax. Sales tax rates differ by state.

13 They range from less than one percent to more than ten percent.

14 So when you buy goods in America, you usually need to pay more than the price on the tag.

15 Jessica: Hi, Mrs. Johnson! Minhee: Hello, Mrs. Johnson!

16 Mrs. Johnson: Hi, Jessica! Hi, Minhee! How are you?

17 Jessica: Fine, thank you. We are here for a burger. Enjoy your meal.

18 Mrs. Johnson: Thank you. You, too!

19 Minhee: Jessica, why did you wave to Mrs Johnson?

20 In America, people often greet each other by waving.

21 Waving to an older person is not regarded as rude.

22 When you come to America, you may feel uncomfortable about it at first, but why don't you try it?

23 You can wave to and smile at an elderly man walking on the street. He may wave back.

24 Andy: Minhee, try this apple pie.

25 Minhee: No, thanks. I don't want to.

26 Andy: Why not? Don't you like apple pie?

27 Minhee: Yes.

28 Andy: Then, try some. It's delicious.

29 Minhee: No. I just said I don't like apple pie.

30 Andy: What?

31 Americans often ask negative questions, such as "Aren't you coming?" and "Didn't you go to the hospital?"

32 It can be difficult to answer negative questions correctly. Here is some advice.

33 In response to negative questions, such as "Don't you like apple pie?" you should answer "No," if you don't like it.

34 And you should answer "Yes," if you like it.

35 These answers are the same as the answers to positive questions, such as "Do you like apple pie?"

36 Which cultural difference is most surprising to you?

37 I have been learning about cultural differences since I came to America.

38 Some surprised me at first, but now I am getting used to them.

Project Step 1

1. on correct English expressions

2. Make sure, instead of eye shopping

3. Make sure you don't say, should say, instead

Project Step 3

1. realized, have been using, incorrect

2. For example, should say, instead of

3. an incorrect expression, Make sure you don't use

Enjoy Writing

1. Can't Miss

2. There are, around the world

3. Among, like to attend

4. have been celebrating, for many years

5. is held in

6. if I go, a lot of things

7. people throwing, on each other

8. will be fantastic

9. to dance with other people

10. taste traditional, dishes

11. going to, exciting

12. can't wait for

Project Step 1

1. A: Can I get your advice on correct English expressions?
2. B: Make sure you say window shopping instead of eye shopping.
3. C: Make sure you don't say Y-shirt. You should say dress shirt instead.

Project Step 3

1. Today, I realized I have been using many incorrect English expressions.
2. For example, we should say dress shirt instead of Y-shirt.
3. Eye shopping is also an incorrect expression. Make sure you don't use it.

Enjoy Writing

1. Holi That I Can't Miss
2. There are many interesting festivals around the world.
3. Among them, I'd like to attend Holi.
4. People in India have been celebrating this festival for many years.
5. Holi is held in March.
6. I think that if I go, I'll experience a lot of things.
7. First, there are people throwing colored powder and water on each other.
8. It will be fantastic!
9. Second, I want to dance with other people on the street.
10. I'll also taste traditional Holi dishes.
11. It's going to be very exciting.
12. I can't wait for the day!

Lesson 3

01 충분히; 충분한	02 분석하다	03 출석하다, 참석하다
04 인물, 형상, 사람 모양의 장난감		
05 진정시키다, 평온하게 하다		06 출연자들
07 성격	08 세부, 세목	09 개발자
10 매우, 대단히	11 플로리스트, 화초 연구가	
12 분석가	13 약함, 약점	14 포함하다
15 ~ 중에서	16 자원	17 지휘하다, 처신하다
18 줄이다, 완화하다	19 전문가	20 다루다
21 생물, 생명체	22 추천하다	23 시인
24 수의사	25 우편집배원	26 선택하다, 고르다
27 화초, 푸른 잎	28 힘, 강점	29 마이크
30 오디션을 보다	31 청진기	32 공연
33 정원사	34 현실적인	35 ~함으로써
36 실현되다	37 ~을 보살피다	38 ~에 만족하다
39 (단체, 조직에) 소속하다, 속하다		
40 ~을 최대한 활용하다		
41 ~처럼 보이다, ~일 것 같다	42 ~을 확신하다	
43 ~을 꿈꾸다		

01 personality	02 analyze	03 cast
04 strength	05 stethoscope	06 conduct
07 veterinarian	08 weakness	09 detail
10 select	11 gardener	12 specialist
13 developer	14 microphone	15 highly
16 among	17 florist	18 audition
19 greenery	20 analyst	21 handle
22 include	23 calm	24 responsibility
25 realistic	26 traditional	27 recommend
28 performance	29 creature	30 resource
31 reduce	32 someday	33 engineer
34 enough	35 care for	36 belong to
37 dream of ~	38 be happy with ~	
39 come true	40 by -ing	41 It seems that ~
42 I'm sure that ~	43 make the best use of	

1 cast, 출연자들   2 data, 자료   3 collect, 모으다
4 lead, 이끌다   5 belong to, 소속하다, 속하다
6 responsibility, 책임   7 analyst, 분석가

8 bank teller, 은행 창구 직원   9 greenery, 푸른 잎, 화초

10 personality, 성격   11 resource, 자원

12 analyze, 분석하다   13 include, 포함하다

14 audition, 오디션을 보다   15 developer, 개발자

16 care for, 보살피다

대화문 TEST Step 1

Listen & Speak 1 A

1 planning, police station, police officer / to become, someday / do, too, dreamed of becoming, since / with, ask, something / are, going to ask / what, to do to become / sure, would like to

2 wrong / animator, drawing skill, enough / Being an animator, a, artist / do to become, animator / a lot of, to make, practice drawing / quite sure that, if, try hard

Listen & Speak 1 B

• interested, technology, Which, right / sure, developer

• interested in writing. Which job, be right for / quite sure, be a good job for

Listen & Speak 2 A

1 glad to meet, what you do / guide, different places, information, visit / else / popular culture, traditional / It seems, knowing a lot, happy with, my job

2 finish, role model / wrote, be like / does, do / how to stretch, also helps, reduce, calm themselves / It seems that, to keep both, and

Listen & Speak 2 B

• program writer, become / seems to, writing, helpful

• social worker, help me become / seems, reading books to kids, be helpful

Real Life Talk

most interested, among / interested in working / most interested, among / working, playing / it seems to me that, belong to, realistic / mean / belong to, personality types, Realistic, one of, types / interesting, What kind of, recommend / police officer, and so on / to be / I'm quite sure, soccer player

Communication Task Step 2

3 Ss, 2 As, 1 E / seems to, belong to / Jobs that, recommended, librarian, counselor / have always wanted / sounds, quite sure that you could

Wrap Up 1

are, doing / looking for, recipe / cook often / to cook, chef someday / make, come true / taking, to think of, creative / I'm quite sure, good chef

대화문 TEST Step 2

Listen & Speak 1 A

1 B: Anne, I'm planning to visit the police station to see my uncle. He is a police officer.

G: Oh, I want to become a police officer someday.

B: You do? Me, too. I have dreamed of becoming a police officer since I was ten.

G: Can I come with you, Matt? I want to meet your uncle and ask him something.

B: Sure. What are you going to ask?

G: I want to ask him what I need to do to become a police officer.

B: I see. I'm sure he would like to meet you.

2 M: What's wrong, Jisu?

G: I want to be an animator, but my drawing skill is not good enough.

M: Hmm... Being an animator is not just about a good artist.

G: What should I do to become an animator?

M: Read a lot of books to make good stories and practice drawing every day.

G: Okay, I'll do so.

M: I'm quite sure that you can be a good animator if you try hard.

G: Thank you very much.

Listen & Speak 1 B

• A: I'm interested in technology. Which job would be right for me?

B: I'm quite sure that an app developer could be a good job for you.

• A: I'm interested in writing. Which job would be right for me?

B: I'm quite sure that a writer could be a good job for you.

Listen & Speak 2 A

1 G: I'm glad to meet you, Mr. Han. Could you please tell me what you do?

M: Okay. I guide travelers to different places in China and give them information about where they should visit.

G: What else do you do?

M: I tell them about popular culture and traditional food in China.

G: It seems to me knowing a lot about China is very important. Are you happy with your job?

M: Yes. I really love my job.

2 B: Did you finish the report about your role model?

G: Yes, I did. I wrote about my role model, Ms.

Shin. I want to be like her.

B: What does she do?

G: She teaches people how to stretch. She also helps them reduce stress and calm themselves.

B: Good. It seems that she helps to keep both their mind and body healthy.

G: Yes, and I think it's great.

Listen & Speak 2 B

• A: I want to be a radio program writer. What would help me become one?

B: It seems to me writing your own stories would be helpful.

• A: I want to be a social worker. What would help me become one?

B: It seems to me reading books to kids at a hospital would be helpful.

Real Life Talk

Bora: What are you most interested in among the things on this list?

Jessie: I'm most interested in working outside and playing sports.

Bora: Well, it seems to me that you belong to the realistic type.

Jessie: What do you mean?

Bora: Most people belong to one of six personality types. Realistic is one of the types.

Jessie: Oh, that's interesting. What kind of jobs do they recommend for realistic types?

Bora: A farmer, a police officer, a soccer player, and so on.

Jessie: Oh, I have always wanted to be a soccer player.

Bora: That's good. I'm quite sure you could become a great soccer player.

Communication Task Step 2

A: I have 3 Ss, 2 As, 1 I, and 1 E.

B: It seems to me that you belong to Type S.

C: Yes. Jobs that are recommended for Type S are teacher, nurse, librarian or counselor.

A: Cool. I have always wanted to be a teacher.

D: That sounds great. I'm quite sure that you could be a good teacher.

Wrap Up 1

B: Hello, what are you doing, Sumi?

G: I'm looking for a good recipe on the Internet. I need it for my family dinner today.

B: That is nice. Do you cook often?

G: Yes, I try to cook every weekend. I want to be a chef someday.

B: What are you doing to make your dream come true?

G: I'm taking a cooking class. I try to think of new and creative dishes.

B: I'm quite sure you could be a good chef.

본문 TEST Step 1 p.58~60

01 florist, who creates, with

02 To become, need, things

03 attended, for, gardeners

04 how to, care for

05 days, lot of different

06 movie sets, decorate, with

07 something colorful, fresh, greenery

08 If, highly recommend, become

09 sport data analyst

10 sounds like, doesn't it

11 In fact, work for

12 watch recorded, run, collect

13 analyze, show, strengths, weaknesses

14 If, understands, do better

15 Since, have been, big

16 work, watch, all, time

17 perfect, because watching, hobby

18 As, director, theater, lot

19 audition, look for, voices

20 selecting, cast, each scene

21 put, cast, together, practice

22 During, performance, area, conduct

23 responsibility, each, played, way

24 direct, to keep, together

25 Conducting, directing, waving, around

26 scientist, big field

27 includes studies, creatures living

28 Among, have studied, living

29 growth ring, that interests

30 By looking, out, born

31 used to, resources, manage

32 because, the best use

본문 TEST Step 2 p.61~63

01 florist, who creates, with

02 To become, need to know many things

03 attended, for, gardeners

04 at this school, how to grow, care for

05 These days, a lot of different

06 movie sets, decorate, with flowers

07 something colorful with, greenery

08 plants, highly recommend

09 sport data analyst

10 sounds like, doesn't it

11 In fact, a lot of fun

12 to watch recorded games, run, to collect

13 analyze, to show, weaknesses

14 understands, strengths, do better

15 Since, have been

16 baseball games all the time

17 perfect job, because watching baseball games, hobby

18 As, a musical theater, a lot of

19 audition, look for, voices

20 selecting the cast, for each scene

21 put, cast, together

22 During, performance, conduct

23 my responsibility, each, played, same way

24 direct, to keep, together

25 Conducting, directing, waving

26 ocean scientist, a big field

27 includes, oceans, creatures living in them

28 Among, have studied, living

29 the growth ring, that interests

30 By looking, find out, was born

31 I get from, is used to understand, manage, oceans better

32 because, makes the best use of

본문 TEST Step 3　　　　　　　p.64~65

1 안녕하세요. 저는 Tom입니다. 플로리스트란 꽃으로 아름다운 것들을 창조하는 사람입니다.

2 플로리스트가 되기 위해서 여러분은 꽃에 관해 많은 것을 알 필요가 있습니다.

3 나는 플로리스트와 정원사를 양성하는 고등학교에 다녔습니다.

4 제가 다양한 종류의 꽃을 기르고 다루는 방법을 배운 곳이 바로 이 학교에서였습니다.

5 오늘날, 플로리스트는 많은 다양한 일을 할 수 있습니다.

6 나는 때때로 영화 세트장을 디자인하고 꽃으로 상점을 꾸밉니다.

7 나는 싱싱한 꽃과 화초로 다채로운 무언가를 창조해 낼 때 행복합니다.

8 만약 당신이 식물과 예술을 좋아한다면, 나는 당신에게 플로리스트가 될 것을 강력히 추천합니다.

9 나는 Emma입니다. 나는 스포츠 데이터 분석가입니다.

---

10 어려운 직업처럼 들리죠, 그렇지 않나요?

11 사실, 그것은 매우 재미있습니다. 나는 야구팀을 위해서 일합니다.

12 나의 일은 녹화된 경기를 보고 자료를 수집하기 위해 컴퓨터 프로그램을 실행하는 것입니다.

13 그리고 나서, 나는 내 팀의 강점과 약점을 보여 주기 위해서 그 자료들을 분석합니다.

14 만약 팀이 자신들의 강점과 약점을 이해하면, 그들은 다음번에 더 잘할 수 있습니다.

15 어렸을 때부터, 나는 야구의 열혈 팬이었습니다.

16 지금, 나는 일하는 중에 내내 야구를 봅니다.

17 야구 경기를 보는 것은 나의 취미이기 때문에 이것은 나에게 완벽한 직업입니다!

18 안녕하세요. 나는 Chris입니다. 뮤지컬 극장 감독으로서 나는 많은 것을 합니다.

19 나는 배우들을 대상으로 오디션을 실시하고, 훌륭하고 강한 목소리를 찾아냅니다.

20 배역에 맞는 배우를 고른 뒤에, 나는 그들에게 각 장면을 위한 노래를 가르칩니다.

21 그리고 나서, 나는 배우와 오케스트라를 함께 연습시킵니다.

22 공연 동안에, 나는 오케스트라 석에 있고 지휘를 합니다.

23 각각의 노래가 매번 동일하게 연주되도록 만드는 것은 나의 책임입니다.

24 나는 공연을 제대로 진행하기 위해 연주자들과 가수들을 감독합니다.

25 지휘하고 감독하는 것은 단지 내 팔을 흔드는 것만이 아닙니다!

26 나는 예지입니다. 나는 해양 과학자입니다. 해양 과학은 거대한 분야입니다.

27 그것은 바다와 그 안에 살고 있는 생물에 관한 연구를 포함합니다.

28 여러 가지 중에서 나는 한국 주변의 바다에 살고 있는 많은 종류의 물고기를 연구해 왔습니다.

29 나의 흥미를 끄는 것은 바로 물고기 안에 있는 나이테입니다.

30 나이테를 살펴봄으로써, 나는 언제 어디서 그 물고기가 태어났는지 알아낼 수 있습니다.

31 내가 물고기에서 얻은 모든 정보는 바다의 자원을 이해하고 바다를 더 잘 관리하기 위해 사용됩니다.

32 내 직업은 자연을 가장 잘 활용할 수 있게 한다는 점에서 중요합니다.

본문 TEST Step 4-Step 5　　　　　　　p.66~70

1 Hi, I am Tom. A florist is someone who creates beautiful things with flowers.

2 To become a florist, you need to know many things about flowers.

3 I attended a high school for florists and gardeners.

4 It was at this school that I learned how to grow

and care for different types of flowers.

5 These days, florists can do a lot of different things.

6 I design movie sets sometimes and I decorate shops with flowers.

7 I am happy when I create something colorful with fresh flowers and greenery.

8 If you like plants and the arts, I highly recommend you become a florist.

9 I am Emma. I am a sport data analyst.

10 It sounds like a difficult job, doesn't it?

11 In fact, it is a lot of fun. I work for a baseball team.

12 My job is to watch recorded games and run a computer program to collect data.

13 Then, I analyze the data to show my team's strengths and weaknesses.

14 If the team understands their strengths and weaknesses, they can do better next time.

15 Since I was young, I have been a big fan of baseball.

16 Now, in my work, I watch baseball games all the time.

17 This is a perfect job for me because watching baseball games is my hobby!

18 Hi, I am Chris. As a director of a musical theater, I do a lot of things.

19 I audition the actors and I look for good, strong voices.

20 After selecting the cast, I teach them the songs for each scene.

21 Then, I put the cast and orchestra together for practice.

22 During the performance, I am in the orchestra area and conduct.

23 It's my responsibility to have each song played the same way every time.

24 I direct the musicians and the singers to keep the show together.

25 Conducting and directing is not just about waving my arms around!

26 My name is Yeji. I am an ocean scientist. Ocean science is a big field.

27 It includes studies of the oceans and the creatures living in them.

28 Among other things, I have studied many kinds of fish living in the seas near Korea.

29 It is the growth ring in a fish that interests me.

30 By looking at it, I can find out when and where the fish was born.

31 All the information I get from fish is used to understand sea resources and manage the oceans better.

32 My job is important because it makes the best use of nature possible.

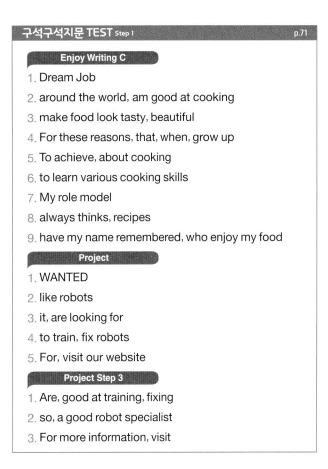

구석구석지문 TEST Step 1   p.71

Enjoy Writing C

1. Dream Job
2. around the world, am good at cooking
3. make food look tasty, beautiful
4. For these reasons, that, when, grow up
5. To achieve, about cooking
6. to learn various cooking skills
7. My role model
8. always thinks, recipes
9. have my name remembered, who enjoy my food

Project

1. WANTED
2. like robots
3. it, are looking for
4. to train, fix robots
5. For, visit our website

Project Step 3

1. Are, good at training, fixing
2. so, a good robot specialist
3. For more information, visit

구석구석지문 TEST Step 2   p.72

Enjoy Writing C

1. My Dream Job
2. I like food from around the world and I am good at cooking.
3. I can also make food look tasty and beautiful.
4. For these reasons, it is a chef that I want to be when I grow up.
5. To achieve my dream, I will read magazines about cooking.
6. Also, I will go to France to learn various cooking skills.
7. My role model is my dad.
8. He always thinks of new recipes and then cooks these new dishes for us.
9. I want to have my name remembered by people who enjoy my food.

Lesson 4

단어 TEST Step 1   p.73

01 점수	02 알람소리, 경보	03 출생, 탄생
04 발언, 논평, 비평	05 연락하다	06 장점, 유리함
07 해독	08 불편한	09 중독
10 단점, 약점, 불리한 점		11 즐거운
12 만들다, 형성시키다		13 필요한
14 시끄러운	15 반, 절반	16 위험한
17 줄이다	18 시민	19 게시하다
20 집중하다	21 대신에	22 창의적인
23 실수	24 ~할 작정이다	25 추측하다
26 제한하다	27 인터넷이나 SNS에 올리는 글	
28 상쾌한	29 존중하다, 존경하다	
30 저작권	31 옥외의, 야외의	32 고통
33 제안하다	34 야기하다, 원인이 되다	
35 사실	36 무료로	37 반면에
38 치우다	39 당장	40 설정하다
41 잠시 동안	42 ~에서 떨어져 있다, ~을 멀리하다	
43 알아내다, 계산하다		

단어 TEST Step 2   p.74

01 addiction	02 birth	03 uncomfortable
04 cause	05 limit	06 post
07 block	08 reduce	09 copyright
10 alert	11 refreshed	12 advantage
13 instead	14 respect	15 noisy
16 disadvantage	17 enjoyable	18 mistake
19 focus	20 comment	21 form
22 intend	23 suggest	24 citizen
25 contact	26 necessary	27 half
28 outdoor	29 pain	30 creative
31 dangerous	32 detox	33 password
34 device	35 for a while	36 put aside
37 such as	38 stay away from	
39 in fact	40 put aside	41 for free
42 figure out	43 on the other hand	

단어 TEST Step 3   p.75

1 birth, 출생   2 half, 반, 절반   3 copyright, 저작권
4 symbol, 상징   5 advantage, 장점
6 comment, 논평, 해설, 비평   7 alert, 경고, 알림
8 device, 기기, 장치   9 intend, ~할 작정이다

10 addiction, 중독　11 message, 메시지

12 contact, 연락하다　13 mistake, 실수

14 digital, 디지털 방식을 쓰는　15 detox, 해독

16 conversation, 대화

대화문 TEST Step 1　　　　p.76~77

Listen & Speak 1 A

1. look tired / until late, so, slept for less than / Playing, is not good for your health / can't stop, addicted / were, would set, to limit

2. spend, much time on / get together, almost, can't help it / If I were you, suggest doing outdoor activities / Outdoor / a lot of, such as / right, suggest

Listen & Speak 2 A

1. are, doing / posting, that, took with / if, could post / because, looks good / not supposed to post, without asking / call, right away

2. let's watch / On / download, for free / supposed to download, from, against, law / Why don't we go, instead, Let's

Real Life Talk

posted strange things on, posted them / figured out, password / What should, do / were, change, password / should / easy to guess / used, birth date / In fact, (You')re not supposed to use, personal information, make a password / change, stronger one

Wrap Up

doing, writing, posting / take / took, from, blog / (you)'re not supposed to post / Why not / Because, owner, right to use

대화문 TEST Step 2　　　　p.78~79

Listen & Speak 1 A

1. G: You look tired, Peter.

B: I played computer games until late, so last night I slept for less than four hours.

G: Playing computer games too much is not good for your health.

B: I know, Jenny, but I can't stop it. I think I'm addicted to it.

G: If I were you, I would set a daily plan to limit game time.

B: That's a good idea. Thanks.

2. W: Tony, you spend too much time on your smartphone.

B: My friends get together on SNS almost every day, so I can't help it, Mom.

W: If I were you, I would suggest doing outdoor activities to your friends.

B: Outdoor activities?

W: Yes. You can do a lot of great activities such as soccer or skating.

B: All right. I will suggest them today.

Listen & Speak 2 A

1. G: James, what are you doing?

B: I'm posting some of the pictures that I took with Sarah today.

G: Did you ask Sarah if you could post them online?

B: No, but I think it's okay because she looks good in the pictures.

G: You're not supposed to post someone's pictures without asking.

B: Oh, maybe you're right. I'll call Sarah and ask her right away.

2. G: David, let's watch this new movie on the computer.

B: On the computer?

G: Yes. I have a website we can download it from for free.

B: You're not supposed to download movies from that website, Catherine. It's against the law.

G: Really? I didn't know that.

B: Why don't we go to the movie theater, instead?

G: Okay. Let's go.

Real Life Talk

Bora: Seho, look! Somebody posted strange things on your SNS. I don't think you posted them.

Seho: Really? Who did this?

Bora: I think someone figured out your password.

Seho: What should I do?

Bora: If I were you, I would change my password.

Seho: I think I should.

Bora: Is your password easy to guess?

Seho: I used my birth date.

Bora: That is not good. In fact, it is a big mistake. You're not supposed to use your personal information when you make a password.

Seho: Okay, I see. I will change it to a stronger one.

Wrap Up

B: What are you doing, Sohee?

G: I'm writing a posting about the restaurant I visited today.

B: Those are great pictures. Did you take all of them?

G: No. I took the pictures from someone's blog.

B: Then you're not supposed to post them on your blog.

G: Why not?

B: Because only the blog owner has the right to use them.

G: Oh, I see.

본문 TEST Step 1　　　　p.80~81

01 When, wake up, first

02 read, postings on, smartphone

03 Imagine, near, How, feel

04 check items on, true

05 Are, addicted to

06 Without, feel uncomfortable

07 take, into, bathroom

08 more, spend, on, than

09 check, postings while studying

10 try, reduce, on, fail

11 right after, sound, alert

12 next to, while, eating

13 score, more than half

14 so, problem with, addiction

15 addiction causes, spend, time

16 focus, studies, pain, neck

17 for you to start

18 staying away, such, while

19 lot, freedom from, noisy

20 focus, work, refreshed, creative

21 help, spend, with, others

22 Living without, however, easy

23 necessary, set, rules, using

24 need to follow

25 form, create rules, using

26 turn off, while studying

27 take, smartphone into, bathroom

28 keep, out of, use

29 spend, playing outside without

30 post fewer, messages on

31 were, reduce, by half

32 would turn off, alerts

33 lives, difficult, use, dangerous

34 With, become, wise, user

본문 TEST Step 2　　　　p.82~83

01 When, wake up in the morning, what

02 read, postings on

03 Imagine, is, near, How

04 check items, that are

05 Are, addicted to

06 Without, feel uncomfortable

07 take, into, bathroom

08 more enjoyable to, on, than with

09 check, postings while studying

10 reduce, I spend on, fail

11 right after, an alert　　　　12 next to, while

13 What, score, check more than half

14 have, with, addiction

15 causes you to spend, on

16 Also, focus on, studies, have a pain in, neck

17 for you to start digital detox

18 means staying away from, for

19 help, a lot, freedom from, noisy

20 focus, on, feel refreshed, creative ideas

21 help, spend, with others

22 Living, however, is

23 necessary for you to set, for using

24 need to follow

25 form, create rules for using

26 turn off, while studying　　　　27 take, into

28 keep, out of the bedroom, them

29 More Time for, spend more time playing outside without

30 Fewer, post fewer, on

31 I were, would reduce, on, by half

32 I were, would, off

33 had, would be more difficult, too much, dangerous

34 With, wise smartphone user

본문 TEST Step 3　　　　p.84~85

1 안녕하세요, 학생 여러분! 여러분은 아침에 일어났을 때, 가장 먼저 하는 일이 무엇인가요?

2 스마트폰으로 SNS 게시물을 읽나요?

3 스마트폰이 여러분 근처에 있지 않다고 상상해 보세요. 기분이 어떤가요?

4 학생 여러분, 이 목록에서 여러분에게 맞는 항목들을 표시해 보세요.

5 너는 스마트폰에 중독되었는가?

6 나는 스마트폰이 없으면, 불편함을 느낀다.

7 나는 스마트폰을 화장실에 가져간다.

8 나는 친구들과 함께 시간을 보내는 것보다 스마트폰을 하면서 보내는 시간이 더 즐겁다.

9 나는 공부하면서 SNS 게시물을 종종 확인한다.

10 나는 스마트폰을 사용하는 시간을 줄이려고 노력하지만, 실패한다.

11 나는 알림음을 듣자마자 스마트폰을 확인한다.

12 나는 식사 중에 스마트폰을 옆에 둔다.

13 여러분의 점수는 어떤가요? 절반보다 더 많이 표시했나요?

14 만약 그렇다면, 여러분은 스마트폰 중독의 문제를 가지고 있을지도 모릅니다.

15 스마트폰 중독은 여러분이 스마트폰에 너무 많은 시간을 보내게 만듭니다.

16 또한 여러분은 학업에 집중할 수 없고 목에 통증이 있을지도 모릅니다.

17 그렇다면 지금 여러분은 디지털 디톡스를 시작할 시간입니다.

18 디지털 디톡스는 스마트폰과 컴퓨터 같은 디지털 기기들로부터 잠시 동안 떨어져 있는 것을 의미합니다.

19 디지털 디톡스는 여러분을 많이 도와줄 것입니다. 여러분은 시끄러운 디지털 세계로부터 자유를 즐길 수 있습니다.

20 여러분은 하는 일에 더욱 집중할 수 있습니다. 종종 여러분은 상쾌함을 느끼고 새롭고 창의적인 아이디어를 얻을 수 있습니다.

21 디지털 디톡스는 또한 여러분이 다른 사람들과 더 많은 시간을 보내도록 도와줄 것입니다.

22 하지만 스마트폰 없이 사는 것은 쉽지 않습니다.

23 그러므로 여러분은 스마트폰을 사용하기 위한 몇 가지 규칙을 정할 필요가 있습니다.

24 그리고 나서 여러분은 그 규칙들을 따라야 합니다.

25 자, 조를 형성하고, 여러분의 조에서, 스마트폰을 사용하기 위한 규칙을 만들어 보세요.

26 우리는 공부하는 동안 스마트폰을 끌 것이다.

27 우리는 화장실에 스마트폰을 가져가지 않을 것이다.

28 우리는 밤에 스마트폰을 침실 밖에 두고 사용하지 않을 것이다.

29 야외 활동을 위한 더 많은 시간 – 우리는 스마트폰 없이 밖에서 노는 데 더 많은 시간을 보낼 것이다.

30 SNS는 더 적게 – 우리는 스마트폰에 SNS 메시지를 더 적게 올릴 것이다.

31 만약 내가 너라면, 나는 스마트폰에 쓰는 시간을 절반으로 줄일 것이다.

32 만약 내가 너라면, 모든 알림을 끌 것이다.

33 잘했어요, 학생 여러분! 만약 스마트폰이 없다면 우리의 삶이 더 힘들겠지만, 스마트폰을 너무 많이 사용하는 것은 위험합니다.

34 디지털 디톡스와 함께, 여러분은 현명한 스마트폰 사용자가 될 수 있습니다.

1 Hi, students! When you wake up in the morning, what is the first thing you do?

2 Do you read SNS postings on your smartphone?

3 Imagine your smartphone is not near you. How do you feel?

4 Students, please check items on the list that are true for you.

5 Are you addicted to your smartphone?

6 Without my smartphone, I feel uncomfortable.

7 I take my smartphone into the bathroom.

8 It is more enjoyable to spend time on my smartphone than with friends.

9 I often check SNS postings while studying.

10 I try to reduce the time I spend on my smartphone, but I fail.

11 I check my smartphone right after I hear the sound of an alert.

12 I have my smartphone next to me while I'm eating.

13 What is your score? Did you check more than half?

14 If so, you may have a problem with smartphone addiction.

15 Smartphone addiction causes you to spend too much time on your smartphone.

16 Also, you cannot focus on your studies and may have a pain in your neck.

17 Then now is the time for you to start digital detox.

18 Digital detox means staying away from digital devices, such as smartphones and computers, for a while.

19 Digital detox will help you a lot. You can enjoy freedom from the noisy digital world.

20 You can focus more on your work. Sometimes you can feel refreshed and have new, creative ideas.

21 Digital detox will also help you spend more time with others.

22 Living without a smartphone, however, is not easy.

23 So, it is necessary for you to set some rules for using your smartphone.

24 You then need to follow the rules.

25 Now, please form groups and, in your group, create rules for using your smartphone.

26 We will turn off our smartphones while studying.

27 We will not take our smartphones into the bathroom.

28 We will keep our smartphones out of the bedroom and not use them at night.

29 More Time for Outside Activities – We will spend more time playing outside without our smartphones.

30 Fewer SNS Messages – We will post fewer SNS messages on our smartphones.

31 If I were you, I would reduce my time on my smartphone by half.

32 If I were you, I would turn off all alerts.

33 You did a good job, students! If we had no smartphones, our lives would be more difficult, but too much use of a smartphone is dangerous.

34 With digital detox, you can become a wise smartphone user.

Enjoy Writing C

1. If There Were

2. would be, advantages, disadvantages, if, were

3. let's talk about

4. If, didn't have, would play outside

5. Plus, would be safe from

6. On the other hand, would be, disadvantages

7. If, would not, for us to contact

8. would take, for us to find information

Project 2

1. It, for us to be, citizens

2. If, Internet, SNS, would be more difficult

3. it, for us to use, wisely

4. respect myself, others

5. share my password with

6. use kind words

7. never use bad words

8. don't spend, much time online

Project 3

1. for everyone to become

2. show, what digital citizens do

3. enjoy

Enjoy Writing C

1. If There Were No Smartphones

2. There would be some advantages and some disadvantagesif there were no smartphones.

3. First, let's talk about some advantages.

4. If we didn't have smartphones, we would play outside more often.

5. Plus, we would be safe from neck pain.

6. On the other hand, there would be some disadvantages.

7. If there were no smartphones, it would not be easy for us to contact people.

8. Also, it would take so long for us to find information.

Project 2

1. It is necessary for us to be digital citizens!

2. If there were no Internet or SNS, our lives would be more difficult.

3. So, it is very important for us to use digital devices wisely as a digital citizen.

4. I respect myself and others on SNS.

5. I never share my password with anyone.

6. I use kind words.

7. I never use bad words.

8. I don't spend too much time online.

Project 3

1. It's very important for everyone to become a digital citizen.

2. Our group will show you what digital citizens do.

3. Please enjoy.

11 burial, 매장, 장례식　12 tomb, 무덤
13 amusement park, 놀이공원　14 crown, 왕관
15 poem, 시　16 flag, 깃발

단어 TEST Step 1　p.92

01 매장, 장례식　02 존경, 경의　03 통치, 지배
04 희생; 희생하다　05 바람, 갈망　06 우편 번호
07 비밀. 비밀의　08 장군　09 정부
10 조화　11 교육시키다　12 전문가
13 퍼지다, 퍼뜨리다　14 먹이를 주다, 먹이다
15 (정치적, 사회적) 운동　16 ~의 도처에, ~ 내내
17 입구　18 보호하다　19 지도자, 리더
20 주된, 주요한　21 임무　22 묘, 무덤
23 조직, 기구　24 궁전　25 보물
26 애국적인　27 안개 낀　28 대통령, 의장
29 독립　30 감독하다. 지휘[총괄]하다
31 조각상　32 묻다, 매장하다　33 공화국
34 끝내다; 완전한　35 전시회　36 ~에 속하다
37 ~을 입다　38 ~에 관해 듣다　39 ~가 필요하다
40 ~을 수행하다　41 ~처럼 보이다　42 ~하기 위해서
43 ~을 기대하다

단어 TEST Step 2　p.93

01 bury　02 secret　03 desire
04 respect　05 government　06 rule
07 educate　08 burial　09 foggy
10 general　11 sacrifice　12 poem
13 independence　14 palace　15 main
16 tomb　17 direct　18 treasure
19 feed　20 patriotic　21 statue
22 protect　23 spread　24 zip code
25 entrance　26 complete　27 leader
28 organization　29 specialist　30 harmony
31 exhibition　32 mission　33 republic
34 throughout　35 movement　36 put on
37 belong to　38 carry out　39 look like+명사
40 be in need　41 hear of
42 so that+주어+동사
43 look forward to+명사/동명사

단어 TEST Step 3　p.94

1 treasure, 보물　2 republic, 공화국
3 exhibition, 전시회　4 mission, 임무　5 palace, 궁전
6 organization, 조직　7 bury, 묻다　8 process, 과정
9 sacrifice, 희생　10 statue, 조각상

대화문 TEST Step 1　p.95~96

Listen & Speak 1 A

1. Look at, huge / looks strong / Because, was built to protect, during / who built / ordered, to direct, process, don't you / heard of, great scientist
2. don't you / national flag, isn't it / what, symbols, mean / Tell me, them / circle, means harmony, peace / lines, corners mean / mean, earth

Listen & Speak 2 A

1. planning to go / museum built by / heard, great things / bought, treasures that, had taken / must be interesting / looking forward to
2. what did you do / to do volunteer work / What kind of / cleaned around, tombs, respect, who died / Sounds, too / planning to go, join / I'm looking forward to

Real Life Talk

reading / Poetry, know, don't you / heard, much / poems when, under, rule, desire, independence, be felt, poems / to read, poems, learn more / In fact, planning to visit / when, going / near, Palace, palace at / Let's meet / looking forward to, visit

Wrap Up

let put on traditional / gifts for, Germany / there are, gift shops / shopping, for lunch / know, don't you / traditional, soup, delicious, make you healthy / looking forward to trying

대화문 TEST Step 2　p.97~98

Listen & Speak 1 A

1. B: Look at Suwon Hawseong. It's huge.
   G: It also looks strong.
   B: Because it was built to protect the people during wars.
   G: Wow. Do you know who built it?
   B: Yes. King Jeongjo ordered Jeong Yakyong to direct the building process. You know about Jeong Yakyong, don't you?
   G: Yes, I've heard of him. He was a great scientist in Joseon.

2. G: Brian, you know Taegeukgi, don't you?

   B: Sure. It's the national flag of Korea, isn't it?

   G: That's right. Do you know what the symbols in Taegeukgi mean?

   B: No, I don't. Tell me about them.

   G: The circle in the middle means harmony and peace.

   B: What do the black lines on the four corners mean?

   G: They mean four things: sky, fire, water, and earth.

1. G: I'm planning to go to the Gansong Museum.

   B: What is the Gansong Museum?

   G: It's a museum built by Gansong Jeon Hyeongpil.

   B: I heard that he did great things for the country.

   G: Yes. He bought many Korean treasures that some Japanese had taken to Japan.

   B: Wow. The museum must be interesting.

   G: Yes. I'm looking forward to it!

2. B: Soyeon, what did you do last weekend?

   G: I went to Hyeonchungwon to do volunteer work.

   B: What kind of volunteer work did you do there?

   G: I cleaned around the tombs. I felt great respect for the people who died for the country.

   B: Sounds great. Can I do it, too?

   G: Sure. I'm planning to go there again next Wednesday. Will you join me?

   B: Sure. I'm looking forward to it.

Andy: Bora, what are you reading?

Bora: I'm reading *Sky, Wind, Star, and Poetry* by Yun Dongju. You know about Yun Dongju, don't you?

Andy: I've heard his name, but I don't know much about him.

Bora: He wrote many beautiful poems when Korea was under Japanese rule. His love for the country and his desire for independence can be felt in his poems.

Andy: Really? I didn't know that. I want to read his poems and learn more about him.

Bora: Great. In fact, I'm planning to visit the Yun Dongju Museum soon. Do you want to come with me?

Andy: Yes, when are you going?

Bora: Next Saturday. It's near Gyeongbok Palace.

Can you meet me at the palace at 2 p.m.?

Andy: Sure. Let's meet there.

Bora: Great. I'm really looking forward to the visit.

B: Tomorrow let's put on traditional Korean clothes, hanbok, and go to Insadong.

G: Good, but I want to buy gifts for my friends in Germany tomorrow.

B: In Insadong, there are many gift shops.

G: Great. After shopping, what should we eat for lunch?

B: Hmm. You know Samgyetang, don't you?

G: No. What is it?

B: It's a traditional Korean soup. It's delicious and will make you healthy.

G: Sounds good. I'm looking forward to trying it.

01 Last week, went to

02 visited, inside, park

03 entrance, museum, saw, statue

04 national hero, fighting, independence

05 helped educate, by building

06 movement, spread throughout, moved

07 joined, later became, president

08 exhibition, shows, lot, life

09 While looking around, stopped

10 formed, secret, fight against

11 belonged to, group

12 place, hall, watches under

13 made, plan, kill, generals

14 directed, carry out, mission

15 left, need, anymore, let

16 carried, so, forget, sacrifice

17 completing, tour, tombs, heroes

18 bodies, been, independence, brought

19 By, deep, respect, sacrifice

20 As, thought, words, exhibition

21 was written in

22 what, wish, say clearly

23 second, would, independence, country

24 what, loudly, complete independence

01 my history club

02 visited, inside the park

03 At, entrance, white statue

04 a great national hero, spent, fighting, independence, from Japanese rule

05 helped educate, by building

06 In, when the independence movement, throughout, moved to

07 joined, later became its president

08 The exhibition hall, shows

09 While looking around, stopped at, Patriotic Organization's

10 formed, secret organization, to fight against

11 belonged to

12 At, saw two watches under

13 In, made a plan to, Japanese generals

14 Patriotic Organization, directed, to carry out

15 left for, wearing a very old watch, Mine, won't, it anymore, take, let, have

16 always carried, so that, would not forget, sacrifice

17 completing, moved to, tombs, three heroes

18 had been, after, independence, them

19 By doing so, deep love, for the sacrifice

20 As, left, thought, words, that, had read, exhibition hall

21 It, written in

22 what my wish is, clearly, Korea's Independence

23 what my second wish, independence

24 asks me what my third wish is, loudly, complete independence

9 우리는 전시관을 둘러보면서 한인 애국단의 단원들 사진 앞에 섰다.

10 김구는 일본에 맞서 싸우기 위해 1931년에 비밀 조직을 형성했다.

11 이봉창과 윤봉길이 그 집단에 속해 있었다.

12 전시관의 한 곳에서, 우리는 김구와 윤봉길의 사진 아래에 있는 시계 두 개를 보았다.

13 1932년에 김구는 상해에 있는 한 공원에서 일본 장군들을 암살하기 위한 계획을 세웠다.

14 한인 애국단의 지도자로서 그는 윤봉길이 임무를 수행하도록 지시했다.

15 윤봉길이 임무를 위해 떠날 때, 그는 김구에게 말했다. "선생님, 당신은 매우 낡은 시계를 차고 계시는군요. 제 것은 새것이나, 저는 그것이 더 이상 필요하지 않을 것입니다. 부디 제 시계를 가져가시고, 제가 선생님 것을 가지도록 해 주십시오."

16 김구는 윤봉길의 희생을 잊지 않기 위해서 윤봉길의 시계를 항상 상의에 넣고 다녔다.

17 기념관 관람을 마치고, 우리는 이봉창, 윤봉길, 그리고 백정기 의사들이 묻힌 삼의사의 묘로 이동했다.

18 그들의 시신은 일본에 있다가 독립이 되고 나서 김구가 그들의 시신을 효창 공원으로 가져왔다.

19 그는 그렇게 함으로써 삼의사들의 희생에 대한 그의 깊은 사랑과 경의를 보여 주었다.

20 내가 효창 공원을 떠날 때, 나는 전시관에서 읽었던 「나의 소원」에 있는 김구의 말을 생각했다.

21 그것은 『백범일지』에 쓰여 있었다.

22 만약 신이 나의 소원이 무엇이냐고 묻는다면, "그것은 대한 독립이오."라고 명확하게 말할 것이다.

23 만약에 그가 나의 두 번째 소원이 무엇이냐고 묻는다면, 나는 "그것은 내 나라의 독립이오."라고 말할 것이다.

24 만약 그가 나의 세 번째 소원이 무엇이냐고 묻는다면, "그것은 내 나라의 완전한 독립이오."라고 큰 소리로 말할 것 이다. 그것이 나의 대답이다.

1 지난주에 우리 역사 동아리는 효창 공원에 갔다.

2 우리는 공원 안에 있는 김구 기념관을 방문했다.

3 기념관 입구에서 우리는 하얀색의 김구 조각상을 보았다.

4 김구는 일본 통치로부터 대한의 독립을 위해 싸우는 데 그의 삶 대부분을 보낸 위대한 국민 영웅이다.

5 1900년대에 그는 학교를 설립함으로써 젊은이들을 교육시키는 것을 도왔다.

6 1919년에 3.1 운동이 나라 전체에 걸쳐 퍼져나갔을 때, 그는 중국 상하이로 이동했다.

7 그곳에서 그는 대한민국 임시정부에 합류했고 나중에는 그것의 대표자가 되었다.

8 기념관 안에 있는 전시관은 김구의 삶에 관한 많은 것을 보여 준다.

1 Last week my history club went to Hyochang Park.

2 We visited the Kim Koo Museum inside the park.

3 At the entrance of the museum, we saw a white statue of Kim Koo.

4 Kim Koo is a great national hero who spent most of his life fighting for the independence of Korea from Japanese rule.

5 In the 1900s, he helped educate young people by building schools.

6 In 1919, when the independence movement had spread throughout the country, he moved to Shanghai, China.

7 There he joined the Government of the Republic of Korea and later became its president.

8 The exhibition hall in the museum shows a lot of things about Kim Koo's life.

9 While looking around the hall, we stopped at a photo of the Korean Patriotic Organization's members.

10 Kim Koo formed the secret organization in 1931 to fight against Japan.

11 Lee Bongchang and Yun Bonggil belonged to the group.

12 At one place in the hall, we saw two watches under a photo of Kim Koo and Yun Bonggil.

13 In 1932, Kim Koo made a plan to kill Japanese generals in a park in Shanghai.

14 As the leader of the Korean Patriotic Organization, he directed Yun to carry out the mission.

15 When Yun left for the mission, he told Kim, "Sir, you are wearing a very old watch. Mine is new, but I won't need it anymore. Please take my watch, and let me have yours."

16 Kim Koo always carried Yun's watch in his jacket so that he would not forget Yun's sacrifice.

17 After completing the tour of the museum, we moved to the tombs of the three heroes, Lee Bongchang, Yun Bonggil, and Baek Jeonggi.

18 Their bodies had been in Japan, but after Korea's independence Kim Koo brought them to Hyochang Park.

19 By doing so, he showed his deep love and respect for the sacrifice of the three heroes.

20 As I left Hyochang Park, I thought about Kim Koo's words in My Wish that I had read in the exhibition hall.

21 It was written in *Baekbeomilji*.

22 If God asks me what my wish is, I would say clearly, "It is Korea's Independence."

23 YIf he asks me what my second wish is, I would say, "It is the independence of my country."

24 If he asks me what my third wish is, I would say loudly, "It is the complete independence of my country." That is my answer.

Real Life Talk Step 3

1. chose, because, were impressed by, sacrifice for

2. can learn more about, by visiting

Enjoy Writing

1. was born in

2. When, in his teens, moved to, went to, there

3. left for, so that, get a better education

4. helped improve the lives, became a respected leader

5. had returned to, founded, to fight for Korea's independence

6. Government of the Republic of Korea

7. built a lot of, to educate, until, died in

Project Step 1

1. to introduce, to foreigners, don't you

2. a temple in

3. one of the most beautiful temples

4. has many treasures like

Real Life Talk Step 3

1. My group members chose An Junggeun because we were impressed by his sacrifice for the country.

2. You can learn more about him by visiting the An Junggeun Museum or An Junggeun Park.

Enjoy Writing

1. An Changho was born in 1878.

2. When he was in his teens, he moved to Seoul and went to school there.

3. In 1902, he left for America so that he could get a better education.

4. In America, An helped improve the lives of the Korean people there and became a respected leader.

5. After he had returned to Korea, he founded the New Korean Society in 1907 to fight for Korea's independence.

6. He also joined the Government of the Republic of Korea in Shanghai in 1919.

7. After that, he built a lot of schools to educate people until he died in 1938.

Project Step 1

1. A: I want to introduce Bulguksa to foreigners. You know Bulguksa, don't you?

2. B: Yes, I do. It's a temple in Gyeongju.

3. C: Yes. It's one of the most beautiful temples in Korea.

4. D: It also has many treasures like the Dabotop.

MEMO

1학기 전과정

적중 100 plus

영어 기출 문제집

정답 및 해설

시사 | 박준언

적중 1OO + 특별부록

Plan B

우리학교
최신기출

시사 · 박준언 교과서를 배우는

학교 시험문제 분석 · 모음 · 해설집

전국단위 학교 시험문제 수집 및 분석
출제 빈도가 높은 문제 위주로 선별
문제 풀이에 필요한 상세한 해설

중3-1
영어

시사 · 박준언

◎ 선택형 문항의 답안은 컴퓨터용 수정 싸인펜을 사용하여 OMR 답안지에 바르게 표기하시오.
◎ 서술형 문제는 답을 답안지에 반드시 검정 볼펜으로 쓰시오.
◎ 총 28문항 100점 만점입니다. 문항별 배점은 각 문항에 표시되어 있습니다.

[충북 ○○중]
1. 다음 영어 표현과 그 의미가 바르게 쓰인 것은? (3점)

① be filled with ~: ~으로 덮여 있다

② be regarded as ~: ~를 추천한다

③ would like to ~: ~하고 싶다

④ in response to: ~와 차이가 나서

⑤ get used to ~: ~로 사용되다

[부산 ○○중]
2. 다음 대화의 빈칸에 가장 알맞은 표현은? (3점)

A: _____
B: Yes. He is humorous and told us some fun stories about math. It was interesting.
A: Good. I hope you enjoy studying math.

① Do you like math?

② What is your favorite subject?

③ Who is your homeroom teacher?

④ Can you tell me more about him?

⑤ How was your first day of third grade?

[충북 ○○중]
3. 주어진 대화 사이에 문장 (A)~(E)를 배열한 것으로 가장 알맞은 것은? (조건: (A)~(E)는 각각 B 혹은 G의 대화임.) (4점)

G: Jiho, how was your first day of third grade?
B: _____
G: _____
B: _____
G: _____
B: _____
G: Cool! I hope you enjoy studying math.

(A) Can you tell me more about him?

(B) My homeroom teacher is Mr. Kim. He teaches math.

(C) Yes. He is humorous and told us some fun stories about math. It was interesting.

(D) It was pretty good. The teachers and my new classmates are all good.

(E) That sounds good. Who is your homeroom teacher?

① (B)-(A)-(C)-(E)-(D)

② (B)-(D)-(E)-(C)-(A)

③ (C)-(A)-(B)-(D)-(E)

④ (D)-(E)-(B)-(A)-(C)

⑤ (D)-(E)-(C)-(A)-(B)

[충북 ○○중]
4. 다음 중 짝지어진 대화가 어색한 것은? (3점)

① A: How was your first day of third grade?
   B: It was pretty good.

② A: Who is your homeroom teacher?
   B: My homeroom teacher is Mr. Kim.

③ A: Can you please introduce yourself to the class?
   B: Yes. I like sports, especially soccer.

④ A: Can you tell me about your plan for this weekend?
   B: My motto is "You can go forward slowly, but never go back."

⑤ A: Is there anything else you want to tell your new friends?
   B: Yes. I want to get along with everyone.

[5~6] 다음 대화를 읽고 물음에 답하시오.

> Amy: (A) Ted, look at this movie poster. I want to see this movie.
> Ted: It looks interesting. (B)
> Amy: Yes. It is about a hero who saves the Earth.
> Ted: It looks like an SF movie.
> Amy: Yes, it is. Actually, SF is my favorite kind of movie. I like the scenes made with computer technology. They are fantastic and look real. (C)
> Ted: That's cool. I am free this weekend. Let's go to see it together. (D)
> Amy: Sounds good. (E)

5. 위 대화에서 알 수 있는 사실은? (3점)

① What is the title of the movie?

② How much is the movie ticket?

③ Why does the hero save the Earth?

④ When are they going to meet to see a movie?

⑤ Where can they learn the computer technology?

6. 위 대화의 (A)~(E) 중 주어진 표현이 들어가기에 가장 알맞은 위치는? (3점)

> Can you tell me about it?

① (A) ② (B) ③ (C) ④ (D) ⑤ (E)

7. 다음 우리말과 같은 의미가 되도록 빈칸에 알맞은 단어를 쓰시오. (4점)

> • 그녀는 집에서 학교까지 정말 걸어다닌다.
> = She _____ _____ from home to school.

→ _____

8. 다음 대화의 내용과 일치하지 않는 것은? (4점)

> S: Nice to meet you. I'd like to join your photo club.
> B: Thank you for your interest in the club. Can you tell me about yourself?
> S: Yes. My name is Kim Seho. I am in the third grade, class 8.
> A: Tell me more. What do you like to do most in your free time?
> S: Well, I like to take pictures most.
> B: That's great. What is your dream for the future?
> S: I want to be a photographer.
> A: Then you made the right choice. You can learn a lot of photo-taking skills here. Welcome to our club.
> S: Thank you. I'm so glad!
>   *S: Seho **B: Bora ***A: Andy

① Seho wants to join a photo club.

② Seho likes to take pictures most in his free time.

③ Bora wants to know about Seho's future dream.

④ Andy taught Seho how to take good pictures.

⑤ Andy thinks Seho can learn a lot of photo-taking skills in the photo club.

9. 다음 대화의 빈칸에 알맞은 말을 쓰시오. (4점)

> A: Please tell me about correct English expressions.
> B: You should say ⓐ_____ _____ instead of eye shopping.
> C: Don't say Y-shirt. You should say ⓑ _____ _____ instead.

ⓐ: _____ _____

ⓑ: _____ _____

[10~11] 다음 대화를 읽고, 물음에 답하시오.

A: Nice to meet you. I'd like to join your photo club.
B: Thank you for your interest in the club.
_____ ⓐ _____
A: Yes. My name is Kim Seho. I am in the third grade, class 8.
C: Tell me more. What do you like to do most in your free time?
A: Well, what I like most is to take pictures.
B: That's great. What is your dream for the future?
A: I want to be a photographer.
C: Then _____ ⓑ _____ You can learn a lot of photo-taking skills here. Welcome to our club.
A: Thank you. I'm so glad!

10. ⓐ에 들어갈 가장 알맞은 말은? (3점)

① Let me introduce myself.
② I am curious about your school.
③ Can you tell me about yourself?
④ I wonder why you chose our club.
⑤ What do you want to learn in our club?

11. ⓑ에 들어갈 가장 알맞은 말은? (3점)

① you made the right choice.
② our club is not easy to join.
③ why do you want to join our club?
④ you should teach us how to take pictures.
⑤ what I recommend to you is a drama club.

12. 다음 문장에서 어법상 어색한 부분을 올바른 문장으로 고쳐 쓰시오. (4점)

• The letter shows what good friends are they.

→ _____

13. 다음 중 어법상 옳은 문장을 모두 고른 것은? (3점)

(A) Ted doesn't like spicy food, but he does likes Gimchi.
(B) My mom did watch the TV show last night.
(C) You don't like exercise much, but you do love playing basketball.
(D) I do wanting to talk with you about our project.
(E) Ms. Kim does teach English in our school.

① (A), (B), (D)　　② (A), (D), (E)
③ (B), (C), (E)　　④ (B), (D), (E)
⑤ (C), (D), (E)

14. 다음 밑줄 친 what에 대하여 바르게 설명하고 있는 친구를 모두 고르면? (정답 2개) (4점)

• <u>What</u> I want to do is to go to travel.

① 갑이: 밑줄 친 What은 관계대명사야.
② 을이: 여기서는 '무엇'이라고 해석하는 거야.
③ 병이: 아니야 '~하는 것'으로 해석하는 거야.
④ 정이: 선행사를 포함하지 않는 관계대명사야.
⑤ 한이: 여기서 what 대신에 the thing who로 바꾸어 쓸 수 있어.

[15~18] 다음 글을 읽고 물음에 답하시오.

Have you ever thought about your dream house? Today, in class, we ㉠created our dream house. Here are some of the dream houses that we made.

A House in Nature – Minho
㉡Nature is my good friend. I feel good when I walk in the forest. I'd like to have a dream house in the countryside. ⓐIt should have a big garden with many flowers and trees. I am always excited by the sound of birds. ⓑIt will be wonderful to wake up in the morning and listen to the songs of the birds. Also, I'd like to have many pets. ⓒIt will be fun ㉢play with them!

A Place for Family – Misun
My family is the most important thing to me. In my dream house, my family feels safe and comfortable. At the gate, you can find a beautifully designed sign with my family's picture on ⓓit. When you ⓔenter the house, you will see a large living room. My family sometimes plays board games and sings there. ⓔIt will have a garden with a large picnic table for family picnics. There we will ㉤enjoy barbecues. Do you like my dream house?

15. 위 글의 Miho와 Misun이의 꿈의 집에서 찾을 수 <u>없는</u> 것은? (3점)

① Minho – 큰 정원
② Minho – 애완동물
③ Misun – 아름답게 디자인된 문패
④ Misun – 바이올린
⑤ Misun – 커다란 피크닉 테이블

16. 위 글의 밑줄 친 ㉠~㉤ 중, 어법상 <u>어색한</u> 것은? (4점)

① ㉠ ② ㉡ ③ ㉢ ④ ㉣ ⑤ ㉤

17. 밑줄 친 ⓐ~ⓔ 중 지칭하는 대상이 바르게 짝지어진 것은? (대·소문자 구분 없음.) (4점)

ⓐ a dream house
ⓑ the sound of birds
ⓒ pets
ⓓ a beautifully designed sign
ⓔ my dream house

① ⓐ, ⓑ   ② ⓐ, ⓒ   ③ ⓐ, ⓔ
④ ⓑ, ⓓ   ⑤ ⓑ, ⓔ

18. 위 글을 읽고 답할 수 <u>없는</u> 것은? (3점)

① Where does Minho want to have his dream house?
② What makes Minho excited?
③ What is the most important thing to Misun?
④ How does Misun's family feel in Misun's dream house?
⑤ Is Misun good at board games?

19. 다음 글의 빈칸에 공통으로 들어갈 말로 가장 적절한 것은? (4점)

To Jina, at some future time
Hi, Jina. What I want to put into this memory box are my soccer ball, my school newspaper, and a letter from my best friend, Semin. I want to put in the soccer ball _____ I spend a lot of time playing soccer. I want to put in the school newspaper _____ I want to remember what happened in my middle school days. Finally, I want to put in the letter from Semin _____ it shows what good friends we are. What I hope from you is to keep these things forever.

From Jina

① but   ② when   ③ because
④ before   ⑤ while

[20~21] 다음 글을 읽고 물음에 답하시오.

Bryan

I am an early adopter of new technology. I do like to use new products and technology before others. When I get near my house, the front door recognizes my face and opens automatically. The furniture checks the weather conditions and advises me on what to wear. The bathroom mirror tells me my weight and the condition of my health. A robot cleans the house and cooks for me. This is what I can imagine about my dream house.

20. 위 글의 제목으로 적절한 것은? (3점)

① A Fun House
② A Place for Friends
③ A House in the Countryside
④ A House with Many Robots
⑤ A House with New Technology

21. 위 글을 읽고, Bryan의 dream house를 그림으로 그렸을 때 찾아 볼 수 없는 것은? (4점)

① Bryan의 얼굴을 인식하고 자동으로 열어주는 문
② 날씨 상태를 체크하는 가구
③ 몸무게와 건강 상태를 말해주는 욕실 체중계
④ 집 청소를 해주는 로봇
⑤ 요리를 해주는 로봇

[22~23] 다음 글을 읽고 물음에 답하시오.

Julie

Welcome to my dream house! ⓐ재미있게 노는 것이 내가 가장 원하는 것이다, so my dream house is full of exciting things. It has a (A)_____ in the basement. There I can eat cookies and enjoy my favorite movies. My dream house has a (B)_____ _____ on the second floor. I can play many different kinds of games there. My house also has a swimming pool. I want to do fun things with my friends in my house. You can be my guest!

22. 위 글의 밑줄 친 ⓐ를 조건에 맞게 영어 문장으로 쓰시오. (5점)

조건

• 관계대명사 what을 포함할 것.
• 7단어의 영어 문장으로 작성할 것.
• 완전한 문장으로 쓸 것.

→ _____ _____ _____ _____
_____ _____ _____

23. 위 글의 빈칸 (A), (B)에 각각 알맞은 단어를 영어로 쓰시오. (4점)

(A): _____

(B): _____ _____

24. 다음 〈보기〉의 단어 중에서 필요한 것을 선택하여 우리말 뜻에 맞게 영어로 쓰시오. (4점)

보기

she / does / her / lost / hers / did / wallet / lose

• Jina는 어제 그녀의 지갑을 정말 잃어버렸어.
→ Jina _____ yesterday.

[25~26] 다음 글을 읽고 물음에 답하시오.

> I am an early adopter of new technology. An early adopter is someone who uses new products and technology (A)_____ others. When I get near my house, the front door recognizes my face and opens automatically. The furniture checks the weather conditions and advises me on (B)_____ to wear. The bathroom mirror tells me my weight and the condition of my health. A robot cleans the house and cooks for me.

25. 위 글의 (A)와 (B)에 문맥상 가장 올바르게 들어갈 단어로 짝지어진 것은? (3점)

	(A)	(B)
①	in front of	what
②	after	how
③	after	what
④	before	how
⑤	before	what

26. 위 글을 읽고 답할 수 없는 것은? (3점)

① How many kinds of furniture does the writer have in the dream house?

② What does the bathroom mirror do in the dream house?

③ What does the front door do in the dream house?

④ What does the robot do in the dream house?

⑤ What does an early adopter do?

[27~28] 다음 글을 읽고 물음에 답하시오.

> Have you ever thought about your dream house? Today, in class, we created our dream house. ⓐHere are some of the dream houses what we made.
>
> A House in Nature - Minho
> Nature is my good friend. ⓑI do feeling good when I walk in the forest. I'd like to have a dream house in the countryside. ⓒIt should have a big garden with many flowers and trees. I am always excited by the sound of birds. ⓓIt will be wonderful to wake up in the morning and listen to the songs of the birds. Also, I'd like to have many pets. ⓔIt will be boring to play with them!

27. 위 글의 밑줄 친 ⓐ~ⓔ 중, 글의 흐름상 또는 어법상 쓰임이 적절하지 않은 문장의 개수는? (4점)

① 1개 ② 2개 ③ 3개 ④ 4개 ⑤ 5개

28. 위 글을 읽고 답할 수 없는 질문은? (4점)

① What did Minho do in class today?

② Where does Minho want to live?

③ What does Minho think about nature?

④ Does Minho like to have many pets in the future?

⑤ What does Minho's dream house have on the second floor?

문항수 : 선택형(24문항) 서술형(4문항)   20 . . .

◎ 선택형 문항의 답안은 컴퓨터용 수정 싸인펜을 사용하여 OMR 답안지에 바르게 표기하시오.
◎ 서술형 문제는 답을 답안지에 반드시 검정 볼펜으로 쓰시오.
◎ 총 28문항 100점 만점입니다. 문항별 배점 은 각 문항에 표시되어 있습니다.

[경기 ㅇㅇ중]

1. 다음 문장의 빈칸 (A), (B)에 들어갈 말로 가장 적절한 것은?   (4점)

- You have to be polite to our (A)_____.
- The USA death (B)_____ from cancer increased last year.

	(A)	(B)
①	guest	rate
②	health	tax
③	forest	state
④	furniture	goods
⑤	basement	weight

[충북 ㅇㅇ중]

2. 다음 중 빈칸에 들어가기에 가장 적절한 표현은?   (3점)

Jina: Jiho, how was your first day of third grade?
Jiho: It was pretty good. The teachers and my new classmates are all good.
Jina: That sounds good. Who is your homeroom teacher?
Jiho: My homeroom teacher is Mr. Kim. He teaches math.
Jina: (A)_____
Jiho: Yes. He is humorous and told us some fun stories about math.

① What is your favorite subject?
② Can you tell me more about him?
③ Is your math class difficult to understand?
④ Why don't you study together tomorrow?
⑤ Could you show me how to solve this math problem?

[강남구 ㅇㅇ중]

[3~4] 다음 대화를 읽고 물음에 답하시오.

G: Ted, look at this movie poster. I want to see this movie.
B: It looks interesting. Can you tell me about it, Amy?
G: Yes, it is about a hero who saves the Earth.
B: It looks like an SF movie.
G: Yes, it is. ⓐ_____, SF is my favorite kind of movie. I like the scenes made with computer technology. They are fantastic and look real.
B: That's cool. I am free this weekend. Let's go to see it together.
G: Sounds good.

3. 위 대화의 내용과 일치하는 것은?   (4점)

① 테드는 포스터 속의 영화를 가장 좋아한다.
② 테드는 포스터 속의 영화를 에이미와 같이 보고 싶지 않다.
③ 테드는 포스터 속의 영화의 내용에 대해 전부터 알고 있었다.
④ 에이미는 테드가 말하기 전까지 포스터 속의 영화 의 장르를 몰랐다.
⑤ 두 사람은 이번 주 주말에 포스터 속의 영화를 보 러 갈 것이다.

4. 위 대화의 빈칸 ⓐ에 들어갈 문맥상 가장 알맞은 말은?   (3점)

① At last   ② In fact
③ By the way   ④ On the other hand
⑤ For example

5. 다음 대화의 내용과 일치하는 것은? (4점)

Amy: Ted, look at this movie poster. I want to see this movie.

Ted: It looks interesting. Can you tell me about it, Amy?

Amy: Yes, it is about a hero who saves the Earth.

Ted: It looks like an SF movie.

Amy: Yes, it is. Actually, SF is my favorite kind of movie. I like the scenes made with computer technology. They are fantastic and look real.

Ted: That's cool. I am free this weekend. Let's go to see it together.

Amy: Sounds good.

① Ted has no interest about the movie.

② Amy and Ted will make an SF movie.

③ Amy and Ted want to join the movie club.

④ Amy doesn't know anything about the movie.

⑤ Amy and Ted will go to see the SF movie this weekend.

6. 다음 대화의 빈칸에 적절하지 않은 것은? (3점)

A: What is your nickname?

B: My nickname is Little Giant because I am small but strong.

A: What do you like most?

B: _____

① To travel is what I like most.

② What I don't like is hamburger.

③ I like to listen to K-pop music most.

④ What I like most is to study English.

⑤ Playing the guitar is what I like most.

7. 다음 질문에 대한 대답으로 적절하지 않은 것은? (3점)

• What do you like to do most in your free time?

① I like to play soccer most.

② What I like most is reading books.

③ Rock is my favorite kind of music.

④ Playing the drums is my favorite activity.

⑤ What I like to do most is to watch a movie.

8. 다음 빈칸에 공통으로 들어갈 말로 가장 적절한 것은? (대·소문자 구분 없음.) (3점)

G: I often go traveling with my family. _____ I like most about traveling is trying new foods.

B: My favorite subject is music. I can play the drums and guitar. Among them, playing the guitar is _____ I like most.

G: This is a picture of Dora. She is my best friend, not just a pet. Playing with her in my free time is _____ I like most.

① why   ② that   ③ what
④ which   ⑤ where

9. 다음 문장이 같은 의미가 되도록 빈칸에 알맞은 말을 쓰시오. (4점)

• She couldn't believe what her friend said to her.

= She couldn't believe _____ _____ _____ her friend said to her.

→ _____ _____ _____

[10~11] 다음 대화를 읽고 물음에 답하시오.

G: Ted, look at this movie poster. I want to see this movie.

(A) It looks like an SF movie.

(B) Yes. It is about a hero who saves the Earth.

(C) It looks interesting. Can you tell me about it, Amy?

G: Yes, it is. Actually, SF is my favorite kind of movie. The scenes in the movie are fantastic and look real.

B: That's cool. I am free this weekend. Let's go to see it together.

G: Sounds good.

10. 위 대화의 올바른 순서는? (3점)

① (A) - (B) - (C) ② (B) - (A) - (C)
③ (B) - (C) - (A) ④ (C) - (A) - (B)
⑤ (C) - (B) - (A)

11. 위 대화의 내용과 일치하지 <u>않는</u> 것은? (3점)

① Amy and Ted are looking at a movie poster.
② The movie is about a hero who saves the Earth.
③ SF movies are Ted's favorite kind of movie.
④ Ted is not busy this weekend.
⑤ Amy and Ted are going to see the movie this weekend

12. 다음 문장에 대하여 <u>어색하게</u> 설명하고 있는 친구는? (4점)

• Mrs. Han does teaches English in our school.

① 갑이: 위의 문장에서 does는 동사를 강조하기 위하여 사용하는 단어야.
② 을이: 맞아. 동사를 강조할 때 사용할 수 있는 것은 do, does, did를 사용할 수 있어.
③ 병이: 그런데 여기서 teaches는 잘못되었어.
④ 정이: 그래. 강조의 does 뒤에는 동사원형을 써야 해.
⑤ 한이: 아니야. 주어가 3인칭 단수이기 때문에 teaches가 맞는 거야.

13. 다음 밑줄 친 부분을 조동사 do/does/did로 강조하여 문장을 다시 쓰시오. (6점)

(1) She <u>lost</u> her wallet in the park.
→ _____

(2) I <u>walk</u> to my house from school every day.
→ _____

(3) He <u>enjoys</u> swimming with me on weekends.
→ _____

(1): _____
(2): _____
(3): _____

14. 〈조건〉에 맞게 다음 문장을 영작하시오. (4점)

• 그가 가장 갖고 싶어 하는 것은 시계야.

조건
• <보기>의 단어를 활용하고 선행사를 포함하는 관계대명사 what을 활용할 것.

보기

most / have / watch

→ _____

[15~17] 다음 글을 읽고 물음에 답하시오.

A Fun Place - Julie
Welcome to my dream house! Having fun is what I want most, so my dream house is full of (A)_____ things. It has a theater in the basement. There, I can eat cookies and enjoy my favorite movies. ⓐMy dream house has a game room on the second floor. I can play many different kinds of games there. My house also has a swimming pool. I want to do fun things with my friends in my house. You can be my guest!

A Place for Family - Misun
My family is the most important thing to me. In my dream house, my family feels safe and (B)_____. At the gate, you can find a beautifully designed sign with my family's picture on it. (C)_____ you enter the house, you will see a large living room. My family sometimes plays board games and sings there. It will have a garden with a large picnic table for family picnics. There, we will enjoy barbecues. Do you like my dream house?

15. 위 글의 문맥상 빈칸 (A), (B), (C)에 알맞은 말이 순서대로 짝지어진 것은? (4점)

	(A)	(B)	(C)
①	fantastic	comfortable	Which
②	exciting	nervous	As
③	exciting	comfortable	When
④	expensive	nervous	When
⑤	expensive	comfortable	Which

16. 위 글의 내용과 일치하는 것은? (3점)

① Julie can watch her favorite movies in the theater of her dream house.
② Julie wants to do fun things with her friends in the public swimming pool near her dream house.
③ There will be a game room with a large picnic table in Misun's dream house.
④ Misun designed the sign with her family's picture on the gate.
⑤ Misun is planning to enjoy barbecues with her friends in her dream house.

17. 위 글의 밑줄 친 ⓐ를 'It ~ that'을 이용하여 'a game room'을 강조하는 문장으로 전환하시오. (4점)

ⓐMy dream house has a game room on the second floor.

→ _____

18. 다음 빈칸에 들어갈 말로 가장 적절한 것은? (3점)

_____ I feel good when I walk in the forest. I'd like to have a dream house in the countryside. It should have a big garden with many flowers and trees. I am always excited by the sound of birds. It will be wonderful to wake up in the morning and listen to the songs of the birds. Also, I'd like to have many pets. It will be fun to play with them!

① Nature is my good friend.
② Pets are my good friends.
③ Birds are my good friends.
④ Nature is not my good friend.
⑤ Birds are not my good friends.

[19~22] 다음 글을 읽고 물음에 답하시오.

My Dream House

Have you ever thought about your dream house? Today, in class, we created our dream house. Here are some of the dream houses that we made.

A House in Nature - Minho
ⓐ<u>Nature is my good friend.</u> I do feel good when I walk in the forest. ⓑ<u>I'd like to have a dream house in the countryside.</u> ⓒ<u>It should have a big garden with many flowers and trees.</u> ⓓ<u>I am always excited by the sound of birds.</u> ⓔ<u>It will be impossible to wake up in the morning and listen to the songs of the birds.</u> Also, I'd like to have many pets. It will be fun to play with them!

A Fun Place - Julie
Welcome to my dream house! (A)<u>Having fun</u> is what I want most, so my dream house is full of (B)<u>excited things</u>. It has a theater in the basement. There, I can eat cookies (C)<u>and enjoy</u> my favorite movies. My dream house has a game room (D)<u>on the second floor</u>. I can play many different kinds of games there. My house also has a swimming pool. I want (E)<u>to do</u> fun things with my friends in my house. You can be my guest!

---

19. 위 글의 밑줄 친 ⓐ~ⓔ 중 내용상 흐름과 거리가 먼 것은? (3점)

① ⓐ   ② ⓑ   ③ ⓒ   ④ ⓓ   ⑤ ⓔ

20. 위 글과 관련된 내용을 묻는 것으로 거리가 먼 것은? (4점)

① What did Minho do in class today?
② When does Minho feel good?
③ What kind of garden does Minho want to have in his dream house?
④ Where is the theater in Julie's dream house?
⑤ How often does Julie play games?

21. 위 글의 Julie에 관한 내용과 일치하지 <u>않는</u> 것은? (3점)

① She can watch movies in her dream house.
② She can play games that she likes in her game room.
③ She can swim in her dream house.
④ She can read a lot of books in her dream house.
⑤ She wants to do fun things with her friends.

22. 위 글의 밑줄 친 (A)~(E) 중 어법상 낱말의 쓰임이 바르지 <u>않은</u> 것은? (3점)

① (A)   ② (B)   ③ (C)   ④ (D)   ⑤ (E)

23. 다음 글의 빈칸에 들어갈 전치사로 가장 적절한 것은? (4점)

I am an early adopter of new technology. I like to use new products and technology _____ others. When I get near my house, the front door recognizes my face and opens automatically. The furniture checks the weather conditions and advises me on what to wear. The bathroom mirror tells me my weight and the condition of my health. A robot cleans the house and cooks for me.

---

① by   ② to   ③ after
④ before   ⑤ among

[24~25] 다음 글을 읽고 물음에 답하시오.

Nature is my good friend. I do feel good when I walk in the forest. I'd like to have a dream house in the countryside. ⓐIt should have a big garden with many flowers and trees. ⓑIn my dream house, my family is the most important thing to me. ⓒI am always excited by the sound of birds. ⓓIt will be wonderful to wake up in the morning and listen to the songs of the birds. ⓔAlso, I'd like to have many pets. It will be fun to play with them!

24. 위 글에서 문맥상 글의 흐름이 어색한 문장은? (4점)

① ⓐ   ② ⓑ   ③ ⓒ   ④ ⓓ   ⑤ ⓔ

25. 위 글의 제목으로 가장 적절한 것은? (3점)

① A Fun Place
② A House in Nature
③ A Place for Friends
④ A House which I Live in
⑤ A House with a New Design

[26~27] 다음 글을 읽고 물음에 답하시오.

Welcome to my dream house! I like having fun, (A)_____ my dream house is full of exciting things. It has a theater in the basement. There I can eat cookies and enjoy my favorite movies. My dream house has a game room on the second floor. I can play many different kinds of games there. My house also has a swimming pool. I want to do fun things with my friends in my house. You can be my guest!

26. 위 글의 내용과 일치하는 것은? (4점)

① 글쓴이는 1층에서 영화를 볼 수 있다.
② 글쓴이는 현재 살고 있는 집을 소개 중이다.
③ 글쓴이는 지하실에서 쿠키를 만들 수 있다.
④ 글쓴이는 수영장에 가서 친구들과 많은 것을 할 수 있다.
⑤ 글쓴이는 2층에서 많은 다른 종류의 게임들을 할 수 있다.

27. 위 글의 빈칸 (A)에 들어갈 단어로 가장 알맞은 것은? (3점)

① because   ② or   ③ so
④ but   ⑤ yet

28. 다음 글에 있는 표현과 뜻이 바르게 짝지어진 것의 개수는? (4점)

I am an early adopter of new technology. I like to use new products and technology before others. When I get near my house, the front door recognizes my face and opens automatically. The furniture checks the weather conditions and advises me on what to wear. The bathroom mirror tells me my weight and the condition of my health. A robot cleans the house and cooks for me.

• mirror - 거울
• weight - 몸무게
• furniture - 대문
• advise on - 인식하다
• recognize - ~에 대해 충고하다

① 1개   ② 2개   ③ 3개   ④ 4개   ⑤ 5개

3학년 영어 1학기 중간고사(2과) 1회

문항수 : 선택형(25문항)   서술형(2문항)   20 . . .

◎ 선택형 문항의 답안은 컴퓨터용 수정 싸인펜을 사용하여 OMR 답안지에 바르게 표기하시오.
◎ 서술형 문제는 답을 답안지에 반드시 검정 볼펜으로 쓰시오.
◎ 총 27문항 100점 만점입니다. 문항별 배점은 각 문항에 표시되어 있습니다.

[충북 ○○중]

1. 다음 밑줄 친 단어의 쓰임이 나머지 넷과 <u>다른</u> 하나는? (3점)

① Some surprised me at first, but now I am getting <u>used</u> to them.
② I am not <u>used</u> to making speeches in public.
③ The taxi driver is <u>used</u> to driving for a long time.
④ Is she getting <u>used</u> to her new house?
⑤ I <u>used</u> to go to school by bus when I was young.

[강남구 ○○중]

2. 다음 단어와 영영 풀이가 알맞게 짝지어진 것의 개수는? (4점)

단어	영영 풀이
fee	things that are made to be sold; merchandise or possessions
attend	an act of giving one thing and receiving another in return
manner	the way in which something is done
advise	to give an opinion or suggestion to someone about what should be done
tax	a quantity or degree measured in proportion to something else

① 1개   ② 2개   ③ 3개
④ 4개   ⑤ 5개

[충북 ○○중]

3. 다음 중 짝지어진 대화가 <u>어색한</u> 것은? (3점)

① A: Which country would you like to visit?
   B: I'd like to visit Australia.
② A: Did you pack everything you need for the trip to Thailand tomorrow?
   B: Not yet. What should I take?
③ A: What will you wear?
   B: That's great. The blue dress looks great on you.
④ A: Can I get your advice on how to write an address in English?
   B: Sure. You should write the street address first.
⑤ A: Make sure you don't ask a person's age in Western cultures.
   B: Okay. I'll keep it in my mind.

[대전 ○○중]

4. 다음 대화의 밑줄 친 말과 바꿔 쓸 수 있는 것은? (3점)

A: I want to send this letter to my aunt in the USA. <u>Would you give me your advice on how to write an address in English?</u>
B: Sure. You should write the street address first.

① Do you know my address?
② I have to write the letter in English.
③ Can I help you write an address in English?
④ Are you good at writing a letter in English?
⑤ Please tell me how to write an address in English.

[5~6] 다음 대화를 읽고 물음에 답하시오.

B: My Chinese friend invited me to his house for dinner this Friday.

G: That's good. I hope you enjoy having dinner at his house.

B: I want to prepare a small gift for him. You lived in China for several years. Can I get your advice on what to bring?

G: How about some tea?

B: Tea?

G: Yes. Most Chinese people like to receive tea as a present. They enjoy drinking tea. Also, they usually serve tea to guests.

B: Oh, thanks. Is there anything else that I need to know?

G: (A)_____
White and black mean death in China.

B: Okay. I'll remember that. Thank you for the advice.

*B: Seho **G: Bora

5. 위 대화의 문맥상 빈칸 (A)에 들어갈 말로 가장 적절한 것은? (4점)

① Make sure you don't give flowers in even numbers.

② Make sure you don't wrap the present in white or black paper.

③ Make sure you don't wear shorts when you visit your Chinese friend's house.

④ Make sure you don't use your left hand to hand something to someone.

⑤ Make sure you use two hands when you hand your present to your Chinese friend.

6. 위 대화의 내용과 일치하는 것은? (3점)

① Seho는 이번 주 금요일 저녁 식사에 중국인 친구를 초대했다.

② Seho는 중국인 친구를 위한 선물을 준비했다.

③ Bora는 중국에서 살고 싶어 한다.

④ Bora는 Seho에게 차를 선물할 것이다.

⑤ 중국인들은 보통 손님에게 차를 대접한다.

7. 다음 두 사람의 대화에 이어질 내용을 순서대로 배열한 것은? (4점)

A: Sena, I bought a present for Ms. Han. I have stayed at her house here in Korea.

B: That's great. What did you buy?

ⓐ Yes. Make sure you use two hands when you hand it to her.

ⓑ Why?

ⓒ I bought a hat. Do you think she'll love it?

ⓓ Because giving something to older people with one hand is regarded as rude in Korea.

ⓔ Okay. I'll remember that.

① ⓒ-ⓐ-ⓑ-ⓓ-ⓔ   ② ⓒ-ⓐ-ⓑ-ⓔ-ⓓ

③ ⓒ-ⓑ-ⓐ-ⓔ-ⓓ   ④ ⓒ-ⓑ-ⓓ-ⓐ-ⓔ

⑤ ⓒ-ⓓ-ⓔ-ⓑ-ⓐ

8. 다음 빈칸에 공통으로 들어갈 말로 알맞은 것은? (3점)

• The unemployment _____ decreased last year.

• Where can I find the best exchange _____ for dollars to won?

• The test has a 90% pass _____.

                      * unemployment 실업

① present   ② rate   ③ sales

④ advice   ⑤ tax

[9~10] 다음 대화를 읽고 물음에 답하시오.

Seho: My Chinese friend invited me to his house for dinner this Friday.

Bora: That's good. I hope you enjoy having dinner at his house. (A)

Seho: I want to prepare a small gift for him. You lived in China for several years. (B)

Bora: How about some tea? (C)

Seho: Tea? (D)

Bora: Yes. Most Chinese people like to receive tea as a present. They enjoy drinking tea. Also, they usually serve tea to guests. (E)

Seho: Oh, thanks. Is there anything else that I need to know?

Bora: ⓐ_____ in white or black paper. White and black mean death in China.

Seho: Okay. I'll remember that. Thank you for the advice.

9. 위 대화의 흐름으로 보아 주어진 문장이 들어가기에 가장 적절한 곳은? (4점)

Can I get your advice on what to bring?

① (A) ② (B) ③ (C) ④ (D) ⑤ (E)

10. 위 대화의 빈칸 ⓐ에 들어갈 말을 <조건>에 맞게 완성하시오. (4점)

조건
• 경고하는 말을 쓸 것.
• 완전한 영어 문장으로 작성할 것.
• make sure, wrap을 반드시 이용할 것.

(A) _____ in white or

black paper.

11. 다음 중 밑줄 친 동사의 형태가 어법상 <u>어색한</u> 것은? (3점)

① I like the boy <u>sitting</u> on the bench.

② Who is the person <u>playing</u> the guitar there?

③ He bought me a pencil case <u>made</u> in China.

④ I'm reading a short novel <u>writing</u> by Sara.

⑤ The movie <u>directed</u> by the actor was interesting.

12. 다음 우리말을 영어로 옮기시오. (5점)

한 시간 동안 기다리고 있는 방문객들은 그들의 식사와 함께 많은 반찬들을 제공받는다.
(※ 현재분사와 수동태를 활용하고, 현재시제로 쓰시오.)

→ _____

13. 다음 중 어법이 올바른 문장의 개수는? (4점)

• It's going to be very excited.
• He is a wearing boy a watch.
• The cat has been slept there.
• I'm going to Busan this weekend.
• I want to stop eating fast food.

① 1개   ② 2개   ③ 3개
④ 4개   ⑤ 5개

[14~17] 다음 글을 읽고 물음에 답하시오.

(A)

Hi! My name is Kim Minhee. I have been living in America for three years. Since my family moved here, I have experienced many cultural differences between Korea and America. I would like to share some of them with you.

(B)

Here in America, in ⓐ_____ states, people pay a tax when they buy something. It is called a sales tax. Sales tax rates ⓑ_____ by state. They range from less than one percent to more than ten percent. So when you buy goods in America, you usually need to pay more than the price on the tag.

(C)

(가) In America, people often greet each other by waving. (나) Waving to an older person is not regarded as rude. (다) When you come to America, you may feel ⓒ_____ about it at first, but why don't you try it? (라) You can wave to and smile at an ⓓ_____ man walking on the street. (마)

(D)

Which cultural difference is most surprising to you? I have been learning about cultural differences since I came to America. Some surprised me at first, but now I am getting ⓔ_____ to them.

---

14. 위 글은 무엇에 대한 이야기인가?   (4점)

① American history
② American students
③ Cultural differences
④ Korean cultures
⑤ Korean school life

15. 위 글 (B)의 빈칸 ⓐ, ⓑ에 알맞은 단어는?   (4점)

	ⓐ	ⓑ
①	one	same
②	two	same
③	some	same
④	some	differ
⑤	most	differ

16. 위 글 (C)에서 다음 문장이 들어갈 알맞은 위치는?
                                    (4점)

He may wave back.

① (가)   ② (나)   ③ (다)   ④ (라)   ⑤ (마)

17. 위 글 (C)와 (D)의 빈칸 ⓒ, ⓓ, ⓔ에 알맞은 단어는?
                                    (4점)

	ⓒ	ⓓ	ⓔ
①	comfortable	young	use
②	comfortable	elderly	using
③	uncomfortable	elderly	used
④	uncomfortable	younger	used
⑤	uncomfortable	younger	using

[18~19] 다음 글을 읽고, 물음에 답하시오.

Jessica: Hi, Mrs. Johnson!

Minhee: Hello, Mrs. Johnson!

Mrs. Johnson: Hi, Jessica! Hi, Minhee! How are you?

Jessica: Fine, thank you. We are here for a burger. Enjoy your meal.

Mrs. Johnson: Thank you. You, too!

Minhee: Jessica, why did you wave to Mrs. Johnson?

In America, people often greet each other by waving. 연장자에게 손을 흔드는 것은 무례하다고 여겨지지 않아. When you come to America, you may feel uncomfortable about it at first, but why don't you try it? You can wave to and smile at an elderly man _____ on the street. He may wave back.

18. 위 글의 빈칸에 들어갈 말로 가장 적절한 것은?

(3점)

① has walked   ② walking

③ walked   ④ walks

⑤ walk

19. 위 글의 밑줄 친 우리말을 바르게 영작한 것은?

(4점)

① Wave to an older person regards as rude.

② Waving to an older person is regarded as rude.

③ Wave to an older person is not regarded rude.

④ Waving to an older person does not regard as rude.

⑤ Waving to an older person is not regarded as rude.

[20~22] 다음 글을 읽고 물음에 답하시오.

Hi! My name is Kim Minhee. I have been living in America ⓐthree years ago. Since my family moved to America, I ⓑhave experienced many cultural differences between Korea and America. (A) I would like to share some of them with you. (B) Here in America, in most states, people pay a tax when they buy goods. (C) It ⓒis called a sales tax. (D) Sales tax rates differ by state. (E) So ⓓwhen you buy goods in America, you usually ⓔneed to pay more than the price on the tag.

20. 위 글의 내용과 일치하지 <u>않는</u> 것은? (4점)

① Minhee's family moved to America.

② There are a lot of cultural differences between Korea and America.

③ In most states in America, Americans pay a sales tax.

④ Sales tax rates are different by state.

⑤ You can pay less money than the price on the tag in America.

21. 위 글의 빈칸 (A)~(E) 중 주어진 문장이 들어갈 위치로 알맞은 곳은? (4점)

They range from less than one percent to more than ten percent.

① (A)   ② (B)   ③ (C)   ④ (D)   ⑤ (E)

22. 위 글의 밑줄 친 ⓐ~ⓔ 중 어법상 <u>어색한</u> 것은? (4점)

① ⓐ   ② ⓑ   ③ ⓒ   ④ ⓓ   ⑤ ⓔ

[23~24] 다음 글을 읽고 물음에 답하시오.

Holi That I Can't Miss

There are many interesting festivals around the world. Among them, I'd like to attend Holi. People in India have been celebrating this festival for many years. Holi is held in March. I think that if I go, I'll experience a lot of things. First, there are _____ _____. It will be fantastic! Second, I want to dance with other people on the street. I'll also taste traditional Holi dishes. It's going to be very exciting.

---

23. 위 글의 빈칸에 들어갈 말로 어순이 알맞은 것은?

(4점)

① people throwing colored powder and water on each other

② people colored powder and water on each other throwing

③ colored powder and water throwing people on each other

④ colored powder and water on each other people throwing

⑤ powder and water colored people on throwing each other

24. 위 글의 내용과 일치하지 <u>않는</u> 것은?　　　(3점)

① 글쓴이는 Holi에 참석하고 싶어 한다.

② 다년간 인도 사람들은 이 축제를 거행해왔다.

③ 이 축제는 5월에 열린다.

④ 사람들과 어울려 춤을 출 수 있다.

⑤ 인도의 전통 음식을 맛볼 기회가 있다.

[25~27] 다음 글을 읽고 물음에 답하시오.

Hi! My name is Kim Minhee. I ⓐ<u>have been living</u> in America for three years. Since my family moved here, I ⓑ<u>have experienced</u> many cultural differences between Korea and America. (A) I would like to share some of them with you. (B) Here in America, in most states, people pay a tax when they buy goods. (C) It ⓒ<u>calls</u> a sales tax. (D) They range from less than one percent to more than ten percent. (E) So ⓓ<u>when</u> you buy goods in America, you usually need to pay ⓔ<u>more</u> than the price on the tag.

---

25. 위 글의 빈칸 (A)~(E) 중 주어진 문장이 들어갈 위치로 알맞은 곳은?　　　(3점)

Sales tax rates differ by state.

① (A)　② (B)　③ (C)　④ (D)　⑤ (E)

26. 위 글의 밑줄 친 ⓐ~ⓔ 중 어법상 <u>어색한</u> 것은?

(4점)

① ⓐ　② ⓑ　③ ⓒ　④ ⓓ　⑤ ⓔ

27. 위 글의 내용과 일치하지 <u>않는</u> 것은?　　(4점)

① Kim Minhee lives in America now.

② There are a lot of cultural differences between Korea and America.

③ In most states in America, Americans pay a sales tax.

④ Sales tax rates are the same across all the states.

⑤ You should pay more money than the price on the tag in America.

반			점수	
이름				

◎ 선택형 문항의 답안은 컴퓨터용 수정 싸인펜을 사용하여 OMR 답안지에 바르게 표기하시오.
◎ 서술형 문제는 답을 답안지에 반드시 검정 볼펜으로 쓰시오.
◎ 총 24문항 100점 만점입니다. 문항별 배점은 각 문항에 표시되어 있습니다.

[부산 ㅇㅇ중]

1. 다음 빈칸 어느 곳에도 들어가지 <u>않는</u> 단어는? (4점)

- We sell top quality _____.
- Please give up your seats to _____ people.
- Sam is _____ as a great doctor. Many people respect him.
- In Western cultures, the number thirteen has a _____ meaning. It means bad luck.

① elderly
② positive
③ negative
④ products
⑤ regarded

[대전 ㅇㅇ중]

2. 다음 (A)~(D)가 자연스러운 대화가 되도록 바르게 배열한 것은? (4점)

I prepared a gift for Ms. Han. Her birthday is coming. Do you think she'll love it?

(A) Because giving something to older people with one hand is rude in Korea.
(B) Can I ask why?
(C) Of course, she will love it. Make sure you use two hands when you hand it to her.
(D) Okay. I'll remember that.

① (A)-(B)-(C)-(D)
② (C)-(B)-(A)-(D)
③ (C)-(D)-(B)-(A)
④ (B)-(D)-(A)-(C)
⑤ (B)-(C)-(A)-(D)

[강남구 ㅇㅇ중]

3. 다음 대화의 빈칸 ⓐ~ⓒ에 들어갈 말이 바르게 연결된 것은? (5점)

B: Did you ⓐ_____ everything you need for the trip to Thailand tomorrow?
G: Not yet. What should I take?
B: Remember to bring a pair of long pants or a long skirt.
G: Why? It's very hot in Thailand, ⓑ_____?
B: Yes, but there are many temples in Thailand. You shouldn't wear shorts when you visit a temple.
G: Okay. Is there anything else?
B: Don't forget to ⓒ_____ Korean won to Thai baht.

	ⓐ	ⓑ	ⓒ
①	bag	is it	give
②	wrap	doesn't it	leave
③	wrap	isn't it	address
④	pack	isn't it	exchange
⑤	pack	doesn't it	exchange

[대전 ㅇㅇ중]

4. 다음 두 문장을 한 문장으로 바르게 바꿔 쓴 것은? (4점)

- I started to learn Spanish one year ago.
- I'm still learning it now.

① I learned Spanish for one year.
② I was learning Spanish one year ago.
③ I am learning Spanish one year ago.
④ I have been learn Spanish for one year.
⑤ I have been learning Spanish for one year.

5. 다음 대화의 빈칸 (A)에 들어갈 가장 적절한 표현은?
(4점)

Seho: My Chinese friend invited me to his house for dinner this Friday.

Bora: That's good. I hope you enjoy having dinner at his house.

Seho: I want to prepare a small gift for him. You lived in China for several years. (A)_____

Bora: How about some tea?

Seho: Tea?

Bora: Yes. Most Chinese people like to receive tea as a present. They enjoy drinking tea. Also, they usually serve tea to guests.

Seho: Oh, thank you very much.

① I want to travel to China.
② China is larger than Korea.
③ Tea is good for your health.
④ Is there anything I should remember?
⑤ Can I get your advice on what to bring?

6. 주어진 문장에 이어질 (A)~(E)의 순서로 가장 적절한 것은? (조건: (A)~(E)는 각각 G 혹은 M의 대화임.)
(4점)

G: Look at the people wearing traditional Moroccan clothes. They are really beautiful. I want to take pictures of them.

(A) Wait. There is an important thing you need to know before taking pictures.

(B) They believe it may have a bad effect on them when someone takes their picture.

(C) Oh, really? Can I get your advice on it?

(D) Yes. You shouldn't take pictures of Moroccan people without asking.

(E) Why?

① (A)-(C)-(D)-(E)-(B)
② (A)-(E)-(D)-(C)-(B)
③ (B)-(C)-(D)-(E)-(A)
④ (C)-(A)-(E)-(D)-(B)
⑤ (C)-(B)-(E)-(A)-(D)

7. 다음 그림에서 계속 진행 중인 일을 바르게 표현한 문장을 모두 고르면? (정답 2개)
(4점)

① Ted has been playing games since 2 p.m.
② Tom has been watching TV for two hours.
③ Jane has been watering the plants for two hours.
④ The cat has been sleeping for an hour.
⑤ Mom has been talking on the phone since 3 p.m.

8. 다음 대화에서 〈보기〉의 문장이 들어갈 가장 알맞은 위치는? (4점)

> **보기**
>
> Can I get your advice on how to write an address in English?

A: I want to send this to my aunt in the USA.
B: What is it? (A)
A: It's her hanbok. (B)
B: Sure. You should write the street address first. (C)
A: Like this? (D)
B: Yes. Then, write the name of the city and the state and then the postal code. Finally write the country.
A: Thanks for your help. (E)

① (A)　② (B)　③ (C)　④ (D)　⑤ (E)

9. 다음 밑줄 친 단어의 쓰임이 어법상 어색한 것은? (4점)

① Michael didn't <u>respond</u> to my question.
② How do people in the USA <u>greet</u> each other?
③ It's very hard to <u>solve</u> this question correctly.
④ Waving to older people is <u>regard</u> as normal in America.
⑤ Some gestures have <u>negative</u> meanings in several countries.

10. 다음 문장에서 어법상 어색한 부분을 올바른 문장으로 고쳐 쓰시오. (4점)

> I am getting used to live in the city.

→ _____

11. 다음 중 어법상 어색한 것은? (4점)

① The newspaper was interesting.
② *Spiderman* is interesting.
③ Frank was bored.
④ The magazine was bored.
⑤ The dog was bored.

12. 다음 두 문장을 현재완료진행형을 이용하여 한 문장으로 바꾸시오. (6점)

> (1) I began to eat pizza two hours ago.
> I'm still eating it.
> → _____
>
> (2) She started to learn flamenco a month ago.
> She is still learning it.
> → _____
>
> (3) My uncle started working for the company three years ago.
> He is still working for it.
> → _____

(1): _____
(2): _____
(3): _____

[13~15] 다음 글을 읽고 물음에 답하시오.

Hi! My name is Kim Minhee. I have been living in America for three years. Since my family moved here, I have experienced many cultural differences between Korea and America. I would like to share some of them with you.

In America, people often greet each other by waving. Waving to a(n) (A)[older / younger] person is not regarded as rude. When you come to America, you may feel (B)[comfortable / uncomfortable] about it at first, but why don't you try it? You can wave (C)[to / for] and smile at an elderly man walking on the street. He may wave back.

Americans often ask negative questions, such as "Aren't you coming?" and "Didn't you go to the hospital?" It can be difficult to answer negative questions correctly. Here is some advice. In response to negative questions, such as "Don't you like apple pie?" you should answer "No," if you don't like it. And you should answer "Yes," if you like it. These answers are the same as the answers to positive questions, such as "Do you like apple pie?"

13. 위 글의 제목으로 알맞은 것은?　　(4점)
① My Life in America
② How to Move to America
③ The Great America Culture
④ Different Ways of Greeting in the World
⑤ Cultural Differences between Korea and America

14. 위 글의 괄호 (A), (B), (C)에 문맥상 들어갈 말이 바르게 짝지어진 것은?　　(4점)

	(A)	(B)	(C)
①	older	uncomfortable	to
②	younger	uncomfortable	to
③	younger	comfortable	for
④	older	uncomfortable	for
⑤	older	comfortable	for

15. 위 글을 읽고 답할 수 없는 것은?　　(4점)
① Where does the writer live now?
② Why did the writer leave Korea?
③ How do people often greet in America?
④ What has the writer experienced in America?
⑤ How do people answer negative questions in America?

16. 다음 글의 밑줄 친 ⓐ~ⓕ 중 어법상 어색한 것끼리 짝지어진 것은?　　(4점)

Holi That I Can't Miss
There are many interesting festivals ⓐaround the world. Among them, I'd like to attend Holi. People in India have been celebrating this festival ⓑfor many years. Holi is held ⓒon March. I think that if I go, I'll experience a lot of things. First, there are people throwing colored powder and water ⓓin each other. It will be fantastic! Second, I want to dance ⓔwith other people on the street. I'll also taste traditional Holi dishes. It's going to be very exciting. I can't wait ⓕfor the day!

① ⓐ, ⓔ　　② ⓑ, ⓒ　　③ ⓑ, ⓓ
④ ⓒ, ⓓ　　⑤ ⓒ, ⓕ

[17~18] 다음 글을 읽고 물음에 답하시오.

Americans often ask negative questions, such as "Aren't you coming?" and "Didn't you go to the hospital?" It can be ⓐdifficult to answer negative questions correctly. Here is some advice.

ⓑIn response to negative questions, such as "Don't you like apple pie?" you should answer "No," if you don't like it. And you should answer "Yes," if you like it. These answers are ⓒthe same as the answers to positive questions, such as "Do you like apple pie?"

Which cultural difference is most surprising to you? Some surprised me at first, but now I am ⓓnot getting used to them.

17. 위 글의 밑줄 친 ⓐ~ⓓ 중, 문맥상 적절한 것의 개수는? (4점)

① 0개　② 1개　③ 2개　④ 3개　⑤ 4개

18. 위 글의 내용을 토대로 승희가 할 대답은? (4점)

승희: I am hungry now. If someone asks me, "Aren't you hungry?" I would answer, "＿＿＿＿＿＿＿＿＿"

① No, I'm hungry!
② Yes, I'm hungry!
③ No, I was hungry!
④ No, I'm not hungry!
⑤ Yes, I'm not hungry!

19. 다음 글의 제목으로 가장 적절한 것은? (4점)

There are many interesting festivals around the world. Among them, I'd like to attend Holi. People in India celebrate this festival every year. Holi is held in March. I think that if I go, I'll experience a lot of things. First,

there are people who throw colored powder and water on each other. It will be fantastic! Second, I want to dance with other people on the street. I'll also taste traditional Holi dishes. It's going to be very exciting. I can't wait for the day!

① Holi That I Can't Miss
② Festivals Around the World
③ Taste Traditional Holi Dishes
④ Dance with People on the Street
⑤ Have a Fantastic Experience in India!

20. 다음 글의 빈칸에 들어갈 가장 알맞은 말은? (4점)

Here in America, in most states, people pay a tax when they buy goods. It is called a sales tax. Sales tax rates differ by state. They range from less than one percent to more than ten percent. They are not included in the price tag. So when you buy goods in America, you usually need to ＿＿＿＿＿＿＿＿＿＿.

① buy products on sale
② pay less than the price on the tag
③ pay more than the price on the tag
④ pay the same price as the price on the tag
⑤ compare the prices with those of other countries

21. 다음 중 밑줄 친 동사의 형태가 어법상 어색한 것은? (4점)

① I like the boy sitting on the ground.
② Who is the man playing the piano there?
③ He bought me a suitcase made in Japan.
④ The movie directing by the director was touching.
⑤ I'm reading a sci-fi novel written by Mike.

[22~23] 다음 글을 읽고 물음에 답하시오.

Andy: Minhee, try this apple pie.

Minhee: No, thanks. I don't want to.

Andy: Why not? Don't you like apple pie?

Minhee: Yes.

Andy: Then, try some. It's delicious.

Minhee: No. I just said I don't like apple pie.

Andy: What?

Americans often ask negative questions, such as "Aren't you coming?" and "Didn't you go to the hospital?" It can be difficult to answer negative questions correctly. Here is some advice.

In response to negative questions, such as "Don't you like apple pie?" you should answer "No," if you don't like it. And you should answer "Yes," if you like it. These answers are the same as the answers to positive questions, such as "Do you like apple pie?"

	Like	Don't like
Do you like apple pie?	Yes, I do.	No, I don't.
Don't you like apple pie?	Yes, I do.	No, I don't.

Which cultural difference is most surprising to you? I have been learning about cultural differences since I came to America. Some surprised me at first, but now I am getting used to them.

---

22. 위 글의 내용과 일치하지 <u>않는</u> 것은? (조건: 위 글의 화자는 Minhee이다.)　　　　　　(4점)

① Minhee는 애플파이를 좋아하지 않는다.

② 영어로 "Don't you like apple pie?"와 같은 부정의문문에 대한 대답으로 만약 그것을 좋아하지 않는다면 "Yes"라고 대답해야 한다.

③ 위 글의 표와 같이 영어의 부정의문문에 대한 대답들과 긍정의문문에 대한 대답들은 같다.

④ Minhee는 미국에 온 이후로 문화적인 차이에 대해 계속 배우고 있다.

⑤ 처음에 몇몇 문화적 차이들이 Minhee를 놀라게 했지만, 지금은 그것들에 익숙해지고 있다.

---

23. 위 글의 Andy와 Minhee의 대화 중, Andy의 마지막 말, "What?"에 나타난 Andy의 심경으로 가장 적절한 것은?　　　　　　(4점)

① confused　　② pleased　　③ relaxed

④ proud　　⑤ bored

---

24. 다음 글의 ⓐ~ⓔ 중 흐름상 옳지 <u>않은</u> 것은? (5점)

Hi! My name is Kim Minhee. ⓐ<u>I have been living in America for three years.</u> ⓑ<u>Since my family moved here, I experienced many cultural differences between Korea and America.</u> I would like to share some of them with you. Here in America, in most states, people pay a tax when they buy goods. ⓒ<u>It is called a sales tax.</u> ⓓ<u>They range from less than one percent to more than ten percent.</u> ⓔ <u>So when you buy goods in America, you need to pay as much as the price on the tag.</u>

① ⓐ　　② ⓑ　　③ ⓒ　　④ ⓓ　　⑤ ⓔ

3학년 영어 1학기 기말고사(3과) 1회

반		점수	
이름			

문항수 : 선택형(26문항) 서술형(4문항)   20 . . .

◎ 선택형 문항의 답안은 컴퓨터용 수정 싸인펜을
  사용하여 OMR 답안지에 바르게 표기하시오.
◎ 서술형 문제는 답을 답안지에 반드시 검정
  볼펜으로 쓰시오.
◎ 총 30문항 100점 만점입니다. 문항별 배점
  음 각 문항에 표시되어 있습니다.

1. 다음 영영 풀이에 해당하는 단어로 알맞은 것은?
                                                    (3점)

> • to suggest that someone should do
>   something

① recommend   ② create
③ include   ④ travel
⑤ express

2. 다음 영영 풀이에 해당하는 단어로 알맞은 것은?
                                                    (4점)

> • to direct the performance of musicians or
>   singers

① analyze   ② conduct
③ belong   ④ design
⑤ conclude

3. 다음 밑줄 친 단어의 뜻이 옳지 않은 것은?   (3점)
① He broke the Olympic record(기록) in
  swimming.
② It's hard for me to solve(미루다) the
  problem.
③ I decorate(장식하다) my house before
  Christmas.
④ John is going to attend(참석하다) the
  meeting.
⑤ We are going to audition(오디션을 하다)
  actors for the musical.

4. 다음 주어진 상황을 고려할 때, 빈칸에 들어갈 말로 알
맞지 않은 것은?   (3점)

> A: I've always wanted to be a social worker.
> B: _____
> A: Thank you very much.

① I'm quite sure you can't become a great
  social worker.
② I'm quite sure you will become a great
  social worker.
③ I'm quite sure you can become a great
  social worker.
④ I think you can become a great social
  worker.
⑤ I'm sure you will become a great social
  worker.

5. 다음 대화의 상황에서 〈조건〉을 만족하는 적절한 대답
을 영어로 쓰시오.   (5점)

> A: Excuse me. You should wear a mask
>   here.
> B: Why?
> A: Wearing a mask protects our health from
>   a virus called COVID-19.
> B: Pardon? What does it protect?
> A: _____

조건
> • It ~ that 강조구문을 활용하여 완전한 문장으로
>   답할 것.

→ _____

[6~7] 다음 대화를 읽고 물음에 답하시오.

B: Hello, what are you doing, Sumi?
G: I'm looking for a good recipe on the Internet. I need it for my family dinner today.
B: That is nice. Do you cook often?
G: Yes, I try to cook every weekend. I want to be a chef someday.
B: What are you doing to make your dream come true?
G: I'm taking a cooking class. I try to think of new and creative dishes.
B: _____

6. 위 대화의 빈칸에 들어갈 응답으로 가장 적절한 것은? (3점)

① It seems to me you are a poet.
② Remember to drink enough water.
③ Make sure you have to grow vegetables.
④ Don't forget to leave the gas stove on.
⑤ I'm quite sure you could be a good chef.

7. 위 대화의 내용과 일치하는 것은? (3점)
① Sumi는 요리책에서 음식 사진을 보고 있다.
② B는 요리사가 되기를 희망한다.
③ B는 매주 가족을 위해서 요리한다.
④ Sumi는 요리 수업을 듣고 있다.
⑤ B는 오늘 가족 식사가 예정되어 있다.

8. 다음 대화가 자연스러운 대화가 되도록 (A)~(C)를 바르게 배열한 것은? (3점)

(A) I'm most interested in working together and playing sports.
(B) What are you most interested in among the things on this list?
(C) Well, it seems to me that you are the outgoing type.

① (A) - (B) - (C)   ② (B) - (A) - (C)
③ (B) - (C) - (A)   ④ (C) - (A) - (B)
⑤ (C) - (B) - (A)

[9~10] 다음 대화를 읽고 물음에 답하시오.

G: I'm glad to meet you, Mr. Han. Could you please tell me what you do? (A)
M: Okay. (B) I guide travelers to different places in China and give them information about where they should visit.
G: What else do you do? (C)
M: (D) I tell them about popular culture and traditional food in China.
G: (E) Are you happy with your job?
M: Yes. I really love my job.

9. 위 대화에서 다음 주어진 글이 들어갈 곳으로 알맞은 것은? (3점)

It seems to me knowing a lot about China is very important.

① (A)   ② (B)   ③ (C)   ④ (D)   ⑤ (E)

10. 위 대화의 내용과 일치하지 않는 것은? (3점)
① Mr. Han's job is a tour guide.
② Mr. Han is not so satisfied with his job.
③ Mr. Han guides tourists to different places in China.
④ Mr. Han makes travelers know where to go in China.
⑤ Mr. Han talks to tourists about popular culture in China.

[11~12] 다음 대화를 읽고 물음에 답하시오.

> Mr. Kim: What's wrong, Jisu?
> Jisu: I want to be an animator, but my drawing skill is not good enough.
> Mr. Kim: Hmm... Being an animator is not just about being a good artist.
> Jisu: What should I do to become an animator?
> Mr. Kim: Read a lot of books to make good stories and practice drawing every day.
> Jisu: Okay, I'll do so.
> Mr. Kim: (A)_____
> Jisu: Thank you very much.

11. 위 대화에 드러난 Jisu의 기분 변화로 가장 적절한 것은? (3점)

① excited → shy
② happy → nervous
③ worried → hopeful
④ bored → surprised
⑤ disappointed → sad

12. 위 대화의 흐름상 빈칸 (A)에 들어가기에 가장 자연스러운 것은? (3점)

① I'm sure that you'll enjoy cooking in the future.
② I'm sure that a photographer could be a good job for you.
③ I'm quite sure that you can be a good animator if you try hard.
④ I'm quite sure that an app developer could be a good job for you.
⑤ I'm quite sure that you'll be a famous soccer player if you practice.

13. 다음 대화의 빈칸에 들어갈 말로 가장 알맞은 것은? (3점)

> A: I want to be a(n) _____. What would help me become one?
> B: It seems to me practicing drawing and studying hard would be helpful.

① banker ② art teacher
③ essay writer ④ soldier
⑤ accountant

14. 다음 중 어법상 어색한 문장은? (3점)

① His story made me laugh.
② It was Jessy that fell down the stairs.
③ Her mom let her goes shopping by herself.
④ It is Young-in that plays the piano well.
⑤ It was last Friday that I had a car accident.

15. 다음 밑줄 친 단어의 쓰임이 어법상 어색한 것은? (3점)

① Lily had her husband <u>washed</u> the car.
② I had my hair <u>cut</u> at the hair salon.
③ My mom had me <u>wash</u> the dishes.
④ Tom had his mobile phone <u>fixed</u>.
⑤ He had his car <u>washed</u>.

16. 다음 밑줄 친 부분을 강조하는 표현이 되도록 주어진 문장을 완성하시오. (4점)

> (1) <u>Steve</u> helps me with my homework.
> (2) I met Tom <u>at the museum</u> yesterday.

→ (1) It _____.
→ (2) It _____.

[17~20] 다음 글을 읽고 물음에 답하시오.

Sport Data Analyst

I am Emma. I am a sport data analyst. It sounds like a difficult job, ⓐisn't it? In fact, it is a lot of fun. (A) I work for a baseball team. (B) My job is to watch ⓑrecorded games and run a computer program to collect data. (C) If the team understands their strengths and weaknesses, they can do better next time. Since I was young, I ⓒwas a big fan of baseball. (D) Now, in my work, I watch baseball games all the time. (E) This is a perfect job for me because watching baseball games ⓓare my hobby!

Director of a Musical Theater

Hi, I am Chris. As a director of a musical theater, I do a lot of things. I audition the actors and I look for good, strong voices. After selecting the cast, I teach them the songs for each scene. Then, I put the cast and orchestra together for practice. During the performance, I am in the orchestra area and conduct. It's my responsibility to have each song ⓔplay the same way every time. I (가)direct the musicians and the singers to keep the show together. Conducting and directing is not just about waving my arms around!

17. 위 글의 밑줄 친 ⓐ~ⓔ 중 어법상 알맞은 것은?

(3점)

① ⓐ ② ⓑ ③ ⓒ ④ ⓓ ⑤ ⓔ

18. 위 글의 흐름상 (A)~(E) 중, 주어진 문장이 들어가기에 가장 적절한 곳은? (4점)

Then, I analyze the data to show my team's strengths and weaknesses.

① (A) ② (B) ③ (C) ④ (D) ⑤ (E)

19. 위 글을 읽고 답할 수 없는 것은? (3점)

① Which sport does Chris like?
② What does Emma do as a sport data analyst?
③ When Chris auditions the actors, what does he look for?
④ After selecting the cast, what does Chris teach?
⑤ What was the responsibility as a director of a musical theater?

20. 위 글의 밑줄 친 (가)와 같은 의미로 쓰인 것은?

(3점)

① Protect your child from direct sunlight.
② Could you direct me to the bus stop?
③ We flew direct to Jeju island.
④ That's a direct question.
⑤ She prefers to act rather than direct the actors.

21. 다음 글의 밑줄 친 (A)가 가리키는 말로 적절한 것은?

(3점)

I am an ocean scientist. Ocean science is a big field. It includes studies of the oceans and the creatures living in them. Among other things, I have studied many kinds of fish living in the seas near Korea. It is the growth ring in a fish that interests me. By looking at (A)it, I can find out when and where the fish was born. All the information I get from fish is used to understand sea resources and manage the oceans better.

① the fish   ② the seas
③ the oceans   ④ the creatures
⑤ the growth ring

[22~23] 다음 글을 읽고 물음에 답하시오.

Hi, I am Tom. A florist is someone who creates beautiful things with flowers. To become a florist, you need to know many things about flowers.

I attended a high school for florists and gardeners. (A)I learned how to grow and care for different types of flowers at this school. These days, florists can do (B)a lot of different things. I design movie sets sometimes and I decorate shops with flowers. I am happy when I create something colorful with fresh flowers and greenery. If you like plants and the arts, I highly recommend you become a florist.

22. 위 글의 밑줄 친 (A) 문장을 다음 주어진 우리말과 가장 비슷한 뜻이 되도록 바르게 고쳐 쓴 것은? (3점)

제가 다양한 종류의 꽃을 기르고 다루는 방법을 배운 곳이 바로 이 학교에서였습니다.

① I did learn how to grow and care for different types of flowers at this school.

② It is at this school what I learned how to grow and care for different types of flowers.

③ It was at this school that I learned how to grow and care for different types of flowers.

④ It is at this school that I did learn how to grow and care for different types of flowers.

⑤ It was at this school when I learned how to grow and care for different types of flowers.

23. 위 글의 밑줄 친 (B)a lot of different things에 해당하는 두 가지 일을 우리말로 쓰시오. (4점)

(1) _____

(2) _____

[24~25] 다음 글을 읽고 물음에 답하시오.

My name is Yeji. I am an ocean scientist. Ocean science is a big field. It includes studies of the oceans and the creatures living in them. Among other things, I have studied many kinds of fish living in the seas near Korea. The growth ring in a fish interests me. By looking at it, I can find out when and where the fish was born. All the information I get from fish is used to understand sea resources and manage the oceans better. My job is important because it makes the best use of nature possible.

24. 위 글을 읽고 답할 수 없는 것은? (3점)

① What is Yeji's job?

② Why is Yeji's job important?

③ Why did Yeji choose her job?

④ How can Yeji find out when and where the fish was born?

⑤ What is used to understand sea resources and manage the oceans better?

25. 위 글을 읽고, 'It ~ that' 강조 구문을 사용하여 질문에 올바르게 답한 것은? (3점)

Q: What interests Yeji?
A: _____

① It is the growth ring in a fish that interests her.

② It is the growth ring that in a fish interest her.

③ It is the growth ring in a fish that interested her.

④ It was the growth ring in a fish that interest her.

⑤ It was the growth ring in a fish that interests her.

[26~27] 다음 글을 읽고 물음에 답하시오.

Hi, I am Tom. A florist is someone (A)[who / whom] creates beautiful things with flowers. To become a florist, you need to know many things about flowers.
I (B)[attended / attended to] a high school for florists and gardeners. It was at this school that I learned how to grow and care for different types of flowers. These days, florists can do a lot of different things. I design movie sets sometimes and I decorate shops with flowers. I am happy when I create (C)[something colorful / colorful something] with fresh flowers and greenery. If you like ⓐ_____ and ⓑ_____, I highly recommend you become a florist.

26. 위 글의 괄호 (A), (B), (C) 안에서 어법에 맞는 표현으로 적절한 것은? (4점)

	(A)	(B)	(C)
①	who	attended	something colorful
②	who	attended	colorful something
③	who	attended to	something colorful
④	whom	attended	colorful something
⑤	whom	attended to	something colorful

27. 위 글의 빈칸 ⓐ, ⓑ에 들어갈 말로 가장 적절한 것은? (3점)

	ⓐ	ⓑ
①	colors	movies
②	gardens	schools
③	plants	the arts
④	jobs	money
⑤	nature	vegetables

[28~30] 다음 글을 읽고 물음에 답하시오.

My name is Yeji. I am an ocean scientist who studies ocean space. Ocean science is a big field. ⓐIt includes studies of the oceans and the creatures living in ⓑthem. Among other things, I have studied many kinds of fish living in the seas near Korea. By looking at the growth ring in a fish, I can find out lots of things about fish. All the information I get from fish uses to understand sea resources and manage the oceans better. My job is important because (A)제 직업은 자연을 가능한 가장 잘 이용할 수 있게 합니다.

28. 위 글의 밑줄 친 ⓐ, ⓑ가 각각 지칭하는 것은? (3점)

	ⓐ	ⓑ
①	Ocean science	the oceans
②	Ocean scientist	the oceans
③	Ocean science	the creatures
④	Ocean space	the scientist
⑤	Ocean scientists	the creatures

29. 위 글의 주어진 우리말과 일치하도록 (A)에 들어갈 문장으로 알맞은 것은? (4점)

① it makes use of nature best possible
② it makes possible use of nature best
③ it makes possible to use of nature best
④ it makes the nature of best use possible
⑤ it makes the best use of nature possible

30. 위 글에서 어법상 적절하지 않은 문장을 찾아 바르게 고친 후 완전한 문장으로 쓰시오. (5점)

→ _____

반 이름		점수	

문항수 : 선택형(27문항) 서술형(3문항)   20 .   .   .

◎ 선택형 문항의 답안은 컴퓨터용 수정 싸인펜을
  사용하여 OMR 답안지에 바르게 표기하시오.
◎ 서술형 문제는 답을 답안지에 반드시 검정
  볼펜으로 쓰시오.
◎ 총 30문항 100점 만점입니다. 문항별 배점
  은 각 문항에 표시되어 있습니다.

[대전 ○○중]

1. 다음 영영 풀이에 해당하는 단어로 알맞은 것은?
                                                    (3점)

> • to study something closely and examine it
>   carefully

① analyze   ② include

③ belong   ④ design

⑤ conduct

[충북 ○○중]

2. 다음 대화의 흐름상 빈칸에 들어갈 단어가 알맞게 짝지
어진 것은?   (4점)

> B: Did you finish the report about your role
>   model?
> G: Yes, I did. I wrote about my role model,
>   Ms. Shin. I want to be like her.
> B: What does she do?
> G: She teaches people how to stretch. She
>   also helps them (A)_____ stress and
>   (B)_____ themselves.
> B: Good. It seems that she helps to keep
>   both their mind and body (C)_____.
> G: Yes, and I think it's great.

	(A)	(B)	(C)
①	reduce	calm	healthy
②	solve	calm	health
③	cut	clear	health
④	recommend	keep	healthy
⑤	reduce	clean	health

[충북 ○○중]

3. 다음 문장의 빈칸 (A)~(C)에 들어갈 단어가 순서대로
알맞게 짝지어진 것은?   (4점)

> • The price (A)_____ breakfast and a drink.
> • Peter could not (B)_____ the class
>   because he was very sick.
> • There are many kinds of natural (C)_____
>   under the sea.

ⓐ resources	ⓑ includes	ⓒ attend
ⓓ care for	ⓔ interest	

	(A)	(B)	(C)
①	ⓐ	ⓓ	ⓑ
②	ⓑ	ⓒ	ⓐ
③	ⓓ	ⓔ	ⓐ
④	ⓔ	ⓐ	ⓓ
⑤	ⓔ	ⓑ	ⓐ

[대전 ○○중]

4. 다음 밑줄 친 단어의 뜻이 옳지 않은 것은?   (3점)

① I decorate(장식하다) my room for Christmas.

② It's difficult for me to collect(수집하다)
   stamps.

③ She broke(기록 등을 깨다) the Olympic
   record in short track.

④ John is out of office to attend(결석하다) the
   business meeting.

⑤ We are going to select(선발하다) singers for
   the musical performance.

5. 다음 대화의 흐름상 (A)~(E)를 바르게 배열한 것은?
(4점)

G: I'm glad to meet you, Mr. Han. Could you please tell me what you do?
(A) Yes. I really love my job.
(B) What else do you do?
(C) Okay, I guide travelers to different places in China and give them information about where they should visit.
(D) It seems to me knowing a lot about China is very important. Are you happy with your job?
(E) I tell them about popular culture and traditional food in China.

① (B)-(D)-(A)-(C)-(E)
② (A)-(B)-(E)-(C)-(D)
③ (B)-(A)-(D)-(C)-(E)
④ (C)-(B)-(E)-(D)-(A)
⑤ (D)-(C)-(E)-(B)-(A)

6. 다음 대화의 빈칸에 들어갈 말로 알맞지 않은 것은?
(3점)

A: I've always wanted to be a baseball player.
B: _____
A: Thank you very much.

① I'm quite sure you can't become a great baseball player.
② I'm quite sure you will become a great baseball player.
③ I'm quite sure you could become a great baseball player.
④ I think you can become a great baseball player.
⑤ I'm sure you can become a great baseball player.

7. 다음 대화의 빈칸에 들어갈 말로 알맞은 것은? (3점)

A: I want to be a(n)_____. What would help me become one?
B: It seems to me practicing writing and drawing would be helpful.

① cook
② animator
③ essay writer
④ nurse
⑤ accountant

8. 다음 짝지어진 대화 중 자연스러운 것은? (3점)

① A: I'm planning to visit the police station to see my uncle. He is a police officer.
   B: I'm quite sure you could be a good police officer.
② A: What should I do to become an animator?
   B: I want to ask him what I need to do to become a good animator.
③ A: Read a lot of books to make good stories and practice drawing every day to be a good painter.
   B: I'm quite sure that you can be a good painter.
④ A: I guide travelers to different places in China and give them information about where they should visit.
   B: It seems that you help to keep both their mind and body healthy.
⑤ A: What are you doing to be a good chef?
   B: I'm taking a baking class and I try to think of new and creative dishes.

9. 다음 질문에 대한 대답을 영어로 쓰시오. (단, 「It ~ that」 강조구문으로 쓸 것.) (3점)

Amy: I heard you'll see Tom tomorrow.
Jenny: I was supposed to, but I changed our meeting time.
Amy: So, did you meet him already?
Jenny: Yes, I saw Tom at the station this morning.

Q: When did Jenny see Tom at the station?

→ _____

10. 다음 문장의 밑줄 친 각 부분을 강조 구문으로 나타낸 것으로 옳은 것은? (4점)

ⓐSally ⓑleft ⓒthe note ⓓin my house ⓔlast Saturday.

① ⓐ: It was Sally which left the note in my house last Saturday.

② ⓑ: Sally do leave the note in my house last Saturday.

③ ⓒ: It was the note who Sally left in my house last Saturday.

④ ⓓ: It was in my house that Sally left the note last Saturday.

⑤ ⓔ: It was last Saturday which Sally left the note in my house.

11. 다음 밑줄 친 단어의 쓰임이 어법상 어색한 것은? (3점)

① Risa made her son <u>clean</u> the room.

② I had my hair <u>cut</u> at the hair salon.

③ My father made me <u>repaired</u> the toys.

④ Tom had his mobile phone <u>fixed</u>.

⑤ She had her car <u>washed</u>.

12. 다음 주어진 단어들을 활용하여 우리말에 해당하는 문장을 쓰시오. (단, 'have/has/had+목적어+과거분사' 구문을 사용할 것.) (4점)

the house / repair

우리는 어제 그 집을 수리시켰다.

→ _____

13. 다음 중 어법상 적절하지 <u>않은</u> 문장은? (3점)

① I found something wrong in his words.

② I want to know where you parked your car.

③ Tebby lived in Paris three years ago, didn't he?

④ I am going to run a computer program after watching recording games.

⑤ Walking your dogs every day keeps them happy and healthy.

14. 다음 문장의 밑줄 친 부분과 부정사의 쓰임이 같은 것은? (3점)

<u>To become</u> a florist, you need to know many things about flowers.

① I have no money <u>to lend</u> to you now.

② <u>To run</u> is good for your health.

③ Her dream is <u>to become</u> a doctor.

④ They decided <u>to visit</u> the house.

⑤ She got up early <u>to eat</u> breakfast.

[15~17] 다음 글을 읽고 물음에 답하시오.

My name is Yeji. I am an ocean scientist. Ocean science is a big field. It includes studies of the oceans and the creatures living in them. Among other things, I have studied many kinds of fish living in the seas near Korea. ⓐThe growth ring in a fish interests me. By looking at ⓑit, I can find out when and where the fish was born. All the information I get from fish is ⓒ_____ to understand sea resources and manage the oceans better. My job is important because it makes the best ⓓ_____ of nature possible.

15. 위 글의 밑줄 친 ⓐ문장에서 'the growth ring in a fish'를 강조하는 구문으로 바르게 만든 것은? (3점)

① It is the growth ring in a fish that interests me.

② It is the growth ring in a fish who interests me.

③ It was the growth ring in a fish who interests me.

④ It is the growth ring in a fish to interests me.

⑤ It was the growth ring in a fish where interests me.

16. 위 글의 밑줄 친 ⓑit이 가리키는 것은? (3점)

① ocean science

② ocean scientists

③ many kinds of fish

④ the growth ring in a fish

⑤ all the information I get from fish

17. 위 글의 빈칸 ⓒ, ⓓ에 알맞은 표현으로 짝지어진 것은? (3점)

	ⓒ	ⓓ
①	used	use
②	used	using
③	used	used
④	using	to use
⑤	using	using

[18~19] 다음 글을 읽고 물음에 답하시오.

I am Emma. I am a sport data analyst. It ⓐsounds like a difficult job, ⓑdoesn't it? In fact, it is a lot of fun. I work for a baseball team. My job is to watch ⓒrecorded games and run a computer program to collect data. Then, I analyze the data to show my team's strengths and weaknesses. If the team understands their strengths and weaknesses, they can (A)_____. Since I was young, I have been a big fan of baseball. Now, in my work, I watch baseball games all the time. This is a perfect job for me ⓓbecause of watching baseball games ⓔis my hobby!

18. 위 글의 밑줄 친 부분 중 어법상 어색한 것은? (4점)

① ⓐ   ② ⓑ   ③ ⓒ   ④ ⓓ   ⑤ ⓔ

19. 위 글의 빈칸 (A)에 들어갈 말로 가장 적절한 것은? (3점)

① do better next time

② make much money

③ have a better job

④ buy a nice computer

⑤ enjoy their hobbies

[20~22] 다음 글을 읽고 물음에 답하시오.

My name is Yeji. I am an ocean scientist. Ocean science is a big field. It (A)_____ studies of the oceans and the creatures living in them. ⓐthings among I other have many studied fish of living kinds in the seas near Korea. It is the growth ring in a fish that interests me. By looking at it, I can find out when and where the fish was born. All the (B)_____ I get from fish is used to understand sea resources and (C)_____ the oceans better. My job is important because it makes the best use of nature (D)_____.

20. 위 글의 빈칸 (A)~(D)에 들어갈 단어가 <u>아닌</u> 것은? (4점)

① includes   ② manage
③ achieve   ④ possible
⑤ information

21. 위 글의 밑줄 친 ⓐ를 글의 흐름에 알맞게 배열하시오. (5점)

→ _____

22. 위 글을 읽고 답할 수 있는 질문 <u>두 개</u>는? (3점)

① What can Yeji find out from the growth ring in a fish?
② When did Yeji become an ocean scientist?
③ Why does Yeji think her job is important?
④ What high school did Yeji attend?
⑤ How can Yeji solve the problem about the ocean pollution?

[23~25] 다음 글을 읽고 물음에 답하시오.

Hi, I am Tom. (A) A florist is someone who creates beautiful things with flowers. (B) ⓐ<u>To become</u> a florist, you need to know many things about flowers. I attended a high school for florists and gardeners. (C) These days, florists can do a lot of different things. (D) I design movie sets sometimes and I decorate shops with flowers. (E) I am happy when I create something colorful with fresh flowers and greenery. If you like plants and the arts, I highly recommend you become a florist.

23. 위 글의 내용과 일치하지 <u>않는</u> 것은? (3점)

① florist는 꽃으로 아름다운 것들을 만든다.
② Tom은 florist가 힘든 직업이라고 생각한다.
③ Tom은 florist와 정원사를 위한 고등학교를 다녔다.
④ 요즘에는 florist들은 다양한 일을 할 수 있다.
⑤ Tom은 영화 세트장을 가끔 디자인한다.

24. 위 글의 빈칸 (A)~(E) 중 주어진 문장이 들어갈 위치로 알맞은 곳은? (3점)

It was at this school that I learned how to grow and care for different types of flowers.

① (A)   ② (B)   ③ (C)   ④ (D)   ⑤ (E)

25. 위 글의 밑줄 친 ⓐ<u>To become</u>과 to부정사의 쓰임이 같은 것은? (3점)

① I need a house <u>to live</u> in.
② <u>To walk</u> is good for your health.
③ They wanted <u>to visit</u> the cafe.
④ His goal is <u>to become</u> a dentist.
⑤ He got up early <u>to exercise</u> in the morning.

[26~27] 다음 글을 읽고 물음에 답하시오.

Hi, I am Chris. As a director of a musical theater, ⓐI do a lot of things. I audition the actors and I look for good, strong voices. After selecting the cast, I teach them the songs for each scene. Then, I put the cast and orchestra together for practice. During the performance, I am in the orchestra area and conduct. It's my responsibility to have each song played the same way every time. I direct the (A)_____ and the singers to keep the show together. Conducting and directing is not just about waving my arms around!

26. 위 글의 빈칸 (A)에 들어갈 단어로 알맞은 것은?

(3점)

① writers   ② musicians   ③ audience

④ conductor   ⑤ director

27. 위 글의 밑줄 친 ⓐ가 포함하는 내용이 <u>아닌</u> 것은?

(3점)

① to audition actors

② to have the cast and orchestra practice

③ to look for good, strong voices

④ to sing the songs on the stage

⑤ to direct the singers during the show

[28~29] 다음 글을 읽고 물음에 답하시오.

Hi, I am Tom. (A) A florist is someone who creates beautiful things with flowers. (B) To become a florist, you need to know many things about flowers. (C) It was at this school that I learned how to grow and care for different types of flowers. (D) These days, florists can do a lot of different things. I design movie sets sometimes and I decorate shops with flowers. (E) I am happy when I create something colorful with fresh flowers and greenery. If you like plants and the arts, I highly recommend you become a florist.

28. 위 글을 읽고 답할 수 없는 질문은?   (3점)

① What is the florist?

② How does Tom come to work?

③ When does Tom feel happy?

④ What does Tom do for a living?

⑤ What did Tom learn at his high school?

29. 위 글의 빈칸 (A)~(E) 중 주어진 문장이 들어갈 위치로 가장 적절한 것은?   (3점)

I attended a high school for florists and gardeners.

① (A)   ② (B)   ③ (C)   ④ (D)   ⑤ (E)

30. 다음 밑줄 친 ⓐ~ⓔ 중, 어법상 적절하게 쓰인 것을 <u>모두</u> 고른 것은?   (4점)

Hi, I am Tom. A florist is someone ⓐ<u>which</u> creates beautiful things with flowers. To become a florist, you need to know many things about flowers. I attended a high school for florists and gardeners. It was at this school ⓑ<u>that</u> I learned how to grow and care for different types of flowers. These days, florists can do a lot of different things. I design movie sets sometimes and I ⓒ<u>to decorate</u> shops with flowers. I am happy when I create ⓓ<u>something colorful</u> with fresh flowers and greenery. If you like plants and the arts, I highly recommend you ⓔ<u>become</u> a florist.

① ⓐ, ⓑ, ⓒ   ② ⓐ, ⓑ, ⓓ

③ ⓐ, ⓒ, ⓓ   ④ ⓑ, ⓓ, ⓔ

⑤ ⓒ, ⓓ, ⓔ

문항수 : 선택형(24문항) 서술형(3문항) 20 . . .

◎ 선택형 문항의 답안은 컴퓨터용 수정 싸인펜을 사용하여 OMR 답안지에 바르게 표기하시오.
◎ 서술형 문제는 답을 답안지에 반드시 검정 볼펜으로 쓰시오.
◎ 총 27문항 100점 만점입니다. 문항별 배점음 각 문항에 표시되어 있습니다.

[대전 ○○중]

1. 다음 영영 풀이에 해당하는 단어로 알맞은 것은? (4점)

• a strong and harmful need to repeatedly have or do something (such as gamble)
• a condition of being unable to stop doing something

① list   ② addiction
③ posting   ④ device
⑤ number

[충북 ○○중]

2. 다음 대화의 밑줄 친 ⓐ~ⓔ의 의미로 옳지 않은 것은? (4점)

Julia: David, ⓐhow about watching this new movie on the computer?
David: On the computer?
Julia: Yes. I have a website we can download it from ⓑfor free.
David: ⓒYou're not supposed to download movies from that website, Julia. It's ⓓagainst the law.
Julia: Really? I didn't know that.
David: ⓔWhy don't we go to the movie theater, instead?
Julia: Okay. Let's go.

① ⓐ ~하는 게 어때?
② ⓑ 무료로
③ ⓒ 너는 ~해서는 안 된다.
④ ⓓ 법에 어긋나다
⑤ ⓔ 그 이유가 무엇이니?

[대전 ○○중]

[3~4] 다음 대화를 읽고 물음에 답하시오.

Bora: Seho, look! Somebody posted strange things on your SNS, I don't think you posted them.
Seho: Really? Who did this?
Bora: I think someone figured out your password.
Seho: What am I supposed to do?
Bora: If I were you, I would change my password.
Seho: I think I should.
Bora: Is your password easy to guess?
Seho: I used my birth date.
Bora: That is not good. In fact, it is a big _____. You're not supposed to use your personal information when you make a password.
Seho: Okay, I see. I will change it to a stronger one.

3. 위 대화의 내용과 일치하지 않는 것은? (3점)

① 누군가 세호의 비밀번호를 알아낸 것 같다.
② 보라는 세호에게 비밀번호를 바꿀 것을 제안한다.
③ 세호는 자신의 비밀번호에 생년월일(생일)을 사용했다.
④ 보라는 비밀번호를 만들 때 개인 정보를 쓰지 말라고 한다.
⑤ 세호는 SNS 계정을 삭제하고 새로 만들 것이다.

4. 위 대화의 빈칸에 들어갈 말로 가장 적절한 것은? (3점)

① SNS   ② problem
③ detox   ④ birth date
⑤ addiction

[5~6] 다음 대화를 읽고 물음에 답하시오.

> G: James, what are you doing?
>
> B: I'm posting some of the pictures that I took with Sarah today.
>
> G: Did you ask Sarah if you could post them online?
>
> B: No, but I think it's okay because she looks good in the pictures.
>
> G: (A)_____
>
> B: Oh, maybe you're right. I'll call Sarah and ask her right away.

5. 위 대화의 빈칸 (A)에 들어갈 말을 〈조건〉에 맞게 영어로 옮기시오. (5점)

> 조건
> • "의무"를 나타내는 말을 쓸 것.
> • supposed, post, without을 사용할 것.
> • 9단어를 쓸 것.

→ _____

6. 위 대화를 읽고 답할 수 <u>없는</u> 질문은? (4점)

① What is James doing?

② Where did James take pictures with Sarah?

③ Does Sarah know that James will post her pictures online?

④ What does James think about posting Sarah's pictures online?

⑤ What will James do right after the conversation?

7. 다음 상황에 적절한 가정법 문장을 만들 때, 어법상 빈칸에 알맞은 것은? (2개) (3점)

> (상황) 나는 그의 이메일 주소를 몰라서 그에게 이메일을 보낼 수 없다.
> → If I knew his e-mail address, I _____ send him an e-mail now.

① will   ② would   ③ can

④ could   ⑤ must

8. 다음 주어진 문장과 같은 뜻이 되도록 빈칸에 알맞은 말을 써서 완성하시오. (단, 가정법으로 쓸 것.) (4점)

> • I don't have a lot of money. So I can't buy the car.

→ If I _____,

I _____ .

9. 다음 대화의 내용과 일치하지 <u>않는</u> 것은? (3점)

> G: You look tired, Peter.
>
> B: I played computer games until late, so last night I slept for less than four hours.
>
> G: Playing computer games too much is not good for your health.
>
> B: I know, Jenny, but I can't stop it. I think I am addicted to it.
>
> G: I advise you to set a daily plan to limit game time.
>
> B: Peter, G: Jenny

① Peter는 피곤해 보인다.

② Peter는 어젯밤 4시간도 못 잤다.

③ Jenny는 게임을 너무 많이 하는 것이 건강에 좋지 않다고 생각한다.

④ Jenny는 Peter에게 하루 일과를 계획해서 게임 시간을 제한하라고 조언했다.

⑤ Jenny는 Peter가 컴퓨터 게임을 멈출 수 없다고 생각한다.

10. 다음 주어진 B의 말에 이어질 대화의 순서로 가장 적절한 것은? (4점)

B: You look tired.

(A) That's a good idea.
(B) Playing computer games too much is not good for your health.
(C) I know, but I can't stop it. I think I'm addicted to it.
(D) I think you should set a daily plan to limit game time.
(E) I played computer games until late, so last night I slept for less than four hours.

① (A)-(E)-(B)-(C)-(D)
② (B)-(D)-(C)-(E)-(A)
③ (B)-(D)-(A)-(C)-(E)
④ (E)-(B)-(C)-(A)-(D)
⑤ (E)-(B)-(C)-(D)-(A)

12. 다음 중 어법상 올바른 것은? (3점)

① Jim would be happier if he is with her.
② It was not easy for she to swim in the sea.
③ If I am you, I would not use a smart phone on the street.
④ It will be possible for them to learn yoga next month.
⑤ If I were a college student, I will travel all around the world.

13. 다음 가정법 문장에서 어법상 어색한 부분을 찾아 바르게 고쳐 쓰시오. (3점)

• Sally could call Mike if she know his phone number.

→ _____

11. 다음 대화의 빈칸에 들어갈 말로 가장 적절한 것은? (4점)

G: You look tired, Peter.
B: I played computer games until late, so last night I slept for less than four hours.
G: Playing computer games too much is not good for your health.
B: I know, Jenny, but I can't stop it. I think I'm _____ to it.
G: If I were you, I would set a daily plan to limit game time.
B: That's a good idea. Thanks.

① added
② applied
③ assigned
④ admired
⑤ addicted

14. 다음 중 어법상 옳은 문장을 고른 것은? (4점)

ⓐ It is important for we drink enough water.
ⓑ It was not easy for her to solve the problem.
ⓒ It was foolish of you to stay up late last night.
ⓓ It is difficult of Jenny to catch fish.
ⓔ It is necessary for you to set some rules for using your smartphone.

① ⓐ, ⓑ, ⓓ
② ⓐ, ⓓ, ⓔ
③ ⓑ, ⓒ, ⓔ
④ ⓑ, ⓓ, ⓔ
⑤ ⓒ, ⓓ, ⓔ

[15~16] 다음 글을 읽고 물음에 답하시오.

Hi, students! When you wake up in the morning, what is the first thing ⓐthat you do? Do you read SNS postings on your smartphone? Imagine your smartphone is not near you. How do you feel?
Students, please check items on the list ⓑwhich are true for you.

Are you addicted to your smartphone?
1. Without my smartphone, I feel ⓒuncomfortably.
2. I take my smartphone into the bathroom.
3. It is more enjoyable to spend time on my smartphone than with friends.
4. I check ⓓoften SNS posting while studying.
5. I try to reduce the time I spend on my smartphone, but I fail.
6. I check my smartphone right after I hear the sound of an alert.
7. I have my smartphone next to me while ⓔeating.

What is your score? Did you check more than half? If so, you may have a problem with smartphone addiction.

15. 위 글의 밑줄 친 ⓐ~ⓔ 중 문법적으로 옳은 것의 개수는? (3점)

① 1개 ② 2개 ③ 3개 ④ 4개 ⑤ 5개

16. 위 글의 목적으로 가장 알맞은 것은? (3점)

① 스마트폰 사용의 편리함을 알려주려고
② 스마트폰 중독의 위험성을 알려주려고
③ 스마트폰을 어떻게 사용하는지 알려주려고
④ 스마트폰 게임을 어떻게 하는지 알려주려고
⑤ 스마트폰 중독인지 아닌지 확인하게 해주려고

[17~18] 다음 글을 읽고 물음에 답하시오.

<By Yerim, Yongmin, and Hojin>
(A) We will turn off our smartphones while studying.
(B) We will not take our smartphones into the bathroom.
(C) We will keep our smartphones out of the bedroom and not use them at night.

<By Jina, Hosung, and Minsu>
More Time for Outside Activities
(D) We will spend more time playing outside without our smartphones.
Fewer SNS Messages
(E) We will post fewer SNS messages on our smartphones.

<By Jiho, Sohee, and Yumin>
• If I (F)_____ you, I (G)_____ turn off all alerts.
• If I (F)_____ you, I (G)_____ reduce my time on my smartphone by half.

17. 위 글의 밑줄 친 (A)~(E)를 우리말로 바르게 옮긴 것은? (4점)

① (A) - 공부하는 동안 폰을 켤 것이다.
② (B) - 폰을 욕실에 가져갈 것이다.
③ (C) - 밤에 잘 때 폰을 침대에 보관하지만 사용하지 않을 것이다.
④ (D) - 스마트폰 없이 밖에서 놀면서 더 많은 시간을 보낼 것이다.
⑤ (E) - SNS 문자 보내는 횟수를 늘릴 것이다.

18. 위 글의 (F), (G)에 각각 들어갈 단어는? (4점)

	(F)	(G)
①	is	will
②	am	would
③	am	will
④	were	will
⑤	were	would

[19~20] 다음 글을 읽고 물음에 답하시오.

Living without a smartphone, however, is not easy. So, <u>it is necessary for you to set some rules for using your smartphone</u>. You then need to follow the rules. Now, please form groups and, in your group, create rules for using your smartphone.

19. 위 글의 뒤에 이어질 내용은? (3점)

① 스마트폰의 문제점

② 스마트폰의 좋은점

③ 디지털 기기 구매 방법

④ 디지털 기기의 중독 증세

⑤ 스마트폰 사용을 위한 규칙

20. 위 글의 밑줄 친 문장에 대해 바르게 설명하고 있는 사람을 모두 고르면? (정답 2개) (4점)

① 갑이: 문장 앞의 it은 비인칭 주어야.

② 을이: 아니야, 가주어 it이야.

③ 병이: to set some rules는 진주어이고 for you 는 to set rules의 의미상의 주어가 되는 거지.

④ 정이: 아니야. 의미상의 주어는 「of+목적격」으로 표현해야 되는 거야.

⑤ 한이: 이 문장을 해석하면 '여러분을 위하여 스마트폰 사용 방법을 정할 필요는 없어'가 되는 거야.

21. 다음 글의 내용과 일치하는 것은? (4점)

Now, please form groups and, in your group, create rules for using your smartphone.

By Yerim, Yongmin, and Hojin
We will turn off our smartphones while we are studying.
We will not take our smartphones into the bathroom.
We will keep our smartphones out of the bedroom and not use them at night.

By Jina, Hosung, and Minsu
More Time for Outside Activities
- We will spend more time playing outside without our smartphones.
Fewer SNS Messages
- We will post fewer SNS messages on our smartphones.

You did a good job, students! Without smartphones, our lives may be more difficult, but too much use of a smartphone is dangerous. With digital detox, you can become a wise smartphone user.

① 선생님이 학생들에게 스마트폰 사용 규칙을 정해 주신다.

② Yongmin은 공부하는 동안 스마트폰을 사용할 것이다.

③ Jina는 실내 활동에 더 많은 시간을 소비할 것이다.

④ Hosung은 SNS에 더 적은 메시지를 올릴 것이다.

⑤ 스마트폰 없이 사는 것은 지루하다.

22. 다음 글의 빈칸에 들어갈 말로 가장 적절한 것은? (4점)

What is your score? Did you check more than half? If so, you may have a problem with smartphone addiction. Smartphone addiction causes you to spend too much time on your smartphone. Also, you cannot focus on your studies and may have a pain in your neck. Then now is the time for you to start digital detox. Digital detox means staying away from digital devices, _____ smartphones and computers, for a while.

① unlike   ② among   ③ because

④ such as   ⑤ except for

25. 위 글의 밑줄 친 ⓐ～ⓔ 중 어법상 옳지 <u>않은</u> 것은?
(4점)

① ⓐ   ② ⓑ   ③ ⓒ   ④ ⓓ   ⑤ ⓔ

[23～25] 다음 글을 읽고 물음에 답하시오.

(A) What is your score? Did you check more than half? If so, you may have a problem with smartphone addiction. Smartphone addiction causes you ⓐ<u>to spend</u> too much time on your smartphone. Also, you cannot focus on your studies and may have a pain in your neck. Then now is the time ⓑ<u>for you</u> to start digital detox. Digital detox means ⓒ <u>staying</u> away from digital devices, such as smartphones and computers, for a while.
(B) Digital detox will help you a lot. You can enjoy freedom from the noisy digital world. You can focus more on your work. Sometimes you can feel ⓓ<u>refresh</u> and have new, creative ideas. Digital detox will also help you ⓔ<u>spend</u> more time with others.

[26～27] 다음 글을 읽고 물음에 답하시오.

Students, please check items on the list (A)<u>which</u> are true for you.

Are you addicted to your smartphone?
- Without my smartphone, I feel (B)<u>uncomfortable</u>.
- It is (C)<u>more enjoyable</u> to spend time on my smartphone than with friends.
- I try (D)<u>reduce</u> the time I spend on my smartphone, but I fail.
- I check my smartphone (가)<u>right</u> after I hear the sound of an alert.
- I have my smartphone next to me while (E)<u>eating</u>.

23. 위 글 (A)에서 언급된 smartphone addiction이 일으키는 문제 중의 하나는? (3점)

① You will start digital detox.
② You can focus more on your studies.
③ You can check what your problem is.
④ You may have a problem with your neck.
⑤ You spend less time on your smartphone than with others.

26. 위 글의 밑줄 친 (A)～(E) 중, 어법상 옳은 표현을 <u>모두</u> 고른 것은? (4점)

① (A), (D)
② (B), (C)
③ (B), (C), (E)
④ (A), (B), (C), (E)
⑤ (A), (C), (D), (E)

24. 위 글 (B)의 주제로 가장 적절한 것은? (4점)

① Digital detox will improve your life in many ways.
② Disadvantages of digital detox help you feel comfortable.
③ You need to get used to living without a smartphone.
④ Digital detox will make you spend more time on your smartphone.
⑤ Staying away from digital devices causes you to focus on your work.

27. 위 글의 밑줄 친 (가)와 의미가 같은 문장은? (4점)

① Turn <u>right</u> at the corner.
② It is important to act <u>right</u>.
③ Did you get the <u>right</u> answer?
④ Jessie was standing <u>right</u> behind him.
⑤ Teens have the <u>right</u> to play online games when they want to.

반		점수	
이름			

문항수 : 선택형(22문항)   서술형(3문항)   20 . . .

◎ 선택형 문항의 답안은 컴퓨터용 수정 싸인펜을 사용하여 OMR 답안지에 바르게 표기하시오.
◎ 서술형 문제는 답을 답안지에 반드시 검정 볼펜으로 쓰시오.
◎ 총 25문항 100점 만점입니다. 문항별 배점은 각 문항에 표시되어 있습니다.

[부산 ㅇㅇ중]

1. 다음 영어 단어와 우리말 뜻이 바르게 연결된 것을 있는 대로 고른 것은?   (4점)

ⓐ barely	완벽하게 하다
ⓑ sneeze	가로채다
ⓒ mess up	망치다
ⓓ in a row	계속해서, 연이어
ⓔ with delight	힘이 들어서
ⓕ on the way back	돌아오는 길에

① ⓐ, ⓑ, ⓓ   ② ⓑ, ⓒ, ⓔ

③ ⓐ, ⓒ, ⓓ, ⓔ   ④ ⓑ, ⓒ, ⓓ, ⓔ

⑤ ⓒ, ⓓ, ⓕ

[경기 ㅇㅇ중]

2. 다음 대화의 밑줄 친 우리말과 일치하도록 〈보기〉의 단어들을 재배열하여 〈조건〉에 맞게 영어 문장을 완성하시오.   (5점)

B: How is Susie doing these days?
G: She is doing a part time job to save money.
B: Oh, that's great. 그녀가 미래를 위해서 돈을 저축하는 것이 현명해.
G: I agree.

보기
it / wise / money / of / her / the / to / is / for / save / future

조건
• 〈보기〉의 단어들을 모두 사용할 것.(단, 단어를 변형하거나 추가하지 말 것.)

→ _____

[대전 ㅇㅇ중]

3. 다음 주어진 우리말에 맞게 영작할 때, 빈칸에 들어갈 알맞은 단어는?   (3점)

• 나는 스마트폰에 소비하는 시간을 줄이려고 노력하지만 실패한다.
→ I try to reduce the time I _____ on my smartphone, but I fail.

① spend   ② refuse   ③ solve

④ decide   ⑤ delete

[부산 ㅇㅇ중]

4. 다음 주어진 대화와 관련된 내용은?   (4점)

B: What are you doing, Kelly?
G: I'm posting some pictures about the restaurant I visited today in my own SNS.
B: Those are great pictures. Did you take all of them?
G: No. I took the pictures from someone's websites.
B: Then you're not supposed to post them on your SNS.
G: Why not?
B: Because only the website owner has the right to use them.
G: Oh, I see.

① copyright

② digital detox

③ A.I. technology

④ power blogger

⑤ private information

5. 다음 주어진 문장 다음에 이어질 문장이 자연스러운 대화가 되도록 바르게 배열한 것은? (4점)

> David, you know Taegeukgi, don't you?

(A) That's right. Do you know what the black lines on the four corners mean?
(B) No, I don't. What do they mean?
(C) Sure, It's the national flag of Korea, isn't it?
(D) They mean sky, fire, water, and earth.

① (B) - (C) - (A) - (D)
② (B) - (D) - (C) - (A)
③ (C) - (A) - (B) - (D)
④ (C) - (B) - (D) - (A)
⑤ (C) - (D) - (B) - (A)

6. 다음 글에서 전체 흐름과 관계<u>없는</u> 문장은? (5점)

> Sujin: You look worried, Tony. What's wrong?
> Tony: I can't reduce the time I spend on my smartphone. ⓐ<u>Without it, I feel nervous and unhappy.</u> I have my smartphone next to me while I'm eating. I even take my smartphone into the bathroom. ⓑ<u>It is much more enjoyable to spend time with friends than on my smartphone.</u> I check my smartphone right after I hear the sound of an alert. And I often check SNS postings while studying.
> Sujin: Oh, that's too bad. ⓒ<u>I think they are the signs of smartphone addiction.</u>
> Tony: Really? Oh, no! Then, what should I do?

> Sujin: Why don't you set some rules for using your smartphone and follow them?
> Tony: That's a great idea. I can make a couple of rules now. First, ⓓ<u>I will keep my smartphone out of the bedroom and not use it at night.</u> Second, I will spend more time playing outside without my smartphone. ⓔ <u>With the rules, I can become a wise smartphone user.</u> I will put them into practice from now on.

① ⓐ　② ⓑ　③ ⓒ　④ ⓓ　⑤ ⓔ

7. 다음 대화의 밑줄 친 부분이 <u>어색한</u> 것은? (3점)

> G: David, let's ⓐ<u>watch</u> this movie on the computer.
> B: On the computer?
> G: Yes. I have a website we can ⓑ<u>download</u> it from ⓒ<u>for free</u>.
> B: ⓓ<u>You're supposed to</u> download movies from that website, Catherine. It's against the law.
> G: Really? I didn't know that.
> B: Why don't we go to ⓔ<u>the movie theater</u>, instead?
> G: Okay. Let's go.

① ⓐ　② ⓑ　③ ⓒ　④ ⓓ　⑤ ⓔ

8. 다음 주어진 단어를 사용하여 우리말과 뜻이 같게 영작하시오. (4점)

> • 만약 내가 애완동물이 있다면, 더 행복할 텐데.

→ ＿＿＿＿＿＿＿, ＿＿＿＿＿＿＿ happier.
(have, a pet)

[9~10] 다음 대화를 읽고 물음에 답하시오.

> A: Jinseon, you ⓐspend too much time on your smartphone.
> B: My friends get together on SNS almost every day, so I can't ⓑhelp it, Mom.
> A: Okay. What are you doing ⓒon SNS?
> B: I'm posting some of the pictures that I took with Jungyoon today.
> A: Did you ask Jungyoon ⓓthat you could post them online?
> B: No, but I think it's okay because she looks good ⓔin the pictures.
> A: ⓕYou're not supposed to post someone's pictures without asking.
> B: Oh, maybe you're right. I'll call her and ask her right away.

9. 위 대화의 밑줄 친 ⓐ~ⓔ 중 문맥상 쓰임이 적절하지 않은 것은? (4점)

① ⓐ ② ⓑ ③ ⓒ ④ ⓓ ⑤ ⓔ

10. 위 대화의 밑줄 친 ⓕ와 바꿔 쓸 수 있는 표현으로 알맞은 것은? (3점)

① You need to
② You'd better
③ Don't forget to
④ I advise you to
⑤ You should not

11. 다음 대화에 대한 설명으로 알맞은 것은? (4점)

> A: It seems that someone is checking my smartphone. <u>What should I do?</u>
> B: If I were you, I would set up screen lock.

① Mike: 누군가가 B의 스마트폰을 체크하는 듯해.
② David: A는 B에게 조언해 주고 있어.
③ Tom: 밑줄 친 <u>What should I do?</u>는 조언을 구하는 표현이야.
④ Susan: B가 한 얘기는 과거의 사실이야.
⑤ Lisa: B가 한 얘기는 "만약 내가 너였다면, 스크린 락을 설정했을 텐데."라고 과거형으로 해석해야 해.

12. 다음 문장의 밑줄 친 부분 중 어법상 옳은 것은? (4점)

① It is so kind <u>for</u> you to help us.
② It was easy <u>of</u> him to run a marathon.
③ Is it necessary <u>of</u> her to learn French?
④ It is nice <u>for</u> them to be polite to everyone.
⑤ It was wise <u>of</u> her to save money for her future.

13. 다음 문장에 대한 어법 설명으로 적절하지 않은 것은? (5점)

> • 만약 Sandy가 그렇게 멀리 떨어져 살지 않는다면, 내가 그녀를 더 자주 방문할 텐데.
> → If Sandy ⓐ<u>did not</u> live ⓑ<u>so</u> far away, I would ⓒ<u>have visited</u> her ⓓ<u>more often</u>.

① Susan: 이 문장은 가정법과거를 쓰고 있다.
② Tom: 가정법과거이므로 ⓐ<u>did not</u>을 사용하는 게 맞아.
③ Mike: far away의 의미를 수식하기 위해 ⓑ<u>so</u>가 '그렇게'라는 의미로 쓰였어.
④ David: ⓒ<u>have visited</u>는 현재완료 형태로 주어진 해석에 알맞게 잘 쓰였어.
⑤ Lisa: ⓓ<u>more often</u>은 비교급으로 쓰였어.

[14~16] 다음 글을 읽고 물음에 답하시오.

Living without a smartphone, however, is not easy. So, it is ⓐunnecessary for you to set some rules for using your smartphone. You then need to ⓑfollow the rules. Now, please form groups and, in your group, create rules for using your smartphone.

Group A
· We will ⓒturn off our smartphones while studying.
· We will not take our smartphones into the bathroom.
· We will keep our smartphones out of the bedroom and not use them at night.

Group B
· More Time for Outside Activities – We will spend more time playing ⓓoutside without our smartphones.
· Fewer SNS Messages – We will post fewer SNS messages on our smartphones.

You did a good job, students! If we had no smartphones, our lives would be more ⓔdifficult, but too much use of a smartphone is dangerous. With digital detox, (A)_____
_____.

14. 위 글을 바탕으로, 스마트폰 사용 규칙을 정한 것 중 가장 거리가 먼 것은? (5점)

① I'll never use my smartphone at the dinner table.
② I'll spend more time using my smartphone.
③ I will not use my smartphone after 9 p.m.
④ I will reduce the time I spend on smartphone games.
⑤ I will post fewer SNS messages on my smartphone.

15. 위 글의 밑줄 친 ⓐ~ⓔ 중 흐름상 어울리지 않는 것은? (4점)

① ⓐ ② ⓑ ③ ⓒ ④ ⓓ ⑤ ⓔ

16. 위 글의 빈칸 (A)에 들어갈 말로 가장 적절한 것은? (3점)

① you can be healthier than before
② you can make a plan for studying
③ you can be addicted to digital detox
④ you can be a smarter smartphone user
⑤ you can decide to do outdoor activities

17. 다음 밑줄 친 ⓐ~ⓔ 중에서 글의 흐름상 어색한 문장은? (4점)

There would be some advantages and some disadvantages if there were no smartphones. First, let's talk about some advantages. ⓐIf we didn't have smartphones, we would play outside more often. ⓑWe would spend more time with our family without smartphones. ⓒPlus, we would be safe from neck pain. On the other hand, there would be some disadvantages. ⓓIf there were no smartphones, it would be easy for us to contact people. Also, it would take so long for us to find information. ⓔIt would be more difficult to check the news, too.

① ⓐ ② ⓑ ③ ⓒ ④ ⓓ ⑤ ⓔ

[18~19] 다음 글을 읽고 물음에 답하시오.

Hi, students! When you wake up in the morning, what is the first thing you do? Do you read SNS postings on your smartphone? Imagine your smartphone is not near you. How do you feel?
Students, please check items on the list (A)[what / that] are true for you.

(가)_____

□ Without my smartphone, I feel uncomfortable.
□ I take my smartphone into the bathroom.
□ It is more enjoyable to spend time on my smartphone than with friends.
□ I often check SNS postings while (B)[study / studying].
□ I try to reduce the time I spend on my smartphone, but I fail.
□ I check my smartphone right after I hear the sound of an alert.
□ I have my smartphone next to me (C)[during / while] I'm eating.

18. 위 글의 괄호 (A), (B), (C) 안에서 어법에 맞는 표현으로 가장 적절한 것은? (4점)

	(A)	(B)	(C)
①	what	studying	while
②	what	study	during
③	that	studying	during
④	that	study	during
⑤	that	studying	while

19. 위 글의 빈칸 (가)에 들어갈 설문 조사의 제목으로 가장 알맞은 것은? (4점)

① The Meaning of Smartphone Addiction
② What Can Be the Rules of Digital Detox?
③ Are You Addicted to Your Smartphone?
④ Create Rules for Using Your Smartphone
⑤ How Often Do You Read SNS Postings on Your Smartphone?

[20~21] 다음 글을 읽고 물음에 답하시오.

Digital detox will help you a lot. (A) You can enjoy freedom from the noisy digital world. (B) You can focus more on your work. (C) Sometimes you can feel refreshed and have new, creative ideas. Digital detox will also help you have more time with others.
(D) Living without a smartphone, however, is not easy. (E) You then need to follow these rules.

20. 위 글의 흐름으로 보아, 주어진 문장이 들어갈 위치로 가장 알맞은 곳은? (4점)

So, it is necessary for you to set some rules for using your smartphone.

① (A) ② (B) ③ (C) ④ (D) ⑤ (E)

21. 위 글의 밑줄 친 'these rules'에 해당하는 것은? (4점)

① I will use my smartphone while I exercise.
② I will turn off all alerts of messages when I study.
③ I will always carry my smartphone, even at dinner table.
④ I will look for free wifi when I use my smartphone.
⑤ I will upload daily SNS postings with my smartphone every day.

[22~24] 다음 글을 읽고 물음에 답하시오.

Smartphone addiction causes you to spend too much time on your smartphone. Also, you cannot focus on your studies and may have a pain in you neck. Then now is the time for you to start digital detox. (A) Digital detox means staying away from digital devices for a while. (B) You can enjoy freedom from the noisy digital world. (C) You can focus more on your work. (D) Sometimes you can feel refreshed and have new, creative ideas. (E) Digital detox will also help you spend more time with others. Living without a smartphone, however, is not easy. So, you need to set some rules for using your smartphone. You then need to follow the rules.

22. 위 글에서 주어진 문장이 들어가기에 가장 적절한 곳은? (4점)

Digital detox will help you a lot.

① (A)　② (B)　③ (C)　④ (D)　⑤ (E)

23. 위 글의 내용과 일치하는 것은? (3점)

① You will do digital detox with computers.

② You can feel refreshed without digital detox.

③ You don't need to do digital detox right now.

④ We need smartphones to set some rules.

⑤ Digital detox helps you spend less time on your smartphones.

24. 위 글에서 다음 빈칸에 해당하는 표현을 찾아 대화를 완성하시오. (5점)

Doctor: Hi, Sujin. What's the matter?
Sujin: I have a neck pain.
Doctor: Do you (A)＿＿＿＿＿＿＿＿＿＿?
　　　(너는 너의 스마트폰에 너무 많은 시간을 쓰니?)
Sujin: Yes. I'm addicted to my smartphone. I cannot focus on my studies.
Doctor: You need digital detox right now.
Sujin: What does that mean?
Doctor: It means (B)＿＿＿＿＿＿＿＿＿＿.
　　　(그건 디지털 기기들로부터 잠시 동안 떨어져 있는 것을 의미한단다.)

(A) ＿＿＿＿＿＿＿＿＿＿＿＿＿＿＿＿＿

(B) ＿＿＿＿＿＿＿＿＿＿＿＿＿＿＿＿＿

25. 다음 글의 흐름으로 보아 주어진 문장이 들어가기에 가장 적절한 곳은? (4점)

Also, you cannot focus on your studies and may have a pain in your neck.

What is your score? Did you check more than half? If so, you may have a problem with smartphone addiction. Smartphone addiction causes you to spend too much time on your smartphone. (A) If you have these problems, now is the time for you to start digital detox. (B) It will help you in many ways. (C) First, you can enjoy freedom from the noisy digital world. You can focus more on your work. (D) Sometimes you can feel refreshed and have new, creative ideas. (E) Digital detox will also help you spend more time with others.

① (A)　② (B)　③ (C)　④ (D)　⑤ (E)

◎ 선택형 문항의 답안은 컴퓨터용 수정 싸인펜을 사용하여 OMR 답안지에 바르게 표기하시오.
◎ 서술형 문제는 답을 답안지에 반드시 검정 볼펜으로 쓰시오.
◎ 총 27문항 100점 만점입니다. 문항별 배점은 각 문항에 표시되어 있습니다.

[대전 ○○중]

1. 다음 영영 풀이에 해당하는 단어로 알맞은 것은? (4점)

someone who has the highest position in an organization or business

① tradition   ② citizen

③ statue   ④ president

⑤ mission

[부산 ○○중]

2. 다음 빈칸에 공통으로 들어갈 것은?   (4점)

· Yun Boggil was willing to _____ his life for his country.
· Father Lee Taeseok spent his life working for poor people in Sudan. They will remember his _____.

① duty   ② mission

③ respect   ④ sacrifice

⑤ independence

[강남구 ○○중]

3. 다음 대화의 빈칸에 들어갈 말로 알맞은 것은? (3점)

A: I'm going to Hyochang Park tomorrow.
B: Wow! That must be interesting.
A: Yes. _____

① I can't wait for you.

② I can't go there alone.

③ I'm just looking around.

④ I'm waiting for my friend.

⑤ I'm looking forward to going there.

[경기 ○○중]

4. 다음 짝지어진 대화가 어색한 것은?   (3점)

① A: You know about Jeong Yakyong, don't you?
   B: Yes, I've heard of him.

② A: You know Taegeukgi, don't you?
   B: Sure. It's the national flag of Korea, isn't it?

③ A: The art museum must be interesting.
   B: Yes. I'm not interested in art.

④ A: What is the Gansong Museum?
   B: It's a museum built by Gansong Jeon Hyeongpil.

⑤ A: I'm planning to go to the museum again next Wednesday.
   B: Great. I also want to go there.

[대전 ○○중]

5. 다음 문장들에 대한 설명으로 올바른 것은?   (4점)

· I'm looking forward ⓐto going there.
· I would like ⓑto learn about Picasso.

① Susan: ⓐto와 ⓑto는 문법적으로 기능이 같아.

② Tom: ⓐto는 to부정사의 to로 뒤에는 동사원형이 와야 해.

③ Mike: look forward to는 '~을 기대하다'라는 뜻이야.

④ David: ⓑto는 전치사로 쓰였어.

⑤ Lisa: ⓐto 뒤에는 명사가 나와야 하기 때문에 동명사가 올 수 없어.

6. 다음 대화의 빈칸 (A), (B)에 들어갈 질문으로 가장 적절한 것을 〈보기〉에서 고른 것은? (4점)

Eugene: Soyeon, what did you do last weekend?

Soyeon: I went to Hyeonchungwon to do volunteer work.

Eugene: (A)_____

Soyeon: I cleaned around the tombs. I felt great respect for the people who died for the country.

Eugene: Sounds great. (B)_____

Soyeon: Sure. I'm planning to go there again next Wednesday. Will you join me?

Eugene: Sure.

보기

ⓐ What is Hyeonchungwon?

ⓑ Can I do it, too?

ⓒ What kind of volunteer work did you do there?

ⓓ Why did you plan to go there?

	(A)	(B)
①	ⓐ	ⓑ
②	ⓑ	ⓒ
③	ⓑ	ⓓ
④	ⓒ	ⓐ
⑤	ⓒ	ⓑ

- No, I don't. Tell me about them.
- (C)_____
- The circle in the middle means harmony and peace.
- (D)_____
- What do the black lines on the four corners mean?
- (E)_____
- They mean four things: sky, fire, water, and earth.

① (A)   ② (B)   ③ (C)   ④ (D)   ⑤ (E)

8. 다음 중 어법상 옳은 것은? (4점)

① When Mom came back home, she found that Mike doesn't clean the window.

② Jinho got up early so that catch the first train to Barcelona.

③ If God asks me what is my wish, I would say clearly, "It is Korea's Independence."

④ I am always confusing when I see Amy with her twin sister.

⑤ What are you looking forward to doing next week?

7. 다음 대화의 흐름으로 보아 주어진 문장이 들어가기에 가장 적절한 곳은? (4점)

That's right. Do you know what the symbols in Taegeukgi mean?

- Brian, you know Taegeukgi, don't you?
- (A)_____
- Sure. It's the national flag of Korea, isn't it?
- (B)_____

9. 다음 중 밑줄 친 부분이 어법상 올바른 것은? (4점)

① The smartphone is a device <u>which</u> performs a lot of work.

② She made many films <u>who</u> are popular.

③ The man <u>which</u> cooks in that restaurant is attractive.

④ They like the book <u>who</u> has many pictures.

⑤ Global citizens are people <u>which</u> try to understand different cultures.

10. 다음 글의 내용과 일치하는 것을 있는 대로 모두 고르면? (4점)

Last week my history club went to Hyochang Park. We visited the Kim Koo Museum inside the park. At the entrance of the museum, we saw a white statue of Kim Koo. Kim Koo is a great national hero who spent most of his life fighting for the independence of Korea from Japanese rule. In the 1900s, he helped educate young people by building schools. In 1919, when the independence movement had spread throughout the country, he moved to Shanghai, China. There he joined the Government of the Republic of Korea and later became its president.

ⓐ The writer is planning to visit the Kim Koo Museum.
ⓑ The color of Kim Koo's statue is white.
ⓒ The statue of Kim Koo is in the exhibition hall.
ⓓ Kim Koo helped educate young people in the 1900s.
ⓔ When the independence movement spread, Kim Koo moved to Japan.

① ⓐ, ⓒ
② ⓑ, ⓓ
③ ⓐ, ⓓ, ⓔ
④ ⓑ, ⓒ, ⓓ
⑤ ⓑ, ⓓ, ⓔ

11. 다음 대화의 흐름상 빈칸 (A)에 들어갈 말로 가장 적절한 것은? (3점)

B: Tomorrow, let's put on traditional Korean clothes, hanbok, and go to Insadong.
G: Great. After shopping, what should we eat for lunch?
B: Hmm. You know Samgyetang, don't you?
G: No. What is it?
B: It's a traditional Korean soup. It's delicious and will make you healthy.
G: Sounds good. (A)_____

① I don't think it's delicious.
② Do you know who built it?
③ What's the name of the food?
④ I am looking forward to trying it.
⑤ What did you do last weekend?

12. 다음 중 문맥상 밑줄 친 'so that'의 쓰임이 가장 자연스러운 것은? (3점)

① Steph practiced his shooting hard so that he could be a great player.
② I read many books so that I couldn't get a lot of information.
③ James studied hard so that he couldn't win the math contest.
④ David went to Spain so that he couldn't learn Spanish.
⑤ He wears a mask so that he catches a bad cold.

13. 다음 글의 밑줄 친 ⓐ~ⓔ 중 어법상 어색한 것은? (4점)

When Yun left for the mission, he told Kim, "Sir, you are wearing a very old watch. Mine is new, but ⓐI won't need it anymore. Please take my watch, and ⓑlet me have yours." Kim Koo always carried Yun's watch in his jacket not to forget Yun's sacrifice. ⓒAfter completing the tour of the museum, we moved to the tombs of the three heroes, Lee Bongchang, Yun Bonggil, and Baek Jeonggi. ⓓTheir bodies have been in Japan, but after Korea's independence ⓔKim Koo brought them to Hyochang Park. By doing so, he showed his deep love and respect for the sacrifice of the three heroes.

① ⓐ
② ⓑ
③ ⓒ
④ ⓓ
⑤ ⓔ

[14~16] 다음 글을 읽고 물음에 답하시오.

When Yun left for the mission, he told Kim Koo, "Sir, I'm wearing a watch I don't need anymore. You are wearing an old watch. I guess the ⓐwatch I have is new, but I won't need ⓑit anymore. Please take ⓒthis." Kim said, "OK, I let you change ⓓyours with ⓔthis." (A)김구는 그의 희생을 잊지 않기 위해 그의 시계를 항상 지니고 있었다.
After completing the tour of the museum, we moved to the tombs of the three heroes, Lee Bongchang, Yun Bonggil, and Baek Joenggi. Their bodies had been in Japan, but after Korea's independence Kim Koo brought them to Hyochange Park. By doing so, he showed (B)_____.

14. 위 글의 빈칸 (B)에 들어갈 말로 가장 적절한 것은? (4점)

① the way heroes fought against Japan
② his deep love and respect for their sacrifice
③ how to donate to a museum secretly
④ Japanese military violence to Koreans
⑤ the possibility of being buried in Korea

15. 위 글의 밑줄 친 ⓐ~ⓔ 중 지칭하는 것이 나머지 넷과 다른 것은? (3점)

① ⓐ　　② ⓑ　　③ ⓒ　　④ ⓓ　　⑤ ⓔ

16. 위 글의 밑줄 친 (A)의 우리말을 주어진 〈조건〉에 맞추어 영작하시오. (4점)

> **조건**
> • so that 구문을 사용할 것.
> • carry, sacrifice를 사용할 것.

→ _____

[17~18] 다음 글을 읽고 물음에 답하시오.

The exhibition hall in the museum shows a lot of things about Kim Koo's life. While looking around the hall, we stopped at a photo of the Korean Patriotic Organization's members. Kim Koo formed the secret organization in 1931 to fight _____ Japan. Lee Bongchang and Yun Bonggil belonged _____ the group.
At one place in the hall, we saw two watches under a photo of Kim Koo and Yun Bonggil. In 1932, Kim Koo made a plan to kill Japanese generals in a park in Shanghai. As the leader of the Korean Patriotic Organization, he directed Yun to carry out the mission.

17. 위 글의 내용과 일치하지 않는 것은? (4점)

① 전시관은 김구 선생의 삶에 대해 많은 것을 보여 준다.
② 글쓴이는 한인 애국단 단원들의 사진 앞에 멈춰 섰다.
③ 한인 애국단은 김구 선생이 1931년도에 만든 비밀 단체이다.
④ 김구 선생은 일본인 장교들을 죽일 계획을 세웠다.
⑤ 한인 애국단의 리더로서, 김구 선생은 직접 임무를 수행했다.

18. 위 글의 빈칸에 들어갈 전치사를 순서대로 짝지은 것은? (3점)

① for – at　　② for – of
③ with – over　　④ against – to
⑤ against – over

[19~20] 다음 글을 읽고 물음에 답하시오.

The exhibition hall in the museum shows a lot of things about Kim Koo's life. We looked around the hall, and we stopped at a photo of the Korean Patriotic Organization's members. Kim Koo formed the secret organization in 1931 to (A)_____ Japan. Lee Bongchang and Yun Bonggil (B)_____ the group.
At one place in the hall, we saw two watches under a photo of Kim Koo and Yun Bonggil. In 1932, Kim Koo made a plan to kill Japanese generals in a park in Shanghai. As the leader of the Korean Patriotic Organization, he directed Yun to (C)_____ the mission.

19. 위 글의 빈칸 (A), (B), (C)에 들어갈 어구로 알맞은 것은? (4점)

	(A)	(B)	(C)
①	fight against	belonged to	carry with
②	fight on	belonged on	carry out
③	fight with	belonged at	carry on
④	fight against	belonged to	carry out
⑤	fight for	belonged in	carry for

20. 위 글에 나오는 단어의 영영 풀이에 해당되지 않는 것은? (4점)

① a showing, or presenting to view
② having or expressing a great love for one's country
③ known by only a few people; kept hidden from others
④ something that you intend to do or achieve
⑤ to make somebody unable to think clearly

[21~22] 다음 글을 읽고, 물음에 답하시오.

An Changho was born in 1878. When he was in his teens, he moved to Seoul and went to school there. In 1902, (A)그는 더 좋은 교육을 받기 위해 미국으로 떠났다. In America, An helped improve the lives of the Korean people there and became a respected leader. After he had returned to Korea, he founded the New Korean Society in 1907 to fight for Korea's independence. He also joined the Government of the Republic of Korea in Shanghai in 1919. After that, he built a lot of schools to educate people until he died in 1938.

21. 위 글의 밑줄 친 (A)의 우리말과 같은 뜻이 되도록 바르게 영작한 것은? (4점)

① he left for America in order to get a better education
② he left America in order to get for a better education
③ he left America in order not to get a better education
④ he leaves for America in order to get a better education
⑤ he leaves America in order to get a better education

22. 위 글을 쓴 목적으로 알맞은 것은? (3점)

① to persuade
② to debate
③ to ask a favor
④ to complain
⑤ to provide information

[23~25] 다음 글을 읽고 물음에 답하시오.

Last week my history club went to Hyochang Park. We visited the Kim Koo Museum inside the park. At the entrance of the museum, we saw a white statue of Kim Koo. Kim Koo is a great national hero who spent most of his life fighting for the independence of Korea from Japanese rule. In the 1900s, he helped educate young people by building schools. In 1919, (A)독립운동이 나라 전체로 퍼져나갔을 때, 그는 중국의 상하이로 옮겨갔다. There he joined the Government of the Republic of Korea and later became its president.

23. 위 글의 종류로 가장 적절한 것은? (3점)
① play ② letter ③ novel
④ poem ⑤ travel essay

24. 위 글의 내용과 일치하지 <u>않는</u> 것은? (4점)
① Japan was ruled by Korea.
② Kim Koo helped educate young people.
③ Kim Koo became the president of the Government of the Republic of Korea in Shanghai, China.
④ The writer visited the Kim Koo Museum in Hyochang Park with his(or her) club members.
⑤ The writer and his(or her) club members saw the white statue of Kim Koo at the entrance of the museum.

25. 위 글의 밑줄 친 (A)를 과거완료시제와 주어진 어휘들을 사용하여 어법에 맞게 영작하시오. (5점)

movement / move / spread / throughout

→ _____

[26~27] 다음 글을 읽고 물음에 답하시오.

After we completed the tour of the museum, we moved to the tombs of the three heroes, Lee Bongchang, Yun Bonggil, and Baek Jeonggi. Their bodies had been in Japan, but after Korea's independence Kim Koo brought ⓐ<u>them</u> to Hyochang Park. By doing so, he showed his deep love and respect for the sacrifice of the three heroes.
ⓑ<u>As</u> I left Hyochang Park, I thought about Kim Koo's words in My Wish ⓒ<u>that</u> I read in the exhibition hall. It was written in *Baekbeomilji*.
If God asks me what my wish is, I would say clearly, "ⓓ<u>It</u> is Korea's Independence." If he asks me what my second wish is, I would say, "It is the independence of my country." If he asks me what my third wish is, I ⓔ<u>would</u> say loudly, "It is the complete independence of my country." That is my answer.

26. 위 글의 밑줄 친 ⓐ~ⓔ에 대한 설명으로 <u>틀린</u> 것을 고르면? (3점)
① ⓐ: '세 영웅의 시신들'을 가리킨다.
② ⓑ: '~ 때문에'로 해석한다.
③ ⓒ: 관계대명사로 생략할 수 있다.
④ ⓓ: 김구의 소원을 지칭한다.
⑤ ⓔ: 현재 상황에서 일어나지 않을 일을 가정하고 있다.

27. 위 글의 내용과 일치하지 <u>않는</u> 것은? (4점)
① 전시관 관람을 마치고 삼의사의 묘지로 이동했다.
② 삼의사의 시신은 독립 전까지 일본에 있었다.
③ 글쓴이는 「나의 소원」을 삼의사의 묘지에서 읽었다.
④ 삼의사는 이봉창, 윤봉길, 백정기를 지칭한다.
⑤ 김구는 「나의 소원」에서 대한의 독립이 자신의 간절한 소원임을 밝히고 있다.

3학년 영어 1학기 기말고사(5과) 2회

문항수 : 선택형(22문항) 서술형(4문항)

반		점수
이름		

20 . . .

◎ 선택형 문항의 답안은 컴퓨터용 수정 싸인펜을
   사용하여 OMR 답안지에 바르게 표기하시오.
◎ 서술형 문제는 답을 답안지에 반드시 검정
   볼펜으로 쓰시오.
◎ 총 26문항 100점 만점입니다. 문항별 배점
   은 각 문항에 표시되어 있습니다.

[대전 ○○중]

1. 다음 영영 풀이에 해당하는 단어로 알맞은 것은?(3점)

> an event where objects such as works of art
> are displayed in a public space for people to
> look at

① government　　　② exhibition

③ market　　　　　④ library

⑤ skill

[대전 ○○중]

2. 다음 영영 풀이에 해당하는 단어로 알맞은 것은?(3점)

> the act of giving up something that you want
> to keep especially in order to get or do
> something else or to help someone

① disrespect　　　② sacrifice

③ silence　　　　④ desire

⑤ duty

[대전 ○○중]

3. 다음 문장의 밑줄 친 부분을 바르게 고친 것은? (3점)

> • Tony didn't want to buy the magazine
>   because he has already buy it.

① already buys

② already buyed

③ had already bought

④ was already bought

⑤ have already bought

[부산 ○○중]

4. 다음 중 두 사람의 대화가 어색한 것은?　　　(3점)

① A: You know about Jeong Yakyong, don't
      you?
   B: No, I've never heard of him. He was a
      great scientist in Joseon.

② A: Do you remember our plan to visit the
      Hanok Village?
   B: Sure. I'm looking forward to visiting
      there.

③ A: Have you ever heard about Yun Dongju?
   B: I've heard about his name, but I don't
      know much about him.

④ A: What kind of volunteer work did you
      do there?
   B: I cleaned around the tombs.

⑤ A: What are you going to do next Monday?
   B: I'm planning to watch a movie with my
      friends.

[충북 ○○중]

5. 다음 대화의 밑줄 친 ⓐ~ⓔ 중 흐름상 어색한 것은?
                                          (4점)

> G: I'm planning to go to the Gansong
>   Museum.
> B: What is the Gansong Museum?
> G: ⓐIt's a museum built by Gansong Jeon
>   Hyeongpil.
> B: ⓑI heard that he did great things for the
>   country.
> G: Yes. ⓒHe sold many Korean treasures to
>   Japan.
> B: Wow. ⓓThe museum must be interesting.
> G: Yes. ⓔI'm looking forward to it!

① ⓐ　　② ⓑ　　③ ⓒ　　④ ⓓ　　⑤ ⓔ

① (A), (E), (G)　　② (B), (C), (G)
③ (A), (E), (F), (G)　④ (C), (D), (E), (H)
⑤ (E), (G), (H)

8. 다음 대화에서 Jiho와 Miller가 내일 하기로 한 일이 <u>아</u>닌 것은? (4점)

Jiho: Tomorrow let's put on traditional Korean clothes, hanbok, and go to Insadong.
Miller: Good, but I want to buy gifts for my friends in Germany tomorrow.
Jiho: In Insadong, there are many gift shops.
Miller: Great. After shopping, what should we eat for lunch?
Jiho: Hmm. You know Samgyetang, don't you?
Miller: No. What is it?
Jiho: It's a traditional Korean soup. It's delicious and will make you healthy.
Miller: Sounds good. I'm looking forward to trying it.

① wearing hanbok
② visiting Insadong
③ buying some presents
④ having lunch together
⑤ trying making Samgyetang

[6~7] 다음 대화를 읽고 물음에 답하시오.

Andy: Bora, what are you reading?
Bora: I'm reading *Sky, Wind, Star, and Poetry* by Yun Dongju. ⓐ<u>You know about Yun Dongju, don't you?</u>
Andy: I've heard his name, but I don't know much about him. ⓑ<u>His poems spread very fast throughout the world.</u>
Bora: He wrote many beautiful poems when Korea was under Japanese rule. ⓒ<u>His love for the country and his desire for independence can be felt in his poems.</u>
Andy: Really? I didn't know that. ⓓ<u>I want to read his poems and learn more about him.</u>
Bora: Great. ⓔ<u>In fact, I'm planning to visit the Yun Dongju Museum soon.</u> Do you want to come with me?
Andy: Yes, when are you going?
Bora: Next Saturday. It's near Gyeongbok Palace. Can you meet me at the palace at 2 p.m.?
Andy: Sure. Let's meet there.
Bora: Great. I'm really looking forward to the visit.

6. 위 대화의 밑줄 친 ⓐ~ⓔ 중 흐름상 <u>어색한</u> 것은? (4점)

① ⓐ　② ⓑ　③ ⓒ　④ ⓓ　⑤ ⓔ

7. 위 대화를 읽고, 〈보기〉의 (A)~(H) 중 답할 수 <u>없는</u> 것을 <u>모두</u> 고른 것은? (4점)

【보기】
(A) How many poems did Yun Dongju write?
(B) What is Bora looking forward to?
(C) When were Yun Dongju's poems written?
(D) When is Bora going to visit the Yun Dongju Museum?
(E) When was Korea under Japanese rule?
(F) What can be felt through Yun Dongju's poems?
(G) Why is Bora planning to visit the Yun Dongju Museum?
(H) About what does Andy want to learn more?

9. 다음 중 문맥상 밑줄 친 'so that'의 쓰임이 자연스러운 것은? (3점)

① I wear a mask <u>so that</u> I catch a cold.
② Jim studied hard <u>so that</u> he got bad grades.
③ David went to China <u>so that</u> he could forget Chinese.
④ I went to the market <u>so that</u> I could buy the food I needed.
⑤ Steve practiced hard <u>so that</u> he could lose the piano competition.

10. 다음 대화의 내용과 일치하는 것은? (4점)

Andy: Bora, what are you reading?

Bora: I'm reading Sky, Wind, Star, and Poetry by Yun Dongju. You know about Yun Dongju, don't you?

Andy: I've heard his name, but I don't know much about him.

Bora: He wrote many beautiful poems when Korea was under Japanese rule. His love for the country and his desire for independence can be felt in his poems.

Andy: Really? I didn't know that. I want to read his poems and learn more about him.

Bora: Great. In fact, I'm planning to visit the Yun Dongju Museum soon. Do you want to come with me?

Andy: Yes, when are you going?

Bora: Next Saturday. It's near Gyeongbok Palace. Can you meet me at the palace at 2 p.m.?

Andy: Sure. Let's meet there.

Bora: Great. I'm really looking forward to the visit.

① Andy is reading Yun Dongju's poems.

② Andy knows quite well about Yun Dongju.

③ Yun Dongju wrote poems during the Korean War.

④ Andy will visit the Yun Dongju Museum next Saturday.

⑤ Andy and Bora will meet at Gyeongbok Palace Station.

11. 다음 중 어법상 어색한 문장은? (4점)

① I have never traveled abroad before I was 20.

② David asked what present I had given to Jane.

③ They had left the restaurant before I got there.

④ I had a stomachache after my mom had gone out.

⑤ When my dad came home, I had just finished my homework.

12. 엄마가 집에 도착하기 전에 일어난 일을 주어진 표현을 이용하여 문장으로 쓰시오. (8점)

To-do list
Mike - clean the windows
Judy - water the plant
Amy - wash the dishes
Steve - feed the dog

Mom found _____ when she came back home.

(A): Mike (B): Judy (C): Amy (D): Steve

(A): _____

(B): _____

(C): _____

(D): _____

13. 다음 영어 질문에 대하여 주어진 〈조건〉에 맞게 영어로 답을 쓰시오. (6점)

조건
• 'so that+주어+동사 …'의 표현을 사용할 것.
• 완전한 문장으로 작성할 것.
• (A)는 communicate, (B)는 stay를 이용할 것.

(A) Q: Why do you study English?
(B) Q: Why do you exercise?

(A): _____

(B): _____

[14~17] 다음 글을 읽고 물음에 답하시오.

Kim Koo is a great national hero ⓐwho spent most of his life fighting for the independence of Korea from Japanese rule. In the 1900s, he helped ⓑeducate young people by building schools. In 1919, when the independence movement spread throughout the country, he moved to Shanghai, China. There he joined the Government of the Republic of Korea and later became its president.

The exhibition hall in the museum shows a lot of things about Kim Koo's life. [(A)] looking around the hall, we stopped at a photo of the Korean Patriotic Organization's members. Kim Koo formed the secret organization in 1931 to fight [(B)] Japan, Lee Bongchang and Yun Bonggil ⓒbelonged the group. At one place in the hall, we saw two watches under a photo of Kim Koo and Yun Bonggil. In 1932, Kim Koo made a plan ⓓto kill Japanese generals in a park in Shanghai. As the leader of the Korean Patriotic Organization, he directed Yun [(C)] the mission.

When Yun left for the mission, he told Kim, "Sir, you are wearing a very old watch. Mine is new, but I ⓔwon't need it anymore. Please take my watch, and let me have yours." Kim Koo always carried Yun's watch in his jacket because he didn't want to forget Yun's sacrifice.

14. 위 글의 ⓐ~ⓔ에 대한 설명으로 틀린 것을 고르면? (3점)

① ⓐ: 'whom'으로 바꿔 쓸 수 있다.

② ⓑ: 'to educate'로 바꿔 쓸 수 있다.

③ ⓒ: 'belonged to'로 고쳐 써야 한다.

④ ⓓ: 앞에 나오는 명사를 꾸미는 형용사적 용법이다.

⑤ ⓔ: 'not ~ anymore'는 '더 이상 ~하지 않다'는 의미이다.

15. 위 글의 흐름상 빈칸 (A), (B), (C)에 들어갈 말로 바르게 짝지어진 것을 고르면? (4점)

	(A)	(B)	(C)
①	As	for	carry over
②	Because	with	carry out
③	As	against	to carry over
④	While	for	carry out
⑤	While	against	to carry out

16. 위 글을 읽고, 〈보기〉 중에서 시간의 순서를 고려할 때, 3번째로 일어난 일을 고르면? (4점)

> **보기**
> Ⓐ 임시 정부 수립
> Ⓑ 학교를 세워서 청년들을 교육
> Ⓒ 김구 선생과 윤봉길 의사의 시계 교환
> Ⓓ 일본 장군 암살 계획
> Ⓔ 한인 애국단 결성

① Ⓐ　② Ⓑ　③ Ⓒ　④ Ⓓ　⑤ Ⓔ

17. 위 글을 읽고, 대답할 수 없는 질문을 2개 고르면? (4점)

① How did Kim Koo get money to build schools?

② What made Lee and Yun become the members of Korean Patriotic Organization?

③ What plan did Kim Koo make in 1932?

④ What organization did Kim Koo establish in 1931?

⑤ Why is Yun's watch so important to Kim Koo?

[18~19] 다음 글을 읽고 물음에 답하시오.

The exhibition hall in the museum shows a lot of things about Kim Koo's life. While looking around the hall, we stopped at a photo of the Korean Patriotic Organization's members. Kim Koo formed the secret organization in 1931 to fight against Japan. Lee Bongchang and Yun Bonggil (A)_____ the group.
At one place in the hall, we saw two watches under a photo of Kim Koo and Yun Bonggil. In 1932, Kim Koo made a plan to kill Japanese generals in a park in Shanghai. As the leader of the Korean Patriotic Organization, he directed Yun (B)_____ the mission.

18. 위 글의 내용상 빈칸 (A), (B)에 알맞은 표현은?
(3점)

	(A)	(B)
①	belonged	to carry
②	belonged to	to carry with
③	belonged to	to carry out
④	were belonged to	to carry out
⑤	were belonged to	to carry with

19. 위 글의 내용과 일치하지 <u>않는</u> 것은? (4점)
① 전시관은 김구의 삶에 관한 많은 것들을 보여준다.
② 김구는 한인 애국단을 결성했다.
③ 전시관의 한 곳에서 우리는 김구와 윤봉길의 사진 아래에 있는 총을 보았다.
④ 김구는 상하이에서 일본 장군들을 암살할 계획을 세웠다.
⑤ 김구는 한인 애국단 지도자였다.

[20~22] 다음 글을 읽고 물음에 답하시오.

When Yun left for the mission, he told Kim, "Sir, you are wearing a very old watch. Mine is new, but I won't need it anymore. ⓐPlease take my watch, and let me has yours." ⓑKim Koo always carried Yun's watch in his jacket not to forget Yun's sacrifice. ⓒAfter completing the tour of the museum, we moved to the tombs of the three heroes, Lee Bongchang, Yun Bonggil, and Baek Jeonggi. ⓓTheir bodies was in Japan, but after Korea's independence Kim Koo brought them to Hyochang Park. ⓔBy doing so, he showed his deep love and respect for the sacrifice of the three heroes.

20. 위 글의 밑줄 친 ⓐ~ⓔ 중 문맥상 두 번째 단락이 시작되는 곳으로 알맞은 것은? (4점)
① ⓐ ② ⓑ ③ ⓒ ④ ⓓ ⑤ ⓔ

21. 위 글에서 어법상 <u>어색한</u> 부분 두 개를 찾아 쓰고, (1)은 한 단어, (2)는 두 단어로 바르게 고치시오. (4점)

	어색한 부분		바르게 고친 표현
(1)	_____	→	_____
(2)	_____	→	_____

22. 위 글을 읽고 다음 질문에 'so that'을 이용하여 대답을 완성하시오. (3점)

Q: Why did Kim Koo always carry Yun's watch in his jacket?

A: Kim Koo always carried it _____ _____.

[23~24] 다음 글을 읽고 물음에 답하시오.

Last week my history club went to Hyochang Park. We visited the Kim Koo Museum inside the park. At the entrance of the museum, we saw a white statue of Kim Koo.

Kim Koo is a great national hero who spent most of his life ⓐ[to fight / fighting] for the independence of Korea from Japanese rule. In the 1900s, he helped ⓑ[educating / educate] young people by building schools. In 1919, when the independence movement had spread throughout the country, he ⓒ [moves /moved] to Shanghai, China. There he joined the Government of the Republic of Korea and later became its president.

23. 위 글의 내용과 일치하지 <u>않는</u> 것은? (4점)

① The writer belongs to the history club.

② The Kim Koo Museum is located in Hyochang Park.

③ Kim Koo fought for the independence of Korea from Japanese rule.

④ Kim Koo became the leader of the Government of the Republic of Korea in Shanghai.

⑤ Kim Koo joined the Government of the Republic of Korea after the independence of Korea from Japanese rule.

24. ⓐ~ⓒ에 들어갈 말이 바르게 짝지어진 것은? (4점)

	ⓐ	ⓑ	ⓒ
①	fighting	educate	moves
②	to fight	educating	moves
③	fighting	educate	moved
④	to fight	educate	moved
⑤	fighting	educating	moved

25. An Changho에 대한 글의 내용과 일치하는 것은? (3점)

An Changho was born in 1878. When he was in his teens, he moved to Seoul and went to school there. In 1902, he left for America in order to get a better education. In America, An helped improve the lives of the Korean people there and became a respected leader. After he had returned to Korea, he founded the New Korean Society in 1907 to fight for Korea's independence. He also joined the Government of the Republic of Korea in Shanghai in 1919. After that, he built a lot of schools to educate people until he died in 1938.

① 서울에서 태어났다.

② 10대 때 미국으로 유학을 떠났다.

③ 미국에서 조국의 독립을 위해 신민회를 설립했다.

④ 조국으로 돌아와 서울에서 정부가 하는 일을 도왔다.

⑤ 많은 학교를 설립하고 사람들의 교육에 힘썼다.

26. 다음 글의 흐름상 적절하지 <u>않은</u> 문장은? (4점)

①In 1932, Kim Koo made a plan to kill Japanese generals in a park in Shanghai. ② There he joined the Government of the Republic of Korea and later became its president. ③As the leader of the Korean Patriotic Organization, he directed Yun to carry out the mission. ④When Yun left for the mission, he told Kim, "Sir, you are wearing a very old watch. ⑤Mine is new, but I won't need it anymore. Please take my watch, and let me have yours."

정답 및 해설

Lesson 1 (중간) 1회

---

01 ③ **02** ④ **03** ④ **04** ④ **05** ④ **06** ②

07 does walk **08** ④

09 ⓐ window shopping ⓑ dress shirt **10** ③ **11** ①

12 The letter shows what good friends they are.

13 ③ **14** ①, ③ **15** ④ **16** ③ **17** ③ **18** ⑤

19 ③ **20** ⑤ **21** ③

22 Having fun is what I want most

23 (A) theater (B) game room **24** did lose her wallet

25 ⑤ **26** ① **27** ③ **28** ⑤

---

01 ① be filled with ~: ~로 가득 차다

　② be regarded as ~: ~로 여겨지다

　④ in response to: ~에 응하여[답하여]

　⑤ get used to ~: ~에 익숙해지다

02 'He is ~'로 he에 대해 언급하고 있으므로 ④번이 적절하다.

03 첫날이 어땠는지 묻자 (D)에서 좋았다고 답하고 (E)에서 담임선생님이 누구인지 묻고 (B)에서 김 선생님이라고 답하고 (A)에서 그에 관해 더 묻자 (C)에서 재미있는 얘기를 많이 해 주신다고 답하는 순서가 적절하다.

04 주말 계획을 물었는데 자신의 좌우명을 답하고 있어 어색하다.

05 'I am free this weekend. Let's go to see it together.'라고 하고 있다.

06 (B) 다음에 'Yes'라고 답하며 주어진 말의 it에 대해 설명하고 있으므로 (B)가 적절하다.

07 '정말 걸어다닌다'라고 동사를 강조하고 있으므로 강조의 조동사 do를 이용하여 동사를 강조한다.

08 Andy가 Seho에게 좋은 사진을 찍는 법을 가르쳐 준 내용은 없다.

09 ⓐ eye shopping의 적절한 표현은 window shopping이고, ⓑ Y-shirt의 적절한 표현은 dress shirt이다.

10 자신에 대한 언급을 하고 있으므로 ③번이 적절하다.

11 사진작가가 되고 싶다는 말에 이어 많은 사진 찍는 기술을 배울 수 있다고 하고 있으므로 ⓑ에는 ①번이 적절하다.

12 '감탄문(what+형용사+명사+주어+동사)'이 shows의 목적어가 되도록 쓰는 것이 적절하다.

13 (A) does likes → does like

　(D) do wanting → do want

14 관계대명사 what은 '~하는 것'으로 해석한다. 선행사를 포함하는 관계대명사로 the thing which[that]로 바꾸어 쓸 수 있다.

15 Misun이는 바이올린에 대해서는 언급하지 않았다.

16 ⓒ은 진주어로 to play가 되어야 한다.

17 ⓑ, ⓒ는 가주어이다. ⓓ는 the gate를 가리킨다.

18 Misun이 보드 게임을 잘하는지는 알 수 없다.

19 뒤에 이유가 나오므로 because가 적절하다.

20 새로운 기술을 적용한 자신의 꿈의 집에 대한 글이므로 ⑤번이 적절하다.

21 'The bathroom mirror tells me my weight and the condition of my health.'라고 했다.

22 재미있게 노는 것: Having fun

　내가 가장 원하는 것: what I want most

23 (A) enjoy my favorite movies라고 했으므로 theater

　(B) play many different kinds of games라고 했으므로 game room이 적절하다.

24 동사를 강조할 때 do, does, did를 사용할 수 있으며 그 다음에는 동사 원형이 나온다. 과거이므로 did lose로 쓴다.

25 (A) '~보다 먼저'가 어울리므로 before

　(B) what to wear: 무엇을 입을지

26 꿈의 집에서 필자가 얼마나 많은 가구를 가지고 있는지는 알 수 없다.

27 ⓐ what → that ⓑ feeling → feel ⓔ boring → fun

28 Minho의 꿈의 집 2층에 무엇이 있는지는 알 수 없다.

Lesson 1 (중간) 2회

---

01 ① **02** ② **03** ⑤ **04** ② **05** ⑤ **06** ② **07** ③

08 ③ **09** the thing(s) that[which] **10** ⑤ **11** ③

12 ⑤

13 (1) She did lose her wallet in the park.

　(2) I do walk to my house from school every day.

　(3) He does enjoy swimming with me on weekends.

14 What he wants to have most is a watch.

15 ③ **16** ①

17 It is a game room that my dream house has on the second floor.

18 ① **19** ⑤ **20** ⑤ **21** ④ **22** ② **23** ④ **24** ②

25 ② **26** ⑤ **27** ③ **28** ②

---

01 (A) guest: 손님 (B) death rate: 사망률

02 'Yes.'라고 한 후 'He is ~'로 he에 대해 언급하고 있으므로 ②번이 적절하다.

03 'I am free this weekend. Let's go to see it together.'라고 했다.

04 앞의 내용에 대해 좀 더 설명하고 있으므로 ②번이 적절하다.

05 Ted가 'I am free this weekend. Let's go to see it together.'라고 하자 Amy가 'Sounds good.'이라고 했다.

06 ②번은 좋아하지 않는 것을 답하고 있다.

07 자유 시간에 무엇을 하는 것을 가장 좋아하는지 물었는데 가장 좋아하는 음악에 대해 말하고 있으므로 어색하다.

08 like의 목적어와 is의 보어 역할을 할 수 있는 what이 적절하다.

09 관계대명사 what은 'the thing(s) that[which]'로 쓸 수 있다.

10 이 영화를 보고 싶다는 말에 이어 (C)에서 그것에 대해 말해 달라고 하고 (B)에서 지구를 구한 영웅에 관한 것이라고 답하자 (A)에서 공상 과학 영화같다고 하는 순서가 적절하다.

11 SF movie는 Amy가 가장 좋아하는 영화이다.

12 동사를 강조할 때 do, does, did를 사용할 수 있으며 그 다음에는 동사 원형이 나온다.

13 동사를 강조할 때 강조하고자 하는 동사 앞에 do, does, did를 쓰고 그 다음에 동사 원형을 쓴다.

14 관계대명사 what이 have의 목적어와 is의 보어 역할을 하도록 쓴다. 그가 가장 갖고 싶어 하는 것: What he wants to have most

15 (A) 즐겁게 지내는 것이 가장 원하는 것이라고 했으므로 '흥미로운', (B) 가족이 가장 중요하다고 했고 앞에서 safe를 언급했으므로 comfortable, (C) 집에 들어서면 보게 될 것이라고 하는 것이 자연스러우므로 When이 적절하다.

16 Julie가 'It has a theater in the basement. There, I can eat cookies and enjoy my favorite movies.'라고 했다.

17 'It is'와 'that' 사이에 강조하고자 하는 것을 쓰고 나머지를 that 다음에 쓴다.

18 자연과 관련된 꿈의 집을 언급하고 있으므로 ①번이 적절하다.

19 ⓔ에서 impossible을 possible로 고치는 것이 적절하다.

20 Julie가 게임을 얼마나 자주 하는지는 알 수 없다.

21 Julie가 집에서 많은 책을 읽을 수 있다는 언급은 없다.

22 '흥미롭게 만들어 주는 것들'이므로 (B)는 exciting things가 되어야 한다.

23 '다른 사람보다 먼저'가 어울리므로 before가 적절하다.

24 자연과 관련된 집을 언급하면서 가족을 언급하는 ⓑ는 어색하다.

25 자연과 관련된 집을 언급하고 있으므로 ②번이 적절하다.

26 'My dream house has a game room on the second floor. I can play many different kinds of games there.'라고 했다.

27 결과를 이끄는 so가 적절하다.

28 • furniture - 가구 • advise on - ~에 대해 충고하다
• recognize - 인식하다

Lesson 2 (중간)

01 ⑤ **02** ② **03** ③ **04** ⑤ **05** ② **06** ⑤ **07** ①
08 ② **09** ②
10 Make sure you don't wrap the present **11** ④
12 The visitors waiting for an hour are served a lot of side dishes with their meal(s).
13 ② **14** ③ **15** ⑤ **16** ⑤ **17** ③ **18** ② **19** ⑤
20 ⑤ **21** ⑤ **22** ① **23** ① **24** ③ **25** ④ **26** ③
27 ④

01 ⑤번은 '~하곤 했다'의 의미로 쓰였지만 나머지는 모두 '~에 익숙해지다'라는 의미로 쓰였다.

02 manner, advise 두 개만 맞음

03 무엇을 입을지 물었는데 파란색 드레스가 너한테 잘 어울린다고 하는 것은 어색하다.

04 영어로 주소 쓰는 법을 묻는 것으로 ⑤번이 적절하다.

05 흰색과 검은색이 죽음을 의미한다고 했으므로 ②번이 적절하다.

06 'Also, they usually serve tea to guests.'라고 했다.

07 무엇을 샀는지 묻자 ⓒ에서 모자를 샀다며 좋아할지 묻고 ⓐ에서 그렇다며 두 손으로 드리라고 말하고 ⓑ에서 그 이유를 묻고 ⓓ에서 이유를 알려주고 ⓔ에서 기억하겠다고 하는 순서가 자연스럽다.

08 rate: 비율, 율 unemployment rate: 실업률
exchange rate: 환율 pass rate: 합격률

09 '무엇을 가져갈지' 충고를 구하는 주어진 문장에 대한 답이 (B) 다음에 '약간의 차가 어때?'라고 나오므로 (B)가

적절하다.

10 'make sure'는 '꼭 ~하라'는 뜻으로 경고하는 말로 쓰인다. wrap: 싸다, 포장하다

11 소설이 Sara에 의해 쓰여진 것이므로 과거분사가 되어야한다.

12 한 시간 동안 기다리고 있는 방문객들: The visitors waiting for an hour 그들의 식사와 함께: with their meal(s) 많은 반찬들을 제공받는다: are served a lot of side dishes

13 · It's going to be very exciting.
· He is a boy wearing a watch.
· The cat has been sleeping there.

14 한국과 미국의 문화 차이에 대해 언급하고 있으므로 ③번이 적절하다.

15 ⓐ 뒤에서 'you usually need to pay more than the price on the tag'라고 했으므로 most가 적절하다. ⓑ 뒤에서 'They range from less than one percent to more than ten percent.'라고 했으므로 differ가 적절하다.

16 (마) 앞에서 '너는 길을 걷고 있는 연세가 많으신 할아버지께 손을 흔들며 미소를 지어도 돼.'라고 했고 주어진 문장의 He가 (마) 앞 문장의 an elderly man을 가리키므로 (마)가 적절하다.

17 ⓒ '나이가 많은 사람에게 손을 흔드는 것은 무례하다고 여겨지지 않는다'고 했으므로 uncomfortable ⓓ 문맥상 elderly ⓔ get used to ~ing: ~에 익숙해지다

18 an elderly man을 수식하는 말로 '능동'의 의미를 지닌 현재분사가 적절하다.

19 연장자에게 손을 흔드는 것: Waving to an older person, 무례하다고 여겨지지 않다: is not regarded as rude

20 'in America, you usually need to pay more than the price on the tag.'라고 했다.

21 주어진 문장의 They가 가리키는 것이 (E) 앞의 Sales tax rates이므로 (E)에 들어가는 것이 적절하다.

22 현재완료나 현재완료진행형의 경우 특정한 과거를 나타내는 부사(구)와 함께 쓰이지 않는다. ⓐ의 three years ago를 for three years로 바꿔야 한다.

23 throwing의 목적어로 'colored powder and water'를 쓰며, 이것이 people을 뒤에서 수식하도록 하고 on each other를 마지막에 쓰는 것이 적절하다.

24 'Holi is held in March.'라고 했다.

25 (D) 다음 문장의 They가 주어진 문장의 Sales tax rates를 가리키므로 (D)에 들어가는 것이 적절하다.

26 It이 주어이므로 ⓒ는 수동태 is called로 쓰는 것이 적절하다.

27 'They range from less than one percent to more than ten percent.'라고 했다.

Lesson 2 (중간)

01 ②	**02** ②	**03** ④	**04** ⑤	**05** ⑤	**06** ①
07 ①, ④		**08** ②	**09** ④		

10 I am getting used to living in the city. **11** ④

12 (1) I have been eating pizza for two hours.
(2) She has been learning flamenco for a month.
(3) My uncle has been working for the company for three years.

13 ⑤	**14** ①	**15** ②	**16** ④	**17** ④	**18** ②	**19** ①
20 ③	**21** ④	**22** ②	**23** ①	**24** ⑤		

01 순서대로 products, elderly, regarded, negative가 들어간다.

02 선물을 준비했다고 한 선생님이 좋아할지 묻자 (C)에서 좋아할 거라며 두 손으로 드리라고 말하고 (B)에서 그 이유를 묻고 (A)에서 이유를 알려주고 (D)에서 기억하겠다고 하는 순서가 자연스럽다.

03 ⓐ 짐을 쌌는지 물어보는 pack, ⓑ 앞에 is 동사가 있고 긍정이므로 isn't it, ⓒ 환전하라는 exchange가 적절하다.

04 일 년 전에 시작해서 아직도 배우는 중이므로 현재완료진행시제를 이용한다.

05 '차가 어떤지' 제안하고 있으므로 ⑤번이 적절하다.

06 사진을 찍고 싶다고 하자 (A)에서 알아야 할 중요한 것이 있다고 하고, (C)에서 충고해 달라고 하고, (D)에서 묻지 않고 사람들 사진을 찍으면 안 된다고 말하고, (E)에서 이유를 묻자 (B)에서 그들은 누군가가 사진을 찍으면 나쁜 영향을 받는다고 믿는다며 이유를 설명하는 순서가 자연스럽다.

07 ② one hours ③ Jane이 얼마동안 식물에 물을 주고 있는지 알 수 없음. ⑤ Mom has been talking on the phone since 2 p.m.

08 (B) 다음에 'Sure.'라고 답하고 '거리 주소를 먼저 써야 한다'고 하고 있으므로 (B)에 들어가는 것이 적절하다.

09 Waving이 주어이므로 수동태로 쓰는 것이 적절하다. regard A as B = A be regarded as B: A를 B로 여기

정답 및 해설 **29**

다

10 get used to ~ing: ~에 익숙해지다

11 감정을 나타내는 동사의 경우 감정을 불러일으키면 현재분사로 쓰고 감정을 느끼면 과거분사로 쓴다.

12 (1) 과거에 시작해서 아직도 하고 있는 것을 현재완료진행형(have/has been ~ing)으로 쓴다.

13 한국과 미국의 문화 차이에 대해 언급하고 있으므로 ⑤번이 적절하다.

14 (A) '나이가 많은 사람에게 손을 흔드는 것은 무례하다고 여겨지지 않는다'라고 하는 것이 적절하므로 older, (B) 문맥상 '불쾌하게 느낄지도 모르므로 uncomfortable, (C) wave to: ~에게 손을 흔들다

15 필자가 왜 한국을 떠났는지는 알 수 없다.

16 ⓒ March라는 달 이름 앞이므로 in, ⓓ throw on: ~에게 던지다

17 ⓓ는 'not getting used to'가 아니라 'getting used to'가 되어야 자연스러운 흐름이 된다.

18 부정의문문으로 물었더라도 긍정의 의문문에서와 같이 답해야 한다.

19 인도의 전통 축제인 Holi를 소개하면서 거기에 가서 하고 싶은 것들을 언급하고 있으므로 ①번이 적절하다.

20 sales tax가 붙으므로 가격표보다 더 많이 지불해야 한다.

21 The movie가 주어이므로 '수동'의 의미를 갖는 과거분사 directed로 써야 한다.

22 'In response to negative questions, such as "Don't you like apple pie?" you should answer "No," if you don't like it. And you should answer "Yes," if you like it.'라고 했다.

23 'Don't you like apple pie?'에 'Yes.'라고 하고서는 'Then, try some. It's delicious.'라는 말에는 'No. I just said I don't like apple pie.'라고 했으므로 'confused(혼란한, 어리둥절한)'가 적절하다.

24 sales tax가 붙으므로 ⓔ에서 as much as를 more than으로 고쳐야 한다.

Lesson 3 (기말)

---

01 ① **02** ② **03** ② **04** ①
05 It is our health that wearing a mask protects from a virus called COVID-19.
06 ⑤ **07** ④ **08** ② **09** ⑤ **10** ② **11** ③ **12** ③
13 ② **14** ③ **15** ①

---

16 (1) is Steve that helps me with my homework
(2) was at the museum that I met Tom yesterday
17 ② **18** ③ **19** ① **20** ⑤ **21** ⑤ **22** ③
23 (1) 영화 세트장을 디자인 함 (2) 꽃들로 가게를 꾸밈
24 ③ **25** ① **26** ① **27** ③ **28** ① **29** ⑤
30 All the information (that) I get from fish is used to understand sea resources and manage the oceans better.

---

01 주어진 풀이는 recommend이다.
 • 누군가에게 어떤 것을 하라고 제안하다

02 음악가나 가수의 공연을 감독하는 것은 'conduct'이다.

03 solve는 '미루다'가 아니라 '풀다, 해결하다'라는 뜻이다.

04 'I'm (quite) sure'로 확실히 될 것이라고 언급하는데 ① 번은 될 수 없다고 말하고 있다.

05 'It is'와 'that' 사이에 강조할 것을 쓰고 나머지는 that 다음에 써서 강조한다. our health를 보호하는 것이므로 'It is'와 'that' 사이에 our health를 쓰고 나머지는 that 다음에 쓴다.

06 요리사가 되기 위해 노력하는 이에게 해 줄 적절한 말은 ⑤번이다.

07 'I'm taking a cooking class.'라고 했다.

08 (B)에서 가장 관심 있는 것이 무엇인지 묻자 (A)에서 함께 일하는 것하고 운동하는 것이라고 답하자 (C)에서 outgoing type이라고 하는 순서가 적절하다.

09 Mr. Han이 중국에 관한 다양한 내용을 언급하자 그에 대한 반응으로 나온 말로 마지막 부분인 (E)에 들어가는 것이 적절하다.

10 G가 'Are you happy with your job?'이라고 묻자 Mr. Han이 'Yes. I really love my job.'이라고 했다.

11 'my drawing skill is not good enough'에서 'worried'를, Mr. Kim의 조언에 'Thank you very much.'라고 한 것에서 'hopeful'을 유추할 수 있다.

12 animator가 되려는 사람에게 ③번이 적절하다.

13 '그림 그리기'와 '열심히 공부하기'가 도움이 될 것 같다는 말에 어울리는 것은 ②번이다.

14 ③에서 사역동사 let의 목적격보어로 동사원형 go가 적절하다.

15 ①에서 사역동사 had의 목적격보어로 목적어인 her husband가 세차를 하는 것이므로 동사원형 wash가 되어야 한다.

16 'It is[was]'와 'that' 사이에 강조하고자 하는 말을 넣고 나머지를 다음에 쓰면 된다.

17 ⓐ doesn't it ⓒ have been ⓓ is ⓔ played

18 녹화된 경기를 보고 자료를 수집하고 나서 분석한다는 것이 자연스러우므로 (C)가 적절하다.

19 Chris가 어떤 운동을 좋아하는지는 알 수 없다.

20 밑줄 친 (가)와 ⑤: 감독하다 ① 직접적인 ② ~에게 길을 가리켜 주다 ③ 직행으로 ④ 직접적인, 솔직한

21 앞 문장에 나온 the growth ring을 가리킨다.

22 '이 학교에서'를 강조하는 것이므로 'It was'와 'that' 사이에 'at this school'을 넣고 나머지를 'that' 다음에 쓴다.

23 'I design movie sets sometimes and I decorate shops with flowers.'라고 했다.

24 왜 Yeji가 그녀의 직업을 선택했는지는 알 수 없다.

25 'The growth ring in a fish interests me.'라고 했으므로 'It is'와 'that' 사이에 'the growth ring in a fish'를 넣고 나머지를 'that' 다음에 쓴다.

26 (A) 선행사가 주어이므로 who, (B) 'attend to'는 '~을 돌보다, ~을 간호하다'라는 의미로 쓰인다. (C) -thing으로 끝나는 부정대명사는 형용사가 뒤에서 수식하므로 something colorful이 적절하다.

27 꽃을 다루며 아름답게 장식하는 일을 주로 하는 florist에게 어울리는 것으로 'plants'와 'the arts'가 적절하다.

28 ⓐ 앞 문장의 Ocean science, ⓑ 바로 앞에 나온 the oceans를 가리킨다.

29 makes의 목적어로 the best use of nature를 쓰고 possible을 목적격보어로 쓴다.

30 'All the information (that) I get from fish'가 주어이므로 수동태로 써야 한다.

Lesson 3 (기말)

> **01** ① **02** ① **03** ② **04** ④ **05** ④ **06** ① **07** ②
> **08** ⑤
> **09** It was this morning that Jenny saw Tom at the station.
> **10** ④ **11** ③
> **12** We had the house repaired yesterday.　　　**13** ④
> **14** ⑤ **15** ① **16** ④ **17** ① **18** ④ **19** ① **20** ③
> **21** Among other things, I have studied many kinds of fish living
> **22** ①, ③　　　**23** ② **24** ③ **25** ⑤ **26** ② **27** ④
> **28** ② **29** ③ **30** ④

01 무언가를 면밀히 연구하고 조심스럽게 조사하는 것은 'analyze'이다.

02 (A) 스트레스를 reduce(줄여준다)
(B) 스스로를 calm(평온해지게 하다)
(C) 몸과 마음을 healthy(건강하게) 유지시킨다

03 각각 (A) includes(포함하다) (B) attend(참석하다) (C) resources(자원)가 적절하다.

04 'attend'는 '참석하다, 출석하다'라는 의미이다.

05 한 선생님에게 무엇을 하는지 말해 달라고 하자 (C)에서 하는 일을 설명하고 (B)에서 그 밖의 하는 일을 묻자 (E)에서 추가로 설명하고 (D)에서 하는 일에 만족하는지 묻자 (A)에서 그렇다고 답하는 순서가 자연스럽다.

06 'I'm (quite) sure'로 확실히 될 것이라고 언급하는데 ① 번은 될 수 없다고 말하고 있다.

07 쓰기와 그리기가 도움이 될 것이라는 말에서 ②번이 적절함을 알 수 있다.

08 훌륭한 요리사가 되려고 무엇을 하는지 묻자 제빵 수업을 듣고 새롭고 창의적인 요리에 대해 생각하려고 노력한다고 답하고 있다.

09 언제인지 물었으므로 답이 되는 시간을 'It was'와 'that' 사이에 넣고 나머지를 'that' 다음에 쓴다.

10 'It is[was]'와 'that' 사이에 강조하고자 하는 말을 넣고 나머지를 다음에 쓰면 된다. 이때 'that' 대신에 강조하는 것이 사람이면 'who나 whom'을, 사물이면 'which', 시간이면 'when', 장소면 'where'를 쓸 수 있다. 동사를 강조할 때는 'do, does, did+동사원형'을 시제와 주어의 수에 맞게 사용한다.

11 내가 장난감을 수리하는 것이므로 '능동'의 의미를 갖도록 사역동사 made의 목적격 보어를 동사 원형으로 써야 한다.

12 집이 수리되는 것이므로 사역동사 had의 목적격 보어를 '수동'의 의미를 가지는 과거분사 repaired로 써야 한다.

13 게임이 녹화된 것이므로 과거분사 recorded로 써야 한다.

14 ⓐ와 ⑤: 부사적 용법의 목적 ① 형용사적 용법 ②, ③, ④: 명사적 용법

15 'It is'와 'that' 사이에 'the growth ring in a fish'를 넣고 나머지를 'that' 다음에 쓴다.

16 바로 앞 문장에 나온 'the growth ring in a fish'이다.

17 ⓒ 'All the information'이 주어이므로 수동태에 쓰이는 used, ⓓ makes의 목적어로 쓰인 명사 use가 적절하다.

18 뒤에 절이 이어지므로 ⓓ의 because of는 because로 고쳐야 한다.

19 약점과 강점을 잘 안다면 다음에 더 잘할 것이다.

20 각각 (A) includes (B) information (C) manage (D) possible이 들어간다.

21 among other things: 다른 여러 가지 중에서 have studied: 연구해 왔다 many kinds of fish: 많은 종류의 물고기 living: 살고 있는

22 'I can find out when and where the fish was born' 과 'My job is important because it makes the best use of nature possible'이라고 했다.

23 Tom이 플로리스트가 힘든 직업이라고 생각한다는 말은 없다.

24 주어진 문장의 this school이 (C) 앞의 a high school이 므로 (C)에 들어가야 한다.

25 ⓐ와 ⑤: 부사적 용법의 목적 ① 형용사적 용법 ②, ③, ④: 명사적 용법

26 'director of a musical theater'라고 했으므로 musicians가 적절하다.

27 무대에서 노래를 부르는 것은 포함되지 않는다.

28 Tom이 어떻게 직장에 오는지 알 수 없다.

29 (C) 다음의 this school이 주어진 문장의 a high school 이므로 (C)에 들어가야 한다.

30 ⓐ 선행사가 사람이므로 who나 that을 써야 한다.
ⓒ 동사가 필요한 자리이므로 decorate로 써야 한다.

Lesson 4 (기말) 1회

> **01** ② **02** ⑤ **03** ⑤ **04** ②
> **05** You're not supposed to post someone's pictures without asking.
> **06** ② **07** ②, ④
> **08** had a lot of money, could buy the car. **09** ⑤
> **10** ⑤ **11** ⑤ **12** ④
> **13** Sally could call Mike if she knew his phone number.
> **14** ③ **15** ③ **16** ⑤ **17** ④ **18** ⑤ **19** ⑤
> **20** ②, ③ **21** ④ **22** ④ **23** ④ **24** ① **25** ④
> **26** ④ **27** ④

01 '반복적으로 어떤 것을 가지거나 하기 위한 강하고 해로운 필요'와 '어떤 것을 하는 것을 멈추지 못하는 상황'을 가리 키는 말은 'addiction(중독)'이다.

02 'Why don't we ~?'는 '~하는 게 어때?'라는 의미로 쓰 였다.

03 'I will change it to a stronger one.'이라고 했다.

04 앞에서 좋지 않다고 하고 뒤에서 개인 정보를 쓰지 말라고 했으므로 'problem'이 적절하다.

05 사진을 물어보지도 않고 올린 후 친구의 말을 듣고 당장 물 어보겠다고 했으므로 불허를 나타내는 표현인 'You're not supposed to ~.'를 이용한다.

06 James가 Sarah와 어디서 사진을 찍었는지는 알 수 없다.

07 현재 상황이므로 가정법과거로 써야 하며 이때 주절에는 'would/should/could/might+동사원형'을 쓴다.

08 현재 상황이므로 가정법과거로 반대의 내용을 쓴다. 가 정법과거는 'If+주어+동사의 과거형 ~, 주어+would/ should/could/might+동사원형'으로 쓴다.'

09 Peter가 'I can't stop it. I think I am addicted to it.' 이라고 말했다.

10 피곤해 보인다는 말에 이어 (E)에서 게임을 늦게까지 해서 잠을 4시간도 못 잤다고 하고 (B)에서 게임을 너무 많이 하는 것은 건강에 좋지 않다고 하자 (C)에서 아는데 멈출 수가 없다고 하자 (D)에서 하루 일과의 계획을 세우라고 하고 (A)에서 좋은 생각이라고 하는 순서가 자연스럽다.

11 게임을 멈출 수 없다고 했으므로 'addicted(중독된)'가 적절하다.

12 ① is → were ② she → her ③ am → were
⑤ will → would

13 현재 사실에 반대되는 가정을 하는 가정법과거에서는 if절 에 동사의 과거형을 쓴다. know를 knew로 고친다.

14 ⓐ we → us ⓓ of → for

15 ⓒ feel의 보어로 형용사 uncomfortable이 와야 한다.
ⓓ often은 동사 check의 앞에 위치해야 한다.

16 'please check items on the list'라고 하고 그 목록에 는 'Are you addicted to your smartphone?'이라고 되어 있으므로 ⑤번이 적절하다.

17 ④번만이 제대로 표현되었다.

18 가정법과거는 'If+주어+동사의 과거형 ~, 주어+would/ should/could/might+동사원형'으로 쓴다.

19 글의 마지막에 'create rules for using your smartphone'이라고 했다.

20 ⑤ 여러분은 스마트폰 사용을 위한 몇 가지 규칙을 정할 필요가 있습니다.

21 'We will post fewer SNS messages on our smartphones.'라고 했다.

22 such as: ~와 같은, 예를 들어

23 'may have a pain in your neck'라고 했다.

24 'Digital detox will help you a lot.'이라고 했다.

25 ⓓ는 주어가 감정을 느끼는 것이므로 과거분사 refreshed가 적절하다.

26 (D)는 try의 목적어로 to reduce가 되어야 한다.

27 (가)와 ④: 바로, 곧 ①: 오른쪽으로 ②: 바르게 ③: 정확한, 틀리지 않은 ⑤: 권리

Lesson 4 (기말)   2회

---
01 ⑤
02 It is wise of her to save money for the future.
03 ① **04** ① **05** ③ **06** ② **07** ④
08 If I had a pet, I would be   **09** ④ **10** ⑤ **11** ③
12 ⑤ **13** ④ **14** ② **15** ① **16** ④ **17** ④ **18** ⑤
19 ③ **20** ⑤ **21** ② **22** ② **23** ⑤
24 (A) spend too much time on your smartphone
　　(B) staying away from digital devices for a while
25 ①
---

01 ⓐ barely: 간신히, 겨우, 거의 … 없는 ⓑ sneeze: 재채기하다 ⓔ with delight: 기꺼이

02 'wise'가 사용됐으므로 의미상의 주어로 'of+목적격'을 쓴다.

03 'the time'을 수식하는 '소비하는'이 필요하므로 spend가 적절하다.

04 website 주인이 사용할 권리를 갖고 있다는 말에서 'copyright(저작권)'에 관한 내용임을 알 수 있다.

05 태극기를 알지 않느냐고 하자 (C)에서 한국의 국기 아니냐고 묻자 (A)에서 맞다며 검은 선들이 의미하는 것을 아는지 묻고 (B)에서 모른다며 무슨 의미인지 묻자 (D)에서 의미하는 바를 알려주는 순서가 적절하다.

06 스마트폰에 중독되어 증상을 말하고 있으므로 ⓑ는 It is much more enjoyable to spend time on my smartphone than with friends.로 쓰는 것이 적절하다.

07 뒤에서 법에 어긋난다고 했으므로 ⓓ는 '불허'를 나타내는 'You're not supposed to ~.'를 쓰는 것이 적절하다.

08 현재 상황이므로 가정법과거로 쓴다. 가정법과거는 'If+주어+동사의 과거형 ~, 주어+would/should/could/might+동사원형'으로 쓴다.

09 사진들을 온라인에 올릴 수 있는지 물었느냐는 뜻이므로 ⓓ는 that이 아니라 if를 써야 적절하다.

10 'You're not supposed to ~'는 불허를 나타내는 표현이므로 ⑤번이 적절하다.

11 'What should I do?'는 조언을 구하는 표현이다.

12 ① for → of ② of → for ③ of → for ④ for → of

13 ⓒ는 현재완료가 아니며 가정법과거에 맞춰 visit로 써야 한다.

14 스마트폰을 덜 사용하자는 내용이어야 하는데 ②번은 더 많은 시간을 보내겠다는 것이므로 거리가 멀다.

15 '스마트폰 없이 사는 것은 쉽지 않다.'고 했으므로 '여러분은 스마트폰 사용에 대한 몇 가지 규칙을 정할 필요가 있다.'고 하는 것이 적절하다.

16 바로 앞에서 '지나친 스마트폰 사용은 위험하다'고 했으므로 ④번이 적절하다.

17 ⓓ는 'If there were no smartphones, it would not be easy for us to contact people.'이 되어야 자연스럽다.

18 (A) the list라는 선행사가 있으므로 관계대명사 that, (B) 접속사 while이 있으므로 '주어+be동사'가 생략된 형태의 studying, (C) 뒤에 절이 이어지므로 while이 적절하다.

19 스마트폰을 얼마나 쓰고 있는지에 대한 내용이 나오므로 '여러분은 스마트폰에 중독되었나요?'가 적절하다.

20 (E) 앞에서 '스마트폰 없이 사는 것은 쉽지 않다.'고 한 후 주어진 문장에서 So로 결과를 이끌어 '여러분은 스마트폰 사용에 대한 몇 가지 규칙을 정할 필요가 있다'라고 하는 것이 자연스러우므로 (E)에 들어가는 것이 적절하다.

21 앞에서 '스마트폰 없이 사는 것'을 언급했으므로 '공부할 때 모든 알림을 끌 거'라는 ②번이 적절하다.

22 주어진 문장의 자세한 내용이 (B) 뒤에 이어지므로 (B)가 적절하다.

23 (B) 뒤에 이어지는 내용이 스마트폰에 시간을 덜 보내게 된다는 것이다.

24 (A) 'spend too much time'이라는 표현을 이용한다.
　　(B) 'staying away from'이라는 표현을 이용한다.

25 주어진 문장의 Also에 주목한다. 비슷한 내용이 앞에 나왔을 것이므로 (A)가 적절함을 알 수 있다.

Lesson 5 (기말)   1회

---
01 ④ **02** ④ **03** ⑤ **04** ③ **05** ③ **06** ⑤ **07** ②
08 ⑤ **09** ① **10** ② **11** ④ **12** ① **13** ④ **14** ②
15 ⑤
16 Kim Koo always carried his watch so that he would not forget his sacrifice.
17 ⑤ **18** ④ **19** ④ **20** ⑤ **21** ① **22** ⑤ **23** ⑤
---

24 ①

25 when the independence movement had spread throughout the country, he moved to Shanghai, China.

26 ② **27** ③

01 '기관이나 사업체에서 가장 높은 지위를 가지고 있는 사람'은 'president(사장)'이다.

02 sacrifice: 희생하다; 희생

03 'look forward to ~ing'는 기대를 나타내는 말이다.

04 박물관이 흥미롭다고 하자 그렇다고 하고 미술에 관심 없다고 하는 것은 어색하다.

05 ⓐto는 전치사, ⓑto는 to부정사의 to이다.

06 (A) 자원 봉사한 내용을 말하고 있으므로 ⓒ (B) 'Sure.' 라고 답하며 'I'm planning to go there again next Wednesday. Will you join me?'라고 하고 있으므로 ⓑ가 적절하다.

07 태극기를 아느냐고 묻자 안다며 한국의 국기 아니냐고 답하고 주어진 문장에서 맞다며 국기의 상징들을 아는지 묻자 모른다고 답한 것이 자연스러우므로 (B)가 적절하다.

08 ① doesn't clean → had not cleaned
② catch → he could catch
③ what is my wish → what my wish is
④ confusing → confused

09 ② who → that[which] ③ which → who[that]
④ who → that[which] ⑤ which → who[that]

10 'we saw a white statue of Kim Koo'라고 했고 'In the 1900s, he helped educate young people by building schools.'라고 했다.

11 기대를 나타내는 ④번이 적절하다.

12 'so that+주어+동사 ~' 구문은 목적을 나타내며 '~하기 위해서'라는 뜻이다.

13 ⓓ는 시신을 모셔온 과거보다 시신이 일본에 있었던 것이 더 이전에 있었던 일이므로 과거완료(had+p.p.) 시제를 사용해야 한다.

14 김구가 그들의 시신을 모셔온 것은 그들의 희생에 대한 그의 사랑과 존경을 보여 주기 위함이었다.

15 ⓔ는 김구의 시계이고 나머지는 모두 윤봉길의 시계이다.

16 'so that+주어+동사 ~(~하기 위해서)'는 목적을 나타낸다.

17 'he directed Yun to carry out the mission'이라고 했다.

18 fight against: ~에 대항하여 싸우다, belong to: ~에 속

19 (A) fight against: ~에 대항하여 싸우다 (B) belong to: ~에 속하다 (C) carry out: ~을 수행하다

20 ⑤번은 'mix up'에 대한 풀이이다.
① exhibition ② patriotic ③ secret ④ plan

21 'so that+주어+동사 ~' 구문은 목적을 나타내며 '~하기 위해서'라는 뜻이다. so that 뒤에는 주어와 동사가 있는 절이 오며, 목적을 나타내는 'to+동사원형' 또는 'in order to+동사원형'으로 바꾸어 쓸 수 있다.

22 안창호에 관해 소개하기 위한 글이다.

23 위 글은 travel essay(기행문)이다.

24 'independence of Korea from Japanese rule'이라고 했다.

25 김구가 상하이로 간 과거보다 독립 운동이 더 이전에 일어난 일이므로 과거완료시제로 쓴다.

26 ⓑ의 As는 '~할 때'라는 뜻의 접속사이다.

27 'I thought about Kim Koo's words in My Wish that I read in the exhibition hall.'이라고 했다.

Lesson 5 (기말)

01 ② **02** ② **03** ③ **04** ① **05** ③ **06** ② **07** ①
08 ⑤ **09** ④ **10** ④ **11** ①
12 (A) Mike had cleaned the windows
(B) Judy had watered the plant
(C) Amy had washed the dishes
(D) Steve had fed the dog
13 (A) I study English so that I can communicate with foreigners.
(B) I exercise so that I stay healthy.
14 ① **15** ⑤ **16** ⑤ **17** ①, ② **18** ③ **19** ③
20 ③ **21** (1) has → have (2) was → had been
22 so that he would not forget Yun's sacrifice
23 ⑤ **24** ③ **25** ⑤ **26** ②

01 '사람들이 볼 수 있도록 공적인 공간에 예술품 같은 물건들이 전시되는 이벤트'는 'exhibition(전시회)'이다.

02 '특히 어떤 것을 하거나 얻기 위하여 또는 누군가를 돕기 위하여 자신이 지키고 싶은 어떤 것을 포기하는 행위'는 'sacrifice(희생)'이다.

03 사고 싶지 않은 시점 이전에 이미 사가지고 있는 것이므로 과거완료로 써야 한다.

04 정약용에 대해 못 들어 봤다면서 조선 시대의 위대한 과학

자라고 하는 것은 어색하다.

05 ⓒ는 'He bought many Korean treasures that some Japanese had taken to Japan.'으로 고치는 것이 적절하다.

06 윤동주에 관해 잘 모른다고 하고 그의 시가 전 세계에 빠르게 퍼졌다고 하는 것은 어색하다.

07 (A) 시를 몇 편이나 썼는지는 알 수 없다.
(E) 한국이 언제 일본의 통치를 받았는지는 알 수 없다.
(G) 보라가 왜 윤동주 박물관에 가려고 하는지는 알 수 없다.

08 삼계탕을 먹기로 한 것이지 만들기로 한 것은 아니다.

09 'so that+주어+동사 ~(~하기 위해서)'는 목적을 나타낸다.

10 Bora가 'I'm planning to visit the Yun Dongju Museum soon. Do you want to come with me?'라고 하자 Andy가 'Yes'라고 했다.

11 ① I had never traveled abroad before I was 20.

12 엄마가 집에 도착하기 전에 일어난 일이므로 과거완료로 쓴다.

13 'so that+주어+동사 ~(~하기 위해서)'는 목적을 나타내므로 'Why'에 맞게 이유를 쓴다.

14 ⓐ의 who는 주격이므로 'whom'으로 바꿔 쓸 수 없다.

15 (A) '~하는 동안'을 의미하는 While (B) '~에 대항하여' 싸우는 것이므로 against (C) directed의 목적격 보어로 to carry out이 적절하다.

16 시간 순서로 보면 ⑧-ⓐ-ⓔ-ⓓ-ⓒ이다.

17 ① 학교를 세우기 위해 어떻게 돈을 구했는지는 알 수 없다. ② 무엇이 이봉창과 윤봉길로 하여금 한인 애국단의 단원이 되도록 했는지는 알 수 없다.

18 (A) belong은 자동사이므로 수동태로 쓰이지 않고 belong to의 형태로 쓰인다. (B) directed의 목적격 보어로 to carry out이 적절하다.

19 'At one place in the hall, we saw two watches under a photo of Kim Koo and Yun Bonggil.'이라고 했다.

20 ⓒ 다음부터 기념관 관람을 마친 후의 이야기가 나온다.

21 사역동사 let의 목적격 보어로 have, 시신을 모셔온 과거보다 시신이 일본에 있었던 것이 더 이전에 있었던 일이므로 과거완료(had+p.p.) 시제를 사용해야 한다.

22 'so that+주어+동사 ~' 구문은 목적을 나타내며 '~하기 위해서'라는 뜻이며 'Kim Koo always carried Yun's watch in his jacket not to forget Yun's sacrifice'라고 했다.

23 'There he joined the Government of the Republic of Korea and later became its president.'라고 했다.

24 ⓐ spend+시간+~ing: ~하는 데 시간을 보내다 ⓑ help는 다음에 동사원형이나 to부정사가 온다. ⓒ 과거의 일이므로 moved가 적절하다.

25 'After that, he built a lot of schools to educate people until he died in 1938.'라고 했다.

26 ②번 문장은 위 글이 시작되기 전에 언급되어야 흐름상 적절하다. There가 'in a park in Shanghai'를 가리키므로 어색하다.

MEMO